Information Seeking Behavior and Challenges in Digital Libraries

Adeyinka Tella
University of Ilorin, Nigeria

A volume in the Advances in Library and Information Science (ALIS) Book Series

Information Science REFERENCE
An Imprint of IGI Global

Published in the United States of America by
Information Science Reference (an imprint of IGI Global)
701 E. Chocolate Avenue
Hershey PA, USA 17033
Tel: 717-533-8845
Fax: 717-533-8661
E-mail: cust@igi-global.com
Web site: http://www.igi-global.com

Library of Congress Cataloging-in-Publication Data

Names: Tella, Adeyinka, 1972- editor.
Title: Information seeking behavior and challenges in digital libraries / Adeyinka Tella, editor.
Description: Hershey, PA : Information Science Reference, [2016] | Includes bibliographical references and index.
Identifiers: LCCN 2016006151| ISBN 9781522502968 (hardcover) | ISBN 9781522502975 (ebook)
Subjects: LCSH: Digital libraries. | Digital libraries--Africa. | Information behavior. | Electronic information resource searching. | Information retrieval. | Copyright--Electronic information resources.
Classification: LCC ZA4080 .I525 2016 | DDC 027--dc23 LC record available at https://lccn.loc.gov/2016006151

This book is published in the IGI Global book series Advances in Library and Information Science (ALIS) (ISSN: 2326-4136; eISSN: 2326-4144)

British Cataloguing in Publication Data
A Cataloguing in Publication record for this book is available from the British Library.

Advances in Library and Information Science (ALIS) Book Series

ISSN: 2326-4136
EISSN: 2326-4144

Mission

The **Advances in Library and Information Science (ALIS) Book Series** is comprised of high quality, research-oriented publications on the continuing developments and trends affecting the public, school, and academic fields, as well as specialized libraries and librarians globally. These discussions on professional and organizational considerations in library and information resource development and management assist in showcasing the latest methodologies and tools in the field.

The **ALIS Book Series** aims to expand the body of library science literature by covering a wide range of topics affecting the profession and field at large. The series also seeks to provide readers with an essential resource for uncovering the latest research in library and information science management, development, and technologies.

Coverage

- Professional Development
- Human resources management
- Journal Collections
- Marketing Library Products and Services
- Future of Computing in Libraries
- Resource Sharing in Libraries
- Green Libraries
- E-Books in Libraries
- Distance Learning and Librarianship
- Ethics of Information

IGI Global is currently accepting manuscripts for publication within this series. To submit a proposal for a volume in this series, please contact our Acquisition Editors at Acquisitions@igi-global.com or visit: http://www.igi-global.com/publish/.

The Advances in Library and Information Science (ALIS) Book Series (ISSN 2326-4136) is published by IGI Global, 701 E. Chocolate Avenue, Hershey, PA 17033-1240, USA, www.igi-global.com. This series is composed of titles available for purchase individually; each title is edited to be contextually exclusive from any other title within the series. For pricing and ordering information please visit http://www.igi-global.com/book-series/advances-library-information-science/73002. Postmaster: Send all address changes to above address.

Titles in this Series

For a list of additional titles in this series, please visit: www.igi-global.com

Technology-Centered Academic Library Partnerships and Collaborations
Brian Doherty (New College of Florida, USA)
Information Science Reference • copyright 2016 • 309pp • H/C (ISBN: 9781522503231) • US $165.00 (our price)

Space and Organizational Considerations in Academic Library Partnerships and Collaborations
Brian Doherty (New College of Florida, USA)
Information Science Reference • copyright 2016 • 366pp • H/C (ISBN: 9781522503262) • US $200.00 (our price)

Special Library Administration, Standardization and Technological Integration
Joseph M. Yap (De La Salle University, Philippines) Martin Julius V. Perez (Department of Foreign Affairs, Philippines) Maria Cecilia I. Ayson (Filipinas Heritage Library, Philippines) and Gladys Joy E. Entico (EastWest Bank, Philippines)
Information Science Reference • copyright 2016 • 373pp • H/C (ISBN: 9781466695429) • US $185.00 (our price)

Handbook of Research on Disaster Management and Contingency Planning in Modern Libraries
Emy Nelson Decker (Atlanta University Center, Robert W. Woodruff Library, USA) and Jennifer A. Townes (Atlanta University Center, Robert W. Woodruff Library, USA)
Information Science Reference • copyright 2016 • 676pp • H/C (ISBN: 9781466686243) • US $345.00 (our price)

Handbook of Research on Inventive Digital Tools for Collection Management and Development in Modern Libraries
S. Thanuskodi (Alagappa University, India)
Information Science Reference • copyright 2015 • 422pp • H/C (ISBN: 9781466681781) • US $295.00 (our price)

Innovative Solutions for Building Community in Academic Libraries
Sheila Bonnand (Montana State University, USA) and Mary Anne Hansen (Montana State University, USA)
Information Science Reference • copyright 2015 • 376pp • H/C (ISBN: 9781466683921) • US $200.00 (our price)

Integrating Video Game Research and Practice in Library and Information Science
Jacob A. Ratliff (Independent Researcher, USA)
Information Science Reference • copyright 2015 • 300pp • H/C (ISBN: 9781466681750) • US $185.00 (our price)

Social Media Strategies for Dynamic Library Service Development
Adeyinka Tella (University of Ilorin, Nigeria)
Information Science Reference • copyright 2015 • 388pp • H/C (ISBN: 9781466674158) • US $245.00 (our price)

IGI GLOBAL
DISSEMINATOR OF KNOWLEDGE
www.igi-global.com

701 E. Chocolate Ave., Hershey, PA 17033
Order online at www.igi-global.com or call 717-533-8845 x100
To place a standing order for titles released in this series, contact: cust@igi-global.com
Mon-Fri 8:00 am - 5:00 pm (est) or fax 24 hours a day 717-533-8661

Editorial Advisory Board

List of Reviewers

Table of Contents

Detailed Table of Contents

The environment in which library services are currently offered has changed drastically. The volume of information has grown enormously; the variety of information, its sources and format of presentation have increased; the speed of information flow has increased; times and places to experience communication media have expanded; the number of information perspectives and points of view has exploded; and the people's interest in and expectation of the availability of information have grown. The information users have also changed and now exhibit remarkably unique information seeking behaviour. They basically want synthesised information with the least effort. They are intolerant to any forms of delay and get bored very fast. Librarians must understand the emerging information seeking behaviour and the resultant expectations to be able to satisfy the users' information needs closely. As they do so, they must acknowledge that the uptake of traditional services has dropped drastically and that it is much easier to follow the library users into their digital echo chambers than try to attract them back to the conventional library spaces.

This chapter addresses the issue of information-seeking behaviour of users in the digital libraries' environment in sub-Saharan Africa. Information-seeking behaviour may be shaped by the environment in which users seek information. A digital library is still relatively new in sub-Saharan Africa and there is not much known about how the digital library environment may shape the information-seeking behaviour and/or information needs of users. The chapter explores the concept of digital libraries and the nature of the collections and services of digital libraries in comparison to traditional libraries. The chapter also discusses what a library is, the services provided by libraries, and the differences between a traditional library and a digital library. Covered in the chapter also is a brief history of digital libraries. Digital literacy as a factor which may shape the information-seeking behavior of users in a digital library environment is also discussed in the chapter. Information literacy has changed drastically. The

There has been an increasing amount of research focus on the development of digital libraries, particularly on information seeking. A variety of information-seeking models used by library and information science (LIS) academics investigate the manner in which information is sought and transformed into knowledge, which should be taken into account during the design of digital libraries. However, in part this reflects the lack of knowledge about how these models explain user information seeking behaviors in a digital library environment. This chapter aims to address this lack of knowledge. It presents a set of information-seeking models that can be used by LIS scholars or experts to comprehend the dynamics of information seeking by users of digital libraries. The major role of this chapter is to provide a review of the existing "models" to date, and also to present a comparative analysis of the notable models that may contribute to ways of understanding the research on information seeking in digital libraries.

This chapter examined digital libraries and copyright issues. It considered several issues such as the meaning of digital libraries, the characteristics, functions, digital scholarship services, copyright and the materials that can be and cannot be copyrighted, fair use of library materials, reservation for general use, access to electronic copies, guidelines for fair use in the digital libraries, library reproduction and re-distribution and inter-library loan. The chapter concludes that, reading through this chapter, undergraduates, academics and other library users will have a good understanding of what the digital libraries are and copyright issue all of which are considered very important and germane as we approach paperless society.

This Chapter presents a study conducted on literature related to information seeking behaviour available on the World Wide Web. The outcome of searching the World Wide Web using Google Scholar were analysed to present the growth of publications; collaboration pattern of authors; most contributing authors; type of publications in which information scientists preferred to publish their works; highly preferred journals in which information seeking behaviour related works are published; and the impact of information seeking behaviour related literature.

Indexing and abstracting are like Siamese twins in the information retrieval process. Indexing and abstracting are the two approaches to distilling information content into an abbreviated, but comprehensive representation of an information resource(s). They are knowledge organisation tools which usually provide detailed and accurate maps and road signs in the information superhighway. Digital libraries are characterised by an electronic stock of information which can be accessed via computers, and are extension and augmentations of physical libraries in digital forms. They are information retrieval systems (a device interposed between a potential user of information and the information itself) which provide opportunities to access and retrieve information that is often accessible for a variety of reasons. This chapter presents a literature review on indexing and abstracting, information retrieval process, digital libraries pointing out the importance of indexing and abstracting in the information retrieving process and then highlighting the roles played by indexing and abstracting as tools for information retrieval in digital libraries. The chapter posits that indexing and abstracting plays a significant role as information retrieval tools in digital libraries.

The chapter considers the importance of demographic and socio-economic factors as well as cognitive skills to information seeking in a digital library environment. Demographic factors such as age and gender were considered. Younger adults were found to respond positively to the demands of information seeking in the digital environment while their older counterparts are still struggling to come to terms with the changes. In the same vein, studies have revealed that the value placed on technology by men and women varies. While men express high level of confidence in navigating the digital environment, women still suffer low self-confidence in doing same. Identified socio-economic factors that also constitute a barrier to information seeking in a digital environment include income level, level of education, non-availability of ICT infrastructures and epileptic power supply especially in Africa among others. Unwillingness to see one's needs as information needs, inability to articulate one's information needs, unawareness of information sources, low self-efficacy, poor search skills among others were identified as cognitive barriers to information seeking in the digital environment. Based on the findings of this chapter, the study recommends that for persons who are adjudged to be the older generation, it is imperative for them to acquire requisite ICT skills that will make it easier for them to navigate the digital environment. There is also a clarion call on African leaders to provide infrastructures that will enable ICT to thrive as the digital environment is fast replacing the hitherto traditional one.

simple sampling technique to select 28 respondents from the population. Structured questionnaire was designed for the collection of data. It was discovered from the findings that majority of the farmers were illiterate of the middle aged group between 31-40. The farmers plant many crops, but it is noticeable that the farmers plant cassava mostly, the area which the farmers indicated they need information most is on agriculture, it was also observed that the farmers access information from colleagues (co-farmers), friends and relatives, agricultural extension workers. The information needs of the farmers in this study on agriculture includes how to prevent diseases for their crops on the farm and after harvesting, the farmers also stated that they need information on how to seek for loan, where to get the best market to sell their farm produce and how to get the best agro-chemical for effective use. In this study it was discovered that the challenges the farmers face in acquiring information includes, the inability to read and write in English language, lack of constant electricity supply, conflict among members of various associations and lack of access to agricultural extension workers. It is recommended that the farmers should be given effective adult education, provision of information centre with necessary personnel and information media to boost information accessibility. Also the government was encouraged to negotiate with mobile telecommunication operators to subsidize services so that the farmers who form majority in the rural areas can access information and communicate easily through their mobile phones.

This chapter discusses how to use social networking tools for information seeking in a digital library environment. Social networking is an evolutionary development of online participation, where people of common interest communicate, share and contribute content on the social cyberspace. The role of social networking for information seeking in libraries, most especially digital library is still evolving and cannot be over-emphasized. There is the need for libraries to exploit the advantages presented by these new media in providing better services. Social networking tools enable librarians and other information professionals to communicate, network and share documents with many clients regardless of location, and at little or no expense and viz. The chapter looks at: information seeking / search process; digital libraries; social networking as a concept; relationship between web 2.0, library 2.0, social media and social networking; role of social networking in digital library environment; role of information professionals in using social networking; social media platforms in digital library environment; challenges and prospects of integrating social networking with digital libraries and ways to improve the use of social networking for information seeking and dissemination in the future.

Adequate knowledge about the information needs and seeking behaviour of users is vital for developing digital library collections, services and facilities to meet their information needs effectively. Information seeking as an underlying feature in research cannot be done without an enabling environment where needed resources and services are provided. The available literature reveals that although librarians have made good progress in adapting primary values of librarianship which are to support intellectual freedom and equitable access to information, information seeking process in the Digital Libraries has,

Foreword

I was very happy when my colleague Adeyinka Tella asked me to write the foreword to this very interesting and significant book. Dr. Tella has been a contributor to the peer-reviewed open access e-journal *Library Philosophy and Practice* (LPP) and to a number of other scholarly journals originating in Africa, North America, Asia, and elsewhere around the globe. The globalization of librarianship is a phenomenon I began to notice in the very early days of LPP, which was founded in 1998. We began to receive submissions from Nigeria, Ghana, Uganda, India, Pakistan, Bangladesh, Iran, Malaysia, and a number of other countries. Those same international authors began to appear in other LIS journals, and a scholarly conversation began among librarian colleagues everywhere in the world. It became apparent that we all faced the same issues and challenges and that we all had the same goals. It has also been an opportunity for librarians in the US to gain a greater understanding of the library and educational environment in countries that are less familiar to many Americans. We gained new friends and colleagues who made us aware that countries like Nigeria, India, Iran, and so on, are very populous and have a large number of tertiary institutions with thousands of students, faculty, and librarians.

This global perspective is essential for understanding and appreciating this volume whose topic is one of the most crucial and perennially interesting in all of LIS: information-seeking behavior of library users, in particular information seeking in a digital age and in digital libraries. These fifteen chapters focus on the general and the particular, on the digital environment and the mixed (print and digital) environment of most libraries, on specific places and individual libraries, on particular occupations and user groups, and on the effect of demographics (such as socioeconomic status) on information-seeking behavior. This book uses many lenses to examine this important topic and provide an array of observations and insights, from authors in Nigeria, Kenya, South Africa, and other places.

Tom Kwanya of the Technical University of Kenya inaugurates the topic of information seeking in digital libraries with a look at the current information environment, exhorting librarians to "follow library users into their digital echo chambers," rather than trying to bring them back to conventional library spaces and services.

Many of the authors in this book present the challenges for digital libraries from an African perspective. E.M. Ondari-Okemwa of the University of Fort Hare in South Africa looks specifically at digital libraries in Sub-Saharan Africa, finding that digital libraries are still a relatively new phenomenon in this region. Ondari-Okemwa looks at "digital literacy" as it contrasts with traditional definitions of literacy and considers the impact of socioeconomic factors on digital literacy in Sub-Saharan Africa.

As in many regions of the world, higher education in Kenya has expanded drastically without increases in infrastructure. This has led to a rise in distance (online) education that requires the use of digital resources. Licensing requirements for these resources have important legal ramifications that librarians must strictly observe. Japhet Otike of Moi University in Kenya considers the legal aspects of using digital resources to support distance learning by universities in Kenya.

Copyright is one of the most crucial legal issues in the provision of digital library resources. Pedro Pina of the Polytechnic Institute of Coimbra, Portugal, explores this important topic. Pina describes the tension between the democratization of information represented by access to digital resources and the rights of authors and publishers to control and profit from their works.

Adeyinka Tella, Saheed Oyeniran, and Olubokola James Ojo of the University of Ilorin, Nigeria also look at copyright and digital libraries, focusing on issues such as fair use, reproduction, and interlibrary loan, which can be challenging in the digital environment.

Three librarians and scholars from the University of Putra, Malaysia, look at different models of information seeking in the context of digital libraries. Zeinab Zaremohzzabieh, Seyedali Ahrari, Prof. Bahaman Abu Samah, and Prof. Jusang Bolong examine existing models and their applicability to the digital environment.

Bibliometrics and scientometrics can reveal interesting patterns in scholarly communication. Akakandelwa Akakandelwa of the University of Zambia takes a bibliometric approach to the literature on information seeking that is available on the Web. The author used Google Scholar to look at the growth of publications, collaboration patterns, impact, and citation patterns.

Like bibliometrics, a review of the literature can also unearth issues and challenges presented from varying perspectives and using different methodologies. Olaronke O. Fagbola of the National Open University of Nigeria presents a literature review on indexing and abstracting and information retrieval for digital libraries, exploring the impact of indexing and abstracting on the retrieval of electronic information.

Barriers to information seeking are an essential part of the study of information-seeking behavior. Felicia Yusuf, Owolabi Sola, Aregbesola Ayooluwa, Sunday Oguntayo, Foluke Okocha, and Eyiolorunse Toluwani of Landmark University, Omu-Aran, Kwara State, Nigeria, look at the barriers to information-seeking in the digital environment. The authors consider demographics, socioeconomic factors, and cognitive skills, all of which may have a negative effect on the ability to seek and retrieve information.

Ajayi Ayo Oluwaseun of the University of Ibadan, Nigeria, also looks at barriers to information seeking, looking more generally at the things that prevent users from accessing information.

Information seeking is different for people in different professions, language communities, age groups, and so on. Joel O. Afolayan of the Michael Imoudu National Institute for Labour Studies, Ilorin, Nigeria looks at the information-seeking behavior of trade unionists and reviews challenges to success and the impact of information on industrial relations and worker satisfaction and productivity.

Femi Titus Akande and Akinade Adebowale Adewojo of the Nigerian Stored Products Research Institute, Ilorin, Kwara State, Nigeria, also look at a particular group of information seekers, in this case farmers. The authors surveyed a group of 28 farmers and found a low rate of literacy that co-exists with a need for information for successful farming.

A case study or survey of one institution can shed light on issues that are generalizable to a larger population. Michael Terver Upev Kwaghga Beetseh, and Joy Asibi Idachaba, of the Federal University of Agriculture Makurdi, Benue State, Nigeria present a study of the usability of digital resources in one particular Nigerian academic library. The authors surveyed library staff and discovered what kinds of resources are digitized by the library and used by its patrons, as well as the challenges to digitization and use of digitized resources. Challenges included a need for more standardization of processes and more sophisticated equipment.

While nearly a generation ago a library website was enough of a digital presence, libraries must now use Web 2.0 tools to interact with library users. Ganiyu Ojo Adigun of Ladoke Akintola University Library, Ogbomoso, Nigeria, explores the use of social networks by libraries.

Prakash Dongardive of Mekelle University, Ethiopia, examines the growth of digital libraries since the1990s and considers whether digital libraries are now the predicted "information super highway."

These fifteen chapters help us assess the current library environment and answer the question, "Is the 'digital library' the same thing as a 'library'?" Have print collections become secondary or even non-existent in some cases, and the electronic resources now the default format and collection for libraries and library users? There is no easy answer to that question, and digital libraries present some significant challenges, including funding, management, access issues, infrastructure, and training for librarians and library users. There are intellectual property issues as well as seemingly-mundane but actually quite pressing problems such as the unreliable power supply experienced by some libraries. The authors of this volume present us with information, analysis, and recommendations that will help us make progress on these issues and do the thing we are all so committed to doing: connect people with the information they need, and in so doing, make their lives better.

Mary K. Bolin
University of Nebraska - Lincoln, Nebraska, USA

Mary K. Bolin, *PhD is Professor and Catalog and Metadata Librarian at the University of Nebraska--Lincoln Libraries, Lincoln, Nebraska USA. She is also an instructor in the School of Information at San Jose State University, San Jose, California, USA, where she teaches beginning cataloging and a metadata seminar. Dr. Bolin received her BA in Linguistics from the University of Nebraska in 1976, her MSLS from the University of Kentucky in 1981, an MA in English from the University of Idaho in 1999, and a PhD in Education from the University of Nebraska in 2007. Along with her colleague, Prof. Gail Eckwright, she is one of the founding editors of the open access, peer-reviewed e-journal, Library Philosophy and Practice, which has been published since 1998.*

Preface

INTRODUCTION

The revolution brought by Information and Communication Technology has led to an increase in the establishment of Digital libraries (DL) around the world. Consequently, the ways and manners of information seeking by users has changed. Users of information services are now faced with highly decentralized, heterogeneous document sources. From the user point of view, document and data structures in Digital Libraries offer a broad variety of new searching and browsing possibilities. In order to guide the user during the search, there is need to familiarize users with the idea of high-level search activities for successful searching and information seeking in digital libraries. In addition to providing information on the low-level functions offered by typical DL systems, strategic support is an important means of tactics and stratagems.

A great deal of information is needed for the Digital Libraries' users to create more awareness on how to research for and gather information in the context of the so-called digital libraries. The idea behind these efforts is to combine different information sources to solve the problem of finding useful information in the borderless world of the internet.

The book 'information seeking behavior in the digital libraries' discusses and addresses the difficulties and challenges that users have faced when sourcing and seeking information through the digital libraries. The book address different aspects of information seeking in digital libraries, ranging from searching through various digital library databases, different types of information seeking behavior in the digital libraries context, the digital libraries and the barrier to information seeking behavior, relation between human computer interaction and seeking information in the digital libraries and other related topics. Additionally, the book explores the impact of seeking information through the digital libraries on the users.

Undoubtedly, this book is expected to appeal to information professionals and researchers working in the fields of library and information science, knowledge management, information management, communication science, social sciences, and information technology, especially, those who specialised in digitization, automation of libraries, electronic/digital resources. At the same time, the book provides insight and support practitioners and experts concerned with the organization, management of knowledge, and information in digital environment.

There are fifteen major chapters in the book. These chapters detailed the contents represented in the book and more importantly, they appeal to readers to read along and enjoy the piece.

The book kick-starts it discussion on a chapter that examines information seeking behaviour in the digital libraries context. The chapter emphsised that the volume of information has grown enormously and the variety of information, sources and format of presentation have increased; the speed of information flow has increased; times and places to experience communication media have expanded; the number of information perspectives and points of view has exploded; and the people's interest in and expectation of the availability of information have grown. The chapter also points out that the information users have also changed and now exhibit remarkably unique information seeking behaviour. They basically want synthesised information with the least effort, they are intolerant to any forms of delay and get bored very fast.

The following chapter addresses the issue of information-seeking behaviour of users in the digital libraries' environment in Sub-Saharan Africa. Information-seeking behaviour may be shaped by the environment in which users seek information. A digital library is still relatively new in Sub-Saharan Africa and there is not much known about how the digital library environment may shape the information-seeking behaviour and/or information needs of users. The chapter also discusses what a library is, the services provided by libraries, and the differences between a traditional library and a digital library. The chapter discusses the extent to which low levels of digital literacy in sub-Saharan Africa may also be responsible for shaping information-seeking behaviour of users in a digital library environment. The chapter concludes that the major differences between the two types of libraries are mainly technology, rather than a fundamental change in the way libraries operate.

The third chapter examines the legal challenges librarians managing university libraries in Kenya experience when providing information services in support of distance learning. Kenya is experiencing enormous socio-economic changes. These changes have exerted serious pressure on higher education resulting to phenomenal expansion of university education. Unfortunately, the demand for university education has not translated into infrastructural expansion of universities. While university intake continues to grow at an alarming rate, funding for universities including libraries continue to diminish. An option taken by many universities to meet increased demand for higher education has been to invest in distance education. This option has its own challenges. Distance learning like residential programmes, require adequate financial investment in print and electronic information resources; and ICT infrastructure. Since libraries in Kenya are underfunded, they are compelled to reproduce the scarce materials available with them to serve distant learners as opposed to acquiring additional materials. The book emphasized that this arrangement has equally serious challenges. Top on the list is copyright infringement. Without adequate exceptions and limitations to copyright restrictions, university authorities and librarians are likely to be charged for infringement.

The next chapter points out that libraries have a strong role to play in promoting culture and knowledge as intermediaries between creators and readers. In the analogical world, such usages didn't have relevant effects on the normal exploitation of copyrighted works. However, digitisation had a strong effect on right holders' interests by facilitating and democratizing access to works, considering that libraries may reproduce them and promote their online accessibility. Litigation regarding the referred actions has dramatically increased in the last years as they may stress the normal exploitation of copyrighted works and the exclusive rights of reproduction and of distribution. Based on the European Union's legislation and jurisprudence, the chapter analyses the lawfulness of public libraries digitisation of books from their collection in order to make them available to users without the right holder's consent, confronting them with the exclusive right of reproduction and the making available right.

The chapter that follows points out that a variety of information-seeking models used by library and information science (LIS) academics investigate the manner in which information is sought and transformed into knowledge, which should be taken into account during the design of digital libraries. However, in part, this reflects the lack of knowledge about how these models explain user information seeking behaviors in a digital library environment. On that note, the chapter addresses the lack of knowledge, and presents a set of information-seeking models that can be used by LIS scholars or experts to comprehend the dynamics of information seeking by users of digital libraries. The chapter also provides a review of the existing "models" to date, and also presents a comparative analysis of the notable models that may contribute to understanding the research on information seeking in digital libraries.

Next to this is the chapter that examined digital libraries and copyright issues. It considered several issues such as the meaning of digital libraries, the characteristics, functions, digital scholarship services, copyright and the materials that can be and cannot be copyrighted, fair use of library materials, reservation for general use, access to electronic copies, guidelines for fair use in the digital libraries, library reproduction and re-distribution and inter-library loan. The chapter concludes that, reading through this chapter, undergraduates, academics and other library users will have a good understanding of what the digital libraries are and copyright issues all of which are considered very important and germane as we approach paperless society.

The chapter that follows presents a study conducted on literature related to information seeking behaviour available on the World Wide Web. The outcome of searching the World Wide Web using Google Scholar were analysed to present the growth of publications; collaboration pattern of authors; most contributing authors; type of publications in which information scientists preferred to publish their works; highly preferred journals in which information seeking behaviour related works are published; and the impact of information seeking behaviour related literature.

Following this is the chapter that presents a literature review on indexing and abstracting, information retrieval process in digital libraries pointing out the importance of indexing and abstracting in the information retrieving process and then highlighting the roles played by indexing and abstracting as tools for information retrieval in digital libraries. The chapter posits that indexing and abstracting plays a significant role as information retrieval tools in digital libraries.

The next chapter considers the importance of demographic and socio-economic factors as well as cognitive skills to information seeking in a digital library environment. Demographic factors such as age and gender were considered. Younger adults were found to respond positively to the demands of information seeking in the digital environment while their older counterparts are still struggling to come to terms with the changes. Based on the findings of in the study, the chapter recommends that for persons who are adjudged to be the older generation, it is imperative for that they acquire requisite ICT skills that will make it easier for them to navigate the digital environment. There is also a clarion call on African leaders to provide infrastructures that will enable ICT to thrive as the digital environment is fast replacing the hitherto traditional one.

The following chapter entrenches trade unionists information needs in terms of capacity building towards organizational productivity as well as the information seeking behavior using digital sources. The chapter through literature review identifies the challenges of meeting up with the needs and management of information by Information Resource Centre of Michael Imoudu National Institute for Labour Studies' (MINILS) in the era of digital divide.

The next chapter examines usability of digital library resources in Francis Sulemanu Idachaba Library University of Agriculture Makurdi, Nigeria. The population for the study comprised of the entire library staff of the Francis Sulemanu Idachaba Library University of Agriculture Makurdi. The chapter identifies criteria used for the selection of digitized library resources while there are challenges associated with the process of digitization of library resources of Francis Sulemanu Idachaba Library of University of Agriculture Makurdi. The chapter concludes that latest advancement in the field of information technology have compelled libraries to embrace automation because the facilities provided by automated libraries go far beyond the activities of traditional libraries. The chapter recommends that the library management should provide effective solution to the problems faced in the digitization unit by purchasing more equipment for the services such as digital camera, Photoshop software, a standby generating set, standardization on the supplied paper size and CD-ROMs, upgrading of the systems in other to meet the needs of modern day's technologies.

The chapter that follows presents the report of a study that examined information needs and seeking behavior of farmers in Laduba community, Kwara State, Nigeria. This study adopted a survey research design using simple random sampling technique to select 28 respondents from the population. Structured questionnaire was designed for the collection of data. It was discovered from the findings that majority of the farmers were illiterate of the middle aged group between 31-40. The chapter reveals the agricultural information needs of the farmers in this study to includes how to prevent diseases for their crops on the farm and after harvesting, information on how to seek for loan, where to get the best market to sell their farm produce and how to get the best agro-chemical for effective use. The chapter recommends that the farmers should be given effective adult education, provision of information centre with necessary personnel and information media to boost information accessibility.

Next in the series of chapter featured in the book is the one that examines the role of social networking for information seeking in a digital library environment; while the next chapter examines the barriers to Information Seeking in the Digital Libraries. The one that preceed these focuses on information overload and copyright infringements: A critical appraisal of postgraduate students' attitude and use of intellectual contents.

The concluding chapter of the book points out that during the decade of 1990s the term digital libraries become a recognized phrase for describing libraries that offer access to digital information by using a variety of networks, including internet and world wide web. It's also emphasized that digital libraries provide remote access to the contents and the services of the libraries and other information sources combining an onsite collection of current and heavily used materials in both print and electronic form with an electronic networks which provide access to and delivery for worldwide libraries and commercial information and knowledge sources. In the light of these therefore, this chapter discussed digital libraries as information superhighway looking at issues like factors responsible for the emergence of digital libraries, influence internet on digital libraries, etc.

ORGANIZATION OF THE BOOK

Chapter 1: Information Seeking Behaviour in Digital Library Contexts, by Tom Kwanya

The environment in which library services are currently offered has changed drastically. The volume of information has grown enormously; the variety of information, its sources and format of presentation have increased; the speed of information flow has increased; times and places to experience communication media have expanded; the number of information perspectives and points of view has exploded; and the people's interest in and expectation of the availability of information have grown. The information users have also changed and now exhibit remarkably unique information seeking behaviour. They basically want synthesised information with the least effort. They are intolerant to any forms of delay and get bored very fast. Librarians must understand the emerging information seeking behaviour and the resultant expectations to be able to satisfy the users' information needs closely. As they do so, they must acknowledge that the uptake of traditional services has dropped drastically and that it is much easier to follow the library users into their digital echo chambers than try to attract them back to the conventional library spaces.

Chapter 2: Information-Seeking Behaviour of Users in the Digital Libraries' Environment in Sub-Saharan Africa, by EM Ondari-Okemwa

This chapter addresses the issue of information-seeking behaviour of users in the digital libraries' environment in sub-Saharan Africa. Information-seeking behaviour may be shaped by the environment in which users seek information. A digital library is still relatively new in sub-Saharan Africa and there is not much known about how the digital library environment may shape the information-seeking behaviour and/or information needs of users. The chapter explores the concept of digital libraries and the nature of the collections and services of digital libraries in comparison to traditional libraries. The chapter also discusses what a library is, the services provided by libraries, and the differences between a traditional library and a digital library. Covered in the chapter also is a brief history of digital libraries. Digital literacy as a factor which may shape the information-seeking behaviour of users in a digital library environment is also discussed in the chapter. Information literacy has changed drastically. The digital information literacy that may play a role in socio-economic development in sub-Saharan Africa is no longer the literacy defined as the ability to read and write at a basic level and sign a document. As society is moving from information age to digital age, new definitions of digital information literacy are evolving which include how to access information in digital formats, and how to evaluate information and use it appropriately. Digital information literacy forms the basis for lifelong learning and is common to all disciplines, to all learning environments and to all levels of education. In sub-Saharan Africa, levels of digital information literacy are low due to numerous factors which are also explored in this chapter. Development of digital information literacy in sub-Saharan Africa has been slow compared to the development of information and communication technologies in the region. The chapter discusses the extent to which low levels of digital literacy in sub-Saharan Africa may also be responsible for shaping information-seeking behaviour of users in a digital library environment. The chapter concludes that the major differences between the two types of libraries are mainly to do with technology, rather than a fundamental change in the way libraries operate. This is because digital libraries are still libraries which largely share the same objectives and purposes of the traditional libraries.

Chapter 3: Legal Considerations of Providing Information in Support of Distance Learning By Digital Libraries in Universities in Kenya, by Japhet Otike

The chapter examines the legal challenges librarians managing university libraries in Kenya experience when providing information services in support of distance learning. Kenya is experiencing enormous socio-economic changes. These changes have exerted serious pressure on higher education resulting to phenomenal expansion of university education. Unfortunately, the demand for university education has not translated into infrastructural expansion of universities. While university intake continues to grow at an alarming rate, funding for universities including libraries continue to diminish. An option taken by many universities to meet increased demand for higher education has been to invest in distance education. This option has its own challenges. Distance learning like residential programmes, require adequate financial investment in print and electronic information resources; and ICT infrastructure. Since libraries in Kenya are underfunded, they are compelled to reproduce the scarce materials available with them to serve distant learners as opposed to acquiring additional materials. This arrangement has equally serious challenges. Top on the list is copyright infringement. Without adequate exceptions and limitations to copyright restrictions, university authorities and librarians are likely to be charged for infringement.

Chapter 4: Copyright Issues in the Context of the Digital Library, by Pedro Pina

Libraries have a strong role on promoting culture and knowledge as intermediaries between creators and readers. In the analogical world, such usages didn't have relevant effects on the normal exploitation of copyrighted works. However, digitisation had a strong effect on right holders' interests by facilitating and democratizing access to works, considering that libraries may reproduce them and promote their online accessibility. Litigation regarding the referred actions has dramatically increased in the last years as they may stress the normal exploitation of copyrighted works and the exclusive rights of reproduction and of distributing. Based on the European Union's legislation and jurisprudence, the present chapter analyses the lawfulness of public libraries digitisation of books from their collection in order to make them available to users without the right holder's consent, confronting them with the exclusive right of reproduction and the making available right.

Chapter 5: Researching Information Seeking in Digital Libraries through Information-Seeking Models, by Zeinab Zaremohzzabieh, Seyedali Ahrari, Bahaman Abu Samah, and Jusang Bolong

There has been an increasing amount of research focus on the development of digital libraries, particularly on information seeking. A variety of information-seeking models used by library and information science (LIS) academics investigate the manner in which information is sought and transformed into knowledge, which should be taken into account during the design of digital libraries. However, in part this reflects the lack of knowledge about how these models explain user information seeking behaviors in a digital library environment. This chapter aims to address this lack of knowledge. It presents a set of information-seeking models that can be used by LIS scholars or experts to comprehend the dynamics of information seeking by users of digital libraries. The major role of this chapter is to provide a review of the existing "models" to date, and also to present a comparative analysis of the notable models that may contribute to ways of understanding the research on information seeking in digital libraries.

Chapter 6: Digital Libraries and Copyright Issues, by Adeyinka Tella, Saheed Oyeniran, and Olubokola James Ojo

The chapter examined digital libraries and copyright issues. It considered several issues such as the meaning of digital libraries, the characteristics, functions, digital scholarship services, copyright and the materials that can be and cannot be copyrighted, fair use of library materials, reservation for general use, access to electronic copies, guidelines for fair use in the digital libraries, library reproduction and re-distribution and inter-library loan. The chapter concludes that, reading through this chapter, undergraduates, academics and other library users will have a good understanding of what the digital libraries are and copyright issue all of which are considered very important and germane as we approach paperless society.

Chapter 7: A Glimpse of the Information Seeking Behaviour Literature on the Web: A Bibliometric Approach, by Akakandelwa Akakandelwa

This Chapter presents a study conducted on literature related to information seeking behaviour available on the World Wide Web. The outcome of searching the World Wide Web using Google Scholar were analysed to present the growth of publications; collaboration pattern of authors; most contributing authors; type of publications in which information scientists preferred to publish their works; highly preferred journals in which information seeking behaviour related works are published; and the impact of information seeking behaviour related literature.

Chapter 8: Indexing and Abstracting as Tools for Information Retrieval in Digital Libraries: A Review of Literature, by Olaronke O. Fagbola

Indexing and abstracting are like siamese twins in the information retrieval process. Indexing and abstracting are the two approaches to distilling information content into an abbreviated, but comprehensive representation of an information resource(s). They are knowledge organisation tools which usually provide detailed and accurate maps and road signs in the information superhighway. Digital libraries are characterised by an electronic stock of information which can be accessed via computers, and are extension and augmentations of physical libraries in digital forms. They are information retrieval systems (a device interposed between a potential user of information and the information itself) which provide opportunities to access and retrieve information that is often accessible for a variety of reasons. This chapter presents a literature review on indexing and abstracting, information retrieval process, digital libraries pointing out the importance of indexing and abstracting in the information retrieving process and then highlighting the roles played by indexing and abstracting as tools for information retrieval in digital libraries. The chapter posits that indexing and abstracting plays a significant role as information retrieval tools in digital libraries.

Chapter 9: Demographics, Socio-economic and Cognitive Skills as Barriers to Information Seeking in a Digital Library Environment, by Felicia Yusuf, Sola Owolabi, Ayooluwa Aregbesola, Sunday Oguntayo, Foluke Okocha, and Toluwani Eyiolorunse

The chapter considers the importance of demographic and socio-economic factors as well as cognitive skills to information seeking in a digital library environment. Demographic factors such as age and gender were considered. Younger adults were found to respond positively to the demands of information seeking in the digital environment while their older counterparts are still struggling to come to terms with the changes. In the same vein, studies have revealed that the value placed on technology by men and women varies. While men express high level of confidence in navigating the digital environment, women still suffer low self-confidence in doing same. Identified socio-economic factors that also constitute a barrier to information seeking in a digital environment include income level, level of education, non-availability of ICT infrastructures and epileptic power supply especially in Africa among others. Unwillingness to see one's needs as information needs, inability to articulate one's information needs, unawareness of information sources, low self-efficacy, poor search skills among others were identified as cognitive barriers to information seeking in the digital environment. Based on the findings of this chapter, the study recommends that for persons who are adjudged to be the older generation, it is imperative for them to acquire requisite ICT skills that will make it easier for them to navigate the digital environment. There is also a clarion call on African leaders to provide infrastructures that will enable ICT to thrive as the digital environment is fast replacing the hitherto traditional one.

Chapter 10: Information Seeking Behaviour of Trade Unionists: A Review of Associated Challenges in Digital Era, by Joel O. Afolayan and Michael Imoudu

Trade Unionism is mostly like a reactive movement rather than proactive. Its activities and programmes have witnessed setbacks overtime, notwithstanding the originality of intent and positivity of disposition to democratic process. Trade union is a major component of the system of modern industrial relations in any nation. Constitutionally, it has own set of objectives or goals to achieve. Change in the political, social and educational environment gives it an interface of a forum that protects and advances workers' interests, improves the quality of life and condition of workforce, enlarges their traditional capacity of establishing terms and conditions of employment. This chapter entrenches trade unionists information needs in terms of capacity building towards organizational productivity as well as the seeking behavior using digital sources. The challenges of meeting up with the needs and management of information by Information Resource Centre of Michael Imoudu National Institute for Labour Studies' (MINILS) in the era of digital divide is review with recommendations.

Chapter 11: Usability of Digital Resources: A Study of Francis Sulemanu Idachaba Library University of Agriculture Makurdi, by Michael Terver Upev, Kwaghga Beetseh, and Joy Asibi Idachaba

This chapter basically examines usability of digital library resources in institutions: A study of Francis Sulemanu Idachaba Library University of Agriculture Makurdi. The population for the study comprised of all the 124 library staff of the Francis Sulemanu Idachaba Library University of Agriculture Makurdi. Sample for the study was 118 respondents. Data was collected using structured question. The data collected was analysed using descriptive statistics; precisely arithmetic mean. Findings revealed that there are little types of library resources digitized in Francis Sulemanu Idachaba library. There are also criteria used for the selection of library resources digitized in Francis Sulemanu Idachaba Library, University of Agriculture Makurdi. The findings also revealed that there are challenges and problems face in the process of digitization of library resources of Francis Sulemanu Idachaba Library of University of Agriculture Makurdi. The study concluded that latest advancement in the field of information technology have compelled libraries to embrace automation as the facilities provided by automated libraries go far beyond the activities of traditional libraries. It was recommended that the library management to provide effective solution to the problems faced in the digitization unit by purchasing more equipment for the services such as digital camera, Photoshop software, a standby generating set, standardization on the supplied paper size and CD-ROMs, upgrading of the systems in other to meet the needs of modern day's technologies.

Chapter 12: Information Need and Seeking Behavior of Farmers In Laduba Community Of Kwara State, Nigeria, by Femi Titus Akande and Akinade Adebowale Adewojo

The study adopts a survey research design using simple random sampling technique to select 28 respondents (farmers). Structured questionnaire was designed for the collection of data. It was discovered that majority of the farmers were illiterate and were of the middle aged group between 31-40. The farmers plant many crops, but it is noticeable that the farmers plant cassava mostly, the area which the farmers indicated they need information most is on agriculture, it was also observed that the farmers access information from colleagues (co-farmers), friends and relatives, agricultural extension workers. The information needs of the farmers includes how to prevent diseases for their crops on the farm and after harvesting, the farmers also stated that they need information on how to seek for loan, where to get the best market to sell their farm produce and how to get the best agro-chemical for effective use. In this study it was discovered that the challenges the farmers face in acquiring information includes, the inability to read and write in English language, lack of constant electricity supply, conflict among members of various associations and lack of access to agricultural extension workers. It is recommended that the farmers should be given effective adult education, provision of information centre with necessary personnel and information media to boost information accessibility. Also the government was encouraged to negotiate with mobile telecommunication operators to subsidize services so that the farmers who form majority in the rural areas can access information and communicate easily through their mobile phones.

Chapter 13: Role of Social Networking for Information Seeking in a Digital Library Environment, by Adigun, Ganiyu Ojo
Chapter 14: Barriers to Information Seeking in the Digital Libraries, by Ayo Oluwaseun Ajayi
Chapter 15: Digital Libraries: Information Superhighway, by Prakash Dongardive

During the decade of 1990s the term digital libraries become a recognized phrase for describing libraries that offer access to digital information by using by using a variety of networks, including internet and world wide web. Other synonyms used interchangeably digital libraries are library without walls and electronic and virtual libraries because every online or virtual source of information is electronic source of information but every electronic information sources are not online or virtual form, so digital or electronic library includes digital contents and that can be delivered any time anywhere to the networked computer. Digital libraries provide remote access to the contents and the services of the libraries and other information sources combining an onsite collection of current and heavily used materials in both print and electronic form with an electronic network which provide access to and delivery for worldwide libraries and commercial information and knowledge sources. Basically the digital libraries are the metaphor for the networked libraries.

Chapter 1
Information Seeking Behaviour in Digital Library Contexts

Tom Kwanya
The Technical University of Kenya, Kenya

ABSTRACT

The environment in which library services are currently offered has changed drastically. The volume of information has grown enormously; the variety of information, its sources and format of presentation have increased; the speed of information flow has increased; times and places to experience communication media have expanded; the number of information perspectives and points of view has exploded; and the people's interest in and expectation of the availability of information have grown. The information users have also changed and now exhibit remarkably unique information seeking behaviour. They basically want synthesised information with the least effort. They are intolerant to any forms of delay and get bored very fast. Librarians must understand the emerging information seeking behaviour and the resultant expectations to be able to satisfy the users' information needs closely. As they do so, they must acknowledge that the uptake of traditional services has dropped drastically and that it is much easier to follow the library users into their digital echo chambers than try to attract them back to the conventional library spaces.

INTRODUCTION

Information seeking is the conscious effort to acquire information in response to a need or gap in knowledge (Case, 2002). It can also be perceived as the process of acquiring, evaluating and using information. Thus, information seeking behaviour encompasses a wide array of actions which individuals or groups take to identify, seek, evaluate, select and use information to fulfil their information needs (Wilson, 2000). Kakai, Ikoja-Odongo and Kigongo-Bukenya (2004) also define information seeking behaviour as an individual's way and manner of gathering and sourcing for information for personal use, knowledge updating, and development. Savolainen (2007) describes information seeking behaviour as how people need, seek, manage, give and use information in different contexts. In this process people normally interact with other people, information systems or tools. Information seeking is a means of gathering or sourcing information necessary for specific or general purposes.

DOI: 10.4018/978-1-5225-0296-8.ch001

Central to information seeking behaviour is the concept of information need. Hjørland (1997) defines an information need as relevant information which individuals or groups require in relation to a given task. In this respect, Weigts *et al.* (1993) explain that people seek information to understand new ideas and issues; elucidate existing information; confirm information held; elucidate beliefs and values held; and to confirm beliefs and values held. Thus, information seeking begins with the realisation of an information need and ends with the satisfaction of that need (Krikelas, 1983). Wilson (1981) argues that information seekers are motivated by physiological, cognitive or affective needs and further suggests that the barriers they face stem from those physiological, cognitive or affective realms.

Libraries must understand the information seeking behaviour of their users to be able design services that closely fit their information needs (Mahajan, 2009). Zhang (1998) agrees with this view and stresses that an understanding of library users' information needs and information seeking behaviour is fundamental to the provision of successful information services. According to Devadason and Lingman (1997), the understanding of information needs and information seeking behaviour of actual and potential library users is essential as it helps in the planning, implementation, and operation of information systems and services. It is no wonder that White (1975) specifically avers that if academic librarians are to realistically serve researchers, they must recognise the changing needs and variations in information gathering and provide services that would be most useful. Therefore, knowledge of the information needs and information seeking behaviour of users is vital for developing library collections, upgrading facilities and improving services to effectively meet the information needs of users (Gunasekera, 2010).

EMERGING TRENDS IN THE MODERN INFOSPHERE

The emergence of the Internet and related technologies has facilitated a momentous change in the way people seek information, communicate and collaborate (Limb, 2004; Casey and Savastinuk, 2006; Miller, 2006; Rothman, 2006; Courtney, 2007). Practically every day seems to bring new techno-applications facilitating their users to do more and more information storage, organisation and communication (Casey and Savastinuk, 2007). As the users become more aware of the possibilities of using technology and find it easier to go to search engines (Google) than drive to the library, the library faces immense challenges on how effectively to offer services to such users. These challenges and emerging possibilities have triggered new conversations on how to discover, invent and/or share knowledge in this age (Casey and Savastinuk, 2007). These applications and conversations have created new expectations for better usability, faster response to customer needs with better products and have exposed the limitations of library services available at a physical building with limited opening hours (Shuman, 2001; Chad and Miller, 2005; Rothman, 2006; Casey and Savastinuk, 2007), strict membership requirements, limited information resources and imperfect user involvement in influencing the services they get (Cohen, 2006). The information environment within which libraries now find themselves is changing, probably faster than ever before (Miller, 2006; Casey and Savastinuk, 2007) and becoming even more complex. As the pace of this change accelerates, the greatest challenge to the libraries and librarians now is how to keep up (Courtney, 2007).

Indeed, statistics provided by the Online Computer Library Center (OCLC, 2005) and Miller (2006) show that there exists a dissonance between the environment and content that libraries provide and the environment and content that information consumers want and use. Preferences for self-service, satisfaction and seamlessness have been identified as some of the indicators of this dissonance in the infosphere.

Therefore, library service characteristics that support self-service or disintermediation, user satisfaction and seamlessness such as ease of use, convenience and availability are now as important to the modern user as quality and trustworthiness of the products (OCLC, 2005).

As libraries struggle to cope with the new demands and challenges, OCLC's (2005) report indicates that they are rapidly relinquishing their place as the top sources of inquiry (Chad and Miller, 2005; Campbell, 2006). Indeed, a sizable number of current library users indicate that they will reduce their library use in due course (OCLC, 2005). Statistics from the Association of Research Libraries (ARL) also indicate that the uptake of traditional library services, such as reference services, dropped by 69 percent between 1991 and 2012 while circulation dropped by 44 percent in the same period (ARL, 2013). This change can be attributed to the constantly shifting expectations of users, especially revolving around time and convenience of use of library services and collection. Fundamentally, modern library users simply expect to be able to access any information they want anytime anywhere. Indeed, they want the library service to fit their lifestyle and not vice versa. They easily note when this is not happening and stop coming to the library.

THE DIGITAL LIBRARY

The digital library model is one of the strategies librarians have embraced to respond to the changing expectations and circumstances of current library users. A digital library is a library where the collection is processed and stored in digital formats facilitating electronic searching and retrieval of the same through digital devices such as computers, mobile phones and other hand-held devices. This model of library service has evolved for many years (Singh, 2003) and is sometimes described as "paperless," "virtual," "library without walls," "electronic library," and "bionic library," among other names (Harter, 1996). Although some scholars also describe digital libraries as those libraries which have more digital collections than physical ones, others assert that digital libraries only offer services electronically; they are virtual and do not have a physical presence. Some literature also reveals the common understanding that most digital libraries contain highly specialised collections. It is also evident that digital libraries do not stock all the information resources locally but often collaborate with content producers to facilitate online access (Harter, 1996; Leiner, 1998; Levy and Marshall, 1994; Miksa and Doty, 1994; Prasad and Swarnalatha, 2005).

Baohua *et al.* (2002) also suggest that the digital library is a major transformation of the traditional library model. They explain that this transformation is evident in the transition of the traditional libraries from passive to active use; from direct to indirect service; from providing information "blindly" to selective and accurate dissemination of information; and the provision of "rich" collections whose quality is enhanced through mixing and remixing by different collaborators such as librarians and users at various levels. On his part, Singh (2003) emphasises that the digital library is more about the digital service environment than the digital content. He asserts that this environment brings together digital collections, people and services that support information processing and sharing. Prasad and Swarnalatha (2005) also describe digital libraries as organisations that provide the resources, including the specialised staff to select and organise; offer intellectual access; interpret, distribute, preserve integrity; and ensure the persistence over time, of collections of digital works so that they are readily and economically available for use by a defined community.

Baohua *et al.* (2002) identify the major characteristics of the digital library as:

1. The digitisation of the information resources making them more durable and easily sharable; 2) digital information transfer through communication technologies such as the Internet;
2. Limitless potential to share information across physical boundaries;
3. Focus on knowledge and not just information resources; and
4. Fast speed of service delivery.

Singh (2003) also adds that digital libraries

1. Have a higher variety of information resources;
2. Provide localised access to distributed content;
3. Enable the same information resource to be shared by many people simultaneously;
4. Have shifted paradigms from collection ownership to mere access;
5. Emphasise quality and usefulness of collection as opposed to quantity; and
6. Presuppose the absence of human intermediaries.

The major benefits of digital libraries include no physical boundary; round the clock availability; multiple access points to services and collection; user-friendly interfaces; longevity of documents; cost-effective use of space; and value addition to services and collection.

EMERGING DIGITAL LIBRARY CONTEXTS

Many studies, as discussed earlier, have demonstrated that the environment in which library services are currently offered has changed drastically. In fact, some scholars have described the situation as the climate of ceaseless change (Giesecke, 1994; Haricombe and Lusher, 1998). For instance, Rainie (2009) points out that the volume of information has grown drastically; the variety of information, its sources and format of presentation have increased; the speed of information flow has increased; times and places to experience communication media have expanded; the number of information perspectives and points of view has exploded; and the people's interest in and expectation of the availability of information have grown. Consequently, all library typologies all over the world are changing; perhaps faster than ever. This rapid pace of change is largely attributed to the constant and far-reaching changes in the environments in which the libraries currently operate.

Chisenga and Rorissa (2001) explain that in the face of shifting library user expectations, there is need for new strategies to design and deliver services and products which match the emerging information needs and seeking behaviour. They recommend the effective use of ICT tools to expand the reach of service, enhance interactivity, improve personalisation of services and leverage mediation. Mostert (2009) also underscores the emerging important place of ICTs in libraries. She explains that the new breed of library users now tend to measure the quality of services and products based on the library's level of investment in ICTs. She also adds that users perceive the library's relevance to their needs based on the currency of the ICT tools available for the users in the facility. Webster (2002) holds a similar view and explains that library users are beginning to evaluate the usefulness of libraries in terms of the availability of ICT tools and how accessible they are to the patrons. Odini, Otike and Kiplang'at (2012) as well as Banda, Mutula and Grand (2004) suggest that in this scenario, librarians should not continue to rely on conventional information systems and services which seem inadequate in meeting the current information needs of the users. They argue that the apparent rigidity of information systems may have resulted from a lack of adequate user information needs assessments by librarians and propose the adoption of user-centric library service models.

To anticipate and effectively respond to the emerging user needs, librarians require ample resources, facilitative policies and supportive institutional structures. Critically, they also need a combination of skills to weave these together into an appropriate fabric of services, systems and products. Kwanya, Stilwell and Underwood (2012) propose a set of competencies that librarians require to be effective. These include technical, personal and interpersonal, ICTs and management. They explain that the technical competencies cover various aspects of the professional and technical role that a librarian is expected to demonstrate. The personal and interpersonal issues comprise personal attributes and attitude, communication, public relations and networking competencies which may be seen to reside in the personal and social dimension. Effective use of ICTs requires competency in ICT systems, hardware and software, the Internet, Web and desktop publishing and digitisation. Management issues cover general management, funds and project management and legal affairs. Chisenga and Rorissa (2001) also propose electronic publishing, digital data management as well as knowledge management as some of the competencies librarians currently require to effectively deliver services to the emerging techno-savvy user population. They emphasise that librarians need to surpass mere library automation and instead embrace technologies to offer superior information experience for the users.

KEY CHARACTERISTICS OF USERS IN DIGITAL LIBRARY CONTEXTS

Many librarianship scholars and practitioners agree that there is an emerging breed of library users which some authors have described as very different from the current users in several perspectives. These character differences are largely manifested through their expectations about access to, availability and retrieval of information; time use; personal efficacy and efforts to enhance their library usage; dependence on emerging ICTs to search, access and use information; acceptance of formal and informal information sources based on a broad definition of "books"; as well as the rewards and challenges of networking for social, economic, political and other purposes (Rainie, 2009; Tanui, 2013).

Libraries all over the world are experiencing a steady growth in the number and interests of this new breed of users. Similarly, they are facing the dilemma of how best to meet their information needs. In Kenya, for instance, Tanui (2013) explains that a new paradigm shift is emerging in knowledge management in academic and research libraries based on reconstructed and redefined user needs as well as a model that views the library as a concept and not a physical place. He further explains that the new breed of users in academic and research libraries in Kenya have developed sophisticated information needs which cannot be satisfied effectively by traditional library services and products. The concerns of the new breed of library users are immediacy, intricacy and interaction. Petros and Rugare (2013) also report that social networking, especially on mobile devices, has enhanced research and information transmission amongst university students in Zimbabwe. On his part, Primrose (2013) recommends that academic libraries should create easy learning spaces which have facilities that enable social interaction to enhance the information experience of students and other users. Aboyade, Oyebamiji and Amusan (2013) suggest that libraries in Nigeria, and indeed the rest of Africa, should embrace new ICT tools and service models not only to meet their user needs but also to attain the standards of world class libraries.

Using the case of Ghana, Laryea (2013) asserts that libraries, just like living organisms, are continuously growing and mutating to fit in the prevailing information and the general socioeconomic environment.

It is evident from the foregoing that libraries are now serving an emerging breed of users whose information seeking behaviour and interests are remarkably different from the past. It is imperative that librarians seek to understand the fundamental characteristics of these users to serve them effectively. Table 1 summarises the key characterisation of the new breed of users currently found in digital library contexts.

INFORMATION SEEKING BEHAVIOUR IN DIGITAL CONTEXTS

One of the outstanding information seeking behaviours of modern library users relates to their relationship with their libraries and librarians. Many studies, as indicated earlier, have found that many of these users will not seek out the assistance of a librarian unless there are obvious indications that available reference help is better than the other options (Katz, 2002). Du Preez and Fourie (2009) also conducted a study which concluded that library users in digital contexts relied less on libraries or librarians to authenticate information but instead validated the information they received through experimentation and informal interactions. This information seeking behaviour confirms the findings of the OCLC (2005) research which investigated the perceptions of library users towards libraries. The key findings of the study were that: 1) A large number of users begin their information searches with search engines, not librarians or catalogues; 2) People who have used both search engines and librarians for information searches admit that both approaches yield results of more or less similar quality; 3) The library is not the first or only stop for many information seekers, and although this is not an entirely new finding, the situation is worse now because more alternatives to the library exist; and 5) Information seekers are not satisfied with the traditional library experience and desire that it should stretch beyond books, crowded and noisy reading areas, limited parking, bureaucratic limitations on the use of resources, need to travel, as well as unfriendly, unavailable and sometimes inadequate library staff.

Table 1. Key attributes of the new breed of users in digital library contexts

Attribute	New Breed of Library Users
Age	Generally young or middle-aged.
Tolerance	Exhibit a know-it-all-attitude and low tolerance for delays in getting the services or products they require.
ICTs	Glorify ICTs, have much trust in ICT tools, generally more knowledgeable in ICTs, and feel the obligation to constantly remain connected.
Level of effort	Instant gratification with least effort; easily bored.
Relationships	Constant links with peers in whom they trust; little relationship with librarians; value feedback.
Library space	Rarely come to the physical library because they are nomadic. However, they are attracted to physical libraries with comfortable seats, space for collaboration, socialising and programming.
Socialisation	They frequent libraries that they find fun to use; they are not generally drawn to the library by its collection per se.
Control	They want to be in charge of their usage; appreciate personalisation and prefer using their own equipment.
Creativity	They are highly creative and prefer to contribute as much content as they consume.
Mentality	Their thought process is in "hypertext", not linear; expect every screen to be a touch screen.

Research evidence has also shown that information users in digital library contexts overwhelmingly prefer informal, human sources when they are looking for information (Case, 2002). They also expect emotional support during their search and tend to return to sources that have served them well in the past (Harris and Dewdney, 1994). This view is supported by the findings of another study conducted by Du Preez and Fourie (2009) in South Africa which revealed that modern information seekers are increasingly relying on interpersonal interaction with colleagues, customers, vendors and contractors for their day-to-day professional and business information needs. In Nigeria, Ukachi (2004) as well as Saleh and Lasisi (2011) conducted separate but similar studies which revealed that interpersonal communication with relatives, friends and neighbours was emerging as an important source of research information. Other studies conducted by Ocholla (1996); Ssendikadiwa (1996) cited by Kakai, Ikoja-Odongo and Kigongo-Bukenya (2004); Ikoja-Odongo and Ocholla (2004); Odini (2005); Ajiboye and Tella (2007); Khati (2009); Adams (2009); Baro, Onyenania and Osaheni (2010); Mnubi-Mchombu and Mostert (2011); Onuoha and Anowiyi (2011); as well as Olorunfemi and Mostert (2012) concluded that library users in Africa are increasingly relying more on their social networks for information than on libraries or librarians. It is important to note that the preferred form of interaction between information seekers and sources, whether human or otherwise, is increasingly digital.

Library users also tend to seek out information sources that they perceive as convenient, or easy to find, rather than the most accurate (Krikelas, 1983). Therefore, they exhibit an information seeking behaviour which involves a kind of skimming activity, where they peruse just one or two pages from an online resource or site and then bounce out, perhaps never to return. A study by Adams (2009) on "Generation Y" students at the Stellenbosch University in South Africa found that they treat the World Wide Web as their information universe; expect to have quick access to information; perceive conventional information searching tools as time consuming and sophisticated; confident in the use of technology to access information; prefer to work in teams, multitask and are tech-savvy. Salwasser and Murray-Rust (2002) as well as Condron, Richards *et al.* (1999) and earlier studies share the same view and reason that digital library users want free and ready access to synthesised information; not just information resources. Similarly, Farkas (2008) found that digital library users would like to have more full-text articles available online so as not to use interlibrary loans, a notion she calls "self-sufficiency".

A study conducted by CIBER (2008), found that the digital library users also exhibit an information seeking behaviour which is perceived as being horizontal, "promiscuous", diverse and volatile. The findings of the study further suggest that these users:

1. Are generally more competent with technology, pick up their skills on the move through trial and error and expect a lot from ICTs;
2. Prefer interactive systems and are turning away from being passive consumers of information;
3. Have drastically shifted to digital forms of communication, such as texting rather than talking;
4. Multitask in most, if not all, aspects of their lives;
5. Prefer info-tainment approaches to traditional information provision;
6. Have limited tolerance of delay in the provision of information services;
7. Find their peers more credible, as sources of information, than authority figures and structures;
8. Feel the need to remain constantly connected;
9. Believe everything is on the web; and
10. Are information format agnostic.

Digital library users are also not just content-consuming users. They also create their own content which augment existing material through annotations (adding tags or comments) or cross-referencing (adding links) within a dynamic and collaborative digital information space (Pienaar and Smith, 2007; Dussin and Ferro, 2009). Searchable tags supplied by the users, and in their own language, could be more useful than those developed through conventional means. Some scholars have also argued that to digital library users, conversations, research and learning never end (Primus, 2009). The users interact and create resources with each other and with the librarians and, thus, blur the lines between the user and librarian, creator and consumer, as well as authority and novice (Maness, 2006). Consequently, they appreciate efforts to empower them to create or manage their own content (Casey and Savastinuk, 2007). Many of them want to create as much content as they consume. Therefore, they want library systems which can support them to share and collaborate in the process of content creation. Such systems should be easy, quick, recognisable and flexible (Pauli, 2008). These users view the library as a platform where user-contributed content is being used to add value, is fun to work in, and has something for everyone (Ayre, 2008).

Digital library users prefer to be given appropriate options for information formats, method of delivery, and fulfilment type, including loan, copy, digital copy, and purchase (Ayre, 2008). These users would also like to be able to personalise their spaces, for instance by choosing the background colours of the website, font sizes and faces, or greetings. Although boundaries are inevitable, these library users prefer experimenting with the widest range of options. Being given options gives these users the feeling that they are in charge of their usage since they relish being in control (Ramos, 2007). It is also a perspective of self-service where the patrons conceptualise, actualise and review their own usage. Basically, digital library users are also described as visual learners; have a low threshold for boredom and memorisation; need customisable learning experiences; enjoy active or hands-on learning; and are hyper-text, non-linear thinkers (Wheeler and Harris, 2006).

These digital information seekers perceive library use as part and parcel of their lives and apply a multiplicity of approaches and technologies to seek and use information. To them, boundaries between social and work information seeking activities are blurred and they apply several different methods of communication to satisfy their information needs. This explains why they are more comfortable with info-tainment than conventional communication. They can play video games, listen to music and use library information, all at the same time. They are adventurous and live on the edge of emerging technologies. Thus, to them, email is dated; Instant Messenger, Twitter, Facebook, YouTube and MySpace are the tools used to seek, use and share information. They also exhibit an expectation or desire to use their own equipment, such as smart phones, laptops and other digital applications. So, they expect the library to have facilities which will enable them to plug in and easily use their own appliances (Primus, 2009; Saecker, 2010). These preferences explain why libraries which provide more social information resources, such as video games, have registered an increment in usage, especially among the younger generation. But again, the same libraries have experienced reduced visits by older patrons (Kirriemuir, 2007).

The library users in digital contexts also appreciate an information experience that is responsive and fuelled by questions, provokes conversation, is built on identity, measures with currency, demands personal investment, and is guided by safely-made mistakes (Warlick, 2010). Significantly, they prefer to remain in constant touch with their colleagues and librarians through myriad communication tools and techniques. They value feedback mechanisms that enable them to provide suggestions and comments about the services and products of the library. So, whether it is rating or reviewing information resources through tagging or responding to user surveys, these library users would like open and seamless communication systems between them (library users) and the library and beyond, encompassing alerts, updates, feeds and social networks (Rainie, 2009). Critically, they also want their suggestions or comments acted on and when the suggestions are not implemented, they would like dialogue on the decision (Casey and Savastinuk, 2007; Kwanya, 2011). Effective feedback mechanisms build relationships with the users and enhance their ability to contribute to and benefit from the library's services. When users understand the library's plans and activities, they fit better with the library's mission and do their part in facilitating its fulfilment (Metz, 2002; Singer and Griffith, 2010).

As explained earlier, the library users in digital environments do not see the library as the centre of their information environment. They rely more on networked information systems, such as the Internet and the World Wide Web. This partly explains why most of these library users now turn to the Internet instead of travelling to the library. However, some librarianship scholars are quick to point out that this apparent overreliance on the Internet, as a trusted source of ready information, may be misguided. For instance, Zimmerman and Tu (2003) explain that these users often utilise inadequate search engines and obviously get a morass of disorganised, incomplete and sometimes inaccurate information. Sadly, they explain, the users seem to be perfectly happy with the results. A better approach, however, would be to balance the use of the different information sources. Librarians in digital contexts should educate the users on how to identify and use credible Internet information sources. Although these users may exhibit a know-it-all-attitude, the librarians should impress upon them the fact that not all the "ready pieces" of information accessible via the World Wide Web and other sources are authoritative, especially on sensitive subjects.

It is also important to observe that information seekers in digital library contexts are accustomed to the notion that "books" and "coffee" go together, just like movies and popcorn. They view the library space as useful for collaboration, entertainment and refreshment. They want information about their friends and submit personal updates to their friends, share events that they could go to, and wish to know what their friends are reading, who their friends know, and what movies their friends are watching. Libraries should, besides the digital spaces, create physical spaces with a warm and welcoming ambiance and decor where users can linger longer. The effective use of such spaces also requires effectual programming to scheduled activities, such as book talks, software demonstrations, discussion groups and performances (stand-up comedies or yoga), which create a platform to engage the users (Dilevko and Gottlieb, 2004; Isaacson, 2006). The greatest challenge in creating these socialising areas is space constraints in most libraries. Nonetheless, some libraries have already begun modifying their structures to accommodate this emerging need (Dilevko and Gottlieb, 2004). But as the libraries take on these new roles, they are apparently admitting that they can no longer attract users with their collections alone. Similarly, debate is still ongoing as to whether attracting more people through social programming would translate to the improved use of the library collections and services. Some scholars have also pointed out that although "coffee" and "books" may go together, they cannot mix together on tables - coffee damages books (Marshall, 1998). Nevertheless, the important issue here is the emerging opinion that library services will soon be established together with other services. Thus, the library will no longer be a standalone institution, but a conglomeration of several entities providing integrated services.

Library users in digital contexts have embraced what some scholars have described as "mobility", drawing them deeper into the digital world to the extent that they feel a sense of obligation to stay connected and cannot afford to be off the grid (Ramos, 2007; Rainie, 2009). They are nomadic and expect services where they are, when they need them. They own mobile devices which have converged technologies, such as video, audio, Geographical Positioning Systems (GPS) and/or wireless Internet connectivity, enabling them to remain connected anytime, anywhere. In essence, the library is where the mobile device is. Whether on the train or in the grocery shop or restaurant, these users can search for and use information from a wide array of mobile computing devices (Morgan, 2009; Tarulli, 2010). It is, therefore, incumbent on the library to deploy services, such as text message (SMS) referencing or mobile search applications and content, which are downloadable on mobile devices, such as iPhones, iPads or Blackberries. Specifically, the library services should take into account the applications, interfaces and connectivity options most of their patrons use. With the soaring uptake of mobile telephony services globally, libraries can no longer ignore these devices. The potential of mobile devices, to extend the reach of the library and enrich its feedback mechanisms, cannot be overemphasised. Already, several libraries in Africa are delivering various library services on mobile devices. For instance, the University of Pretoria in South Africa and International Livestock Research Institute (ILRI) in Kenya and Ethiopia, are using social networking applications to deliver references, provide access to downloadable research publications, and disseminate library notifications, among other services, on mobile devices.

Table 2 summarises the information seeking behaviour of library users in digital contexts.

Table 2. The information seeking behaviour of library users in digital contexts

Information Seeking Issue	Information Seeking Behaviour
Place of library	Neither the first nor the only point of information seeking.
Reliance on librarians	Overwhelming reliance on peers; help sought from librarians as a last resort.
Information validation	Through experimentation, trial and error, and social interaction with peers, friends or friends of friends, among others.
Information sources	Informal, human sources in digital platforms and spaces superseding books and conventional materials.
Level of effort	Least effort; convenient, easy to access and use sources; skimming and bouncing off; and instant gratification.
Information universe	The Internet and the World Wide Web; everything is online; if it is not on the Web then it does not exist.
Searching approach	Diverse, volatile, team work, multi-tasking and "promiscuous"; low tolerance for delay.
Information preference	Synthesised, free, full-text, readily accessible information; not just information sources or links to sources.
Content creation	Strive to create as much content as they consume; original and experiential content.
Technology	Techno-savvy; obligated to remain constantly connected; heavily dependent on technology; exhibit technostress and technolust.
Control	In charge of their own information seeking processes, tools, sources and lexicon using own equipment.
Information space	Digital, boundless, personalisable, customisable, free, interactive, comfortable and safe space.
Learning orientation	Visual learning with low threshold for memorisation; active, hands-on learning.
Information sphere	Hypertext, non-linear mentality; every screen is touch-screen; infinitely federated networks of information pathways.
Mobility	Nomadic; constant access to personal information space and portfolio; the library is where the mobile device is whether on the train, restaurant or church.

INFORMATION SEEKING MODEL IN DIGITAL LIBRARY CONTEXTS

People generally seek information to solve a problem. Consequently, information seeking behaviour begins with the identification of a problem that needs to be solved. This is ordinarily followed by an articulation of the information needed to aid the solution of the problem encountered. The success of any information seeking behaviour depends greatly on an accurate articulation of the information need which is often exemplified by a knowledge gap. People's ability to articulate their information needs is an important facet of their information competency. Once an information need has been properly identified and articulated, an appropriate information seeking behaviour follows. In digital library environments, the time lapse between need articulation and information seeking behaviour is quite short compared to the situation in the physical environments. This scenario is due to the ready access of information sources in digital environments. If the information seeking behaviour is successful, then the seeker uses, disseminates or stores the information found. If the seeker is satisfied, then he/she ends the information seeking process otherwise he/she repeats the information seeking behaviour with adjustments as necessary. On the other hand, if the information seeking fails, the seeker makes further demands on the information sources or redefines the information need and changes information seeking behaviour accordingly. If the process fails after several attempts, then the information seeker may end it. The Figure 1 summarises this information seeking behaviour.

Figure 1. Information seeking model in digital library environments

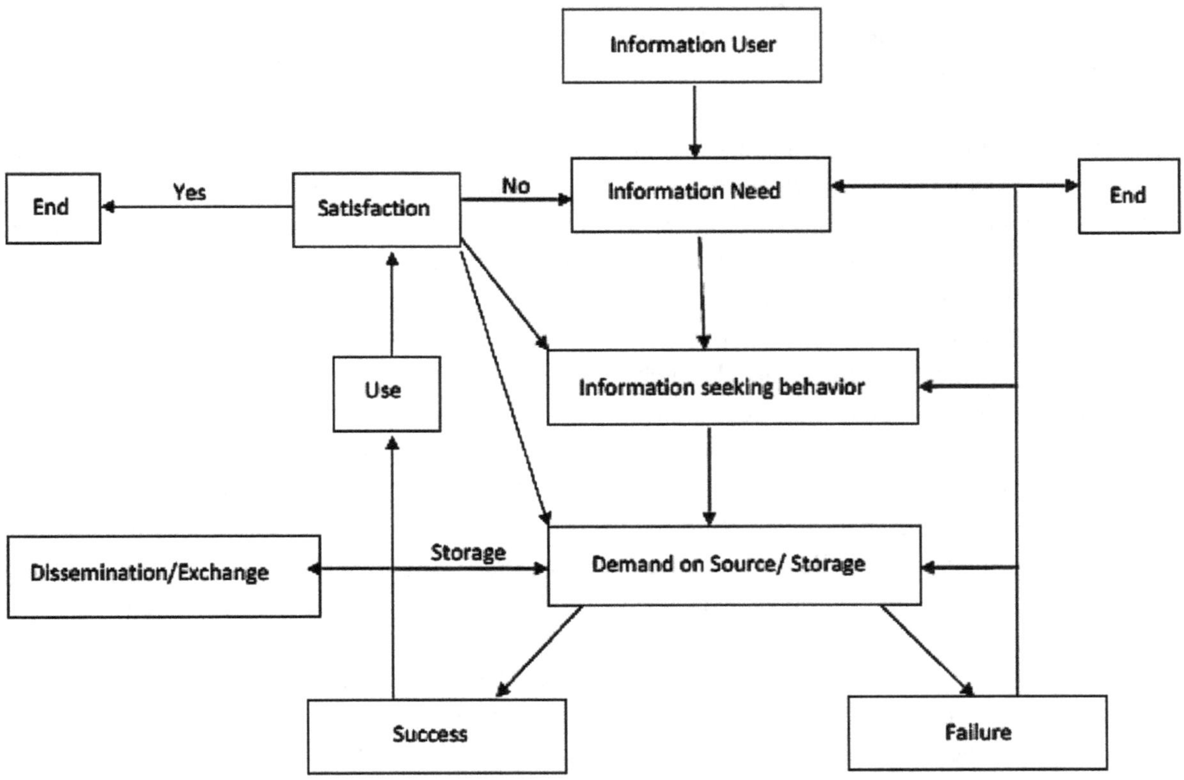

IMPACT OF INFORMATION SEEKING BEHAVIOUR IN DIGITAL CONTEXTS

One of the most important impacts of the new information seeking behaviour in digital library environments is decreasing appreciation of the traditional library. Indeed, a study conducted by Electronic Information for Libraries (EIFL) in 2011 in six countries in sub-Saharan Africa revealed that many libraries are not attracting repeat users any more (EIFL, 2011). These findings underpin the view that many people seem to struggle to find the justification to continue using libraries when perceivably better alternatives exist. This view is anchored on the understanding that many people do not use libraries willingly. Many have to be attracted by good services or prodded by unavoidable events such as examinations (Kwanya, 2011). The study by EIFL (2011) revealed that potential library users visit the library less because they are either too busy to visit the physical libraries or are unaware of the library services in their locale. Given that the modern lifestyle is likely to continue being more demanding and leaving little time for people to do other things, bringing the libraries closer to the users through technology and other means has the potential of increasing library use.

This information seeking behaviour has also resulted in the creation of informal information networks of peers using social networking and communication technology. These networks serve as the first stop for information searching. Information users will only venture outside these networks if they miss the information they need. Often, they do not make effort to confirm information available on the network. They seem to apply a form of bandwagon mentality that if the majority of their peers believe the information as true then it is actually true. Such users lack the patience or skills to confirm the veracity of the available information. In case the information sought is not already on the network, the user would seek it elsewhere and deposit it on the network for later reference and possible use by the peers. Although relying on peers to find relevant information may work in certain circumstances, this information seeking approach may lead to inaccurate information being accessed and applied. This situation may lead to what Stebbins (2015) describes as false certainty fortified by information echo chambers. She explains that an information echo chamber occurs when information is amplified by repetition inside an enclosed system, such as one's Facebook or Twitter feed, where different or competing views are not provided. Thus echo chambers may sometimes have "wisdom of the crowd" which is not credible but abundant. Wisdom of the crowd in information echo chambers inhibits the creation and sharing of new knowledge and sustains the status quo. This situation is exacerbated by the fact that information users in digital library contexts desire instant gratification and are intolerant to any forms of delay. Therefore, they use shortcuts to satisfy their information needs. Such users apply least cognitive effort as they seek synthesised information and do not take time to doubt, query, hesitate or qualify information in the echo chamber.

Another impact of the new information seeking behaviour thriving in digital library environments is the increase in the prevalence of technostress. This emanates from overreliance on technology. The term technostress was introduced by Craig Brod in his book *Technostress: the human cost of the computer revolution* published in 1984 (Brod, 1984; Kupersmith, 1998). He argued that the computerisation of society can change people's attitudes and norms via the socialisation process, since the computer is held in high esteem. He emphasised that people should be aware of the impact of machines so that they control the machines rather than the machines socialising them. He described technostress as a modern disease of adaptation caused by an inability to cope with the new computer technologies in a healthy manner. He explained that technostress manifests itself in two distinct and related ways: in the struggle to accept computer technology, and in the more specialised form of over-identification with computer technology. Kupersmith (1998) adds that technostress is part of the price the modern generation pays for living in a time of revolutionary and dramatic change. Technostress has also been described as a feeling of anxiety or mental pressure from overexposure or involvement with technology. It is any negative impact on attitudes, thoughts, behaviours, or body physiology that is caused either directly or indirectly by technology. One well-documented form of technostress is the escalating problem of information overload, colloquially called "data smog" (Kupersmith, 2003). Technostress can also be associated with technology related performance anxiety (the feeling that one cannot use technology systems effectively or help others to do so), role conflicts (uncertainty about one's role), and disparity between increasing demands and decreasing resources (Kupersmith, 1998). Poor user interfaces, lack of standardisation, networking and security issues, hardware and ergonomic problems may also cause technostress (Kupersmith, 2003). Technostress is people's reaction to technology and its impact on them. It is becoming more prevalent with the increasing ubiquity of technology. Its impact permeates all spheres of life. Prabhakaran and Mishra (2012) also explain that technostress results from poor technological change management. They explain that technostress is manifested by multitasking madness (inability to multitask efficiently), burnout, fatigue, frustration, withdrawal, and information overload.

The digitised, techno-based information seeking behaviour in digital library environments may also lead to technolust which is defined as the constant desire to have the newest, flashiest, fastest, shiniest technological gadget available even if one does not need it. Technolust can also be perceived as a passionate desire for technological fulfilment. Stephens (2008) adds that technolust is an irrational love for new technology combined with unrealistic expectations for the solutions it brings. He emphasised that new technologies cannot, on their own, save any library. He advises libraries not to make new technologies to become the centre of their missions. Technolust drives people to acquire new technologies without careful planning, an environmental scan of the current landscape, and a complete road map for training, roll out, buy-in and evaluation. People exhibiting technolust are in a rush to add new technologies as soon as they hit the shelves just to boost the coolness factor (Stephens, 2004) even if they cannot afford it. Technolust is a form of obsession or addiction to new technologies; it is a compelling desire to get the coolest technology. Technolust is perceived as one of the desires that have nothing to do with people's real wants and needs or the reality in which they live. It is an extreme form of consumerism fanned by an abundance of "must-get" gadgets flooding the market. New terms such as techno-shame, techno-hesitation, techno-banality and techno-phobia have also sprung up to describe behaviour contrary to technolust. The terms generally refer to the tendency to keep using the technology one has, as long as it is still useful, before acquiring emerging technologies. Techno-banality is the extreme opposite of technolust. People exhibiting techno-banality have been described as dunce (technologically) and possessing obsolete gadgets. Such people fear to adventure and experiment with emerging technologies and prefer to keep with the tested.

Since information seekers in digital library environments create some of the content they consume, the growth in the volume of information in cyberspace is exponential. To illustrate this immense growth rate, consider what happens on the Internet in just one minute. Lepi (2014) suggests that in one Internet minute 639,800GB of global IP data gets transferred; 133 botnet infections occur; six new Wikipedia articles get published; 1,300 new mobile users get registered; 20 identity thefts occur; 204 million emails are sent; 47,000 apps get downloaded; transactions worth $83,000 in Amazon sales are completed; 61,141 hours of music are played on Pandora; 100 new LinkedIn accounts are created; 20 million photos are viewed on flickr while 3,000 other photos are uploaded; 320 new Twitter accounts are created; 100,000 new tweets are sent; 277,000 Facebook logins occur; 6 million Facebook views happen; 2 million Google search queries are initiated; 30 hours of video are uploaded to YouTube; while 1.3 million videos are also viewed on the same platform. She also estimates that the current number of networked devices equals the global population and predicts that the number will be double the global population in due course. Furthermore, Rainie (2009) notes that the volume of information has grown drastically; the variety of information, its sources and format of presentation have increased; the speed of information flow has increased; times and places to experience communication media have expanded; the number of information perspectives and points of view has exploded; and people's interest in and alertness to the need for ready information has grown. This change is largely attributed to the fact that digital information is easier to reproduce and distribute. The ease of production enables even the most ephemeral information to be captured and shared (Stahl, 1995). This information explosion has complicated the infosphere making it difficult for the users to identify, select, access, and use authoritative information. This complexity works against the expectations of the users who generally seek simplicity. For instance, Head (2008) explains that students in the digital age are overwhelmed, challenged, confused, and frustrated by the research process, despite the convenience, relative ease, or ubiquity of the Internet. This frustration is perceived to be a result of the effects of information overload and being inundated with resources. Burke (2010) also explains that most library users report having difficulty traversing a vast and ever-changing information landscape. While information overload is an old concept its manifestations in the digital age present slightly different and more overbearing challenges for librarians.

As users become more aware of ICT tools prevalent in digital contexts and as the competition between libraries and other alternative sources of research information increases, the need to promote library services is similarly becoming even more of a necessity than ever. Although library promotion has been an issue of concern for some time, the way it needs to be done as well as the tools to be used have changed. Sharma and Bhardwaj (2009) assert that information professionals must now consider promotion of library services as an important element of modern librarianship. They add that a library, regardless of typology, should adequately promote its services, collection, and physical space. Marketing of the library, its services and products creates awareness of its existence and what it can offer, thus increasing library usage. One of the major promotional challenges facing librarians is the negative attitudes commonly held by the library users. In some settings librarians are considered as lesser professionals whose work is largely clerical (Sharma and Bhardwaj, 2009). Several such stereotypes about librarians exist. Some of these include the portrayal of librarians as socially inept, lacking ambition and failing in other fields of endeavour (Piper and Collamer, 2001). To change this perception, librarians should demonstrate that they are competent and knowledgeable (Sharma and Bhardwaj, 2009) in ways that resonate with contemporary users and their needs. Several library promotion options exist. The Special Libraries Association (SLA) (1999) suggests using library newsletters, current awareness services, word of mouth, library events, timely service and user empowerment as some of the ways libraries can promote themselves. However, one of the unique possibilities libraries can harness to build a good image in this era is Corporate Social Responsibility (CSR). Pachat and Manjula (2011) suggest, for instance, that some of the CSR activities academic and research libraries can engage in include setting up a school library in a remote rural area, adult literacy drives and content development for prison services. Sharma and Bhardwaj (2009) also suggest that librarians should work to create a welcoming environment in the libraries to build confidence of the potential users in the library services. They assert that users will be attracted to libraries where librarians are helpful and driven away from libraries where the librarians are unfriendly or lazy. Another opportunity for promotion of library services is programming. Several studies have shown that library users come to the library for more than books or use of the Internet. Many people can be attracted to the library to listen to poets, meet authors, watch performances, and listen to live musical performances, or listen to public lectures. More users may also come to the library to meet and talk with the other library users and build community. Consequently, the demand for programming is rising (Youngman, 2002). Besides attracting more users to the libraries, programming also puts the library in the spotlight (media attention) and has the potential to attract additional funding and support. All libraries in this era should prioritise the promotion of their services and products.

The need for accountability by libraries and librarians has also increased, especially in light of the fact that funding sources are dwindling. Against all expectations of most institutions, libraries do not seem to be prioritised in many instances and are considered as non-essential compared to infrastructure and corporate staffing needs. As library communities get more complex, institutions seem to be asking that the libraries should justify why they should be entrusted with the stewardship of organisational knowledge management. CLIR (2008) warns that if libraries are not careful, they will be left with "low-margin" services which no other institution would like to offer while leaving the "high-margin" services to the private and commercial sectors. Even research institutions which have traditionally valued libraries now also seem to be asking librarians to justify their position in the research cycle. This trend is critical because such institutions measure their success in terms of their research output and most of the time libraries are evaluated using profit-based commercial metrics. CLIR (2008) further cautions that evaluating the academic and research libraries using a return on investment rather than a public good (social contract) model could drive decisions which are at odds with the stated institutional missions. Indeed, this trend calls for a review of the performance indicators librarians collect and how they are reported. Troll (2001) points out that the traditional approaches to library performance management and reporting do not sufficiently capture the issues of concern to modern library users.

Information seeking behaviour in digital library environments has also let to what some scholars have called the "McDonaldisation of libraries". Larney (1996) explains that the term McDonaldisation is used to describe how the aspects that characterise the American hamburger chain McDonald's are finding their way into and impacting on various patterns of modern society. He identifies the dimensions of McDonaldisation as efficiency, calculability, predictability and control. Manley (1990) explains that the principles by which McDonald's has been known, such as its service to a wide range of customers, cost effectiveness, filling a pertinent need, and having employees who always smile, can find easy application in libraries. Quinn (2000) suggests that the fast-service approach of the McDonald's can be applied in libraries as many more users appear to be less willing to wait for services. He further explains that fast-food joints achieve fast service by letting the customer perform part of the work and points out that the same approach is finding its way into some libraries where users are now expected to self-serve some of the services. Similarly, he explains that "just in time" collection development approach has been influenced by the efficiency element of McDonaldisation. Quinn (2000) further explains that libraries can achieve McDonald's predictability and control attributes through standardisation of services, products, tools and processes. However, Larney (1996) cautions that the application of these principles casually can lead to oversimplification of the information delivery process. He also points out that the McDonald's does not cater for special interests nor does it claim to serve nutritious food. He further explains that the penchant for fast-food efficiency may not apply in academic and research libraries simply because information is not a commodity. He cautions that information cannot be treated as if it was a "large Coke and fries" and points out that effective user-centred information delivery takes longer than assembling the informational equivalent of some "combo" meal.

The prevalent information seeking behaviour in digital library environments has also brought the mediation by librarians into focus. This has given prominence to a new mediation approach known as apomediation. The term apomediation is a scholarly socio-technological concept used to describe the social mediation of information. The term, which originated in the health discipline, is derived from a combination of Latin words 'apo' which means to stand by or next to, and "mediare" which means to be in the middle (Eysenbach, 2008; O'Connor, 2010). Apomediation is an information search strategy where users bypass formal intermediaries but instead of acting completely independently, are guided by peers and web tools to find credible and relevant information (Eysenbach, 2008). The concept of apomediation emanated from the view that intermediaries, as middlemen or gatekeepers, often stand in between the library users and the information they need (Eysenbach, 2008). This situation is undesirable because it restricts direct access to information. Intermediation also affects the quality of the information users receive because it is influenced heavily by the qualities of the intermediary. Apomediation seeks to bridge the gap created by disintermediation, the elimination of intermediaries in the information demand and supply chain, which implies that users may get lost in the vast reservoirs of information available in infosphere. Users who lose their way in the infosphere may end up accessing inaccurate information, leading them to wrong conclusions and application. Apomediaries offer guidance to users to obtain trustworthy information using less traditional methods or sources. Essentially, apomediation is a shift from the reliance on gatekeepers to networked approaches for identifying, locating and using trustworthy information. With the rising popularisation of social networks where content is passed along by users, any user can act as an apomediary or informal knowledge broker, although the credibility and quality of information will vary (Eysenbach, 2008). One of the key qualities of an apomediary is trustworthiness which Eysenbach (2007) suggests is bestowed by the peers and opinion leaders. He further explains that in an apomediated environment, apomediary credibility is more important than the source or message credibility. This concept seems to support the view of the librarians that library users left alone, through disintermediation, may not make the best use of the library systems. Apomediaries do not leave users alone but also do not stand in between them and information. Conversely, apomediaries stand by the users and guide them to high quality information and services without being overbearing on them (Eysenbach, 2008). The application of the advice, intervention and direction of apomediaries by the users is largely optional. Apomediaries can influence action without being there in person or having a stake in the issue; they are peripheral mediators. Apomediation signifies subtle content filtering processes and techniques which lead library users to readily access authoritative information. Apomediaries provide cues and meta-information which enable information users to navigate the infosphere and locate credible information. Thus, apomediaries direct users from valueless information sources through a combination of collaborative and distributed tools and techniques that facilitate learning. Hetland (2011) explains that apomediation involves a voluntary collaboration between experts and amateurs in the generation, location, access and use of credible information. O'Connor (2010) suggests that social media play a significant part in apomediation.

CONCLUSION

The environment in which digital libraries operate is unique. The digital generation of library users who commonly operate in these digital library environments have developed equally unique information seeking behaviour. The key characteristic of this behaviour is the desire to get synthesised information conveniently using the least effort. They are currently exploiting the potential of the emerging information and communication technologies to minimise limitations to information searching, access, sharing and use. Critically, they treat information seeking just like any other current socioeconomic activities they are involved in; it is part and parcel of their daily norms and lifestyle. Consequently, they build and seek the support of online communities to collaboratively create, rate and recommend information necessary for their myriad endeavours. Due to the existing information overload, some of them merely rely on the recommendations of their peers and hardly experience primary information sources firsthand. Importantly, they operate in "fortified" information echo chambers with a know-it-all, impatient and intolerant attitude which further limit their exposure to new information. It is incumbent on libraries operating in these digital contexts to devise and implement strategies to penetrate these echo chambers to deliver information services and products which can be found through the prevailing digital information seeking behaviour.

RECOMMENDATIONS

To meet the needs of this breed of information seekers, librarians should similarly adopt a new service delivery paradigm integrating user participation and the removal of various human, physical and technological barriers to information flow. A good understanding of the information seeking behaviour as well as its determinants is the first step towards the realisation of such a service. In their efforts to unravel this behaviour, the librarians should accept that libraries exist to serve users and not vice versa. Therefore, they should not fear to change so as to accommodate the emerging behaviour of the users even if they do not seem reasonable to the librarians. The librarians must accept the reality that the uptake of traditional library services is dwindling and that it is much easier to reach the library users where they currently are, the way they are, than try to draw them back into the traditional library spaces controlled by the librarians. The best strategy to achieve this is to embrace apomediation whereby the users control their information activities as the librarians stand by to offer essential support at the point of need. For this approach to succeed, the librarians need to empower the users with the essential skills to operate as independently as possible.

SUGGESTIONS FOR FURTHER RESEARCH

It would be interesting to find out the gender influence on the information seeking behaviours in digital environments. It would also be important to compare and contrast the information seeking behaviours of information users in different library typologies. A study on the essential competencies digital information users require to succeed in the modern infosphere may also be useful. Libraries in specific geographical areas may also benefit from a comparative study of the information seeking behaviour of users in different locations.

REFERENCES

Adams, L. E. (2009). Information seeking behaviour of Generation Y students at the Stellenbosch University Library and Information Service. Retrieved from http://etd.uwc.ac.za/usrfiles/modules/etd/docs/etd_gen8Srv25Nme4_7779_1275522114.pdf

Ajiboye, J. O., & Tella, A. (2007). University undergraduate students' information seeking behaviour: implications for quality in higher education in Africa. *The Turkish Online Journal of Educational Technology,* 6(1). Retrieved from http://www.tojet.net/articles/v6i1/614.pdf

Albanese, A. R. (2001). Revolution or evolution. Retrieved from http://www.libraryjournal.com/article/CA178186.html

Anwar, M. A., Al-Ansari, H., & Abdullah, A. (2004). Information seeking behaviour of Kuwaiti journalists. *Libri*, *54*(4), 228–236. doi:10.1515/LIBR.2004.228

Applegate, R. (2008). Whose Decline? Which Academic Libraries are "Deserted" in Terms of Reference Transactions? *Reference and User Services Quarterly*, *40*(2), 176–188.

Ayre, L. B. (2008). The extensible library: library 2.0 and patron 2.0. Retrieved from http://galecia.com/included/docs/2007/LoriAyre_SSP_june8_2007.pdf

Baro, E. E., Onyenania, G. O., & Osaheni, O. (2010). Information seeking behaviour of undergraduate students in the humanities in three universities in Nigeria. *South African Journal of Library and Information Science*, *76*(2), 109–117. doi:10.7553/76-2-74

Belkin, N. J. (1980). Anomalous states of knowledge as a basis for information retrieval. *The Canadian Journal of Information Science*, *5*, 133–143.

Bernal, J. D. (1960). Scientific information and its users. *Aslib Proceedings*, *12*(12), 423–438. doi:10.1108/eb049779

Blazek, R., & Aversa, E. (1994). The humanities: A selective guide to information resources. (4th ed.). Library Science Text Series. Englewood, CO: Libraries Unlimited.

Burke, J. (2010), Discovery versus disintermediation: the new reality driven by today's end-user. Retrieved from http://www.vala.org.au/vala2010/papers2010/VALA2010_57_Burke_Final.pdf

Campbell, J. D. (2006). Changing a cultural icon: The academic library as a virtual destination. *EDUCAUSE Review*, *41*(1), 16–31. Retrieved from http://www.educause.edu/EDUCAUSE+Review/EDUCAUSEReviewMagazineVolume41/ChangingaCulturalIconTheAcadem/158029

Case, D. O. (2002). *Looking for information: a survey of research on information seeking, needs, and behavior*. Amsterdam: Academic Press.

Case, D. O. (2007). *Looking for Information: A Survey of Research on Information Seeking, Needs, and Behavior* (2nd ed.). Amsterdam: Elsevier.

Casey, M., & Savastinuk, L. C. (2006). Library 2.0: service for the next generation library. Retrieved from http://www.libraryjournal.com/article/CA6365200.html

Casey, M., & Savastinuk, L. C. (2007). *Library 2.0: a guide to participatory library service*. Medford: Information Today.

Chad, K., & Miller, P. (2005). Do libraries matter? The rise of library 2.0. Retrieved from http://www.talis.com/downloads/white_papers/DoLibrariesMatter.pdf

Challener, J. (1999). *Information seeking behaviour of professors of art history and studio art* [Unpublished Master's Thesis]. Kent State University.

CIBER. (2008). Information behaviour of the researcher of the future. Retrieved from http://www.ucl.ac.uk/infostudies/research/ciber/downloads/ggexecutive.pdf

CLIR. (2008). No brief candle: reconceiving research libraries for the 21st century. Retrieved from http://www.clir.org/pubs/reports/pub142/pub142.pdf

Cohen, L.B. (2006). A librarian's 2.0 manifesto. Retrieved from http://liblogs.albany.edu/library20/2006/11/a_librarians_20_manifesto.html

Courtney, N. (2007). *Library 2.0 and beyond*. London: Libraries Unlimited.

Dervin, B. (1992). From the mind's eye of the user: The sense-making qualitative-quantitative methodology. In J.D. Glazier & R.R. Powell (Eds.), Qualitative Research in Information Management (pp. 68-70). Englewood, CO: Libraries Unlimited.

Devadason, F. J., & Lingman, P. P. (1997). A methodology for the identification of information needs of users. *IFLA Journal*, *23*(1), 41–51. doi:10.1177/034003529702300109

Du Preez, M., & Fourie, I. (2009). The information behaviour of consulting engineers in South Africa. *Mousaion*, *27*(1), 137–158.

Dussin, M., & Ferro, N. (2009). Managing the knowledge creation process of large scale evaluation campaigns. Retrieved from http://lekythos.lib.ucy.ac.cy/bitstream/handle/10797/13871/ECDL015.pdf?sequence=1

Eysenbach, G. (2007). From intermediation to disintermediation to apomediation: New models for consumers to access and assess the credibility of health information in the age of Web 2.0. *Studies in Health Technology and Informatics*, *129*(1), 162–166. PMID:17911699

Eysenbach, G. (2008). Medicine 2.0: Social networking, collaboration, participation, apomediation, and openness. *Journal of Medical Internet Research*, *10*(3), e22. Retrieved from http://www.ncbi.nlm.nih.gov/pmc/articles/PMC2626430/ doi:10.2196/jmir.1030 PMID:18725354

Farkas, M. (2008). The essence of library 2.0. Retrieved from http://meredith.wolfwater.com/wordpress/index.php/2008/01/24/the-essence-of-library-20/

Fialkoff, F. (2012). Libraries should be what users want - with a little help from librarians. *Library Journal*, Retrieved from http://lj.libraryjournal.com/2012/05/opinion/editorial/owning-up-to-the-future-libraries-should-be-what-users-want-with-a-little-help-from-librarians/

Green, A. (2011). Africa: failure to adopt technology in libraries results in fewer users. Retrieved from http://www.globalissues.org/news/2011/11/11/11841

Gunasekera, C. (2010). Students' usage of an academic library: A user survey conducted at the main library, University of Peradeniya. *Journal of the University Librarians Association of Sri Lanka*, *14*(1), 43–60.

Harris, R. M., & Dewdney, P. (1994). *Barriers to information: how formal help systems fail battered women*. Westport, CT: Greenwood Press.

Head, A. (2008). Information literacy from the trenches: How do humanities and social science majors conduct academic research? *College & Research Libraries*, *69*(5), 427–446. doi:10.5860/crl.69.5.427

Hetland, P. (2011). Science 2.0: bridging science and the public. *Nordic Journal of Digital Literacy* 6(Special Issue), 326-339. Retrieved from http://www.uv.uio.no/intermedia/personer/adm/perhet/dokumenter/dk_2011_special_issue_art05_Norwegian.pdf

Hopkins, R. (1989). The information seeking behaviour of literary scholars. *Canadian Library Journal*, *46*(2), 113–115.

Ikoja-Odongo, R., & Ocholla, D. N. (2004). Information seeking behavior of the informal sector entrepreneurs: The Uganda experience. *Libri*, *54*(1), 54–66. doi:10.1515/LIBR.2004.54

Isaacson, D. (2006). BackTalk: serve their needs, not their wants. Retrieved from http://www.libraryjournal.com/article/CA6396343.html

Kakai, J. M., Ikoja-Odongo, R., & Kigongo-Bukenya, I. M. N. (2004). A study of the information seeking behavior of undergraduate students of Makerere University, Uganda. *World Libraries*, 14(1). Retrieved from http://www.worlib.org/vol14no1/print/kakai_print.html

Katz, W. A. (2002). *Introduction to reference work* (Vol. II). Boston: McGraw-Hill.

Khati, P. (2009). Information seeking behavior of undergraduate students at the University of Western Cape. Retrieved from http://www.slideshare.net/2548233/info-seeking-behaviour-of-students-at-uwc

Kirriemuir, J. (2007). Digital games in libraries in information science. Retrieved from http://www.slideshare.net/silversprite/digital-games-in-libraries-and-information-science

Krikelas, J. (1983). Information seeking behavior: Patterns and concepts. *Drexel Library Quarterly*, *19*, 5–20.

Kuhlthau, C. (2004). *Seeking meaning: A process approach to library and information services* (2nd ed.). Westport, CT: Greenwood Press.

Kuhlthau, C. C. (1991). Inside the search process: Information seeking from the user's perspective. *Journal of the American Society for Information Science*, *42*(5), 361–371. doi:10.1002/(SICI)1097-4571(199106)42:5<361::AID-ASI6>3.0.CO;2-#

Kuhlthau, C. C. (1993). A principle of uncertainty for information seeking. *The Journal of Documentation*, *49*(4), 339–355. doi:10.1108/eb026918

Kupersmith, J. (1998). Technostress in the bionic library. Retrieved from http://www.jkup.net/bionic.html

Kupersmith, J. (2003). Library technostress. Retrieved from http://www.jkup.net/tstress-survey-2003.html

Kwanya, T. (2011). The potential of Library 2.0 for research libraries in Kenya. Retrieved from http://researchspace.ukzn.ac.za/xmlui/bitstream/handle/10413/5025/Kwanya_Tom_Joseph_Mboya_2011.pdf?sequence=1

Larney, T. (1996), The McDonaldisation of information. Retrieved from http://web.simmons.edu/~chen/nit/NIT%2796/96–171-Larney.html

Laryea, K. A. (2013, June 25-29). Mutation is a must: a perspective on collection development for academic libraries. *Paper presented at 2nd Annual International Interdisciplinary Conference*, Catholic University of Eastern Africa (CUEA), Nairobi, Kenya.

Lepi, K. (2014). What happens in an Internet minute. Retrieved from http://www.edudemic.com/internet-minute-infographic/

Limb, P. (2004). *Digital dilemmas and solutions*. Oxford: Chandos Publishing. doi:10.1533/9781780630649

Line, M. B. (1969). Information requirements in the social sciences: Some preliminary considerations. *Journal of Librarianship*, *1*(1), 1–19. doi:10.1177/096100066900100101

Mahajan, P. (2009). Information seeking behaviour: a study of Punjab University, India. Library Philosophy and Practice. Retrieved from http://www.webpages.uidaho.edu/~mbolin/mahajan4.htm

Majid, S., & Kassim, G. M. (2000). Information-seeking behaviour of International Islamic University Malaysia Law Faculty Members. *Malaysian Journal of Library & Information Science*, *5*(2), 1–17.

Maness, J. A. (2006). Library 2.0 theory: web 2.0 and its implications for libraries. *Webology,* 3(2). Retrieved from http://www.webology.ir/2006/v3n2/a25.html

Manley, W. (1981). Facing the public'. *Wilson Library Bulletin*, *55*(10), 762–763, 798.

Marshall, A. B. (1998). *Trafficking in old books*. Ann Arbor: Lost Domain.

Metz, R. F. (2002). *Coaching in the library: a management strategy for achieving excellence*. Chicago: American Library Association.

Miller, P. (2005). Web 2.0: building the new library. Retrieved from http://www.ariadne.ac.uk/issue45/miller/

Miller, P. (2006). Library 2.0 – the challenge of disruptive innovation. Retrieved from http://www.talis.com/resources/documents/447_Library_2_prf1.pdf

Mnubi-Mchombu, C., & Mostert, J. (2011). Information seeking behaviour of orphaned and vulnerable children's caregivers in Namibia. *Library Review*, *60*(5), 396–408. doi:10.1108/00242531111135308

Morgan, E. L. (2009). Technology trends and libraries: so many opportunities. Retrieved from http://infomotions.com/musings/trends-and-opportunities/

O'Connor, D. (2010). Apomediation and ancillary care: Researchers' responsibilities in health-related online communities. *International Journal of Internet Research Ethics*, *3*(12). Retrieved from http://ijire.net/issue_3.1/7_OConnor.pdf

Odini, C. (2005). Information seeking and communication behaviour of Kenya Railways' engineers. *University of Dar es Salaam. Library Journal*, *7*(2), 98–111.

Olorunfemi, D. Y., & Mostert, J. (2012). Information seeking behaviour of law students in a developing country: a literature review. Retrieved from http://www.lis.uzulu.ac.za/research/2012/Yemisi%20and%20Mostert%20SCECSAL,%20UZ,%207.pdf

Pachat, J., & Manjula, M. (2011). Collaboration in corporate libraries. In L. E. Kelsey & M. J. Porter (Eds.), *Best practices for corporate libraries* (pp. 65–79). Santa Barbara: Libraries Unlimited.

Petros, M. F., & Rugare, M. (2013, June 25-29). The impact of social networks on teaching and learning: the Great Zimbabwe University experience. *Paper presented at 2nd Annual International Interdisciplinary Conference, held at the Catholic University of Eastern Africa CUEA)*, Nairobi, Kenya.

Pienaar, H., & Smith, I. 2007). Development of a Library 2.0 service model for an African library. *Proceedings of the73rd IFLA General Conference and Council*, Durban, South Africa.

Piper, P. S., & Collamer, B. E. (2001). Male librarians. *Journal of Academic Librarianship*, *27*(5), 406–411. doi:10.1016/S0099-1333(01)00226-9

Prabhakaran, A., & Mishra, H. K. (2012). Technological change in libraries: the evolution of technostress. Journal of Arts, Science & Commerce, 2(1), 131-135. Retrieved from http://www.researchersworld.com/vol3/Paper_14.pdf

Primus, S. (2009). Distance learning library services: Keeping up with the times. *Distance Learning*, *6*(1), 22–30.

Quinn, B. (2000). The McDonaldisation of Academic Libraries?'. *College & Research Libraries*, *61*(3), 248–261. Retrieved from http://crl.acrl.org/content/61/3/248.full.pdf doi:10.5860/crl.61.3.248

Rainie, L. (2009). The nine tribes of the Internet. Retrieved from http://www.slideshare.net/lrainie/the-nine-tribes-of-the-internet-1555624

Ramos, M. M. (2007). The role of librarians in the 21st century. Retrieved from http://www.slideshare.net/plaistrlc/the-role-of-librarians-in-the-21st-century

Rothman, D. (2006). Library 2.0. Retrieved from http://davidrothman.net/2006/11/30/library-20/

Saleh, A. G., & Lasisi, F. I. (2011). Information needs and information seeking behavior of rural women in Borno State, Nigeria. Retrieved from http://www.webpages.uidaho.edu/~mbolin/saleh-lasisi2.pdf

Salwasser, J., & Murray-Rust, C. (2002). Assessing the need for a natural resources digital library. Retrieved from http://www.istl.org/02-winter/article2.html

Savolainen, R. (2007). Information behavior and information practice: Reviewing the 'umbrella concepts' of information-seeking studies. *The Library Quarterly*, *77*(2), 109–127. doi:10.1086/517840

Sharma, A. K., & Bhardwaj, S. (2009). Marketing and promotion of library services. Retrieved from http://crl.du.ac.in/ical09/papers/index_files/ical-79_73_172_2_RV.pdf

Shuman, B. A. (2001). *Issues for libraries and information science in the internet age*. Englewood: Libraries Unlimited.

Singer, P. M., & Griffith, G. (2010). *Succession planning in the library: developing leaders, managing change*. Chicago: American Library Association.

SLA (Special Libraries Association). (1999). Seven easy ways to promote your library. Retrieved from http://units.sla.org/division/dleg/Newsletter/v5no3_seven.htm

Stahl, B. (1995). Trends and challenges for academic libraries and information services. *CAUSE/EFFECT,* 18(1). Retrieved from http://www.educause.edu/ir/library/text/cem951a.txt

Stebbins, L. (2015). Markers of quality: the role of librarians in everyday life information literacy – peer to peer review. Retrieved from http://lj.libraryjournal.com/2015/12/academic-libraries/markers-of-quality-the-role-of-librarians-in-everyday-life-information-literacy-peer-to-peer-review/#_

Stephens, M. (2004). Technoplans vs. technolust. *Library Journal*. Retrieved from http://www.libraryjournal.com/article/CA474999.html

Stephens, M. (2008). Taming technolust: Ten steps for planning in a 2.0 world. *Reference and User Services Quarterly*, *47*(4), 314–317. doi:10.5860/rusq.47n4.314

Supply and Demand in ARL Libraries, 1986-2011. (2011). Association of Research Libraries.

Tanui, T. (2013, June 25-29). Reconstructing and redefining the university library: the exploitation of underlying library resources. *Paper presented at 2nd Annual International Interdisciplinary Conference, held at the Catholic University of Eastern Africa (CUEA)*, Nairobi, Kenya.

Tarulli, L. (2010). Mobile devices and library catalogues. Retrieved from http://laureltarulli.wordpress.com/2010/06/21/mobile-devices-and-library-catalogues/

Taylor, R. S. (1968). Question negotiation and information seeking in libraries. *Journal of College and Research Libraries*, *29*(3), 178–194. doi:10.5860/crl_29_03_178

Troll, D. A. (2001). How and why are libraries changing. Retrieved from http://old.diglib.org/use/whitepaper.htm

Ukachi, N. B. (2004). Information needs, sources, and information seeking behaviour of rural women in Badagry, Lagos, Nigeria. Retrieved from http://www.unilag.edu.ng/opendoc.php?sno=15750&doctype=doc&docname=$

Warlick, D. (2010). Patron 2.0. Retrieved from http://davidwarlick.com/wordpress/?p=1143

Weigts, W., Widdershoven, G., Kok, G., & Tomlow, P. (1993). Patients' information seeking actions and physicians' responses in gynaecological consultations. *Qualitative Health Research*, *3*(4), 398–429. doi:10.1177/104973239300300402

Wheeler, A., & Harris, P. (2006). Creativity & personalization: freshman orientation for the millennial generation. Retrieved from http://www.emich.edu/public/loex/handouts/wheeler/FreshmanOrientationSlides.pdf

White, M. D. (1975). The communication behavior of academic economists in research phases. *The Library Quarterly*, *45*(5), 337–354.

Wilson, T. D. (1981). On user studies and information needs. *The Journal of Documentation*, *37*(1), 3–15. doi:10.1108/eb026702

Wilson, T. D. (1999). Models in information behavior research. *The Journal of Documentation*, *55*(3), 249–270. doi:10.1108/EUM0000000007145

Wilson, T. D. (2000). Human information behaviour. *Informing Science*, *3*(2), 49–55.

Youngman, D. C. (2002). Re-shaping library service programming: new strategies for the new millennium. Retrieved from http://www.iatul.org/doclibrary/public/Conf_Proceedings/2002/Youngman.pdf

Zhang, W. (1998). Analyzing faculty and staff's information needs and use of electronic technologies: A liberal arts college's experience. *Journal of Education Media and Library Sciences*, *35*(3), 218–241.

Zimmerman, N., & Tu, F. (2003). It is not just a matter of ethics II: an examination of issues related to the ethical provision of consumer health services in public libraries. In B. Rockenbach, T. Mendina, & S. Almagno (Eds.), *Ethics and electronic information: a festschrift for Stephen Almagno* (pp. 119–130). Jefferson: McFarland.

KEY TERMS AND DEFINITIONS

Apomediation: A scholarly socio-technological concept used to describe the social mediation of information. The term, which originated in the health discipline, is derived from a combination of Latin words 'apo' which means to stand by or next to, and "mediare" which means to be in the middle. It is used in this chapter to refer to a mediation approach in which librarians stand by the information users to offer support only at the point of need. It is contrasted with intermediation which implies that the librarians stand between the users and the information they seek and disintermediation which implies the absence of the librarians in infosphere.

Digital Library: A library where the collection is processed and stored in digital formats facilitating electronic searching and retrieval of the same through digital devices such as computers, mobile phones and other hand-held devices. It is sometimes described as "paperless," "virtual," "library without walls," "electronic library," and "bionic library," among other names. Digital libraries only offer services electronically; they are virtual and do not have a physical presence.

Echo Chamber: An environment created when information is amplified by repetition inside an enclosed system, such as one's Facebook or Twitter feed, where different or competing views are not provided. Thus echo chambers may sometimes have "wisdom of the crowd" which is not credible but abundant. Wisdom of the crowd in information echo chambers inhibits the creation and sharing of new knowledge and sustains the status quo.

Information Need: Relevant information which individuals or groups require in relation to a given task. People seek information to understand new ideas and issues; elucidate existing information; confirm information held; elucidate beliefs and values held; and to confirm beliefs and values held.

Information Seeking Behaviour: The conscious effort to acquire information in response to a need or gap in knowledge. It can also be perceived as the process of acquiring, evaluating and using information. It encompasses a wide array of actions which individuals or groups take to identify, seek, evaluate, select and use information to fulfil their information needs. It is how people need, seek, manage, give and use information in different contexts. In this process people normally interact with other people, information systems or tools.

Infosphere: An environment constituted by informational entities as well as their properties, interactions, processes and relations. Infosphere covers both offline and online information spaces.

McDonaldisation: The term used to explain how the aspects that characterise the American hamburger chain McDonald's are finding their way into and impacting on various patterns of modern society. The dimensions of McDonaldisation include efficiency, calculability, predictability and control.

Technolust: The constant desire to have the newest, flashiest, fastest, shiniest technological gadget available even if one does not need it. Technolust can also be perceived as a passionate desire for technological fulfilment. It is an irrational love for new technology *combined with unrealistic expectations for the solutions it brings.*

Chapter 2
Information-Seeking Behaviour of Users in the Digital Libraries' Environment in Sub-Saharan Africa

E.M. Ondari-Okemwa
University of Fort Hare, South Africa

ABSTRACT

This chapter addresses the issue of information-seeking behaviour of users in the digital libraries' environment in sub-Saharan Africa. Information-seeking behaviour may be shaped by the environment in which users seek information. A digital library is still relatively new in sub-Saharan Africa and there is not much known about how the digital library environment may shape the information-seeking behaviour and/or information needs of users. The chapter explores the concept of digital libraries and the nature of the collections and services of digital libraries in comparison to traditional libraries. The chapter also discusses what a library is, the services provided by libraries, and the differences between a traditional library and a digital library. Covered in the chapter also is a brief history of digital libraries. Digital literacy as a factor which may shape the information-seeking behavior of users in a digital library environment is also discussed in the chapter. Information literacy has changed drastically. The digital information literacy that may play a role in socio-economic development in sub-Saharan Africa is no longer the literacy defined as the ability to read and write at a basic level and sign a document. As society is moving from information age to digital age, new definitions of digital information literacy are evolving which include how to access information in digital formats, and how to evaluate information and use it appropriately. Digital information literacy forms the basis for lifelong learning and is common to all disciplines, to all learning environments and to all levels of education. In sub-Saharan Africa, levels of digital information literacy are low due to numerous factors which are also explored in this chapter. Development of digital information literacy in sub-Saharan Africa has been slow compared to the development of information and communication technologies in the region. The chapter discusses the extent to which low levels of digital literacy in sub-Saharan Africa may also be responsible for shaping information-seeking behaviour of users in a digital library environment. The chapter concludes that the major differences between the two types of libraries are mainly to do with technology, rather than a fundamental change in the way libraries operate. This is because digital libraries are still libraries which largely share the same objectives and purposes of the traditional libraries.

DOI: 10.4018/978-1-5225-0296-8.ch002

INTRODUCTION

Digital libraries are still relatively new in the sub-Saharan Africa region and in the larger Africa. It is still not clear to the users of digital libraries in sub-Saharan Africa whether the new models of libraries are the same of different from the traditional libraries. It is equally not clear the extent to which the digital library environments shape the information-seeking behavior of users in sub-Saharan Africa. According to (Wells, 1938) the concept behind digital libraries has its roots in libraries disseminating 'knowledge for all'. Digital libraries have been known to break the barriers of geographical boundaries to give access to information to all domains and communities (Fox, Suleman, Madalli, & Cassel, 2004). Access to information to all domains and communities in Sub-Saharan Africa is a major challenge. Digital libraries may hold hope for users in sub-Saharan Africa for enabling all to access information though they also have their own challenges unique to sub-Saharan Africa.

Information-Seeking Behavior

Information-seeking behaviour as a broad term that encompasses a set of actions taken by individuals or groups to show their information need, seek information, check and select the information to fulfil their information needs ((Pareek & Rana, 2013). Digital libraries largely depend on information and communication technologies. Modern modes of technology have changed the information environment in which researchers access information and work. (Ge, 2010). Ge further argues that the pursuit of knowledge has been revolutionized, mainly through the vast expansion of data accessible via the Internet. There is no doubt that increased knowledge of the information-seeking behaviours and information environment in which researchers access information is crucial to meeting their information needs. Knowledge of information-seeking behaviour and the environment may enable librarians to design information services which may satisfy information needs of users.

In sub-Saharan Africa, the younger generations seem to have more familiarity with information and communication technologies than the older generations. This perhaps may be applicable everywhere in the world. Dresang (1999) thinks that the environment for youth has changed dramatically in the digital age, but to date, the paradigm for studying the information-seeking behaviour of the youth remains static. Researchers must seek out 'with new eyes' productive informal information seeking behaviour of the youth population. Apparently, the digital environment has drastically shaped the information-seeking behaviour of the youth. Dresang contends thus:

Our current research paradigm suggests that adults study information-seeking strategies of youth for the benefit of youth. We conduct research in situations we create to which youth often come compelled as a "last resort," in which youth may be neither comfortable nor competent, and in which we define the terms of success.... adults might more appropriately study the tactics of already-engaged and experienced youth in informal information-seeking situations to predict successful negotiation for all information seekers. (Dresang, 1999, p. 1123)

Digital Library

What is a digital library and how different is it from the "traditional library?" The term "digital library" seems to be a problematic one (Borgman, 2003) in the sense that as yet, there is no universally accepted complex relationship between electronic information collections and libraries as institutions (Lynch, 1993) and it is viewed as an oxymoron, meaning if a library is a library, it can't be digital and if (Borgman, 2003) a library is digital, then it is not a library (Greenberg, 1998). Still, another definition of a digital library is that "a digital library is a system that provides a community of users with coherent access to a large, organized repository of information and knowledge" (Lynch and Garcia-Molina, 1995). A rather popular definition is that a digital library as an organized and focused collection of digital objects, including text, images, video and audio, with the methods of access and retrieval and for the selection, creation, organization, maintenance and sharing of collection it (Smith, 2001).

There is no doubt that the concept of a digital library is new in sub-Saharan Africa and relatively new in other regions of the world. If national and global information infrastructure are meant to serve every citizen, then digital libraries should be easy to understand and even easier to use (Europe and the Global Information, 1994; Computer Science and Telecommunications Board, 1997). This sounds more or less like what the traditional libraries are designed to do. However, traditional libraries and digital libraries in sub-Saharan Africa are not at that stage where they may serve every citizen and/or may be easy to understand and to use. The shift from traditional libraries to the digital libraries is not merely a technological evolution, but a shift which requires a change in the paradigm by which people access and interact with information. Digital libraries are Internet-based. The Internet and other online technologies have transformed the possibilities of what a library is capable of doing (O'Day and Nardi, 2003). As a result, boundaries among sites, tools, collections, and service for information gathering have become less than clear.

Traditional Library vs. Digital Library

What may be seen as a 'traditional' library? Libraries have always been centred in some kind of physical space with physical collections (Harris M., 2012). Over time, the nature of library collections has changed (starting from clay tablets, paper items (books etc.), through to microfilm, tapes, and CDs), but the collections have still remained located in space (Troll, 2002). However, since the advent of modern ICT, libraries started offering services via computer; some of which do not require physical access to the library (Harris, 2012). These services included not just non-essential, but 'nice-to-haves' (like the catalogue becoming online and publicly accessible), but digital *resources,* such as bibliographic databases, first available on CD-ROM and then online, and then full-text databases, electronic journals and so on. The origin of "traditional libraries" becoming "digital" may be traced to this time. In other words, this is when 'traditional' libraries started becoming 'digital'. Some of the characteristics which differentiate traditional libraries from digital libraries as identified by Trivedi (2010) are shown in Table 1.

Sub-Saharan Africa

Sub-Saharan Africa is made up of 48 independent nations, 42 of which are located on the mainland and six are island nations (see Table 2). The island nations include Madagascar, Seychelles, Comoros, Cape Verde and Sao Tome and Principe. In some quarters, Mauritius is generally not considered a sub-Saharan island nation as the ethnic makeup of the country is predominantly East Indian, Chinese and French. However, it is always counted as one of the sub-Saharan African countries.

Table 1. Characteristics of traditional library and digital library

Print collection	All resources in digital form.
Stable, with slow evolution	Dynamic and ephemeral
Individual objects not directly linked with each other.	Multi-media and fractal objects
Flat structure with minimal contextual metadata	Scaffolding of data structures and richer contextual metadata.
Scholarly content with validation process	More than scholarly content with various validation processes
Limited access points and centralized management	Unlimited access points, distributed collections and access control
The physical and logical organization correlated.	The physical and logical organization may be virtually
One way interactions	Dynamic real time dialogue
Free and universal access.	Free as well as fee based.

Source: Trivedi, 2010: http://www.webpages.uidaho.edu/~mbolin/trivedi-diglib.htm.

Table 2. Other emerging characteristics which differentiate digital libraries from traditional libraries

Traditional Library	Digital Library
Emphasis on storage and preservation of physical items, particularly books and periodicals	Emphasis on access to digitized materials wherever they may be located, with digitization eliminating the need to own or store a physical item
Cataloguing at a high level rather than one of detail, e.g., author and subject indexes as opposed to full text	Cataloguing down to individual words or glyphs
Browsing based on physical proximity of related materials, e.g., books on sociology are near one another on the shelves	Browsing based on hyperlinks, keyword, or any defined measure of relatedness; materials on the same subject do not need to be near one another in any physical sense
Passivity; information is physically assembled in one place; users must travel to the library to learn what is there and make use of it	Broadcast technology; users need not visit a digital library except electronically; for them, the library exists at any place they can access it, e.g., home, school, office, or in a car.

The sub-Saharan region has an estimated population of about 800 million (World Bank, 2013). Some countries in the region are very large with large populations. Nigeria for example has a population approximated to be 150 million. Some other countries are small with populations not exceeding 500,000. Cape Verde has an estimated population of 420,979. Djibouti has an estimated population of 486,530. Sub-Saharan Africa is classified as the poorest region of the world (Table 3). Development agencies describe the region as collectively suffering from the legacies of native corruption, interethnic conflicts, overall ignorance of the indigenous populations, violence and perpetual political strive (World Bank, 2013). Life expectance in sub-Saharan Africa is probably the lowest in the world. The region is well endowed with natural resources but still lags behind in economic development. Literacy rates are low, medical care low and technological development lags behind other regions of the world. Power supply in sub-Saharan Africa is unstable to the extent that it emerges as the most limiting factor, being cited by more than half of firms in more than half of African countries as a major business obstacle. Deficiencies in broader transport infrastructure and infrastructure for information and communication technologies (ICT) are less prevalent, but nonetheless substantial in some cases (World Bank, 2013).

Table 3. Sub-Saharan African countries listed alphabetically

Angola
Benin
Botswana
Burkina Faso
Burundi
Cameroon
Cape Verde
Central African Republic
Chad
Comoros
Congo (Brazzaville)
Congo (Democratic Republic)
Côte d'Ivoire
Djibouti
Equatorial Guinea
Eritrea
Ethiopia
Gabon
The Gambia
Ghana
Guinea
Guinea-Bissau
Kenya
Lesotho
Liberia Madagascar
Malawi
Mali
Mauritania
Mauritius
Mozambique
Namibia
Niger
Nigeria
Réunion
Rwanda
Sao Tome and Principe
Senegal
Seychelles
Sierra Leone
Somalia
South Africa
Sudan
Swaziland
Tanzania
Togo
Uganda
Western Sahara
Zambia
Zimbabwe

Source: Library of Congress: https://www.loc.gov/rr/amed/guide/afr-countrylist.html.

The Nature of Digital Libraries

A relatively new development in sub-Saharan Africa and other regions of the world, digital libraries are seen as representing the confluence of many interdisciplinary fields, from data management, information retrieval, library sciences, document management to web services, information systems, image processing, artificial intelligence, human-computer interaction, and digital curation (Candela & Nardi, 2011). The concept has a multi-faceted nature which has led researchers to come up with a variety of definitions as to what a digital library is, in most cases touching on numerous disciplinary perspectives (Borgman, 2000), (Fox & Marchionini, Towards a world-wide digital library, 1998), (Fox, Akscy, Furuta, & Legget, 1995), (Bertino, et al., 2001), (Ioannidis, 2005), (Ioannidis, et al., 2005), (Lagoze & Van de Sompel, 2001). Gonçalves et al. have explained that the lack of well-defined and agreed boundaries of the term "digital library" arises because digital libraries are essentially complex multi-dimensional applications (Goncalves, Fox, Watson, & Kipp, 2004). Ross pinpointed those aspects by characterizing a digital library as "the infrastructure, policies and procedures, and organisational, political and economic mechanisms necessary to enable access to and preservation of digital content" (Ross, 2003). Some of the aspects Ross points out may not be very favourable in sub-Saharan Africa to enable implementation of digital libraries and to enable users to access information without facing many problems. For example, there would be very few countries in sub-Saharan Africa, if any which have policies and procedures in place to guide the development of digital libraries.

Regarding policy, Odedra et al. (n. d.) argue that "in many sub-Saharan African countries, there exists a blind notion that if the more developed countries use the technology and tell us to do so as well, then we should." However, no IT policies or strategic buying plans exist which clearly identify the needs that are likely to bring overall benefit to a nation, or which determine what may be achieved with the available resources. Odedra et al. further argue that some regulatory policies covering procedures for the acquisition of hardware and software do exist in a few places. Such regulations typically mandate centralized acquisition for the public sector and tax private companies and non-governmental organizations in order to discourage imports or to raise convertible currency for the state. Such taxes range from 0% in Mauritius to over 100% in Kenya. However, a number of countries such as Botswana, Zimbabwe, Nigeria and Mauritius have recently taken initiatives to formulate more comprehensive IT policies.

Some of the countries in sub-Saharan Africa do not have steady policies. In the year 2009, the Government of Kenya zero-rated ICTs among other basic goods and services in order to make them more affordable and in particular for mobile technology, expand the subscriber penetration (Omwansa, 2014). The tax break was meant to stimulate the development of the ICT industry, a policy-action that has had a significant effect on the Kenyan economy. Later in 2013, the Government reversed the decision, impacting negatively on the growth of the information and communication technologies sector and on Kenya's role as a leading digital economy in Sub-Saharan Africa.

The information infrastructure in most sub-Saharan African countries is still shaky and largely unreliable. Political and economic mechanisms in sub-Saharan Africa may be improving but not to the extent of supporting the smooth development and thriving of digital libraries in the region. Many governments in sub-Saharan Africa view free and quick access to information as a threat to governments. Digital libraries are supposed to enable quick and free access to information. Among the current digital library implementations, there is a variety in character and type of content. Some are homogeneous collections on particular topics or media whereas others have a heterogeneous character (Ross, 2003). In addition to that, there is a variety also in services offered over digital library content and audience served. All digital libraries are information systems, and they instantiate particular software systems and information architectures. The lack of agreement on the best design of digital library systems reflects, in part, a lack of agreement on the nature, functionality, and architecture of such information systems.

Benefits of Digital Libraries

Traditional libraries have been around for a long time and their benefits are well documented and known. What then are the benefits of digital libraries and how may such benefits shape the information-seeking behavior of users in sub-Saharan Africa? Besides shaping the information-seeking behavior, what benefits may users in sub-Saharan Africa derive from digital libraries? Lesk (n. d.) is of the opinion that so far, digitisation of library information sources has been described as "something that avoids problems." In addition, electronics can offer many advantages to libraries. Such advantages include both better access to traditional materials, easier preservation, and extension of library collections. Bawden and Vilar (2006) see some of the benefits of a digital library as including: *comprehensive* – include everything; *accessible* – everything immediately available; *immediate gratification* – speed of response; *followability of data* – seamless; *ease of use* – single interface; *multiple formats* – text, images, sound.

According to the Digital Library Federation (1998), digital libraries are organizations that provide the resources, including the specialized staff, to select, structure, offer intellectual access to, interpret, distribute, preserve the integrity of, and ensure the persistence over time of collections of digital works so that they are readily and economically available for use by a defined community or set of communities.

Ding (2000) identifies a number of benefits of a digital library including:

1. Digitization means no new buildings are required; information sharing can be enhanced and redundancy of collections reduced.
2. Digitization leads to the development of Internet in digitalized based libraries. As Internet is now the preferred form of publication and dissemination.
3. Digital materials can be sorted, transmitted and retrieved easily and quickly.
4. Access to electronic information is cheaper than its print counterpart when all the files are stored in an electronic warehouse with compatible facilities and equipment.
5. Digital texts can be linked, thus made interactive; besides, it enhances the retrieval of more information (Ding, 2000: 26-32).

Kumar and Rao (2014) contend that digital libraries bring significant benefits to the users through the following features:

1. **Improved Access:** Digital libraries are typically accessed through the Internet and Compact Disc-Read Only Memory (CD-ROM). Digitization of Library Resources and they can be accessed virtually from anywhere and at any time. They are not tied to the physical location and operating hours of traditional library.
2. **Wider Access:** A digital library can meet simultaneous access requests for a document by easily creating multiple instances or copies of the requested document. It can also meet the requirements of a larger population of users easily.
3. **Improved Information Sharing:** Through the appropriate metadata and information exchange protocols, the digital libraries can easily share information with other similar digital libraries and provide enhanced access to users.
4. **Improved Preservation:** Since the electronic documents are not prone to physical wear and tear, their exact copies can easily be made, the digital libraries facilitate preservation of special and rare documents and artefacts by providing access (Kumar & Rao, 2014).

Benefits of digital libraries may be summarized as improved access, wider access, improved information sharing and improved preservation of information. In light of the benefits of digital libraries, it is natural today to find more information being digitized and uploaded into the Internet or Compact-Disc Read Only Memory (CD-ROM) in order to be made correspondingly accessible globally (Kumar & Rao, 2014). Improved access to information and improved sharing of information as well as improved preservation of information all key to information services in sub-Saharan Africa where access to information is very limited.

INFORMATION-SEEKING BEHAVIOR OF USERS IN THE DIGITAL LIBRARY ENVIRONMENT IN SUB-SAHARAN AFRICA

Many factors may contribute to the information-seeking behavior of digital library users in sub-Saharan Africa. Library and information scientists, practitioners and scholars have for some time been conducting research on information-seeking behavior, information behavior and information needs of users. The context of information-seeking behavior and information needs may not be static. If anything, the context of information-seeking behavior has shifted to what Al-Suqri and Al-Aufi (2015) call the "digital planet," a result of which electronic resources have largely replaced print documents. Scholarship in Library and Information Science has recently changed dramatically due to the impact of technology and the changing nature user needs and information-seeking behavior as they adapt to the new information environment (Al-Suqri and Al-Aufi, 2015). Digital libraries may be seen as part of the new information environment that may shape information-seeking behavior of users in sub-Saharan Africa as they adapt to the new information environment in their quest to find information which may satisfy their needs.

The digital environment has led to changes in the creation, storage, distribution, access and delivery of information (Bawden and Vilar, 2006). The digital information environment has changed the way information is created, collected, consolidated, and communicated. Library services have been automated and information services have become electronic. Libraries have to acquire, organize, distribute and preserve information in digital formats.

Library Services in the digital environment have automated and continue to automate library system services for e-onsite resources: CDROMs, e-journals on subscription, e-books, etc. The Internet services Information services: SICT has greatly affected the information environment in which the researcher seeks information. The information-seeking process has remained the same but the tools accessing have changed. Consequently, the information-seeking behaviour of researchers has changed to include new tools and new formats of information. Librarians and other users of information in sub-Saharan Africa must adapt to the changing technological environment to be able to use electronic resources and access tools so as to be able to respond to new user information needs and information-seeking behaviours of users to be able to participate in the national, regional and global information infrastructure. Repackaging of information and information resources sharing activities have all changed. Interlibrary loans and document delivery are now done differently in a digital library environment.

The changes which have taken place in the information environment notwithstanding, the concerns of researchers, scholars and practitioners in the field of information-seeking behavior largely remain the same: to understand and build knowledge about the needs of information seekers and the ways in which they think and behave in the process of meeting their information needs (Al-Suqri and Al-Aufi, 2015).

The essence of understanding and building knowledge about needs of information seekers is to develop information systems, services, tools and resources which may facilitate information searching, transfer, sharing and retrieval. Suffice to say that digital libraries in sub-Saharan Africa and other regions of the world require information systems, services, tools and resources which may enable users to share, access, transfer and retrieve information with ease.

According to Wilson (1999), information-seeking behaviour arises as a consequence of a need perceived by an information user, who, in order to satisfy that need, makes demands upon formal or informal information sources or services, which result in success or failure to find relevant information. If successful, the individual then makes use of the information found and may either fully or partially satisfy the perceived need – or, indeed, fail to satisfy the need and have to repeat the search process. Wilson's (1999) model in Figure 1 shows that part of the information seeking behaviour may involve other people through information exchange and that information perceived as useful may be passed to other people, as well as being used (or instead of being used) by the person himself or herself.

Ellis's (1989) model framework of information-seeking behaviour is based on empirical research, initially among social scientists, but subsequently tested in other groups, which included academic researchers (Ellis, 1993), physicists and chemists (Ellis, Cox, & Hall, 1993), and engineers and scientists in an oil company (Ellis and Haugan, 1997). The model framework has also been tested by other researchers studying social scientists (Meho and Tibbo, 2003), web users in industry (Choo, Detlor & Tumbull, 2000) and lawyers (Makri, Blandford and Cox, 2008a, b). Ellis explained that the complexities of information behaviour could be described by a small number of different types of activity:

Figure 1. Information-seeking behavior
Source: Wilson, 1999: 251.

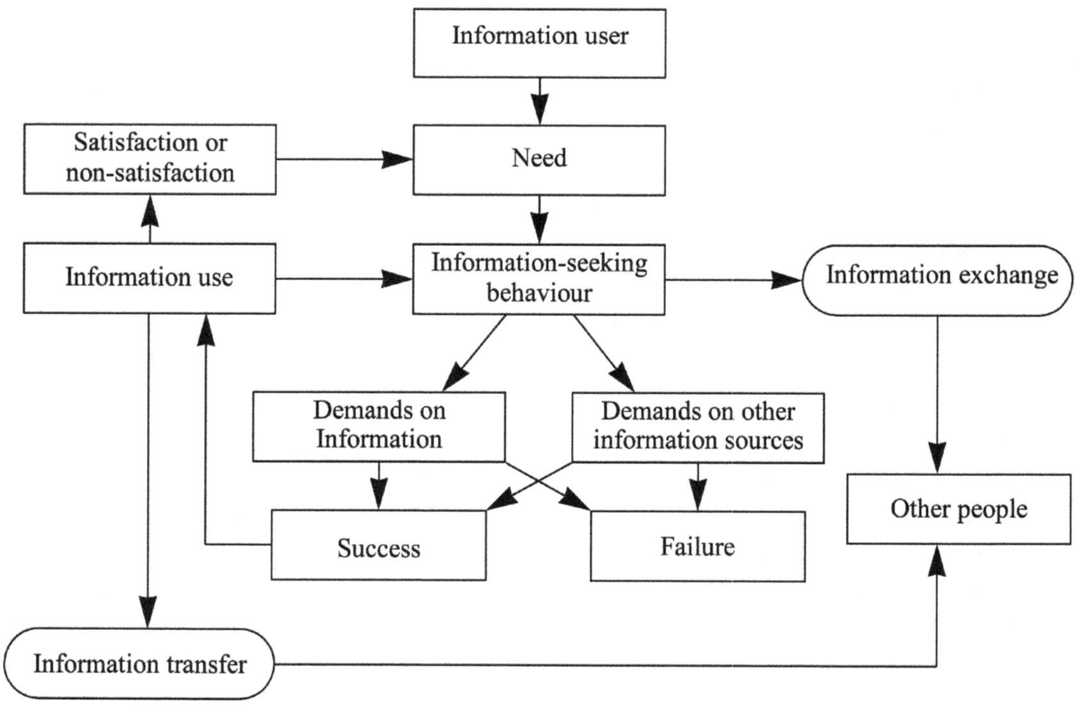

- **Starting:** The initial activities undertaken when seeking information on a topic.
- **Chaining:** Following up references cited in sources consulted (backward chaining), or identifying material that cites those sources (forward chaining).
- **Browsing:** Semi-directed or semi-structured searching in an area of potential interest.
- **Differentiating:** Filtering sources by judging their quality, relevance and other characteristics.
- **Monitoring:** Maintaining awareness of developments in a field of interest.
- **Extracting:** Systematically searching through a source to identify relevant material.

After the initial framework had been described (Ellis, 1989), Ellis identified additional activities, notably "verifying" (checking the accuracy of information) and "ending" (completing information-seeking activities) (Ellis, Cox and Hall, 1993). Ellis refers to his behavioural model as "the relation between these characteristics or components. These can interact in various ways in different information-seeking patterns. It does not represent a set of stages or phases that any or all researchers follow when seeking information" (Ellis, 2005). The model is intended to describe the information-seeking activities of individuals. As such, the model does not in any way include the role and activities of information providers. Nor does it consider the individual's information needs or the context, such as work environment, in which such needs would arise.

There may be no doubt that availability of electronic access to information has brought major changes to human information-seeking behaviour-related to sources and services and their use. Such changes are so drastic that library and information professionals have been prompted to study information-seeking behaviour, and its place in the process of accessing information.

Krikelas (1983) identifies the elements of user studies and presents them as unified concepts within a model of information-seeking behaviour. The concept of information-seeking behaviour, information needs, information gathering, information giving and source preference are discussed. The user Information seeking behaviour and the user characteristics in seeking information are two entities. These two entities are studied and seem to emphasize on the correlation of the two entities in information-seeking behaviour study conducted by Sridhar (1987). Sridhar (1989) examined various aspects of information-seeking behaviour which included the motives and purposes of seeking information, nature and type of information sought, delegation of information gathering work, and the time spent on in gathering information.

Marchionini (1995) explains the concept of information seeking behaviour and the changing information environment. Bates (1996) conducted a survey on decades of research on information needs and information-seeking behaviour. Findings of the survey showed that in the 1950s and the 1960s, the emphasis was on the information needs of scientists and engineers. In the 1970s, the needs shifted to the social sciences and humanities.

The information seeking is not restricted with the libraries only but is also seen in the local council offices, professional people, post office, advice agencies, family and friends depending on the information they need to seek. Marcella and Baxter (1999b) report the results of their survey of information needs and information seeking behaviour of a national sample of the UK population. The major findings include that majority of respondents had sought information in the past and that an even greater number predicted a future need for information. This shows the trend towards the new technology to access the information.

The World Wide Web is a tool for partial information gathering and learning for students. Fidel et al. (1999) conducted an analysis on web searching behaviour of high school students. In their findings, they point out that the web can be envisioned through user training on web resources and systems design which accommodates users' information seeking and searching behaviour. Searching the World Wide Web was the principal Internet activity while use was generally conservative in character.

Nicholas, Huntington, Willians and Dobrowolski (2004) conducted a study on the impact of the Internet on information seeking in the British Media. The focus was largely on the newspapers. They surveyed the Journalists and Media Librarians. They concluded that the web publishing had made many changes in the information access process. There are two main platforms used for searching the Web – directories and search engines. Green (2000) explored the relationship between Web publishing and information retrieval technologies. Most of the libraries have their sites to explain about library resources, products and services. The level of end user satisfaction with information technology (IT) has widely been accepted as an indicator of IT success. Mahmood and Burn (2000) focused on the relationships between end user satisfaction and some of the variables such as perceived usefulness, ease of use, user expectations, user attitude towards information systems (IS) in widely divergent settings and the user skills as shown in Figure 2.

All digital library service providers need strategies to cope up with this diversity. Some, if not virtually all of the factors identified by Mahmood et al. (2000) Mahmood, Burn, Geornoets, & Jacquez, 2000) as determining as affecting IT end-user satisfaction may be responsible for shaping information-seeking behaviour of digital library users in sub-Saharan Africa. Factors like user expectations, user experience,

Figure 2. Factors affecting IT end-user satisfaction
Source: Mahmood et al., 2000: 753

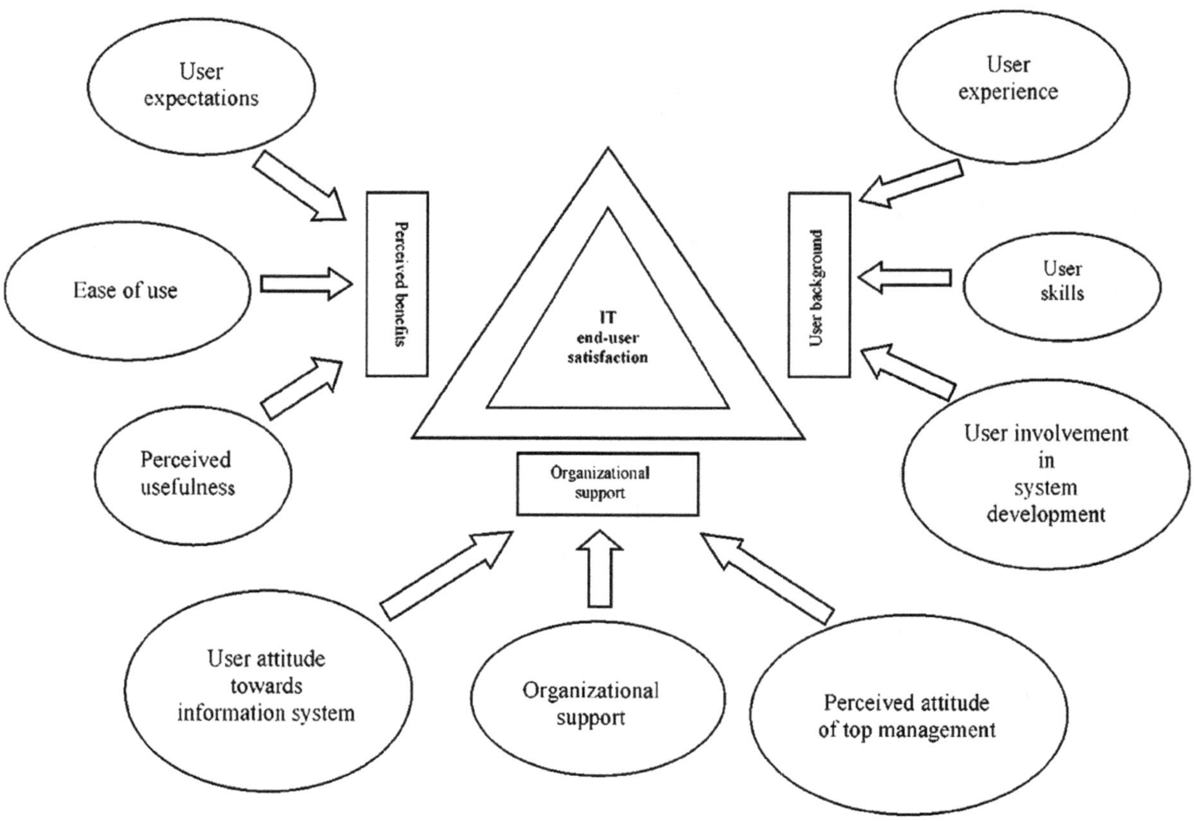

user skills, user involvement in system development, perceived attitude of top management may shape the information seeking behaviour of digital library users in sub-Saharan Africa. Many users are not skilled; they are not involved in system development and may not always find it easy to use the system. Electronic journals may be largely seen as forming part of the digital library. Eason, Richardson, & Yu (2000) also analyse the patterns of use of electronic journals (Hargittai, 2001).

In sub-Saharan Africa, members of the general user population lack the basics of surfing the Web. Sub-Saharan Africa's army of Internet users is still a relatively small one at 12 percent of the total population, and it remains very focused on immediately practical, low-cost, mobile web applications (TNS, 2012). However, significant opportunities exist for organisations that can adapt digital communications strategies to fit this pattern of web use. Even with that, the ordinary users barely know what a back button is and thus find it incredibly hard moving from screen to screen. In sub-Saharan Africa, many users don't know about search engines and solely rely on functions of their browsers or Internet service providers. Hanani and Frank (2000) (Hanani & Frank, 2000) define a search engine as an interface/tool that enables the search engine clients to launch a basic search on the search engine's database and get back a list of web pages of (supposedly) relevant resource URLs, or to recursively descend the branches of the search engine's directory in search of sites of interest. Hanani and Frank (2000) closely link search engines to digital libraries as shown in Figure 3.

Many users in sub-Saharan Africa face problems entering valid search terms. Invalid search terms yield no results and a user may get frustrated to the extent of giving up on conducting a search on the Internet. In sub-Saharan Africa, many users happen to be inexperienced Internet users who are unable to distinguish between a browser Address/Location bar and a search engine text input. Inexperience Internet users asked for example to visit "www.foo.com", might go to the Yahoo! home page and enter "www.foo.com" into the Yahoo search engine (Fluid Dynamics Software Corperation, 2015). This causes confusion when the given site is not in the search index; the users often report that "the site is not coming up". Some respondents also had a hard time entering valid search terms.

Figure 3. Relationship between search engines and digital libraries
Source: Hanani and Frank, 2000: http://u.cs.biu.ac.il/~ariel/download/ird665/kyoto.pdf.

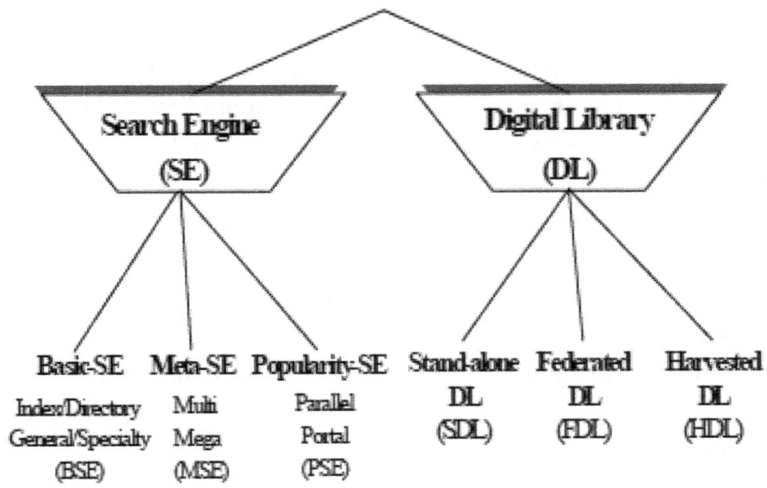

In a study conducted by Hargittai (2001), it was found out that one recurring mistake was entering multiple term queries without any spaces. Respondents to the study seemed to believe that it was not necessary to use spaces on the Web, thus the exclusion of spaces in between search terms. Some other respondents typed search terms in the location bar itself. This kind of information-seeking behaviour is quite common among users of digital libraries in the sub-Saharan Africa region. However, given that most browsers now automatically redirect those terms into a search engine, this seems to cause fewer serious problems among users of digital libraries in sub-Saharan Africa. In general, Hargittai discovered that young people (late teens and twenties) had a much easier time getting around online than their older counterparts (whether people in their 30s or 60s). Hargatti's finding collaborates with findings by Appelbaum (1990); Brosnan (1999); Harris & Davison (1999) that according to technology adoption theory and research on technology use, one of the factors normally used to profile individuals is age. However, Davis (1989) does not totally agree with age as an absolute determinant of user information seeking behaviour. Age may be a determinant of information seeking behaviour of users in sub-Saharan Africa. Users born before information technology was common place in sub-Saharan Africa may not be very comfortable accessing information in a digital library environment.

Other factors used to profile individuals' information seeking behaviour include – education level (Bramley, 1989; Bunning, 1992; Mullen & Lyles, 1993; Alavi, 1994; Davis, 2000; Piccoli, Ahmad, & Ives, 2001) and gender (Agarwal, Krudys, & Tanniru, 1997; Gefen & Straub, 1997; Venkatesh & Morris, 2000; Ono & Zavodnty, 2003). Culture may also influence a user's information seeking behaviour as it may determine acceptable usage of the technology and perceived reliability (Walshman & Sahay, 1999; Walshman, 2002; Kim, 2003; Rose, Evaristo, & Straub, 2003; Anandarajan, Igbaria, & Anakwe, 2000; Venkatesh & Morris, 2000). Gender may also influence the information seeking behavior of users in a digital library environment (Gefen et al., 1997; Gefen, 2003; Legris, Ingham, & Collerette, 2003). There has also been the thinking that access could perhaps be the most accepted determinant of individual use and perhaps a major determinant of information seeking behaviour of users in digital library environment (Anandarajan, Igbaria, & Anakwe, 2000; Majchrzak et al., 2000; Agarwal & Venkatesh, 2002). Access to information in sub-Saharan Africa is a major issue. Access refers to the breaking of long-standing information barriers, bringing entrée to a wide diversity of opinion and opportunity (Dresang, 1999). The digital environment may facilitate or inhibit access. Kibirge and DePalo (2001) look at access to digital library remote collections as a perennial problem similar to earlier online public access online catalogues (OPACs) connections via Gopher, the end-user will be faced the idiosyncrasies of the system to which he or she connects. Kibirige and DePalo explain that when utilizing electronic resources at the local library, one may have a degree of hand holding which may have the luxury of either voice or e-mail. The remote site identifies the user as "external" and by definition not entitled to human intervention type of help, unless done by special arrangement. In addition, remote site digital collections have a "transience element" which the end-user should be made aware of. Frequent users of the Internet would probably discover through trial and error and experience that some material on remote links have a way of disappearing without apparent notice to external users. The onus will be on the host library to explain the vicissitudes of external digital collections to its users during training sessions. In sub-Saharan Africa, majority of users lack adequate skills to enable them navigate through the digital library when attempting to access information. Training of users is rare and not guaranteed, making access even more complicated.

Language barrier is another major problem that people ordinary users face in searching for, retrieving, and understanding multilingual collections on the Internet (Bian & Chen, 2000) (Bian & Chen, 2000).

It is accepted that the Internet and digital libraries make available heterogeneous collections in various languages. They make available many useful and powerful information dissemination services. However, about 80 percent of Web sites are in English and about 40 percent of Internet users do not speak English (Grimes, 1996) (Grimes, 1996). Language barrier becomes the major problem in searching, retrieving, and understanding materials in different languages. Most residents of sub-Saharan Africa who would be ordinary users of digital libraries still speak their native tongue, even if they also understand certain European languages like French, English, Spanish, etc. or/and live in nations that have "English" or "French" as their official language (Phil, 2014) (Phil, 2014). Although there are thousands of languages spoken in SSA, the historical setting and a need to adopt a common language in a country, often, European origin language, such as English, French or Portuguese is used as an official language (Hayashi, 2013) (Hayashi, 2013). Even to the extent that residents of sub-Saharan Africa can understand English, French, etc., they almost always learned such languages as a second language, and have a better grasp on their tribal language. Figure 4 shows the distribution languages adopted as official languages in sub-Saharan Africa (English, French and Portuguese).

It is all about acceptance and ease of using technology. Research has shown that individuals' perceptions about a technology influence their acceptance and subsequent adoption of the technology. The key constructs for examining individuals' perceptions in past adoption studies have been perceived usefulness and perceived ease of use (Rose & Straub, 1998; Grover & Rammanlal, 1999; Venkatesh, 1999; Gefen, Karahana and Straub, 2003). These two factors are taken from the Technology Acceptance Model (TAM),

Figure 4. Map of official languages in Sub-Saharan Africa
Source: Hayashi, 2013: http://iussp.org/sites/default/files/event_call_for_papers/LongAbstract%20iussp1308%20MobilitySSA%20Reiko%20Hayashi130813.pdf.

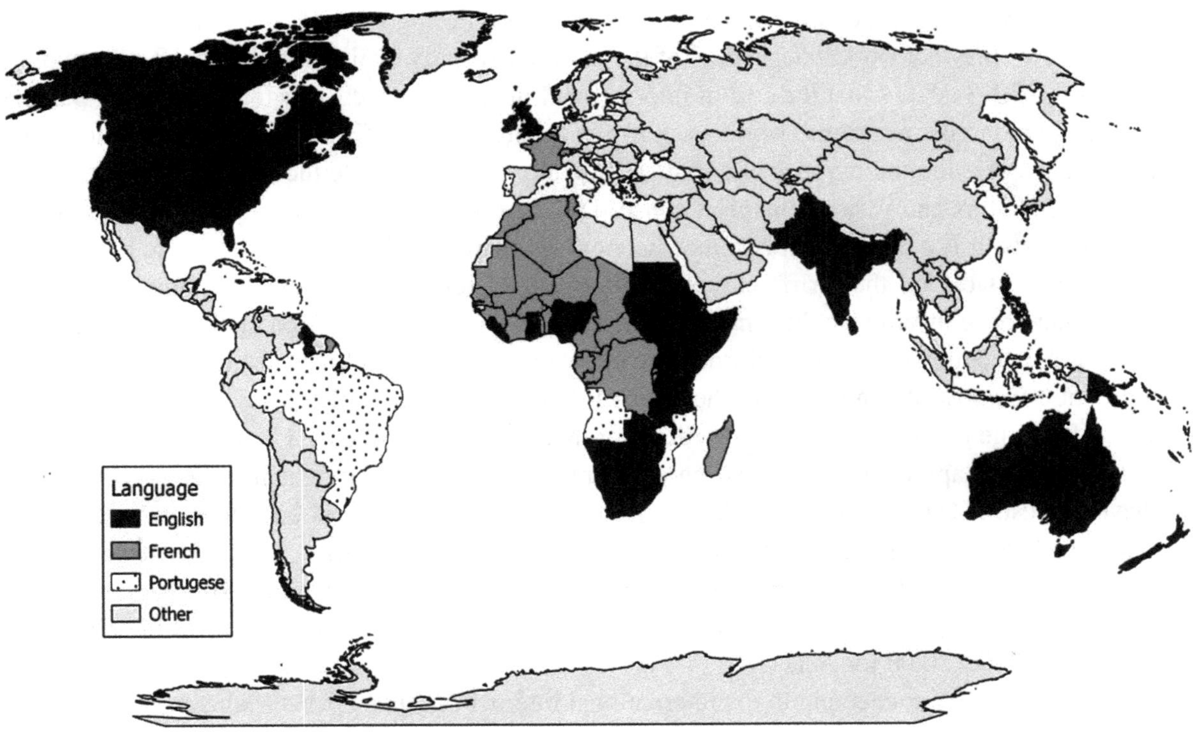

developed by Davis (1989), and having its theoretical underpinnings in the Theory of Reasoned Action (Davis, 1989). TAM specifies causal linkages between two key sets of constructs:

1. Perceived Usefulness (PU) and Perceived Ease of Use (PEOU); and
2. Actual usage behaviour (U) (Davis, 1989).

PU is defined as the user's 'subjective probability that using a specific application system will increase his or her job performance within an organization. Some of this is clearly based on comfort with the technology they are using and not necessarily based on elaborate techniques they have mastered specifically with respect to the Web. In a study conducted by Meso, Musa, & Mbarika (2005) on consumer use of mobile information and communication technology in sub-Saharan Africa, many factors which may also affect the information seeking behaviour of digital library users were identified. Some of the factors are those which have been identified by other scholars as being responsible for the information seeking behaviour of users of digital libraries. The major factors Meso, Musa & Mbarika (2005) identified as shown in Figure 5 include level of education, age, gender, culture, perceived technology reliability, accessibility, perceived ease of use and perceived usefulness of ICTs. In sub-Saharan Africa, ordinary users and other mobile technologies would also find it prestigious accessing information through digital libraries and other related mobile information and communication technologies.

SOME CHALLENGES TO ACCESSING INFORMATION THROUGH DIGITAL LIBRARIES IN SUB-SAHARAN AFRICA

It may not look like there are any challenges confronting users of digital libraries in sub-Saharan Africa, but there are several challenges. One of the major challenges is the high cost of connecting to the Internet. Digital libraries may not work independent of the Internet. A study by the International Telecommunication Union (2013) shows that the cost of international Internet connection is too high in sub-Saharan Africa compared to the rest of the world as shown in Figure 6. The ITU (2013) reports that the market is in the hands of a limited number of commercial groups which include the major operators, former incumbent operators and various financial consortia. Censorship and tight regulations may contribute to the high costs. It is a market that is somewhat non-transparent and monopolistic. There is very little information available on the tariffs charged in this market for leasing available bandwidth. This is more so when those in authority become interested parties in companies which facilitate the leasing of bandwidth. Such companies would allocate free or next to free shares to those in authority and nobody may question the cost of connecting to the Internet. Not "very friendly" companies may altogether be excluded from the deals made secretly by denying them operating licenses. Competition may also be stifled by delaying approval and processing of licenses for companies in which those in authority do not have interest. ITU (2013) has used data collected from some incumbent operators, Internet service providers and national regulatory authorities to draw a map showing charges for leasing bandwidth on the SAT 3 submarine cable. In sub-Saharan Africa, the cost for leasing bandwidth on the SAT 3 is shown as USD 5000.00 compared to the North America and Europe, where the cost is shown as USD 2,5 and a maximum of USD 30.00 for Asia.

Overall, the cost of connecting to the international Internet is highest in sub-Saharan Africa.

Figure 5. Factors influencing information seeking behaviour of digital library users in SSA
Source: Meso, Musa & Mbaruka, 2005:122.

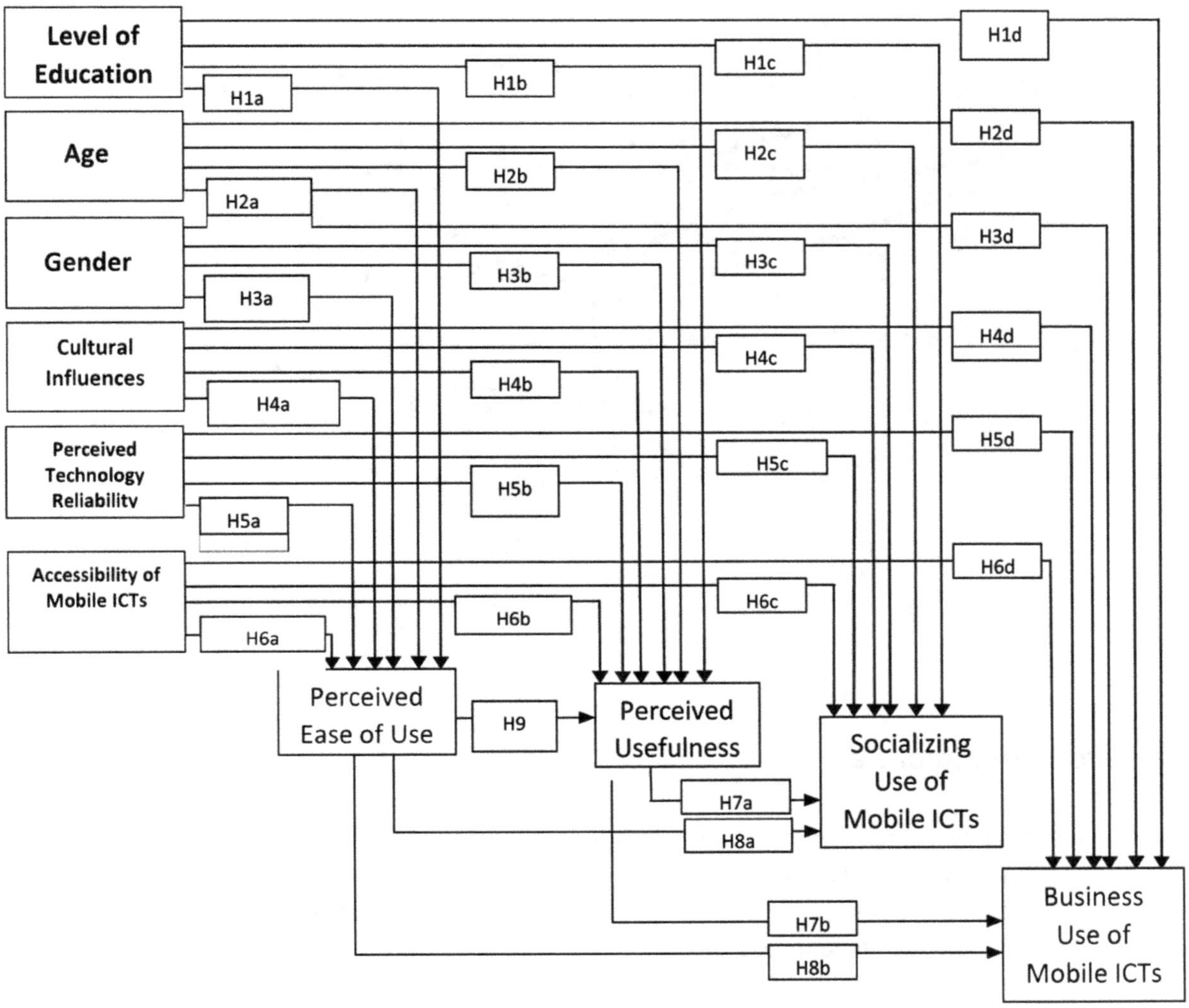

Building Digital Libraries

Building a digital library in sub-Saharan Africa is easier said than done. The optimism and hype from the early 1990's has been replaced by a realization that building digital libraries will be a difficult, expensive, and long-term effort (Lynch & Garcia-Molina, 1995). Creating effective digital libraries in sub-Saharan Africa may not be an easy task. The integration of digital media into traditional collections will not be straightforward, like previous new media (e.g., video and audio tapes), because of the unique nature of digital information--it is less fixed, easily copied, and remotely accessible by multiple users simultaneously. Some the more serious issues facing the development of digital libraries are outlined below

Figure 6. Cost of connecting to the international Internet in different regions of the world
Source: ITU, 2013: https://www.itu.int/en/ITU-D/Regulatory-Market/Documents/IIC_Africa_Final-en.pdf.

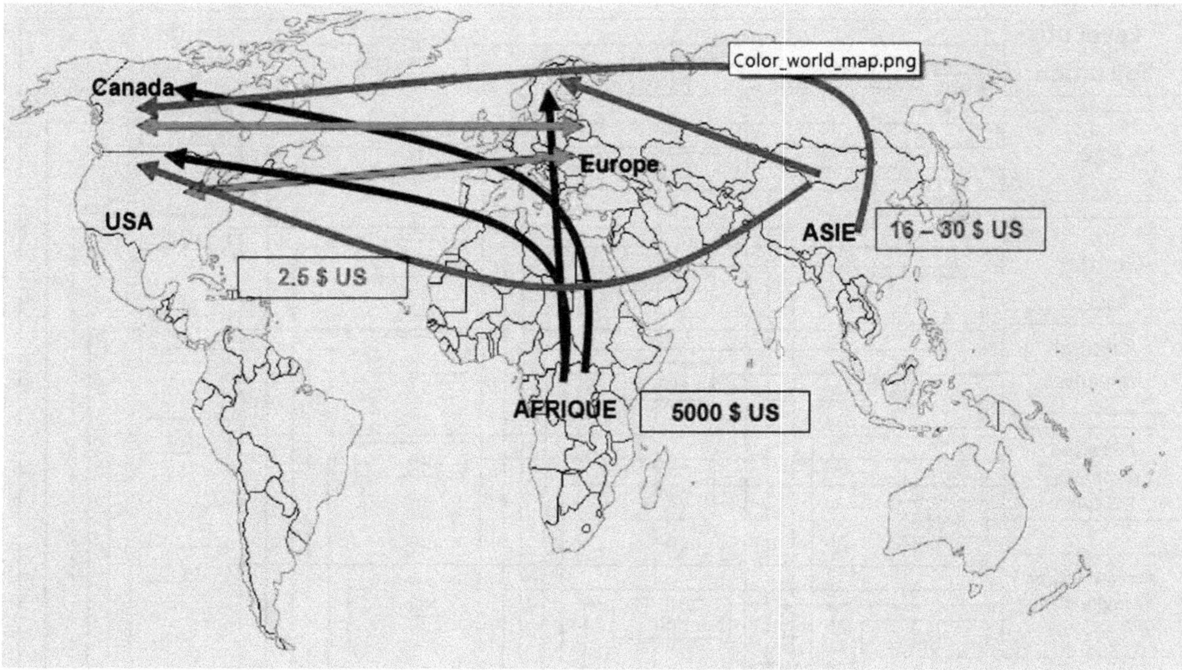

Technical Architecture

Cleveland (1998) identifies technical architecture as a major challenge to establishing a digital library. The first issue is that of the technical architecture that underlies any digital library system. Libraries may need to enhance and upgrade current technical architectures to accommodate digital materials. The architecture will include components such as:

- High-speed local networks and fast connections to the Internet – in most sub-Saharan African countries, Internet connections are very slow.
- Relational databases that support a variety of digital formats.
- Full text search engines to index and provide access to resources.
- A variety of servers, such as Web servers and FTP servers.
- Electronic document management functions that will aid in the overall management of digital resources.

(Cleveland, 1998) Cleveland (1998) points out that one important thing about technical architectures for digital libraries is that they won't be monolithic systems like the turn-key, single box OPAC's with which librarians are most familiar. Instead, they will be a collection of disparate systems and resources connected through a network, and integrated within one interface, most likely a Web interface or one of its descendants. For example, the resources supported by the architecture could include:

- Bibliographic databases that point to both paper and digital materials.
- Indexes and finding tools.
- Collections of pointers to Internet resources.
- Directories.
- Primary materials in various digital formats.
- Photographs.
- Numerical data sets.
- Electronic journals.

Though these resources may reside on different systems and in different databases, they would appear as though there were one single system to the users of a particular community.

Expectations of Users

This is yet another challenge of establishing and running digital libraries in sub-Saharan Africa to the satisfaction of users. Boawden and Vilar (2006) suggest that typical expectations of digital library services include:

- **Comprehensive:** Include everything;
- **Accessible:** Everything immediately available;
- **Immediate Gratification:** Speed of response;
- **Followability of Data:** Seamless;
- **Ease of Use:** Single interface;
- **Multiple Formats:** Text, images, sound.

These expectations and capabilities are certainly not expected from conventional or a digital library services in sub-Saharan Africa in the near future. The reason is clear. Expectations of digital libraries are strongly colored by experience with the ubiquitous digital information environment, the World Wide Web. Fast and Campbell (2004) put it thus:

Web searching is shaping user expectations of what an information retrieval system looks like, how it behaves, and how to interact with it… [Digital libraries] are now being used by people who have extensive experience on systems that require almost no training, and which produce immediate, if not completely satisfying, results. (Fast and Campbell, 2004: 138)

These expectations and several more others can be a major challenge to digital libraries in sub-Saharan Africa. Users may expect the digital library to meet all their information needs they would expect information to be delivered in all formats, information to be immediately accessible through simple searching, etc. It is unrealistic for a digital library in sub-Saharan Africa to meet the expectations. The expectations are far too high and unrealistic.

One may summarize major challenges of digital libraries in sub-Saharan Africa as:

- Shrinking library budgets and sometimes non-existent of library budgets that force the library management to struggle to maintain a minimum standard of services, leaving no room for new ventures and developments.
- Lack of financial support specifically for establishing and maintaining digital libraries as well as conducting research and development.
- Absence of fully developed and up to date OPACs, and little access to online information resources – online databases, e-journals, etc.
- Poor information infrastructure – computers and networks.
- Poor facilities for access to ICT, especially the Internet.
- Unnecessarily stringent government and institutional policies on access to the Internet.
- Lack of trained manpower.
- Poor information and digital literacy rates which lead to lack of appreciation of modern information services and their use.

Digital Divide

The digital divide is the gap between those communities that have access to the Internet and those communities that do not. Often, this gap falls along racial, economic, and geographical lines (Digital divide basics fact sheet, 2015) (Fact Sheet, 2015). The digital divide typically exists between those in cities and those in rural areas; between the educated and the uneducated; between socioeconomic groups; and, globally, between the more and less industrially developed nations (Rouse, 2005). Even among populations with some access to technology, the digital divide can be evident in the form of lower-performance computers, lower-speed wireless connections, lower-priced connections such as dial-up, and limited access to subscription-based content. Digital divide is a challenge to the development, operation and maintenance of digital libraries in sub-Saharan Africa. Majority of the users of digital libraries have low levels of digital and information literacies for one and access to information is not guaranteed.

THE WAY FORWARD AND RECOMMENDATIONS

Providers of information and users of information may agree that the concept of a digital library is still a new phenomenon in the sub-Saharan Africa region. However, the digital library is now a reality which may not be wished away. The digital library comes with numerous advantages which may benefit users in sub-Saharan Africa. Major among the benefits of digital libraries include comprehensiveness, accessibility of information, immediate gratification, followability of data and ease of use. The following recommendations are suggested as the way forward for establishing digital libraries in sub-Saharan Africa:

Understanding of Digital Library Users' Information Needs and Information-Seeking Behavior

It would be important to invest in research on understanding users' information needs and information seeking behavior in the sub-Saharan African context. Basic understanding of information needs and information seeking behavior of users would enable information professionals in sub-Saharan Africa to design digital library systems which may satisfy information needs of users as well as understand the factors which determine their information seeking behavior (Al-Suqri and Al-Aufi, 2015).

Training

Digital libraries are new in sub-Saharan Africa. Very few users of digital libraries in the sub-Saharan Africa region may optimally and competently use digital libraries without requiring any initial training. Most academic libraries and librarians in sub-Saharan Africa have for decades recognized their education function and developed elaborate bibliographical instruction programs for the benefit of users. However, current technological innovations demand new operational paradigms. For instance, in the days of the card catalog, access knowledge acquired lasted a long time before it became obsolete. In the digital age however, an ever-changing information technology complicates assimilation and retention of the requisite access language information (Kibirige & DePalo, 2001). Consequently, an information seeker in a digital library environment needs initial training and constant guidance on how to access information. Many of the library users in sub-Saharan Africa do not have access to computers at home and even at work and thus do not have the basic computer access skills before coming to the library. Digital library users in sub-Saharan Africa need to understand the basics of the equipment for getting on the system and logging off, how to download and/or e-mail the downloadable material to one's e-mail address. The simple act of downloading images and animated video material requires knowing the capacity of the equipment user may be working with. If remotely accessed from the office or home, the equipment – computer and telecommunications links must have the capacity to accommodate the type of image desired. In sub-Saharan Africa, users find it frustrating when the home or office equipment does not have enough memory or storage on the hard disk to manipulate an animated graphic vital to his or her work. The meaning here then is that the user must thus be apprised of the limitations of the equipment to be used for access whether at home, office or in the host library. Many are cases where the access computer may not have the appropriate software for the graphics the user needs to manipulate.

It is important that the user also understands the nature of digital collections. Users may have the impression that a digital library to provide all the information that is available in the world. Several issues may come into play here. One, a user may have to use more than one interface to access dissimilar digital collections within one and the same library. A research conducted by the USA Library of Congress demonstrated that a single, all-purpose interface may not be appropriate for all digital collections, especially in large research libraries (Marchionini, 1998). Second, by way of training, a digital library user in sub-Saharan Africa may also need to know the nature of the content of the digital collection(s), whether text, graphics, or both and their characteristics. Third, the licensing issue for particularly proprietary databases may baffle the user, as some vendors may insist that their products can only be used within the library. Fourth, links to digital resources have to be clearly differentiated, internal as distinct from external. Some of the external links to digital resources may need user ID in contrast to internal collections.

Kibirige and DePalo (2001) are of the opinion that users of a digital library must clearly understand digitized multimedia before accessing it. This definitely implies training prior to accessing the digital library. Training of users of digital libraries may be a major challenge in sub-Saharan Africa considering that there are very few librarians who are trained and well-versed in operations of digital libraries. For sound/voice recordings, a major component of a digital library, an appropriate sound card and speakers must be available in order to take full advantage of the recordings. Likewise, digitized artwork requires an appropriate video card for near-original-image reproduction. If the multimedia has to be imported into a text document for presentation or publication, image handling software must be accessible to the end-user. Currently, several relatively inexpensive image editors are available on the market for example, PhotoShop Pro. Some software suites like the Microsoft Office 2000 have these utilities bundled into their generalized offerings, for instance, Microsoft Photo Editor. The facilities may be available in the market but may not be easily available for use in the digital libraries in sub-Saharan Africa because of affordability issues. In sub-Saharan Africa, digital library users who in most cases are not trained on how to access the information may not be able to access the information they need. Not being able to access information would lead to dissatisfaction with the digital libraries.

Building and Linking Local Digital Libraries

Building digital libraries of local and indigenous materials, is an important step in bridging the digital divide. A number of such digital libraries are now being built in sub-Saharan African countries. Projects on building digital libraries of indigenous resources in sub-Saharan African countries may be initiated and funded by institutions and governments locally, while some may be developed though international collaboration. Carnegie Mellon Foundation of the USA has for long time assisted in developing and equipping libraries in developing regions.

Digital Outsourcing

Information professionals in the sub-Saharan African countries should spend time on outsourcing of free digital information sources and services. Selection *may* include:

1. Identification of the appropriate sources and services based on the subject, sources/authority, user requirements, etc.
2. Evaluation of the sources in order to assess the relevancy of the selected sources and services in light of the user requirements vis-à-vis the technical requirements to access and use them, and
3. To create some sort of surrogate for each source and service to facilitate organization, etc.
    - **Organisation of the Digital Information Sources and Services:** This may require basic web design skills which may be acquired easily, and a number of free courses and guides for web design are available on the web. Major professional skills may be required in the organisation of the identified digital resources and services. An understanding of the users and their information needs vis-à-vis the content, format, etc., of the selected sources and services may help the information professionals in sub-Saharan Africa organise them properly. Appropriate tools used for information organisation in traditional libraries (classification schemes, thesauri, etc.) may be used for the purpose.
    - **Using Freely Available Digital Library Software and Support:** Digital library software may be costly but free software and support are available from a number of international digital library research groups, such as NDLTD, GDL, etc., which may be used for building local digital libraries in sub-Saharan Africa.
    - **Improving Information Use:** Information use rather than access is a major problem in sub-Saharan African countries. Paul (2002) contends that 'a major issue in debating the digital divide in ASEAN countries centres more on usage than on wired access or computer

ownership.' There are many reasons for poor information usage despite having good access. One of the major reasons is poor information literacy. The other most important reason is the work culture and habits. In many sub-Saharan African countries, the work culture does not allow people to spend more time on the Internet, and the day-to-day activities are based more on the traditional approach through the use of paper documents and telephone or written communications.

- **Improving Information and Digital Literacy Skills:** Poor information and digital literacy is a major problem in sub-Saharan African countries. Widharto (2002) while discussing the problems facing information services in Indonesia opines that training remains a key to the future of the Indonesian libraries. This statement can be generalised for sub-Saharan African countries as well. Information or digital literacy training may be organised at different levels. Because of the limitation of resources, in sub-Saharan Africa, information professionals may begin with a simple approach of providing training to the users at different levels – basic levels, middle levels, advanced levels, etc. Nevertheless, to keep pace with the rapid changes in ICT and digital library systems and services, such training should be provided on a regular basis in order to help the users keep up to date and thereby make the optimum use of the sources and services made available to them. The digital divide can only be reduced in sub-Saharan Africa if the users actually make use of the information for the purpose of making informed decisions, and in every aspect of their daily lives. Paul (2002) is of the opinion that the digital divide can be bridged by improved: access, measured by access indicators usage, measured by usage indicators, and outcome, measured by impact indicators. In sub-Saharan Africa, these may not be easy parameters to measure, and may call for painstaking research to develop the measuring yardsticks and best practice standards.

CONCLUSION

The concept of a digital library is still relatively new in sub-Saharan Africa. Not much research has been conducted on the management of digital libraries and/or factors responsible for shaping information-seeking behaviour of users of digital libraries in the sub-Saharan Africa region context. It may be assumed rightly or wrongly that principles of managing traditional libraries are applicable to the management of digital libraries and that factor responsible for shaping information seeking behaviour of users of traditional libraries and digital libraries are the similar. Many ordinary users in sub-Saharan Africa are still comfortable with the traditional libraries. Some academic libraries in sub-Saharan Africa have tried to go digital, but still try to exist side by side with the traditional libraries. Objectives of the traditional libraries and the digital libraries are similar. The major objectives are to collect information, process the information, store it and enable users access to the information. The major differences between the two types of libraries are mainly to do with technology, rather than a fundamental change in the way libraries operate. Digital libraries are still libraries which largely share the same objectives and purposes of the traditional libraries. A user can access a digital library anywhere, which is not possible with the traditional library. Some of the factors responsible for shaping information-seeking behavior of digital library users include but not limited to low levels of information and digital literacy, digital divide, culture, education levels, gender and weak information infrastructures.

While information professionals and in sub-Saharan African countries may feel threatened by the growing digital divide, and users feel that they are lagging behind the digital library revolution due to the high cost of digital library research and development, as well as due to other factors such as the lack of technology, manpower, and other resources, many new developments are taking place that may reverse the situation if they are used properly. However, the pre-requisite to these services is the availability of basic ICT and Internet facilities. Since this is one of the major problems in in sub-Saharan Africa and many users may not have reliable and affordable Internet access from home, or even from work, library and information centres can play a very important role.

REFERENCES

Agarwal, R., Krudys, G., & Tanniru, M. (1997). Infusing learning into the information systems organization. *European Journal of Information Systems*, *6*(1), 25–40. doi:10.1057/palgrave.ejis.3000257

Agarwal, R., & Venkatesh, V. (2002). Assessing a firm's web presence: A heuristic evaluation procedure for the measurement of usability. *Information Systems Research*, *13*(2), 168–186. doi:10.1287/isre.13.2.168.84

Al-Suqri, M., & Al-Aufi. (2015). Information-seeking behavior and technology adoption: theories and trends. Hershey, Pennsylvania, USA: IGI Global.

Alavi, M. (1994). Computer-mediated collaborative learning: An empirical investigation. *Management Information Systems Quarterly*, *8*(4), 159–174. doi:10.2307/249763

Anandarajan, M., Igbaria, M., & Anakwe, U. (2000). Technology acceptance in the banking industry: A perspective from a less developed country. *Information Technology & People*, *13*(4), 298–312. doi:10.1108/09593840010359491

Appelbaum, S. (1990). Training managers to reduce fear and love the machines. *Industrial and commercial training*, 22(6), 9-16.

Bates, M. (1996). Learning about the information seeking of interdisciplinary scholars and students. *Library Trends*, *45*(2), 155–164.

Bawden, D., & Vilar, P. (2006). Digital libraries: To meet or manage user expectations. *Aslib Proceedings*, *58*(4), 346–354. doi:10.1108/00012530610687713

Bertino, E., Casarosa, V., Crane, G., Croft, B., Del Bimbo, A., & Fellner, D. (2001). Digital libraries: future directions for a European Research Programme. San, Cassiano: DELOS.

Bian, G., & Chen, H. (2000). Cross-language information access to multilingual collections on the Internet. *American society for information science*, 51(3), 281-296.

Borgman, C. (2003). Designing digital libraries for usability. In *A. Bishop, N. Van House, & B. Buttenfield, Digital library use: social practice in design and evaluation* (pp. 85–118). Cambridge, Massachusetts: MIT Press.

Bramley, P. (1989). Effective training. *Journal of European Industrial Training*, *13*(7), 2–33. doi:10.1108/EUM0000000000203

Brosnan, M. (1999). Modelling technophopia: A case for word processing. *Computers in Human Behavior*, *15*(2), 105–121. doi:10.1016/S0747-5632(98)00020-X

Bunning, C. (1992). The reflective practitioner: A case study. *Journal of Management Development*, *11*(1), 25–38. doi:10.1108/EUM0000000001388

Candela, L., & Nardi, D. (2011). Digital library technology cookbook: an introperability framework best practices and solutions. Brussels: European Commission Information Society and Media. Retrieved from http://www.dlorg.eu

Choo, C., Detlor, B., & Tumbull, D. (2000). Information Seeking on the Web: an integrated model of browsing and searching. First Monday, 5(2). Retrieved from http://firstmonday.org/ojs/index.php/fm/article/view/729/638

Cleveland, G. (2003). Digital libraries: definitions, issues and challenges. Retrieved from http://www.ifla.org/archive/udt/op/udtop8/udtop8.htm

Computer Science and Telecommunications Board. (1997). *More than Screen Deep: Toward every-citizen interfaces to the nation's information infrastructure*. Washington, DC: National Academy Press.

Davis, C. (2000). Managing expert power in information technology. *Journal of Database Management*, *11*(2), 34–36.

Davis, F. (1989). Perceived usefulness, perceived ease of use and user acceptance of information technology. *Management Information Systems Quarterly*, *13*(3), 319–340. doi:10.2307/249008

Digital divide basics fact sheet. (2015). Retrieved from Lifeline Fact-Sheet: http://centerformediajustice.org/wp-content/uploads/2015/12/lifelinefact-sheet-1.pdf

Digital library Federation. (1998). Retrieved from https://old.diglib.org/about/dldefinition.htm

Ding, C. (2000). Access to digital information: Some breakthroughs and obstacles. *Journal of Librarianship and Information Science*, *32*(1), 26–32. doi:10.1177/096100060003200104

Dresang, E. (1999). More research needed: Informal information-seeking behavior of youth on the Internet. *Journal of the American Society for Information Science*, *50*(12), 1123–1124. doi:10.1002/(SICI)1097-4571(1999)50:12<1123::AID-ASI14>3.0.CO;2-F

Eason, K., Richardson, S., & Yu, L. (2000). Patterns of use of electronic journals. *The Journal of Documentation*, *56*(5), 477–504. doi:10.1108/EUM0000000007124

Ellis, D. (1989). A behavioral approach to information retrieval system design. *The Journal of Documentation*, *45*(3), 171–212. doi:10.1108/eb026843

Ellis, D. (1993). Modelling the information-seeking patterns of academic researchers: A grounded theory approach. *The Library Quarterly*, *63*(4), 469–486. doi:10.1086/602622

Ellis, D. (2005). Ellis's model of information-seeking behavior. In *K. Fisher, S. Erdeles, & L. MacKechnie, Theories of information behavior* (pp. 138–142). Medford, New Jersey: Information Today.

Ellis, D., Cox, D., & Hall, K. (1993). A comparison of information-seeking patterns of researchers in the physical and social sciences. *The Journal of Documentation*, *49*(4), 356–369. doi:10.1108/eb026919

Ellis, D., & Haugan, M. (1997). Modelling the information-seeking behavior of engineers and research scientists in an industrial environment. *The Journal of Documentation*, *53*(4), 384–403. doi:10.1108/EUM0000000007204

Europe and the Global Information Society. (1994). *Recommendations to the European Council ("the Bangemann Report")*. Brussels: European Council.

Fast, K., & Campbell, D. (2004). I still like Google: university student perceptions of searching OPACs and the web. *Proceedings of the 67th American Society for Information Science and Technology*, 4(1), 138-146. Retrieved from http://onlinelibrary.wiley.com/doi/10.1002/meet.1450410116/pdf

Fidel, R., Davies, R., Douglass, M., Holder, J., Hopkins, C., Kushner, E., & Toney, C. et al. (1999). A visit to the information mall: Web searching behavior of high school students. *Journal of the American Society for Information Science*, *50*(1), 24–37. doi:10.1002/(SICI)1097-4571(1999)50:1<24::AID-ASI5>3.0.CO;2-W

Fluid Dynamics Software Corporation. (2015). FDSC. Retrieved from https://www.xav.com/scripts/search/help/1123.html

Fox, E., Akscy, R., Furuta, R. L., & Legget, J. (1995). Digital libraries. *Communications of the ACM*, *38*(4), 23–28. doi:10.1145/205323.205325

Fox, E., & Marchionini, G. (1998). Towards a world-wide digital library. *Communications of the ACM*, *41*(4), 29–32. doi:10.1145/273035.273043

Fox, E., Suleman, H., Madalli, D., & Cassel, L. (2004). Digital libraries. In M. Singh (Ed.), *Practical handbook of Internet computing* (pp. 61–76). New York: CRC. doi:10.1201/9780203507223.ch4

Ge, X. (2010). Information-seeking behavior in the digital age: A multidisciplinary study of academic researchers. *College & Research Libraries*, *71*(5), 435–455. doi:10.5860/crl-34r2

Gefen, D., Karahanna, E., & Straub, D. (2003). Trust and TAM in online shopping: An integrated model. *Management Information Systems Quarterly*, *27*(1), 51–90.

Gefen, D., & Straub, D. (1997). Gender difference in the perception and use of e-mail: An extension to the technology acceptance model. *Management Information Systems Quarterly*, *21*(4), 389–400. doi:10.2307/249720

Goncalves, M., Fox, E., Watson, L., & Kipp, N. (2004). Streams, structures, spaces, scenarios, societies (5S): a formal model for digital libraries. ACM transactions on information systems (TOIS), 22(2), 270-312.

Green, D. (2000). The evolution of web searching. *Online Information Review*, *24*(2), 124–137. doi:10.1108/14684520010330283

Greenberg, D. (1998). Camel drivers and gatecrashers: quality control in the digital research library. In B. Hawkins & P. Battin (Eds.), *The mirage of continuity: reconfiguring academic information resources for the 21st century* (pp. 105–116). Washington, DC: Council on Library and Information Resources and Association of American Universities.

Grimes, B. F. (1996). *Ethnologue: Language of the world* (13th ed.). Dallas: Summer Institute of Linguistics.

Grover, V., & Rammanlal, P. (1999). Six myths of information and market information technology networks, electronic commerce and the battle for consumer surplus. *Management Information Systems Quarterly*, *23*(4), 465–495. doi:10.2307/249486

Hanani, U., & Frank, A. (2000). The parallel evolution of search engines and digital libraries: their mega portal. *Proceedings of the Kyoto International Conference on Digital Libraries* (pp. 269-276). Kyoto: Kyoto University. Retrieved from http://u.cs.biu.ac.il/~ariel/download/ird665/kyoto.pdf

Hargittai, E. (2001). Second-level digital divide: Mapping differences in people's online skills. TPRC. Retrieved from http://arxiv.org/ftp/cs/papers/0109/0109068.pdf

Harris, M. (2012, March). What is a digital library? Retrieved from Writing on information studies. Retrieved from next-nexus.info/writing/infostudies/digital_libraries.php

Harris, R., & Davison, R. (1999). Anxiety and involvement: Cultural dimensions of attitudes towards computers in developing societies. *Journal of Global Information Management*, *7*(1), 26–38. doi:10.4018/jgim.1999010103

Hayashi, R. (2013). Language specific mobility difference in sub-Saharan Africa. *Proceedings of the XXVII IUSSP International Population Conference.* Tokyo: National Institute of Population and Social Security Research. Retrieved from http://iussp.org/sites/default/files/event_call_for_papers/LongAbstract%20iussp1308%20MobilitySSA%20Reiko%20Hayashi130813.pdf

International Telecommunication Union. (2013). Study on international Internet connectivity in sub-Saharan Africa. Geneva. Retrieved from https://www.itu.int/en/ITU-D/Regulatory-Market/Documents/IIC_Africa_Final-en.pdf

Ioannidis, Y. (2005). Digital libraries at crossroads. *International Journal on Digital Libraries*, *5*(4), 255–265. doi:10.1007/s00799-004-0098-4

Ioannidis, Y., Mair, D., Abiteboul, S., Buneman, P., Davidson, S., & Fox, E. (2005). Digital library information-technology infrastructures. *International Journal on Digital Libraries*, *5*(4), 266–274. doi:10.1007/s00799-004-0094-8

Kibirige, H., & DePalo, L. (2001). The education function in a digital library environment: A challenge for college and research libraries. *The Electronic Library*, *19*(5), 283–295. doi:10.1108/02640470110408869

Kim, C. (2003). A comparison of perceived importance of information systems development strategies by developers from the United States and Korea. *Information resources management*, 16(2), 1-18.

Krikelas, J. (1983). Information-seeking behavior: Patterns and concepts. *Drexel Library Quarterly*, *19*(2), 5–20.

Kumar, V., & Rao, p. (2014). Digitization of library resources and the formation of digital libraries: a practical approach. *International Journal and Magazine of Engineering, Technology, Management and Research*, 1(12). Retrieved from http://www.ijmetmr.com/oldecember2014/VVijayKumar-DrPRama-MohanRao-14.pdf

Lagoze, C., & Van de Sompel, H. (2001). The open archives initiative: building a low-barrier interoperability framework. *Proceedings of the 1st ACM/IEEE-CS Joint Conference on Digital Libraries, Virginia, United States of America* (pp. 54-62). New York: ACM. Retrieved from http://www.openarchives.org

Legris, P., Ingham, J., & Collerette, P. (2003). Why do people use information technology? A critical review of the technology acceptance model. *Information & Management*, *40*(3), 191–204. doi:10.1016/S0378-7206(01)00143-4

Lesk, M. (n. d.). (B. a. London, Producer) Retrieved from http://lesk.com/mlesk/follett/follett.html

Lynch, C. (1993). *Accessibility and integrity of networked information collections. Background Paper No. BP-109*. Washington, DC: Office of Technology Assessment.

Lynch, C., & Garcia-Molina, H. (1995). Interoperability, scaling, and the digital libraries research agenda (Research workshop). Retrieved from http://www.hpcc.gov/reports-nco/iita-dlw/main.html

Lynch, C., & Garcia-Molina. (1995, May 18-19). Interoperability, scaling and the digital libraries. *Proceedings of the 1995 IITA Digital Libraries Workshop*. Retrieved from http://www-diglib.stanford.edu/diglib/pub/reports/iita-dlw/main.html

Mahmood, M., Burn, J., Geornoets, L., & Jacquez, C. (2000). Information technology end-user satisfaction: A meta-analysis of the empirical literature. *International Journal of Human-Computer Studies*, *52*(4), 751–771. doi:10.1006/ijhc.1999.0353

Majchrzak, A., Rice, R., Malhotra, A., King, N., & Ba, S. (2000). Technology adaptation: The case of a computer-supported inter-organizational virtual team. *Management Information Systems Quarterly*, *24*(4), 569–600. doi:10.2307/3250948

Makri, S., Blandford, A., & Cox, A. (2008a). Using information behaviors to evaluate the functionality and usability of electronic resources: From Ellis's model to evaluation. *Journal of the American Society for Information Science and Technology*, *59*(14), 2244–2267. doi:10.1002/asi.20927

Makri, S., Blandford, A., & Cox, A. (2008b). Investigating the information-seeking behavior of academic lawyers: From Ellis's model to design. *Information Processing & Management*, *44*(2), 613–634. doi:10.1016/j.ipm.2007.05.001

Marcella, R., & Baxter, G. (1999). The information needs and information-seeking behavior of a national sample of the population in the United Kingdom. *The Journal of Documentation*, *55*(2), 159–183. doi:10.1108/EUM0000000007142

Marchionini, G. (1995). *Information seeking in electronic environment*. Cambridge: Cambridge University Press. doi:10.1017/CBO9780511626388

Marchionini, G., Plaisant, C., & Komlodi, A. (1998). Interfaces and tools for the Library of Congress National Digital Library program. *Information Processing & Management*, *34*(5), 535–555. doi:10.1016/S0306-4573(98)00020-X

Meho, L., & Tibbo, H. (2003). Modelling the information-seeking behavior of social scientists: Ellis's study revisited. *American Journal of the society for Information and Technology*, 54(6), 570-587.

Meso, P., Musa, P., & Mbarika, V. (2005). Towards a model of consumer use of mobile information and communication technology LDCs: The case of sub-Saharan Africa. *Information Systems Journal*, *115*(2), 119–146. doi:10.1111/j.1365-2575.2005.00190.x

Mullen, T., & Lyles, M. (1993). Toward improving management development's contribution to organizational learning. *Human resources planning[HRP]*, 16(2), 35-49.

Nicholas, D., Huntington, P., Willians, P., & Dobrowolski, T. (2004). Re-appraising information seeking behavior in a digital environment: Bouncers, checkers, returnees and the like. *The Journal of Documentation*, *60*(1), 24–43. doi:10.1108/00220410410516635

O'Day, V., & Nardi, B. (2003). An ecological perspective on digital libraries. In *A. Bishop, N. Van House, & B. Buttenfield, Digital library use: social practice in design and evaluation* (pp. 65–82). Cambridge, Massachusetts: MIT Press.

Odedra, M., Lawrie, M., Bennet, M., & Goodman, S. (n. d.). University of Pennsylvania - African Studies. Retrieved from http://www.africa.upenn.edu/Comp_Articles/Information_Technology_117.html

Odedra, M., Lawrie, M. B., & Goodman, S. (n. d.). University of Pennsylvania- African Studies. Retrieved http://www.africa.upenn.edu/Comp_Articles/Information_Technology_117.html

Omwansa, T. (2014). Re-introduction of VAT on ICT equipment in Kenya: special focus on mobile phones. School of Computing and Informatics, University of Nairobi, Nairobi, Kenya. Retrieved from http://www.c4dlab.ac.ke/wp-content/uploads/2014/04/VAT_TKO.pdf

Ono, H., & Zavodnty, M. (2003). Gender and the Internet. *Social Science Quarterly*, *84*(1), 111–121. doi:10.1111/1540-6237.t01-1-8401007

Pareek, A., & Rana, M. (2013). Study of information seeking behavior and library use pattern of researchers in the s University. Library philosophy and practice. Retrieved from http://digitalcommons.unl.edu/librphilprac/887

Paul, J. (2002). Narrowing the digital divide: Initiatives undertaken by the Association of South-East Asian Nations. *Program*, *36*(1), 13–22. doi:10.1108/00330330210426085

Phil, P. (2014, January 22). City-Data Forum. Retrieved from http://www.city-data.com/forum/africa/2035113-language-sub-saharan-africa.html#ixzz3wCUAxBlz

Piccoli, G., Ahmad, R., & Ives, B. (2001). Web based virtual learning environments: A research framework and a preliminary assessment of effectiveness in basic IT skills training. *Management Information Systems Quarterly*, *25*(4), 401–426. doi:10.2307/3250989

Rose, G., Evaristo, R., & Straub, D. (2003). Consumer responses to web download time: A four-continent study of mono and polychronism. *IEEE Transactions on Engineering Management*, *50*(1), 31–44. doi:10.1109/TEM.2002.808262

Rose, G., & Straub, D. (1998). Predicting general IT use: Applying TAM to the Arabic world. *Journal of Global Information Management*, *6*(3), 39–46. doi:10.4018/jgim.1998070104

Ross, S. (2003). *Digital library development review*. Wellington: National Library of New Zealand.

Rouse, M. (2005, April). Wireless definition. Retrieved from http://whatis.techtarget.com/definition/digital

Smith, A. (2001). Strategies for building digitized collections.: Digital Library Federation, Council on Library and Information Resources, Washington, DC. Retrieved from http://www.clir.org

Sridhar, M. (1987). Information-seeking behavior of the Indian space technologists. Retrieved from http://elis.da.ulcc.ac.uk/10887/2/J_26_ISB_OF_IST.pdf

Sridhar, M. (1989). Information-seeking behavior of the Indian space technologists. *Library Science*, *26*(2), 127–132.

TNS Global. (2012, June 15). Connected world. Retrieved from http://www.tnsglobal.be/sites/default/files/whitepaper/TNS_In_Focus_digital_media_SSA.pdf

Trivedi, M. (2010). Digital libraries: functionality, usability and accessibility. Library philosophy and practice. Retrieved from http://www.webpages.uidaho.edu/~mbolin/trivedi-diglib.htm

Troll, D. (2002). How and why libraries are changing: What we know and what we need to know. Portal. *Libraries and the Academy*, *2*(1), 99–123. doi:10.1353/pla.2002.0023

Venkatesh, V., & Morris, M. (2000). Why don't men ever stop to ask for directions? Gender, social influence, and their role in technology acceptance usage behavior. *Management Information Systems Quarterly*, *24*(1), 115–139. doi:10.2307/3250981

Walshman, G. (2002). Cross-cultural software production and use: A structurational analysis. *Management Information Systems Quarterly*, *26*(4), 350–380.

Walshman, G., & Sahay, S. (1999). GIS for district-level administration in India: Problems and opportunities. *Management Information Systems Quarterly*, *23*(1), 39–65. doi:10.2307/249409

Wells, H. (1938). *World brain*. New York: Doubleday.

Widharto, L. (2002). Challenges in accessing information in Indonesia during the economic crisis. *Bulletin of the American Society for Information Science and Technology*, *28*(4), 25–27. doi:10.1002/bult.243

Wilson, T. (1999). Models in information behavior research. *The Journal of Documentation*, *55*(3), 249–270. doi:10.1108/EUM0000000007145

World Bank. (2013). Fact sheet: infrastructure in sub-Saharan Africa. Washington, DC: World Bank. Retrieved from http://go.worldbank.org/SWDECPM5S0

ADDITIONAL READING

Agusto, D. E. (2002). Bounded rationality and satisficing in young people's web-based decision-making. *Journal of the American Society for Information Science and Technology*, *53*(1), 16–27. doi:10.1002/asi.10024

Andrews, J., & Law, D. (Eds.). (2004). *Digital Libraries: Policy, Planning and Practice*. Aldershot: Ashgate.

Auster, E., & Chan, D. C. (2004). Reference librarians and keeping up to date: A question of priorities. *Reference and User Services Quarterly*, *44*(1), 57–66.

Babu, B. R., & O'Brien, A. (2000). Web OPAC interfaces: An overview. *The Electronic Library*, *18*(5), 316–327. doi:10.1108/02640470010354572

Bishop, A. P. (1999). Document structure and digital libraries: How researchers mobilize information in journal articles. *Information Processing & Management*, *35*(3), 255–279. doi:10.1016/S0306-4573(98)00061-2

Bishop, A. P. Van House, NA & Buttenfield, B (Eds.), (2003). Digital library use: social Practice in design and evaluation. Cambridge: Massachusetts Institute of Technology.

Borgman, C. L. (2000). Digital *libraries and the continuum of scholarly communication. The Journal of Documentation*, *56*(4), 412–430. doi:10.1108/EUM0000000007121

Griffiths, J. R., & Brophy, P. (2005). Student searching behavior and the web: Use of academic resources and Google. *Library Trends*, *53*(4), 539–554.

Levy, D. M., & Marshall, C. C. (1995). Going digital: A look at assumptions underlying digital libraries. *Communications of the ACM*, *38*(4), 77–84. doi:10.1145/205323.205346

Ondari-Okemwa, E. 2013. Educating and training knowledge workers on management and valuation of intangible assets in a knowledge economy. In S. Buckley & Jackvljevic (Eds.), Knowledge management innovations for interdisciplinary education: Organizational applications (pp. 233-253). Hershey, PA, USA: IGI Global.

Xia, W. (2003). Digital library services: perceptions and expectations of user communities and librarians in a New Zealand academic library. *Australian Academic and Research Libraries*, 34(1), 56-70. Retrieved from http://alia.org.au/publishing/aarl/34.1/full.text/xia.htm

KEY TERMS AND DEFINITIONS

Digital Divide: A term that refers to the gap between demographics and regions that have access to modern information and communications technology, and those that don't or have restricted access. This technology can include the telephone, television, personal computers and the Internet.

Digital Libraries: An organized and focused collection of digital objects, including text, images, video and audio, with the methods of access and retrieval and for the selection, creation, organization, maintenance and sharing of collection.

Digital Literacy: Using technologies to find, use and disseminate information. A digitally literate person should have skills to analyse and evaluate information to complete a range of activities, and transmit knowledge, skills and ideas to other people.

Information and Communications Technologies: An umbrella term that includes any communication device or application, encompassing: radio, television, cellular phones, computer and network hardware and software, satellite systems and so on, as well as the various services and applications associated with them, such as videoconferencing and distance learning. ICTs are often spoken of in a particular context, such as ICTs in education, health care, or libraries.

Information Literacy: The ability to recognize when information is needed and being able to efficiently locate, accurately evaluate, effectively use, and clearly communicate information in various formats.

Information-Seeking Behavior: What people do or how they behave when they are purposively seeking information as a consequence of a need to satisfy some goal. In the course of seeking, the seeker may interact with manual information system (such as a newspaper, a journal or a library), or with computer-based systems such as World Wide Web. An information seeker may make inquiries from information professionals, from friends, from work colleagues or from family members in the course of seeking information.

Library User: Anybody who visits the library with the purpose of exploiting its resources to satisfy his/her information needs. The underlined word "visits" as it is used in the 21st century, include remote access to the library portal or website. User may also include all those who avail themselves of the services offered by a library. The term encompasses various terms such as patrons, clients, information users, information seekers, consumers, readers, etc. these terms can be used interchangeably, because they all apply to those seeking the services of a library.

Sub-Saharan Africa: African region south of the Sahara Desert. The region is made up of 48 independent nations, 42 of which are located on the mainland and six are island nations. The island nations include Madagascar, Seychelles, Comoros, Cape Verde and Sao Tome and Principe. In some quarters, Mauritius is generally not considered a sub-Saharan island nation as the ethnic makeup of the country is predominantly East Indian, Chinese and French. However, it is always counted as one of the sub-Saharan African countries.

Traditional Library: A building or a physical fixed space which emphasizes physical collections and often invoked as a counterpoint to the modern or digital library. The traditional library is equivalent to the physical library: it is driven by a focus on physical items and physical spaces. The priority in such a library, as reflected in traditional library building design, is the housing and protection of the current and future print collection.

Chapter 3

Legal Considerations of Providing Information in Support of Distance Learning by Digital Libraries in Universities in Kenya

Japhet Otike
Moi University, Kenya

ABSTRACT

This paper examines the legal challenges librarians managing university libraries in Kenya experience when providing information services in support of distance learning. Kenya is experiencing enormous socio-economic changes. These changes have exerted serious pressure on higher education resulting to phenomenal expansion of university education. Unfortunately, the demand for university education has not translated into infrastructural expansion of universities. While university intake continues to grow at an alarming rate, funding for universities including libraries continue to diminish. An option taken by many universities to meet increased demand for higher education has been to invest in distance education. This option has its own challenges. Distance learning like residential programmes, require adequate financial investment in print and electronic information resources; and ICT infrastructure. Since libraries in Kenya are underfunded, they are compelled to reproduce the scarce materials available with them to serve distant learners as opposed to acquiring additional materials. This arrangement has equally serious challenges. Top on the list is copyright infringement. Without adequate exceptions and limitations to copyright restrictions, university authorities and librarians are likely to be charged for infringement.

DOI: 10.4018/978-1-5225-0296-8.ch003

INTRODUCTION

The growth of higher education in Kenya has been phenomenal. At independence in 1963, the country did not have a full-fledged university. The only institution of higher learning was the University College of Nairobi which was a constituent college of the University of East Africa. The student population in this constituent college was less than 1000. By March 2013, the number of universities in Kenya had shot up to over 55 universities. Out of this number, 22 comprised public universities. The total number of students in these universities has skyrocketed to over 200,000. The majority of these students are to be found in public universities. Of the public universities, Kenyatta University leads with a student enrolment of 61,928, followed by University of Nairobi (57162) and Moi University (34,477). The huge number of university enrolment has made the cost of funding university education unbearable to the government. This has forced public universities to look elsewhere for additional sources of funding to supplement the meager funds available from the government.

One of the areas that has suffered seriously from the financial crunch is the library. Ideally, a university library is supposed to receive a minimum of five percent of the total funding from the government. In Kenya, this rarely happens. The result has been that university libraries particularly in government funded universities have been seriously underfunded to the extent that it is difficult to access any popular title or issue of a journal on the library shelves. Shortage of information materials is the order of the day in public university libraries. This scarcity has been worsened by the presence of a growing number of university library staff who have decided to go back to class to improve on their papers. Many staff take advantage of their position to keep popular materials for themselves. In an impromptu exercise carried out in one public university library, a senior staff was found with over 150 titles in his office both processed and unprocessed!

In the absence of adequate and current information materials in the library, students have tended to rely very heavily on notes and handouts made available to them by lecturers. Lecturers, too, have tended to re-circle the same handouts year in and out. Photocopy shops have mushroomed in and around university libraries to take advantage of the high demand for reprographic services. To ensure that each student has access to handouts, lecturers deposit copies of their materials with copy shops to enable students to make copies at their convenience. This approach of imparting knowledge is not the best as it narrows students thinking and makes them to reproduce whatever they have been given. This is totally contrary to university teaching which seeks to make students creators of knowledge. Unfortunately, students can not generate knowledge when they have access to limited sources of information.

DISTANCE LEARNING IN KENYA

Distance learning is a mode of educational delivery where the instructor and the learner are separated by space and time; the instructions are delivered through specially designed materials and methods, supported by organizational and administrative structures; and arrangements. It uses a combination of learning methods varying from print, non-print to internet resources.

Distance learning is not new on the African continent and in Kenya in particular. It is something that existed long before independence. However, the kind of distance learning that existed in the pre-independence days was different from the one that exists presently. In the pre-independence days, it was conducted through correspondence by schools stationed essentially in Britain. Students were given modules complete with course packs to study. At the end of each topic, students were given questions to attempt. In the present era, many of these programmes are conducted by universities. A number of universities particularly public universities, have embraced this option as the most cost effective way of meeting increased demand for university education without spending heavily on physical infrastructure such as student hostels and classrooms. In Kenya, Kenyatta University leads in this approach. It is argued that much of the funds solicited from the government goes to the welfare of students, namely, providing adequate bed space, sporting and other recreation facilities. Distance learning can save this by investing the funds into academic programmes such as libraries, ICTs and improving on the quality of staff essential for its success.

Distance learning requires a number of things to succeed. One consideration is competent, well qualified and highly motivated staff. This is so because the staff have to provide personalized attention to the students something that is not common with residential programmes. Second is a well-stocked and staffed library. In the absence of class room lectures, students have to rely very heavily on the services in the library. At the same time, some materials will need to be reproduced and made available to students in the form of course packs. Some materials may be digitized. The library will need to subscribe to digital information resources. Thirdly, there will be need for excellent ICT infrastructure. ICT is required to facilitate faster communication between the lecturers and students. Unlike in the past where communication was by mail post, the present system calls for electronic communication. Much of the instructions and resources will need to be digitized and communicated electronically. Time is of essence here. Fourthly, there will be need for adequate funding. Funds determine the success of any information service. Adequate funds will be required to acquire the above resources. It thefore goes without saying that distance learning requires a fully functional digital library.

THE ROLE OF COPYRIGHT IN DISTANCE LEARNING

Since distance learning relies very heavily on electronic communication, copyright issues need to be taken very seriously. This is so because nearly all the information materials conveyed to the students in the form of course packs and the materials the students will access in the library will be in digital form. Reproduction of these materials will require the university and in particular, the library to obtain clearance from copyright holders or their agents.

The above issue compels us to find out more about copyright. Copyright is a legal right accorded to creators of intellectual property such as books, journal articles, etc. in whatever form, to protect them from being reproduced without their authority. This law requires that any person or organization wishing to reproduce a copyrighted work must obtain permission or a reproduction license from the copyright owner or his agent. The agent in most cases, is a Reprographic Rights Organization (RRO). In Kenya, this organization is known as KOPIKEN. KOPIKEN is mandated by copyright holders to issue out reproduction license and collect license fee on their behalf. Despite the role that KOPIKEN plays in this regard, it does not have a legal mandate to enforce copyright law. This role is played by the Kenya Copyright Board (KECOBO). The best KOPIKEN can do is to report the defaulters to KECOBO for legal redress.

What Does Copyright Do?

- Copyright empowers the creators or rights holders to exclude others from certain uses of their work.
- It grants the copyright owner the exclusive right or monopoly which cannot be enjoyed by anybody else without his/her permission.
- It gives the author a say on the issue of reproduction license. Only the owner or his/her agent can issue reproduction license.
- It protects the copyright owner from unfair competition, particularly those who have invested a lot of money or effort into the venture.
- It facilitates creativity and innovation. The monopoly the owner obtains motivates him/her to be even more creative. This alone leads to accelerated development.

Works Protected by Copyright

In Kenya, the following works are eligible for copyright protection:

- Literary works such as printed as well as non-printed materials such as books, journals, magazines, newspapers, computer programmes.
- Musical works.
- Artistic works: paintings, drawings, engravings, maps, plans, works of sculpture, architectural drawings, etc.
- Audio-visual works.
- Sound recordings.
- Broadcasts.

COPYRIGHT EXCEPTIONS AND LIMITATIONS

Copyright laws in many countries provide exemptions to some copyright restrictions. With these exemptions, people using copyrighted works for certain cases and in particular, non-profit purposes, do not need to obtain permission from the copyright owner. These exemptions are often referred to as "Exceptions and Limitations" to copyright restriction. In England and much of the commonwealth states, they are known as "Far Dealing" while in the United States, the law recognizes them as "Fair Use". Countries that are signatories to the Berne Copyright Convention are required to incorporate these exemptions in their national copyright laws. Kenya has these exemptions in its copyright legislation.

The exemptions are not supposed to economically or monetarily disadvantage the copyright owner. They are only applicable where certain circumstances permit. These conditions appear in the 1967 revision of the Berne Copyright Convention in the form of "Three -Step Test." According to this arrangement, reproduction of copyrighted work can only be carried out:

1. In certain special cases.
2. That do not conflict with the normal exploitation of the work.
3. Do not unreasonably prejudice the legitimate interest of the authors/rights holders.

In the United States, the American copyright law provides four conditions under which reproduction can be carried out (Murunga, 2009).

1. **The Purpose and Character of the Use:** This focuses on whether the use under consideration achieves the purposes of copyright, which is to stimulate creativity for the enhancement of the general public.
2. **The Nature of Copyrighted Work:** This focuses on the character of the work: whether the work is based on the fact alone or is a mixture of fact and imagination; and whether the work has been published.
3. **The Amount and Substantiality of the Portion Used in Relation to Copyrighted Work as a Whole:** Generally, the less the work reproduced in relation to the entre work the more the likelihood it will be treated as fair use.
4. **Whether the INFRINGING Use of the Work Has Significantly Harmed the Copyright Owner's Business:** The exemption is considered fair use if less or insignificant damage is done to the owner's business or monetary returns.

Importance of Exceptions and Limitations

Exemptions are important both to the library and information user because:

1. Without them, rights holders would have an almost complete monopoly relating to access to their work. As a result, every use would be subject to permission from the rights holders or license. Access to information would be severely hampered. The core functions of a library in disseminating information would be affected.
2. They facilitate easier and faster access to information and knowledge. Without these exemptions, information users including among others, writers, authors, researchers, etc., would be compelled to obtain written permission every time they cite or refer to a work from authors or publishers who may not be easy to locate.
3. Authors and publishers would be flooded with too many requests which they may not be able to cope with. This could affect timely use of information.
4. Exemptions enable information to be disseminated to wider audience including those in the farthest corners of the country through controlled reproduction, inter-library lending, etc.
5. Both writers and publishers stand to benefit from exemptions in their official capacity as consumers or users of information. Without them, they would equally be handicapped.
6. Exemptions discourage information censorship. Without them censorship would be the order of the day. Copyright owners would restrict certain information from being reproduced. Librarians by virtue of their training, are required to fight information censorship in whatever form it comes.
7. The library is supposed to provide current, accurate and timely information to users wherever they happen to be. Without exemptions, their work would be hampered.

8. Exceptions and limitations strike a balance between the interests of the authors on one hand, and the interests of the users on the other hand.
9. Without exemptions, the creation of new works would be impeded. Writers like other users, are serious users of information and by extension, library services.
10. On copyright exceptions, IFLA (2004) maintains that unless libraries and citizens are granted exceptions which allow reasonable access and fair use for purposes which do not harm the interests of rights holders, and which are in the public interest and in line with fair practice such as education and research, there is a danger that only those who can afford information will be able to take advantage of the benefits of the information society. If there were no effective public interest exceptions, especially in the digital environment, this would lead to an even greater divide than already exists between the information rich and the information poor in both the developed and developing nations. This is not to say that rights owners should be persuaded to give their works away freely. Once a work has been legitimately obtained, e.g. purchased by a library or an individual, there should be some exceptions allowed under national laws, which are in line with the Berne three-step test. Further, there should be no discrimination in copyright laws against visually, aurally or learning disabled persons. Reformatting of materials to make it accessible should not be considered an infringement of copyright and should be considered as reasonable access. In countries with many languages and dialects, there is a greater need for exceptions to allow translation and reproduction of materials for literacy and learning purposes.

Why Are Exceptions and Limitations Required in Kenya?

A number of factors can be advanced for exceptions and limitations in the country. Among these are:

1. Researchers may need to make copies of copyrighted materials to use them in the field to assist them to carry out experiments. Materials such as journals are normally not lent out by libraries. The only way out is to reproduce the required articles.
2. The skyrocketing cost of information materials has made it very difficult for libraries and users in developing countries to acquire all what they need. Without these exemptions, it would be difficult for libraries to serve the public.
3. The increasing number of students enrolling in institutions of higher learning has made it hard for libraries both public and universities, to maintain a steady flow of information materials to meet the increasing needs of patrons. This has prompted libraries to use every legal means to address their information needs.
4. The increasing need for information has compelled users to maximize the limited resources in the library by copying what they need. Libraries have responded to this phenomenon by participating in inter-library lending.
5. The rising population or enrollment in schools vis-a-vis diminishing funding for schools and universities:
    a. has placed serious strain on the scarce information resources available in libraries leading to loss and mutilation of materials
    b. libraries have responded to this phenomenon by replacing lost and damaged copies through photocopying or borrowing from other libraries.

6. Some materials available in libraries are either out of print or out of stock. Such materials cannot be available through the book trade. Reproduction and inter-library lending appear to be the only way out.
7. The problem with orphan works. Since the origin of most of these materials cannot be ascertained, it is difficult to obtain permission from the copyright owners to reproduce them. Restriction of these materials seriously hampers their use.
8. Use of copyrighted materials for distance learning. Many universities in Africa and Kenya in particular, are embracing the concept of Open and Distance Learning (ODL) as the only way to take higher education to all corners of the country. The success of this programme requires digitization and transmission of this information through the internet.
9. Development of the National Collection. In an attempt to develop the national collection or national imprint, a library should be allowed to fill up gaps in its national collection by reproducing documents from other sources. This should also apply to the National Archives' effort to acquire migrated archives to fill up gaps existing in their stock.

EXCEPTIONS AND LIMITATIONS TO COPYRIGHT RESTRICTIONS IN KENYA

In Kenya, exceptions and limitations to copyright restrictions are covered by sections 25 – 29 of the Copyright Act, 2001. These exemptions apply strictly for non-commercial purposes. They include:

1. Use of copyrighted work for: scientific research; private study; criticism or review; or reporting of current events for subject to acknowledgement of the source;
2. The inclusion in a collection of literary or musical works of not more than two short passages from the work in question for use in a school registered under the Education Act, or any university. Where this is done, acknowledgement of the source is required.
3. Reproduction of a work by or under the direction or control of the government or by such public libraries, non-commercial documentation centres and scientific institutions for public use.

It does appear that the above exemptions are not comprehensive enough and therefore, do not cater for the information needs of all people in Kenya. To improve this shortfall, Sihanya (nd) proposed the following additions:

1. Reproduction of published work in Braille for the exclusive use of the visually handicapped
2. Exception to the Technological Protection Measures (TPMs) that may be used by the rights holders especially in the digital environment. The law in Kenya does not allow circumvention of the TPMs.
3. Making of not more than three copies of a book by or under the direction of a person in charge of a public library for use by the library if such a work is not available in Kenya
4. Provision for making copies for educational purposes to allow access to learning materials in an attempt to boost teaching and learning activities in academic institutions in the country.

TO WHAT EXTENT DOES THE EXCEPTIONS AND LIMITATIONS PROVISION IN THE COPYRIGHT ACT MEET DISTANCE LEARNING IN KENYA

It appears from the above discussion that the Copyright Act does not support distance learning. The following arguments can be advanced:

1. Distance or e-learning does not appear to be a major objective of the exceptions and limitations. Although distance learning has been in existence long before the present legislation came into existence in 2001, the law does not take it seriously. In some countries such as Uganda (Kawooya,2010) and Ghana (Adusei, 2010), although distance learning has not been mentioned, there are very generous provisions for learning and teaching which can be extended to distance learning. In Uganda, there is no limit on reproducing copyrighted materials for teaching purposes. Since the law is not specific on printed materials, this can also be extended to cover digitization for e-learning.
2. Reproduction of materials in support of teaching in schools and universities. This area has been poorly covered by the law. Reproduction under exceptions and limitations is confined to producing not more than two short passages from a copyrighted work. With this kind of restriction, it would be illegal and impracticable for teaching and library staff to produce course packs for class room use or distance learning. With diminishing funding for university education coupled with increased enrolment, there is need to improve this section to allow reproduction of multiple copies to facilitate teaching and learning.
3. Reproduction of materials considered out of print (Otike, 2011). Libraries and information users should be allowed to reproduce materials which are either out of print or out of stock. This is a normal practice in many countries. If the required materials are not available through the book trade, it is proper that people in need and in particular, libraries, should be allowed to reproduce them for use by their patrons. Libraries as custodians and disseminators of information have a duty to their patrons to meet their information needs.
4. Reproduction of multiple copies for use by libraries and archives. The two institutions play a very important role in national development. They serve as repositories of knowledge for posterity. The two institutions serve not only students, academic staff and the general public, but also the rights holders, namely authors, writers, and publishers in their official capacity as information consumers. Authors and writers like any users, need information to generate new information products for the book market. Without libraries, their work would equally be hampered. This being the case, it is important that they should support the library in its endeavour of making information and knowledge available to those in need. Unfortunately, the law in Kenya does not allow libraries to reproduce copies of copyrighted works for the purpose of replacing lost or damaged copies. Nor does the law permit the library to produce copies for preservation purposes. In developed countries of the west, this role is supported by both the government and rights holders. Some materials published at the beginning of colonialism in this country are very rare. There is therefore need to preserve these materials to be used in the distant future. Cambridge and Oxford university libraries for instance, boast of some of the oldest and rarest literature collection published as far back as AD 1200.
5. Reproduction of materials for people with disabilities. The exceptions and limitations in the copyright law in Kenya does not cover people with disabilities. Any person or organization wishing to reproduce the materials in let's say, Braille form, must obtain a license from the rights holders. A number of countries such as the United States provide this exception but strictly for domestic

use. The Braille materials so reproduced under fair use cannot be exported. It has been the view of many people in Kenya and in particular, librarians, that reproduction of Braille materials be covered under exceptions and limitations to enable the disadvantaged members of the society to have equal access to information.

6. Reproduction of materials in support of inter-library lending. It is now clear that however well-funded a library is, it cannot acquire all the information materials it requires. No single library has ever done this. To address the increasing information needs for a fast growing population, libraries in Kenya, like those in the developed countries, have to participate in resource sharing. This includes among others, inter-library lending. This may include reproducing copyrighted documents and passing them to libraries that do not have. It may also include lending out the original materials to cooperating libraries to be passed on to their users. Copyright holders in Kenya are opposed to this practice. They argue that it eats into their profits. Copyright law in Kenya does not cover this practice which is considered key to the work of librarians. Inter-library lending is crucial in the success of distance learning. Libraries in Kenya need to be accorded this right to enable them to serve a huge student population. Distance learning can only succeed with support from other libraries through inter-library cooperation.
7. Reproduction to facilitate document supply service. This service enables library users to be kept up to date with latest information pertaining to their immediate areas of interest. The service may involve reproducing by way of photocopying or digitization, contents pages of journals or journal articles and passing them to the users in need both within the library and outside who may include distance learners. Unfortunately, this option is not covered by exceptions and limitations in Kenya. Any library that endeavours to do this, is likely to infringe the law. Yet this is one service that is likely to benefit distance learners who may be a great distance away.
8. Permission to circumvent Technological Protection Measures (TPMs). In addition to print literature, some information is available in digital form. Much of this electronic or digital information is found in digital databases. Since the information is copyrighted, access to the information is protected by password. This ensures that those authorized can access the information. TPM is a protective measure instituted by the rights holders that restricts unauthorized people from accessing the databases to reproduce the information in them. Any unauthorized library or person who does so infringes copyright. Librarians feel that libraries should be allowed to circumvent this protective measure or device to provide information to a wider public. In Kenya, TPMs are not covered by exceptions and limitations. However, the general tendency in the world is towards this direction. Since the world is heading towards a paperless society, librarians are becoming increasingly concerned that if this exception is not allowed by law, rights holders are likely to use TPMs to permanently bar libraries from disseminating information in the digital media.
9. In support of the above argument, Ouma and Sihanya (2010) observed that TPMs are problematic. They pose serious consequences to access to information. They are already limiting access to e-books, articles, databases, newspapers and other educational materials. They however admit that this is not a problem that can be sorted out soon. Nearly all major international treaties still support TPMs.
10. Permission to allow parallel importation of information materials. Parallel importation arises in a situation where the library, for instance, imports information materials such as books from a cheaper

but restricted source instead of importing them from the original and therefore, more official source where the materials appear to be more expensive. Generally, materials produced in a restricted source under a special license from the original publisher for a specific market are not meant to be re-exported although some unscrupulous suppliers do it. So buying materials from a restricted source is illegal in Kenya as it is in many countries because it infringes copyright law as it denies the original publisher an income. There is however a feeling among the library fraternity that this practice should be allowed under exceptions and limitations to make information materials more affordable and widely available. International conventions are still opposed to parallel importation because it denies rights holders a good income.

LEGAL IMPLICATIONS FOR THE DIGITAL LIBRARY

In an attempt to provide information to distant learners, the librarian managing the digital library is likely to come across insurmountable challenges. Among these are copyright hurdles. As stated earlier, the Copyright Act in Kenya does not have generous provision for reproducing copyrighted works for educational purposes under exceptions and limitations. The Act allows reproduction of only two short passages under fair use. Anything beyond that amounts to copyright infringement. This makes it hard for the librarian to digitize library materials into course packs and pass them to distant learners. In addition, many publishers and authors in Kenya do not support the idea of reproducing their materials by libraries. They argue that the exercise deprives them of an income and therefore, a livelihood. Inter-library cooperation in which the resources of one library are made available to other libraries on the network are seriously resisted. The law in Kenya has no provision for inter-library lending of materials.

Another challenge relates to digital information in data bases maintained by publishers or their agents. Although digital libraries can access these internet-based resources through subscription, the license could limit the frequency of access by users. Furthermore, access to the data bases may be restricted by technology protection measures. So any person who accesses the content by circumventing these measures such as passwords, is considered to have infringed the law. This could result in the data base being denied to the entire library.

An institutional digital repository is an important component of a digital library. A repository is an institutional archive that brings together all digital materials produced by members of the university fraternity. The materials may comprise theses and dissertations produced by students and staff, conference papers, research reports, copies of articles published in learned journals, staff CVs, past exam papers, etc. A university hosting distance programmes must have a comprehensive institutional repository. However, putting up a repository has its own challenges. A large percentage of the deposited materials are likely to be copyrighted. These may include theses produced in other universities, papers in conference proceedings, articles from learned journals, etc. Publishers in particular do not support the idea of academic authors depositing their materials in repositories. This is so because publishers consider repositories as their rivals. It does not matter whether the materials were deposited by the authors. The reason is that the authors may not own the copyright. Some journals require authors to transfer their right to copyright before the papers are published. So whereas a person may be a proud author of an article, he may not own the copyright. Before a donor deposits his material, the librarian must ensure that copyright issues have been sorted out with the publishers or else the librarian could be charged for copyright infringement.

Another precaution the digital librarian will need to take is to ensure that the materials deposited are neither defamatory nor prohibited. This requires the digital librarian to keep abreast of the law. In Kenya such materials may attract severe penalties. It does not even help the librarian to state that he was not aware the materials were illegal because the law assumes that every individual in the country is legally literate and that ignorance of the law is no defense.

CONCLUSION

In view of the foregoing, it can be concluded that the only way to improve access to information to distant learners is to overhaul the Copyright Act, 2001. This Act was conceived, drafted and managed by rights holders with the technical assistance of legal draftsmen in the government. It is for all intents and purposes, the rights holders' baby. Librarians did not play any role in its enactment. The result is that the law is one sided. What makes the situation appear even worse is the fact that the Kenya Copyright Board, a body that manages copyright in the country established by this Act, is dominated almost totally by rights holders. The chair of the board has since its inception been headed by publishers. Publishers have been very critical about librarians. They argue that librarians do not support their cause. There is need to review the composition of this body to represent the interests of rights holders, information users; and librarians and archivists. Otherwise the way it is now, the board can easily pass out as "the rights holders' exclusive club."

In support of the above view, an international NGO, Electronic Information for Libraries (EIFL, 2006) argues that copyright law directly affects library services providing access to learning resources, scientific and research information critical to education and training in every country. Librarians and their representative organizations are important stakeholders in any national debate and must be consulted when the law on copyright, related rights or enforcement is being discussed. This means that library representatives should maintain regular contact with government copyright officials and should be kept informed of any national developments. Librarians can submit position papers, attend hearings and put forward suggestions for amendments.

There is also need for librarians and information users to be fully informed about issues relating to copyright. Legal awareness is important to enable them to discharge their duties without being scared by rights holders or their agents about copyright infringement. This is so because staff from the Reproduction Rights Organisation (RRO) in the country have a tendency of making impromptu visits to libraries and threatening them to pay reproduction fee knowing very well that libraries are covered by copyright exceptions and limitations. A few libraries particularly those owned by private universities have started paying up. In developed countries where librarians are knowledgeable about copyright, such incidences do not happen. Otike (1997) affirmed that every member of the public needs to be legally informed. The law in every country pre-supposes that every citizen despite his/her age, education is legally literate. In a similar study, it was found that even those staying in rural areas need to be exposed to the law and that the law should not be considered a domain of the legal fraternity alone (Otike, 1996).

Librarians need to network. Networking enables them to share ideas and problems pertaining to their work, and in particular, issues relating to copyright. The best way out is to form consortia or work closely with the national library organization, Kenya Library Association. As long as librarians remain united, RROs will be kept at bay.

REFERENCES

Adusei, P. (2010). Ghana. In C. Armstrong (Ed.), *Access to knowledge in Africa: the role of copyright* (pp. 57–82). UCT Press.

Aguirre, V. V. (2010). Ensuring access to information: A librarian's dilemma. *Journal of Philippine Librarianship*, *30*(1), 10–21.

Ayamunda, J., & Nwabachili, C. (2015). Copyright exceptions and use of educational materials in universities in Kenya. *Journal of Law. Policy and Globalization*, *39*, 104–116.

Berkman Centre for internet and Society. (2012). Copyright for librarians: the essential handbook.

Budapest Open Access Initiative. (2012). Retrieved from http://www.soros.org/openaccess/read.shtml

Chahale, S. (n. d.). The publishing industry in Kenya. *Copyright News*, 9, 3.

Christian, G. E. (2008). Issues and challenges to the development of open access institutional repositories in academic and research institutions in Nigeria. Available at: http//idl-bnc.idrc.ca/dspace/bitstream/10625/36986/1/127792pdf

Durkey, E. (2008). Academic libraries and copyright issues in Ghana. *International Journal of Legal information*, 36, 432-448.

Electronic Information for Libraries (EIFL). (2006). EIFL-IP handbook on copyright and related issues for libraries.

IFLA. (2004). Limitations and exceptions to copyright and neighbouring rights in the digital environment: an international library perspective. Retrieved from http://archive.ifla.org/III/clm/p1/ilp.htm

Jain, P. (2012). Promoting open access to research in academic libraries. Retrieved from llunllib.unl.edu/LLP/

John-Okeke, R. (2008). Developing institutional repositories: Considering copyright issues. *Journal of Applied Information Science and Technology*, *2*(8), 11–18.

Kaddu, S. (2007). Information Ethics: A student perspective. *International Review of information. Ethics*, *7*, 2–6.

Kawooya, D. et al.. (2010). Uganda. In C. Armstrong (Ed.), *Access to knowledge in Africa: the role of copyright* (pp. 281–316). UCT Press.

Medical Library Association. (2007). The copyright law and the health sciences librarian. Available at: www.mlanet.org

Mwita, D. (1999, September 22). Freedom of information access in Kenya: a publishing perspective in a changing environment. *Paper presented at the13th Kenya Library Association Annual Seminar.*

Otike, J. (1996). Provision of legal information to rural populations in Anglophone Africa. *Libri*, *46*(4), 228–231. doi:10.1515/libr.1996.46.4.226

Otike, J. (1997). Legal information needs of the general public; with special reference to developing countries. *Library Review*, *46*(1), 28–33. doi:10.1108/00242539710160866

Otike, J. (2011, August 24-26). Kenya Libraries and Information Services Consortium (KLISC). *Presented at the Copyright Advocacy Workshop*, Nairobi, Kenya.

Otike, J. (2012, June 4 – 8). Copyright: the challenges posed by Reproduction Rights organizations (RROs) in the provision of information to users with special reference to Kenya. *Presented at the Standing Conference for East, Central and Southern African Librarians (SCESCAL)*, Nairobi, Kenya.

Otike, J. (2012, June 4-8). Copyright: challenges posed by reprographic rights organizations (RROs) in the provision of information to users with special reference to Kenya. *Presented at the Standing Conference of East, Central and Southern African Librarians (SCECSAL)*, Nairobi, Kenya.

Ouma, E., & Sihanya, M. (2010). Kenya. In C. Armstrong (Ed.), *Access to knowledge in Africa: the role of copyright* (pp. 83–125). UCT Press.

Sihanya (n. d.). Promoting access through legal reform: Kenya case study. *Presented in a workshop on exceptions and limitations for education and research environments in Ghana.*

Chapter 4
Copyright Issues in the Context of the Digital Library

Pedro Pina
Polytechnic Institute of Coimbra, Portugal

ABSTRACT

Libraries have a strong role on promoting culture and knowledge as intermediaries between creators and readers. In the analogical world, such usages didn't have relevant effects on the normal exploitation of copyrighted works. However, digitisation had a strong effect on rightholders' interests by facilitating and democratizing access to works, considering that libraries may reproduce them and promote their online accessibility. Litigation regarding the referred actions has dramatically increased in the last years as they may stress the normal exploitation of copyrighted works and the exclusive rights of reproduction and of distributing. Based on the European Union's legislation and jurisprudence, the present chapter analyses the lawfulness of public libraries digitisation of books from their collection in order to make them available to users without the right holder's consent, confronting them with the exclusive right of reproduction and the making available right.

INTRODUCTION

Digital libraries are one of the most central and impressive battlegrounds in the clash between copyright and access to knowledge and culture promoted by digital technology. Digital libraries are organized collections of information stored in digital formats and accessible over a network. The creation of the collection implies, except for works that originally have a digital format, massive operations of digitisation, meaning the "conversion of analogue information in any form to digital form with suitable electronic devices (such as a scanner), so that the information can be processed, stored, and transmitted through digital circuits, equipment and networks" (Lucas-Schloetter. 2011. 159). Digitisation and subsequent transmission of works in a digital support may conflict with core powers granted by copyright law to authors: the exclusive patrimonial rights to reproduce, to distribute or to communicate their works to the public or to authorize such usages by others.

DOI: 10.4018/978-1-5225-0296-8.ch004

From the perspective of the public interest, the benefits derived from digitisation and from online accessibility of intellectual works are undeniable. Access to works from people with low income, from remote regions or access to rare or out of market works is facilitated, which potentiate the growth of direct knowledge of the works and the creation of new or derivative works based on the former. Large scale initiatives and projects like *Google Books*, the *World Digital Library* or *Europeana* could act like a celestial library allowing users to store copies of works, to reproduce them wherever they have an internet broadband connection or to share it with other people. On a smaller scale, physical libraries may digitise their corporeal collection making it available to their users. Full democratization of knowledge faces, however, the obstacle of copyright infringement, which leads libraries to refrain their activities by making available only works from the public domain or small parts of copyrighted works that don't affect their normal economic exploitation.

As the European Commission declares in the Green paper on Copyright in the Knowledge Economy,

Under the current legal framework, libraries or archives do not enjoy a blanket exception from the right of reproduction. Reproductions are only allowed in specific cases, which arguably would cover certain acts necessary for the preservation of works contained in the libraries' catalogues. On the other hand, the library exception and national rules implementing it are not always clear on issues such as "format-shifting" or the number of copies that can be made under this exception. Detailed regulations in this respect result from legislative policy decisions undertaken at the national level. Some Member States have restrictive rules with respect to reproductions that can be made by libraries. In recent years, libraries and other public interest establishments have become increasingly interested not only in preserving (digitising) works but also in making their collections accessible online. If that were to take place, libraries argue, researchers would no longer have to go to the premises of libraries or archives but would easily be able to find and retrieve the required information on the Internet. Also, publishers state that they are digitising their own catalogues with a view to setting up interactive online databases where this material can be easily retrieved from the user's desktop. These services require payment of a subscription fee. (2008, p. 7)

It is therefore crucial to take into account the benefits of digitisation and the specific nature of digital copies to find an adequate balance between the protection of rights and legitimate interests of creators and the public interest in democratizing access to culture and knowledge by means of digital libraries.

Copyright is today recognized not as a mere economic privilege on the exploitation of intellectual aesthetic creations but as a human right. In Article 27 of the Universal Declaration of Human Rights, after being proclaimed that "everyone has the right freely to participate in the cultural life of the community, to enjoy the arts and to share in scientific advancement and its benefits", it is granted by § 2 that "everyone has the right to the protection of the moral and material interests resulting from any scientific, literary or artistic production of which he is the author".

Similarly, the International Covenant on Economic, Social and Cultural Rights provides in its article 15, § 1, that

States Parties recognize the right of everyone:

1. *To take part in cultural life;*
2. *To enjoy the benefits of scientific progress and its applications;*

3. *To benefit from the protection of the moral and material interests resulting from any scientific, literary or artistic production of which he is the author.*

It is not a mere coincidence that copyright is granted the dignity of a fundamental right side by side with the other fundamental right of access to cultural and scientific information. As it is pointed out by Akester,

... the rights that underpin access to information and copyright protection are linked within a perpetual cycle of discovery, enlightenment and creation. Freedom of expression, information, science and art promotes this cycle and, as such, is not only an essential element of man's spiritual freedom and of a democratic society, but also vital for the existence of a dynamic and self-renewing environment of information, knowledge and culture. (2010, p. 2)

Both copyright law and libraries have a strong role on promoting culture, science and knowledge, renewing the cycle with the creation of new cultural works and scientific discoveries. Libraries work as catalysts on the dissemination of intellectual creations, since they act as intermediaries between creators and readers, preserving works or making them available to the public.

Copyright is a branch of law traditionally related to the promotion of culture and science. Pursuant to most copyright laws, right holders are granted moral rights, like the right to paternity or the right to integrity of the work, and also the exclusive patrimonial rights to reproduce, to distribute or to communicate their works to the public or to authorize such usages. For such reason, by rewarding or incentivizing authors to create, protection of authorship and copyright are seen as indispensable means to the private and free production of cultural and scientific works without the risks of public censorship that are inherent to a system of public subsidies.

Copyright law protects original intellectual aesthetic creations which are non-tangible or immaterial goods. Therefore, the externalization of such intangible reality needs the mediation of a physical support which may transform and evolve according to the known technology. That is the foundation for the dichotomy between the *corpus mysticum*, the copyrighted creative expression, and the *corpus mechanicum* that discloses the former. For that reason, it can be considered that copyright, *per se*, was not conceptually constructed as a tangible right, but as an intangible *sui generis quasi*-property right over intellectual creations embodied in tangible objects such as books or records. In the analog world, the *corpus mechanicum* is truly corporeal, which makes it relatively easy for rightholders to control the usages of their works, considering that material objects are scarce by nature and it is expensive to embody works in physical objects (e. g., editing books) and to distribute them. For that reason, standing in a position where they cannot cause major damages to right holders, final consumers have a minor role in pre-digital copyright laws.

Digital technology has generated a major change in the field of copyright as it permitted consumers to experience and to share creative works without a corporeal fixation, just by reading online, watching movies or listening to music via streaming on video or music portals on the internet or by downloading or uploading protected content in peer-to-peer and file-sharing platforms. Digital technology has, thus, favoured an enormous, global and almost uncontrolled flow of intangible information, including copyrighted content, which could easily escape right holders' control. From the right holders' perspective, digitisation, although lowering the cost of fixation and distribution, has changed in quality and in quantity the possibilities of infringement and of other unauthorized uses: it is possible to make huge amounts of perfect copies of digitised works and to easily share and spread them globally throughout the internet, since no corporeal body is needed, unlike what happened in the analogical era. The referred state of things permitted the establishment of parallel economies based on counterfeiting and unauthorized but economically significant non-commercial uses, such as the exchange of digital files through p2p networks which have grown to such an extent that they are competing with the normal exploitation of works and challenging established commercial models (Geiger, 2010, p. 4).

Nonetheless, the core of copyright patrimonial protection remains the same today as in the pre-digital era since rightholders have the power to exclusively exploit all the non-private usages of their creations, excluding others from using it without proper authorization and, normally, remuneration. Legislators adapted copyright law maintaining the system of exclusive rights on different usages of the works and creating new forms of exploitation, granting the exclusive right to making the work accessible to the public. In the European Union, the referred right was introduced by the article 3 of the Directive 2001/29/EC of the European Parliament and of the Council of 22 May 2001 on the harmonisation of certain aspects of copyright and related rights in the information society (InfoSoc Directive). According to recital 24, the making available right "should be understood as covering all acts of making available such subject-matter to members of the public not present at the place where the act of making available originates, and as not covering any other acts". The enactment of new exclusive rights wasn't enough from the point of view of rightholders, considering the possibility of massive and global infringement and the inefficiency of analog legal tools for copyright enforcement, the reactive nature of courts and the lack of jurisdictional sovereignty in cases of transnational infringements. For such reason, rightholders, as reflected on the famous Clark slogan "the answer to the machine is in the machine" (1996, p. 139), started developing self-help systems based on technological protection measures (TPM) such as steganography, encryption or electronic agents like web crawlers or spy-bots able to hinder online infringements and economic losses and, at the same time, to provide them to manage digital rights in their contractual relations with intermediaries and consumers. Digital rights management (DRM) systems based on the combination of different TPM allow rightholders to potentially control all the utilizations of digital copyrighted works, including, *inter alia*, access to contents or even to some personal data of the users. The idea of a technological perfect control (Lessig, 2006, p. 183) of digital contents made some rightholders think that they could dismiss or to underrate copyright law's protection. Combining TPM and contracts, they unilaterally set the conditions for end users to access to protected contents. According to Guibault and Helberger,

DRM systems [...] create an environment in which various types of use, including copying, are only practically possible in compliance with the terms set by the right holders. Therefore, they usually do not deny access but rather manage access to content by combining technical measures with a payment mechanism. DRM-based business models ensure that consumers pay for actual use of content, and that the content is protected and cannot be accessed by unauthorized users. (2005, p. 9)

The referred approach wasn't sufficient *per se* considering that TPM could be circumvented by other technological devices or software and so, as a result, the information and communication technologies (ICT) industry started lobbying for the enactment of new laws whereby both copyright and technology protection measures were recognized. The goal was to technologically transform the copyright legal by internalizing and recognizing self-help digital systems.

Several international treaties and digital copyright national laws – from the Agreement on Trade Related Aspects of Intellectual Property Rights (TRIPS) or the World Intellectual Property Organization (WIPO) Copyright Treaty and the WIPO Performances and Phonograms Treaty, at the international level, to the Digital Millennium Copyright Act (DMCA), in the USA, or the InfoSoc Directive in the European Union, followed by subsequent transpositions into member state laws –, adopted the legal-technological approach for protecting creative expression by recognizing that the use of TPM was a lawful means to a digital rights management system. Moreover, the referred new generation of copyright laws provided that circumvention acts and the creation or dissemination of circumvention devices were forbidden and punished as criminal offenses. In this context, it is proper to conclude with Werra (2001) that rightholders are entitled to:

... three levels of cumulative protection: the first is the legal protection by copyright. The second level is the technical protection of works through measures protection techniques. The third level is the new legal protection against circumvention of TPM introduced by the WIPO Treaties. (p. 77)

According to the current legal background, technology can be combined with contractual provisions included in end user license agreements consequently creating what can apparently be the perfect digital rights management system taking into consideration that licensors can contractually predict which users' behaviours are lawful or not and have the means to digitally control it. That is to say that in these specific cases, copyright may be partially overridden and substituted by the combination of technology and contract law. Since this kind of provisions had substantially more to with copyright enforcement than to the material regulation of creative expression, some authors distinguish it from primary substantive copyright and called it *paracopyright* (Jaszi, 1988) or *übercopyright* (Helberger and Hugenholtz, 2007). As a starting point, full lock-up of protected content is today foreseen in copyright law, marginalizing practices that were seen in the analog world as free, like private non-commercial uses.

In what is related to access to culture and knowledge, balance within copyright law may be endangered if no exceptions or limitations are foreseen. Following article 10 of the WIPO Copyright Treaty, the InfoSoc Directive predicts some limitations or exceptions to the granted exclusive rights. According to Recital (34),

Member States should be given the option of providing for certain exceptions or limitations for cases such as educational and scientific purposes, for the benefit of public institutions such as libraries and archives, for purposes of news reporting, for quotations, for use by people with disabilities, for public security uses and for uses in administrative and judicial proceedings.

From the public interest point of view, it is unequivocally important to understand how such kind of limitations was implemented.

COPYRIGHT LIMITATIONS AND DIGITAL LIBRARIES

Before the digital technology era, a reasonable internal balance between rightholders' and users' interests could be found in copyright, since the law recognized some limitations to the powers granted to the formers. In the first place, limitations defining the protected object of copyright were foreseen, granting protection only to the original exteriorization of one idea, not to the idea itself or to pure information. The well-known idea-expression dichotomy is an objective limitation on creators' rights.

Secondly, copyright protection is time limited, which means that, once it has exceeded its term – currently, in the European Union, according to article 1 of the Directive 2006/116/EC of the European Parliament and of the Council of 12 December 2006 on the term of protection of copyright and certain related rights, the life of the author and for 70 years after his death –, the once protected work enters into the public domain.

Furthermore, copyright acts normally preview exemptions or limitations on exclusive rights, allowing free usages of copyrighted works, like fair use or fair dealing in common law copyright systems or, in the continental European systems, the statutory exemptions explicitly listed in legal instruments, combined with the three-step test rule foreseen in the Berne Convention for the Protection of Literary and Artistic Works, according to which an exception to exclusive rights can only be accepted in specific cases where it is not in conflict with the normal exploitation of the work and does not unreasonably prejudice the legitimate interests of rightholders.

The fair use doctrine is codified at 17 U.S.C. § 107 and is foreseen as a limitation on holders'rights for purposes such as criticism, comment, news reporting, teaching, scholarship, or research. Considering that fair use is an open concept, which may cause some uncertainty in its application, determining if a use is fair, must consider some factors like:

1. The purpose and character of the use, including whether such use is of a commercial nature or is for nonprofit educational purposes;
2. The nature of the copyrighted work;
3. The amount and substantiality of the portion used in relation to the copyrighted work as a whole; and
4. The effect of the use upon the potential market for or value of the copyrighted work.

The fair use defense is, therefore, appreciated a posteriori, leaving short certainty and security to unauthorized users of copyrighted content over the legality of their actions. In fact, the judgment on, for instance, the extension and the substantiality of the original work's portion that is used can only be made on casuistic terms, which increases "the economic risk inherent in relying on the doctrine — not to mention the up-front costs of defending a lawsuit or seeking a declaratory judgment" (Hayes, 2008, p. 569). In the European Union, the InfoSoc Directive starts, in its Article 2, by imposing Member States the obligation to provide for the exclusive right to authorize or prohibit direct or indirect, temporary or permanent reproduction by any means and in any form, in whole or in part:

1. For authors, of their works;
2. For performers, of fixations of their performances;
3. For phonogram producers, of their phonograms;
4. For the producers of the first fixations of films, in respect of the original and copies of their films;
5. For broadcasting organizations, of fixations of their broadcasts, whether those broadcasts are transmitted by wire or over the air, including by cable or satellite.

In Article 3 of the referred Directive, the European Union legislator predicts the author's exclusive right to authorize or prohibit any communication to the public of their works, by wire or wireless means, including the making available to the public of their works in such a way that members of the public may access them from a place and at a time individually chosen by them. Member States shall provide for the exclusive right to authorize or prohibit the making available to the public, by wire or wireless means, in such a way that members of the public may access them from a place and at a time individually chosen by them:

1. For performers, of fixations of their performances;
2. For phonogram producers, of their phonograms;
3. For the producers of the first fixations of films, of the original and copies of their films;
4. For broadcasting organizations, of fixations of their broadcasts, whether these broadcasts are transmitted by wire or over the air, including by cable or satellite.

Contrary to what is foreseen in analog copyright laws, the referred exclusive right shall not be exhausted by any act of communication to the public or making available to the public.

Cultural and scientific information protected by copyright law seems to be fully locked-up by the legislator. However, exceptions to that principle of exclusivity were foreseen. In Article 5 (2), the InfoSoc Directive imposes to Member States a list of mandatory exceptions to reproduction rights, to the right of communication to the public of works and to the right of making available to the public other subject-matter that are basically regarded to educational or scientific purposes, including "(c) specific acts of reproduction made by publicly accessible libraries, educational establishments or museums, or by archives, which are not for direct or indirect economic or commercial advantage". Furthermore, it predicted in article 5 (3) (n) that Member States may provide for limitations on the reproduction right and on the make available right in case of use by communication or making available, for the purpose of research or private study, to individual members of the public by dedicated terminals on the premises of establishments referred to in paragraph 2(c) of works and other subject-matter not subject to purchase or licensing terms which are contained in their collections.

After setting the referred exhaustive list of limitations on exclusive rights, the InfoSoc Directive foresaw the existence of limits on the recognition of limitations, since they shall only be applied in certain special cases which do not conflict with a normal exploitation of the work or other subject-matter and do not unreasonably harm the legitimate interests of the rightholder. In other words, the InfoSoc Directive imposes that limitations must respect the three-step test, when, in its original sense, predicted in Article 9 (2) of the Berne Convention, it was a sort of general clause of internal limitations on exclusive rights.

In fact, according to the identified provision, a use of copyrighted content shall only be free in certain special cases that don't conflict with a normal exploitation of the work and don't unreasonably prejudice the legitimate interests of the author. This solution is also predicted in article 10 of the WIPO Copyright Treaty, in article 13 of the Agreement on trade-related aspects of intellectual property rights (TRIPS). Senftleben (2004) points out that, in its origins, the three-step test formula reflected a compromise between the formal and harmonized recognition of the holders' reproduction right and the preservation of existing limitations in different national legislations. The option that was then taken consisted not in enumerating exhaustively a list of existing free uses, but in the formulation of a general clause and abstract criteria that, "due to its openness, [...] gains the capacity to encompass a wide range of exceptions and forms a proper basis for the reconciliation of contrary opinions" (p. 51).

However, contrary to its original purpose, the three-step test was introduced by article 5 (5) of the InfoSoc Directive, in a rather curious manner: the test was presented as a restriction to the exhaustive list of limitations of the exclusive rights over the work granted to the holders. Furthermore, Article 6 (4) of the InfoSoc Directive expressly admits the possibility of escaping from copyright law and its exceptions to contract law, since Member States only have to ensure that rightholders take appropriate measures to make available to beneficiaries the means of benefiting from those exceptions or limitations in the absence of voluntary measures, including agreements between rightholders and other parties concerned at the limitations.

The European Union two-levelled filter of copyright's internal limitations on exclusive rights leaves short space to unauthorized uses, despite the principle declared in the first part of the InfoSoc Directive's Recital (40):

Member States may provide for an exception or limitation for the benefit of certain non-profit making establishments, such as publicly accessible libraries and equivalent institutions, as well as archives. However, this should be limited to certain special cases covered by the reproduction right. Such an exception or limitation should not cover uses made in the context of on-line delivery of protected works or other subject-matter. This Directive should be without prejudice to the Member States' option to derogate from the exclusive public lending right in accordance with Article 5 of Directive 92/100/EEC. Therefore, specific contracts or licenses should be promoted which, without creating imbalances, favour such establishments and the disseminative purposes they serve.

THE *TECHNISCHE UNIVERSITÄT DARMSTADT VS ULMER* CASE

The dispute was between the *Technische Universität Darmstadt* (TU Darmstadt) and a publisher, *Eugen Ulmer KG*, regarding the digitisation by the former of the textbook of Schulze W., *Einführung in die neuere Geschichte*, contained in its academic library's collection, whose rights were held by the latter. TU Darmstadt did not take up Ulmer's offer of an opportunity to purchase and use the textbooks it publishes as electronic books, including the textbook at issue. After digitising the physical textbook from its collection, TU Darmstadt made its digital copy available to the public, by terminals installed on the premises of the library, always without Ulmer's authorization. Furthermore, TU Darmstadt permitted users to make partial or full paper copies and to store digital copies on USB pen drives.

Ulmer sued TU Darmstadt for copyright infringement, claiming that the library could no longer exercise its right to use the textbook by communication or making available for the purpose of research or private study after declining the contractual offer to purchase the electronic book. The *Landgericht Frankfurt am Main*, the competent Regional Court, decided that that the rightholder and the public establishment must have reached prior agreement on the digital use of the work concerned for the exception not to apply. The court also rejected Ulmer's application pursuing TU Darmstadt's prohibition from digitising the textbook at issue or having it digitised. Nonetheless, the court granted Ulmer's request to prohibit users of the TU Darmstadt library from being able, at electronic reading points installed therein, to print out the work and/or store it on a USB stick and/or take such reproductions out of the library.

Judging the appeal, the *Bundesgerichtshof* (Federal Court of Justice) requested the Court of Justice of the European Union (CJEU) for a preliminary ruling under Article 267 TFEU on the interpretation of Article 5(3)(n) of the InfoSoc Directive. After the transposition of the InfoSoc Directive, at the time of the facts, Article 52b of the *Gesetz über Urheberrecht und verwandte Schutzrechte*, the German law on copyright and related rights, stated on the matter of reproduction of works at electronic reading points in public libraries, museums and archives:

So far as there are no contractual provisions to the contrary, it shall be permissible to make available published works from the holdings of publicly accessible libraries, museums or archives which neither directly nor indirectly serve economic or commercial purposes, exclusively on the premises of the relevant establishment at dedicated electronic reading points for the purpose of research and private study. The number of copies of a work made available at electronic reading points shall not, in principle, be higher than the number held by the establishment. Equitable remuneration shall be paid in consideration of their being made available. The right in question may be asserted only by a collecting society.

Having doubts on the consistency of the German law with the InfoSoc Directive, the *Bundesgerichtshof* decided to stay the proceedings and refer the following questions to the Court for a preliminary ruling:

1. *Is a work subject to purchase or licensing terms, within the meaning of Article 5(3)(n) of Directive 2001/29, where the rightholder offers to conclude with the establishments referred to therein licensing agreements for the use of that work on appropriate terms?*
2. *Does Article 5(3)(n) of Directive 2001/29 entitle the Member States to confer on those establishments the right to digitise the works contained in their collections, if that is necessary in order to make those works available on terminals?*
3. *May the rights which the Member States lay down pursuant to Article 5(3)(n) of Directive 2001/29 go so far as to enable users of the terminals to print out on paper or store on a USB stick the works made available there?*

Answering the first question, the CJEU, after remembering that the limitation under Article 5(3)(n) of the InfoSoc Directive aims to promote the public interest in sponsoring research and private study, through the dissemination of knowledge, which constitutes, moreover, the core mission of publicly accessible libraries, concluded that the mere act of offering unilaterally to conclude a licensing agreement is not sufficient, since the concept of "work subject to purchase or licensing terms" refers to "contractual terms actually agreed as opposed to mere contractual offers".

The CJUE followed the Opinion of Advocate General Jääskinen, according to whom, "being satisfied with a simple offer by the copyright holder would allow the application of that exception to be made subject to unilateral decisions, which would therefore deprive the exception of its effectiveness for the establishments concerned. A teleological interpretation also requires, in view of the general interest objective pursued by the Union legislature, namely to promote learning and culture, that the user is able to rely on that exception" (CJUE, 2014, pp. 5-6).

The answer to the second question implied to determine whether the exception under article 5(3)(n) of the InfoSoc Directive, related to the making available right, allows libraries to digitise the works contained in their collections or not, since the act of reproduction isn't literally foreseen in the legal text. The CJUE, after declaring that TU Darmstadt, by giving access to the work in its terminals, practices an act of communication or of making the work available, recalled that public libraries have an ancillary right to digitise. Without such right, the exception for the making available right would be rendered largely meaningless or ineffective. The CJUE remembers that the library's right to digitise for ulterior making available to users fulfils the requirement of specificity foreseen in the Three-step test envisaged in Article 5 (5) of the InfoSoc Directive, since it is only applicable to "some of the works of a collection" when it is necessary for the purposes outlined in Article 5(3)(n). In other words, the exception does not provide space to allow a library to digitise its entire collection but only individual works.

About the third question, the CJUE classifies the acts of printing or storing works in USB disks as acts of reproduction involving the creation of a new analogue or digital copy of the work that an establishment makes available to users by means of dedicated terminals. Therefore, they fall out from the scope of the exception foreseen in Article 5(3)(n) of the InfoSoc Directive. Nevertheless, such acts may be permitted by Member States under the exception of private copy provided for in Article 5(2)(a) or (b) of the InfoSoc Directive if the rightholders receive a fair compensation.

FUTURE RESEARCH DIRECTIONS

The Technische Universität Darmstadt vs. Ulmer case (C-117/13) - was a test case and, as so, may function as a landmark for posterior decisions. It is clear in the judicial decision that the court tried to conciliate rights and exceptions or limitations in order to promote public interest in dissemination of knowledge and culture and to guarantee rightholders' legitimate interests at the same time. Still, some answers remain blurry, which may bring unsafety and inefficiency when it is certain that "unrestricted access to information will hamper copyright protection and excessive copyright protection will encumber the reception of the information contained in protected works. (Akester, 2010, p.2)

Regarding the answer to the first of the three questions, the CJEU did not examine the meaning and the scope of the expression "works (…) not subject to purchase or licensing terms". It would be important to analyse the validity and the enforceability of general contractual terms and conditions and copyright disclaimers contained in the works, considering that contractual arrangements may override copyright exceptions. If, in the past, copyright law held internally the balance between divergent rights and interests, the current legal system and the combination of contract law with digital management systems "may override copyright's escape valves – the idea-expression dichotomy, fair use, statutory exemptions – which are as much a part of copyright as are the exclusive right's themselves" (Goldstein, 2003, p. 170).

However, as Ascensão notes, "it is an historical constant that when internal limitations are missing, external limitations emerge" (2008, p. 55). That idea reflects the growing recognition of external limitations on copyright as the expansion of this branch of law has put it in collision with other fundamental rights of similar or greater importance. If users can't find protection inside the boundaries of copyright law, they will seek it outside, like in consumers' law, competition law, privacy law or directly in fundamental liberties, like the freedom of speech. The second answer raises one major problem that may endanger the scope of the exception. When the CJUE confirms the respect for the requirement of specificity of the exception,

… explicitly underscores that the ancillary right of digitisation does not allow publicly accessible libraries to digitise their entire collections. What the Court did not consider though, is that the outcome

of the application of the 3-step test to the digitisation of each individual work for the purposes of making it available for research and private study purposes may conflict with the absolute prohibition of digitising the entire collection. It remains unclear if, provided the conditions of the 3-step test are met, digitisation of a substantial volume of the works in the library's collection is lawful. (Yakovleva, 2014)

At the same time, from the rightholders' point of view, the second answer may also be criticized, because of the lithe interpretation of the second of the three-step test, the non-conflict with a normal exploitation of the work, considering that there is today a relevant market for electronic books that seemed to be forgotten in the court's analysis. A narrow and strict interpretation of the three-step test is not the only alternative to the court's interpretative methodology. It would be interesting to analyse the case under the light of a balanced interpretation of the three-step test, like the one proposed by a group of some of the most important copyright scholars in the European Union from the Max Planck Institute for Intellectual Property, Competition and Tax Law who drew some guiding principles to take into account when interpreting and applying the Three-Step Test. According to their advised opinion, not disregarding that

... account should be taken of the interests of original rightholders, as well as of those of subsequent rightholders [...], the Three-Step Test should be interpreted in a manner that respects the legitimate interests of third parties, including interests deriving from human rights and fundamental freedoms; interests in competition, notably on secondary markets; and other public interests, notably in scientific progress and cultural, social, or economic development" (Geiger, Hilty, Griffiths & Suthersanen, 2010, p. 121).

For that purpose,

... the Three-Step Test requires a comprehensive overall assessment, rather than the step-by-step application that its usual, but misleading, description implies. No single step is to be prioritized. As a result, the Test does not undermine the necessary balancing of interests between different classes of rightholders or between rightholders and the larger general public. Any contradictory results arising from the application of the individual steps of the test in a particular case must be accommodated within this comprehensive, overall assessment. (Geiger, Hilty, Griffiths & Suthersanen, 2010, p. 119)

Considering that the three-step test, as defined by the Berne Convention, must be interpreted by national legislators, when foreseeing limitations on exclusive rights, and by the judiciary, interpretation under these principles prevents reductionist results that are achieved when one focuses restrictively on one of the steps, especially on the second. In fact, reducing copyright only to its economic reflex implies forgetting its social and collective function and its public interest based justification, converting it into a body of law that merely seeks to protect investments. The answer to the last question also presents some problems as it is not clear on the lawfulness of the library's behaviour: if private copying made by users may be legal under some conditions, it is not clear if the library may enable users to the reproduction. If they are not, "the users' right to reprography and private use with respect to works available through dedicated terminals, without relevant functionality of the terminals, are simply theoretical" (Yakovleva, 2014).

CONCLUSION

The core of copyright law from the pre-digital world, where works had to be embodied in corporeal supports, remains today although it has to deal with digitisation. The survival of the economic models created for the exploitation of copyrighted corporeal works must not be the purpose of copyright law, but the respect for rightholders economic and moral interests considering the potential of the digital world. Today, copyright law recognizes more limitations to exclusive rights on analog works than on digital works, favouring the lock-up of digital information, which seems to be a paradox, considering its huge potential especially when it strengthens the exercise of the right of access to culture and to knowledge. Digitisation by libraries of works from their collection for ulterior online accessibility by their users in their internal terminals is an activity that stands precisely at the centre of the paradox. Legal uncertainty over the lawfulness of such activity must not mean that libraries become a mere repository of analog works. Access to culture and to knowledge is a part of a dialectic system where freedom of expression and protection by copyright take also place, envisaging more and more creative production. It's up to legislators and to jurisprudence to create a solution of conceptual and practical agreement focusing both rights on their complementarity and avoiding reductionist solutions where the strengthening of one directly hinders the other. The CJUE tried to do so by permitting digitisation by an academic library of copyrighted works for purposes of research and education and the subsequent accessibility of the digital copy in internal terminals, recognizing that such activity fell under the exception foreseen in Article 5 (3) of the InfoSoc Directive, but emphasizing the specificity of such act and its teleological explanation.

Some of the appointed interpretative weaknesses of the court decision may find plausible justification in the contradictory nature of the legal solutions that it has to execute. It is hard to respect the right of access to knowledge and to culture, which requires free movements of ideas and of their creative expressions when there is a system constructed to lock-up information and copyrighted content that, paradoxically, is fed by other works. No one puts new wine into old wineskins; or else the new wine will burst the wineskins and be spilled, and the wineskins will be ruined.

RECOMMENDATIONS

The present chapter discloses the existing paradox between the information highway that digital technology permitted and the informational lock-up that legislative public regulation created when trying to ensure a high level of protection of intellectual property rights.

It is recommended that legislators foresee new normative solutions that, protecting authors and rightholders on the one side, recognize, on the other side, free digital usages of protected works by public libraries in the strict pursuit of their functional finalities of democratizing access to science and culture and also by their users when acting without commercial intentions.

Access to knowledge and to culture cannot be overridden by a copyright legal author-centric system that disremembers the public interest when this should be one of the former's justifications. The core of exclusive rights granted to rightholders must be kept when dealing with private libraries with commercial purposes. However, a specific and more open legal framework for public digital libraries must be erected allowing a completely free digitization of analog works or the unauthorized distribution of digital copies of works to the libraries' users only for academic, research or private purposes, punishing ulterior distribution in a commercial scale.

Copyright law's new internal balance between public and rightholders' interests needs to be achieved and, for such purpose, a clear line defining what is a commercial or a non-commercial use, especially for academic and research purposes within the context of public digital libraries, must be drawn, creating a safe harbour for researchers or readers that seek only access to knowledge and the creation of new works.

REFERENCES

Akester, P. (2010). *The new challenges of striking the right balance between copyright protection and access to knowledge, information and culture*. Intergovernmental Copyright Committee, UNESCO. Retrieved from http://unesdoc.unesco.org/images/0018/001876/187683E.pdf

Ascensão. José de Oliveira. (2008). Sociedade da informação e liberdade de expressão. In Direito da Sociedade da Informação (7th ed., Coimbra ed., pp. 51-73).

CJEU. (2014). Court of Justice of the European Union - opinion of Advocate General Jääskinen - Case C-117/13, Retrieved from http://curia.europa.eu/juris/document/document.jsf?text=&docid=153306&pageIndex=0&doclang=en&mode=lst&dir=&occ=first&part=1&cid=77241

Clark, C. (1996). The answer to the machine is in the machine. In P. Bernt Hugenholtz (Ed.), *The future of copyright in a digital environment*. The Hague: Kluwer Law International.

Geiger, C. (2010). The future of copyright in Europe: Striking a fair balance between protection and access to information. *Intellectual Property Quarterly*, *1*, 1–14.

Geiger, C., ... (2008). A balanced interpretation of the "three-step test" in copyright law. Max Planck Institute for Intellectual Property, Competition and Tax Law. Retrieved from http://www.ip.mpg.de/shared/data/pdf/declaration_three_step_test_final_english.pdf

Geiger, C., Hilty, R., Griffiths, J., & Suthersanen, U. (2010). Declaration: A Balanced Interpretation of The "Three-Step Test" In Copyright Law. Journal of Intellectual Property, Information Technology and E-Commerce Law, 1(2), 119-122.

Goldstein, P. (2003). *Copyright's highway: from Gutenberg to the celestial jukebox*. Stanford University Press.

Hayes, C. J. (2008). Changing the rules of the game: How video game publishers are embracing user-generated derivative works. *Harvard Journal of Law & Technology*, *21*(2), 567–587.

Helberger, N., & Hugenholtz, P. B. (2007). No place like home for making a copy: Private copying in European copyright law and consumer law. *Berkeley Technology Law Journal*, *22*, 1061–1098.

Lucas-Schloetter, A. (2011). Digital Libraries and Copyright Issues: Digitisation of Contents and the Economic Rights of the Authors. In I. Iglezakis, T. Synodinou, & S. Kapidakis (Eds.), *E-Publishing and Digital Libraries: Legal and Organizational Issues* (pp. 159–179). Hershey, PA, USA: IGI Global. doi:10.4018/978-1-60960-031-0.ch009

Senftleben, M. (2004). *Copyright, Limitations and the three-step Test. An Analysis of the Three-Step Test in International and EC Copyright Law*. The Hague: Kluwer Law International.

Werra, J. (2001). Le régime juridique des mesures techniques de protection des oeuvres selon les Traités de l'OMPI, le Digital Millennium Copyright Act, les Directives Européennes et d'autres legislations (Japon, Australie). *Revue Internationale du Droit d'Auteur*, *189*, 66–213.

Yakovleva, S. (2014). Public libraries: the right to digitise and the right of reproduction. *Kluwer Copyright Blog*. Retrieved from http://kluwercopyrightblog.com/2014/10/17/public-libraries-the-right-to-digitise-and-the-right-of-reproduction/

KEY TERMS AND DEFINITIONS

Copyright: The set of exclusive moral and economic rights granted to the author or creator of an original intellectual work, including the right to copy, distribute and adapt the work.

Digital Libraries: Organized collections of information stored in digital formats and accessible over a network.

Digital Rights Management (DRM): A copyrighted work's management system based on digital technology that, amongst other powers, allows copyright holders to control access to works or to prevent unauthorized copies.

Digitization: The process of converting analog information of any form into a digital format that can be understood by computer systems or electronic devices, making it easier to store, to access and to disseminate.

Distribution (Right of): The exclusive right of a copyright owner to distribute copies of the original work to the public by sale, lease, or rental, physically or by wire or wireless means.

File-Sharing: The practice of sharing computer data or space on a network.

Information and Communication Technologies (ICT): An umbrella term reflecting a set of technological and digital tools and resources used to communicate, to create, to disseminate, to store and to manage information, including computer hardware and software, the Internet, and broadcasting technologies.

Limitations (on Copyright): A set of free uses of copyrighted works that escape rightholders control, mainly because of public interests related to research, study, freedom of speech or the respect for privacy rights.

Peer-to-Peer (P2P): A computer network designed so that computers can send information directly to one another without passing through a centralized server.

Private Copy: A copy of a copyrighted work that is made for personal and non-commercial use.

Reproduction (Right of): The exclusive right of a copyright owner to make copies of the original work.

Technological Protection Measures: Digital technology-based tools idealized to control third parties access to works or subsequent unauthorized uses.

Chapter 5
Researching Information Seeking in Digital Libraries through Information-Seeking Models

Zeinab Zaremohzzabieh
Universiti Putra Malaysia, Malaysia

Bahaman Abu Samah
Universiti Putra Malaysia, Malaysia

Seyedali Ahrari
Universiti Putra Malaysia, Malaysia

Jusang Bolong
Universiti Putra Malaysia, Malaysia

ABSTRACT

There has been an increasing amount of research focus on the development of digital libraries, particularly on information seeking. A variety of information-seeking models used by library and information science (LIS) academics investigate the manner in which information is sought and transformed into knowledge, which should be taken into account during the design of digital libraries. However, in part this reflects the lack of knowledge about how these models explain user information seeking behaviors in a digital library environment. This chapter aims to address this lack of knowledge. It presents a set of information-seeking models that can be used by LIS scholars or experts to comprehend the dynamics of information seeking by users of digital libraries. The major role of this chapter is to provide a review of the existing "models" to date, and also to present a comparative analysis of the notable models that may contribute to ways of understanding the research on information seeking in digital libraries.

INTRODUCTION

During the past couple of years, Information Technologies (ITs) have been an inspiration to the transformation in the way people have conventionally gone about seeking and retrieving information. Libraries have been fast to react to this change to the need for Web-based information. Users currently have readily available access to a plethora of Web-based information services, comprising digital libraries. The modern digital library has progressively carried some key alterations to person-information behavior

DOI: 10.4018/978-1-5225-0296-8.ch005

related sources and services. However, users of traditional libraries have dealt with only a small range of information sources: basic reference sources, manuscripts, magazines, main papers, tabloids, and academic journals. The digital library environment offers novel opportunities to collect, establish, and retrieve massive volumes of information from numerous sources, while making distributed diverse resources spread through the network seem like a single uniform federated source (Chen & Schatz, 1999). In fact, digital libraries are becoming an alternative to traditional information systems for providing access to needed information because they are able to transcend the traditional boundaries of time, space, and physicality that are typically associated with 'brick-and-mortar' libraries (Lesk, 2005, pp. 2–3; Witten, Bainbridge, & Nichols, 2010).

These digital library features are further divided to cover aspects of interface design, as well as system functionality. Since the recent past, there has been a wealth of research on the development of digital libraries, particularly regarding information seeking behavior (Fidel & Pejtersen, 2004; Pharo, 2004; Wang, Hawk, & Tenopir, 2000). These studies have demonstrated the evolution and maturing of digital libraries from information search support systems to powerful mechanisms that support an entire range of information management activities. Dania Bilal and Joe Kirby (2001) stated that information seeking research maintains the notion that customers exhibit shared features of information actions at dissimilar phases of the information seeking procedure. In addition, the changes in the area of information retrieval (IR) systems, users and information limited in IR systems raise issues for researchers to be able to gain a better understanding of information-seeking strategies in new information milieus, and posture contests for creators to design IR systems that effectively simplify user-system interactions.

In this regard, research on digital library evaluation has also made possible the emergence of a variety of the related information seeking models for evaluating the performance of digital libraries (Belkin's episode model 1996; Ingwersen's cognitive model, 1996; Kuhlthau's ISP model, 1991; Wilson's model, 1999). These information seeking models explain specific problems and processes. The procedure of information searching can be modelled in a variety of different ways based on the viewpoint employed, and thus has been defined in a variety of models. Wilson (1999) mentioned that models of information seeking may be described as frameworks to conceptualize a particular problem, and in turn may change into a statement of the association amongst theoretical suggestions.

Though, many of these models utilized by library and information science (LIS) academics concentrate on how info is sought and transformed into knowledge, and how this should influence digital library design. To some degree it reflects the lack of knowledge about the manner in which these models are able to explain user information seeking behaviors in digital library environments. As Fox and Urs (2002) emphasized, digital library research is in despairing need of effective theoretical models. Without a suitable theoretical model embracing an extensive setting of information resource uses, awareness of the real usage of digital information sources is incomplete, and thus the design of digital libraries will continue to follow the "build-it-and-they-will-come" mind set. Thus, a central theme of this chapter is to address this lack of knowledge. It begins with an evaluation of previous investigations on the information seeking behavior in the basis of a digital library setting. It then summarizes some models in the past studies and literature on information-seeking in digital libraries. Finally, this chapter also provides a conclusion, not in terms of specific data-gathering methods, but in terms of "models", and presents a comparative analysis of all the models that may contribute to ways of understanding the research on information seeking in digital libraries.

INFORMATION SEEKING BEHAVIOR IN DIGITAL LIBRARIES

Efficient information seeking has become vital in today's information society with the fast development of digitally recorded information and multifaceted information management systems. With the traditional library environment changing to that of a digital one, instructional support through web services has more potential than in the past to cope with users' needs. As Lynch (1997) mentioned, the function of the common library is changing to cope with today's networked information environment. Bordeianu, Carter and Dennis (2000) also describe Web OPACs and other web-based libraries as doorway processes for planning digital enter to library resources and collections.

The internet is a powerful tool for delivering entree to a vast series of information services from automatic databases. Ajiboye and Tella (2006), in their study on information searching behavior of university students in the University of Botswana, exposed that the internet is the most referred source by them. This was validated by the vast mainstream of participants (1089; 54.4%) using the internet. Similarly, G. T. Shakeel and P. Vinayagamoorthy (2013) inspected the information seeking behavior of Business School students in Academic City, Dubai, UAE. A major finding from the current study was that the internet and electronic resources are the most vital sources of academic information. According to Chu et al. (2008), well-structured content in e-libraries facilitate access to a vast amount of digital information on the internet. Furthermore, Ogba (2013), in their study on the information seeking behavior of final year law students in Nigeria, revealed that the respondents use Google as the first, and Wikepedia as the second, popularly used electronic resource for information seeking.

Additionaly, results from several studies stated that users' information seeking behaviors are being improved by the accessibility of digital library environments. Ellis and Oldman (2005) conducted a study on researchers' information-seeking behaviors in an English literature course at British universities, and suggested the use of electronic resources in relation to browsing and information literacy for further study. Buchanan et al., (2006) explored the information seeking behavior of undergraduate students in the field of humanities. They mentioned that a few basic policies and strategies had a crucial role in digital library use by these library users. Furthermore, the Online Computer Library Center (OCLC) conducted an online survey of university and college students in 2002, which was described in the OCLC White Paper entitled "Web-based Information Habits of College Students". The scope of this study is to explain participants' opinion about successful information delivery. This study also concentrated on issues and challenges that answer the following questions: Why do students consider information in the library and on the internet? How do they access the information they need? What do they value?

A number of studies have focused on the information seeking behaviors of professionals and students (Fidzani, 1998; Foster, 2004; Kerins, Madden, & Fulton, 2004; Steinerová & Susol, 2006). The objective of several studies was to describe how professionals and/or undergraduate students in particular fields search for information, and the related challenge and issues involved. A few of them have concentrated on the information seeking process of graduate students. Turner (2007) further investigated Information retrieval (IR), information seeking, new capability of storing and reading behavior of library clients. In the interest of digital library environments, he advised designers to be aware of user behavior in such systems. He provided detailed guidance to designers for a better understanding of digital library clients. Meanwhile, another study investigated information seeking habits of academic education faculties in public research universities (Rupp-Serrano & Robbins, 2013). The search comprises a consideration of how regularly human science faculties (e.g., eucational faculty) access and seek information, and how they keeping up-to-date on the latest developments in the field. This study also highlights the importance of electronic resources. The education faculty stresses online access to library databases, and the continuing value of printed books and e-books, for meeting researchers' information needs. Urquhart et al. (2003) explained the reasons why undergraduate students use a library's electronic databases. The study found that participants use electronic resources for coursework, which could comprise making lecture notes or preparing for a presentation. Nonetheless, the modularization effect was clear in the dominance of the use of the library's electronic resources to assist in preparing to write preps.

The discussion above shows that library users greatly benefit from a large volume of high-quality materials that have been carefully authored and stored in the digital library environment, and that information seeking in a digital library adds additional challenges to the seeker, who must also study the details of the information system being applied.

UNDERSTANDING INFORMATION-SEEKING MODELS

One way to understand the very complicated phenomenon of information seeking in a digital library is to look into the related theories or models of information seeking behaviors. Many information-seeking models and theories exist for understanding the general processes, as well as specific problems, of information seeking. Currently, utilizing information seeking models have been the main tactic within the area of library and information science educations. In addition, information-seeking models are valuable to information science and library studies, as they predict the ways in which information-seekers attempt to satisfy their needs for information, enabling information providers to develop services and resources tailored to these behaviors. Järvelin & Wilsonn (2003) stated that the strength of these models is that they provide a shortened illustration of a system which is useful for several distinctive rationales, which include the analysis of relationships, generation of hypotheses and generalisation about and prediction of phenomena. Thus, some of the most cited models in the literature on information-seeking that are frequently employed as a foundation for showing information seeking behaviors of users in digital library environments are: the Information Search Process Model (ISP) by Kuhlthau (1983), Information Seeking Model by Ellis (1989b), and the Model of Information Behavior by Wilson (1999).

A set of criteria is also presented to aid the selection of evaluation models for analysis. Therefore, for each of the models, the chapter entry covers:

- **The Name of the Model:** The name of the model is detailed in this chapter.
- **The Organisation/Author(s) that Have Developed It:** The organisation or author(s) that have established the model are indicated in this chapter. This can range from development organisations and the government, to individual researchers and academics.
- **Summary:** A one-paragraph overview of the model.
- **Initiative Focus:** An explanation of the origins and content of the particular approach, explaining how the models can be classified according to the following keys: library or information center context, approach, and stages or components.
- **SW Analysis:** The models reviewed have distinct characteristics, as well as strengths and weaknesses, while concurrently sharing commonalities as well. These characteristics of the seeking of information are used to investigate information seeking behaviors.

- **Variants:** Variations in the main models that may be used in outlining information seeking models and other information behavior aspects.
- **Examples of Use:** Summarized examples of applying the model to show the relationship between information seeking behavior and digital libraries.

KUHLTHAU'S INFORMATION SEARCH PROCESS (ISP) MODEL

Carol Kuhlthau developed the Information Seeking Process (ISP) model in 1991 based on the information search process of undergraduates and secondary students in a traditional library. Her ISP model realizes information searching as a complex route of intellectual and sentimental aspects of library users. Initially, the ISP model has adapted its roots from past models, namely, Kelly's Phases of Construction (1963), Taylor's Levels of Needs as hypothetical centres (1968), and Belkin's Anomalous States of Knowledge (1980). Kuhlthau (2005) also takes into account that the ISP model is illustrative, documenting shared behavior patterns in users' knowledge about the information seeking process for composite jobs requiring construction and learning, with a discrete beginning and ending (Kuhlthau, 2005). The ISP model is one of the greatest habitually cited models in the field of libraries and information science studies (Pettigrew & McKechnie, 2001). To date, the ISP model is helpful to those working in these fields, mainly because it draws attention to the users of information, what these users do with the information, and how these users feel when seeking for information.

Stages of Information Search Process (ISP) Model

The ISP model be made up of six specific steps, namely, task initiation, selection, exploration, focus formulation, collection and presentation, which together illustrate not only the information seeking tasks, but also how users actually feel when they conduct information searches (see Table 1 for details).

1. **Task Initiation:** This is the first stage of the information search procedure. The user seeks background information and becomes aware of an information need, in which the user may have feel-

Table 1. Concepts for information search process (ISP) model

Stages in ISP	Task Initiation	Selection	Exploration	Focus Formulation	Collection	Presentation/ Search Closure
Feelings experienced (Common to all six stages)	Uncertainty	Optimism	Frustration/ doubt Confusion	Clarity	Confidence/ sense of adaptation	satisfaction/ dissatisfaction
Actions (Common to all six stages)	Ambiguous/General			Closer/ Narrowed	Increasing interest	Directed or Clearer
Actions (Common to all six stages)	seeking background related to information		Seeking for relevant information	Formulate	Focused information	
Appropriate Task based on ISP Model	Understand	Identity	Examine		Gather	Compete

Adapted from Kuhlthau, 1991.

ings of improbability and vague thoughts. At this stage, the job is only to identify the need for information.

2. **Selection:** In this stage, the approach to be followed is identified, and the general topic for seeking information is selected. The feeling of uncertainty turns to optimism after this stage, and the user is ready to begin searching. If the approach to be followed or selection fails to retrieve appropriate materials, feelings of anxiety may arise again until the problem is solved.
3. **Exploration:** In this stage, the user investigates information about the generality of the selected topic, and seeks relevant information. However, the user may not be certain about the exact information he/she needs, and thus may feel confusion, frustration, doubt and a dip in confidence.
4. **Focus Formulation:** This stage marks the process of information search in which users resolve their uncertainty. As it becomes obvious to users which information they need, they can focus on that information, and thus, their confidence level increases.
5. **Collection:** Interaction among the user and the information systems begins in this stage. The user's task is to collect all the relevant information recognized in the previous step. Since he/she now has a clear sense of direction, the user easily identifies the information to collect, and his/her confidence continues to increase as involvement deepens and uncertainty subsides.
6. **Presentation/Search Closure:** This is the last stage in the ISP. After the information search process is complete with a new understanding, it empowers users to describe their learning to other people, or, in some such tactic, lay the learning to utilize ISP stages. The next task is to prepare the outcome for presentation, or however the individual chooses to use the information. If the presentation of the results is successful, the user feels relieved.

The six stages in the ISP model include three realms of activity in searching for information: the affective (feelings experienced), the cognitive (thoughts about content and process), and the physical (real actions taken) (see Table 1).

SW Analysis

The ISP model has strengths and weaknesses:

Strengths:

- The model can be examined in a diversity of college and school library locations.
- It is the primary mode to concentrate on affective states in library and information science (LIS).
- The model may be more descriptive, analytical, and testable.
- The model is for the most part a linear process.
- The model is more general.
- A novel facet of the ISP model was the enclosure of the affective, the cognitive, and the physical aspects.
- The model reveals not only the user-centered, action-oriented process of interaction, but also the returning and unscrupulous nature of the information seeking behavior as well.

Weaknesses:

- The ISP model does not highlight the task of the information provider, nor does it draw attention to the users' information need or the background and context in which they rise.
- The ISP model focuses significantly on feelings or affecting dimensions, so methods (e.g., qualitative and quantitative) for evaluating the model are not sufficient to detect these aspects.
- The stages are most often presented and conducted in a linear fashion that does not seem to explain information seeking in a constantly shifting and non-linear environment.

VARISTIONS IN INFORMATION SEARCH PROCESS (ISP) MODEL

Task-Based Information Retrieval (IR) Process

Some versions of the IR model alter some aspects of the ISP model. In 2001, Vakkari polished the ISP model in the framework of IR within a model of the task-based IR process, based on data from a longitudinal study with student participants (Vakkari, 2001). He improved the stages used by Kuhlthau in the task performance context, and categorized the six stages of the ISP model into three main stages: pre-focus (the ISP model's 1st, 2nd, and 3rd stages), focus formulation (the ISP model's 4th stage), and post-focus (the ISP model's 5ht and 6th stages; see Table 2 for details).

Similar to ISP the model, Vakkari's model is a longitudinal information searching process relating to writing an academic paper. Preparing the information searching process to its context, Vakkari's model outlines key components of continual searches, comprising the process of task performance, coherence and specificity of information, estimated contribution, actions on running searches, choice channels, questions and relevance judgements to keep the references retrieved, documents gained and applied, and application of information in documents. The model also defines the relations among these components, normally in a one-way task in linear ordering, search actions, information action, and evaluation action (see Table 3).

ELLIS' MODEL OF INFORMATION-SEEKING BEHAVIOR

In 1984, David Ellis first published his Information-Seeking Behavior model in 1984. Ellis (1989a) described his model as the information seeking patterns of social scientists, and categorized the patterns into their basic behavioral features. He believes that, when the IR system includes these patterns, researchers will find the IR system easier to apply; and adapt the IR systems to each person's preferred

Table 2. Core principles of the task-based IR process

Components	Description
Pre-Focus Phase	Thoughts about process and content are ambiguous and general, and this makes it difficult for researchers to state concretely what information is required.
Focus Formulation	Once establishing the pre-focus phase, the search is directed, heading to more relevant information being accepted.
Post-Focus	Searches are more exact; this phase can include rechecking for extra information.

Table 3. Examples of use – Information search process model

Reference	Focus and Aim	Method	Model Application	Finding on Digital Library Environment
C.C. Kuhlthau, J.Heinström and R. J. Todd (2008)	• **Focus of this Study:** Digital library environments (e.g., electronic sources and databases). • **The Aim:** Examines the continued usefulness of Kuhlthau ISP model in digital library environments at ten new Jersey public schools	Qualitative and quantitative methods	Kuhlthau ISP model	• **Findings Rely on the Stages of the ISP Model:** The findings of this study support the progression of feelings, thoughts and actions and validate the ISP model in the altering information environment for clarifying students' information behavior process. • **Findings Rely on the Stages of the ISP Model:** The formulation and exploration stages are the most challenging stages of students' behavior search process
L. E. Adams (2009)	• **Focus of this Study:** Library Websites (i.e., library catalogues and databases compete with Google). • **The Aim:** Examine the gaps between current library IR systems and the information seeking habits of Gen Y Students at the Stellenbosch University	Qualitative study • **Data Gathering Methods:** Interviews, journal writings and surveys	Kuhlthau ISP model • **The Reason:** Gen Y students follow the stages of ISP model with regard to feeling, thought, and actions when searching information in the digital library environment	Findings rely on the stages of the ISP model: **1. Initiation:** Knowledge of participants declined when starting to seek information on a particular topic. **2. Selection:** The participants did not make harder to select a topic, however that they hesitate that they did not know how to prepare to write assignments **3. Exploration:** The participants did not complete the stage of discovering and gathering information for an assignment and experienced vagueness **4. Focus Formulation:** The participants did complete the stage **5. Collection:** The participants felt excited, focused and certain about the information they collected for their topic. **6. Presentation:** The students complete their assignment **7. Result:** Expected that not all of the participants went through all the ISP model' s stages

style of seeking information (D. Ellis, 1989b). Ellis was the first to develop the features of information-seeking habits of social scientists, and how they seek information and relate to the materials, as opposed to the information they apply and the way in which materials are acquired. According to Ellis (1989a), the model is based on the experience of social scientists from their own information seeking activities. He has developed the model further in other information seeking studies of several groups of researchers from different disciplines, including engineers (D. Ellis, 1993), scientists (D. Ellis & Haugan, 1997), and physicists and chemists (D. Ellis, Cox, & Hall, 1993). The model has also been verified by other academics, including social scientists (Meho and Tibbo, 2003), lawyers (Makri, Blandford, & Cox, 2008), and Web users in industry (Choo, Detlor, & Turnbull, 2000).

Features of Information Seeking Behavior Model

The Information Seeking Behavior model consists of eight specific features, including Starting, Chaining, Browsing, Differentiating, Monitoring, Extracting, Verifying, and Ending (see Figure 1 for details).

- **Starting/Surveying:** The first feature of Ellis's model. It starts with searching information and gathering the initial information for the search, as well as selecting early points for the search.

Figure 1. A stage process version of Ellis' (1994) behavioral framework
Source: Wilson, 1999, p. 255.

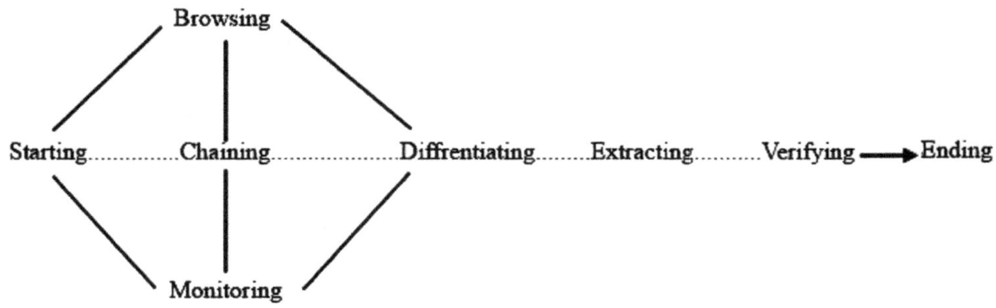

- **Chaining:** When the users follow strings of citations or other methods of referential links between materials to recognize different sources of information. Chaining can be a forward or backward activity. A forward activity can occur when users search different sources that relate to the first search or follow citations in the source of information. It could also be a backward activity when a reference from an early source is tracked.
- **Browsing:** Includes semi-structured or semi-directed searching in the way of potential interest as a monitoring action through screening and scanning of tables of contents, and journals to uncover something of specific interest.
- **Differentiating/Distinguishing:** Considered an activity in which information seekers categorize the sources of information based on their value and applicability to their information need.
- **Monitoring:** Like seeking information for existing awareness purposes, where the user keeps an awareness of progresses in his field of interest within the monitoring of specific sources.
- **Extracting:** In this feature, the user works systematically within a specific source to place materials of interest in the extracting manner. This suggests the selective recognition of related material in the source of information, and is characterized as a key part of the information-seeking behavior of many academics.
- **Verifying and Ending:** These two last features of Ellis's model were added to the 1993 model. They are activities used to confirm the information accuracy, and activities occurring at the end of researching the topic, such as preparing a paper for presentation or publication (D. Ellis et al., 1993).
- **Notice:** Ellis notes that "the specified interrelation of the structures in any user's information seeking behavior will vary from the unique environments of the information seeking behaviors of the user related to that specific point in time".

SW Analysis

Strengths:

- The suitability of applying the model to specify design insights by providing activities for those users who want to accomplish tasks within the systems.
- The model is more generic.
- Ellis is one of the first to model the information-seeking habits of social scientists.

- The model functions at many levels of the overall information seeking process.
- The mode is applicable and valid over a variety of empirical fields.
- The model is established on practical studies and has been tested in numerous succeeding studies, and with many sets of users.

Weakness:

- The model does not consider many variables and factors normally intricate in information seeking.
- The model does not directly suggest analysable relations.
- The model itself is static in that it does not provide a feedback loop between the various behaviors.
- The features of the model do not signify a set of phases that any searches follow when searching information.
- The model does not comprise the activities of information bringers.
- The model does not consider the user's information need or the context in which those needs rise.

Variations in Information-Seeking Behavior Model

Ellis has been qualified with creating one of the greatest key models of information-seeking processes in the social sciences field. Ellis claims that his model can be potentially combined with a flexible IR system. He anticipated to include hypertext links, bibliographic images, citation searching skills, and graphic imageries of pages of contents. His idea could be named a prediction, considering the way the digital library environment has eased his ideas. Many researchers verified and extended the model for information-seeking patterns of social sciences and humanities researchers in the digital age. In 2005, Xuemei Ge (2005) refined the model to come up with a new model with more features. The overall aim of this model was to evaluate how technology adds to the information-seeking habits in social studies at the University of Tennessee, Knoxville; and how well Ellis's model works with new technologies. His study investigates the information-seeking behavior of academics in these disciplines, and covers the David Ellis model for social scientists.

In his study, Ellis's model was upgraded by comprising two extra features, along with the six initial features of the Ellis model: starting, chaining, browsing, monitoring, differentiation, and extracting. Ge (2005) proposes two additional features: "preparation and planning" and "information management", as the analysis of his study showed that some improvements to the basic model are needed because several activities relate to information-seeking, or tasks that cannot be sorted into only the six features of Ellis's model (See Tables 4 and 5 for details).

WILSON'S MODELS OF INFORMATION BEHAVIOR

Thomas D. Wilson has put forth a series of models of information searching over many years, more specifically, 1981, 1996, 1997, and 1999. Wilson (1999) distinguishes his models of information behavior from previous models of information seeking since he stated that information behavior models are more related to user behavior surrounding the actual beginning of information-seeking. They also have a broader viewpoint of the information search than using computer-based IR systems (e.g., the World Wide Web) or manual information systems (e.g., a library or a newspaper). Wilson's (1999) model also

Table 4. The features of information-seeking behavior model in the digital age

Features	Type of Activities
Starting	Start research and collecting the initial materials to research through electronic information resources.
Chaining	For some participants, the most significant feature of the Elis's model is "chaining.
Browsing	"Browsing" e-journals or Web pages does not seem completely different in nature from browsing the table of contents in book chapters or journal articles.
Monitoring	Monitoring almost precedes starting through the Web and other electronic resources.
Differentiation	The feature has become a lot more complex. Assessing, relying on where you get the resources from, can be problematic.
Extracting	
Preparation & Planning	Seeking information needs planning, attention to a variety of technology and tools that allow information to be recognized, situated and obtained.
Information Management	It could possibly qualify as a new feature, as the academic can deal with large amounts of information via a variety of approaches and resources.

Ge, 2005, 2010.

Table 5. Examples of use – information-seeking behavior model

Reference	Focus and Aim	Method	Model Application	Finding on Digital Library Environment
Makri, Blandford, Cox (2008)	• **Focus of This Study:** Electronic legal resources. • **The Aim:** Analysis information-searching habits of 27 academic lawyers, who were asked to think clearly whilst using digital legal materials to find information for their work.	Qualitative method • **Data Gathering Methods:** A naturalistic observational part in addition to an in-depth interview part	Ellis's model in low-level by using it as a lens rather than as a validation of the model • **The Reason:** Ellis's features do not provide any direct design specifications for interactive systems, so 'leap' between ensuing design decisions and kinds of activities are less of a leap than that needed	Findings refined the model by the levels that behavior was observed to conduct at (i.e. the source, materials, content, and search result levels) and characters of the three higher-level activities of 'identifying and locating', 'accessing', and 'selecting and processing.' 'Identifying and locating' resources might be enabled by one or many of a main set of lower-level behaviors (surveying, monitoring, searching, surfing, extracting and binding).
Azami and Fattahi (2010)	• **Focus of This Study:** Four database user interfaces (i.e., Emerald, Science Direct, ProQuest, and Ebsco) • **The Aim:** Recognize the key features as well as the weaknesses and strengths of database interfaces in relation to users' information seeking behaviors.	Qualitative method based on heuristic evaluation[1] • **Data Gathering Methods:** Checklist and direct observation	Ellis' information seeking behavior model • **The Reason:** The model takes into account as the most appropriate model in new digital environments (e.g., the Web and various online databases.	Results rely on the features of the Ellis model **1. Starting:** This feature is very common among the databases (e.g., provide various key icons in their interfaces to assist the users for the search of necessary information. **2.Chaining:** Was verified on the database graphic interfaces in different modes. **3. Browsing:** The function of this icon is not matched with the intentions of "browsing" and the users' need (e.g., Ebsco database has completely ignored this feature) **4. Differentiation:** Recognizing among various sources for users through items **5. Monitoring:** Databases offer suitable sources along with relevant facilities in order to maintain users up-to-date with relevant and different information **6. Extracting:** Databases are able to assist their users to emphasize sources they need within the "extracting" feature

clarifies three phases of information seeking. 1) Why is information seeking expected to occur more in reply to some requirements than others? 2) Why is a source of the information applied more than others? 3) Why do users' views of their own ability and value affect their success in meeting the goal of information? His model highlights "information process" and appeals a feedback loop in which way information seeking is thought of as iterative operation at several stages, rather than a consecutive one (Wilson, 1999).

Wilson's (1999) Model of Information Behavior

Wilson's 1999 model (see Figure 2) is a main review of that of 1981, drawing on inquiry from a range of disciplines and fields other than Information Science (Ingwersen & Järvelin, 2005; Wilson, 1999). These fields include psychology, health communication, innovation, decision-making theory, psychology, and consumer research. The model evokes the cycle of information activities, from the rise of the context of information need to the stage when information is being applied (use and information administering) (Niedzwiedzka, 2003).

The 1996 model introduces some new components to the older model. First, the barriers in the earlier model are now defined as intervening variables, which comprise demographic, psychological, role-related or social, environmental, and source features. Several forms of information-seeking behavior are identified as passive attention, passive, active, and ongoing search.

Figure 2. Wilson's model of information behavior (1999), demographic, role-related, or social

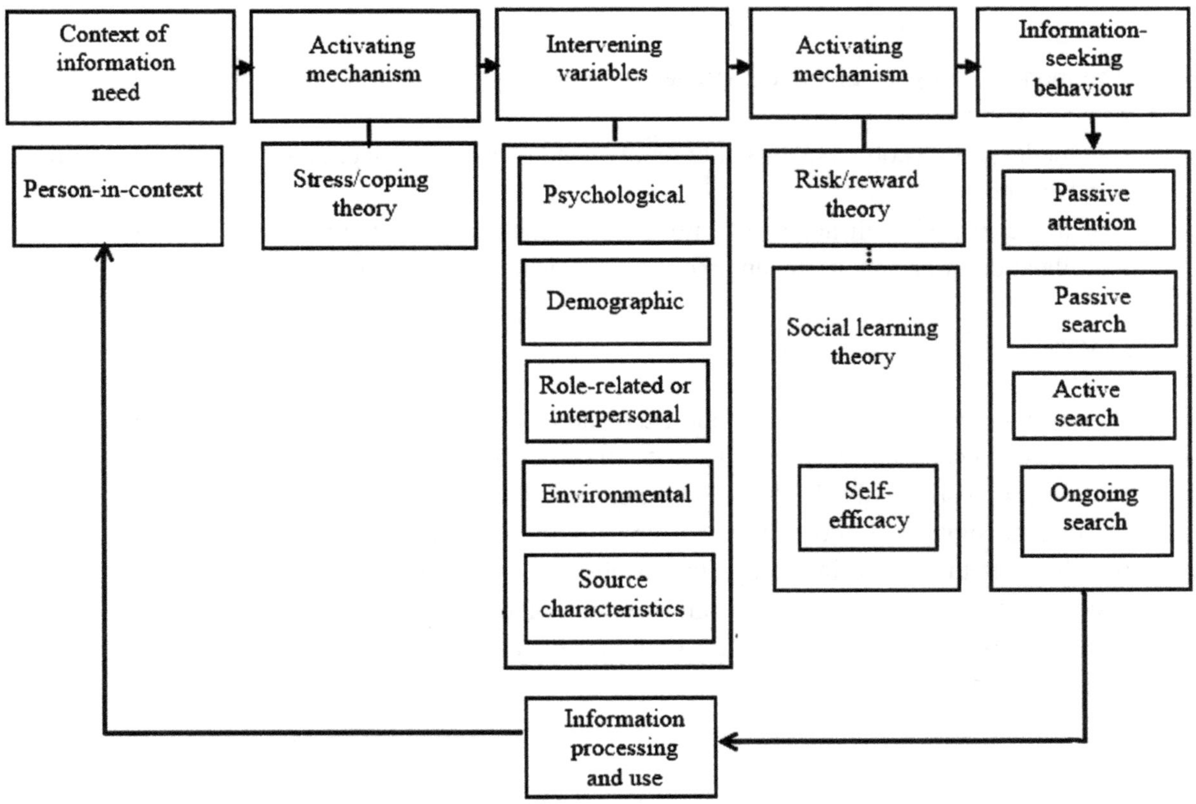

- **Passive Attention:** Obtaining information without seeking for it.
- **Passive Search:** Almost unintentional when the user obtains related information.
- **Active Search:** Seeker dynamically seeks information.
- **On-Going Search:** An extension of what the user has studied within Active Search, allowing improved information behavior.

Furthermore, two other notions were outlined. The first one, activating structures related to the subsequent theories:

- **Stress/Coping Theory:** Which may label why specific needs lead to information seeking behaviors that others do not.
- **Risk and Reward Theory:** For example, the users may be concerned to seek information if the risk of not having it looks high.
- **Social Learning Theory:** Which includes the perception of self-efficacy, or the users' belief in their capability to complete a specific task.

The second concept concerns information processing and use. Consequently, the model continues through macro-behavior. However, its growth and the presence of other theoretic behavior models makes it a stronger foundation of hypotheses and additional research than Wilson's previous model.

SW Analysis

Strengths:

- The model has a general and comprehensive range in that it can be used for all kinds of seekers of information.
- The model gives a complete insight of opinion and ideas or a map of areas in revaluating information behavior.
- The model includes all angles of information behavior, from individual in environment, need identification information use, and mediating variables to information gaining.

Weakness:

- It does not have organized power and explanatory power in that it does not put forward clearly organized concepts and relationships that can be examined and calculated.
- Every hypothesis is only absolute, and is not made unambiguous.
- There is no sign of the procedures whereby environment has its consequence on the user, nor of the elements that result in the opinion of obstacles and barriers, nor of whether the numerous expected barriers have different or similar effects on the motivation of users to seek information.
- There are no clear parts that stimulate thinking about the sorts of features that a more comprehensive model should contain.

Variations in Wilson's 1996 Model of Information Behavior

Sandra Tury, Lyn Robinson, and David Bawden, (2015) extended the version of the Wilson's 1999 model for effectively supporting the library and information needs of distance learners in the digital age, using the students of the International Programmes of the University of London as part of a case study (see Figure 3). This model was chosen because the concept of 'intervening variables' in the Wilson's 1999 model can enhance or hinder the whole process of information-seeking behavior, including acquisition and use. According to Thórsteinsdóttir (2005), the model is important for distance learning, as often learners are confronted with numerous barriers, such as poor information and computer literacy.

In light of the findings, a revised version of this model can be derived, specifically for considering the distance learning context. This variant of the model, shown in Figure 3, extends some of the generic variables of the original (e.g., mediating variables, activating methods, context of information need, and person-in-context) to make them more specifically relevant to distance learning studies.

Figure 3. An extension of Wilson's model for the information behaviors of distance learners
Tury et al., 2015.

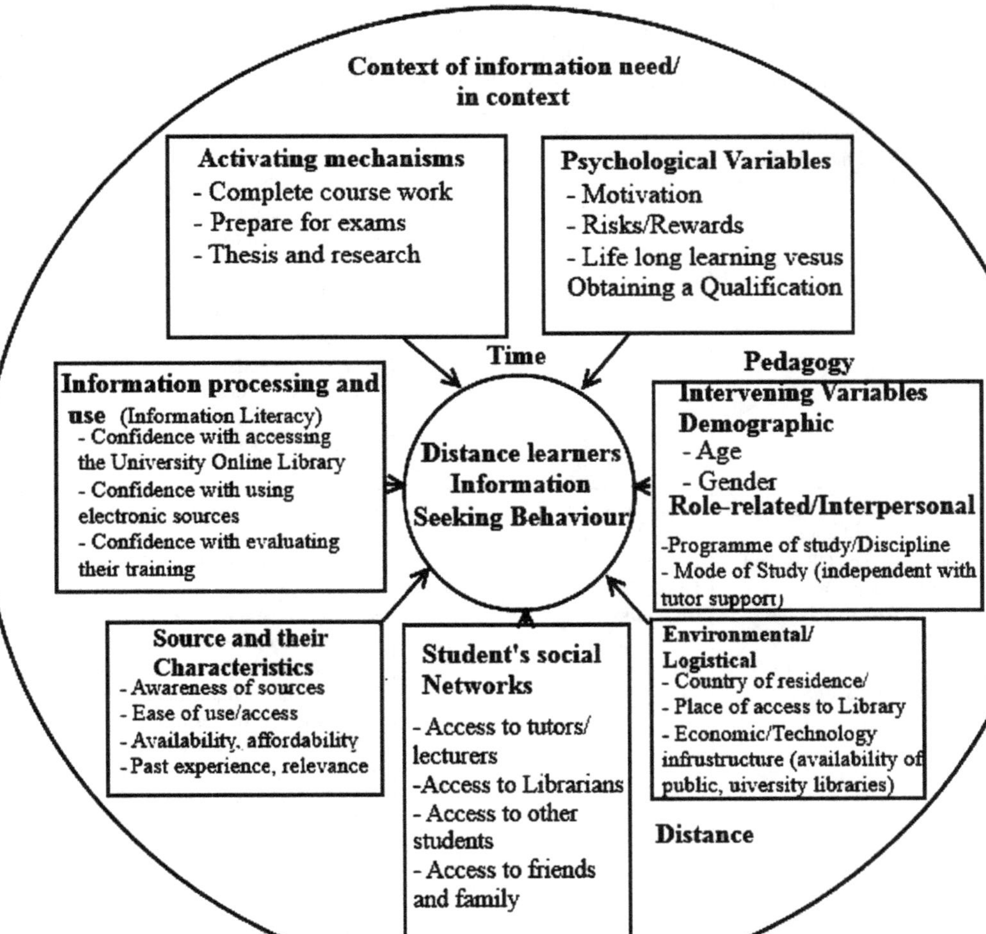

This extension leaves unchanged the basic structure of Wilson's model in 1999, expressing the process of information seeking, while allowing a concentration on the aspects of most importance for distance learners (see Table 6).

VARIATIONS IN ISP MODEL, ELLIS MODEL, AND WILSON'S MODEL

Mohammed Nasser Al-Suqri (2011) refined the ISP model, Ellis model, and Wilson's 1999 model, and gives a novel model of information-seeking behavior. He analyses the ability of this model to portray contemporary information-seeking through e-resources between social researchers at Sultan Qaboos University in Oman. The results of the study provided support for new additional factors relating to the

Table 6. Examples of use – Wilson's 1999 model of information behavior

Reference	Focus and Aim	Method	Model Application	Finding on Digital Library Environment
Mostert & Ocholla (2005)	• **Focus of This Study:** Digital sources in libraries of Parliaments • **The Aim:** Examine the parliamentary info, sources, and facilities in South African libraries and control the role that is acted by parliamentary information services.	Quantitative study • **Data Gathering Methods:** Survey	Wilson' 1999 model **The Reason:** To help our thinking of the environment on information seeking habits of parliamentarians in South Africa	Results depend on the intervening variables of the Wilson' 1999 model: 1. Use of electronic sources almost matching that of print sources /they access information across individual sources and have academic qualifications/ education 2. The barriers they meet while seeking for information: 3. Limited ICT knowledge and skills for exploiting technology and insufficient information of the searching and retrieval technology. 4. Does not fulfil their information demands because of inadequate marketing of their services 5. Lack of innovative information services; unawareness of the users of their information provision potential. 6. Low-level information services provided 7. The complexity of information behavior among parliamentarians in relationship to human intermediaries
Ogba (2013)	• **Focus of This Study:** E-library and online database (i.e., OPAC and card catalogue) • **The Aim:** Study the information seeking behavior of last year law students in Ekiti State University	Qualitative method • **Data Gathering Methods:** Face to face interview technique	Wilson's 1999 model of information seeking behavior.	Findings rely on the intervening variables of the Wilson' 1999 model: 1. No use of library digital facilities. 2. Use Google website. 3. Many of the respondents did not know that reference resources were parts of materials 4. Avoids seeking assistance from library staff 5. The obstacles found in this study 6. Insufficient sources from internet surfing, 7. Incapability to choose perfect resources required for research, 8. Lack of data on positions to apply for information seeking, 9. Lack of Nigerian online resources 10. These barriers to be affected by 11. Dearth of skills, thinking of library team, information, 12. Ease in getting sources, bad practices from earlier research.

location and format of the source of information, since these appropriate factors were located to have a main influence on the information-seeking process among the participants (see in Figure 4), and that the model can be useful to up-to-date information-seeking regardless of the variations in the information setting.

CONCLUSION

Information-seeking models enjoy widespread usage in the field of information and library sciences, but they have so far been rarely used in the context of the digital library, partly because of the lack of a proper information seeking model covering a broad context of information online resource uses, and because understanding of the actual usage of digital library environment is limited. However, the digital library seems to have an important influence on the information seeking behavior of library users. The developing digital library requires users to have a refined model of information seeking in order to be able to properly employ the wide variety of online resources accessible, and also to transfer among users who need, seek, manage, give and employ information in different contexts.

Accordingly, this chapter provides a good summation of information seeking behavior in digital libraries through general models of information-seeking. There is a large gap in our knowledge when users have limitations and difficulties in research on digital libraries. The present chapter first addressed a variety of viewpoints of information seeking in digital library environments in previous researches (e.g., seeking through numerous digital library databases, information seeking through online resources in

Figure 4. Social science scholars' information-seeking behavior

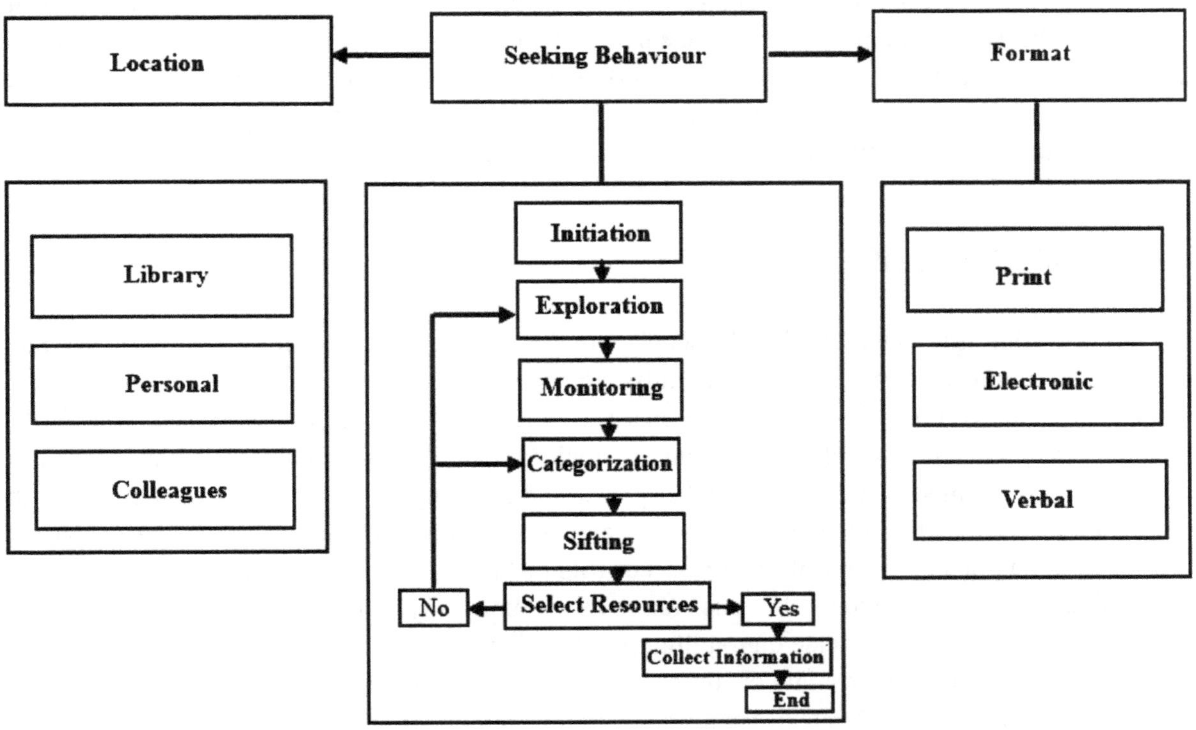

different types of university and school library settings, and why library users search through a number of digital libraries databases). The second part of chapter then discusses models of information seeking in the context of information science and library studies, including Kuhlthau's (1993) Information Search Process Model, Ellis' (1994) Model of Information-Seeking Behavior, and Wilson's (1999) Model of Information Behavior. These three models were summarized and discussed as they are relevant to the investigation on the information needs and information-seeking behavior of digital library users. However, the entire scope of these models is complex, requiring a number of diverse strategies for accomplishing a specified goal. These three models in the field of information behavior do not try to explain the same set of activities or phenomena: some, as in the case of Kuhlthau's (1993) model, present six specific stages of activity in which the behavioral patterns may happen; others, like Ellis (1994) model, are involved with behavioral patterns in the real search activity. In addition, Ellis's model is a set of activities inside what Kuhlthau brands a 'collection', and that all of these are rooted within information behavior model of Wilson's (1999) in overall.

From the above discussion, it is apparent that all model denotes a different, but also parallel or an coinciding, approach to information-seeking behavior investigation. Currently, we illustrated the use of the models through the discussion of several detailed examples of how the models can be employed to assess both the functionality and usability of the information seeking behavior of users in the digital library context. The chapter then ensued to present two other novel models that may be beneficial in understanding the influence of seeking and searching information over digital libraries. In the meantime, there have been several models that were presented in the chapter, including the models of Tury, Robinson and Bawden (2015), and Nasser Al-Suqri (2011), signifying digital library evaluation notions, tactics, and models variations in the main models that may be employed in outlining models of information seeking and other aspects of information behavior.

In summary, this chapter helps to confirm that the library and information science discipline is based on models which are usually robust and of continuing value. Together, there is a clear need to adapt these, as in the existing examples and models in this chapter, so that they altogether reveal the present-day information-seeking environment in today's digital age. These future research efforts could further our understanding of the uses of information-seeking models, as well as the range of geographical and cultural contexts in which other academic scholars conduct their research.

RECOMMENDATIONS

In this viewpoint, it is suggested that the scholars in the area of library and information science must concentrate on information seeking model in the context of the digital library. These models must be used as the key instrument to deliver a rational and empirical approach from which to build further theoretical and realistic research. Further epistemological, theoretical and empirical studies of the relation between these models are also compulsory. It would be thought-provoking to investigate how the interrelations between these models are valuable and beneficial to analyse specific and particular user groups' information seeking and information need in digital library setting. What's more, both quantitative and qualitative research is required in this area so as to empirically validate and confirm these models of information-seeking for diverse digital libraries. To learn more about information seeking behavior activities or searching methods, and the development of novel information seeking model are required that actually observe search strategies and tactics used by digital library users. This type of model will help to determine true information seeking abilities and to instruct and teach searchers how to search and evaluate information found on the Internet. As a final point, the use models of information-seeking have been conducted in this area in the past, nonetheless this is vital in order to identify best practice in the digital library so they can be more broadly accepted.

REFERENCES

Adams, L.E. (2009). *Information seeking behaviour of Generation Y students at the Stellenbosch University Library and Information Service* (Magister Bibliothecologiae). University of the Western Cape. Retrieved from http://etd.uwc.ac.za/handle/11394/2715

Ajiboye, J.O., & Tella, A. (2006). Class attendance and gender effects on undergraduate students' achievement in a social studies course in Botswana. *Essays in Education*, *18*(1), 1–11.

Al-Suqri, M. N. (2011). Information-seeking behavior of social science scholars in developing countries: A proposed model. *The International Information & Library Review*, *43*(1), 1–14. doi:10.1080/10572317.2011.10762875

Azami, M., & Fattahi, R. (2010). Matching database user interfaces with Ellis model of information seeking behavior: results of a qualitative survey. *Proceedings of the QQML2010*, Chania, Crete, Greece. Retrieved from http://www.researchgate.net/profile/Mohammad_Azami/publication/228965938_Matching_database_user_interfaces_with_Ellis_model_of_information_seeking_behavior_results_of_a_qualitative_survey/links/00b7d521cf0b43da95000000.pdf

Belkin, N. J. (1980). Anomalous states of knowledge as a basis for information-retrieval. *Revue Canadienne Des Sciences De L Information [Canadian Journal of Information Science]*, 5(May), 133–143.

Belkin, N. J. (1996). Intelligent information retrieval: whose intelligence? In Proceedings of the Fifth International Symposium for Information Science (Vol. 96, pp. 25–31). Konstanz: Universitätsverlag Konstanz. Retrieved from http://core.kmi.open.ac.uk/download/pdf/11540431.pdf#page=23

Bilal, D., & Kirby, J. (2001). Factors Influencing Children's and Adults' Information Seeking on the Web: Results of Two Studies. *Proceedings of the ASIST Annual Meeting* (Vol. 38, pp. 126–40). Retrieved from http://eric.ed.gov/?id=EJ637598

Bordeianu, S., Carter, C. E., & Dennis, N. K. (2000). Delivering electronic resources with Web OPACs and other Web-based tools: Needs of reference librarians. *RSR. Reference Services Review*, *28*(2), 111–119. doi:10.1108/00907320010326683

Buchanan, G., Cunningham, S. J., Blandford, A., Rimmer, J., & Warwick, C. (2006). Information seeking by humanities scholars. Retrieved from www.ucl.ac.uk/slais/claire-warwick/articles/ECDL2.doc

Chen, H., & Schatz, B. (1999). Guest Editors' Introduction: Digital Libraries—Technological Advances and Social Impacts. *Computer, 32*(2), 0045–50.

Choo, C. W., Detlor, B., & Turnbull, D. (2000). Information seeking on the Web: An integrated model of browsing and searching. *First Monday*, *5*(2). doi:10.5210/fm.v5i2.729

Chu, H. C., Hwang, G. J., Huang, S. X., & Wu, T. T. (2008). A knowledge engineering approach to developing e-libraries for mobile learning. *The Electronic Library*, *26*(3), 303–317. doi:10.1108/02640470810879464

Ellis, A. (1994). *Reason and emotion in psychotherapy*. Secaucus, NJ: Birch Lane.

Ellis, D. (1989a). A behavioural approach to information retrieval system design. *The Journal of Documentation*, *45*(3), 171–212. doi:10.1108/eb026843

Ellis, D. (1989b). Behavioural approach to information retrieval system design. *The Journal of Documentation*, *46*, 191–213.

Ellis, D. (1993). Modeling the information-seeking patterns of academic researchers: A grounded theory approach. *The Library Quarterly*, *63*(4), 469–486. doi:10.1086/602622

Ellis, D., Cox, D., & Hall, K. (1993). A comparison of the information seeking patterns of researchers in the physical and social sciences. *The Journal of Documentation*, *49*(4), 356–369. doi:10.1108/eb026919

Ellis, D., & Haugan, M. (1997). Modelling the information seeking patterns of engineers and research scientists in an industrial environment. *The Journal of Documentation*, *53*(4), 384–403. doi:10.1108/EUM0000000007204

Ellis, D., & Oldman, H. (2005). The English literature researcher in the age of the Internet. *Journal of Information Science*, *31*(1), 29–36. doi:10.1177/0165551505049256

Entezaryan, N., & Fattahi, R. (2009). The study of user`s understanding of the interface environment of database on the basis of Nilson models. *Library & Information Science Research*, *47*(3), 43–64.

Fidel, R., & Pejtersen, A. M. (2004). From information behaviour research to the design of information systems: The Cognitive Work Analysis framework. *Information Research*, *10*(1), 10–11.

Fidzani, B. T. (1998). Information needs and information-seeking behaviour of graduate students at the University of Botswana. *Library Review*, *47*(7), 329–340. doi:10.1108/00242539810233459

Foster, A. (2004). A nonlinear model of information-seeking behavior. *Journal of the American Society for Information Science and Technology*, *55*(3), 228–237. doi:10.1002/asi.10359

Fox, E. A., & Urs, S. R. (2002). Digital Libraries. In B. Cronin (Ed.), *Annual Review of Information Science and Technology* (Vol. 36, pp. 503–589).

Ge, X. (2005). Information-seeking Behavior of Social Sciences and Humanities Researchers in the Internet Age [Master Thesis]. University of Tennessee, Knoxville. Retrieved from http://trace.tennessee.edu/utk_gradthes/1899/

Ge, X. (2010). Information-seeking behavior in the digital age: A multidisciplinary study of academic researchers. *College & Research Libraries*, *71*(5), 435–455. doi:10.5860/crl-34r2

Ingwersen, P. (1996). Cognitive perspectives of information retrieval interaction: Elements of a cognitive IR theory. *The Journal of Documentation*, *52*(1), 3–50. doi:10.1108/eb026960

Ingwersen, P., & Järvelin, K. (2005). Information retrieval in context: IRiX. In ACM SIGIR Forum (Vol. 39, pp. 31–39). ACM. Retrieved from http://dl.acm.org/citation.cfm?id=1113351

Järvelin, K., & Wilson, T. D. (2003). On conceptual models for information seeking and retrieval research. *Information Research, 9*(1). Retrieved from http://InformationR.net/ir/9-1/paperl63. html

Kelly, G. (1963). *A theory of personality: The psychology of personal constructs*. New York, NY: Norton.

Kerins, G., Madden, R., & Fulton, C. (2004). Information Seeking and Students Studying for Professional Careers: the Cases of Engineering and Law Students in Ireland. *Information Research: An International Journal, 10*(1). Retrieved from http://arrow.dit.ie/ittsupart/3/

Kuhlthau, C. C. (1983). *The research process: Case studies and interventions with high school seniors in advanced placement English classes using Kelly's theory of constructs* [PhD dissertation]. Rutgers University, New Brunswick.

Kuhlthau, C. C. (1991). Inside the search process: Information seeking from the user's perspective. *Journal of the American Society for Information Science*, *42*(5), 361–371. doi:10.1002/(SICI)1097-4571(199106)42:5<361::AID-ASI6>3.0.CO;2-#

Kuhlthau, C. C. (1993). A principle of uncertainty for information seeking. *The Journal of Documentation*, *49*(4), 339–355. doi:10.1108/eb026918

Kuhlthau, C. C. (2005). Towards collaboration between information seeking and information retrieval. *Information Research*, *10*(2), 10–12.

Kuhlthau, C. C., Heinström, J., & Todd, R. J. (2008). The 'information search process' revisited: is the model still useful? *Information Research, 13*(4).

Lesk, M. (2005). *Understanding digital libraries* (2nd ed.). San Francisco, CA: Morgan Kaufman.

Lynch, C. (1997). Searching the Internet. *Scientific American*, *276*(3), 52–56. doi:10.1038/scientificamerican0397-52 PMID:8972618

Makri, S., Blandford, A., & Cox, A. L. (2008). Investigating the information-seeking behaviour of academic lawyers: From Ellis's model to design. *Information Processing & Management*, *44*(2), 613–634. doi:10.1016/j.ipm.2007.05.001

Mostert, B. J., & Ocholla, D. N. (2005). Information needs and information seeking behavior of parliamentarians in South Africa. *South African Journal of Libraries and Information Science, 71*(2), 136.

Niedzwiedzka, B. (2003). A proposed general model of information behaviour. *Information Research*, *9*(1), 9–1.

OCLC. (2002). *How Academic Librarians can Influence Students' Web-Based Information Choices*. Retrieved from http://www.mnstate.edu/schwartz/informationhabits.pdf

Ogba, C. O. (2013). Information Seeking Behaviour of Final Year Law Students in South Western Nigerian Universities. *Information & Knowledge Management*, 3(5).

Pettigrew, K. E., & McKechnie, L. E. F. (2001). The use of theory in information science research. *Journal of the American Society for Information Science and Technology*, *52*(1), 62–73. doi:10.1002/1532-2890(2000)52:1<62::AID-ASI1061>3.0.CO;2-J

Pharo, N. (2004). A new model of information behaviour based on the search situation transition schema. *Information Research*, *10*(1), 10–11.

Rupp-Serrano, K., & Robbins, S. (2013). Information-seeking habits of education faculty. *College & Research Libraries*, *74*(2), 131–142. doi:10.5860/crl-322

Shakeel, G. T., & Vinayagamoorthy, P. (2013). Information seeking behaviour of business school students: A special study of universities and colleges located in Academic City, Dubai, UAE. *International Journal of Library and Information Science*, *5*(11), 447–456.

Steinerová, J., & Susol, J. (2006). Users' information behaviour-a gender perspective. *Information Research*, *12*(3), 13.

Taylor, R. (1968). Question-negotiation and information-seeking in libraries. *College & Research Libraries News*, *29*(1), 178–194. doi:10.5860/crl_29_03_178

Thórsteinsdóttir, G. (2005). The information seeking behaviour of distance students: a study of twenty Swedish library and information science students (PhD dissertation). Sweden: University of Boras; Retrieved from http://bada.hb.se/handle/2320/2573

Turner, K. (2007). Information seeking, retrieving, reading and storing behaviour of library-users. Retrieved from http://std.kku.ac.th/4830802252/Programme/Greenstone/examplegreenstone/Word_and_PDF/Documents/rtf02.rtf

Tury, S., Robinson, L., & Bawden, D. (2015). The Information Seeking Behaviour of Distance Learners: A Case Study of the University of London International Programmes. *The Journal of Academic Librarianship*.

Urquhart, C., Thomas, R., Lonsdale, R., Spink, S., Yeoman, A., Fenton, R., & Armstrong, C. (2003). Uptake and use of electronic information services: Trends in UK higher education from the JUSTEIS project. *Program*, *37*(3), 168–180.

Vakkari, P. (2001). A theory of the task-based information retrieval process: A summary and generalisation of a longitudinal study. *The Journal of Documentation*, *57*(1), 44–60. doi:10.1108/EUM0000000007075

Wang, P., Hawk, W. B., & Tenopir, C. (2000). Users' interaction with World Wide Web resources: An exploratory study using a holistic approach. *Information Processing & Management*, *36*(2), 229–251. doi:10.1016/S0306-4573(99)00059-X

Wilson, T. D. (1999). Models in information behaviour research. *The Journal of Documentation*, *55*(3), 249–270. doi:10.1108/EUM0000000007145

Witten, I. H., Bainbridge, D., & Nichols, D. M. (2010). *How to Build a Digital Library* (2nd ed.). Burlington, MA: Morgan Kaufmann.

ADDITIONAL READING

Al-Muomen, N., Morris, A., & Maynard, S. (2012). Modelling information-seeking behaviour of graduate students at Kuwait University. *The Journal of Documentation*, *68*(4), 430–459. doi:10.1108/00220411211239057

Bates, R. (2005). Can We Live Together? Towards a global curriculum. *Arts and Humanities in Higher Education*, *4*(1), 95–109. doi:10.1177/1474022205048760

Choo, C. W., Detlor, B., & Turnbull, D. (1998). A Behavioral Model of Information Seeking on the Web–Preliminary Results of a Study of How Managers and IT Specialists Use the Web. *Presented at the 61st Annual Meeting of the American Society for Information Science*, Pittsburgh, PA. Retrieved from http://eric.ed.gov/?id=ED438799

Kostagiolas, P. A., Lavranos, C., Korfiatis, N., Papadatos, J., & Papavlasopoulos, S. (2015). Music, musicians and information seeking behaviour: A case study on a community concert band. *The Journal of Documentation*, *71*(1), 3–24. doi:10.1108/JD-07-2013-0083

Nicholas, D., & Huntington, P. Μονόπωλη, M., & Watkinson, A. (2015). Engaging with scholarly digital libraries (publisher platforms). Retrieved from http://hypatia.teiath.gr/xmlui/handle/11400/8426

Robson, A., & Robinson, L. (2013). Building on models of information behaviour: Linking information seeking and communication. *The Journal of Documentation*, *69*(2), 169–193. doi:10.1108/00220411311300039

Sinha, M. K. (2015). A Study on Information Needs and Information Seeking Behaviour of Rural Population with Special Reference to Barak Valley, South Assam (North East India): A Survey. In *Sinha, Manoj Kumar and Das, Pulak (2015). A Study on Information Needs and Information Seeking Behaviour of Rural Population with Special Reference to Barak Valley, South Assam (North East India): A Survey.* Retrieved from http://papers.ssrn.com/sol3/papers.cfm?abstract_id=2602153

Urquhart, C., & Rowley, J. (2007). Understanding student information behavior in relation to electronic information services: Lessons from longitudinal monitoring and evaluation, Part 2. *Journal of the American Society for Information Science and Technology*, *58*(8), 1188–1197. doi:10.1002/asi.20562

Wang, P., Dervos, D. A., Zhang, Y., & Wu, L. (2007). Information-seeking behaviors of academic researchers in the internet age: A user study in the United States, China and Greece. *Proceedings of the American Society for Information Science and Technology*, *44*(1), 1–29.

Wilson, T. D. (2010). *Information behavior models Encyclopaedia of information science and technology* (3rd ed.). London, Britain: Taylor and Francis.

KEY TERMS AND DEFINITIONS

Digital Library: A group of documents in organized electronic method, available on the Internet or on CD-ROM (compact-disk read-only memory) disks. Depending on the specific library, a user may be capable to access journal articles, records, documents, pictures, mp3, and mp4. "An informal meaning of a digital library is a controlled gathering of information, with linked services, where the information is kept in digital arrangements and easy to use over a network. A vital part of this definition is that the information is controlled. A flow of data sent to earth from a satellite is not a library. The same data, when organized scientifically, becomes a digital library collection. The majority of individuals would not consider a database containing monetary records of one company to be a digital library, but would admit a collection of such information from many companies as part of a library. Digital libraries cover varied information for use by many diverse operators. Digital libraries vary in size from small to gigantic. They can employ any kind of computing tools and any appropriate software. The uniting matter is that information is organized on computers and available over a network, with procedures to select the material in the collections, to organize it, to make it obtainable to operators, and to archive it."

Ellis' Model: An overall model of information seeking behaviours based on revisions of the information seeking patterns of social researcher, research physicists, and chemists, and engineers and research experts in a manufacturing firm. Ellis, employing Glaser and Strauss's 'grounded theory' approach, originated six general features of the information seeking blueprints of social scientists.

ICTs: Employed as instruments and as well as means used for collection, capture, process, storage, transmission and distribution of information. ICTs (information and communications technology - or technologies) are an umbrella word that comprises any communication tool or function, including: radio, TV, mobile phones, CPU and network hardware and software, cable systems and so on, in addition to the numerous services and applications related with them, such as videoconferencing and distance learning. ICTs are frequently spoken of in a specific setting and background, for instance ICTs in learning, health care, or libraries.

Information and Library Sciences: An interdisciplinary or multidisciplinary area that applies the practices, viewpoints, and tools of management, information technology, education, and other areas to libraries; the collection, organization, conservation, and distribution of information resources; and the political economy of information. It also means the study of the organization and administration of a library and it is technical, informational, and reference facilities.

Information Seeking: The method or action of trying to gain information in both human and technological contexts. Information seeking is related to, but dissimilar from, information retrieval (IR).

Information Seeking Models: Have been generated to deliver a theoretical source in the comprehending of attitudes and behaviours of seekers.

Internet-Based Digital Libraries: On the Internet, the use of a digital library is improved by a broadband connection like cable modem or DSL. Dial-up connections can be employed to access plain-text documents and some documents containing images, but for complicated files and those with animated video content, a downstream data speed of as a minimum several hundred kilobits per second (Kbps) can make the user's feeling less boring, in addition to more informative. Internet-based digital libraries can be updated on a daily basis. This is one of the utmost assets of this emerging technology.

ISP Model: Shows a complete vision of information seeking from the user's viewpoint in six phases: task initiation, selection, exploration, focus formulation, collection and presentation. The six phase model of the ISP joins three realms of experience: the affective (feelings) the cognitive (thoughts) and the physical (actions) common to each phase (1). The ISP reveals information seeking as a procedure of structure influenced by Kelly's personal construct theory (2) with information cumulative uncertainty in the early stages of the ISP.

Wilson's Model: Described as a macro-model or a model of the gross information-seeking behaviour and it proposes how information needs result from and what may prevent (and, by implication, aid) the real search for information. It also represents, indirectly, a set of hypotheses about information behaviour that are testable: for instance, the proposal that information needs in dissimilar work roles will be diverse, or that private traits may constrain or aid information seeking. As a result, the model can be considered as a basis of hypotheses, which is a general function of models of this kind.

ENDNOTE

1 Heuristic method points to classify usability difficulties based on human aspects in designing user interface (Entezaryan & Fattahi, 2009).

Chapter 6
Digital Libraries and Copyright Issues

Adeyinka Tella
University of Ilorin, Nigeria

Saheed Oyeniran
University of Ilorin, Nigeria

Olubukola James Ojo
University of Ilorin, Nigeria

ABSTRACT

This chapter examined digital libraries and copyright issues. It considered several issues such as the meaning of digital libraries, the characteristics, functions, digital scholarship services, copyright and the materials that can be and cannot be copyrighted, fair use of library materials, reservation for general use, access to electronic copies, guidelines for fair use in the digital libraries, library reproduction and re-distribution and inter-library loan. The chapter concludes that, reading through this chapter, undergraduates, academics and other library users will have a good understanding of what the digital libraries are and copyright issue all of which are considered very important and germane as we approach paperless society.

INTRODUCTION

Networks of libraries and information services are important channels of communication in the society. They are gateways to the universe of knowledge accumulated over centuries and recorded until recently and majorly on print media. Libraries have been instrumental in all aspects of development in society by providing continual information back-up services to sustain economic growth of nations, emancipation of the masses and their education. Without the provision of library services and materials to support education, research and the supply of information for the improvement of trade, social and economic progress would not have been on such scale.

DOI: 10.4018/978-1-5225-0296-8.ch006

As a transmission agency for communication of knowledge, ideas and information from creators to end users, libraries are definitely concerned with copyright legislations. They have been for years collecting and processing works of authors and making these available to the library patrons. Even in our electronic era, libraries are continuing to provide access to the mass of electronic materials published world-wide. However, rigid copyright legislations aiming exclusively to bring commercial benefits to copyright holders without considerations to other social issues are counter-productive. This requires some explanation. It is an undisputed fact that authors have to be rewarded for their works which are their intellectual properties. Others should not be permitted to derive commercial benefits illegally from their works. However, the same works need to be brought to the notice of users and made accessible to everyone - students, researchers and the public - without infringing on the rights of the creators of the works. The copyright legislations protect the rights of the creators while access to the materials is provided by libraries under certain conditions. The two imperative needs of safeguarding the rights of the creators and providing access to the work by the public are satisfied when copyright legislations ensure sufficiently the protection of owners' rights and at the same time provide exception clauses for users and more particularly to libraries and archives. The doctrine of "fair use" in the USA which allows copying of copyrighted materials for educational and non-profit purposes is aligned on this progressive approach to copyright. It is important for society to allow users access to the ideas, knowledge and information contained in copyrighted materials. Just like the creators have access to other materials in creating their work, new researchers should equally have access to ensure progress and continuity in the pursuit of new knowledge and for the advancement of science. Scholarly research and communication are impaired if all copyrighted materials are inaccessible or are exclusively available through purchase of the rights for use. For developing countries, the case may be even more catastrophic as lack of funds dramatically limits their acquisition programmes.

Many libraries (digital, electronic, hybrid and virtual) have developed guidelines for the use of copyrighted materials. These guidelines address library and educational fair use as well as fair use exceptions for research and scholarly work. The purpose of this chapter is to help undergraduates, other categories of students and academics understand copyright and fair use in the classroom.

Nowadays, we see libraries especially the academic libraries addressing copyright and intellectual property issues because of their role in teaching and promoting information literacy. In the previous chapter, Information literacy is defined as a set of abilities requiring individuals to "recognize when information is needed and have the ability to locate, evaluate, and *use effectively* the needed information" (Association of College and Research Libraries, 2010, p. 1). According to this association, one of the information literacy competency standards concerning the *effective use of information* states that "an information literate individual is able to ... understand the economic, legal, and social surrounding the use of information, and *access and use information ethically and legally*" (ACRL, 2010, p. 2). Using information ethically and legally is what copyright issues is all about and these must be understood by the undergraduate students at this age. To continue the discussion in this chapter, issues such as what digital libraries is, its characteristics and function, what copyright entails, materials that can be and cannot be copyrighted, the fair use issues and others will be considered.

LITERATURE REVIEW

Digital Libraries

The term 'digital library' serves as a convenient and familiar shorthand to refer to electronic collections and conveys a sense of richer content and fuller capabilities than do terms such as 'database' or 'information retrieval system'. At the same time, such uses of the term convey a far narrower sense of a library than one of a full-service institution with long-term responsibilities. Lynch (1993) was prescient in noting that the term 'digital library' is problematic because it obscures the complex relationship between electronic information collections and libraries as institutions. Two complementary ideas were identified by Boorgman et al (1996) to broaden our understanding of digital libraries. These are fully discussed as follows:

1. Digital libraries are a set of electronic resources and associated technical capabilities for creating, searching and using information. In this sense they are an extension and enhancement of information storage and retrieval systems that manipulate digital data in any medium (text, images, sounds; static or dynamic images) and exist in distributed networks. The content of digital libraries includes data, metadata that describe various aspects of the data (e.g. representation, creator, owner, reproduction rights) and metadata that consist of links or relationships to other data or metadata, whether internal or external to the digital library.
2. Digital libraries are constructed, collected and organized, by (and for) a community of users and their functional capabilities support the information needs and uses of that community. They are a component of communities in which individuals and groups interact with each other, using data, information and knowledge resources and systems. In this sense they are an extension, enhancement and integration of a variety of information institutions as physical places where resources are selected, collected, organized, preserved and accessed in support of a user community. These information institutions include, among others, libraries, museums, archives and schools, but digital libraries also extend and serve other community settings, including classrooms, offices, laboratories, homes and public spaces. The above dentitions extend the scope of digital libraries in several directions, based on the contributions of scholars from many disciplines. It moves beyond information retrieval to include the full life cycle of creating, searching and using information. Rather than simply collecting content on behalf of user communities, it embeds digital libraries in the activities of those communities and it encompasses information-related activities of multiple information institutions.

Digital libraries should be understood in terms of electronic collection of real or virtual resources, which may also be available elsewhere. These resources must be whole works, with which humans can have a complete cognitive or affective engagement. A digital library may allow either online or offline access to the elements it organizes and houses, and may include multimedia as well as multilingual data.

IFLA (2010) defines *digital libraries* (DLs) as "online collection of digital objects, of assured quality, that are created or collected and managed according to internationally accepted principles for collection development and made accessible in a coherent and sustainable manner, supported by services necessary to allow users to retrieve and exploit the resources." In this perspective, digital library is viewed "as an organized collection of information, a focused collection of digital objects, including text, video, and audio, along with methods for access and retrieval, and for selection, organisation, and maintenance of the collection." (Witten & Bainbridge, 2003)

In simple term, Digital Libraries (DLs) are collections of information that have associated services delivered to user communities using a variety of technologies. The collections of information can be scientific, business or personal data and can be represented as a digital text, image, audio, video or other media. Due to the amount and great variety of information stored by DLs, they have become, with search engines in general, one of the major web services with a diverse population of users who have heterogeneous background, skills, and preferences.

To sum up the above definitions, there is need to emphasised that there are many definitions of a "digital libraries." Terms such as "electronic library" and "virtual library" are often used synonymously. The elements that have been identified as common to these definitions are:

- The digital libraries are not a single entity;
- The digital libraries require technology to link the resources of many;
- The linkages between the many digital libraries and information services are transparent to the end users;
- Universal access to digital libraries and information services is a goal;
- Digital libraries collections are not limited to document surrogates: they extend to digital artefacts that cannot be represented or distributed in printed formats.

The aim and objectives of most digital libraries system are:

- To expedite the systematic development of: the means to collect, store, and organize information and knowledge in digital form; and of digital library collections;
- To promote the economical and efficient delivery of information to all sectors of society;
- To encourage co-operative efforts which leverage the considerable investment in research resources, computing and communications network;
- To strengthen communication and collaboration between and among the
- research, business, government, and educational communities;
- To take an international leadership role in the generation and dissemination of knowledge in areas of strategic importance to the society;
- To contribute to the lifelong learning opportunities of all people in the society.

Characteristics of Digital Libraries

The characteristics of digital libraries highlighted below have been gleaned from various discussions about digital libraries, both online and in print (e.g. Chepesuik, 1997; Lynch and Garcia-Molina, 1995):

- Digital libraries are the digital face of traditional libraries that include both digital collections and traditional, fixed media collections. So they encompass both electronic and paper materials.

- Digital libraries will also include digital materials that exist outside the physical and administrative bounds of any one digital library
- Digital libraries will include all the processes and services that are the backbone and nervous system of libraries. However, such traditional processes, though forming the basis digital library work, will have to be revised and enhanced to accommodate the differences between new digital media and traditional fixed media.
- Digital libraries ideally provide a coherent view of all of the information contained within a library, no matter its form or format
- Digital libraries will serve particular communities or constituencies, as traditional libraries do now, though those communities may be widely dispersed throughout the network.
- Digital libraries will require both the skills of librarians and well as those of computer scientists to be viable.

Other characteristics could include but may not limit to:

- Emphasis on access to digitized materials wherever they may be located, with digitization eliminating the need to own or store a physical item
- Cataloging down to individual words or glyphs
- Browsing based on hyperlinks, keyword, or any defined measure of relatedness; materials on the same subject do not need to be near one another in any physical sense
- Broadcast technology; users need not visit a digital library except electronically; for them the library exists at any place they can access it, e.g., home, school, office, or in a car

One thing digital libraries will not be is a single, completely digital system that provides instant access to all information, for all sectors of society, from anywhere in the world. This is simply unrealistic. This concept comes from the early days when people were unaware of the complexities of building digital libraries. Instead, they will most likely be a collection of disparate resources and disparate systems, catering for specific communities and user groups, created for specific purposes. They also will include, perhaps indefinitely, paper-based collections. Further, interoperability across digital libraries of technical architectures, metadata, and document formats will also only likely possible within relatively bounded systems developed for those specific purposes and communities.

Functions of Digital Libraries

Many digital libraries and learning environments adapt the interface to the user. Some of the systems also implement personalization, i.e. adaptation of the content, personalized listings of content, recommendations to content of interest to the user etc. At the moment, users have to express their interest in certain topics via different user interfaces for every system. If interests change, users must change their user profiles on every system. This task is as tedious and ridiculous as the manual distribution of search-queries discussed above. A common understanding of user profiles is therefore absolutely essential.

Another very powerful service of a digital library is a push-service, known as alerting service. Many journals use different alert mechanisms to notify registered users. For example, a user may be interested in all newly arrived articles, or articles matching some query in the full-text, abstract, category/classification, or title, or in new articles written by some particular author. Unfortunately, such a feature is presented in different ways by differing systems.

A navigation function could read the user's profile and allow collection browsing according to a preferred view. The navigation function could solicit the services of a recommender function on the user's behalf to guide browsing. It might utilize the users past browsing history, or those of other users whose preferences are judged similar, in forming the structure the user sees of the library. The navigation function also might call upon the services of a query function which, in turn, would utilize the previous output of an indexer.

Other important functions/services of digital libraries are (Tella, 2012):

1. **Storage and Organization:** Physical libraries are well known for storing information and organizing information. Digital libraries have so far exceeded the capacity of storage in a physical library, by offering space saving techniques for storing and displaying data electronically in the form of:
    a. Library catalogues;
    b. Text based e-resources, e.g. databases, books and periodicals;
    c. Digitized rare and special collections;
    d. Multimedia collections, e.g. video, sound, film, graphics, pictures, maps etc.;
    e. Services for acquiring and organizing library information resources.
2. **Search and Browsing Capabilities:** Another outstanding technique about digital libraries is the capability to search it without any physical or time constraints. Examples are:
    a. Library catalogue search, i.e. OPAC;
    b. Searching for rare and preserved sources;
    c. Searching for national repositories (e.g. national archives) through an online portal and cross domain searching;
    d. Searching for a variety of e-resources within one portal;
    e. Browsing the entire range of resources in the DL.
3. **Retrieval:** Retrieval depends on the manipulation service availed by the DL. It is heavily influenced by:
    a. Interface and interaction with the system, e.g.,
        i. How search results are displayed;
        ii. What graphic user interfaces are used to deliver quality web-based library user services.
    b. Architecture, navigation, and overall design.
4. **Virtual Reference:** Through digital libraries the use of instant messaging service using electronic Inter Library Loans System and access to all electronic resources for all e-reserves for all popular teaching materials; self-Issue and return facilities to enable users to issue, renew and return books and journals without the need to queue at a busy service desk are made possible. Additionally, Online Reference Services; e.g. ask a librarian, Instant messaging (IM) and a federated one-stop search engine for all library catalogues and databases (including the IRs) are all embedded under virtual reference function of digital libraries.
5. **Security:** This is yet another important function/service in a digital libraries environment. The users of a DL enter their personal details, this need to be secure. The DL carries copyrighted materials, this also need to be secure from manipulation by the wrong people. The nature of digital material makes it vulnerable to hackers and virus attacks, this call for security.

6. **Digital Scholarship Services:** Digital scholarship has been associated with academic libraries. The term has been commonly used for the application of modern technology to carry out teaching, learning and research activities. These are services that support users' digital scholarship from the inception of task until the completion. At task inception, the user searches for relevant information using all the services mentioned so far (interface, navigation, searching, manipulation etc.). After successfully getting the information, to complete the task, the user might want to:
    a. Annotate the sources used;
    b. Summarize sources consulted;
    c. Create new information by combining text and multimedia sources across all available information;
    d. Digital scholarship encourages the manipulation and use of information in a non-traditional way.

Copyright

To put very simply, copyright is a legal device that provides the creator of a work of art or literature, or a work that conveys information or ideas, the right to control how the work is used" (Fishman, 2008, p. 6). The intent of copyright is to advance the progress of knowledge by giving an author of a work an economic incentive to create new works (Loren, 2000, p. 12).

Copyright is a form of protection provided to the authors of "original works" and includes such things as literary, dramatic, musical, artistic, and certain other intellectual creations, both published and unpublished. Copyright does not protect ideas. It only protects the specific and original expression of the idea. As soon as an idea is given physical form, e.g. a piece of writing, a photograph, music, a film, a web page, it is protected by copyright. There is no need for registration or to claim copyright in some way, protection is automatic at the point of creation. Both published and unpublished works are protected by copyright.

Copyright is a type of property that is founded on a person's creative skill and labour. It is designed to prevent the unauthorised use by others of a work, that is, the original form in which an idea or information has been expressed by the creator. These rights include the right to copy, publish, communicate (e.g. broadcast, make available online) and publicly perform the copyright material.

Copyright is normally owned by the creator(s) of the work, e.g. an author, composer, artist, photographer etc. Copyright is a property right and can be sold or transferred to others. Authors of articles in academic journals, for example, frequently transfer the copyright in those articles to the journal's publisher. It is important not to confuse ownership of a work with ownership of the copyright in it: a person may have acquired an original copyright work, e.g. a painting, letter or photograph, but unless the copyright in it has expressly also been transferred, it will remain with the creator. If the work is created in the course of a person's employment, then the copyright holder is usually the employer.

Copyright provides authors fairly substantial control over their work. According to (U.S. Copyright Office, 2008, p. 1), four basic protections were identified. These are:

- The right to make copies of the work.
- The right to sell or otherwise distribute copies of the work.
- The right to prepare new works based on the protected work.
- The right to perform the protected work (such as a stage play or painting) in public.

With the above various definitions and explanations, it is assumed the meaning of copyright is well understood. Another important question is what exactly can be copyrighted and exactly cannot be copyrighted? The following content provides answer to this question.

Material that Can Be Copyrighted

Materials or information that can be copyrighted are tangible, original expressions. For example, a verbal presentation that is not recorded or written down cannot be copyrighted. However, anything that is tangible can be copyrighted. There are three fundamental requirements for something to be copyrighted, according to the United States Copyright Office (2008, p. 3):

1. **Fixation:** The item must be fixed in some way. The manner of fixation may be just about anything. For example, fixation occurs if something is written on a piece of paper, posted online, or stored on a computer or phone, or on an audio or video device.
2. **Originality:** The work must be original. Originality includes a novel or a student's e-mail message to a professor. Both are considered examples of original expression. It is not necessary for the work to be completely original. Works may be combined, adapted, or transformed in new ways that would make them eligible for copyright protection.
3. **Minimal Creativity:** The work must include something that is above and beyond the original. Verbatim use is not considered original. Reference to the original work that is used to discuss a new concept would be considered original, however. Creativity need only be extremely slight for the work to be eligible for protection. The law merely states this is "original works of authorship" (United States Copyright Office, 2008, p. 3).

Materials that Cannot Be Copyrighted

As there are materials or information that can be protected so also are those that cannot be protected. Those that cannot be protected are:

1. **Works in the Public Domain:** These include: Ideas are in the public domain; Facts are in the public domain; Words, names, slogans, or other short phrases also cannot be copyrighted. However, slogans, for example, can be protected by trademark law; Blank forms.
2. **Government Works:** These include judicial opinions; public ordinances; administrative rulings; works created by federal government employees as part of their official responsibility; works for which copyright was not obtained or copyright has expired; however, this is extremely rare! (U.S. Copyright Office, 2008, p. 3).

It is a common misperception that state employees and contractors performing work on behalf of the federal government cannot copyright their work. Unless it is explicitly stated in the contract between the government and a contractor, federal government contractors are permitted to copyright their works as can state employees (Commerce, Energy, NASA, Defense Information Managers Group, 2008, p. 19).

Fair Use of Library Copyright Materials

Libraries, like individuals, have rights to make fair uses of copyrighted works. Most commonly they exercise these rights in one or another form of what used to be called the Reserve Room. Fair use is the most significant limitation on the copyright holder's exclusive rights (United States Copyright Office, 2010, p. 1). There are no set guidelines that are universally accepted. Instead, the individual who wants to use a copyrighted work must weigh four factors (NOLO, 2010):

1. **The Purpose and Character of the Use:**
    a. Is the new work merely a copy of the original? If it is simply a copy, it is not as likely to be considered fair use.
    b. Does the new work offer something above and beyond the original?
    c. Does it transform the original work in some way? If the work is altered significantly, used for another purpose, appeals to a different audience, it more likely to be considered fair use (NOLO, 2010, p. 6).
    d. Is the use of the copyrighted work for nonprofit or educational purposes? The use of copyrighted works for nonprofit or educational purposes is more likely to be considered fair use (NOLO, 2010, p. 6).
2. **The Nature of the Copyrighted Work:**
    a. Is the copyrighted work a published or unpublished work? Unpublished works are less likely to be considered fair use.
    b. Is the copyrighted work out of print? If it is, it is more likely to be considered fair use.
    c. Is the work factual or artistic? The more a work tends toward artistic expression, the less likely it will be considered fair use (NOLO, 2010, p. 9).
3. **The Amount and Substantiality of the Portion Used:**
    a. The more you use, the less likely it will be considered fair use.
    b. Does the amount you use exceed a reasonable expectation? If it approaches 50 percent of the entire work, it is not likely to be considered a fair use of the copyrighted work.
    c. Is the particular portion used likely to adversely affect the author's economic gain? If you use the "heart" or "essence" of a work, it is less likely your use will be considered fair (NOLO, 2010, p. 13).
4. **The Effect of Use on the Potential Market for the Copyrighted Work:**
    a. The more the new work differs from the original, the less likely it will be considered an infringement.
    b. Does the work appeal to the same audience as the original? If the answer is yes, it will likely be considered an infringement.
    c. Does the new work contain anything original? If it does, it is more likely the use of the copyrighted material will be seen as fair use (NOLO, 2010, p. 11).

Reserving Works for Limited Use Generally

Lecturers often make supplemental reading assignments or recommend additional readings that all their students cannot complete given normal loan periods. Placing the reading materials on reserve gives each student time-limited access, but sometimes even severe restrictions on the loan period will not guarantee full access. The students need more copies. Lecturers may provide their own copies or ask the library to make or acquire additional copies.

Since the Reserve Room is an extension of the classroom, its copying must conform to fair use principles. Complying with fair use is not an easy task because fair use can be hard to understand. For example, the practice of making multiple copies for classroom use is an example of fair use, but the provision also requires the user to consider at least the famous "four factors" that are stated in the statute before deciding whether a particular use is fair (NOLO, 2010):

1. The purpose and character of the use, including whether such use is of a commercial nature or is for non-profit educational purposes;
2. The nature of the copyrighted work;
3. The amount and substantiality of the portion used in relation to the copyrighted work as a whole; and
4. The effect of the use upon the potential market for or value of the copyrighted work.

Discussion on Fair Use

Reserve rooms for print copies explains the basis for this assumption and how such activities on our campuses may be different from the activities of commercial for-profit copy shops. The range of opinion on this issue is broad, however. Some universities advise their on-campus copy centers that course materials containing single chapters from books, single articles from journals and no more than a few charts, graphs or illustrations would generally qualify as fair use for the first semester of use by the same professor for the same class. Requests beyond these would require either a more involved fair use analysis or permission from the publisher. Others believe that all reserve uses require permission if it can be easily obtained, for example, from the Copyright Clearance Center. Others believe that substantially all educational uses are fair.

Print Copies in The Reserve Room

Libraries, like individuals, have rights under 1997 'Copyright Law Section 107' to make fair use of copyrighted works. They commonly exercise these rights in the Reserve Room. Let now analyse the four fair use factors with reference to articles and book chapters and then discuss each one individually.

1. **Purpose and Character of the Use:** The first factor usually weighs in favour of non-profits' universities because the library and faculty are making non-profit educational uses of materials copied for classroom use.
2. **Nature of the Copyrighted Work:** The second factor will weigh in favour of fair use if the material to be copied is factual (texts, journal articles, treatises), rather than creative and fanciful (novels, short stories, plays or similar works).
3. **Amount and Substantiality of the Part Copied:** The third factor may weigh against fair use if each article is considered a whole work. Generally, as the amount copied increases, fair use decreases, but our being a non-profit entity helps us with this factor. Several courts have held that copying all of a work is not fatal to a fair use defence, especially in the non-profit context. If the amount

copied is appropriate in light of the intended use, it will not weigh heavily against you, even if you copy the entire work.

4. **Effect of the Use on the Market for the Copyrighted Work:** This factor responds to changes in the market for permissions and reprints. Publishers have managed to persuade courts to consider this market, rather than the market for the original work, when assessing the economic impact of the proposed copying. The fourth factor may weigh against a finding of fair use if publishers can show that they are losing licensing and royalty fees as a result of copying.

It should be noted that a publisher's willingness to license copies or the existence of easy ways to assess and collect royalties is not by itself enough to defeat a fair use defence in a non-profit setting.

Given the examples above, in the first three factors, only the third factor arguably weighs against a finding of fair use, but in the non-profit context, and with an amount that is appropriate in the light of the intended use, there is ample basis under a finding of fair use whatever the case. Considering the fourth factor, the use would have to be described as otherwise fair use, so we could expect that for a first time use at least, a court might disregard potential licensing or permission fees, not permitting them to convert this otherwise fair use into an unfair use. On the other hand, if these same materials were copied over and over and over again, semester after semester, by the same professor for the same course, a court might be more inclined to wish to take those lost revenues into account.

Reserve Rooms for Images, Audio and Audio-Visual Works

Academic and special libraries still receive occasional requests to reserve audio and video recordings and photographic or slide images similar to the requests described in the discussion of print copies. Although these materials are quickly migrating to digital media in most libraries, it is still of value as a foundation for analysis of electronic reserves to consider a request to reserve analogue excerpts from six commercially recorded musical works, a set of architectural slides and a commercial video showing a musical performance.

The audio reserve request probably will involve combining parts of the six works into a single sound recording. Visual image requests often require that slides be made from photographs or other slides. Finally, the audio-visual reserve request would typically involve making a copy of an entire video.

In addition to the exclusive right to make copies, copyright owners also have the exclusive rights to publicly perform and display their works. As with all the exclusive rights, however, these rights are limited. We will address other limitations in addition to fair use that may protect public performances and displays in the library.

- **Making a Master Recording:** The fair use analysis for copying six musical excerpts is exactly like the analysis for copying six articles. In this case, however, the second factor, the nature of the copyrighted work, will probably weigh against fair use because the work is creative and fanciful rather than factual. Still, with the first factor in favour of fair use, an amount that is appropriate in light of the intended use, and the favourable effect those two have on consideration of the fourth factors, even though this is a harder case than a print example, it seems reasonable to expect that it would be fair.

- **Making Slides from Photographs in a Book:** The request to make slides from a book is similar to the request to make a master recording. Again, the second factor weighs against a finding of fair use since photographic works are not factually based as are journal articles. But, given an educational use and a modest request (a small number of images to be copied from any one book), this request still should qualify as a fair use. It is encouraging to note that this would also be the result under the fair use guidelines for educational multimedia and the guidelines for the use of images. Both sets of guidelines address the application of fair use in the electronic environment, but are helpful, by analogy, to the analogue environment too.
- **Making Duplicate Slides:** This kind of request seems more troubling than making slides from photographs in a book for several reasons. Slides are usually images of creative rather than factual works, making the second factor weigh against fair use (as discussed above). Further, a slide is likely to be considered a whole work, not part of something, thus making the third factor weigh against fair use as well. As discussed in connection with print copies. When two out of the first three factors weigh against fair use, the fourth factor can become problematic because its weight can depend upon whether the use is *otherwise fair*. Even in the non-profit context, once the second and third factors weigh against a finding of fair use, one must seriously consider the possibility that a court would weigh the fourth factor against a finding of fair use as well. The less clearly fair the use is by the time the court considers the fourth factor, the more likely the court is to take the publisher's "lost revenues" into consideration. As most libraries are aware, slide providers often have policies against duplication and expect that the need for additional slides will be filled with additional orders. Note, however, that if the original slides are no longer available or permission to copy them cannot easily be obtained, the fourth factor tips towards fair use.
- **Making a Copy of an Entire Video Recording:** This copying request is difficult for the same reasons as discussed above in duplicating slides. As well as being an entire work, it is a creative work and so the second and third factors weigh against a finding of fair use. That would bring the fourth factor into question, making reliance upon fair use risky, were it not for the fact that permission to make a copy of a movie for non-profit educational use is nearly impossible to obtain. Especially when we are careful to institute limits on the use of the copied movie, we have a reasonable, if not an overwhelming fair use argument.
- **Performing the Copyrighted Work:** The right to make a copy is only one of the rights we need to permit students to listen to or watch a music performance, or view slides in the library. The copyright owner has the exclusive right to publicly perform his work, so we must get his permission unless an exemption covers what we want to do. First we ask, *is the performance public?* Section 101 of the copyright law says that a performance is public if it is in a public place or in any place if "a substantial number of persons outside of a normal circle of a family and its acquaintances" are gathered there.

One must consider whether the place is public and the size and composition of the audience. For example, if the performance takes place in a place open to the public, how many and what kind of people attend is not important. By definition it is a public performance. If the public can be excluded; the size and composition of the audience determine the result.

Most university libraries may not be open to the public, but they are open to considerably more people than a normal circle of a family and its acquaintances. Thus, the displays and performances that take place in the libraries are public performances.

- **Exemptions:** Even if a performance is a public performance, it still may not be an infringement because the copyright law places limits upon the performance right of copyright owners in Section 110 (1) and (2). Section 110(1) says that public performances that take place in the face-to-face teaching activities of a non-profit educational institution are not an infringement.

The legislative history of Section(s) 110(1) and (2) (for distance education) indicates that the legislators thought these two exemptions would cover all performances and displays necessary to teach in public institutions. They specifically include libraries as examples of classrooms or areas devoted to systematic instructional activity. Section 110(1) covers live and recorded performances: The teacher does not have to be in the same room as the students, only in the same general area. Thus, since our audio selections, slides and videotaped music performance would all qualify under these descriptions for the face-to-face classroom exemption, they can be displayed and performed (watched and listened to) in the library without permission.

In addition, fair use applies to all of the exclusive rights of copyright owners, not just to making copies, so a performance may also be a fair use depending upon the results of weighing the four fair use factors, just as described above for analyzing making copies of copyrighted works. Further, it seems likely that if making a copy of a recording or videotape in a particular instance is a fair use, exercising performance rights needed to utilize the copy should also be a fair use. Similarly, if the right to perform or display is covered by Section 110(1), the right to make a copy required for that permitted display or performance should be a fair use.

Providing Access to Electronic Copies

Electronic reserve systems are commonplace. Together with course management systems and faculty and departmental Web servers, e-reserves as they are called, have all but replaced paper course materials on our university campuses. The obvious convenience of electronic storage and access makes this medium very attractive. E-reserves can involve all of the rights of the copyright holder discussed in connection with print copies, sound and video recordings and supplication of images, depending upon the work to be reserved. E-reserves will always involve copying, but will also involve at least one and perhaps both the performance rights (public display and/or performance), and a pubic distribution.

With only minor modifications, we could rely on the fair use analyses described for print copies and sound and video recordings and photographic image duplication to make six articles and a chapter from a book, audio and video recordings and photographic images available to students through e-reserves. We will, however, modify our approach to e-reserves somewhat, in recognition of the additional risks to copyright owners' interests that electronic copies create: the ease of further duplication and distribution. As always, the hallmarks of fair use involve adequate protection of the copyright owner's interests. In electronic reserves, this usually means password protected storage; streaming media when practical; and getting permission after first semester use where there's a functional permissions market, as there is for text. It can also mean purchasing licensed materials that are appropriate for your institution, such as image collections (ARTstor, Saskia).

Guidelines for Fair Use in the Electronic Environment: Digital Libraries

The National Information Infrastructure Task Force Working Group on Intellectual Property Rights established a conference on fair use in the fall of 1994, which met monthly for more than two years. Its purpose was to bring together the interested parties (publishers, authors, libraries, etc.) to negotiate fair use guidelines for the use of materials in a variety of contexts: electronic reserves, use of image archives, interlibrary loan, distance learning and multimedia.

The draft electronic reserve guidelines were not agreed upon widely; nevertheless, they provide a good framework for thinking about what is fair use in the reserve context. As is the case with all Guidelines, they are not the law, but only at best, a statement of certain parties about what they believe would be fair use. As such they represent considerable compromise The Electronic Reserve Guidelines permit us to place small parts of others' works on reserve for one semester without permission. Thereafter, if the same faculty member requests the same materials for the same class, we should get permission. They also require that only students in the class should have access to the materials. These limitations illustrate the kind of consideration given to the copyright owner's interests.

The four factors of fair use test also balance the interests of both the users and the owners of copyrighted works. The analyses set forth in the companion articles on print copies and sound and video recordings and photographic image duplication show how fair use achieves balanced results. For example, the easy availability of a license to use a work, or the lack thereof, influences the fourth factor. The scope of fair use is broader for media such as movies, music and images; narrower for text. This scope is implemented in time (the amount of time one may use materials without permission) and in the amount of the materials that can be used. So, continued educational uses of materials for which permission is difficult or impossible to obtain are likely fair uses; continued educational uses of materials for which permission can easily be obtained are less likely fair uses.

One note of caution: Because reserve materials are suggested or required course readings are exempted from the coverage of the provisions of the Digital Millennium Copyright Act ("DMCA") that limit the liability of Internet service providers (ISPs), the DMCA ISP provisions do not apply to them. This means that if reserve materials are found to infringe a copyright owner's rights, the library or the University of which it is a part will not be able to take advantage of the special protections set forth in the DMCA and will not have to follow its detailed notice and take-down procedures, but must rely instead on all the other defences that are available under the rest of the copyright law, including but not limited to fair use and the good faith fair use defence.

Library Copying for Patrons and for The Library's Collection

The Copyright Act 1997 (Section 16) makes provision for libraries and Archives to make a single copy of a copyright work under certain conditions where:

1. *The work reproduced is a published article or other short extract of a writing, with or without illustrations, and where the purpose of the reproduction is to satisfy the request of a physical person, if:*
    a. *The library or archive is satisfied that the copy will be used solely for the purpose of study, scholarship or private research;*

   b. *The act of reproduction is an isolated case occurring, if repeated, on separate and unrelated occasions; and*
   c. *There is no license available, offered by a collective administration organisation in a way that the library or archive is aware or should be aware of the availability of the license, under which such copies can be made; or*
2. *The making of such copy is in order to preserve and, if necessary in the event that it is lost, destroyed or rendered unusable, replace a copy or to replace, in the permanent collection of another similar library or archive, a copy which has been lost, destroyed or rendered unusable, if:*
   a. *It is impossible to obtain such a copy under reasonable conditions; and*
   b. *The act of reprographic reproduction is an isolated case occurring, if repeated, on separate and unrelated occasions.*

The Copyright Act however does not define reprography as comprehensively as it is understood today as a process of duplicating a work through printing, photocopying, scanning, burning on CDs or DVDs and electronic storage for dissemination or distribution over networks.

It is understood that libraries are allowed to make photocopies or make reprographic reproduction of any copyrighted materials if the legal conditions authorizing these are respected. By so doing, libraries are not infringing the rights of owners or breaching the Copyright Act 1997. However, it is suggested that libraries need to obtain a license to do this now. Section 15 (b) (iii) and Section 16 (a) (iii) of the Copyright Act 1997 is pressing libraries and educational institutions to apply for a license for reprographic reproduction of copyrighted materials.

LIBRARY REPRODUCTION AND DISTRIBUTION

Archiving

Section 108, Subsection (b) of the 1997 copyright law gives libraries the right to archive unpublished materials; subsection (c) addresses archiving published materials. The requirements for the two kinds of materials are different: to make a copy of an unpublished work, a library's purpose must be preservation or security and it must have a copy of the work in its collection; to make a copy of a published work, a library's purpose can only be to replace a copy it has or used to have in its collection, because the copy has been damaged, is deteriorating, lost or stolen, or the format has become obsolete. Such published works also must be out of print.

Patron Requests

Section 108 authorizes libraries to make copies requested by patrons. The is neutral regarding the medium of reproduction, thus, "copies" are not so narrowly defined as they are in the archive provisions. One may make a photocopy or a digital copy or send a fax.

If a patron requests part of a book or an article that the library has in its collection, the library can make the copy so long as it complies with the provisions of Section 108(**d**):

- The copy must become the property of the patron;
- The library should have no notice that the copy will be used for a purpose other than private study, scholarship or research;
- The library should display and have on its order form a standard 'Warning of Copyright'.

If a patron requests a copy of an entire work, the library can make the copy so long as it complies with the provisions of Section 108(**e**):

- Determine that a copy (even a used copy) cannot be obtained at a fair price;
- If you make a copy, it must become the property of the patron;
- The library should have no notice that the copy will be used for a purpose other than private study, scholarship or research;
- The library should display and have on its order form a 'Warning of copyright'.

The warning governs the making of photocopies or other reproductions of copyrighted material. is that under certain conditions specified in the law, libraries and archives are authorized to furnish a photocopy or other reproduction. One of these specified conditions is that the photocopy or reproduction is not to be "used for any purpose other than private study, scholarship, or research." If a user makes a request for, or later uses, a photocopy or reproduction for purposes in excess of "fair use," that user may be liable for copyright infringement. This institution reserves the right to refuse to accept a copying order if, in its judgment, fulfilment of the order would involve violation of copyright law (The copyright law of the United States (title 17, United States Code)

Unsupervised Copying, News Programs, and Contractual Imitations on Acquisitions

Libraries are permitted to make a limited number of copies of audio-visual news programs. Unlike other sections of the law that permit copying for patrons, section (f)(3) does not require that the copy become the property of the patron, so the library can retain and lend its copies. Audio-visual news programs include local, regional and national network newscasts, interviews concerning current events and on-the-spot news coverage of news events. The provision was not, however, intended to apply to news-magazines and documentaries

Section 108(f) (4) says that if you enter into a contract in the process of acquiring a work for your collection, and the contract limits your rights to copy in some way, the contract prevails over your statutory rights. In other words, you can contract away your rights under Section 108 as you might, for example, in acquiring private manuscripts or electronic databases.

Even if a contract eliminates the library's rights under Section 108, the bigger controversy is whether libraries may contractually eliminate either their own or their patrons' fair use rights. For example, a database license may:

- Require the library to prevent patrons from making copies by requiring the library to post a notice that copying is prohibited;
- Prohibit the library's making a reserve copy; or
- Require that permitted copies include a notice that further copying is prohibited.

Would these prohibitions and requirements have any legal effect upon a patron's right to make copies under Section 107? The patron, after all, is not a party to the contract and even a vociferous copyright notice should not unilaterally extinguish a statutory privilege like fair use that embodies a fundamental principal of copyright law

Interlibrary Loan

The library may be either a requestor or responder in the interlibrary loan context ("IL"). Requestors are responsible for compliance with copyright law where applicable. Responders only have to ask whether the requestor has complied. Further, the guidelines only apply to newer articles, those published fewer than five (5) years before the date of the request, and small parts of other works, and do not define what would substitute for subscriptions to older materials or entire works under Section 108(e). There are no guidelines for these.

CONCLUSION

This chapter has examined digital libraries and copyright issues. It is has considered several issues such as the meaning of digital libraries, the characteristics, functions, digital scholarship services, copyright and the materials that can be and cannot be copyrighted, fair use of library materials, reservation for general use, access to electronic copies, guidelines for fair use in the digital libraries, library reproduction and re-distribution and inter-library loan. It is the expectation that reading through this chapter undergraduates and other library users will have a good understanding of what the digital libraries are and copyright issue all of which are considered very important as we approach paperless society.

REFERENCES

Association of College and Research Libraries. (2010). *Information literacy competency standards for higher education.* Retrieved from http://www.ala.org/ala/mgrps/divs/acrl/standards/informationliteracycompet ncy.cfm

Borgman, C. L., Bates, M. J., Cloonan, M. V., Efthimiadis, E. N., Gilliland-Swetland, A., Kafai, Y., Maddox, A. (1996). Social aspects of digital libraries. Final report to the National Science Foundation. http://dli.grainger.uiuc.edu/national.htm

Chepesuik, R. (1997). The future is here: America's go digital. *American Libraries*, *2*(1), 47–49.

Copyright Working Group. (2008). Works created under a federal contract or grant. *Frequently asked questions about copyright issues: Issues affecting the S. government.* Retrieved from http://www.cendi.gov/publications/04 8copyright.pdf

Fishman, S. (2008). *The copyright handbook: What every writer needs to know.* Berkeley, CA: Nolo.

Harper, G. K. (2001). The Copyright Crash Course. The University of Texas Library. Retrieved from http://copyright.lib.utexas.edu/l-108abc.html

Hauroo, P. (nd*). Copyright issues for Libraries in Mauritius.

IFLA. (2010). *IFLA Manifesto for Digital Libraries*. Retrieved from http://www.ifla.org/en/publications/ifla-manifesto-for-digital-libraries

Loren, L. P. (2000). The purpose of copyright. *Open Spaces Quarterly, 2*(1). Retrieved from http://www.open-spaces.com/

Lynch, C., & Garcia-Molina, H. (1995). Interoperability, scaling, and the digital libraries research agenda http://www.hpcc.gov/reports/reports-nco/iita-dlw/main.html

Lynch, C. A. (1993). Accessibility and integrity of networked information collections (Background Paper No. BP- TCT-109). Office of Technology Assessment, Washington.

NOLO. (2010). *The 'fair use' rule: When use of copyrighted material is acceptable*. Retrieved from http://www.nolo.com/legal-encyclopedia/article30100.html

United States Copyright Office. (2008). *Copyright basics*. (Circular 1). Retrieved from http://www.copyright.gov/circs/circ01.pdf

United States Copyright Office. (2010). *Fair use*. (Circular FL-102). Retrieved from http://www.copyright.gov/fls/fl102.html

Witten, I., & Bainbridge, D. (2003). *How to build a digital library*. San Francisco: Morgan Kaufmann Publishers.

ADDITIONAL READING

Fadayomi, J. A. Tella, Adeyinka, & Adesina, O.F. (2013). Application of Information and Communication Technology to Library services. In J.O. Omoniyi, F.A. Adekola, & W. Fola-Adio (Eds.), Effective Communication in Higher Education: The Use of Library (pp. 54-60). Ilorin: University of Ilorin Press.

Tella, A., Olasina, G.E. & Baskaran, C. (2010). The Global Information Infrastructure-Digital Library: Roles and Challenges in Educational Development. In B. Ramesh Babu & R. Rajendran (Eds.), *Proceedings of the International Conference on Innovation Driven Librarianship* (pp. 693-700). Delhi: M/S Nisha Graphics.

Tella, A. (2012). Digital Libraries. In B.L Adeleke & W.B. Adeoti-Adekeye (Eds.), Effective Communication in Higher Education: The Use of Libraries (pp. 66-72). Ilorin: University of Ilorin Press.

KEY TERMS AND DEFINITIONS

Copyright: A set of rights in certain creative works such as text, artistic works, music, computer programs, sound recordings and films. These rights are granted exclusively to the copyright owner to reproduce the material and for some materials the right to perform or show the work to the public. Copyright is a legal right created by the law of a country that grants the creator of an original work exclusive right for its use and distribution. This is usually only for a limited time. The exclusive rights are not absolute but limited by limitations and exceptions to copyright law, including fair use. *Copyright* is just one form of intellectual property. It's not the same as trademark, which protects brand names, mottos, logos, and other source identifiers from being used by others for certain purposes.

Copyright Issues: All issues that concern the copyright of information and contents in digital library. The issue range from rent, lend or issue copies of the work to the public, Copying, duplication, reproduction, selling, hiring, distribution, commercial, personal and educational usage.

Digital Libraries: A collection of digitized documents, images and sounds that can be accessed and read by the use of computers. It is an online collection of digital objects, of assured quality, that are created or collected and managed according to internationally accepted principles for collection development and made accessible in a coherent sustainable manner, supported by services necessary to allow clients to retrieve and utilize the resources.

Electronic Database: An organised collection of information on a particular subject or multi-disciplinary subject areas where information can be searched and retrieved electronically and the coverage contents include journals articles, newspaper articles, book review, conference proceedings and so on. In other words, it is searchable electronic collection of resources which may hold a range of different types of information including journals, books, or newspaper articles and abstracts, reports, pictures and e-books.

Electronic Information: The information provided in electronic form and includes researches available on the internet such as e-books, e-journals; online database, CD-ROM databases and other computer based electronic networks.

Electronic Libraries: A type of the library that is heterogeneous system which information is available in hard copy on magnetic type and discs, CD-ROMs and videodiscs, and also from online sources. Storage and copying of information are done either by downloading or by printing from a master file. In other words, it an electronic or online library where users can have access to books, journals, novels, articles or any other information over the internet.

Virtual Library: A digital space that keeps and organizes virtual books and their associated documents or in other words, it is refers to a space where book can be read including computers, mobile devices and the internet, the access can either be for free while others require subscriptions.

Chapter 7
A Glimpse of the Information Seeking Behaviour Literature on the Web:
A Bibliometric Approach

Akakandelwa Akakandelwa
University of Zambia, Zambia

ABSTRACT

This Chapter presents a study conducted on literature related to information seeking behaviour available on the World Wide Web. The outcome of searching the World Wide Web using Google Scholar were analysed to present the growth of publications; collaboration pattern of authors; most contributing authors; type of publications in which information scientists preferred to publish their works; highly preferred journals in which information seeking behaviour related works are published; and the impact of information seeking behaviour related literature.

INTRODUCTION

Information is a basic resource like any other resource such as raw materials, land, equipment, labour, capital, and energy, which are required to carry out day to day activities. As such information plays a vital role in human kind's life. At individual level information, affects our personal and professional lives as it is needed to make decisions and various choices. Timely access to relevant, accurate and current information has become more critical, especially in this globalized society which is daily increasingly becoming more and more competitive and complex. Since information is a critical resource it must be managed effectively and efficiently.

Information seeking behaviour (ISB) is an umbrella term for every human interaction with information (Bates, 2010). It is a very important concept in library and information science and occupies a central part of research in library and information studies (Järvelin, 1987). It deals with behaviours and actions exhibited by human beings in their search for information to satisfy diverse information needs.

DOI: 10.4018/978-1-5225-0296-8.ch007

Wilson (2008) articulates that "information seeking behavior is the purposive seeking for information as a consequence of a need to satisfy some goal. In the course of seeking information an individual may interact with a manual information system (such as newspapers or library) or with a computer based system (such as the World Wide Web)." Mutshewa (2007) cautioned that the term 'information seeking behaviour' could be misleading because it implies the behaviour of information rather than the behaviour of people. Therefore, several researchers (Spink and Cole, 2006; Sonnenwald and Iivonen, 1999; Wilson, 2000) have preferred the term 'human information behaviour' to the term 'information seeking behaviour'; but the majority of researchers still use the term information seeking behaviour. However, Bates (2010) observes that information seeking behaviour is the 'official' term used in the *Encyclopaedia of Library and Information Science* and the term used by the *Information Behaviour Conference* (ISIC).

Wilson (1999) proposed a nested model of ISB to explain what information seeking behaviour research encompasses. He describes ISB as an onion, which consists of at least three layers. The inner layer depicts information searching, which is generally understood as information retrieval or interactive information retrieval, such as occurs in a database. The next layer consists of information seeking, which can occur everywhere else. The outermost layer (the all-embracing layer), comprises information behaviour that embraces all kinds of human interactions with information. Active research is an exchange between the layers, in particular between information retrieval and information, but also between information seeking and the more general behavioural research groups (Tamine-Lechani *et al.*, 2010).

According to cognitive psychology human beings are fundamentally active and goal-oriented and willing to get information about themselves and the world (Eskola, 1998). Their actions are directed by intentions, expectations and response. They maintain knowledge in memory in hierarchically organized structures, schemes, and new knowledge is constructed on the basis of previously learned knowledge. This process of construction has features in common for every human being but the contents are individual. Learning occurs in connection with action and is part of the cognitive process. During the last decades the cognitive approach has emphasized aspects in the contents and the context of learning (von Wright 1994, 16-18).

The library is the most widely-used source of information available to literate societies. Therefore, librarians must be aware of the kind of information being sought and how it can be obtained. Furthermore, because of the rapidly escalating cost of purchasing and archiving print journals and electronic media, the library has the duty to provide and maintain efficient services (Thanuskodi, 2009). Technological advancements and innovations have changed modern libraries from store houses to gateways of information. Information and communication technologies (ICTs) have completely changed the setup of libraries and have transformed and expanded their roles, and the services they provide, beyond storage, preservation and dissemination of information.

Fourie (2006) observes that information-seeking behaviour differs significantly according to background, culture, conditions, needs, and requirements. It is therefore difficult to predict the actual behaviour that a person might exhibit in a quest for information. In order to understand the behaviour of human beings better, there is a need for multidisciplinary research using multidimensional approaches. Fourie further (2006) observes that "information seeking is a complex, dynamic, social human behaviour that needs as rich a picture as possible to truly understand the phenomenon-and even then there will be many unanswered questions". It is therefore important to study the information-seeking behaviour of various groups of people, in order to serve them better.

Studies of information seeking behavior and related areas were very limited till the early second half of the 20th century. Information seeking behavior has been a focus of research within the library and information profession. A review of 'information need and uses' was conducted annually and contained in the *Annual Review of Information Science and Technology (ARIST).* Information seeking behavior has become a major area of research in many library schools and continues to be a topical issue at many library and information science professional association conferences. Studies on information seeking behavior are conducted in all branches of knowledge including science, medicine, technology, humanities and social sciences. Today information seeking behaviour has become an independent subdomain of library and information science. Furthermore, studies in information seeking behaviour have resulted into the development of many models and theories among which are the Wilson's Model of Information Seeking, Ellis Model of Information Seeking, Kuhlthau's Model of the Information Search Process, and Belkin's Information Seeking Process Model. Models of information seeking attempt to describe the processes a user follows to satisfy an information need.

Earlier studies in information seeking behaviour concentrated on information systems. This research tradition has been called the system oriented paradigm. In those studies, the aim has been to obtain knowledge to support organizational development and administrative decision-making. The approach has been criticised because of insufficient theories, concepts and research methods and because it has not taken into consideration the needs of the information-seeking persons. Quantitative data analysis techniques were predominantly used in these early studies (Dervin & Nilan 1986; Ginman 1995; Järvelin & Vakkari 1981; Wilson 1994).

At the end of 1970s and at the beginning of 1980s, researchers began to realize that questions in information needs, information seeking and information use could not be seen only from the systems' point of view. Therefore, the user of the information and his/her needs came into focus and research in cognitive science was applied in the studies. The new view was called the new paradigm or the cognitive view (Dervin & Nilan 1986; Ginman 1995, 14).

In the digital era, research on information-seeking behaviour has taken on even more importance worldwide (Rafiq and Ameen, 2009). Most of the literature on information-seeking behavior comes from developed countries, while conditions in developing countries vary significantly.

Importance of Information Seeking Behaviour Research

According to Agosto and Hughes-Hassell (2005, p. 141), understanding information seeking behaviour is a vital component in providing high quality library service. Allen (1997, 111) also observes that understanding the information needs of users is the first and most indispensable step in designing and building effective information systems. When LIS professionals understand human information-seeking behaviours and preferences, they can transform their services and resources to correspond to these patterns, to better serve users' information needs. People from all walks of life seek out and utilize information every day (Lorica, 2010). Lorica further observes that information regarding studies and research, work, entertainment, health, money matters, family, and other topics, is obtained from various sources. Knowledge of reasons and motivation why people seek information and the types of information they seek in their everyday lives can impact "collection development, reference services, programming, and budget allotment practices" (Agosto & Hughes-Hassell, 2005, p. 142).

Results of information seeking studies can be used for improving collection development (Lorica, 2010). Agosto and Hughes-Hassell (2005) contend that librarians would be better able to match their collections to young adults' information-seeking practices if given an understanding and appreciation of young adults' source/channel preferences (p. 142). Haines, Light, O'Malley and Delwiche (2010) observed that library resources and services can be modified and made more valuable to patrons in response to findings of information-seeking studies. Similarly, Fourie (2006, pp. 20-21) observes that results from web information-seeking studies can assist library and information science professionals in knowledge representation, in the design of web sites and portals, in the development of training and web-based information retrieval systems (IRS), the design and administration of online information literacy, electronic customer relationship management (CRM) and in the improvement of the quality of online information services. Fourie (2002, 62) is of the view that substantial Web information seeking/searching studies are necessary to refine our knowledge of Web information spaces, their design and maintenance, and training-related issues. In the emerging electronic environment, knowledge about the information seeking behaviour of students and staff on the Web is crucial for those wishing to help them effectively meet their information needs online.

Bibliometrics

This study has employed bibliometrics to study the information seeking behaviour literature available on the Web. It employs a snapshot modality, i.e. exploring a situation at a particular point in time. Bibliometrics is the application of statistical and mathematical methods in Library and Information Sciences. Bibliometrics is a flexible and growing research methodology that lends itself to many approaches. It is concerned with measuring the output of scientific publications using multiple approaches such as author productivity, contextual analysis, citation analysis, data clustering, and bibliographic coupling. Bibliometrics, as a tool to measure scientific research output, has seen major changes over the last five decades and has emerged as an established filed of research in library and information schools. Bibliometrics is an important field of the informational science because it represents a unique set of techniques for the monitoring and analysis of the informational resources and for the management of knowledge in social and organizational context.

A Brief Review of Bibliometrics Studies in ISB

There are very few studies in the literature that are closely related to this research. McKecnnie, Goodall, Lajoie-Paquette, and Julien (2005) did a citation analysis on the ISB literature. Their dataset was 155 English-language ISB articles published from 1993 to 2000 in six prominent library and information science (LIS) journals. Their citation and content analysis showed that ISB literature was cited mainly (81.5%) by LIS authors. Some other fields such as engineering, psychology, education and medicine also cited ISB literature. Using content analysis, they categorised reasons of citing ISB literature and showed that they were cited generally (36.0%), for findings (28.5%) and for theory (25.3%) with few citations for method (6.0%). They concluded that ISB "literature is yet to have a significant impact on other disciplines. It appears to be a second stage discipline, marked by theoretical consistency and exponential growth in publications and new researchers".

Julien et al (1996) conducted three longitudinal studies of information needs and use literature. Julien (1996) covered the articles published between 1990 and 1994. She showed that 20 per cent of the citations were to the literature of fields outside LIS. Julien and Duggan (2000) covered the two periods of 1984-1989 and 1995-1998. They showed that the literature was rather focused inward and relied on work conducted within LIS. Part of the literature was interdisciplinary. The third study (Julien et al., 2011) covered 1999-2008 and it again confirmed the interdisciplinary nature of the information behaviour domain. It also showed that compared to the past, the number of papers by academic researchers compared to papers by information professionals, had increased.

Parmar, Kumar and Prakash (2004) conducted a study on literature related to information seeking behaviour from *LISA Plus*. The objectives of their study were to investigate the growth of publications; collaboration pattern of authors; most contributed authors; languages in which maximum number of articles are published; type of publications in which information scientists preferred to publish their works; highly preferred journals in which information seeking behaviour related works are published; and the contents of information seeking behaviour related literature through subject descriptors. A steady growth in number of publications was observed starting from 1967 to 2001, with a maximum number of publications being produced in 1999. The last ten years of the study period witnessed a sudden growth in number of publications. Single-authored publications were the most predominant followed by two-authored, three-authored and four-authored publications, respectively. It was further observed that as collaboration increased the recency is decreased. English was the most prominent language in which 512 (86.77%) of information seeking behaviour related works are published followed by 14 (2.37%) in Finnish language and 8 (1.36%) in Chinese language. Journals were the most preferred type of channel in which researchers working in studies related to information seeking behaviour publish their works followed by conference/seminar/symposia proceedings and books. Most of the literature was published in the following journals: *Journal of the American Society for Information Science, Information Processing and Management*, *Bulletin of the Medical Library Association*, *Kirjastotiede ja Informatiika*, *Library and Information Science Research*, *Information Research* (11articles), and *Reference Librarian*. The most occurring subject keywords were: 'Searching, 'online information retrieval', and 'information storage and retrieval'.

Abubakar (2010) conducted a study to explore the contributions of the field of information-seeking behavior in the literature of health sciences from 2000-2007. The findings indicate that the literature recorded exponential growth from 2004 onward. It also found that 66.9 percent were multi-authored, showing the collaborative approach of scientists in the field. This approach opens doors for interaction among experts in different areas of the health sciences, leading to learning and sharing of information resources. Collaborative research enhanced the productivity of authors as well as their visibility. Bradford's distribution was found to be applicable to this study, even though the graph does not take the Bradford "S" shape.

Jamali (2013) carried out a study of citation relations of 51 works that have proposed an ISB model or theory. The aim was to find out how models and theories of information seeking behaviour are interrelated, whether they have any common roots, and to what extent they are indebted to the fields other than library and information science. Interrelation of models and theories of human information behaviour (HIB), their common roots, and the extent to which they are indebted to the fields other than library and information science (LIS) were investigated. Fifty-one theories were selected and their bibliographic information was obtained from Web of Science and then citation analysis and bibliographic coupling analysis were performed. Pajek, HistCite, Sci2 Tool and VOSViewer software were used for analysis and visualization. The results showed that most of the theories were proposed by information scientists. A few of the theories were proposed by scientists from the fields of sociology, psychology, computer science and a few other disciplines. Citation analysis showed that LIS literature has been used extensively in HIB theories; however, there were also citations to the sources of 29 other fields especially to sociology, communication, psychology, management, educational science and computer science. This is an indication of the interdisciplinary nature of HIB domain. Bibliographic coupling map showed that about four fifths of the theories were linked to each other as a whole network. The development of a large number of theories within the field of LIS is an indication for the increasing maturity of the interdisciplinary research area of HIB as well as the maturity of LIS field.

As observed earlier, few bibliometric studies have been done on the ISB literature, more especially on ISB theories and models. It is therefore hoped that this study will make a contributing to existing knowledge in this area and will inspire further research in this field.

Google Scholar: A Source for Bibliometric Data

Traditionally, the most commonly used source of bibliometric data is Thomson ISI Web of Knowledge, in particular the Web of Science and the Journal Citation Reports (JCR) (Harzing and Wal, 2008). For journals, the most commonly used metric is the Journal Impact Factor (JIF), as calculated in the JCRs, whilst for individual academics it is the number of citations as reported in the Thomson ISI Web of Science. Citing (Bosman et al. 2006) Haring and Wal (2008) observe that an important practical advantage of GS is that it is freely available to anyone with an Internet connection and is generally praised for its speed (Bosman et al. 2006). On the other hand, the WoS is only available to those academics whose institutions are able and willing to bear the (quite substantial) subscription costs of the WoS and other databases in Thomson ISI's Web of Knowledge. This is amplified by Pauly & Stergiou (2005, p. 34) who contend that:

Free access to [...] data provided by GS provides an avenue for more transparency in tenure reviews, funding and other science policy issues, as it allows citation counts, and analyses based thereon, to be performed and duplicated by anyone.

Pauly and Stergiou (2005) further point to the advantage of the no-cost GS option for research and academic institutions not only in developing countries, but also for modestly endowed institutions in developed countries.

It has been established that Google Scholar provides higher citation counts than either Scopus or Web of Science (WoS) due to better coverage of social sciences, free Internet access, and better indexing of proceedings (Noruzi, 2005; Vaughan & Shaw, 2008). This is because Google Scholar have access to doctoral dissertations, master's theses, books, book chapters, and conference papers, etc. (Khey, et al, 2011).

Although for reasons discussed above GS generally provides a higher citation count than ISI, this might not be true for all fields of study. The social sciences, arts and humanities, and engineering in particular seem to benefit from GS's better coverage of (citations in) books, conference proceedings and a wider range of journals. The natural and health sciences are generally well covered in ISI and hence GS might not provide higher citation counts. In addition, user feedback received for Publish or Perish seems to indicate that for some disciplines in the natural and health sciences GS's journal coverage is very patchy. This leads to citation counts in these areas that might actually be much *lower* than those in ISI. In a systematic comparison of 64 articles in different disciplines, Bosman et al. (2006) found overall coverage of GS to be comparable with both WoS and Scopus and slightly better for articles published in 2000 than in 1995.

However, Bosman et al. (2006) report that huge variations were apparent between disciplines, with chemistry and physics in particular showing very low GS coverage and science and medicine also showing lower coverage than in WoS (Bosman et al. 2006). Bosman et al. (2006) observe that more detailed and recent comparisons by academics working in the respective areas would be necessary before we can draw general conclusions. However, they conclude that as a general rule of thumb, that using GS might be most beneficial for 3 of the GS categories:

1. Business, administration, finance & economics;
2. Engineering, computer science & mathematics;
3. Social sciences, arts & humanities.

Bosman et al. (2006) further observe that GS does not perform as well for older publications, as these publications and the sources that cite them have not (yet) been posted on the web. Pauly & Stergiou (2005) found that GS had less than half of the citations of the WoS for a specific set of papers published in a variety of disciplines (mostly in the sciences) between 1925 and 1989. However, for papers published in the 1990 to 2004 period both sources gave similar citation counts. The authors expect GS' performance to improve for old articles as journals' back issues are posted on the web. Meho & Yang (2007) found the majority of the citations from journals and conference papers in GS to belong publications that were published after 1993. Belew (2005) found GS to be competitive in terms of coverage for references published in the last 20 years, but the WoS was superior before then. This means that GS might underestimate the impact of scholars who have mainly published before 1990.

Objectives of the Study

The scope of the study restricted to the literature pertaining to information seeking behaviour from Google Scholar. The analysis of the information seeking behaviour related literature has been done on the basis of some of the following objectives:

1. To depict the growth of publications on the Web;
2. To explore the type of publications in which information scientists preferred to publish their works;
3. To investigate the collaboration pattern of authors;
4. To document highly preferred journals in which information seeking behaviour related works are published; and
5. Establish the extent to which the papers were being cited.

Materials and Methods

Sources of Data and Data Collection Method

Therefore, the Google Scholar database was selected to collect and calculate the citation indices for the ranking of the information seeking behaviour related literature. Harzing's *Publish or Perish* (PoP) software (Harzing, 2009) was used to obtain citation records and index values from Google Scholar. The programme interfaces with Google Scholar, collects data from it and calculates multiple metrics from that data. Some of the advantages of using PoP are that: it has a wide coverage coming from Google Scholar;

it covers a wide variety of information sources such as books, book chapters, conference proceedings, journal articles, theses, dissertations, technical reports, available on the Web. It also covers material published in various languages other than English. Furthermore, it uses the h-index as a measure of citation activity for both authors and journals. It is therefore an appropriate tool to demonstrate evidence of international impact of an author. PoP is used to analysis publications to provide the following statistics:

- Total number of papers,
- Total number of citations,
- Average number of citations per article,
- Average number of citations per author,
- Total number of papers of the author,
- Average number of citations per year,
- Hirsch indicator and link parameters,
- Egghe's g indicator,
- Contemporary h indicator,
- Importance of age in citing rate,
- Two variations of the individual indicator h.

Data was retrieved using a general search phrase "information seeking behaviour in the search field of PoP. The software returned a list of papers attributed to search phrase, ranked by number of recorded citations and displayed in a table with author(s), title, year of publication, and publisher. Each entry in the list had a checkbox that could be toggled to exclude (or include) that entry. Above the list, a table displayed a selection of statistics including number of publications, number of citations, *h* and *g* index values. Where the data appeared to be unreliable the publication was not included for further analysis. The irrelevant and duplicate results were deleted. The publications which had received zero citations were also removed. Finally, the results for each author were copied for further analysis and comparisons. The data were collected on the 16th of October 2015. The data copied into an MS Excel spread sheet and later transferred to SPSS 20 for analysis. A large array of statistics was calculated such as:

1. Total number of papers,
2. Total number of citations,
3. Average number of citations per paper,
4. Average number of citations per author,
5. Average number of papers per author,
6. Average number of citations per year,
7. Hirsch's h-index and related parameters,
8. Egghe's g-index,
9. Contemporary h-index,
10. Age-weighted citation rate,
11. Two variations of individual h-indices, and
12. Analysis of the number of authors per paper.

However, an initial search using Google Scholar only retrieved 13 ISB articles with African origin. This prompted the researcher to conduct a separate search on African ISB publication from AJOL using

Google Scholar. This search retrieved over 2,500 articles. After filtering through the results, 176 relevant articles were selected for a separate data analysis.

Hirsch's h-Index

The h-index, also called Hirsch-index, introduced by J.E. Hirsch in 2005, quantifies the impact of an author's contribution. A scientist has index h if h of his/her Np (total papers) papers have at least h citations each, and the other (Np−h) papers have no more than h citations (Hirsch, 2005). In other words, if a researcher has h-index of 5 it means that he has written five papers each of which (on average) has been cited at least five times by other researchers. Thus h-index determines a researcher's academic impact by using the quantity (total number of his/her papers) and quality (impact or citations to his/her papers). In spite of some shortcomings, the h-index has been considered as a good tool for comparing the researchers of the same field.

Limitations of the Study

The study has a few limitations. This study considered only papers that were retrieved from the Web on the 16th of October 2015. Furthermore, the citation counts are limited by the sampling frame used by Google Scholar. Therefore, publications of the authors not indexed by Google, though they may be available online, could not be retrieved.

RESULTS

Growth of Publications

The total number of information seeking behaviour related publications collected from the Web using PoP was 976. The chronological growth of publications is depicted in Figure 1. A slow growth in number of publications has been observed starting from 1962 to 1996. An exponential growth of literature has been observed from 1997 to 2014 with a peak in 2006. These results show the growing importance of the Internet as a major communication tool for research. The growth of ISB literature is expected to increasing in the forthcoming years.

Age of the ISB Publications

Figure 2 shows the distribution of publications by age of publication. The publication age ranged from 1 to 53 years. The mean age was 15.67 with a standard deviation of 10.695. The mode was 9 years. Twenty-five percent of the publications were aged 8 years and below; 50% were aged 13 years and below; 75% of the publications were aged 20 years and below. These results show that most of the publications on ISB retrieved by Google Scholar were relatively young. Based on age, ISB literature retrieved from Google Scholar can be divided into three categories: publications aged 1-20 years, publications aged 21-40 years, and publications aged 41 years and above.

Publications aged 41 years and above can be termed classics. This category includes Mote, LJB (1962). This category received citations ranging from 6 to 656 with a mean of 99.42 (SD=150.195). *Reasons*

Figure 1. Growth of ISB research publications on Web

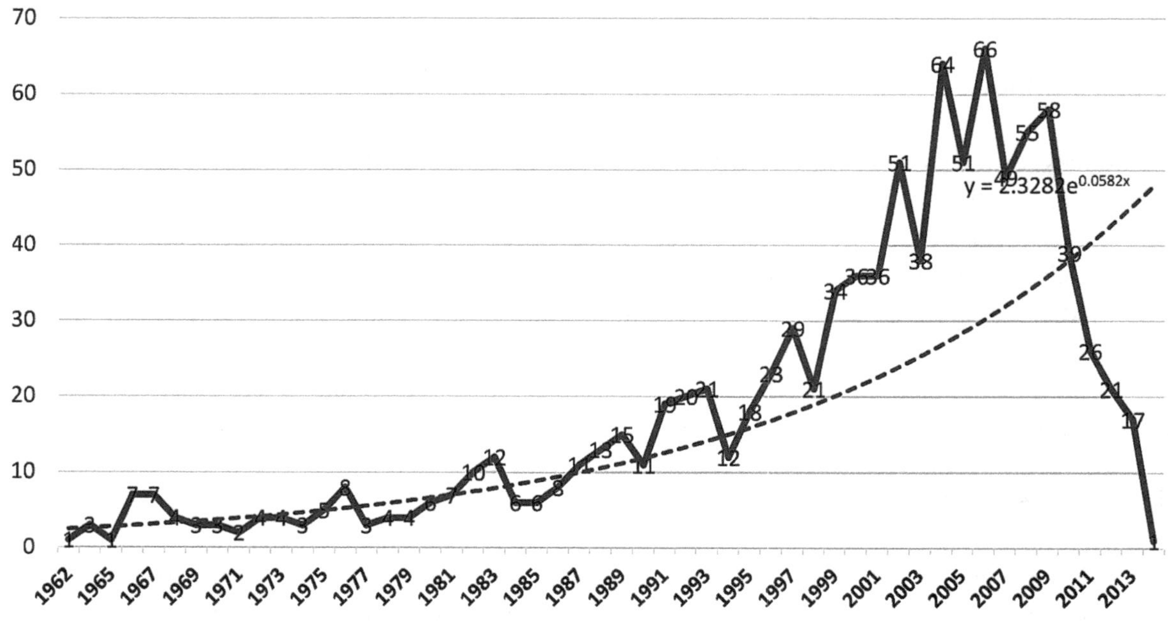

Figure 2. Distribution of ISB publications by age

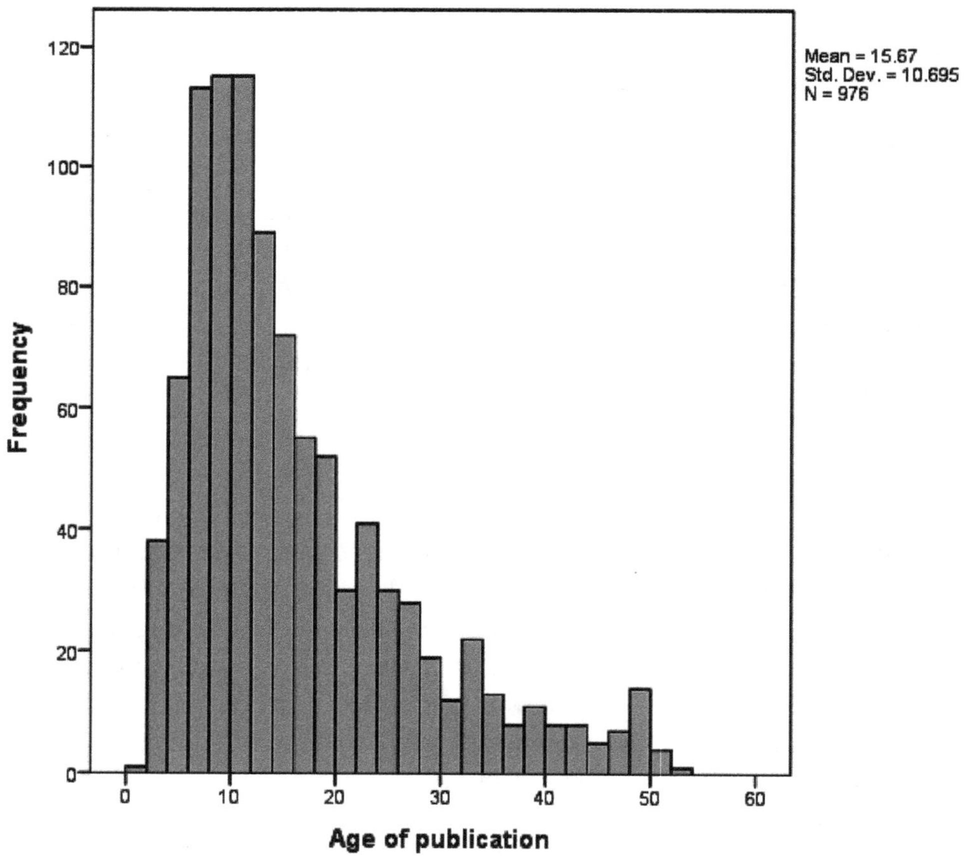

for the variations in the information needs of scientists; Krumboltz, JD & Thoresen, CE (1964). *The effect of behavioral counseling in group and individual settings on information-seeking behaviour*; WW Schroeder (1964). *The effect of reinforcement counseling and model-reinforcement counseling upon the information-seeking behavior of high school students*; Katz, WA (1969). *Introduction to Reference Work*; L Donohew & L Tipton (1973). *A conceptual model of information seeking, avoiding, and processing*; JN Sheth & PS Raju (1974). *Sequential and cyclical nature of information processing models in repetitive choice behaviour*; L Donohew & L Tipton (1973). *A conceptual model of information seeking, avoiding, and processing*; and NT Feather (1967). *An expectancy-value model of information-seeking behavior.*

Publications aged between 21 and 40 years comprised the second category. There were 201 publications in this category. The publications in this group were published from 1975 to 1994. This category consisted of most of publications with the highest citation rates. The mean citation rate was 198.11 (SD=334.31; the minimum was 4 while the maximum was 1833. Some of the prominent publications in this category include M Brucks (1985). *The effects of product class knowledge on information search behaviour*; NJ Belkin & WB Croft (1992). *Information filtering and information retrieval: Two sides of the same coin?*; MJ Bates (1989). *The design of browsing and berrypicking techniques for the online search interface*; KB Murray (1991). *A test of services marketing theory: consumer information acquisition activities*; SE Beatty & SM Smith (1987). *External search effort: An investigation across several product categories*; TD Wilson (1981). *On user studies and information needs*; NJ Belkin, RN Oddy & HM Brooks (1982). *ASK for information retrieval: Part I. Background and theory*; and LF Feick & LL Price (1987). *The market maven: A diffuser of marketplace information.*

Publications aged below 21 years' category constituted the largest category. There were 733 publications in this category. The publications in this group were published from 1995 to 2014. This category consisted of most of publications with the second highest citation rates. The mean citation rate was 99.99 (SD=150.195; the minimum was 6 while the maximum was 2110. Some of the prominent publications in this category were G Marchionini (1997). *Information seeking in electronic environments*; DO Case (1985). *Looking for information: A survey of research on information seeking, needs and behaviour*; TD Wilson (2012). *Models in information behaviour research*; SP Borgatti & R Cross (1992). *A relational view of information seeking and learning in social networks*; TD Wilson (1992). *Human information behaviour*; P Ingwersen & K Järvelin (1999). *The turn: Integration of information seeking and retrieval in context*; DE Rose & D Levinson (1989). *Understanding user goals in web search*; C Hölscher & G Strube (1991). *Web search behavior of Internet experts and newbies*; and MC Gilly, JL Graham & MF Wolfinbarger (1991). *A dyadic study of interpersonal information search.*

Article URLs (Top Level Domain)

Figure 3 shows categories of domains from which the publications of ISB were sourced. The majority (73.9%) of the publications were obtained from commercial websites; 15.5% were obtained from websites of non-governmental organizations; 6.4% of the publications were obtained from government websites; 1.8% of the publications were obtained from websites of educational institutions; and 2.4% of the publications were obtained from websites of other institutions and organizations such as military websites, websites of organizations offering information services, etc.

Figure 3. Distribution of ISB literature by URL

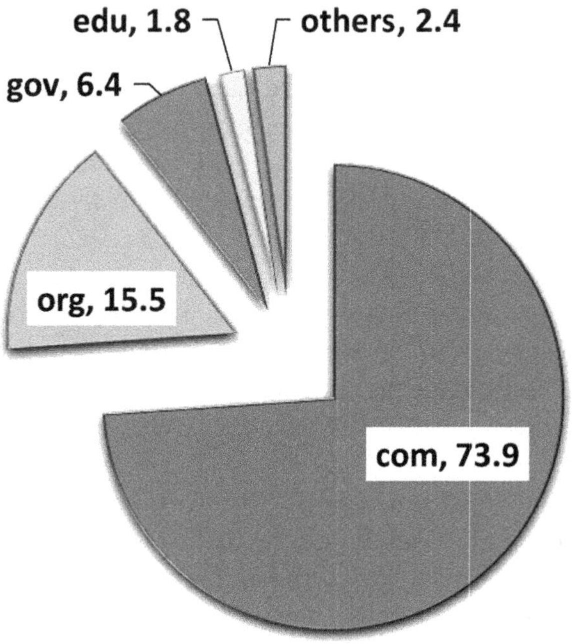

Source of Literature on ISB

Table 1 shows a list of 29 leading journals in which scholars publish literature on information seeking behaviour, ranked in descending order from the most contributing journal to the least contributing journal. These journals have contributed a total of 26.1% (30426) of a total of 116638 citations produced by the dataset.

Major Publishers of ISB Literature

Table 2 shows the distribution of top 19 publishers that have produced 75.0% of the information seeking behavior literature retrieved from Google Scholar. These publishers are led by *Elsevier* (19.2%), *Wiley Online Library* (10.7%), *Taylor and Francis* (7.8%), *Emerald Insight* (6.0%), *National Centre for Biotechnology Information* (4.6%), *JSTOR* (4.3%), *Digital Library ACM* (4.2%), *ERIC* (3.4%). Together these publishers have produced 60.0% of the publications on information seeking behavior retrieved from Google Scholar. Other publishers are *American Psychological Association* (APA) *PsychNET* (3.4%), *Google Books* (2.3%), *Springer* (2.3%), *Wolters Kluwer* (journals.lww.com) (1.6%), *ProQuest* (1.2%), *Citeseer* (0.9%), *Mary Ann Libert* (0.8%), *College and Research Libraries* [CRL] (0.7%), *Digital Commons* (0.7%), *De Gruyter* (0.5%), and *Europe PubMed Central* (0.5%). These results are contrary to the earlier assertion that Elsevier journals are not included in Google Scholar (Meho & Yang 2007) because Elsevier has a competing commercial product in Scopus.

Table 1.

Rank	Title
1	Journal of the American Society for Information Technology
2	Library & Information Science Research
3	Information Processing & Management
4	Journal of Documentation
5	Journal of the Medical Library Association
6	Journal of Health Communication
7	The Journal of Academic Librarianship
8	Bulletin of the Medical Library Association
9	Proceedings of the ASIS Annual Meeting
10	The Library Quarterly
11	College & Research Libraries
12	Human Communication Research
13	Libri
14	Research Strategies
15	School Libraries Worldwide
16	Communication Research
17	Computers in Human Behavior
18	Information Research
19	International Journal of Medical Informatics
20	Library Trends
21	New Directions in Human Information Behavior
22	Reference & User Services Quarterly
23	The Reference Librarian
24	Annual Review of Information Science & Technology
25	Aslib proceedings
26	CyberPsychology & Behavior
27	Library Review
28	School Library Media Quarterly
29	Science & Technology Libraries

Authorship Pattern and Most Contributed Authors

The collaboration pattern of the scientists working in the information seeking behaviour field has been presented in Table 3. There are 376 single authored publications. Two-authored, three-authored and four-authored publications are 326 (38.52%), 155 (33.40%) and 87 (8.91%), respectively. There are 30 (3.07%) papers with a collaboration of five authors and there are only two (0.20%) papers with maximum collaboration of six authors. The mean number of authors per publication was 2.05; the median was 2.0; while the mode was 1. Although there still persistence single authorship among researchers in ISB,

Table 2. Distribution of top publishers contributing to Google Scholar

sn	Publisher	Frequency	Percent	Cumulative Percent
1	Elsevier	187	19.2	19.2
2	Wiley Online Library	104	10.7	29.8
3	Taylor & Francis	76	7.8	37.6
4	emeraldinsight.com	59	6.0	43.6
5	ncbi.nlm.nih.gov	45	4.6	48.3
6	JSTOR	42	4.3	52.6
7	dl.acm.org	41	4.2	56.8
8	ERIC	33	3.4	60.1
9	psycnet.apa.org	33	3.4	63.5
10	books.google.com	22	2.3	65.8
11	Springer	22	2.3	68.1
12	journals.lww.com	16	1.6	69.7
13	search.proquest.com	12	1.2	70.9
14	Citeseer	9	0.9	71.8
15	online.liebertpub.com	8	0.8	72.6
16	crl.acrl.org	7	0.7	73.3
17	digitalcommons.unl.edu	7	0.7	74.0
18	degruyter.com	5	0.5	74.5
19	europepmc.org	5	0.5	75.0

Table 3. Authorship pattern observed in the information seeking behaviour related research publications of Web (1968-2001)

	Frequency	Percent	Cumulative Percent
1 author papers	376	38.52	38.52
2 author papers	326	33.40	71.92
3 author papers	155	15.88	87.80
4 author papers	87	8.91	96.71
5 author papers	30	3.07	99.78
6 author papers	2	0.20	100.00
	976	100.00	

the study has revealed a growing collaborative trend among researchers. The Collaboration coefficient (0.615) indicates almost 62 percent of total authors working in the ISB field are collaborating each other. Collaborative research enhances the productivity of authors as well as their visibility. Subramanyam (1983) states that collaboration has also been found to affect the visibility and productivity of scientists. Zainab (2007) emphasizes the importance of collaboration for effective information seeking, arguing that "Collaboration and professional intermediation therefore becomes necessary to support purposeful bibliographic compilations to support effective information seeking amongst library and information users and researchers."

Figure 4 shows dominancy of single authored ISB publications during the period 1962-2001 period. The years following 2001 have seen a rapid increase of multiple authored publications.

Table 4 documents the most contributed authors to the literature related to information seeking behaviour in Google Scholar. The credit for the most productive author is held C.C. Kuhlthau (6 publications) followed by JL Branch and R. Savolainen with 5publications each; A. Spink and C. Cole, E. Whitmire, J. Kim, K.S. Kim, N.J. Belkin, and T.D. Wilson with 4 publications each; followed by A.K. Shenton and P. Dixon, C. C. Metoryer-Duran, D. Bilal, D. Kelly, J. Hallmark, M. Gross, M.J. Bates, and T. Saracevic with 3 publication.

Figure 4. Collaborations trends in the ISB field at global level

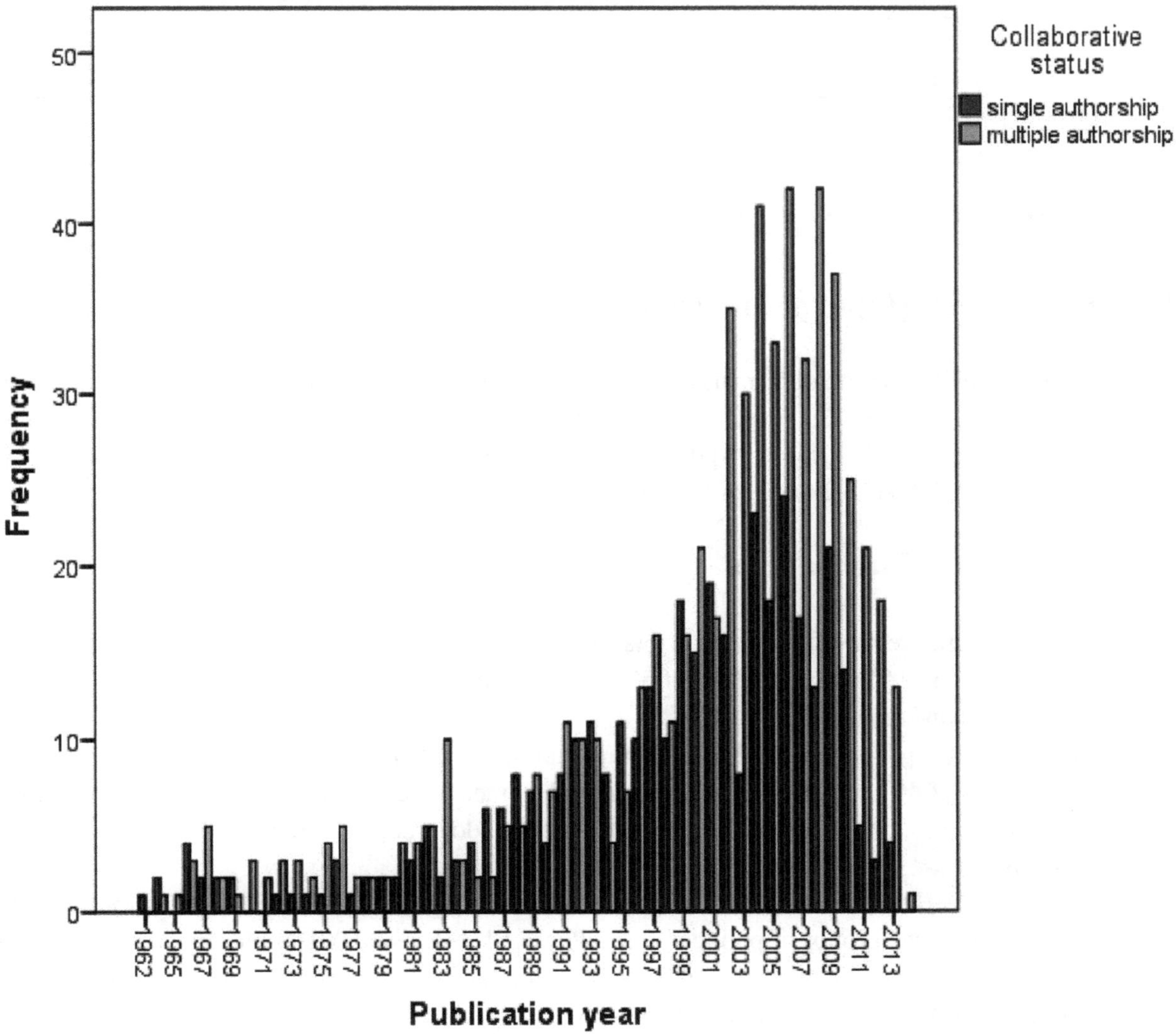

Table 4. Most productive authors

sn	Authors	Frequency	Percent
1	CC Kuhlthau	6	0.7
2	JL Branch	5	0.6
3	R Savolainen	5	0.6
4	A Spink, C Cole	4	0.5
5	E Whitmire	4	0.5
6	J Kim	4	0.5
7	KS Kim	4	0.5
8	NJ Belkin	4	0.5
9	TD Wilson	4	0.5
10	AK Shenton &P Dixon	3	0.4
11	C Metoyer-Duran	3	0.4
12	D Bilal	3	0.4
13	D Kelly	3	0.4
14	J Hallmark	3	0.4
15	M Gross	3	0.4
16	MJ Bates	3	0.4
17	T Saracevic	3	0.4

Preferred Format (Type) of Publications

Figure 5 shows the distribution of formats of publications retrieved from Google Scholar on information seeking behaviour literature. The format of 737 (75.5%) publications were not specified. Of the remaining 239 publications, 39.33% (94) were pdf, 30.13% (72) were citations, 22.18% (53) were html, 7.53% (18) were books, and 0.84% (2) were in MS Word documents.

Impact of the ISB Publications

The 976 ISB literature retrieved produced a total of 116638 citations. The average number of citations per publication was 119.51 with a median of 52.0 and 6 citations as a mode. Sixty-three percent of the publications had an average h-index of 166.

It was observed that pdf documents had an average citation of 214.65 (SD=337.188), citations received an average citation of 46.10 (SD=120.010) and html documents received an average of 75.00 citations (SD=73.056) (Table 5). These results have revealed that pdf documents are the most cited publications followed by html.

A Kruskal-Wallis H test showed that there was a statistically significant difference in citation received between the different age groups of publications, $\chi2(3) = 51.394$, $p = 0.001$, with a mean rank citation score of 146.56 for PDF publications, 72.06 for publications accessed through citations, 126.58 for html publications, and 140.53 book (monographic publications) (Table 6). These results reveal that 21.8% of the variation in the citation of publications is explained by the format of the document.

Figure 5. Distribution of ISB literature by format (type) of publication

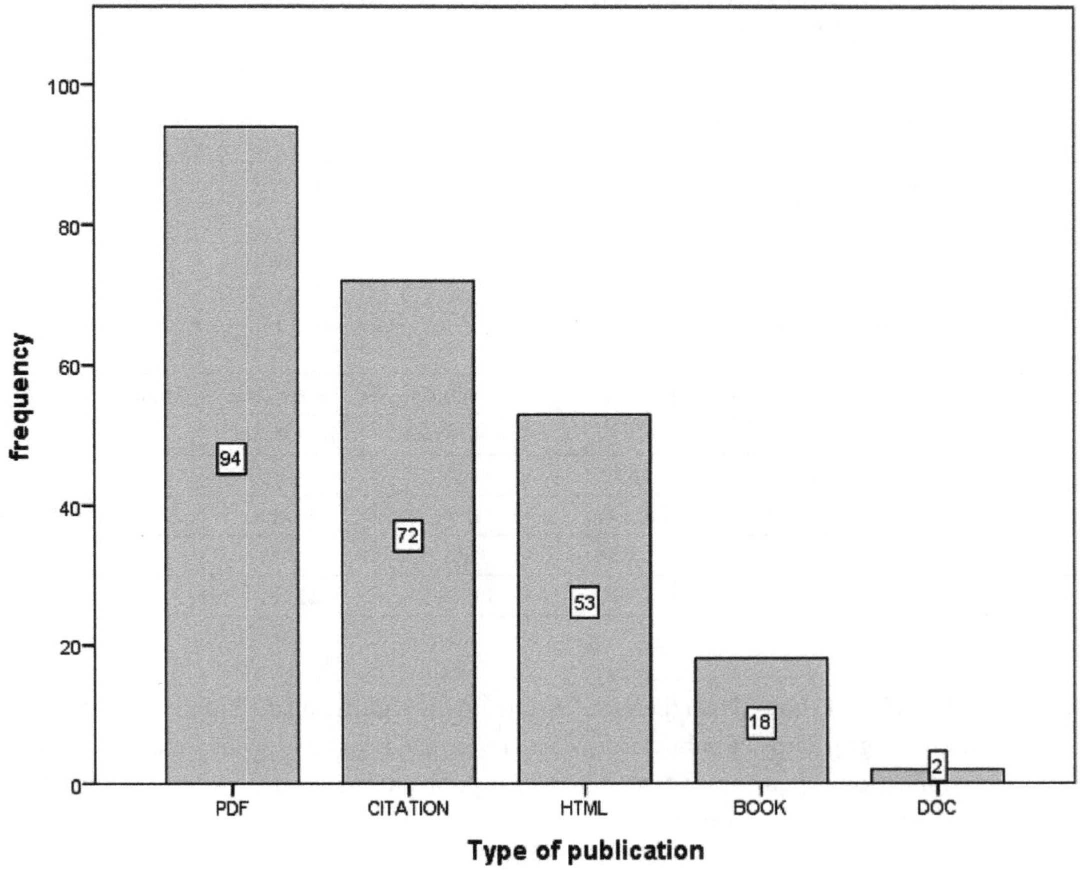

Table 5. Summary mean age of ISB literature across format categories

	N	Mean	Std. Deviation	Std. Error	95% Confidence Interval for Mean		Minimum	Maximum
					Lower Bound	Upper Bound		
Pdf	94	214.65	337.188	34.778	145.59	283.71	4	1833
Citation	72	46.10	120.010	14.143	17.90	74.30	5	836
HTML	53	75.00	73.056	10.035	54.86	95.14	6	316
Total	219	125.44	246.163	16.634	92.65	158.22	4	1833

Further analyses were conducted to establish whether there significant differences existed in the ISB literature with regard to their age categories. Previous studies have shown that older publications receive more citations than younger publications. Table 7 shows that publications aged 1-20 years had 99.36 mean citation with 171.364 standard deviation; publications aged 21-40 years had 198.11 mean with 332.314 standard deviation; and publications aged above 40 had 94.95 mean citation with 135.835 standard deviation.

Table 6. Multiple comparisons mean citations of ISB publications across format categories

Format of Document	Frequency	Mean Rank
Pdf	94	146.56
Citation	72	72.06
HTML	53	126.58
Book	18	140.53
Total	237	

Table 7. Descriptive statistics of citations of ISB publications across age categories

	N	Mean	Std. Deviation	Std. Error	95% Confidence Interval for Mean		Minimum	Maximum
					Lower Bound	Upper Bound		
1-20 years	733	99.36	171.364	6.329	86.93	111.78	4	2110
21-40 years	201	198.11	332.314	23.440	151.89	244.33	4	1833
41 years +	42	94.95	135.835	20.960	52.62	137.28	6	656
Total	976	119.51	216.981	6.945	105.88	133.14	4	2110

A Kruskal-Wallis H test showed that there was a statistically significant difference in citation received between the different age groups of publications, $\chi2(2) = 6.019$, $p = 0.049$, with a mean rank pain score of 478.97 for publications aged 1-20 years, 430.71 for publications aged 21-40 years and 452.82 for publications aged 41 years and above (Table 8).

A Close Look at African ISB Literature

This section takes a brief look at the ISB researches available on the Web retrieved from the African Online Journal (AJOL) database (http://www.ajol.info/). AJOL provides a facility to search for articles on its site using Google. Search terms used were "information seeking behaviour" and "information seeking behaviour". Over 1560 results were recorded. Out of these a sample of 176 relevant articles was selected. Bibliometric data was collected on these publications using PoP.

Figure 6 shows the distribution of the publications by age. The oldest publication was 23 years (i.e. a paper published in 1962) whilst the youngest publications were less than one year (i.e. papers published in 2015). The mean age was 6.04 years, the median was 5 years and the modes were 2 and 5 years. Seventy-five percent of the publications were less than ten years old.

Table 8. Mean rank citations of publications by age category

Age of Publications	Frequency	Mean Rank
1-20 years	733	478.97
21-40 years	201	530.71
41 years +	42	452.82
Total	976	

Figure 6. Age of the African ISB publications on the Web

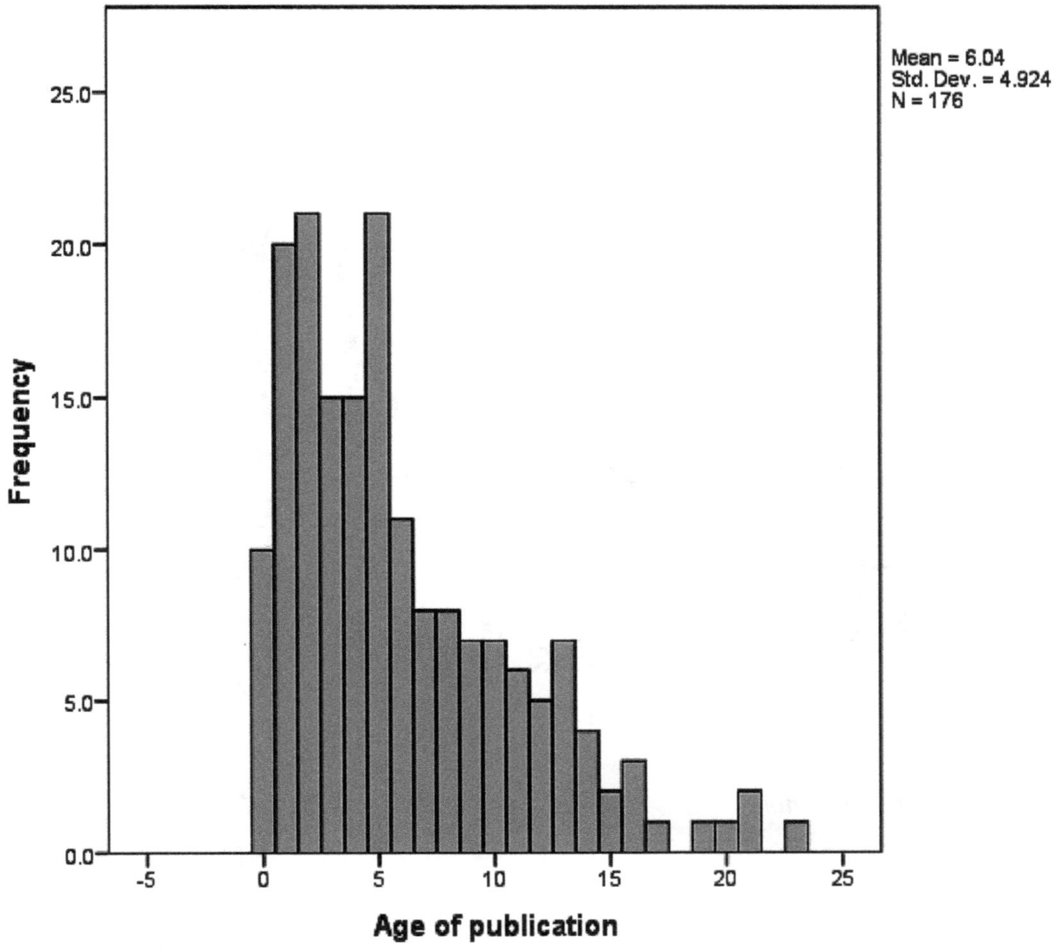

Figure 7 shows the growth of the African ISB publications on the Web as collected using Google Scholar. There was a very slow growth from 1992 to 2008. A rapid increase is observed from 2009 onwards, with a decline in 2011 and 2012. The highest productivity years are 2010 and 2013.

Sixty-four percent of the publications were in PDF format, 27.69% were citations, and 7.69% were html (Figure 8).

Table 9 shows eight leading publishers of African publications on ISB available on the Web. These publishers contributed 76 (43.2%) out of the total of 176 publications. The leading publisher was Reference Sabinet (13.1%, followed by AJOL (8.5%), Taylor and Francis (5.7%), Digital Commons (4.0%), Emerald Insight (3.4%), Degruyter (2.8%), Sage (2.8%), and University of Zululand Department of Library and Information Studies (2.8%).

Table 10 shows the pattern of authorship among African ISB publications. The collaboration pattern of the African scientists working in the ISB field has been presented in Table 9. There were 79 single authored publications, making 44.9% of the total. Two-authored, three-authored and four-authored publications were 78 (44.3%), 17 (9.7%) and 2 (1.1%), respectively. There were no papers with a collaboration above four authors. The mean number of authors per publication was 1.64; the median was

Figure 7. Growth of African ISB publications on the Web

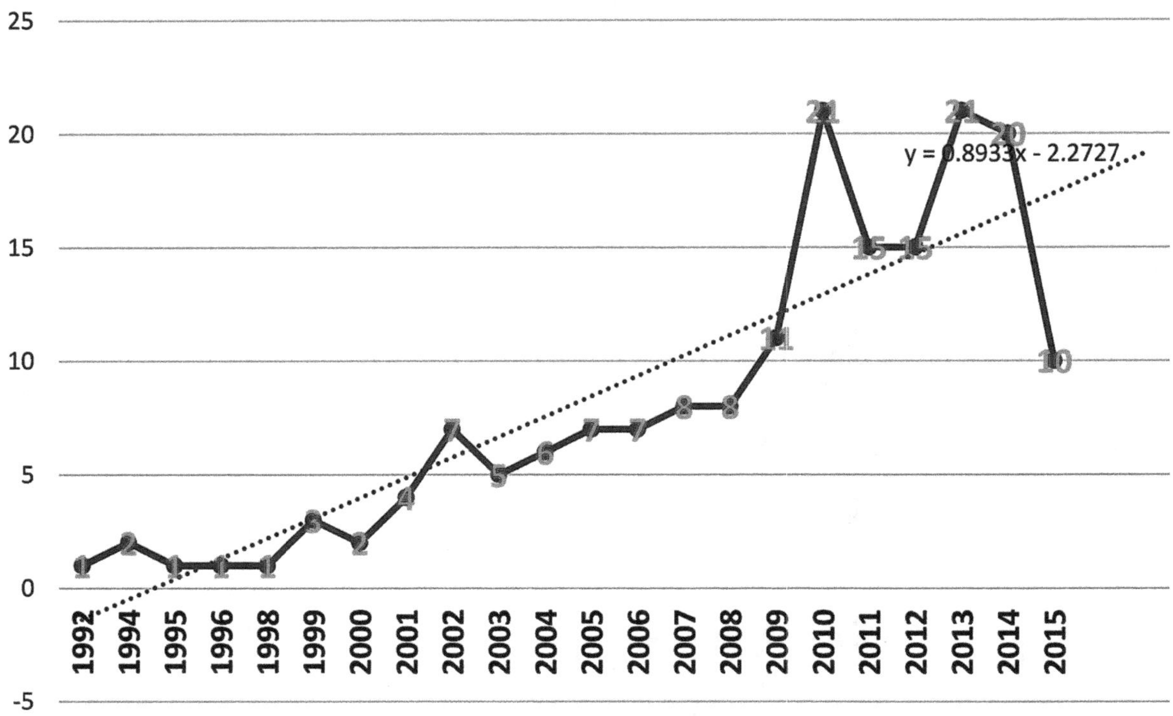

Figure 8. Format of publication

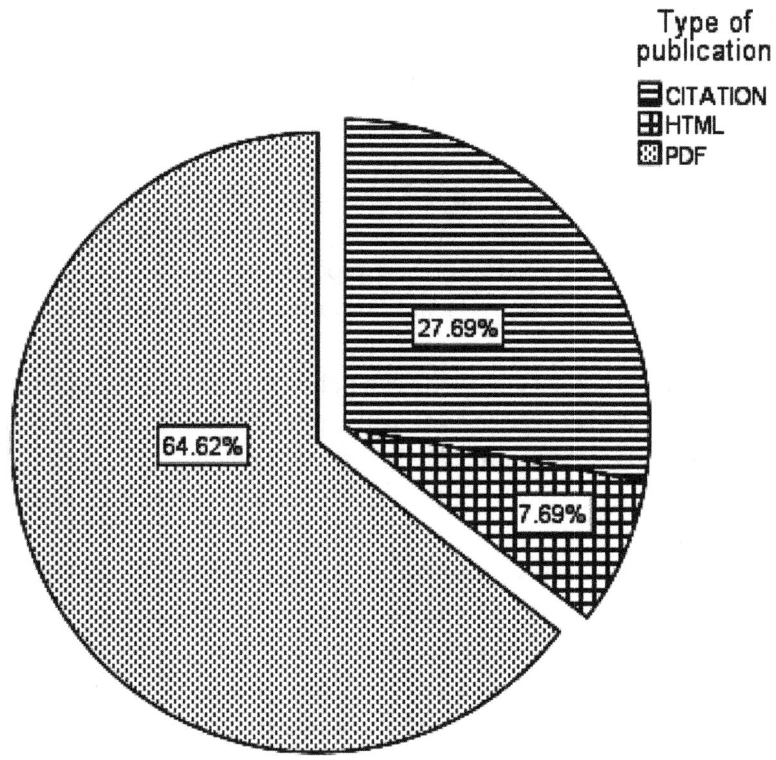

Table 9. Leading publishers of African ISB publication on the Web

	Frequency	Percent
reference.sabinet.co.za	23	13.1
ajol.info	15	8.5
Taylor & Francis	10	5.7
digitalcommons.unl.edu	7	4.0
emeraldinsight.com	6	3.4
degruyter.com	5	2.8
idv.sagepub.com	5	2.8
lis.uzulu.ac.za	5	2.8
Total	76	43.2

2.0; while the mode was 1. The study has revealed a dominance of single authorship, closely followed by two author publications among African researchers in ISB. The Collaboration coefficient (0.551) indicates almost 55.1% percent of total authors working in the ISB field are collaborating with each other. As noted earlier collaborative research enhances the productivity of authors as well as their visibility.

One would expect that because of the ease of collaboration using e-mail and groupware technologies, the number of multiple- authored articles has risen in recent years at a more rapid rate than the number of single-authored articles. In an attempt to test this hypothesis, the publication dates of the single-authored and multiple-authored e-journal articles were compared. Figure 9 shows that the African research landscape in ISB field in the years 1992 to 2006 were dominated by single authored publications while the years 2007 onwards have recorded a steady increase in collaboration with strong persistence of single authorship.

Impact of the ISB Publications

The 176 African ISB literature retrieved produced a total of 1345 citations. The average number of citations per publication was 7.64 with a median of 2.0. Forty-six (26.1%) publications did not receive any citations. The most cited publication received 161 citations. Fifty percent of the publications received a maximum of 2 citations while 75% of the publications received citations ranging from 0 to 9 citations.

It was observed that pdf documents had an average citation of 2.57 (SD=3.858) while citations received an average citation of 7.44 (SD=7.090). These results have revealed that African ISB researchers cited

Table 10. Number of authors

	Frequency	Percent	Cumulative Percent
1 author papers	79	44.9	44.9
2 author papers	78	44.3	89.2
3 author papers	17	9.7	98.9
4 author papers	2	1.1	100.0
Total	176	100.0	

Figure 9. Collaboration trends in African authored ISB publications

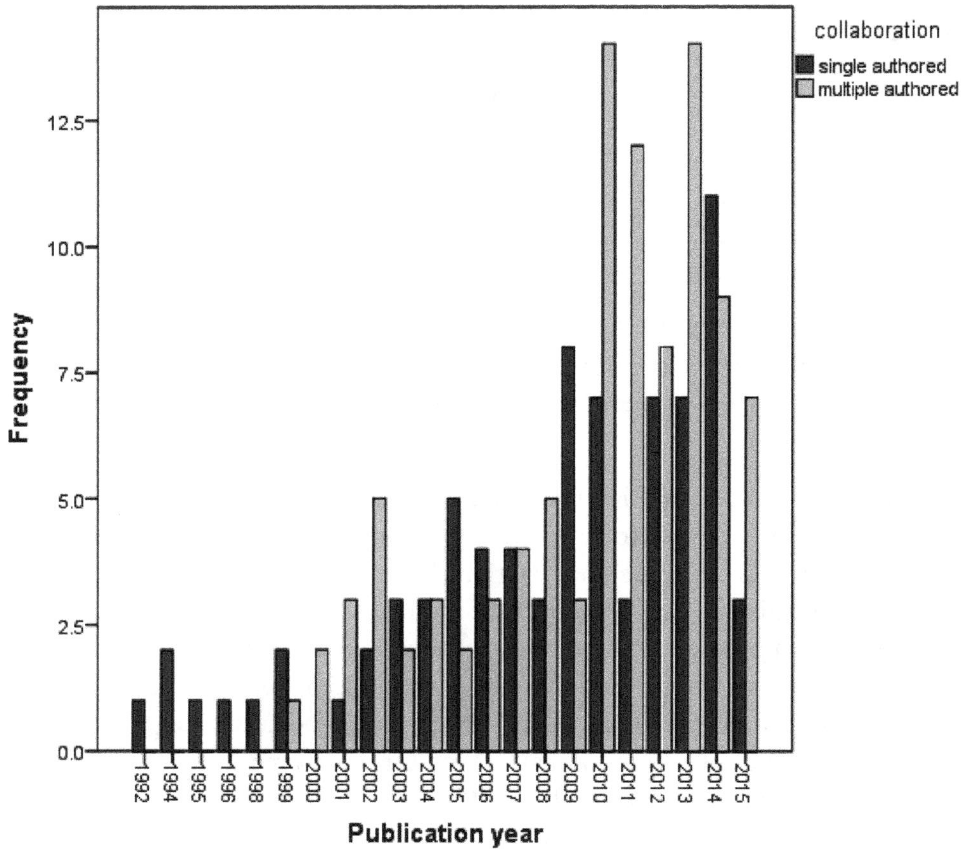

more documents that were not available yet available on the Web. A Mann Whitney U test showed that there was a statistically significant difference in citation received between pdf publications and publications retrieved through citations (U = 163.500, p = 0.001), with a mean rank citation score of 25.39 for PDF publications and 42.42 for publications retrieved through citations (Table 11). These results revealed that older publications retrieved through citation had a higher impact than pdf publications.

Further analyses established that there was a significant correlation between age of publication and citations received (rho=.419, p=.001). Number of citations increased with age of publications, i.e. publications that were older had more citations.

Table 11. Mean rank citation of publications by format

Type of Publication	Frequency	Mean Rank
Pdf	42	25.39
Citation	18	42.42
Total	60	

DISCUSSIONS

The advent of electronic publishing has widened the scope for researchers worldwide to publish their work. Many research institutions maintain pages on their websites that upload research findings. The uploaded material, from research proceedings to published work, contributes to the visibility of research in the world. Consequently, the Internet has provided a critical platform for publishing research publications and has increased their visibility and impact.

This study sought to explore the contributions of library and information science researchers to literature in the field of information seeking behaviour available on the Internet. The study used bibliometrics techniques to depict the growth of publications on the Web, to explore the types of publications in which information scientists preferred to publish their works, to investigate the collaboration patterns, and to document highly preferred journals.

The findings of the study have revealed that the literature in information seeking behaviour available on the Web has recorded a slow growth during the period before 1997. Most of the publications in the field of ISB available on the Internet are relatively of a young age (mean age=15.67). This emphasizes the fact that most of the older publications are still not available on the Internet. The oldest publication retrieved was published in 1962. The mean age of African ISB publications is even much younger (mean age = 6.04 years). This reflects the reality of the online publishing's being a new phenomenon. This slow growth rate before 1997 could be attributed the slow adoption of online publishing by researchers and publishers in most parts of the world.

However, an exponential growth of ISB literature from 1997onward is a strong indicator of the rapid adoption of online publishing in the past two decades. These results attest to the fact that the Internet/WWW has become a critical global publishing platform and scholarly communication. Consequently, electronic journals, databases and institutional repositories covering a wide range of subject areas are now increasing becoming more and more available. Library and information science is no exception, and we now find a significant portion of its literature appearing in e-journals (Hawkins, 2001). As awareness of e-journals spreads and as authors begin to regard them as legitimate publication media, we can expect the number of e-journal articles to grow (Hawkins, 2001).

The findings have also revealed a rapid increase in collaboration among authors of ISB publications at global level from 2001 onwards. This may be attributed to the ease of collaboration brought about by advent of information and communication technologies (for instance, availability of email and groupware). A similar trend is observed at the African level, although at very slow rate. The African authorship landscape is still dominated by single authorship in the ISB field, with notable increase in two authored publications.

The study has revealed that most of the publications in ISB available on the Web are found on "commercial" websites (.com) followed by websites of organizations (.org). Most of these publishers are based in United States of America and Europe. Another phenomenon observed that ISB publications are scattered in a wide range of e-journals and e-databases, including those belonging to fields of science apart from library and information science.

A separate of ISB of African origin has revealed that African information scientists in the ISB field are steadily embracing the Internet as publishing platform. However, the number of publications is relatively small and is largely dominated by a few countries, mainly South Africa and Nigeria. Furthermore, this study has revealed the preponderance of academic organizations (mainly universities) in the production of research publications on ISB. Most of the African researchers concentrate studying information seeking behaviour of students in higher institutions of learning.

The impact of African ISB publications is comparatively lower than their counterparts in Europe and America. However, the study indicates that advent of online publishing has provided opportunities for situation to improve. African publications are steadily receiving more visibility.

CONCLUSION

This study is an exploratory snapshot of the contributions in information-seeking behavior available on the Web and collected using Google Scholar. This study has revealed an exponential growth of ISB literature on the Internet and an increasing trend towards collaborative research. Most of the publications are produced from commercial websites and non-governmental organizations. ISB publications are mainly presented in PDF, Citation and html formats. Very few books are available. The findings indicate that the literature recorded exponential growth from 1997 onward. It also found that 61.5 percent were multi-authored, showing the collaborative approach of scientists in the field. This approach opens doors for interaction among experts in different areas of ISB, leading to learning and sharing of information resources. The results have also showed that ISB literature has a relatively high impact factor (h-index = 166 (63%). PDF documents had the highest visibility followed by html publications. Furthermore, publications aged 21-40 had the highest visibility. These results can be useful in many areas of library and information science such identifying and Prioritising publications to acquire or read; informing the choice of targets for planned publications; contributing to the demonstration of academic impact; and locating potential collaborators.

RECOMMENDATION

The study makes the following recommendations:

1. African research institutions should step efforts to encourage electronic publishing among its researchers and academics and scholars. More researcher should be encouraged to publish in open access journals.
2. African institutions of higher learning should strive to improve the global visibility of their research outputs through acceptance and recognition of electronic publishing in such as areas as promotion and recruitment processes.
3. African institutions should encourage establishment of more electronic institutional repositories, e-databases and e-journals. This will increase availability of local content on the Internet.
4. African research institutions should promote the use of bibliometrics as an evaluation tool of their research productivity.
5. In order to obtain a more comprehensive picture, further studies on availability of African ISB publications available in particular databases which may not be adequately covered by Google Scholar.

REFERENCES

Agosto, D.E., & Hughes-Hassell, S. (2005). People, places, and questions: An investigation of the everyday life information-seeking behaviors of urban young adults. *Library & Information Science Research*, 27(2), 141–63.

Allen, B. (1997). Information Needs: A Person in-Situation Approach. *Proceedings of an international conference on Information seeking in context ISIC '96*, Tampere, Finland (pp. 111–122). London: Taylor Graham Publishing. doi:doi:10.1108/S1876-0562(1996)0000096004 doi:10.1108/S1876-0562(1996)0000096004

Andrup, S., Fagerjord, K., & Magnussen, M. T. (1995). Fagbibliotekets rolle i problembasert læring (PBL). Oslo: RBT/Riksbibliotektjenesten. (Skrifter fra RBT/Riksbibliotektjenesten, Nr. 69).

Bates, M. J. (2010). Information behavior. In M. J. Bates & M. N. Maack (Eds.), *Encyclopedia of Library and Information Sciences* (pp. 2381–2391). New York: CRC Press.

Case, D. O. (2008). *Looking for information: A survey of research on information seeking, needs, and behavior* (2nd ed.). Bingley, UK: Emerald.

Dervin, B., & Nilam, M. (1986). Information needs and uses. *Annual Review of Information Science*, *21*, 3–33.

Dervin, B., & Nilan, M. (1986). Information needs and uses. In M. E. Williams (Ed.), *Annual Review of Information Science and Technology* (Vol. 21, pp. 3–33). New York: Knowledge Industry Publications.

Egghe, L. (2006). Theory and practice of the g-index. *Scientometrics*, *69*(1), 131–152. doi:10.1007/s11192-006-0144-7

Eskola, E. (1998). University students' information seeking behaviour in a changing learning environment - How are students' information needs, seeking and use affected by new teaching methods? *Information Research*, 4(2). Retrieved from http://www.shef.ac.uk/~is/publications/infres/isic/eeskola.html

Fourie, I. (2002, October 24–25). A Review of Web Information-Seeking/Searching Studies (2000-2002): Implications for Research in the South African Context. In T. Bothma & A. Kaniki (Eds.), *Progress in Library and Information Science in South Africa:Proceedings of the Second Biennial DISSAnet Conference* (pp. 49–75). Pretoria: Infuse.

Fourie, I. (2006). Learning from web information seeking studies: some suggestions for LIS practitioners. *The Electronic Library*, 24(1), 20-37. doi:10.1108/02640470610649227

Ginman, M. (1995). Paradigm och trender inom biblioteks- och informationsvetenskap. In: Biblioteken, kulturen och den sociala intelligensen. Aktuell forskning inom biblioteks- och informationsvetenskap. Ed. Lars Höglund. Stockholm: Forskningsrådsnämnden, FNM, 9-18.

Harzing, A.W. (2009). Harzing's Publish or Perish. *Herpetology Notes*, *3*, 239–245.

Harzing, A.W.K., & Wal, R. (2008). Google Scholar as a new source for citation analysis. *Ethics in Science and Environmental Politics*, *8*, 61–73. doi:10.3354/esep00076

Hawkins, D.T. (2001). Bibliometrics of electronic journals in information science. *Information Research*, 7(1). Retrieved from http://www.informationr.net/ir/7-1/paper120.html

Hewins, E.T. (1990). Information need and use studies. *Annual Review of Information Science*, *25*, 145–172.

Hirsch, J. E. (2005). An index to quantify an individual's scientific research output. Retrieved from http://arxiv.org/pdf/physics/0508025v5.pdf

Jamali, H. R. (2013). Citation relations of theories of human information behaviour." Webology, 10(1). Retrieved from http://www.webology.org/2013/v10n1/a106.html

Järvelin, K. (1987). Kaksi yksinkertaista jäsennystä tiedon hankinnan tutkimista varten. *Kirjastotiede ja informatiikka*, 6(1); 18-24.

Järvelin, K. & Vakkari, P. (1981). Tiedontarpeiden ja kirjaston käytön tutkimisesta. Kaksi tutkielmaa. Tamperen yliopisto. Kirjastotieteen ja informatiikan laitos. Julkaisuja A Tutkimusraportit nro 15.

Julien, H. (1996). A content analysis of recent information needs and uses literature. *Library & Information Science Research*, *18*(1), 53–65. doi:10.1016/S0740-8188(96)90030-4

Julien, H., & Duggan, L. J. (2000). A longitudinal analysis of the information needs and uses literature. *Library & Information Science Research*, *22*(3), 291–309. doi:10.1016/S0740-8188(99)00057-2

Julien, H., Pecoskie, J., & Reed, K. (2011). Trends in information behavior research, 1999-2008: A content analysis. *Library & Information Science Research*, *33*(1), 19–34. doi:10.1016/j.lisr.2010.07.014

Khey, D. N., Jennings, W. G., Higgins, G. E., Schoepfer, A., & Langton, L. (2011). Reranking the top female academic "Stars" in criminology and criminal justice using an alternative method: A research note. *Journal of Criminal Justice Education*, *22*(1), 118–129. doi:10.1080/10511253.2010.517655

Lorica, M. D. V. (2010). Information Seeking Behavior: Its relevance to the LIS Profession. Retrieved from http://mlorica.blogspot.com/2011/02/introduction-this-paper-aims-to-provide.html

McKechnie, E.F., Goodall, G.R., Lajoie-Paquette, D. and Julien, H. (2005). How human information behaviour researchers use each other's work: a basic citation analysis study. *Information Research*, 10(2). Retrieved from http://InformationR.net/ir/10-2/paper220.html

Mutshewa, A. (2007). A theoretical exploration of information behaviour: A power perspective. *Aslib Proceedings: New Information Perspectives*, *59*(3), 249–263. doi:10.1108/00012530710752043

Noruzi, A. (2005). Google Scholar: The New Generation of Citation Indexes. *Libri*, *55*(4), 170–180. doi:10.1515/LIBR.2005.170

Parmar, Arvind Kumar, S., Sanghmitra, A. & Prakash, T. (2004). *Bibliometric analysis of information seeking behaviour related literature.*

Pauly, D., & Stergiou, K. I. (2005). Equivalence of results from two citation analyses: Thomson ISI's Citation Index and Google's Scholar service. In *Ethics in Science and Environmental Politics* (pp. 33–35). Retrieved from www.int-res.com/articles/esep/2005/E65.pdf

Rafiq, M., & Ameen, K. (2009). Information Seeking Behavior and User Satisfaction of University Instructors: *A Case Study. Library Philosophy and Practice*. Retrieved from http://www.webpages.uidaho.edu/~mbolin/rafiq-ameen.htm

Spink, A., & Cole, C. (2006). Human information behavior: Integrating diverse approaches and information use. *Journal of the American Society for Information Science and Technology*, *57*(1), 25–35. doi:10.1002/asi.20249

Tamine-Lechani, L., Boughanem, M., & Daoud, M. (2010). Evaluation of contextual information retrieval effectiveness: Overview of issues and Research. *Knowledge and Information Systems*, *24*(1), 1–34. doi:10.1007/s10115-009-0231-1

Thanuskodi, S. (2009). *(June). Information-Seeking Behavior of Law Faculty at Central Law College*. Salem: Library Philosophy and Practice.

Vakkari, P. (2008). Trends and approaches in information behaviour research. *Information Research, 13*(4). Retrieved from http://www.informationr.net/ir/13-4/paper361.html

Vaughan, L., & Shaw, D. (2008). A new look at evidence of scholarly citation in citation indexes and from web sources. *Scientometrics*, *74*(2), 317–330. doi:10.1007/s11192-008-0220-2

Von Wright, J. (1994). *Oppimiskäsitysten historiaa ja pedagogisia seurauksia. 2. muuttamaton p*. Helsinki: Opetushallitus.

Wikipedia. (2015, October 27). Information needs. Retrieved from https://en.wikipedia.org/wiki/Information_needs

Wilson, T. (1981). On user studies and information needs. *The Journal of Documentation*, *37*(1), 3–15. doi:10.1108/eb026702

Wilson, T. (1999). Models in information behaviour research. *The Journal of Documentation*, *55*(3), 249–270. doi:10.1108/EUM0000000007145

Wilson, T. (2000). Human information behavior. *Informing Science*, *3*(2), 49–55.

Wilson, T. D. (1994). Information needs and uses: Fifty years of process? A Journal of Documentation Review, 1994, 15-51.

Wilson, T. D. (2000). Human information behavior. *Informing Science*, *3*(2), 49–55.

Wilson, T. D. (2006). A re-examination of information seeking behavior in the context of activity theory. *Information Research*, *11*, 4.

Wilson, T. D. (2008). Human information behavior. Retrieved from http://inform.nu/Articles/vol.3/v3n2

Yazit, N., & Zainab, A. N. (2007). Malaysian publication contributions to the field of Library and Information Science. In Abdullah, A., et al. (Eds.), Proceedings of ICOLIS '07, Kuala Lumpur (pp. 407-420).

Zainab, A. N. (2007). Women's studies in Malaysia: A bibliometric study with implications for its bibliographical control. In Abdullah, A., et al. (Eds.), Proceedings of ICOLIS '07, Kuala Lumpur (pp. 385-396).

ADDITIONAL READING

Ankem, K. (2006a). Factors influencing information needs among cancer patients: A meta-analysis. *Library & Information Science Research*, *28*(1), 7–23. doi:10.1016/j.lisr.2005.11.003

Archambault, E., & Gagné, E. V. (2004). *The use of bibliometrics in social sciences and humanities*. Montreal: Social Sciences and Humanities Research Council of Canada.

Bates, M. J. (2005a). An introduction to metatheories, theories, and models. In K. E. Fisher, S. Erdelez, & E. F. McKechnie (Eds.), *Theories of information behavior* (pp. 1–24). Medford, NJ: Information Today.

Belew, R. K. (2005). Scientific impact quantity and quality: analysis of two sources of bibliographic data. Retrieved from www.cogsci.ucsd.edu/~rik/papers/belew05-iqq.pdf

Bornmann, L., & Daniel, H. D. (2005). Does the h-index for ranking of scientists really work? *Scientometrics*, *65*(3), 391–392. doi:10.1007/s11192-005-0281-4

Bornmann, L., & Daniel, H. D. (2007). What do we know about the h index? *Journal of America Information Science and Technology*, *58*(9), 1381–1385. doi:10.1002/asi.20609

Bosman, J., Mourik, I., van Rasch, M., Sieverts, E., & Verhoeff, H. (2006) Scopus reviewed and compared. The coverage and functionality of the citation database Scopus, including comparisons with Web of Science and Google Scholar. Utrecht University Library. Retrieved from http://igiturarchive.library.uu.nl/DARLIN/2006-1220-200432/Scopus20doorgelicht%20%26%20vergeleken%20-%20translated.pdf

Egghe, L. (2006). Theory and practice of the g-index. *Scientometrics*, *69*(1), 131–152. doi:10.1007/s11192-006-0144-7

Wilson, T. D. (1981). On user studies and information needs. *The Journal of Documentation*, *37*(1), 3–15. doi:10.1108/eb026702

KEY TERMS AND DEFINITIONS

Bibliometrics: Bibliometrics is the statistical evaluation or quantitative analysis of publications and other research output of researchers, and research institutions. Bibliometrics is used worldwide especially in university and government labs, and also by policymakers, research directors and administrators, information specialists and librarians, and researchers.

Citation Analysis: Citation analysis is the examination of the frequency, patterns, and graphs of citations in articles, books and other publications to establish links to other works or other researchers and to establish the impact or influence of scholarly works.

Information Need: It is often understood as an individual or group's desire to locate and obtain information to satisfy a conscious or unconscious need. The 'information' and 'need' in 'information need' are an inseparable interconnection. Needs and interests call forth information (Wikipedia, 2015).

Information Seeking: Information seeking is "a conscious effort to acquire information in response to a need or gap in your knowledge" Case (2008, p. 8).

Information Seeking Behaviour: "Information Seeking Behavior is the purposive seeking for information as a consequence of a need to satisfy some goal. In the course of seeking, the individual may interact with manual information systems (such as a newspaper or a library), or with computer-based systems (such as the World Wide Web)" (Wilson, 2000, p. 49).

Chapter 8
Indexing and Abstracting as Tools for Information Retrieval in Digital Libraries: A Review of Literature

Olaronke O. Fagbola
National Open University of Nigeria, Nigeria

ABSTRACT

Indexing and abstracting are like Siamese twins in the information retrieval process. Indexing and abstracting are the two approaches to distilling information content into an abbreviated, but comprehensive representation of an information resource(s). They are knowledge organisation tools which usually provide detailed and accurate maps and road signs in the information superhighway. Digital libraries are characterised by an electronic stock of information which can be accessed via computers, and are extension and augmentations of physical libraries in digital forms. They are information retrieval systems (a device interposed between a potential user of information and the information itself) which provide opportunities to access and retrieve information that is often accessible for a variety of reasons. This chapter presents a literature review on indexing and abstracting, information retrieval process, digital libraries pointing out the importance of indexing and abstracting in the information retrieving process and then highlighting the roles played by indexing and abstracting as tools for information retrieval in digital libraries. The chapter posits that indexing and abstracting plays a significant role as information retrieval tools in digital libraries.

INTRODUCTION

The world today, as a thousand years ago has two basic needs: wealth and knowledge. The most generous, efficient and effective information manager may not be able to make available to others what does not exist. Likewise, the most gifted intellects may not be able to apply the powers of reasoning and imaginative deduction to information they do not possess. Hence as the dire need for information drives

DOI: 10.4018/978-1-5225-0296-8.ch008

the individual so also it goads the societies. The Web and wireless technologies have indelibly altered our lives (Tensen, 2013).

Rapid developments witnessed in telecommunications, computer technologies and other related technologies (Internet) have made it possible to store and retrieve information in many different forms and from diverse location. The first use of computers in information management in libraries opened the door to new ways of accessing and using information, making it possible to create and access electronic index to collections, electronic databases of journal article, conference papers and so on (Chowdhury and Chowdhury, 2003). Libraries are repositories of information and knowledge. However, more recently, libraries are understood as extending beyond the physical walls of a building, to serving as a 'gateway' or 'information superhighways' to stored information and knowledge. Such libraries are known and referred to as digital libraries. Libraries connect people and information; digital libraries amplify and augment these connections (Badhusha, 2008). It is pertinent for one to say that one of the most important contributions of web technology has been the creation of digital libraries which gave the means for having unhindered access to diverse information resources irrespective of location.

In digital repositories, the organisation, and access to information, information materials and tremendous amounts of knowledge is guarantee with the aid of information retrieval tools. These tools are indexing and abstracting. They are ancient and dependable information retrieval tools and plays a significant role in the information retrieval process of any information retrieval system be it digital, hybrid or traditional libraries. The indexing and abstracting method guarantees unhindered access to stored information and knowledge and at the same time allow for precision and high recall of information in an information retrieval system.

Indexing and abstracting are like Siamese twins. They are pioneer schemes of early civilization of knowledge classification and document arrangement and are still relevant and serve as the legacy to information retrieval system of the twenty-first Century. According to Cleveland and Cleveland (2000), indexing and abstracting have their distant origins somewhere and at some time when someone realised that written records need to be organised to enhance accessibility. Rubin (2010) describes indexing and abstracting as knowledge organisation tools which usually provide detailed and accurate maps and road signs in the information superhighway.

Traditionally, information retrieval has been a task for professional librarians, however, the availability of the Internet made literature searching directly available to widespread groups of researchers (Schatz, 1997). Information retrieval is the term commonly used to describe many types of literature searching. It is the science of searching for information in documents, searching for documents themselves, searching for metadata which describe documents or searching within databases whether relational stand-alone databases or hypertexually networked databases such as World Wide Web, digital libraries.

Basically, information retrieval system is concerned more with retrieving information about a subject than with retrieving data that satisfies a given query. The major functions of an information retrieval system are organisation and retrieval of information. However, for fast retrieval and ranking, documents in the central repository which provides access and management capabilities to collections and catalogue need to be indexed (Baeza-Yates and Ribeiro-Neto, 2011; Goncalves, 2011).

Digital libraries are a metaphor for access to collections of electronic documents through a network while the classic research area dealing with the electronic search for documents is information retrieval (Ferber and Thiel, 1996). Digital libraries can be seen as new tools for achieving human goals by changing the way information is used in the world. The main channel of access to digital libraries, through which information is created, discovered, enriched, accessed and ultimately used is service (Goncalves, 2011).

The advent of digital libraries, has not led to the replacing libraries of printed material, but instead, it has enhanced information access and use by exploiting information and communication technologies. A digital library is a new kind of institution, a library without walls, largely distinct from modern library in its materials, practices and personnel. Digital libraries are organised collections of information, and the information revolution not only supplies the technological horsepower that drives it, but also fuels an unprecedented demand for storing, organising and accessing information (Witten, Bainbridge and Nichols, 2010). Taylor and Joudrey (2009) submits that digital libraries vary greatly in content and methods of organisation, as they all have some kind of organisation, although not necessarily traditional library organisation.

Digital, 'electronic', 'virtual', 'library without walls' all refers to the vast collection of information to which people gain access over the Internet, cable television, or some other types of remote electronic connections. They are characterised by an electronic stock of information which can be accessed via computers, and are extension and augmentations of physical libraries in digital forms; it provides opportunities to access and retrieve information that is often inaccessible for a variety of reasons in developing countries (Park, Roman, Lee and Chung, 2009). Digital libraries offer unique ways of recording, preserving, collecting, organising and propagating culture in various multi-media forms and enable users to interact effectively with information distributed across a network (Schatz, 1997).

Digital libraries include collections of books, journal articles, graphics, newspapers and other material in digital format; in sum, collections of digitized content. To be a library, that collections should be organised according to some standard so as to allow for easy retrieval of information with information retrieval tools. In the digital library environment, emphasis is on providing integrated access to diversity of modules for information retrieval (Rasmussen, 2011). Essentially, this chapter presents a literature review on indexing and abstracting as information retrieval tools in digital libraries focusing on the concept of indexing and abstracting, the concept of information retrieval, evolution and meaning of digital libraries, essential features and importance; and finally highlighting the role of indexing and abstracting as information retrieval tools in digital libraries.

INDEXING AND ABSTRACTING

Indexing and abstracting are information retrieval and knowledge organisation tools that make it easier for information/library users to retrieve relevant documents from a large collection (print and electronics). Indexing and abstracting are the two approaches to distilling information content into an abbreviated, but comprehensive representation of an information resource(s) (Taylor and Jourdrey, 2009). Also, Cleveland and Cleveland (2000) explains that indexing and abstracting transform document space into an index/abstract space and their goal is to accurately represent the content of an item with the terms that are explicit to the information searchers and give value to documents which are essential aids to information-seeking in libraries.

The processes of indexing and abstracting allows information professionals to provide advanced organisation of information carriers (books, serials, digital materials, manuscripts, and so on) in the library, documentation or information centres (Aina, 2004). Indexing creates a surrogate (substitute) of information items together with abstracting (Cleveland and Cleveland, 2000). Indexing and abstracting is a category of database that provides bibliographic citations and or abstracts for the literature of a discipline or broad subject area, as distinct from a retrieval service that provides information sources in full text. Its general purpose is to minimize the time and effort expended in searching and maximizes the searching success (Feather and Sturges, 1997).

Also, the Encyclopaedia of Library and Information Science states that "indexing and abstracting as a practical art, is a way of representing an actual document or textual item. They are miniature version of the actual thing. It explains further that while indexing is used to locate desired information, abstracting is a medium that helps the searcher to decide which of the apparently correct items s/he wishes to study further. It is pertinent to state here that there is the possibility of seeing indexing and abstracting only as a service. Howbeit, it must be stated at this juncture that this paper will like to emphasis on the power of indexing and abstracting as an effective and efficient retrieval tools in information retrieval systems generally, and in digital libraries in particular.

CONCEPT OF INDEXING

Indexing is the process of providing a guide to the intellectual content of documents in the library collection; the process of creating the entries in an index. It involves any type of subject specification assigned to documents in order to assist with their retrieval (Chakrabortty and Chakrabarti, 1984). Taylor and Jourdrey (2009) explain that indexing is the process by which the content of an information resource is analysed, and the aboutness of that item is determined and expressed in a concise manner. Taylor and Joudrey proceeds to say that indexing is concerned with describing the information resource in such a way that users are aware of the basic attribute of a document such as author, title, length and the location of the content.

Indexing is the process of associating one or more keywords with each document they are about. It is the process whereby subject metadata can be added to information objects or their surrogates to support more effective and efficient retrieval of information (Rowley and Hartley, 2008). Chowdury, 2010) notes that indexing is the process of assigning a subject heading to an information source of whatever form be it books, periodical, multi-media et cetera so as to serve as a retrieval tool for the information source being analysed. Fidel (1986) observes that indexing is the intellectual process of preparing a surrogate record to represent a bibliographic item in information storage and retrieval process. According to Davis and Shaw (2011), indexing is the representation of a document (or part of a document or an information object in a record or an index for the purpose of retrieval. Some common examples include library catalogues, bibliographical databases and back-of-the-book indexes.

Indexing involves methods for providing access to document collections, single document and parts of documents without regard to the location of these documents. It is the fundamental method for organizing knowledge. It always involves the description of the document or document collections that contains messages of interest, unless the document or collection is self-evident, as in back-of-the-book-index (Feather and Sturges, 1997). Indexing is one of the best known of 'traditional' library / information activities. Its importance has not diminished in the digital age. On the contrary, indexing is of even more importance in digital environments, so that information can be efficiently found from sources such as the internet or intranets. It is an important part of the broader process of metadata creation (Anoy). Aina (2004) notes that the basic purpose of indexing is to match the ideas expressed in a document with the ideas embedded in a chosen heading(s) from a prescribed list of subject headings.

Indexing: A Brief History

In order to have a deeper appreciation for indexing being a critical tool for finding information in digital libraries, it is important to understand a bit of the background and history of indexing. Indexes have been used for years to help information users quickly locate pieces of information of interest to them (Skyes, 2001). According to the Encyclopaedia of Library and Information Science, indexes are as old as published writing and exist virtually in every language. It explains that the early indexes were limited to personal names or indexes to the occurrences of words in the text indexed (concordance, rather than topical (subject, concept), indexes. Word indexes were used frequently with religious writings; they constituted an important tool in the mystics' interpretation of the Talmud. Topical indexes are found more frequently beginning with 18th century literature but the choice of terms, and even the order of entries in the index, remained haphazard for a long time. The late 19th century brought with it the development of taxonomy in library work and documentation, this made subject indexing to become systematic and wide spread. Although indexing is often clearly differentiated from cataloguing and classification, a considerable overlap is noticed in practice and the development of new cataloguing technique or new classification system is bound to affect indexing practices.

Despite the obvious need for indexes in searching the literature and other collections, there were no concerted movements to assure the creation of indexes of high quality wherever they were needed. The presence of an index was generally taken for granted, its absence ignored, its quality rarely the subject of comment by publishers and users alike. However, the noticeable changes in the attitude of publishers, librarians and information users came about as a result of the "information explosion" during and immediately following World War II. Suddenly, the dramatic increase in the amount of information to be processed and disseminated coupled with the dramatic decrease in the time allowable for processing and disseminating the information caused a vast concentration of effort and attention on the humble practice of indexing.

What Is an Index?

An index is a systematic guide designed to indicate topics or features of documents in order to facilitate retrieval of documents or parts of documents. It is a distinct knowledge record with its own internal validity and consistency and a metadata which indicates the characteristics and relationships of the information in the data items and other data items that are similar basically to serve two main purposes viz to:

- Minimize the time and effort in finding information; and
- Maximize the searching success of the user (Chakrabortty and Chakrabarti, 1984; Cleveland and Cleveland, 2000).

Indexes are retrieval tools which provide access to the analyzed contents of information resources (articles in journals, short stories in collections, papers in conference proceeding (Taylor and Jourdrey, 2009). An index is a bridge over troubled information explosion waters for seekers of information, a device that connects a potential user of information to a potentially useful information store. Indexes can provide retrieval information for most types of materials: books, periodical articles, and dissertation (Cleveland and Cleveland, 2000; Rubin, 2010).

Indexes gives the thought content of documentary and non-documentary sources and can provide substantial information or direct the user(s) to a library file, a bound volume, a microfilm, a computer file or a database of information. All indexes consist of a series of lead terms, arranged usually in alphabetical order. At this point it is pertinent to state that indexes allow for effective access mechanism and retrieval to an information storage system such as digital libraries.

Types of Indexes

Basically, there are two major categories of indexes. These are:

- **Automated Indexes:** This is a method of indexing in which an algorithm is applied by a computer to the title and/or text of a work to identify and extract words and phrases representing subjects, for use as headings under which entries are made in index. They are usually generated by machine. Examples include search engines, OPAC and so on. (Reitz, 2004).
- **Manual Indexes:** These are indexes that are physically compiled by human beings e.g. back of book index.
- **Book Index:** Most indexes are manually compiled and the most popular is the book index. These are indexes found at the end of a book directing users to the page number of the indexed terms. Other common types include:
- **Periodical Indexes:** These are indexes to a single or several journals. It is generally an index of authors and subject discussed in all the issues for a year. Indexing terms are usually selected from the title of each article in the journal example include LISA.
- **Chain Indexes:** These are indexed terms generated from a classification scheme. The principle is based on the classification theory of Ranganathan.
- **Precis Indexes (Preserved Context Indexing System):** A special type of index that provides a summary of the content of a document. It involves providing a link to the index term in the context in which the author of the document has used the term. There is usually a lead term and other terms. This type of index saves the time of the users from having false starts.
- **Citation Index:** A special type of index that lists all citing articles under a cited paper. For example, for each article cited in the index it would list all other articles that have cited it. This is the basis of Science Citation Index. They are useful to researchers.
- **Subject Indexing:** Subject indexing is the art of describing a document by index terms (often selected from some controlled vocabulary) to indicate what the document is about or to summarize its content. Subject indexing systems are the tools with which subject indexes are prepared. It is the index concepts found in a collection of documents. Subject index is used in information retrieval specially to create bibliographic database to retrieve documents on a particular subject.

Indexing Terms

These are standard terms used for indexing information put into a system (Chakrabortty and Chakrabarti, 1984). Example includes the following:

- **See Reference:** Leads from a term that was not used as index entry to synonym that is used.
- **See Also Reference:** Leads the reader to related information under another heading.

- **BT:** Broader term.
- **NT:** Narrower term.
- **RT:** Related term.

```
Example using BT, NT, and RT
BT: Legumes
      NT:  Cowpea
            RT: Soya beans
```

- **UF/US (Use or Used for):** Directs user to preferred term. Example:

```
         Frocks
            Use Dresses
              Dresses
                    Use for
                           Gowns
                            Frocks
```

- **Scope Note (SN):** It defines the way a term has been used when there is the possibility of ambiguity. It is a standard thesaurus feature.
- **Indexer Note (IN):** These are notes that contain information specifically for indexers using the thesaurus assigned to subject terms. It is often more specific and informal than scope notes and are generally not displayed except internally.
- **History Note (HN):** Another type of internal note that tells when a term was changed or added to the thesaurus
- **Thesaurus Note (TN):** These are informal notes used by the lexicographer in the course of thesaurus development about areas that need additional research and refinement. They are notes by and for the thesaurus developer.

Indexing Language

Indexing language can be defined as the terms or codes that might be used as access points in index (Rowley and Hartley, 2008). They are artificial language consisting of subject headings or content descriptors selected to facilitate information retrieval by serving as access points in a catalogue or index. This includes any lead-in vocabulary and rules governing form of entry, syntax and so on (Reitz, 2004). Reitz explains further that indexing language are list of indexing terms used to represent topics or features of documents and the rules for combining or using those terms. An indexing language allows the indexer to represent the subject matter of a document in a consistent way

The function of an indexing language is to take whatever a natural language does and in addition organize the semantics content through a different expression, providing a point of access to the seekers of information. It is a system for naming subjects and has controlled vocabulary which may be verbal or coded. These are terms or codes that might be used as access points in an index. Some common attributes of indexing language are that it should use a vocabulary and syntax; format, syntax and vocabulary must be comprehensible to computer; the indexing language should be able to sufficiently describe and be precise at the same time and must contain provisions for its own modification, as the language of document or user changes (Chakrabortty and Chakrabarti, 1984; Cleveland and Cleveland, 2000; and Aina, 2004).

The Structure of an Indexing Language

The structures of an indexing language include a set of:

- Index terms (standard terms used for indexing information e.g. BT, NT, See Ref).
- Code terms (set rules that define a limit to the kind of data that can be indexed).
- Entry terms (word by which the entry is arranged in the index other than an article).
- Devices used in association with the index terms to broaden or restrict class definition.
- Rules for use of index language.

Types of Indexing Languages

There are three types of indexing languages; and a complete indexing language will include devices which are used to achieve either high recall or high precision in both indexing and search operations (Chakrabortty and Chakrabarti, 1984; Cleveland and Cleveland, 2000; and Aina, 2004). These include:

- **Controlled Vocabulary (Artificial Language):** This is an indexing language with a standardized set of terms and phrases authorised for use in an indexing system to describe a subject area or information domain (Sykes, 2001). It is a consistent set of words, along with rules of usage, to be followed strictly when indexing. The indexer usually exercises some control over the terms that are to be used as index terms because the indexer assigns only terms that have been listed as possible index terms. Usually, there is generally a pre-conceived standard list of terms used for a given system. Common example includes Thesauri, the Subject Headings List (Sears List, Library of Congress Subject Heading List), the Classification Scheme (DDC, LC, Faceted Scheme and so on). It is only the approved terms that can be used by the indexer to describe the document at hand. It allows for the use of concept indexing
- **Natural Language:** This involves the use of words directly from the text of a document as written by the author of the item been indexed. The indexer makes use of the exact words and phrases used by the author of the document. It is very easy to use by the indexer and the searcher but the major problem is that there is no discrimination between synonyms, semantics, and homograph. This type of indexing language tends to scatter documents on the same subject, where the authors have used different terms. They are used mainly in the back of book index and computerized indexes such as Keyword in Context (KWIC) and Keyword out of Context (KWOC) indexes.
- **Free Vocabulary:** This does not consist of a list of terms distinct from those used to describe a concept in a subject area. No restriction as to the words or phrases to be used as index terms. They may be the exact words and phrases used by the authors or some other words. Mostly used in a computer indexing environment.

The Indexing Process

According to Cleveland and Cleveland (2000), indexing is the process of identifying information in a knowledge record and organising the pointers to that information into a searchable file. Aina (2004) explains that the technique for producing an index is called indexing and indexing is the process of providing a guide to the intellectual content of a document or collection of documents. The indexing process includes not only selecting terms to be indexed but also adding qualifiers as sub-entries where appropriate. In indexing a document, the indexer decides the level of indexing exhausitivity, which is the level of details in which the document is described. For example when using low indexing exhausitivity, minor aspects of the work will not be described with index terms, and so generally, the higher the indexing exhausitivity, the more terms indexed for each document.

The essential operations concerned are:

- Scanning the collection.
- Analyzing the content, this is done based on pre-determined criteria of use of the collection and the index.
- Tagging discrete items in the collection with appropriate identifiers.
- Adding to each identifier the precise location within the collection where the terms occur, so that it may be retrieved.
- Editing the index after a first draft to improve its cohesiveness, consistency, accuracy and usefulness to the reader.

Aina (2004) notes that indexing is an art that involves the following stages:

- **The Familiarization Stage:** This stage involves having a general idea of the document to be indexed by going through the title, preface, foreword, content pages and possibly the introduction.
- **The Analysis Stage:** It involves the indexer using his intellectual judgment by identifying the concepts the book has treated. At times, the indexer may use the exact term used by the author or formulate an appropriate term to accurately describe the entire document.
- **Translation Stage:** At this stage, the identified terms have to be translated into an indexing language used by the system and the searcher(s). Example includes Library of Congress Subject Headings list, Thesaurus, etc. Also subject descriptors earlier chosen from the controlled language that the users of the discipline are familiar with are assigned by the indexer

THE INDEXING SYSTEM

These are the pre-coordinate and post-coordinate indexing system.

Pre-Coordinate Indexing

This is a method of indexing in which concepts are combined by the indexer to form subject headings or descriptors assigned to documents to facilitate the retrieval of information on complex subject. It entails the indexer describing a document's subject with phrases e.g. 'learning disability'. In this type of indexing, a subject term is usually chosen to represent a document which will serve as the lead term to a document. This may contain one or more subject terms. The coordination terms is usually done before searching by the user.

In pre-coordinate indexing, the words are combined by the indexer rather than by the person searching for the information. This type of indexing is commonly used in back-of-the-book indexes, library catalogue and some bibliographic databases. It is equally useful in helping the searcher locate information on a topic while avoiding documents that use the same words but with other meanings otherwise referred to as false drops (Davis and Shaw, 2011).

Post-Coordinate Indexing

This allows searchers to coordinate index terms of their own choosing (within the bounds of the controlled vocabulary) at the time of searching. It permits great flexibility when using electronic indexes. This method is most common in electronic information retrieval systems in which the searcher selects combinations of search terms when using a database. The searcher uses Boolean logic (AND, OR, NOT) to combine words to express the information needed.

Post-coordinate indexing allows searchers to choose words and combine them in ways an indexer may not have anticipated which increases the flexibility of searching and often the number of documents retrieved otherwise known as recall (Davis and Shaw, 2011).

However, the advent of digital libraries, digitization, and electronic databases led to the creation of other indexing system. It includes:

- **Keyword Indexing:** This is a kind of automatic indexing. It extracts words from a document in order to describe its subject. This can be key word in context (KWIC) which forms a column near the middle of the page and portions of the author or key word out of context (KWOC). This forms a column at the left side of a page.
- **Citation Indexing:** Citation indexes are databases of documents' bibliographic references which allow searchers to search by citation chaining, locating newer documents that cite an older one. It is more than an aid to users seeking information but also a research tool for studying the behavioural characteristics of the literature.

TYPES OF INDEXING

Indexes can be categorised into many types: by example, arrangement, searching structure or specific fields or purpose.

- **Descriptive Indexing:** This usually emphasises physical properties such as originator, publisher, date and place of publication while subject indexing emphasises what the document is about (Cleveland and Cleveland, 2000; www.anzsi.org, 2015). Other types of indexing are:
- **Bibliographic and Database Indexing:** Bibliographic database indexes provide records for items such as journal articles. The database provides online access to a body of literature (e.g medical journal articles). Citation and subject details are described according to set rules specifically for that database.

- **Subject Gateways:** These are new forms of electronic indexing (online information) in which indexers create subject gateways on the internet in order to classify links to web pages of interest.
- **Website and Metadata Indexing:** This is a form of indexing that enhances access to information on the World Wide Web. They are similar in style to back of book indexes or can be designed as hierarchical pages to form a direct link to the information required. They complement other navigational tools such as site maps and search engines. Metadata indexes helps to improve the precision of access to web documents through search engines by the use of standard elements similar to those used in database indexes and library catalogues.
- **Genealogical Indexing:** Genealogical indexes allow users to look up people's names and find information about personal and family relationships. They often eliminate the need to access original source materials
- **Geographical Indexing:** Geographic index create indexes to maps, atlases and other cartographic material. Geographical indexes may include place names, topics, historical details, mathematical qualities (for example scale and coordinates) and artistic features.
- **Book Indexing:** This type of index creates indexes to provide access to detailed contents of books. Back-of-book indexes are made for all types of non-fiction books, including textbooks, multi-volume works, technical reports and annual reports. Books that are online, PDF books and ebooks also need indexes. It links directly to points in the text.
- **Legal Indexing:** Legal indexing involves indexing of legal materials by form and content to enhance access.
- **Periodical and Newspaper Indexing:** Periodical and newspaper indexes give access to the contents of individual articles and other items in serialised publications. Many periodical and newspaper indexes are based on a controlled vocabulary to ensure consistent use of terms from year to year. Newspaper and periodical indexes can be annual or cumulative.
- **Pictorial Indexing:** Indexes to images help users identify relevant pictures in collections of photographs, art works, videos and films. Pictorial indexers are skilled in identifying and describing images in visual collections.

Functions of Indexes

Some of the basic functions of an index include the following:

- Directing the reader to a specific topic.
- It enables the reader to find topics according to the reader's way of thinking.
- Allows readers with different degrees of knowledge to locate topics; it does this by showing how a topic is related to other topics in the document-is the topic a subdivision of another topic or does it encompass other topics; is it independent of other topics.
- It helps a reader use a document even if the reader has topics, confused or is unaware of an equivalent topic or is accustomed to different terminologies.
- It indicates relationships among topics.
- Indexes save time and make practical searches that would otherwise be given up possible.
- Suggest users of a topic to lookup related topics also by means of see also reference e.g. dress see also frock.
- Index arranges entries into a systematic and helpful order.

- Analyse concepts treated in a document so as to produce suitable index headings based on its terminology.
- Arrange entries into a systematic and helpful order.
- An index is a valuable aid selection.
- It limits wear and tear on a document because it saves a reader from having to flip through the complete text each time a piece of information is sought.
- Indexing aids the understanding of foreign language material.
- It provides a kind of solution to information glut (information explosion).
- It groups together related topics scattered by the arrangement on the collection.

Indexing Steps

Indexing cannot be reduced to a set of steps that can be followed strictly because it is not a mechanical process but a form of writing. However, Cleveland and Cleveland (2000) explained that document indexing includes a number of steps. These include:

- Content analysis.
- Assigning content indicators.
- Adding location indicators.
- Assembling the resulting entries.

CONCEPT OF ABSTRACTING

Abstracting is a process that consists of analysing the content of an information resource and then writing a succinct summary of that work (Taylor and Joudrey, 2009; Davis and Shaw, 2011). It is a process that provides an added value to the documents being sought (Aina, 2004). Reitz (2004) defines abstracting "as the preparation of a brief, objective statement of the content of a written work to enable the researcher(s) to quickly determine whether reading the entire text might satisfy the specific information need. Reitz proceeds to say that "abstracting is usually limited to the literature of a specific discipline or group of related disciplines and it is performed by an individual or commercial entity, such as an indexing and abstracting service, which provides abstracts regularly to a list of subscribers".

An abstract is a type of surrogate and complement indexes by summarising the actual contents of a document so that readers can determine if the document is appropriate for their purposes (Rubin, 2010). Abstracts have even been viewed as substitutes for original documents and are important facilitators of free-text searching in most online bibliographic databases (Fidel, 1986). An abstract is not an extract, a summary, annotation, terse literature, precise, summary, resume, epitome, paraphrase, digest, or a synopsis. It is like the juice of a lemon (Anoy). Instead, they provide the skeletal representation of a document.

Abstracts can serve as a current awareness tool and aid in the decision of which articles need to be read in full. They equally enable information seekers to access a large body of literature that can be scanned quickly (Rubin, 2010; David and Shaw, 2011). An abstract usually includes a bibliographic citation indicating where the entire text of an item can be located. For abstracts to be used, they need to be indexed (Cleveland and Cleveland, 2000).

Types of Abstracts

Generally, there are three varieties of abstracts (Cleveland and Cleveland, 2000; Reitz, 2004; and David and Shaw, 2011 citing ANSI/NISO, 1997). These are:

- **Informative Abstract:** This is an abstract that summarises as much of the essential content of a work as possible, within the limits of a single paragraph. It presents the actual data and information contained in the original, thereby giving enough details to enable a user to have sufficient knowledge present in the original document, a true surrogate of the original document. Informative abstract represent and summarise the content of all major aspects of the material.
- **Indicative or Descriptive Abstract:** This is an abstract that describes the type and form of the work abstracted, indicating the main topics covered and providing a brief description of the treatment, but does not summarise the content or evaluate quality. It applies generally to non-research papers. Indicative abstract cannot be used in place of the original document. However, it tells the user what can be found in the document rather than the actual data and information written to help the user understand the scope of the original document. The advent of bibliographic databases online changed the role of abstracts as an important enhancement for information retrieval (Stoan, 1991).
- **Informative-Indicative Abstract:** This a combination of the two types above and usually the only solution when space prohibits full report of findings.

Other types of abstract include:

- **Critical Abstracts**: This is a type of abstract that makes an evaluative judgment of the content of the document. It indicates the depth and extent of the content, and the comment on the various aspects of the document.
- **Mission-Oriented Abstracts**: This is a type of abstract whereby the document being abstracted is inter-disciplinary in nature and it is meant for a particular assignment such as food production.
- **Discipline-Oriented Abstracts:** These are concerned with abstracting documents devoted to a particular discipline e.g. Library and Information Science Abstract (LISA).
- **Professional Abstracts:** These are abstract written by skilled professionals who may not necessarily be experts in the subject field but are able to produce high quality abstracts as a result of the skills they possess.
- **Author Abstracts:** These are abstracts prepared by the author(s) of the original document.

It is important to state at this juncture that indexing and abstract forms the basis of any information retrieval system be it the traditional library system (where diverse information resources are located through the use of catalogue, subject heading list), digital or virtual libraries where information are access with the aid of an online public access catalogue (OPAC) because they serve as access tools to the entire holdings of any information repository. In the light of the above discussion on indexing and abstracting, the next section discusses the concept of information retrieval and highlights the role of indexing and abstracting in the retrieval of information from digital libraries.

INFORMATION RETRIEVAL

Information is an indispensable aspect of modern society and information processing is an integral part of every human activity. Information retrieval is a method of storing, organising and offering access to information sources in information repositories (Selvam, 2014). Information retrieval is generally concerned with what an information object is about rather than what it means (Rowley and Hartley, 2008). According to Reitz (2004), information retrieval is the process, methods and procedure used to selectively recall recorded information from a file of data.

Information retrieval includes operations performed by the hardware and software used in indexing whenever a user queries the system (manual or automated) for information relevant to a specific topic. Reitz explains further that for records to be retrieved, the search statement must be expressed in syntax that is executable by the computer (automated) or user (manual). The main purpose of information retrieval is to find desired information in a store of information or a database and it involves the searching and retrieval from storage of information by subject specification (Chowdhury and Chowdhury, 2003).

An information retrieval system is a system designed to analyse, process, store sources of information and retrieve those that match a particular user's requirements (Chowdhury, 2010). Bajpai (1999) sees it as a device interposed between a potential user of information and the information itself. However, Taylor and Joudrey (2009) opine that retrieval of information is dependent upon its having been organised.

The information retrieval process may either involve a citation record with fields of information for author, title, subject headings, or full–text of an article plus the citation information. In any of this, indexing and abstracting plays an important role in ensuring that the query pose by the user is met with a high recall and precision, and the ability to ensure that the information needs of the user is met with desired satisfaction. The information retrieval process is usually enhanced by controlled vocabularies. These are carefully selected list of words and phrases used to tag units of information (document or work) to allow for easy retrieval of document(s).

Information Retrieval Components

- The information user(s) with goal, problem, task, knowledge;
- Information resources (digital library) with information objects selected, organized and represented; and
- The mediator i.e. information personnel that helps to support the interaction between the user(s) and the information resource.

Goals of Information Retrieval System

The goal of any information retrieval system is basically to:

- Support the user in managing the problem(s), achieving the goal;
- Support the user in appropriate resolution of the problematic situation;
- Support the user in effective interaction with information objects or resources; and
- Support in finding information.

Information Retrieval Phases

According to Bajpai (1999), there are four phases in the entire process of information retrieval. These are:

- Word retrieval in which the exact word that will adequately describe the information sought are identified;
- Reference retrieval where reference that are pertinent to the inquiry are identified;
- Document retrieval where the actual documents are located; and
- Data retrieval in which the sought information is extracted from the document.

Functions of Information Retrieval System

An information retrieval system is a mechanism for carrying out the information retrieval process which involves some basic functions (Cleveland and Cleveland, 2000). These functions include:

1. **Information Creation and Acquisition:** This involves the creation and acquisition of information for the system (data, reference or text retrieval) such that no information system can retrieve relevant information if it does not have access to such information. Also to be considered when acquiring information for a system is the user needs and the system's designer should focus on the user's needs at the individual level and the needs of the institution as a whole.
2. **Analysis of Records:** Knowledge records are analysed and tagged by sets of index terms. Documents are represented with proxies (through cataloguing, classifying, indexing, abstracting) so as to reduce the number of actual document that the user is exposed to when conducting a search.
3. **Storage of Knowledge Records:** The knowledge records are stored physically and the index terms are stored into a structured file. The two files form the storage part of an information retrieval system.
4. **Tagging of User's Query:** The user's query is tagged with sets of index terms and then is matched against the tagged records. This is the searching stage, in which the user's needs are expressed with the same representation language and also are coded by the same process.
5. **Matching of Documents:** Matched documents are retrieved for review and the results are presented to the user for her judgement of usefulness. Ambiguity may set in at this point because determining relevance is herculean.
6. **Feedback:** Feedback may lead to several reiterations of the search. This is a crucial and central element in an information retrieval system.

With all that have been said above, it is pertinent to state that indexing, abstracting and information retrieval are inseparable. Good indexing is closely related to the searching stage of information retrieval. An index and an abstract are searching device. The goal of indexing and abstracting is to accurately represent the content of an item with terms that are explicit to the information searcher. Equally, the user must form a query that reflects as closely as possible the content of the searching question or information problem.

CONCEPT OF DIGITAL LIBRARY

One of the most important contributions of web technology has been the creation of digital libraries, which allow users to access digital information resources from virtually anywhere in the world (Chowdhury and Chowdhury, 2003). The advent of information and communication technology (ICT) to support such access has gradually improved as the necessary ICT infrastructure required for the effective utilisation of digital libraries has improved. Digital libraries can be seen as new tools for achieving human goals by changing the way information is used in the world.

Digital libraries are organised collections of different forms of electronic information resources created for a specified community and with capabilities that distinguish them from other information retrieval systems (Marchionini and Mauer, 1995 cited in Fatoki, 2012).

Witten, Bainbridge and Nichols (2010) describe digital libraries as organised collections of information and the information revolution not only supplies the technological horsepower that drives it, but also fuels an unprecedented demand for storing, organising and accessing information.

Digital libraries vary greatly in content and methods of organisation, as they all have some kind of organisation, although not necessarily traditional library organisation (Taylor and Joudrey, 2009). Digital libraries offer unique ways of recording, preserving, collecting, organising and propagating culture in various multi-media forms and enable users to interact effectively with information distributed across a network (Schatz, 1997). Wu-Jun and Peng (2010) explain that the core task of digital libraries is to provide good information retrieval system for the users.

According to Fidel (1986), digital libraries helps users to interact effectively with information distributed across a network. Badhusha (2009) notes that libraries connect people and information; digital libraries amplify and augment these connections. It is pertinent to state at this point that retrieving information in digital libraries requires the possession of certain skills and familiarity with the various information retrieval tools such as indexes and abstracts.

What Is Digital Library?

Digital libraries constitute one of the most advanced and complex types of information systems (Goncalves, 2011). They are usually referring to as 'libraries without walls' but differ from the World Wide Web in that digital collections are carefully selected and organised. Digital libraries are collections in which a site provides digitised information resources with architecture and a service for the retrieval of such resources (Taylor and Joudrey, 2009); they consist of focused collection of digital objects, including text, video and audio, along with methods for access, retrieval, selection, organisation and maintenance (Witten, et al., 2010).

Digital libraries are a set of electronic resources and associated technical capabilities for creating, searching and using information. They are an extension, enhancement and integration of information storage and retrieval systems and multiple information institutions that manipulate digital data in any medium (text, images and sounds, static or dynamic images) and exist in distributed network (Borgman, 2007; Taylor and Joudrey, 2009). Badhusha (2008) further describes digital libraries as organised collection accessible over a network which employs procedures to select, organise, make available and archive information. The primary purpose of digital libraries is to enable searching of electronic collections distributed across networks, rather than merely creating electronic repositories from digitised physical materials.

Moreover, a digital library usually comprised a collection of digital objects (data, digital documents, images); a catalogue of metadata to facilitate the identification, location, retrieval, manipulation and use of digital objects in a networked environment (e.g. representation, creator, owner, reproduction rights) records that serve either to describe, organise, or to specify how the objects in the collection can be used (Borgman, 2000; Chowdhury and Chowdhury, 2003; and Goncalves, 2011). Digital libraries basically are information system comprising totally of digitised collections. However, the fundamental problem common to all information systems is that of providing for the nearest possible coincidence between the description of a topic by a user and the description of the topic in the system's database. The information storehouse must be properly organised (manually or an algorithmic procedure) before the system can use a search procedure to locate the information in the database or digital library (Cleveland and Cleveland, 2000). They emphasise that good indexing is closely related to the searching stage of information retrieval; and that an index and an abstract are devices for searching.

Digital libraries offer many other valued services such as document preservation and recommendation, reference services, selective information dissemination, among others (Goncalves, 2011) which are far more accessible than physical ones. They are an all-encompassing information medium that will empower the mind of users. Users of digital libraries usually vary in terms of their information needs, characteristics, capabilities (literacy and ICT skills) and environment. While, some digital libraries were established to cater for homogenous group of users, others were designed specifically to support a defined group of users. Examples include mostly university libraries (Chowdhury and Chowdhury, 2003). Accessing information in a digital library entails connectivity to a computer network, available content in usable and useful format and lastly, the user exhibiting the requisite skill and knowledge to interact with the digital library. Examples of available digital libraries are: Networked Digital Library of Theses and Dissertations (NDLTD); the Greenstone Library and California Digital Library and so on.

Advantages of digital libraries are that large amount of information in digital formats can be consulted, shared by multiple users simultaneously, updated quickly and available always. Also with the increasing capacities and portability of computers and the growth of high-speed networks, digital libraries are everywhere (Rubin, 2010). The two most prominent features of digital libraries are information retrieval and user interfaces. Citing other authors, Chowdhury and Chowdhury (2003) listed some of the specific features that distinguish digital libraries from other forms of libraries to include:

- Digital libraries are portable and more flexible than conventional ones.
- Relatively easy to extract portions of digital items and re-use them without affecting the original content.
- Digital libraries occupy less tangible world of computers, of magnetic and optical storage mechanism, network connections and Web sites.
- Access to full digital content which allows users to work far outside the library walls.
- Digital libraries have help services available to anyone who can find them.
- Digital libraries allows for effective collaboration as people find it useful to share their lists, either publicly or with specific groups of friend.
- Digital libraries reduce the direct involvement of human intermediaries in the process of information access by end-users.
- It allows for user involvement in knowledge creation and distribution.

- Digital libraries allow for rapid searching with the help of computer systems and the ability to search full text adds great value when large document collections are involved.
- Several users can use the same information resource at the same time, which is not possible in conventional ones.
- Digital libraries break time, space and language barriers as users from anywhere in the world should be able to use a digital library at any time and in any language.

Importance of Digital Libraries

Importance of digital libraries is that:

- A digital library brings information to the user.
- It improves searching and manipulation of information.
- Allow and improve facilities for information sharing.
- Digital libraries allow for timely access to and improve use of information.
- Improve collaboration and reduction of the digital divide.
- Information in digital libraries is explicitly organised, described and managed.
- Digital libraries are usually built for targeted community of users with specific information needs and task.
- Digital libraries eliminate almost completely access and dissemination restrictions inherent to the physical world.

Information Retrieval Process in Digital Library

In a digital library environment, for any user(s) to effectively retrieve information, they are expected to possess certain skills such as the ability to construct appropriate information search strategies, locate and access information, ability to compare and evaluate information obtained from various sources etc. The combination of these skills is what is referred to as information literacy skills (Bajpai, 1999; Chowdhury and Chowdhury, 2003). The information retrieval process usually begins with a user query. A user with information need interact with the information retrieval system through the user interface and submits a query. A search query may contain a simple keyword, multiple keyword or phrase. The retrieval system matches each search term with the inverted index file and retrieves the matching items.

Information Search in a Digital library environment

Information searching is a complex process and it involves a number of stages, at each stage a number of actions is taken and decisions made. In digital libraries, users can have access to information through browsing and searching. Also, the search interface (simple or advanced search screen) varies significantly in terms of the search features and provided facilities, design, layout, fonts, colour et cetera. The only link between a digital library and its user is the user interface which serves as the only gateway and tool through which the user can gain access to and retrieve desired information in digital libraries since they are designed for end users without the involvement of intermediaries (Chowdhury and Chowdhury, 2003).

Framework for Information Search in a Digital Library

The framework for information search in a digital library comprises of the following phases:

- **Formulation Phase:** This phase is usually triggered by an information need, and it entails decision-making with regards to sources selection, fields, what to search for and search variants which may be presented in a variety of ways.
- **Action Phase:** To conduct a search, a search button needs to be pressed by the user of the digital library, and every time a search button is clicked in a navigator, some type of indexing, from rudimentary to sophisticated, is evolved while the user wait patiently till the search process ends.
- **Review of Result Phase:** The information retrieval interface in any digital library usually offers the user with various choices for result viewing, for example some interface return with helpful messages to explain the results such as degree of relevance.
- **Refinement Phase:** Different search interfaces provide different facilities for search query modification and refinement. At times, user(s) may be prompted to to reformulate the search statement and conduct a new search (Chowdhury and Chowdhury, 2003).

THE ROLE OF INDEXING AND ABSTRACTING AS INFORMATION RETRIEVAL TOOLS IN DIGITAL LIBRARY

Indexes and abstracts are cornerstones in the global information infrastructure and their importance is increasing in manifolds as digital libraries fills up with information and with users who need access to this information. Indexes and abstracts are knowledge organisation tools which help users find the information needed to solve problems and also extend retrieval capabilities beyond those of the classified collection or catalogue (Rubin, 2010). The function of an index is to give users systematic and effective shortcuts to the information required. Infact, without an index, the retrieval of information would be impractical (Cleveland and Cleveland, 2000). The roles played by indexing and abstracting in the retrieval of information in digital libraries as highlighted by some authors (Fidel, 1986; Bajpai, 1999; Cleveland and Cleveland, 2000; and Chowdhury and Chowdhury, 2003; Taylor and Jourdney, 2009; and Rubin, 2010) are listed below:

- Indexing facilitates effective and efficient retrieval of information; while abstracting facilitates judgements about the relevance of the retrieved information. The information retrieval process is closely tied to the indexing process because an index record of a document is a concise representation of the original document from a particular angle.
- In digital libraries, indexing and abstracting serve as information retrieval system to the millions of subjects housed by such library which helps or assist a user with a collection of published materials as it relate to a given discipline be it in the sciences, social sciences, education, agricultural sciences and so on.
- Indexing is not as an end in itself; rather, it is one of several approaches to information retrieval process. The success or failure of any retrieval system depends mainly on the adequacy of the in-

dexing and the closely related searching procedures. On the other hand, abstracts are written to decrease the time and effort it takes to read the overwhelming output from research and scholarship around the world. In digital libraries, an index points the user to the pool of available information while the abstract serves as the guide on the exact one to retrieve.

- Just as the less exotic information country roads requires maps and road signs, indexing and abstracting provides detailed and accurate maps and road sign which users deploy when navigating the information super highways or conducting searches in digital libraries.
- Indexes and abstracts are not ends in themselves but are tools, with which users find the information they need to solve their problems. While indexes point to possible useful information, abstracts allow efficient judgement of the relevance and pertinence of that information. In other words, an index is a bridge over troubled information explosion waters for seekers of information just as it serves as a device that connects a potential user of information to a potentially useful information store. A good index allows a swift and quiet trip over the troubled waters.
- Also, indexes identify locations where information may be found, but do not deal with validity, fairness or the morality of that information. Abstracts on the other hand, serve to let the user have a better indication of what will be found in the paper.
- Indexes and abstracts acts as a link between a source of information and its user and if the size of a collection is quite large, they play a major role to retrieve relevant information.
- In a digital library (information retrieval system), index and abstracts will guide or project itself as a guide to the concepts in a collection of documents, minimize the search efforts and ensure optimum results.
- Indexes and abstracts are a systematic guide to concepts derived from a collection of documents represented by entries arranged in a known and searchable alphabetical, numerical classified order.
- They inform the existence of documents containing documents surrogated, such as author, title, imprint, and call number and so on.
- In digital libraries (information retrieval system), index and abstract performs two simultaneous functions: retrieving information from documents that are required and holding back information about required documents based on a particular subject.
- Indexes and abstracts organise the literature so as to allow a specialist identify documents of interest easily in a digital library.

CONCLUSION

Digital libraries are information retrieval systems. There is no doubting the fact that indexing and abstracting are among the major techniques used by information professionals in retrieving relevant information contained in documents stored in the digital libraries. However, while the subject access points of cataloguing are limited, they generally tend to be more in indexes and abstracts as the documents are analysed in order to bring out the subject terms that have been sufficiently treated. This allow for easy retrieval of the document in relation to more subject terms rather than cataloguing which looked only for the dominant theme in a digital library environment. In addition, when the contents of digital libraries are properly organised and indexed, information retrieval will be greatly enhanced.

REFERENCES

Aina, L. O. (2004). *Library and information science text for Africa*. Ibadan: Third World Services Limited.

Anzsi.org. (2015). Types of indexing. Retrieved from https://anzsi.org/resources/about-indexers-and-indexing/types-indexing/

Arm, W.Y. (n. d.). *Digital Libraries*. Cambridge: MIT Press.

Badhusha, K. N. (2008). *Digital library architecture*. New Delhi: Ane Books.

Baeza-Yates, R., & Ribeiro-Neto, B. (Eds.), (2011). *Modern information retrieval: the concepts and technology behind search* (2nd ed.). England: Pearson Education Limited.

Bajpai, S. K. (1999). *Modern information retrieval*. New Delhi: Ess Ess Publications.

Borgman, C. L. (2000). *From Gutenberg to the global information infrastructure: Access to information in the networked world*. Cambridge: M.I.T. Press.

Chakrabortty, A. R., & Chakrabarti, B. (1984). *Indexing: Principles, Processes and Products*. Calcutta: The World Press Private Limited.

Chowdhury, G. G. (2010). *Introduction to Modern Information Retrieval* (3rd ed.). London: Facet Publishing.

Chowdhury, G. G., & Chowdhury, S. (2003). *Introduction to digital libraries*. London: Facet Publishing.

Cleveland, D. B., & Cleveland, A. D. (2000). *Introduction to indexing and abstracting* (3rd ed.). U.S.A.: Libraries Unlimited.

Davis, C. H., & Shaw, D. (Eds.). (2011). *Introduction to information science and technology*. New Jersey: Association for Information Science and Technology.

Encyclopedia of Library and Information Science. (1974). In A. Kent & H. Lancour (Eds.), Vol. I, pp. 16–37). New York: Marcel Dekker Inc.

Encyclopedia of Library and Information Science. (1974). In H. Lancour & J. E. Daily (Eds.), *Kent, A* (Vol. II, pp. 286–298). New York: Marcel Dekker Inc.

Fatoki, O. C. (2012). *Individual and system factors predicting user acceptance of digital libraries in Nigerian universities of agriculture* [Unpublished M.Phil Thesis]. University of Ibadan.

Ferber, R., & Thiel, U. (1996). Digital libraries and information retrieval. *ERCIM News No.27*. Retrieved from http://www.ercim.eu/publication/Ercim_News/enw27/ferber.html

Fidel, R. (1986). The possible effect of abstracting guidelines on retrieval performance of free-text searching. *Information Processing and Management*. 22(4), 309-316. Retrieved from faculty.washington.edu/fidelr/RayaPubs/PossibleEffectofAbstractingGuidelines.pdf

Goncalves, M. (2011). Digital Libraries. In R. Baeza-Yates & B. Ribeiro-Neto (Eds.), *Modern information retrieval: the concept and technology behind search* (2nd ed.). England: Pearson Education Limited.

International Encyclopedia of Information and Library Science. (1997). In J. Feather & P. Sturges, Eds.). London: Routledge.

Lester, J., & Koehler, W. C. (2007). *Fundamentals of information studies: understanding information and its environment*. New York: Neal-Schuman Pub. Inc.

Park, N., Roman, R., Lee, S., & Chung, J. E. (2009). User acceptance of a digital library system in developing countries: An application of the TAM. *International Journal of Information Management*, *29*, 196–209. doi:10.1016/j.ijinfomgt.2008.07.001

Rasmussen, E. (2011). Library systems. In R. Baeza-Yates & B. Ribeiro-Neto (Eds.), *Modern information retrieval: the concept and technology behind search.* (2nd ed.). England: Pearson Education Limited.

Reitz, J. M. (2004). *Dictionary for Library and Information Science*. Westport: Libraries Unlimited.

Rowley, J., & Farrow, J. (2000). *Organizing knowledge: An introduction to managing access to information*. USA: Ashgate Publishing Ltd.

Rowley, J., & Hartley, R. (2008). *Organizing knowledge: an introduction to managing access to information* (4th ed.). England: Ashgate Publishing Limited.

Rubin, R. E. (2010). *Foundations of library and information science* (3rd ed.). New York: Neal-Schuman Publishers, Inc.

Schatz, B. R. (1997). Information retrieval in digital libraries: Bringing search to the net. *Science*, *275*(5298), 327–333. Retrieved from www.canis.illinoi.edu/archive/papers/science-irdl-journal.pdf doi:10.1126/science.275.5298.327 PMID:8994022

Selvam, M. (2014). An introduction to semantic information retrieval in digital libraries. Retrieved from http://www.liscom.org/postContent/fullPaper/pdf/paper%20presented/P%20O%2014%20An%20 Introduction%20to%20Semantic%20Information%20Retrieval%20in%20Digital%20libraries.pdf

Skyes, J. (2001). The value of indexing. A white paper prepared for Factiva, a Dow Jones and Reuters Company. Retrieved from www.4info-management.com/pdf/indexingwhitepaper.pdf

Stoan, S. K. (1991). Research and information retrieval among academic researchers: Implications for library instructions. *Library Trends*, *39*(3), 238–257.

Taylor, A. G. (2004). The organization of information (2nd ed.). Library and Information Science text series. Westport: Libraries Unlimited Inc.

Taylor, A. G., & Joudrey, D. N. (2009). *The organization of information* (3rd ed.). Cincinnati: Libraries Unlimited.

Witten, I. H., Bainbridge, D., & Nichols, D. M. (2010). *How to build a digital library* (2nd ed.). Amsterdam: Morgan Kaufmann Publishers.

Wu-Jun, Y., & Peng, Z. (2010). Computer application and system modelling. *ICCASM, International conference.* Retrieved from ieeexplore.ieee.org/xpi/login.jsp?tp=&arnumber=5622829*url=http%3A%2F%Fieeexplore.ieee.org%Fxpls%2Fabs_ail_jsp%3Farnum

KEY TERMS AND DEFINITIONS

Abstract: A brief, objective summary of the essential content of a book, article, speech, report, dissertation or other work that presents the main points in the same order as the original but has no independent literary value.

Abstracting: Abstracting is a process that consists of analysing the content of an information resource and then writing a succinct summary of that work.

Digital Library: Digital libraries are organized collections of different forms of electronic information resources created for a specified community and with capabilities that distinguish them from other information retrieval systems.

Index: An index is a systematic guide designed to indicate topics or features of documents in order to facilitate retrieval of documents or parts of documents.

Indexing: The process of identifying information in a knowledge record and organizing the pointers to that information into a searchable file.

Information Retrieval: Information retrieval is the process, methods and procedure used to selectively recall recorded information from a file of data. It entails operations performed by the hardware and software used in indexing whenever a user queries the system (manual or automated) for information relevant to a specific topic. It is a method of storing, organising and offering access to information sources.

Chapter 9
Demographics, Socio-Economic and Cognitive Skills as Barriers to Information Seeking in a Digital Library Environment

Felicia Yusuf
Landmark University, Nigeria

Sunday Oguntayo
Landmark University, Nigeria

Sola Owolabi
Landmark University, Nigeria

Foluke Okocha
Landmark University, Nigeria

Ayooluwa Aregbesola
Landmark University, Nigeria

Toluwani Eyiolorunse
Landmark University, Nigeria

ABSTRACT

The chapter considers the importance of demographic and socio-economic factors as well as cognitive skills to information seeking in a digital library environment. Demographic factors such as age and gender were considered. Younger adults were found to respond positively to the demands of information seeking in the digital environment while their older counterparts are still struggling to come to terms with the changes. In the same vein, studies have revealed that the value placed on technology by men and women varies. While men express high level of confidence in navigating the digital environment, women still suffer low self-confidence in doing same. Identified socio-economic factors that also constitute a barrier to information seeking in a digital environment include income level, level of education, non-availability of ICT infrastructures and epileptic power supply especially in Africa among others. Unwillingness to see one's needs as information needs, inability to articulate one's information needs, unawareness of information sources, low self-efficacy, poor search skills among others were identified as cognitive barriers to information seeking in the digital environment. Based on the findings of this chapter, the study recommends that for persons who are adjudged to be the older generation, it is imperative for them to acquire requisite ICT skills that will make it easier for them to navigate the digital environment. There is also a clarion call on African leaders to provide infrastructures that will enable ICT to thrive as the digital environment is fast replacing the hitherto traditional one.

DOI: 10.4018/978-1-5225-0296-8.ch009

INTRODUCTION

Demand for information is traceable to its importance and relevance to production of goods and services. The relevance of information to human existence has positioned it as a factor of production in addition to land, labour and capital. Organizational decision making and management in the 21st Century depend on information. In social parlance, treasure is sought for its worth, none seeks rot. Information is treasure sought after by many. Military operations and intelligence reports depend on information. Investments in shares, oil and gas explorations even marriages require information for decision making process. Kaye (1995) explained that good information is essential for effective operation and decision making at all levels in businesses, affirming that managers use of information in decision-making processes (strategic and operational).

The progressive speed of information acquisition, processing and dissemination has given birth to information society referred to as a society characterized by a high level of information intensity in the everyday life of most citizens, in most organizations and workplaces; by the use of common or compatible technology for a wide range of personal, social, educational and business activities, and by the ability to transmit, receive and exchange digital data rapidly between places irrespective of distance (http://whatis.techtarget.com/definition/Information-Society).

Furthermore, an information society is such in which the creation, distribution, and manipulation of information has become the most significant economic and cultural activity. It has therefore become pertinent to study barriers to digital information seeking considering the transformational capability of information accompanied by technologies which have given birth to the digital age. Digital libraries house millions or innumerable collections in the virtual space with the aim of meeting the information seeker's need but the aim may be truncated by certain intervening variables conversant with users.

These intervening variables are the focus of this discourse. We shall critically examine demographic, socio-economic and cognitive barriers that may limit information seekers from maximally benefiting from unlimited access to the information commonwealth that characterizes the 21st Century. Information rich and information poor are a new way of classifying nations and people around the world. The rich have greater access to available right information and are capable of using them to achieve economic, social and other survival needs, while the poor are limited due to one intervening variable or the other which serve as barrier to ease of access and use.

INFORMATION NEEDS AS PRECEDENCE OF INFORMATION SEEKING

Information seeking is preceded by information needs. Without a specific need information seeking process will not have proper definition and seeker behavior that typifies the information seeking process. Thompson & Zeynep (2004) conceptualized need as a discoverable matter or fact. He further asserted that needs are objectives in the sense that they are what one must look for to support his or her profession. Needs are a matter of priority, what we need is overriding reason. Information needs could be seen as demand (requirement) and want (desire). Haruna and Mabawunku (2001) explained that needs arise when the state of possessed knowledge is less than what is needed to deal with some issues, and that information needs are diverse, consistently changing and not amenable to generalization. The uses of information vary among individuals, groups and society. Krikelas (1983) defined information need as the recognition of the existence of uncertainty in decision making. Information need is also referred to as the extent to which information is required to solve problems as well as the degree of expressed satisfaction or dissatisfaction with the information (Ehikhamenor, 1990).

According to Taylor (2007), information need has four levels:

- The conscious and unconscious need for information not existing in the remembered experience of the investigator. In terms of the query range, this level might be called the "ideal question" — the question which would bring from the ideal system exactly what the inquirer wants, if he could state his need. It is the actual, but unexpressed, need for information.
- The conscious mental description of an ill-defined area. In this level, the inquirer might talk to someone else in the field to get an answer.
- A researcher forms a rational statement of his question. This statement is a rational and unambiguous description of the inquirer's doubts.
- The question as presented to the information system.

Miranda and Tarapanoff (2008) defined information need as a state or process started when one perceives that there is a gap between the information and knowledge available to solve a problem and the actual solution of the problem. Information competencies are defined as the capabilities developed to reach the solution of a problem by searching for new information or knowledge that could fill the perceived gap.

INFORMATION SEEKING AND BEHAVIOR IN A DIGITAL ENVIRONMENT

Information seeking outcome in a digital library environment is influenced by many factors. An information user has specific distinguishing attributes which to a good extent, influence the information search process. Demographic, socio-economic and cognitive factors among others are critical elements this study focuses on in relation to information seeking behavior in a digital library environment. Information seekers are either propelled or inhibited by these identified factors. While access to information in the traditional environment places much emphasis on the skills of the librarian, that of the ICT age has graduated from a 'Librarian-dependent' to a 'Librarian/ICT-dependent' process where both the users' skills as well as that of the librarian are required.

Information seeking is a basic activity practiced by all people and manifested through a particular behavior (Kakai, Ikoja-Odongo & Kigongo-Bukeny, 2004). Information-seeking behavior stems from a perceived need for information by the user according to Wilson's model (Wilson, 1981; Wilson & Walsh, 1996). In order to satisfy this need, the model suggests that the user makes demands upon formal or informal information sources which results in success or failure in the information seeking process. If successful, the individual then makes use of the information found and may either fully or partially satisfy the perceived need or, indeed, fail to satisfy the need and have to repeat the search process. The model also shows that part of the information-seeking behavior may involve other people through information exchange and that information perceived as useful may be passed to other people, as well as being used (or instead of being used) by the person himself or herself.

Information seeking behavior involves personal reasons for seeking information, the kinds of information which are being sought, and the ways and sources with which needed information is being sought.

This is expressed in various forms, from reading printed materials to research and experimentation. Scholars, students and faculty actively seek current information from the various media available in libraries, e.g. encyclopedias, journals and more currently, electronic media (Alemna & Skouby, 2000). Information seeking behavior deals with the psychological cognitive behavior of the seeker. It involves the searching, locating, retrieving and using of information.

Tella (2009) investigated correlates of information seeking beaviour of undergraduate students of University of Bostwana. He asserted that the role that information plays in the academic activities of learners in this digital era is difficult to measure. According to him, any learner who wants to excel in academics needs to be highly informed, well equipped, and relentless in seeking information. The study found the cardinality of self-efficacy to information seeking. Information seeking behavior is an individual's way and manner of gathering and sourcing for information for personal use, knowledge updating and development. It involves complex patterns of actions and interactions which people engage in when seeing information of whatever kind and for whatever purpose. Leckie, Pettigrew and Sylvan (2006) opined that information seeking behavior is expressed in various media available in libraries e.g. encyclopedia, journals and more currently electronic media. Aina (2004) argued that the information seeking behavior of a user depends on education, access to library and the length of a time user wishes to devote to information seeking, no matter how comprehensive the resources and services of a library are.

Wilson (2000) theorized information seeking behavior as that which involves personal reasons for seeking information, the kinds of information which are being sought and the ways and sources with which needed information is being sought. He opined that information needs are influenced by a variety of factors such as the range of information sources available; the uses to which the information will be put; the background, motivation, professional orientation and individual characteristics of user. Other factors are socio-political, economic, legal and regulatory systems surrounding the users as well as the consequences of information use.

The quality of sources of information available to the users is also important because relevant sources are most likely to produce useful information. He also perceives information seeking behavior as the purposive seeking for information as a consequence of need to satisfy some goals. He added further that in the cause of seeking, the individual might interact with several information sources available. Information seekers have specific needs that determine their desire to hunt for such information. Likewise, the importance of such information will regulate their behavior. Igwe (2012) also categorized the information needs into the following:

1. Educational and academics information needs.
2. Political information needs.
3. Job opportunities and business information needs.
4. Economic information needs.
5. Social and entertainment (arts) information needs.
6. Agricultural, geographical and environmental information needs.
7. Medical and health information needs.
8. Scientific and technological information needs.
9. Religious and cultural information needs.
10. Legal and human rights information needs.
11. International and global information needs.

Information seeking behavior is usually affected by some factors as pointed out by Boyol (2006). He stated that information seeking is situation dependent activity where a seeker's action are influenced by access to information perceived quality and trust in the information sources. Information seeking behavior is expressed in various forms, from reading printed materials, to asking friends or colleagues.

Information seeking behavior is also an aspect of scholarly work of most of the academic libraries who strive to develop collections, services and organizational structures that facilitate information seeking behavior. Ellis et al (2003) attempted to propose a general model of information seeking behavior based on studies of the information seeking patterns of social scientists in an industry firm. Ellis elaboration model describes the features of information seeking activities as generic.

According to Kingrey (2002), the term information seeking often serves as an umbrella overarching a set of related concepts and issues. In the library world, discussions of database construction and management, community information needs, reference services and many other topics, resonate with the term. Information seeking is a cognitive exercise and it involves search, retrieval, recognition and application of meaningful content. It has also been viewed as a social and cultural exchange, as discrete strategies applied when confronting uncertainty and as a basic condition of humanity in which all individuals exist. Information seeking behavior describes the multifaceted in relationship of information in the lives of human beings a relationship that can include both active searching through formal information channels such and a variety of other attitudes and actions.

Razak et al (2010) posits that information seeking behavior is a complex activity requiring access to diverse information resources to deal with work related, personal and social information problems. Information seeking behavior refers to strategies for locating information and has three elements; people, information and systems. The study of individual information seeking behavior requires the psychological state of the user that may lead to insight into their expectations and make it possible to predict information selecting activities.

In the words of Uhegbu (2007), information seeking behavior can be described as the way an information user conducts himself or acts when looking for, receiving or acquiring information; the utterance, gesture, anger, anxiety, eagerness, reluctance, zeal or any other attributes displayed by an information user in his effort to purchase, acquire or receive news, data, stories or anything that may inform or misinform his knowledge or understanding of something constitute seeking behavior.

DEMYSTIFYING THE DIGITAL LIBRARY

Digital library has been sandwiched between conventional libraries and unstructured online information resources which have brought about the so called information explosion. There exists a dichotomy which should be clearly identified. Digital libraries are organizations that provide the resources, including the specialized staff, to select, structure, offer intellectual access to, interpret, distribute, preserve the integrity of, and ensure the persistence over time of collections of digital works so that they are readily and economically available for use by a defined community or set of communities (Waters, 1998). Digital library is fast becoming a 'slogan' instead of a professional term for librarians. Access to internet that contains jumbled information, in an unorganized manner has given effrontery to many individuals to conceptualize the World Wide Web as the digital library of the 21st Century. This necessitates the need to demystify it. In the word Lynch (1997):

One sometimes hears the Internet characterized as the world's library for the digital age. This description does not stand up under even casual examination. The Internet--and particularly its collection of multimedia resources known as the World Wide Web--was not designed to support the organized publication and retrieval of information as libraries are. It has evolved into what might be thought of as a chaotic repository for the collective output of the world's digital "printing presses." In short, the Net is not a digital library.

Digital libraries have been argued to be resident in the confines of librarians who are the professionals that mediate in the business of acquisition, processing, organization, storage, preservation and dissemination of information resources. These arguments have produced certain characteristics that should be adopted in defining a digital library (Arms, 1995; Graham, 1995; Chepesuik, 1997; Lynch and Garcia-Molina, 1995):

- Digital libraries are the digital face of traditional libraries that include both digital collections and traditional, fixed media collections. So they encompass both electronic and paper materials.
- Digital libraries will also include digital materials that exist outside the physical and administrative bounds of any one digital library.
- Digital libraries will include all the processes and services that are the backbone and nervous system of libraries. However, such traditional processes, though forming the basic digital library work, will have to be revised and enhanced to accommodate the differences between new digital media and traditional fixed media.
- Digital libraries ideally provide a coherent view of all of the information contained within a library, no matter its form or format.
- Digital libraries will serve particular communities or constituencies, as traditional libraries do now, though those communities may be widely dispersed throughout the network.
- Digital libraries will require both the skills of librarians and well as those of computer scientists to be viable.

A digital library connotes an organized rich and comprehensive content, usually in electronic format and somewhat hosted in virtual space, managed and preserved for long term, and offers its user communities specialized functionality on that content according to agreed policies. Digital resources which are offshoots of Information and Communication Technologies have reshaped information retrieval process and access. In the past, information was transferred from librarians to the user, but presently, most of the communication and transfer of information is between the users and the computers/associated devices and this is due to the existence of digital library and its management. The digital library provides more choices, enhances flexibility and will often provide the learner with instant feedback. It allows retrieval of learning materials faster and conveniently at any time and at any place (Lee, 2005).

Otubelu (2011) explained that digital resources range from archival documents to historical images and other primary sources emanating from scientific field researches. Electronic formats suitable for digital library materials include text formats, such as RTF (Rich Text Format), Markup languages –HTML and XML, PDF (Portable document format) and Image formats –MPEG, JPEG etc. Digital library collections contain permanent documents hosted in a digital environment and it enables quick handling of information resources. Digital libraries are based on digital technologies which aid compression of library materials that already existed in hard copies thereby saving physical space in the library.

The 21st century information landscape continues to experience a shift from the traditional to a more sophisticated ICT based. To maximize the use of resources in the digital library environment, a lot of the users' characteristics come to play. This chapter therefore considers some of these characteristics which include the demographic make-up, socio-economic and cognitive skills of a user as they affect his/her information seeking behavior in a digital library environment. A digital library implies a collection of electronic information resources or service, in which resources and functions (such as acquisitions, preservation, retrieval etc.) are in digital form and performed using information technologies respectively. Borgman (2000) defines digital libraries as sets of electronic resources and associated technologies for creating, searching and using information. They are developed and organized for a particular community of users in support their information needs and use of that community. It involves a wide range of functioning and research outputs, collections of information and documents, and technologies. In this sense they enhance and add to information retrieval systems, presented in diverse forms (text, images, sounds, multimedia, etc.) and accessible online. In other words, users can have access to resources in a digital environment over a computer network either via the internet or institutional intranets from any location within the library or remotely.

Marchionini (1998) observed that practically, a digital library makes its digital resources accessible remotely through computer networks. The content of digital libraries includes data and metadata. Metadata which are traditionally called bibliographic information are data that describes various aspects of other data. It may consist of links to other data within or outside the digital library (such as author's name, titles, year of publication, and subject coverage). Digital library should contain information and documents in digital form. It may be text, images, audio files, or multimedia. The term 'hybrid library' rather than 'digital library' has been used in some literatures, to emphasize that the collection may include non-digital alongside digitized documents.

Libraries that have huge electronic resources (e-journal and e-books) together with sizeable print collections may be considered a digital library. With reference to the content of a digital library, Bawden and Rowlands (1999) stated that for a library to be referred to as a digital library a "significant proportion of the resources available to users" must exist in digital form. Marchionini (1998) observed that a digital library must have some electronic resources and services. Realistically, a digital library is a managed collection of information, with associated services, where the information is stored in digital formats and accessible over a network.

In summary, digital libraries, irrespective of content location, are accessible virtually, searched or browsed, and information retrieved by users from every part of the world. Its content which has been selected and assembled as a cohesive digital collection may physically be stored on computers in different parts of the world. In a completely digital library, nothing need ever reach paper. Furthermore, being a cheap and effective process, digitization offers diverse cultures the opportunity to organize, preserve and make available to users their own local text, image and sound files in ways that were previously inconceivable (Worcman, 2002). They are accessed and used remotely, at different location and concurrently. Its resources are defined by access, technically and economically as compared with a traditional library where resources are by their physical presence.

Trivedi (2010) observed that a digital library is not a single entity. It requires technology link the resources of many collections. The links between digital libraries and their resources are transparent to users. Digital libraries combine technology and information resources to allow remote access, breaking down the physical barriers between resources thereby allowing learners of all types to share resources, time and energy, and expertise to their mutual benefits. Remote access allows possibilities for vicarious field trips, virtual guest speakers, and access to rare and unique materials in classrooms and at home. Digital libraries also bring together facets of many disciplines, and experts with different backgrounds and different approaches.

Digital library collections are not limited to document surrogates (bibliographic records. They are the actual digital objects such as images, texts, etc. Lynch (1994) observed that digital Libraries provide users with coherent access to a very large, organized repository of information and knowledge. According to Berkeley Digital Library Project, University of California, the digital library will be a collection of distributed information sources. The contrast between traditional and digital libraries is presented in Table 1.

It is evident that digital libraries are very different from traditional libraries, but sometimes they are could be have some similarities especially in libraries that are engaged in retrospective conversion of paper-based resources. It should be noted that people do not change because new technology is invented. They still create information that has to be organized, stored, and distributed. They still need to find information that others have created, and use it for study, reference, or entertainment. However, the form in which the information is expressed and the methods that are used to manage it are greatly influenced by technology and this creates change.

Arms (2000) explaining the cardinality of digital libraries affirmed that the doors of the digital library never close; a recent study at a British university found that about half the usage of a library's digital collections was at hours when the library buildings were closed. Materials are never checked out to other readers, miss-shelved or stolen; they are never in an off-campus warehouse. The scope of the collections expands beyond the walls of the library. Private papers in an office or the collections of a library on the other side of the world are as easy to use as materials in the local library. Digital libraries are not perfect. Computer systems can fail and networks may be slow or unreliable, but, compared with a traditional library, information is much more likely to be available when and where the user wants it.

FUNCTIONS OF DIGITAL LIBRARY

Digital libraries have set the stage for the principle of information access which is the real essence of a library. The opening and closing hours that characterize the traditional libraries are eliminated with

Table 1. Traditional vs. digital libraries

Traditional Libraries	Digital or Electronic Library
Print collection	All resources in digital form.
Stable, with slow evolution	Dynamic and ephemeral
Individual objects not directly linked with each other.	Multi-media and fractal objects
Flat structure with minimal contextual metadata	Scaffolding of data structures and richer contextual metadata.
Scholarly content with validation process	More than scholarly content with various validation processes
Limited access points and centralized management	Unlimited access points, distributed collections and access control
The physical and logical organization correlated.	The physical and logical organization may be virtually
One way interactions	Dynamic real-time dialogue
Free and universal access.	Free as well as fee based.

the use of digital libraries. A digital library brings the information to the user's desk, either at work or at home, making it easier to use and hence increasing its usage. With a digital library on the desk top, a user need never visit a library building. The library is wherever there is a personal computer and a network connection.

The digital library exists to perform certain functions which include:

- Providing access to large amounts of information to users wherever they are and whenever they need it.
- Enabling access to primary information sources.
- Supporting multimedia content along with text.
- Enhancing network accessibility on Intranet and Internet.
- Possessing user-friendly interface.
- Making available hypertext links for navigation.
- Possessing Advanced search and retrieval.
- Integrating with other digital libraries.

PURPOSE OF DIGITAL LIBRARY

Digital libraries are beneficial to users due to qualities that distinguish them from traditional libraries. Users of digital libraries have access to an array of information because of interconnectivity achieved through the internet. Digital libraries serve the following purposes:

- Expedite the systematic development of procedures to collect, store, and organize, information in digital form.
- Promote efficient delivery of information economically to all users.
- Encourage co-operative efforts in research resource, computing, and communication networks.
- Strengthen communication and collaboration between and among educational institutions.
- Empowers librarians to take leadership role in the generation and dissemination of knowledge.

Other potential benefits of digital libraries have been viewed by Arms (2000):

- **The Digital Library Brings the Library to the User:** To use a library requires access. Traditional methods require that the user goes to the library. In a university, the walk to a library takes a few minutes, but not many people are member of universities or have a nearby library. Many engineers or physicians carry out their work with depressingly poor access to the latest information. A digital library brings the information to the user's desk, either at work or at home, making it easier to use and hence increasing its usage. With a digital library on the desk top, a user need never visit a library building. The library is wherever there is a personal computer and a network connection.
- **Computer Power Is Used for Searching and Browsing:** Computing power can be used to find information. Paper documents are convenient to read, but finding information that is stored on paper can be difficult. Despite the myriad of secondary tools and the skill of reference librarians, using a large library can be a tough challenge. A claim that used to be made for traditional libraries

is that they stimulate serendipity, because readers stumble across unexpected items of value. The truth is that libraries are full of useful materials that readers discover only by accident. In most aspects, computer systems are already better than manual methods for finding information. They are not as good as everybody would like, but they are good and improving steadily. Computers are particularly useful for reference work that involves repeated leaps from one source of information to another.

- **Information Can Be Shared:** Libraries and archives contain much information that is unique. Placing digital information on a network makes it available to everybody. Many digital libraries or electronic publications are maintained at a single central site, perhaps with a few duplicate copies strategically placed around the world. This is a vast improvement over expensive physical duplication of little used material, or the inconvenience of unique material that is inaccessible without traveling to the location where it is stored.
- **Information Is Easier to Keep Current:** Much important information needs to be brought up to date continually. Printed materials are awkward to update, since the entire document must be reprinted; all copies of the old version must be tracked down and replaced. Keeping information current is much less of a problem when the definitive version is in digital format and stored on a central computer. Many libraries provide online the text of reference works, such as directories or encyclopedias. Whenever revisions are received from the publisher, they are installed on the library's computer. The new versions are available immediately. The Library of Congress has an online collection, called Thomas, that contains the latest drafts of all legislation currently before the U.S. Congress; it changes continually.
- **The Information Is Always Available:** The doors of the digital library never close; a recent study at a British university found that about half the usage of a library's digital collections was at hours when the library buildings were closed. Materials are never checked out to other readers, miss-shelved or stolen; they are never in an off-campus warehouse. The scope of the collections expands beyond the walls of the library. Private papers in an office or the collections of a library on the other side of the world are as easy to use as materials in the local library. Digital libraries are not perfect. Computer systems can fail and networks may be slow or unreliable, but, compared with a traditional library, information is much more likely to be available when and where the user wants it.
- **New Forms of Information Become Possible:** Most of what is stored in a conventional library is printed on paper, yet print is not always the best way to record and disseminate information. A database may be the best way to store census data, so that it can be analyzed by computer; satellite data can be rendered in many different ways; a mathematics library can store mathematical expressions, not as ink marks on paper but as computer symbols to be manipulated by programs such as Mathematica or Maple. Even when the formats are similar, materials that are created explicitly for the digital world are not the same as materials originally designed for paper or other media. Words that are spoken have a different impact from words that are written, and online textual materials are subtly different from either the spoken or printed word. Good authors use words differently when they write for different media and users find new ways to use the information. Materials created for the digital world can have a vitality that is lacking in material that has been mechanically converted to digital formats, just as a feature film never looks quite right when shown on television.

DEMOGRAPHIC FACTORS

Inequality characterizes digital information seekers. It has been established by Olatokun (2009) that there exists a measure of variance in individuals' access and use of information and communication technology due to socio-demographic factors. This discourse specifically focuses on age and gender as demographic barriers to information seeking in digital library environment. Islam et al. (2011) conducted a research on demographic influence concerned with inclusion of digital library on e-learning in the Faculty of Information Management at Universiti Teknologi Mara, Malaysia. According to the research, demographic factors such as level of education and gender assist in understanding and appreciating e-learning. Owolabi and Adebayo (2013) found that ease of use, accessibility and use of ICT were significantly predicted by level of education, age, gender, and income.

Age as Barrier to Information Seeking in Digital Libraries

Age is a progressive natural phenomenon that has predictable influence on humans. The older an individual gets, the higher the rate of certain physiological and psychological changes. The tendency is high for persons below twenty years of age to have lesser responsibilities and be less encumbered compared to adults who have to attend to work, family and other social responsibilities which they feel are mandatory for them. Constituents of interest change as age develops and likewise the energy and speed to match up with the dynamic world in which technology has taken over. Carmen (2006) and Idowu (2004) pointed out the significance of age in relation to digital information use. Their works affirmed that younger age group appears more technology enthusiastic than their older counterpart who are slow in technology adoption and most often are too busy to experiment with new technology innovations. Young adults are more technology savvy and can easily contend with the challenges and complexities of innovations.

Age has also been found to correlate with computers and the use of electronic resources as observed by Okiki and Ashiru (2011) when they noted that younger generations are brought up with computers. They also found that there were significant age differences on the computer tasks performed by younger people compared to the older ones. While younger adults make quick decisions with the aid of computers, the older adults make few correct decisions taking longer time than their younger counterparts. Mungania (2003) while describing the e-learning users asserted that middle-aged people account for the greater part of use of digital information.

Gender Barriers to Information Seeking in Digital Libraries

Within social psychological approach, personality is viewed as a complex of biological, mental and social factors (Nakonecny, 1999) which can influence human information behavior. It is certain that male and female have different personalities which are biological and also portray psychological manifestations which ultimately have influence on their performances in specific tasks. The above describes sexual differences which is different from social inclination of male and female gender. Essentially, gender refers to sets of relationships attributes, roles, beliefs and attitudes that define what being a man or a woman is within the society. It is a socially ascribed attribute as opposed to sex which is a biological attribute. As a result of gender roles assigned by different cultures many women have been brought up to see technology and its use as reserved for on the male gender.

Gender studies in relation to digital information seeking revealed men and women value technologies differently (Fallows, 2005 & Agosto, 2001). In the use of technologies, women prefer social collaboration, contextual information and personal identification. Men's use of information and technologies are determined by preferences of individual work and competition. Manda and Mulkangara (2007) report that gender is associated with the use of electronic information resources, and that male postgraduate students were more likely to use e-resources than female students. They further report that even when there was controlled for attitude towards the use of e-resources or training in the use of e-resources the relationship between gender and e-resources was maintained.

For men, new technologies represent an intellectual challenge and play, while with women, more emotional perception occurs. In learning, women make use of personal identification and imagination and for them, it is important to include the information into a broader context or story (Agosto,2001). Based on men's preferences for logical and analytical thinking, they find it easier to use Boolean logic for query formulation (Agosto, 2001). A study by Kennedy et al. (2003) has also proved that women suffer from lower self-confidence in managing technologies than their male counterparts. Ford, Miller, and Moss (2001) found that women tend to experience more difficulty in finding information online than men, and men have high preference for the Internet as the first source of information. It has also been found that due to domestic responsibilities, women are found to lag behind in the use of digital information resources in comparison to their male counterparts (Rana, 2009; Bailin & grafstein, 2005).

The Place of Socio-Economic Factors in Determining Information Seeking Behavior

One of the most remarkable developments in the modern society has been what is variously described as information explosion, information revolution, or the advent of information age or society (Tiamiyu, 2003). The catalyst of the growth has been rapid adoption and innovations in electronic technologies for creating, processing, communicating and using information. Consequently, libraries are required to provide electronic resources such as e-books, e-journals/journal articles retrieved from online databases, CD-ROMs etc which are accessed through computer-related technologies (Jerabek, Meyer, & Kordinak, 2001) and recently mobile communication devices.

Information accessed within a digital environment, which has e-books among other materials as its collection is becoming important to satisfy users' needs. To a large extent, there is a growth in the global e-book market evident since the last few years (Book Industry Study Group, 2010; Guenette, Trippe, & Golden, 2010; International Digital Publishing Forum, 2010) with predictions for even higher growth in the near future (British Library, 2010; May, 2010) and accompanied with a range of portable devices such as e-book readers, or multi-purpose devices for accessing the resources.

The emergence of these e-resources and their integration into the collections of libraries have generated a wide range of issues and challenges ranging from formation of collection development policy, up to the access point including establishment of budget and adequate funds for acquisitions. Some socio-economic factors have however been found to impede access and use of information communication technologies. As observed by the International Telecommunication Union (2003) there are digital divide in the access and use of ICTs because of sociocultural and economic factors (income and education) around the world. That is, there are gaps in access to and use of ICT among skilled and unskilled (education), high income earners and low income earners (income level), rural and urban (location) and so on.

Although several studies (ALA, 2008; Bertot, 2009; Brindley, 2009; McClure, Bertot, & Jaeger, 2011) have discussed barriers to internet access in libraries, this section will focus mainly on barriers from the perspective of the library patrons in a digital environment. Information seeking in a digital environment from a socio-economic perspective includes research approaches such as ethnographic, cultural and economic studies. Identified socio-economic factors that constitute barriers to information seeking and access in a digital environment will therefore be considered under the following headings.

Level of Education and Income

The internet is an important platform for providing access to information and consequently has been the platform for deploying digital libraries. It has therefore become imperative to access resources in a digital environment using ICTs. The level of education has been found to have the strongest influence on the capability to use computer with internet services in Nigeria (Olatokun, 2009). Olatokun also discovered that income was significantly related to the amount of education a person receives which could be seen as a key "individual difference" that influences the capabilities and functioning that relate to ICTs.

Also, household income plays a very significant role with respect to the ability to use ICTs. Those with lower income tend to have less ownership and capability to use ICTs as their income may not able to accommodate access to or ownership of ICT facilities. It should however be noted that income alone is not enough to measure people's capacity to own and use ICTs, but that their level of education is also of great significance. A study carried out in the United States showed that "2.7% of families with incomes under $15,000 own computers compared to 77.7% of families with incomes over $75,000; and among all families with incomes under $35,000 computer ownership of white families was three times that of African-American families and four times that of Hispanic families" (Kirk & Zander, 2004, p. 171). A study by Valletta and MacDonald (2003) also confirmed that information seekers having less education are being more disadvantaged in using ICTs facilities.

DeBell and Chapman (2006) found that parental educational level directly correlates with the percentage of students who used the internet in their own home to seek information. In the United States, census data showed a similarly strong correlation of level of education and home internet access. In view of Okuwa's (2007) study that showed that educational status influences income, it is expected that students whose parents are highly educated will use internet more compared with students whose parents are not. Education is therefore important, not only with respect to gaining the needed skills to use ICTs that provide the platform to interact with resources in a digital library environment, but also with respect to people's motivation to even use an ICT.

Information and Communication Infrastructure

With the aid of relevant ICTs, interconnectivity of libraries which was unimaginable in the era of traditional information resource management has been made possible. Databases of other libraries can be accessed remotely thereby ensuring effectiveness and efficiency in the process of information dissemination. Also there is access to more current information and extensive links to additional resources in a digital environment. Despite these inherent benefits however, infrastructural limitations such as slow internet speed resulting from inadequate bandwidth to enhance effective access to online based resources, insufficient workstations and required devices to meet the growing demands of the users as well as network security inhibit information seeking.

Infrastructural development in Africa has been the bane of successful deployment of ICT in the region. Africa is regarded as a region with highest concentration of countries with low ICT opportunity, measured by indices related to ICT networks, education and skills, uptake and intensity of its use (International Telecommunication Union, 2007). Understanding the barriers that impede access can help library administrators allocate the limited resources more effectively to balance the needs of patrons seeking information in a digital environment.

Other socio-economic factors that affects information seeking include erratic power supply, as some electronic devices such as computers and other ICT infrastructures needed to access resources in a digital environment depend on electricity to function. This is however epileptic in many African countries which in turn constitutes a barrier to information seekers impeding them from gaining timely access to needed information, apprehension expressed when seeking for information in a digital environment especially those that are not computer literate and accustomed to traditional library, prohibitive cost mostly in developing countries to gain access (Adomi, 2005), irregularities in subscription to electronic resources (Igbo & Imo, 2010), and frustration that accompanies prolonged e-book reading causing a strain to the eyes (Aregbesola & Oguntayo, 2014).

BARRIERS TO INFORMATION SEEKING IN A DIGITAL LIBRARY VIS-À-VIS COGNITIVE SKILLS

The incapability of technology to recognise the existing dichotomy in users' heterogeneous characteristics is a major limitation. There are variables which determine ease of access and use of technology by users. One of these distinguishing attributes subsists in their cognitive skills. Brennan, Kelly & Arguello (2014) observed that although search engines are designed as one-size-fits-all tool, people do not come in one size, but instead vary across many different attributes. Information seeking is predominantly a cognitive task, hence the probability of cognitive variations among users could be viable determinants of astuteness or mediocrity in the search process.

'User-centeredness' is sine qua non to effective and efficient information delivery in the 21st century unlike the past when information users relied solely on experts for information retrieval. Advancement in information and communication technology (ICT) has heralded availability of a plethora of information resources leading to information explosion. Information explosion is not just a cliché but an existing challenge that puts information seekers in the midst of a sea of relevant and irrelevant electronic information resources; a term referred to as high recall, low precision. The Google search engine alone controls an index of more than 8 billion Web pages (Google, 2005), therefore in the myriad of available information sources and resources, cognitive skills become paramount to achieving specificity or precision in the process of information seeking in the digital environment.

The World Wide Web has made the world a global village but the need for the village to speak one language has not been achieved. Each member of the village has to possess the ability to recognize and reconcile (decode) messages to satisfy information needs. On this premise, the need to intricately discuss users' cognitive skills becomes imperative.

Cognitive Skills

Cognitive skills represent mental capabilities and developments associated with knowledge, attention, memory, judgment and evaluation, reasoning and computation, problem solving and decision making, comprehension and production of language, etc. Cognitive processes use existing knowledge and generate new knowledge. It encompasses the mental functions, mental processes (thoughts), and state of intelligent entities (humans, collaborative groups, human organizations, highly autonomous machines, and artificial intelligences). The word cognition comes from the Latin verb *cognosco* (*con* 'with' and *gnosco* 'know').

Carroll (1993) explained that cognitive abilities are comprised of higher mental functions such as reasoning, remembering, understanding and problem solving. Cognitive skills vary, depending on phenomenon of study or task to be accomplished, but it is constant that they are mental activities. The following are some but not all features describing cognitive skills:

- **Attention Skills:** Ability to attend to incoming information and process for a specified need. It can be viewed in three dimensions.
- **Memory:** The ability to store and recall information.
- **Logic and Reasoning:** The ability to reason, form concepts, and solve problems using unfamiliar information or novel procedures.
- **Auditory Processing:** The ability to analyze, blend, and segment sounds.
- **Visual Processing:** The ability to perceive, analyze, and think in visual images. This includes visualization, which is the ability to create a picture in your mind of words or concepts.
- **Processing Speed:** The ability to perform simple or complex cognitive tasks quickly. This skill also measures the ability of the brain to work quickly and accurately while ignoring distracting stimuli (http://www.learningrx.com/what-are-cognitive-skills.htm).

Wilson's 1995 model of information seeking brings to the fore the complexity of information seeking and intervening variables (barriers) which includes cognitive skills (Figure 1).

Information use depends on the individual evaluation of the cognitive and emotional relevance of the information received. Information seeking characteristically places demand on cognitive abilities such as working memory, spatial ability, and reasoning. For information seeking, Sutcliffe and Ennis (1998) proposed theoretical framework which consists of four recurrent cognitive activities: problem identification, need articulation, query formulation and result evaluation.

- **Problem Identification:** Involves identifying the information need from a problem statement.
- **Need Articulation:** The information seeker expresses information need by selecting low-level terms from long-term memory, which may lead to a refinement or restatement of the information need.
- **Query Formulation:** The process of generating queries and depends on the information seeker's skill level and on the capabilities and possibilities of the IR system.
- **Results Evaluation:** A decision-making process whereby the information seeker decides whether to accept the retrieved results or continue searching for more results.

The intellectual processes engaged during search are controlled by the cognitive abilities possessed by the user. When an information user is inhibited in the use of cognitive skills, it constitutes a barrier

Figure 1. Wilson's model of cognitive skills

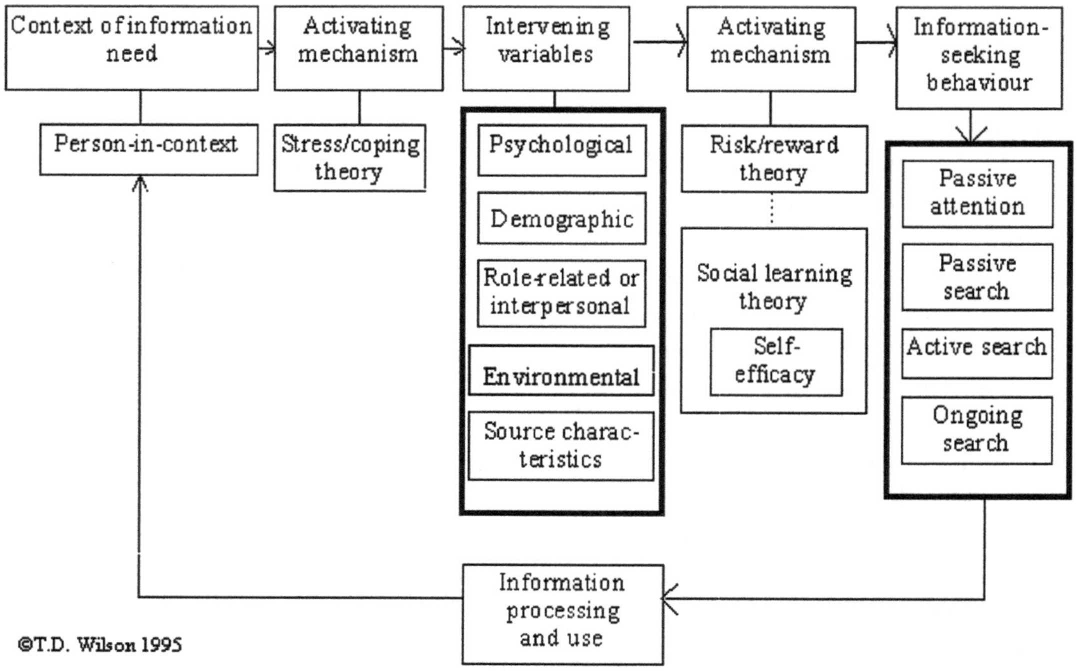

in the process of information seeking which could lead to frustration or outright abandonment of the search endeavors. Cognitive ability has been recognized to have bearing on individuals' behavior towards information seeking. It refers to human ability to perform mental processing of activities which involves full engagement of the brain to achieve a required task (Carroll 1993). It is quite interesting to see identical twins that are very hard to differentiate in many physical ways but cognitive styles.

Riding and Rayner (1998) defined cognitive styles as person's preferred and habitual approach to organizing information. Xie (2000) asserted that information users such as university undergraduates normally employ their general cognitive skills and knowledge in three ways:

1. To represent their problem task;
2. To establish a set of sub-goals to fulfil the overall goals; and
3. To develop techniques and strategies that help to seek the required information.

Gwizdka (2002) examined the relationships between selected cognitive abilities (memory span, visual memory, flexibility of closure, and speed of closure), information presentation in graphical email user interface, and information scanning tasks. A number of cognitive ability effects on user interaction were found. For example, people with lower ability to extract visual patterns tended to move information from their email inboxes to places outside email and were slower on the textual email interfaces than on the visual email interface (Gwizdka, 2004); people who had lower level of working memory (Mw) took more time to locate information in the email inbox and sorted email messages more often (Gwizdka & Chignell, 2004).

Information seeking behavior is greatly influenced by cognitive characteristics. For example, the concept of *cognitive dissonance* as a motivation for behavior proposes that conflicting cognitions make people uncomfortable and that, consequently, they will seek to resolve the conflict in one way or another (Festinger, 1957). One of the ways in which dissonance may be reduced is by seeking information either to support existing knowledge, values or beliefs, or to find sufficient cause to change these factors. Accordingly, Aaker, Batra & Myers (1992) reporting work on advertising and its effects on changes in attitudes towards products, note that where an advertisement matches the belief held by a person, that person is more likely to advance supporting arguments for choosing the product. However, where there are discrepancies between the communication and the previously held belief, the person is likely to bring forward counter-arguments to the claims being made in the advertisement.

On the other hand, Sorrentino and Short (1986) suggested that many people are simply not interested in finding out information about themselves or the world, do not conduct causal searches and do not give a hoot for resolving discrepancies or inconsistencies about the self. This seems to return us to the idea of people having different levels of *cognitive need,* which may be the ultimate driver of information behavior. In the same vein, Rogers (1983) suggested that individuals generally tend to expose themselves to ideas that are in accordance with their interests, needs or existing attitudes. We consciously or unconsciously avoid messages that are in conflict with our predispositions.

Johnson and Macrae (1994) tested the proposition that people are more likely to bias their information search towards information that matches their stereotypical image of a group rather than towards that which does not match their stereotype. They demonstrated that when a group of students, '...could control the amount and nature of information they received about a group, they displayed the anticipated preference for stereotype-matching information.' However, when the students' information acquisition was controlled by the researcher, '...a reduction in their stereotype-based impression of the group' was observed.

Krishnan and Jones (2005) studied how people differ with respect to their preference of information presentation. They found that some people preferred to access files via folders shown in a spatial representation, while others preferred textual keyword-based search to access their files. Other studies have demonstrated reduction of the performance gap between different population groups through appropriate design modifications. Zhang and Salvendy (2001) investigated the effects of users' visualization ability and website structure display design on web browsing performance. They found that structure preview reduced the differences in performance between high and low visualization ability users.

Savolainen (2009) based on the conceptual analysis, examined the features of cognitive barriers and their impact on information seeking. The study resulted in a typology specifying six sub-types of cognitive barriers: unwillingness to see one's needs as information needs, inability to articulate one's information needs, unawareness of information sources, low self-efficacy, poor search skills and inability to deal with information overload. The sub-types were reviewed at two stages of the information-seeking process: identifying and articulating information needs; and selecting and accessing information sources. According to Savolainen, the impact of cognitive barriers is mainly negative. They block, limit or hamper information seeking, or give rise to negative reactions such as frustration. Cognitive barriers can also impact positively by helping the individual to concentrate on a few, good enough sources of information.

CONCLUSION

Information has been adjudged to be a factor of production, hence the demand for it. The orbits of complexities that revolve around each information seeker in digital library environment have been discussed as barriers to timely access to information. Information in digital formats allow for remote accessibility which characterizes the 21st Century information service provision. The factors examined in this study are germane to information seeking in digital libraries. Demographic factors (age and gender); level of income and education, ICT infrastructure and power supply considered under socio-economic; and cognitive factors which pointed out problem identification, need articulation, query formulation and result evaluation, have the capacity to restrict scope of search, delay or block access and ultimately frustrate the information seeking process. Inability to surmount these barriers by information seekers could also hamper effectiveness and efficiency among digital information seekers.

RECOMMENDATIONS

Having examined these inhibiting factors, the authors recommend the following ameliorating approaches to information seeking: The dispensational change in access and use of information should be recognized by older persons who are not favorably disposed to digital information and consciously embrace the change by demonstrating willingness to learn and relearn relevant technologies that will aid their access to digital information. There is a need to educate the populace against the cultural believe of superiority of the male gender over the female. The focus should rather be on cognitive capabilities of individuals and how to improve on them. The need for information users to constantly upgrade knowledge in relation to the dynamic nature of the digital library and ICT infrastructure becomes paramount.

REFERENCES

Aaker, D. A., Batra, R., & Myers, J. G. (1992). *Advertising Management* (4th ed.). Englewood Cliffs, NJ: Prentice Hall.

Adomi, E. E. (2005). The effects of a price increase on cybercafés in Abraka, Nigeria: The bottom-line. *Managing Library Finances*, *18*(2), 78–86. doi:10.1108/08880450510597523

Agosto, D. E. (2001). Propelling young women into Cyber Age: gender considerations in the evaluation of Web-based information. *School Library Media Research* 4. Retrieved from http://www.ala.org/ala/aasl/aaslpubsandjournals/slmrb/slmrcontents/volume42001/agosto.htm

Aina, L. O. (2004). *Library and information science text.* Ibadan: Stirlin-Horden.

Alemna, A. A., & Skouby, K. E. (2000). An investigation into the information needs and information seeking behavior of members of Ghana's legislature. *Library Management*, *21*(5), 235–240. doi:10.1108/01435120010324815

American Library Association. (2008). Serving non-English speakers: 2007 Analysis of library demographics, services and programs. Retrieved from http://www.ala.org/offices/olos/nonenglishspeakers

Aregbesola, A., & Oguntayo, S. (2014). Use of Electronic Resources by Faculty Members in Landmark University. *Computing, Information Systems. Development Informatics and Allied Research Journal*, *5*(2), 53–58.

Arms, W. (2000). *Digital libraries*. Cambridge: M.I.T. Press.

Arms, W. Y. (1995). Key concepts in the architecture of the digital library. *D-lib Magazine*, URL: http://www.dlib.org/dlib/July95/07arms.html

Bailin, A., & Grafstein, A. (2005). The Evolution of Academic Libraries: The Networked Environment. *Journal of Academic Librarianship*, *31*(4), 317–323. doi:10.1016/j.acalib.2005.04.004

Bawden, D., & Rowlands, I. (1999). Digital libraries: Assumptions and concepts. *Libri*, *49*(4), 181–191. doi:10.1515/libr.1999.49.4.181

Bertot, J. C. (2009). Public access technologies in public libraries: Effects and implications. *Information Technology and Libraries*, *28*(2), 81–92.

Blomberg, O. (2011). Concepts of cognition for cognitive engineering. *The International Journal of Aviation Psychology*, *21*(1), 85–104. doi:10.1080/10508414.2011.537561

Book Industry Study Group. (2010). *Consumer attitudes toward e-book reading*. New York, NY: The Author.

Borgman, C. L. (2000). *From Gutenberg to the Global Information Infrastructure: Access to Information in the Networked World*. Cambridge: MIT Press.

Brennan, K., Kelly, D. & Arguello, J. (2014). The Effect of Cognitive Abilities on Information Search for Tasks of Varying Levels of Complexity. ACM. doi:10.1145/2637002.2637022

Brindley, D. L. J. (2009). *Challenges for great libraries in the age of the digital native*. Amsterdam: IOS Press.

British Library. (2010). *2020 vision*. London, UK: The British Library Board. Retrieved from http://www.bl.uk/aboutus/stratpolprog/2020vision/2020A3.pdf

Carmen, L. (2006). My Computer, My Doctor: A Constitutional Call for Federal Regulation of Cyber-medicine. *American Journal of Law & Medicine*, *32*(4), 585–609. PMID:17240732

Carroll, J. B. (1993). *Human cognitive abilities: a summary of factor-analytic studies*. N.Y.: Cambridge University press. doi:10.1017/CBO9780511571312

Chepesuik, R. (1997). The future is here: America's libraries go digital. *American Libraries*, *2*(1), 47–49.

David, K. (1995). The importance of information. *Library Management*, *16*(5), 6–15. doi:10.1108/01435129510772283

DeBell, M., & Chapman, C. (2006). *Computer and internet use by students in 2003 (NCES 2006-065). U.S. Department of Education*. Washington, DC: National Center for Education Statistics.

Fallows, D. (2005). How women and men use the Internet. Washington, DC: Pew Internet & American Life Project. Retrieved from http://www.pewInternet.org/pdfs/PIP_Women_and_Men_online.pdf

Festinger, L. (1957). *A Theory of Cognitive Dissonance*. Stanford, California: Stanford University Press.

Ford, N., Miller, D., & Moss, N. (2001). The Role of Individual Difference in Internet Searching: An Empirical Study. *Journal of the American Society for Information Science and Technology*, *52*(12), 1049–1066. doi:10.1002/asi.1165

Glossary of Cognitive Skills. (n. d.). Retrieved from http://www.learningrx.com/what-are-cognitive-skills.htm

Graham, P. S. (1995). *Requirements for the Digital Research Library*. Retrieved from http://aultnis.rutgers.edu/texts/DRC.html

Guenette, D. R., Trippe, B., & Golden, K. (2010). *A blueprint for book publishing transformation: Seven essential processes to re-invent publishing*. Cambridge, MA: Gilbane Group.

Gwizdka, J. (2002). TaskView - Design and Evaluation of a Task-based Email Interface. CASCON Conference. *IBM*.

Gwizdka, J. (2004). Email Task Management Styles: The Cleaners and the Keepers. In *Extended Abstracts of ACM Conference on Human Factors in Computing Systems CHI'2004* (pp. 1235 – 1238). ACM Press.

Gwizdka, J., & Chignell, M. H. (2004). Individual differences and task-based user interface evaluation: A case study of pending tasks in email. *Interacting with Computers*, *16*(4), 769–797. doi:10.1016/j.intcom.2004.04.008

Haruna, I., & Mabawonku, I. (2001). Information Needs and Seeking Behavior of Legal Practitioners and the Challenges to Law Libraries in Lagos, Nigeria. *The International Information & Library Review*, 2011, 33.

Idowu, B., Adagunodo, R., & Idowu, B. (2004). Gender difference in computer literacy among Nigerian undergraduate students: A case study of Obafemi Awolowo University students, Nigeria.*The African Symposium: An Online Educational Research Journal,* 4(3), 24-30.

Igbo, U. H., & Imo, N. T. (2010). Challenges of Accessibility of Information Resources by the Post Graduate Library Users of a Nigeria University. *An International Journal of Information and Communication Technology*, *7*(2), 1–10.

Igwe, K. N. (2012). A Survey of the Information Literacy Skills of Students in Federal Polytechnic Offa, Kwara State, Nigeria. *Information Technologist*, *9*(2), 8–19.

International Digital Publishing Forum. (2010). *Industry statistics.* Seattle, WA: The Author. Retrieved from http://www.idpf.org/doc_library/industrystats.htm

International Telecommunications Union (ITU). (2003). World telecommunication development report. In Access Indicators for the information society (pp. 12-30).

International Telecommunications Union (ITU). (2007). ICT Statistics Database, Geneva: ITU. Retrieved from http://www.itu.int/ITU-D/icteye/Indicators/Indicators.aspx

Islam, M. A., Abdul Rahim, A., Tan, C. L., & Momtaz, H. (2011). Effect of demographic factors on e-learning effectiveness in a higher learning Institution in Malaysia. *International Education Studies, 4*(1), 4–7. doi:10.5539/ies.v4n1p112

Jerabek, A. J., Meyer, L. S., & Kordinak, T. S. (2001). Library anxiety and computer anxiety: Measures, validity, and research implications. *Library & Information Science Research, 23*(3), 277–289. doi:10.1016/S0740-8188(01)00083-4

Johnson, J. D., & Meischke, H. (1991b). Cancer Information: Women's Source and Content Preferences. *Journal of Health Care Marketing, 11*, 37–44. PMID:10110080

Kakai, M., Ikoja-Odongo, R., & Kigongo-Bukeny, I. M. N. (2004). A study of the information seeking behavior of undergraduate students of Makerere University, Uganda. *World Libraries, 14*, 544–564.

Kennedy, T., Wellman, B., & Klement, K. (2003). Gendering the digital divide. *IT and Society*, 1(5), 72-96. Retrieved from http://www.stanford.edu/group/siqss/itandsociety/v01i05/v01i05a05.pdf

Kirk, M., & Zander, C. (2004). Narrowing the digital divide: In search of a map to mend the gap. *Journal of Computing Sciences in Colleges, 20*(2), 168–175.

Krikelas, J. (1983). Information-Seeking Behaviour: Patterns and Concepts. *Drexel Library Quarterly, 19*(2), 5–20.

Leckie, G. J., Pettigrew, K. E., & Sylvain, C. (1996). Modeling the Information Seeking of Professionals and Lawyers. *The Library Quarterly, 66*(2), 161–193. doi:10.1086/602864

Lee, G. T., & Dahlan, N. (2005). Impact of Interface Characteristics on Digital Libraries Usage. *Malaysian Online Journal of Instructional Technology, 2*(1), 10–15.

Lynch, C. A. (1994). *The integrity of digital information: Mechanism and definitional issues*. Silver Spring, MD: ASIS.

Lynch, C. A. (1997). Searching the Internet. *Scientific American*, 52-56. Retrieved from http://www.sciam.com/0397issue/0397lynch.html

Lynch, C. A., & Garcia-Molina, H. (1995). *Interoperability, Scaling, and the Digital Libraries Research Agenda: A Report on the May 18-19, 1995 IITA Digital Libraries Workshop*. Retrieved from http://www-diglib.stanford.edu/diglib/pub/reports/iita-dlw/main.html

Manda, P. A., & Mulkangara, F. (2007). Gender Analysis of Electronic Information Resources Use: A Case of the University of Dares Salaam Tanzania. *University of Dares Salaam Library Journal, 9*(1), 31–52.

Marchionini, G. (1998). *Research and development in digital libraries. Encyclopedia of Library and Information Science* (Vol. 63). New York: Dekker.

McClure, C. R., Bertot, J. C., & Jaeger, P. T. (2011). The ever changing impacts of internet access on libraries and their communities. In J. C. Bertot, C. R. McClure, & P. T. Jaeger (Eds.), *Public libraries and the internet: Roles, perspectives, and implications* (pp. 261–281). Santa Barbara, CA: Libraries Unlimited.

Nakonecny, M. (1998). *Psychologie osobnosti. 2. vyd.* Prague, Czech Republic: Academia.

Okiki, O.C and Asiru, S.M. (2011). Use of Electronic Information Sources by Postgraduate Students in Nigeria: Influencing Factors. *Library Philosophy and Practice 2011.*

Olatokun, M. W. (2009). Analysing Socio-Demographic Differences in Access and Use of ICTs in Nigeria Using the Capability Approach. *Issues in Informing Science and Information Technology*, *6*(3), 34–40.

Otubelu, N. J. (2011). E-Learning through digital libraries: the case of National Open University. *Library Philosophy and Practice.* Retrieved from unllib.unl.edu/LPP/

Owolabi, S. E. (2013). Socio-demographic factors as determinants of access and use of ICT by staff of university libraries in Oyo State. *Library Philosophy and Practice.* Retrieved from http://digitalcommons.unl.edu/libphilprac/947

Phillips, D. (2006). *Quality of Life: Concept, Policy and Practice* (pp. 1–39). Oxon: Routledge. doi:10.4324/9780203356630

Rana, H. K. (2009). Impact of Information and Communication Technology on Academic Libraries in Punjab. Retrieved from http/www.goarticles.com/cgi-bin/showa/cgi=1239032

Riding, R., & Rayner, S. G. (1998). *Cognitive styles and learning strategies.* London: David Fulton Publisher.

Rogers, E. M. (1983). *Diffusion of Innovation* (3rd ed.). New York: The Free Press.

Sorrentino, R., & Short, J. (1986). Uncertainty Orientation, Motivation, and Cognition. In R. Sorrentino & E. Higgins (Eds.), *Handbook of Motivation and Cognition.* New York: The Guilford Press.

Sternberg, R. J., & Sternberg, K. (2009). *Cognitive psychology* (6th ed.). Belmont, CA: Wadsworth, Cengage Learning.

Taylor, R. S. (1962). The Process of Asking Questions. *American Documentation*, *13*(4), 391–396. doi:10.1002/asi.5090130405

Tella, A. (2009). Correlates of Undergraduates' Information-Seeking Behavior. *College & Undergraduate Libraries*, *16*(1), 1–19. doi:10.1080/10691310902754221

Thompson, C. J., & Zeynep, A. (2004). The Starbucks Brandscape and Consumers' (Anticorporate) Experiences of Glocalization. *The Journal of Consumer Research*, *31*(12), 631–642. doi:10.1086/425098

Trivedi, M. (2010). Digital Libraries: Functionality, Usability, and Accessibility. *Library Philosophy and Practice. ISSN 1522-0222.*

Uhegbu, A. H. (2007). *The Information User: Issues and Themes.* Okigwe Whytem Publishers.

Waters, D. J. (1998). What are Digital Libraries? *CLIR Issues*, July/August. Retrieved from http://www.clir.org/pubs/issues/issues04.HTML

Wilson, T. D. (1981). On user studies and information needs. *The Journal of Documentation*, *37*(1), 3–15. doi:10.1108/eb026702

Wilson, T. D. (1997). Information behavior: An interdisciplinary perspective. *Information Processing & Management*, *33*(4), 551–572. doi:10.1016/S0306-4573(97)00028-9

Wilson, T. D. (2000). Recent Trends in User Studies: Action Research and Qualitative Methods. *Information Research, 5*(3). Retrieved from http://information.net/ir/5-3/paper76html

Worcman, K. (2002). Digital division is cultural exclusion. But is digital inclusion cultural inclusion? *D-Lib Magazine, 8*(3). Retrieved from http://www.dlib.org/dlib/march02/worcman/03worcman.html doi:10.1045/march2002-worcman

Xie, H. (2000). Shifts of interactive intentions and information-seeking strategies in interactive information retrieval. *Journal of the American Society for Information Science, 51*(9), 841–857. doi:10.1002/(SICI)1097-4571(2000)51:9<841::AID-ASI70>3.0.CO;2-0

Zhang, H., & Salvendy, G. (2001). The Implication of Visualization Ability and Structure Preview Design for Web Information Search Tasks. *International Journal of Human-Computer Interaction, 13*(1), 75–95. doi:10.1207/S15327590IJHC1301_5

ADDITIONAL READING

Arms, W. Y. (2000). *Digital Libraries.* Cambridge, MA, USA: MIT Press.

Bhargava, B. K. (2000). *Digital Libraries and Multimedia.* Hingham, MA, USA: Kluwer Academic Publishers.

Bishop, A. P., Van, H. N. A., & Buttenfield, B. P. (Eds.). (2003). *Digital Library Use: Social Practice in Design and Evaluation.* Cambridge, MA, USA: MIT Press.

Kresh, D. (2007). Whole Digital Library Handbook. Chicago, IL, USA: ALA Editions. Retrieved from http://www.ebrary.com

Matthews, G., & Walton, G. (Eds.). (2013). University Libraries and Space in the Digital World. Farnham, GBR: Ashgate Publishing Group.

Nitecki, D. A., & Abels, E. G. (Eds.). (2008). Advances in Librarianship (Vol. 31). Bradford, GBR: Emerald Group Publishing Ltd.

Ralhan, P. (2009). Advancement in Library and Information Science. Jaipur, IND: Oxford Book Co.

Tedd, L.A. (2005). Digital Libraries: Principles and Practice in a Global Environment. Berlin, DEU: K. G. Saur.

KEY TERMS AND DEFINITIONS

Cognition: The set of all mental abilities and processes related to knowledge, attention, memory and working memory, judgment and evaluation, reasoning and computation, problem solving and decision making, comprehension and production of language, etc. Human cognition is conscious and unconscious, concrete or abstract, as well as intuitive (like knowledge of a language) and conceptual (like a model of a language). Cognitive processes use existing knowledge and generate new knowledge.

Demographics: Investigating a population with focus on factors such as age, race, gender, economic status, level of education, income level, marital status and employment amongst others. Demographics are used by researchers, government agencies and non-governmental organizations for decision making, policy formulation, etc.

User: A person or a group of persons who uses the digital library resources. They are not expected to have the technical expertise possessed by librarians. Their main concern is to know if certain information is available and how they will access it. They are not interested in the process of acquisition, processing, storage and preservation of digital resources.

Virtual Space: A generic term for the online world of the Internet. It also encompasses radio, television, phone and video calls, texting, e-mail, blogs, forums, chat rooms, instant messaging, social media interactions, as well as access to corporate data.

Chapter 10
Information Seeking Behaviour of Trade Unionists:
A Review of Associated Challenges in Digital Era

Joel O. Afolayan
Michael Imoudu National Institute for Labour Studies, Nigeria

ABSTRACT

Trade Unionism is mostly like a reactive movement rather than proactive. Its activities and programmes have witnessed setbacks overtime, notwithstanding the originality of intent and positivity of disposition to democratic process. Trade union is a major component of the system of modern industrial relations in any nation. Constitutionally, it has own set of objectives or goals to achieve. Change in the political, social and educational environment gives it an interface of a forum that protects and advances workers' interests, improves the quality of life and condition of workforce, enlarges their traditional capacity of establishing terms and conditions of employment. This chapter entrenches trade unionists' information needs in terms of capacity building towards organizational productivity as well as the seeking behavior using digital sources. The challenges of meeting up with the needs and management of information by Information Resource Centre of Michael Imoudu National Institute for Labour Studies' (MINILS) in the era of digital divide is review with recommendations.

INTRODUCTION

The increasing pressure to explore relevant information resources to better the lot of Trade Union has been the subject of a number of studies (Imbun and Ngangan, 2001). It is obvious that knowledge-based resources determine the rating of the growth and development of an organization in the contemporary society. The scope of the factors of production- Land, Labour, Capital and Entrepreneur has been logically expanded to accommodate 'knowledge'. Knowledge, as it were, is considered worth added to existing four factors of production (Azubuike, 2012). Trade unions are a major component of the system of modern industrial relations in any nation, each having their own set of objectives or goals to achieve

DOI: 10.4018/978-1-5225-0296-8.ch010

according to their constitution. It also has its own master plan toward achieving those goals. This is in line with the International Labour Convention of International Labour Organization, ratified by Nigeria thus: 'Workers and employers without distinction whatsoever shall have the right to establish and, subject only to the rules of the organization concerned to join organization of their choosing without previous authorization; they must have the right to draw up their constitution and rules, to elect their representatives in full freedom, to organize their administration and activities and to formulate their programmes and public authority must refrain from interference which would restrict these rights or impede their lawful exercise, their organization must not be liable to be dissolved or suspended by administrative authority and their organizations must have the right to establish and join federations and confederations and to affiliate with international organizations of employees and employers (Abiala, 2011)

A trade union is an organization formed by workers to protect their interests and improve their working conditions, among other goals. It is a continuous association of wage earners for the purpose of maintaining and improving working conditions. In the developing countries, the exclusive right to form a union and bargain collectively protects workers from exploitative tendencies of employer(s) at work and mounts pressure on employers to share productivity gains with their employees. This therefore necessitates unionization, in the developing countries and even beyond, so that the working population can reap the benefits of economic growth stemming from wealth created by the work force. It will surely cost the trade union greatly if little or no attention is paid to Information. Information as the physical surrogate of knowledge (Aina, 2004) is therefore indispensable. It is though viewed as been ambiguous yet described as a 'process'; as a 'knowledge'; and as a 'thing' by Buckland (1991). Information is a process when it is performing the function of informing, which involves transmitting idea from the source to a recipient. It is knowledge when it is performing the role of imparting knowledge to an individual, where it reduces uncertainty. Information is a thing when it is packaged, thereby making it tangible as record or document. The information need and seeking behavior of Trade Unionists shall be assessed with the view to identify relational challenges in the digital era for possible improvement to exact the indispensability of effective and proportionate information resources so as to strategically position trade unionists for the challenges of globalization. Looking at the development of ICT from general perspectives therefore, the impact felt is varied in certain field of human endeavor from others. However, it is evidence that is a vast and increasing gap.

Every work organization is made up of human beings. Consequent upon this, there is the tendency to be interactions among the stake holders that relate to the organization. Labour relation is simply defined as the web of interactions that exist among actors in the work place. In other words, it is concerned with how workers and the constituted authorities relate among themselves within a work place. It is therefore concerned with the study of confliction and harmonious dimensions of relationships or interactions within a work environment. Labour relations from this perspective and in this context of trade unionism covers: the interplay between workers and government - being the largest employer of work force; interactions between the work force and the management – being the representative of either the government as employer or the proprietor of the employing organization; and interrelationships among workers (inter - union and intra – union relations). Consequently, in this chapter, the terms labour relations and industrial relations shall be used relatively as components of trade unionism

There will always be conflicts and disagreements between employers and employees, either on wages or on the general condition of service of the workers. This chapter is to ascertain the degree of information need assessment in trade unionism, as well as application of the identified information by the trade union officials while interfacing with other stakeholders in the world of work to primarily advance the condition of the work force. The issues that are critical to the mandate of trade unionism include but not limited to the wages and its associated matters e.g. salary and wage rate, allowances and bonus, benefits, welfare packages and so on; conditions and schemes of service like hours of work, promotion issues, redeployment, casualization of work force and job status; consolidation policy leading to segregation and discrepancies in the salary structures e.g. Consolidated Research and Allied Institutions Salary Structure (CONRAISS), Consolidated Tertiary Institutions Salary Structure (CONTISS), Consolidated University Academic Salary Structure (CONUASS), Consolidated Medical and Health Salary Structure (CONMEHSS) etc.; industrial relations like anti-unionism, violation of agreement, impunity etc.; government legislations like Federal Character principle, National Minimum Wage Act (1981), Trade Disputes Act (2004), Trade Disputes (Essential Services) Act (2004), Trade Union (Amendment) Act (2005), National Industrial Court Act (2006), Employee Compensation act (2011); In some cases government policies on general matters also bring about dispute between government and the working population, for example, in June 27, 1986 President Babangida (the then military President) announced a Structural Adjustment Programme (SAP). This programme set government on one side and the working population on the other. Another case was that of 1996 when the Academic Staff Union of Universities embarked on a six months strike during the regime of the late despot Sanni Abacha (the late military President of Nigeria) more than one conflict arises between union and government; Other issues are gender mainstreaming, national economy, labour migration, domesticated conventions of International Labour Organization (ILO), international labour standard, social security, social dialogue, freedom of association, occupational safety and health etc.

The world of work is no doubt, laced with developmental controversies, hence finding solutions to the associated problem arising there-from is a major pre-occupation of peace and development as well as industrial relations practitioners, which include - trade unionist, entrepreneurs, government, non-government, investors and scholars. Conspicuously, the new economic order, that borders on technological drive and environmental dictates so necessitate investigations into the management-related approach to the identified conflicts. In a bid to check these conflicts, workers come together and form unions - Trade Union. They come together having realized the amount of influence they can wield as a group for effective industrial relations. Industrial relations, (also known as labour relations) is the interdisciplinary and somewhat diffuse study of the institutions and rule-fixing processes of the labour It's core subject-matter has always been collective bargaining between trade unions or analogous organizations on the other hand. The term "employee relation" found increasingly in management writing, was once a synonym for industrial relations; it now usually denotes part of the field in which management- trade union relationship either plays a smaller role or is argued to be inappropriate.

ORGANIZATION AND INSTITUTE FOR LABOUR ADMINISTRATION

International Labour Organization (ILO)

Institutionalization of industrial and labour administration is basically traceable to the strategic recognition of industrial peace and harmony in the world of work by the United Nations. International Labour Organization (ILO) is a specialized agency of the United Nations. The ILO was created in 1919, as part of the Treaty of Versailles that ended World War I, to reflect the belief that universal and lasting peace can be accomplished only if it is based on social justice. The Constitution was drafted between January and April, 1919, by the Labour Commission set up by the Peace Conference, which first met in Paris and then in Versailles. The Commission, chaired by Samuel Gompers, head of the American Federation of Labour (AFL) in the United States, was composed of representatives from nine countries: Belgium, Cuba, Czechoslovakia, France, Italy, Japan, Poland, the United Kingdom and the United States. It resulted in a tripartite organization, the only one of its kind bringing together representatives of governments, employers and workers in its executive bodies.

The Constitution contained ideas tested within the International Association for Labour Legislation, founded in Basel in 1901. Advocacy for an international organization dealing with labour issues began in the nineteenth century, led by two industrialists, Robert Owen (1771-1853) of Wales and Daniel Legrand (1783-1859) of France. The driving forces for ILO's creation arose from security, humanitarian, political and economic considerations. Summarizing them, the ILO Constitution's Preamble says the High Contracting Parties were 'moved by sentiments of justice and humanity as well as by the desire to secure the permanent peace of the world...'

There was keen appreciation of the importance of social justice in securing peace, against a background of exploitation of workers in the industrializing nations of that time. There was also increasing understanding of the world's economic interdependence and the need for cooperation to obtain similarity of working conditions in countries competing for markets. Reflecting these ideas, the Preamble states:

Whereas universal and lasting peace can be established only if it is based upon social justice;

And whereas conditions of labour exist involving such injustice hardship and privation to large numbers of people as to produce unrest so great that the peace and harmony of the world are imperiled; and an improvement of those conditions is urgently required;

Whereas also the failure of any nation to adopt humane conditions of labour is an obstacle in the way of other nations which desire to improve the conditions in their own countries.

The areas of improvement listed in the Preamble remain relevant today, for example:

Regulation of the hours of work including the establishment of a maximum working day and week;

Regulation of labour supply, prevention of unemployment and provision of an adequate living wage;

Protection of the worker against sickness, disease and injury arising out of his employment;

Protection of children, young persons and women;

Provision for old age and injury, protection of the interests of workers when employed in countries other than their own;

Recognition of the principle of equal remuneration for work of equal value;

Recognition of the principle of freedom of association;

Organization of vocational and technical education, and other measures. (ILO, 2015)

Social security protection is clearly stressed in ILO conventions and UN instruments as a basic human right – albeit one that a small proportion of the people on our planet actually enjoy. It is, though very broad a concept. However, it could be defined as a system of contribution-based health, pension and unemployment protection, along with tax-financed social benefits. Social security has become a universal challenge in a globalizing world. Relatively low percent of the world's population has adequate social security coverage, while a reasonably percentage lacks any kind of social security protection at all. Those without coverage tend to be part of the informal economy – they are generally not protected in old age by social security, and they cannot afford to pay their health care bill. In addition, many people have insufficient coverage – that is, they may lack significant elements of protection (such as health care or pension) or what protection they do have is low or declining. Experience shows that people are willing to contribute to social security benefits that satisfy their priority needs.

It was once assumed that an increasing proportion of the labour force in developing countries would end up in formal-sector employment covered by social security. However, experience has shown that the growing incidence of informal work has led to stagnant or declining rates of coverage. Even in countries with high economic growth, increasing numbers of workers – often women – are in less secure employment, such as casual labour, homework and certain types of self-employment lacking social security coverage. The most vulnerable groups outside the labour force are people with disabilities and old people who cannot count on family support, and who have not been able to make provisions for their own pensions.

Social security was established as a basic human right in the ILO's Declaration of Philadelphia (1944) and its Income Security Recommendation, 1944 (No. 67). This right is upheld in the Universal Declaration of Human Rights, 1948, and the International Covenant on Economic, Social and Cultural Rights, 1966.

ILO conventions and recommendations relevant to social security extension policies are shown in Table 1.

In 2001, the International Labour Conference adopted the Resolution and Conclusions concerning Social Security.

Social security has a powerful impact at all levels of society. It provides workers and their families with access to health care and with protection against loss of income, whether it is for short periods

Table 1.

S/N	Title	Conventions/Recommendations
1.	The Social Security (Minimum Standards)	Convention, 1952 (No. 102)
2.	The Equality of Treatment (Social Security)	Convention, 1962 (No. 118)
3.	The Employment Injury Benefits	Convention, 1964 Schedule I amended in 1980 (No.121)
4.	Invalidity, Old-Age and Survivors' Benefits	Convention, 1967 (No. 128)
5.	The Medical Care and Sickness Benefits	Convention, 1969 (No.130)
6.	The Maintenance of Social Security Rights	Convention, 1982 (No. 157)
7.	The Employment Promotion and Protection against Unemployment	Convention, 1988 (No.168)
8.	The Job Creation in Small and Medium-Sized Enterprises	Recommendation, 1998 (No. 189)
9.	Maternity Protection	Convention (Revised) 2000 (No. 183)

of unemployment or sickness or maternity or for a longer time due to invalidity or employment injury. It provides older people with income security in their retirement years. Children benefit from social security programmes designed to help their families cope with the cost of education. For employers and enterprises, social security helps maintain stable labour relations and a productive workforce. And social security can contribute to social cohesion and to a country's overall growth and development by bolstering living standards, cushioning the effects of structural and technological change on people and thereby providing the basis for a more positive approach toward globalization.

Social security therefore becomes an issue in the trade unionism simply because it is the end product of all industrial and labour relations, such that practical reflection of all variables of the tripartite (i.e. employers, employees and government) factors are in actionable plan for implementations. This plan, when implemented is substantial, verifiable and measurable. It could be reviewed to shape up with the socio-economic reality of the moment. The plan in question could come up in form of policy, even law that could be enforced, and sustained as governance of a nation transits. Notably, in Nigeria, are the Education Trust Fund (ETF), Industrial Training Fund (ITF), National Health Insurance Scheme (NHIS), Scholarship Board, Pension Reform, National Housing Fund (NHF), Subsidy Reinvestment Programme (SURE-P) to list but a few. It is important that the interests of the stakeholders are counterpoised (Figure 1).

In the recognition of the processes leading to organizational effectiveness and individual well-being, the above chat flow portrays, distinctly the scientific approach to the study of individual (employee) processes, group (trade union) processes and organization (employer-related environmental) processes. The trio processes eventually lead to operational information that could either be structured or unstructured but primarily tend towards enhancing organizational effectiveness as well as the well-being of individuals - social security. A stage that cannot be skipped in the process is the knowledge management (KM) stage. Knowledge Management is the matured stage of information stage. Knowledge management refers to tools, techniques and strategies used to generate, organize, analyze, leverage and share knowledge. Knowledge management is based on existing resources in an organization. The heart of KM is the extreme applicability of information. Knowledge occupies an important position in the information continuum. It is derived from data and information.

Michael Imoudu National Institute for Labout Studies (MINILS)

The idea to establish a Labour Institute of National repute is dated back to the third National Development Plan 1975 – 1980 when the Federal Government of Nigeria took over the Patrice Lumumba Labour Institute (LLI) and Trade Union Institute for Economic and Social Development (TUIESD) established

Figure 1.

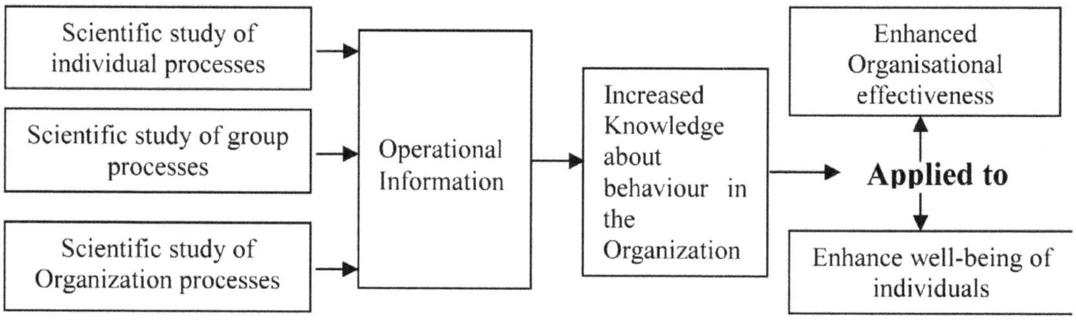

by the banned Nigerian Trade Union Congress (NTUC) and United Labour Congress of Nigeria (ULCN) respectively. The antecedents and rationale behind the establishment of the National Institute for Labour Studies were therefore articulated in the 1975 National Labour Policy and Plan. The objective was pursued with vigor during the second republic when the foundation stone of the Institute was laid in Ilorin by the then Civilian President, Shehu Shagari on May 4, 1983. The Institute has its legal backing in Act Cap. 261 of the Laws of the Federation of Nigeria, 1990 (formerly, Decree No. 5 of 1986). The National Institute for Labour Studies (NILS) was renamed Michael Imoudu Institute for Labour Studies (MIILS), Ilorin by the then Military President, General Ibrahim Babangida, on May 1, 1992 in honour of the Nigeria's foremost labour leader and stout defender of workers' rights, Pa Michael Aitokhaimen Omiunu Imoudu and later Michael Imoudu National institute for Labour Studies (MINILS) to reflect the national status of the Institute.

MINILS is Nigeria's foremost institute for labour education. The Institute is administered under a seminal and inclusive arrangement involving Government, Labour and Employers. MINILS mandate is to provide workers' education. Pursuant to this, the Institute is involved in several activities in the areas of research, training, education, publication and consultancy. The Institute undertakes extensive initiatives aimed at building the capacity of workers and their unions; promoting exchange between industrial relations parties in the interest of industrial harmony; developing international linkages to encourage best practices and global solidarity; and advancing the frontiers of knowledge in labour matters. (MINILS, 2015)

The objectives of the MINILS are:

1. To provide workers' education generally so as to enhance the role of trade unions in the social and economic development of the country and equip trade union officials and managers with skills normally required for collective bargaining and joint consultation in fostering the growth of better labour and management relations
2. To provide opportunities for policy makers in the field of labour and social policy in industry, in the trade unions and in government to acquire, by personal experience, a full understanding of the issues which confront them in their day to day work
3. To provide and arrange comparative study and investigation of the principles and techniques of trade unionism and thereby assist Government in evolving a virile and well organized trade union movement capable of giving full and responsible expression to the needs of workers and the aspirations of the country
4. To undertake, organize and facilitate study course, conferences, lectures, seminers and the like with a view to improving the standard of the trade union administration and infusing a sense of direction and accountability
5. To promote research through collaboration with universities and Institute concerned with industrial and labour matters
6. To award grants, scholarships or travel fellowships for research in labour studies and allied subjects
7. To undertake and provide for publication of journals, research papers and books in furtherance of the aforesaid objectives

The Institute undertakes, organizes and facilitates study courses, conferences, lectures, seminars, and research through collaboration with Universities and Institutes concerned with socio-economic issues, with a view to strengthening tripartite relationship and social dialogue in the workplace.

TEMPLATES OF TRADE UNION IN NIGERIA

Organized trade unions officially started on Monday, 19 August 1912 in Nigeria when workers in the then civil service organized themselves into trade unions as was done in Sierra Leone (Egboh, 1968 in George, Owoyemi & Onokala, 2012). One Mr Henry Libert – a Sierra Leonean- summoned a meeting of about thirty-three indigenous workers, and by the fifth meeting on 15 November 1912 after advice was received from Sierra Leone, the aim of the union was decided and this was to promote the welfare and interests of the indigenous workers of the Nigerian Civil Service (Okonkwo, 1993). It was known then as the Civil Service British Workers Union but later changed to the Nigerian Civil Service Union shortly before independent.

It remained an exclusive union of Africans of 1st class workers until the outbreak of the First World War in 1914. This brought about an astronomical rise in cost of living and the union had to seek the support of other workers outside the 1st class to agitate for 30% increase in basic salaries as the war bonus which was granted by the colonial administrators (Ananaba, 1979). The union later discussed other grievances which included: discrimination in salary scale in favor of Europeans against African workers performing same jobs, and abolition of the 'frequent imposition of fines as a measure of discipline' (Yesufu, 1982).

In 1931, the Railway Workers Union and the Nigeria Union of Teachers were formed; before this time, railway workers were under the Nigerian Civil Service Union (*Ibid*). The 1930 economic crisis aided the coming out of the then Mechanic Union out of the Nigerian Civil Service Union; although the former claimed to embrace all employees of the railway; the clerical workers chose to remain with the later. With the passing of the Nigerian Trade Union Ordinance in 1938, the numbers of registered trade unions as well as memberships increased for example, in 1940 only 14 unions were registered with 4,629 members but by 1944 this had increased to 91 registered unions with over thirty thousand members (Nigeria Department of Labour Annual Reports, 1945).

According to Fashoyin, (1980), by 1975, under the military regime of General Murtala Muhamed one thousand trade unions were registered. In the same year, his government established a Commission of Enquiry to look into the past activities of the unions. Administrators were appointed to manage the unions as the unions were polarized and ideologically divided therefore creating labour problems for the country. The unions were restructured into 42 along industrial lines and a Labour centre was created (Nigerian Federal Ministry of Labour and Productivity, 1976) the parent ministry of today's National Institute for Labour Studies. The Nigerian Labour Congress (NLC) was created in 1978 and the 42 industrial unions became affiliates. This was given a legal backing through the Trade Union Decree. In 1989, the trade union was restructured again with 29 industrial unions affiliated to NLC through the Trade Union (Amendment) Decree 22 of 1978. While the workers were multiplying their unions, a new development came up in 1960; this was the urgent need for a different union for the employees of related employments and job descriptions. A few of them is reviewed below:

Academic Staff Union of Universities (ASUU)

Out of all the categories of trade and workers' union in the Nigerian economy, the academic members of staff were the first to organize themselves into a trade union. The academic staff in Nigerian Universities first organizes themselves into a trade union to promote their interest in 1965 when they formed the Nigerian Association of University Teachers (NAUT). The union then existed in the five universities (i.e. first and second generation universities) that were founded around 1960s namely; the University of

Ibadan (UI) though established in 1948 as University College Ibadan (UCI), but became a full-fledged university in 1962, the Ahmadu Bello Univeristy (ABU), Zaria 1962, University of Lagos (UNILAG), 1962, University of Nigeria Nsukka (UNN), 1955 and the University of Ife (now) Obafemi Awolowo University (OAU), Ile Ife, (1962). The union then had a total of 1,209 members (FMOE) cited in Jega, 1994). Its pioneer chairman was Professor Olumbe Basir of the University of Ibadan. According to Jega (ibid) the main focus of NAUT's activities in its formative years was limited to the welfare of its members. But by early 1970s with the increase in the number of universities in the country new issues crept into the demands of university academic staff among which were not only welfare matters, but also personal and collective intellectual integrity and perceptions of national self-reliance and good governance. Consequently, the Academic Staff Union of Universities (ASUU) was formed in 1978 and was registered in March 1978 under the Trade Union Decree of 1978. The union during the transition period from NAUT to ASUU was led by Dr. I. O Agbede from the University of Ife. By the time he took off in 1978, it had a total of 5,805 members drawn from ten branches. The objectives of the union were: First is organization of academic staff who is qualifies for membership; secondly, regulation of relationship between academic staff and employers, as well as among members; thirdly, establishment and maintenance of a high standard of academic performance and professional practice; fourthly, establishment and maintenance of just and proper conditions of service for its members.

Others are: advancement of the education and training of its members; provision of benefits and other assistance to the members as provided for in the constitution; encouragement of participation of its members in the affairs of the University system and of the nation at large; protection and advancement of the socio-economic and cultural interests of the nation and such other objects as lawful and are not inconsistent with the spirit and practice of trade unionism. Again, the goals and objectives of this union also transcend the particular interests of members.

All these and other objects have been at the center of ASUU struggle over the years. Like most trade unions, ASUU has employed strike on many occasions in the pursuit of its goals and objectives. For example, it went on strike in 1988, 1989, 1992, 2003, and so on. However, the use of strike by the union in pursuit of its goals has brought it into collision with the Federal Government and consequently earned it proscription. For instance, the union was proscribed in 1988, 1992 and 1996. Following its ban in 1992, it was operating, though illegally, under the name Academic Staff Union of Nigerian Universities (ASUNU). When the ban was lifted in 1993, it reverted to its former name, (ASUU). The ASUU is of course the most formidable union in Nigerian Universities. Its strength lies in the fact that whenever its members go on strike, the whole academic activities in the universities usually ground to a halt.

Senior Staff Association of Nigerian Universities (SSANU)

Another trade union in Nigerian universities is the Senior Staff Association of Nigerian Universities. It is an off shoot of the Senior Staff Association of Universities, Teaching Hospitals, Research Institutes and Associated Institutions of Nigeria (SSAUTHRAI). The SSAUTHRAI was formed at the national level in August 1978 by the non-teaching, senior staff of Universities, Polytechnics, Colleges of Educations, Research Institutes, Teaching Hospitals and Allied Institutions. The major aim of the union is to protect the interests of members on matters that border on work pay, conditions of service and professional development. In its early years through the early 1990s, it was the umbrella union for all non-teaching staff in the tertiary education sector. However, in 1985, there emerged the perception among University members of SSAUTHRAI that the Union was too unwieldy and could not therefore proficiently cater for their interests (Suowari, 2005). This perception was anchored on the fact that: The union was a gargantuan union serving the manifold interests of a plurality of unions with disparate conditions of service and orientations; it lacked homogeneity, unity of command and purpose, because of the character of its composition, and different salary structure, conditions of service were not easy to negotiate and industrial actions were difficult to coordinate. In spite of this emerging perception about the union in the middle of 1980s, it was still able to keep the various component sectors together. In the early 1990s however, the unity of the union could not be sustained. Owing to this, the divisive tendency which first reared its head in the mid-1980s became apparent and obvious. This eventually led to the formation of Senior Staff Association of Nigerian Polytechnics (SSANIP) in the year 2000 and the Senior Staff Union of Colleges of Education (SSUCOE) same year. In November, 2001 at the 5th National delegate Conference of SSUCOE held at the Niger State College of Education, Minna, the National President of the Union (Obawusi, 2001) puts the basis of their put out thus: It would be ridiculous for us to remain with SSAUTHRIAI which had bitten more than it can (*sic*) chew and which consisted of various establishments with dissimilar peculiarities, when in actual fact the name "Colleges of Education" does not feature in its letters. He further submitted, "we do not have or share conditions and schemes of service with Teaching Hospitals, Research Institutions, Fiber Institutions, Leather Institutions, National Library or Agricultural Centres. We do not also belong to allied institutions as was the case in SSAUTHRIAI because the positions of the Colleges of Education, the statues of the Provosts, Governing Councils and the Supervisory body – National Council for Colleges of Education (NCCE) are distinct in the Education industry in Nigeria. Thus, aliens can no longer be allowed to lead the staff unions in our sixty-four Colleges of Education in the present millennium and political dispensation in Nigeria" With the breakaway of all these sectors, the SSAUTHRIAI is only active in the Research Institutions, Allied Institutions and the Monotechnics in the country.

Non-Academic Staff Union (NASU) of Educational and Associated Institutions

The Non-Academic Union of Allied and Education Institutions (NASU) is the association that represents the non-teaching staff in Nigerian universities. The union came into existence in 1977 as one of the house unions, and in 1978 it was strengthened by decree No. 22 (Davison 1977). It was formally recognized as one of the 42 registered unions affiliated to Nigerian Labour Congress (NLC). Before the eventual birth of the union at the national level, three separate meetings were held by some founding members at the Cocoa Research Institute of Nigeria (CRIN) Ibadan in 1976, the Ahmadu Bello University, Zaria in 1977 and the University of Nigeria, Enugu campus in 1977. The follow up to these meetings was a submission of draft constitution on the 7th of November, 1977 to the Administrator of Trade Union in Nigeria. Thereafter, a registration certificate number 0063 dated 15th August, 1978 was issued to the union (Adebisi, 2010). The principal objectives of the union are the regulation of relations between workers and the Governing Councils of the university. The Governing Councils and workers or their union works toward eliminating exploitation in the workplace, as well as providing benefits to members. In the history of NASU, the union has fought a number of battles that have contributed to the welfare of their members. Osang (2002) says that in December 1992, when Prof Babatunde Fafunwa was Education Minister, the federal government approved a separate University salary table that favoured members of the Academic Staff Union of Nigerian Universities (ASUU), when NASU heard of the disparity in the salary table, they embarked on a 42-day nationwide strike to demonstrate their disapproval of the action of the federal government, favoured the academic staff over the non-teaching staff, who are a majority of the workforce. Osang states further that in 1999, NASU presented a memorandum to the federal government to press home their demand for improved terms and conditions of services that will correct the problem created by the National Minimum Wages of General Abubakar on Elongated University Salary Scale (EUSS) in favour of the civil service salary table. The EUSS was restyled as the Harmonized Tertiary Institutions Salary Structure (HATISS).

When President Olusegun Obasanjo assumed the mantle of leadership in Nigeria, the minimum wage was negotiated with the trade unions under the umbrella of the Nigeria Labour Congress (NLC). Individual workers are in a weak bargaining position with their employers when negotiating issue that affect them, but the union played dominant role of strengthening the position of workers in relation to employers The unions at the university negotiate for the welfare of their members and serve as a platform for social interaction and education among members, by organizing seminars, lectures, conference, and workshops. In addition, unions operate special loan plans to assist members in getting financial aid for emergency domestic needs Moreover, NASU has also improved working conditions and raised the dignity of members through schemes such as the welfare system that the union operates by deducting a percentage from members' salaries. The scheme assists members after retirement before. Some unions operate cooperative shops where essential commodities are sold at regulated prices. Some operate thrifts and credit societies where members can obtain loans with minimal interest and a convenient means of repaying.

TRADE UNION AND INFORMATION NEED

Union is an institution of representatives of employees formed for the purpose of maintaining and improving the employment conditions of its members. Trade Union has been severally defined by different authorities and scholars. I have realized that there may not be an all-encompassing perfect definition for Trade Union, however attempt by the Trade Union Act descriptively considerable thus: Trade Union is any combination of workers or employers, whether temporary or permanent, the purpose of which is to regulate the terms and conditions of employment of workers, whether the combination in question would or would not be an unlawful combination by reason of any of its purposes being in restraint of trade, and whether its purposes do or do not include the provision of benefits for its members. In a bid to further ascertain the legality of such 'combination, as described above, the Act provided for mandatory registration of same. Trade Union can safely be viewed as organization of workers who comes together with the aim of bettering their lots. Okafor and Malizu (2013) identified five major substantive issues which are at the heart of the workers' quest in uniting which include: wages and others material remuneration; working conditions; job security, working time and; respect and dignity.

By and large, Trade Union therefore, as organized group of employees in any nation plays several roles in alteration of sectors of economy and as contributor to dynamic and equitable growth. Hence the urgent need for it to be furnished with information resources in the right proportion. The economic value of trade union makes it suitable to categorize it with civil organizations and non-governmental organization. Furthermore, some of the perceived characteristics of trade union include the following:

1. It is an organization, which is expected to so function.
2. There must be employer and employees.
3. There must be a legal tool or documents regulation her activities.

4. There must be human mechanics (membership, leadership and followership).
5. Contractual framework.
6. There must be a 'databank' from where information is to be drawn for operations.

Trade unionists are the drivers of system or principles and theory of labour relations, the 'audible' and silent variables inclusive.

The most valuable resource of any growing organization is knowledge, which stems from data as demonstrated in the continuum in Figure 2.

The fundamentals and tenets of communication give rise to the need for carefulness in information handling at all levels, which its transfer is required. Information need could be occasioned by a number of reasons. Issa (2011) opined that information is fundamental to the life chances of the individual and the community. From the development perspective, society and people require at least six types of information thus: 'What', 'Who', 'When', 'Where', 'Why' and 'How'. Meanwhile, all these can be brought under three main categories as obtainable in Trade Unionism, thus: Legal information, operational information and administrative information.

1. **Legal Information (Foundation):** In a civil society, it is a wise to consider the legal implication of any action and inaction. It has the fundamental potency to make or mar the process and the resources committed therein a project. The trade union stakeholders will have need of this information so as not to play into the hand of the law. No matter how highly placed an institution is, a step in the wrong direction, particularly against the law is enough to humble such and strip it off the reputation and respect accordingly. Trade union has a good number of individuals, structures and institutions to contend with but within the confinement of law. The versatility and complexity of law therefore compel serious minds in trade union to embrace and value its currency, analysis and applications. There are legislations that regulate and affect the operations of trade unionists in Nigeria. They include but not limited to the followings: Constitution of the Federal republic of Nigeria; Trade Union Act; Trade Union (International Affiliation) Act; Trade Dispute Act; Workmen's Compensation Act; National Minimum Wage Act; Pension Reform Act; Nigeria Police Act; Personal Income Tax Act; Labour Act; Public Service Rule; Employee Compensation Act; National Industrial Court Act; Factory Act; International Labour Organization Conventions et.

Figure 2. Information management continuum

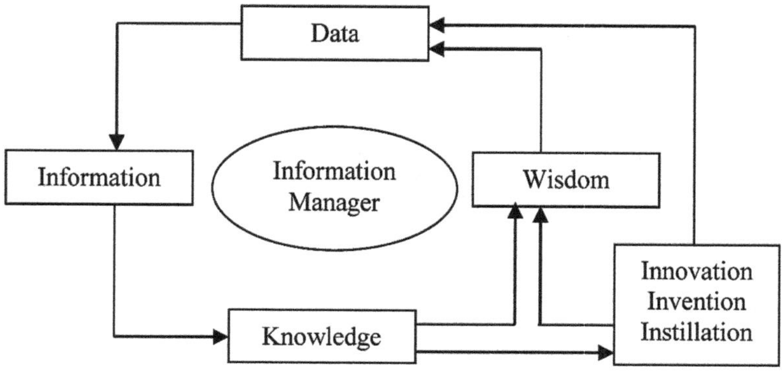

2. **Operational Information (Structure):** An ideal organization is expected to be up and running. The level of activities determines the degree of liveliness the members will put into the discharge of their responsibilities. To attain and sustain feat, there is a need for 'community' analysis of the existing programmes of the union vis-à-vis the members' disposition to it and how to improve on the same to carry everyone along in the Union. Hamzat (2012) asserted that every organization generates information, which they use for the daily running of the organization, as well as for projecting and planning purposes. There must be an avenue to pull the interest of everyone together in readiness for the array of activities. What will require the operational information is not far from that of the legal information as they cannot be separated. The former laid the foundation while the latter put in place a suitable structure and platform for operation. Operationally, it is necessary to compare note with sister unions within and outside the country, hence affiliation, partnership, globalization and internationalization. International Labour Organization is poised as the good platform for network and regulates the best practices in the world of trade unionism.
3. **Administrative Information (Furnish):** Trade unions have not only organized the masses with a view to improving material situation and condition of labour in general, but have taken a more revolutionary step to unite, disciple and educate masses with the view to abolish capitalism. In all of these, it is expedient that trade union generate records which are documents that institutions or individuals create or receive in the course of administrative and executive transactions. Many records are kept by an organization for only a short time, to provide evidence or information for the organization. Other records have a longer value, as evidence of or information about the actions or functions of the organization over time. However, those records worth preserving for their enduring value are called 'archives'. It is on this note that the managerial responsibilities in trade union which transcend human and finance is to be coordinated in a serious manner. Information created in the course of day to day activities may have to be tracked to technically furnish trade union administratively.

INFORMATION MANAGEMENT IN TRADE UNIONISM

Information Management (IM) was conceptualized when the need to mobilize intellectual resources for organizational productivity and profitability stared administrators in the face. As seemingly new as the concept appears, IM practice and fundamentals have been in existence from antiquities. The revolution trend of writing supports this analogy i.e. the transiting from papyrus to machine readable (Salman, 2009). Communication of information and ideals constitutes a major task of the contemporary society. Information Management is still the application of systematic and scientific control over identification, selection, acquisition and dispense of the refined data. Haastrup (2012) noted that open and close mechanisms as ingredients of communication system. A closed communication system according to him, is a rigid communication which does not encourage free information flow, while an open system is a flexible and unambiguous communication which allows for clarity of message and free information flow. The system helps to strengthen the employer-employee relationship. It is therefore structurally suicidal and organizationally insensitive to presume Trade Union can strive without effective Information Management. Information must be readily available to the right person at the prerequisite time and in the form it is required in order to balance the deficit of institutional and leadership defect. This is the exigent need of the moment in Trade Unionism.

INFORMATION SEEKING BEHAVIOR

The information seeking is more relative than absolute. It is not only seen in the local council offices, among professional people, post office, advice agencies, family and friends depending on the information they need to seek but also transcends these. Information seeking can be vied as a continuous process, involving active and passive behaviors; formal and informal communication. It is obvious in a cycle of creating, using and seeking information which can be viewed as series of stages which people move back and forth, and they may be actively, creating, using and seeking information concurrently (Borgman, 2000) Therefore, information seeking behavior refers to the pattern of response to the information need by person or group of persons.

The Information behavior is a sub-discipline within the field of information science. It describes how people need, seek, manage, give and use information in different contexts. It may also be described as information-seeking behavior or human information behaviour. Regardless of the nomenclature, Information carriers may include a variety based on the information seeking behavior and information-needs studies of various groups, in which the Trade Unionists are not an exception. The Information carriers may include a variety of channels, a variety of sources within the channels, and a variety of messages contained within these sources

According to general model of the information search process (ISP) by Kuhlthau (1993), The ISP consists of 6 stages thus: initiation stage, selection stage, exploration stage, formulation stage, collection stage and presentation stage. Wilson (1999) corroborated Kuhlthau's models as they are based on empirical research and have been tested in subsequent studies. It is important to examine the information seeking models as what users or seekers actually do when searching for information may be very different from what the information managers think they do.

SPECIALIZED INFORMATION SERVICES

The innovations in information communication technology have influenced libraries to serve better and adapt to the changes which has now become inevitable. The information institutions also changed drastically with service provision, collection development, human resource planning and training. It therefore becomes more necessary than ever to have a changed mind set towards service and the management of libraries. One of the major developments in the libraries and information services in lately has been the introduction and spread of electronic information sources (EIS) that is the product of Information and Communication Technology. The progress in information technology has offered today's information seekers different opportunities to access information resources in an increasing array, format and varied location.

Over times, it has been observed that conflicts capable of causing crisis are traceable to 'mis-information', 'information overload', 'insufficient information' or 'wrong information'. No conflict ever existed without having its root in, at least one of these. It is not enough to have well packaged information, until it gets to the right person in right format at the time; it does the society no good. The philosophy of 'censorship in librarianship' is literarily subsumed in "all good information materials are not good for all". This is another notion that explains further the significance of personalized users' identity management (PIM). PIM serves as a springboard for effectiveness and efficiency of specialized information service (SIS) particularly for the Trade Unionists. It is against this backdrop that special libraries with related mandate, especially Michael Imoudu National Institute of Labour Studies (MINILS) Information Resource Centre (Library), are poised to strategically identify and relevant information package for its users and potential users in the right format such services include but not limited to, Current Awareness Services (CAS), Selective Dissemination of Information (SDI), Book Reservation Service (BRS), Reference Service (RcS), Referral Service (RrS), Document Delivery Service (DDS), Indexing and Abstracting Services (IAS), Interlibrary Research and Resource Sharing Archival Service (AS), Reprographic Service (RS).These services are designed and dispensed in accordance with "terms and conditions" applicable i.e. there are conditions (majorly, category of membership) under which some of these services can be enjoyed by users, while there are services that everyone is entitled to equally.

THE CHALLENGES OF TRADE UNIONISM

There are challenges facing the trade union of late. They are so enormous that it has been of concern to the generality of the stakeholders in the sub-sector. Below is the highlight of those challenges.

1. Strong anti-union sentiments in national politics.
2. Lack of institutional support from the government systems.
3. Human resources capacity constraints to initiate and implement specialized projects in such areas like research, education, organizing, law, etc.
4. Weak leadership which fails to grow the movement using current potential. This also encourages the infiltration of the ideals of unionism by capitalists whose survival is under a serious threat.
5. Absence of Union consciousness and solidarity and the dominance of business unionism, which leads to divisions.
6. Restrictive legislative framework.
7. Weak trade union education programmes.
8. Poor structural linkages and networking between affiliates.

THE CHALLENGES OF DIGITAL SOURCES OF INFORMATION

Altering the outlook of source of information in trade unionism is a great deal of issue. In other words, creating effective digital source of information poses serious challenges for existing and future stakeholders. The integration of digital media into the handling of the traditional operations will not be straight jacket exercise. This is certainly because of the unique nature of digital information, which is less fixed, easily copied, and remotely accessible by multiple users simultaneously. Traditional library processes such as collection development and reference, though forming a potential basis for digital syndication, but will have to be revised and enhanced to accommodate the identified variance. Taking what we know about libraries and information centers as a starting point, we can begin to examine in more detail what the specific challenges might be.

Resource Discovery is one of the areas of challenges of the digital sources. Digital information on the Internet is characterized by the fact that digital documents can exist in several formats, possibly in several versions, in locations that are not yet fixed (cloud). A document or resource may exist at one network location one day and disappears the following day. Services spring up increasingly day in day out. These indexing services with unstructured "indexing languages" provide an essential service in assisting users to find information while the users are already noting that these services are becoming overburdened and that obtaining meaningful results can be frustratingly elusive, considering the growing concern of chaotic world of information leading undue information overload.

The Collection Development of digital contents is another area of challenge. Information resources' gatekeepers have considerable experience in digitization, although the profession has tended to call it something else. The "retrospective conversion" or 'retro-conversion" of printed library cards into machine-readable catalog (MARC) records represents one of the earliest widespread, digitization efforts. A lesson learnt here is surely that conversion of paper into digital is expensive, and requires high level of technical know-how and time-consuming. The cost/benefit analysis to provider and consumer of digital information resources for enhanced bibliographic access established the benefit of the expense, but it was acknowledged that the costs involved were higher than anticipated. Considerable study of what users – trade unionists need; how they use information, and whether digital formats serve their needs effectively is still required. Undertaking digitization initiatives without a fundamental understanding of user needs constitute misconceptions. Being digital is not necessarily commensurate with being useable.

There remains a significant challenge inherent in the preservation of digital sources. Pre-digital libraries have had to worry about climate control and the de-acidification of books, but the preservation of digital information will make these time-consuming and costly problems look easy. Digital storage media are "fragile", with a limited shelf life. Yet, the digital information on those storage media, even if they do survive will be rendered unreadable by obsolescence of technology. The fact that as information technology evolves, older systems disappear taking with them the ability to read the information they managed. To preserve digital information, digital libraries will continually have to "migrate" information from one digital hardware and software configuration to another. This by implication pre-exposes the content of this digital information bearing technologies to obsoleteness as well as the inestimable cost of further migration and transfer to catch up with the trends in the ever changing world of information and communication technology (ICT). Other areas are digital information administration, cost, copyright and licensing (Kuny and Cleveland, 2008)

The globalized era is characterized by speed, accuracy and precision in the production, organization, transfer, access, storage, retrieval and use of information contents, resources and knowledge assets. It is the world other where the influence, power, wealth and position of organization entirely depend on ability and capacity to create, use and translate information contents to socio-economic and infrastructural value. This therefore, among nations of the world is one of the most important factors through which the lapsing window period for Millennium Development Goals (MDGs) and Nigeria's projection of emerging as one of the twenty largest economies by the year 2020 (Vision 20-2020) are attainable.

Considering it nature, digital sources offer new levels of access to broader audience of users and new opportunities for library and information resources profession to advance in theory and practice. They contain information collections predominantly in electronic form. Electronic documents and resources have some special management requirements as compared to printed document, though one could be the function of the other. Yet they include infrastructure, acceptability, compatibility, access restrictions, readability, standardization, authorization, preservation, copyright, intractability, security etc. Increasingly emerging technologies and their program applications are surreptitiously taking over the scene in the creation, handling, transfer, storage, retrieval and deployment of knowledge contents. These technologies interface with human beings day in day out. The multifariousness and multi-functionality of these devices make the consciousness of content creation evasive to the creator, thereby making the bibliographic control of electronic resources cumbersome.

The new technologies and trade unionism's relationship have evolved rapidly in recent years. At the same time, ICT as across-cutting technology is characterized by its unique effects on everyday life, on scientific and technological developments, the economy in general and, last but not least, on work organization. As such, the impact of ICT goes well beyond the sector itself. As the International Labour Organization has observed: "While much attention has surrounded the volatile new world of the 'dot. com', this isa distraction: the true portent of ICT is how it will transform the 'old economy'" (ILO 2001).

The major challenges faced by the labour movement are:

1. There is dearth of comprehensive affiliates" database which can inform stakeholders and researchers about membership data.
2. Defect in the generation, coordination and storage of information to support policy advocacy, solidarity and lobbing. Therefore, ICT is not used to inform trade union strategies.
3. Absence of fulltime research office and capacity.
4. Lack of education on the explorative capacity of information and communication technology (ICT) equipment and application.
5. No effective interaction of Unions and their members through intranets or networking.
6. Insufficient fund to ensure full participation of members in trade union education.
7. No link between ICT and Labour Education (information and knowledge base) and ideological orientation of union representatives.
8. Filing is another problem in trade unions. Manually filing leads to shortage of space.
9. No generic software packages in use.
10. It is a free-market affair, where there is a free entry and exit. This can be tracked using ICT.
11. Leadership has poor ICT skills and a poor appreciation of the role of ICT in trade union work. Leaders still using manual systems to run.

CONCLUSION

Trade union positively impacts on the Nigeria society. Its influence is not only been enjoyed by its members alone but also been felt in all the nation's sectors; educationally, politically and economically. Recognizing the immense potent of information management and optimizing ICT in projecting good image of an organization. The marriage of the duo is therefore expedient on our drift towards an ideal society. ICT have emphatically increase productivity and profitability in small, medium and macroeconomic, whose employees constitute the membership of trade union. It is therefore a no push away for the trade union to holistically adopt and deplore, in full capacity, the use of ICT to facilitate effective administration, thereby attaining the feat of best practices.

RECOMMENDATIONS

Having attended to the sundry and affiliated issues in the information and the seeking behavior in the trade unionism, it was noted that the major players and observers in trade unionism have been predisposed to contemporary and future challenges of creation, storage, administration, retrieval, accessibility and evaluation of digital information contents as well as the quality control in the digital collection development and management. The recommendations thereafter are presented thus:

The indexing service developers are should intensify effort to establish a cost recovery model that will allow them to match capabilities with the growth of information on the Web. This could be done through advertising. Still, there is no guarantee that these services will provide high quality service to the general trade unionists for indefinite return on investment. A reasonable expectation is that there will be structural levels of service established. At a base level, anyone can access the database without charge but the results will be of limited usefulness and good information will be swamped by a flood of the bad, which is the practice anyway, whereby searching is not efficient. A higher level of use will attract a pay for better service such that there will be increased search functionality, better algorithms for ranking information, and higher speed access.

The techno-peasants are expected to taste "digital cake." This is the category of technologically-inclined user with relatively low skill. There are also important questions as to whether the existing technologies can scale sufficiently to accommodate growth in the number of users and the volume of information on the Internet. Users are discovering the quality of information retrieved from large heterogeneous databases may be lost in a flood of irrelevant results. Large centralized databases represent single points of failure and bottlenecks. Hence, there is the need to have a decentralized database to provide for specific subject area for efficiency and effectiveness.

Librarians organize knowledge through the processes of subject analysis and cataloguing-creating information about information or what is known as "metadata". A major challenge exists to develop methods of consistently and uniquely identifying and retrieving networked information, no matter what format they are or where they reside. Metadata standards are still in their infancy. The scope of initiatives and research coverage should focus more on expanding the capacity of metadata to provide promising ways forward. Meanwhile, given to the complexity of metadata issues, solution to the global resource discovery and digital content management problems remains distant.

Information resources professionals provide another role in supporting resource discovery, one in which digital technologies play only a small role. This is in providing a "trusted" service. This trust and authority is based upon making choices, evaluating information as a part of collection development and with a thorough understanding of what users need. The Librarians do not only create pathfinders and guides for their users, they *are* the pathfinders and guides. This is not far fetch from the fact that the roles of the information resource managers have totally change. Technology has redefined professional roles.

REFERENCES

Abiala, E. O. (2011). *Trade Union Laws and Practice in Nigeria: The Travails*. Ibadan: St Paul's Publishing House.

Adebisi, A. (2010). Labour Relations and Industrial Harmony in Nigerian Tertiary Educational Institutions In Omotoso Femi, Agagu A. A. and Abegunde Ola (Eds.), Governance, Politics and Policies in Nigeria: An Essay in Honour of Prof. Dipo Kolawole (pp. 438-464). Porto Novo: Editions SONOU d'Afrique.

Aina, L. O. (2004). *Library and Information Science Text for Africa*. Ibadan: Third World Information Services Limited.

Ananaba, W. (1979). The Trade Union in Africa. C. Nigeria: Nwamife Publishers Ltd..

Borgman, C. L. (2000). *From Gutenberg to the Global Information Infrastructure: Access to Information in the Network World*. Cambridge, MA: MIT Press.

Buckland, M. (1991). *Information and Information System*. New York: Praeger.

Davison, R. B. (1977). *Industrial Relations Decree: Questions and Answers to Explain the Law* (pp. 2–6). Zaria: Ahmadu Bello University Press.

Fashoyin, T. (1980). *Collective Bargaining in the Public Sector in Nigeria*. Nigeria: Macmillan Publishers.

Haastrup, A. A. (2012). Current Trends in Employee and Industrial Relations in Nigeria: Challenges for HR.

Hamzat, D. (2012). Fundamentals of Archives Management. Proceedings of Records and Information Management Awareness Foundation Quarterly Training (Q3), Lagos.

Inbun, B. Y., & Ngangan, K. (2012). The Disclosure of Information in Paupa New Guinea. *Labour Management in Development,* 2(4). Retrieved from http://ncdsnet.anu.edu.au

International Labour Organization. (2001). *World Employment Report 2001: Life at Work in the Information Society*. Geneva: International Labour Office.

Issa, A. O. (2011). A Study of Public Library status in Rural Information Dissemination. Retrieved from http://unilorin.edu.ng/publications/issaao

Jaja, C.A. (2012). Knowledge Management and its Enabling Resources for Transformative Development. *Proceedings of the Annual National Workshop of NLA*, Ilorin.

Jega, M. (1994). *Nigerian Academics under Military Rule*. Stockholm: Department of Political Science, Stockholm University.

Kuhlthau, C. C. (1993). *Seeking Meaning: A Process Approach to Library and Information Services*. Norwood, NJ: Ablex Publishing.

Kuny, T., & Cleveland, G. (2008). The Digital Library: Myths and Challenges. Retrieved from http://web.simmons.edu/~chen/488_sp2008/kuny.pdf

Nigeria Department of Labour. (1955). Annual Report *1954/55*

Obawusi, L. (2001). An Address" Delivered at the opening ceremony of The 5th National Delegate Conference of the Senior Staff Union of Colleges of Education held at the Niger State College of Education, Minna. November 7.

Okafor, G. O., & Malizu, C. F. (2013). The Media, Democracy and Trade Unionism in Nigeria. *Challenges and Prospects New Media and Mass Communication*, *17*, 2224–3275.

Okonkwo, R. (1993). The Nigeria Civil Service Union, 1919-*1922. The International Journal of African Studies*, *26*(3), 609–622.

Olusoji , J.G. , Oluwakemi , O. , & Uche , O. (2012). Trade Unions and Unionism in Nigeria: A Historical Perspective.

Osang, W. (2002). *The Trade Unions and their Impact on University Education in Nigeria* [M.Ed. Thesis]. University of Ibadan.

Suowari, D. U. (2005). *Contribution to Sectoral Development. The Roles and Responsibilities of the Senior Staff Association of Nigerian Universities*. SSANU.

Trade Union (Amendment) Act 2005. (2005).

Wilson, T. D. (1999). Models in Information Behaviour Research. *The Journal of Documentation*, *55*(3), 249–270. doi:10.1108/EUM0000000007145

Yesufu, T. M. (1982). *The Dynamics of Industrial Relations: The Nigerian Experience*. Ibadan: University Press Limited.

ADDITIONAL READING

Abrigo, C. M. (2009). *From Raw Materials to End Product*. Developing an Online Resource for the International Labour Organization.

Ahmed, I. B. (2009). Managing Research Libraries in Developing Economy. *The Information Manager*, *9*(2), 44–48.

Aina, L. O. (2004). *Library and Information Science Text for Africa*. Ibadan: Third World Information Services Limited.

Aliyu, M. B. (2012). An Introductory Text on the Types of Libraries. Offa: Correctman Printing Production

Kumar Ashish (2013). Assessing the Information Need and Information Seeking Behavior of Research Scholars of M.B.P.G. College: A Case Study.

Brown-Syed, C. (2011). Parents of Invention: The Development of Library Automation System in the Late 20th Century. *International Journal of Information Dissemination and Technology*, *2*(2).

Clooman, M. V., & Berger, S. E. (2003). The Continuing Development of Special Collections Librarianship. *Library Trends*, *52*(1).

Igwe, K. N., & Uzuegbu, C. P. (2013). Automation of Libraries and Information Centre. Lagos: Waltodany Visual Concepts International Labour Organization (2014). ILO Programme Implementation 2012 – 13: Report of the Director General (Appended to the Report of the Chairperson of the Governing Body). Geveva: International Labour Office.

Issa, A. O., Igwe, K. N., & Uzueghu, C. P. (2013). *Provision of Library and Information Services to Users in the Era of Globalization*. Lagos: Waltodanny Visual Concept.

Issa, A. O., Uzuegbu, C. P. & Nwosu, M. C. (2014). Entrepreneurship Studies and Practices in Library and Information Science. Umuahia: Zeh Communications

Modiredi, G. (2009). State of Information Technology in the Botswana Federation of Trade Unions: Challenges, Opportunities and Needs. Presented at International Training Centre of the ILO Program for Workers Activities (ACTRAV) on Trade Union Training on Information Management for Trade Union Organization, Research and Education Course, Turin, Italy.

Prensky, M. (2001). Digital Native, Digital Immigrants. *On the Horizon*, *9*(5), 1–6. Retrieved from http://www.marcprensky.com doi:10.1108/10748120110424816

Reitz, J. M. (2005). Dictionary for Library and Information Science. Westport: libraries Limited.

Tella, A., & Issa, A. O. (2012). *Library and Information Science in Developing Countries: Contemporary Issues. United State of America*. IGI Global. doi:10.4018/978-1-61350-335-5

Uhegbu, A. N. (2007). *The Information User: Issues and Themes*. Okigwe, Nigeria: Whytem Press.

KEYWORDS AND DEFINITIONS

Capacity Building: The planned identification, exploration, development and strengthening of human, financial and institutional resources towards an improved out rate, management, skills and other capabilities of an organization.

Collective Bargaining: Collective bargaining is a negotiation process between employer(s) and trade union targeted at agreeing to regulate working conditions.

Employee Welfare: The facilities, benefits, services offered by employer(s) to employees which need not be monetary but in any form that include allowances, housing, mobility, insurance, food, training etc. primarily to make life worthwhile for the employees.

International Labour Organization (ILO): ILO is a unique international tripartite structure which gives an equal voice to workers, employers and governments in ensuring that the views of social partners are closely reflected in labour standards and in shaping policies and programmes.

Social Security: A concept, policy or programme of government that focuses on the provision of economic assistance, usually monetary, to people faced with unemployment, disability, agedness and other forms of socio-economic threats.

Trade Union: The organization of workers, who unite to protect their common interests which include wages negotiation, working condition terms, regulation of relations between employees (its members) and employer, taking of collective action to enforce the terms of collective bargaining, raising new demands on behalf of its members and helping settle their grievances.

Chapter 11
Usability of Digital Resources: A Study of Francis Sulemanu Idachaba Library University of Agriculture Makurdi

Michael Terver Upev
University of Agriculture, Nigeria

Kwaghga Beetseh
University of Agriculture, Nigeria

Joy Asibi Idachaba
University of Agriculture, Nigeria

ABSTRACT

The chapter basically examined usability of digital library resources in Francis Sulemanu Idachaba Library University of Agriculture Makurdi, Nigeria. The population for the study comprised of the entire library staff of the Francis Sulemanu Idachaba Library University of Agriculture Makurdi. Sample for the study was 118 respondents drew from population of the library staff. Data was collected using structured question. The data collected was analysed using descriptive statistics; precisely arithmetic mean. Findings revealed that there are different types of library resources digitized in Francis Sulemanu Idachaba library. There are also criteria used for the selection of digitized library resources while there are challenges associated with the process of digitization of library resources of Francis Sulemanu Idachaba Library of University of Agriculture Makurdi. The chapter concluded that latest advancement in the field of information technology have compelled libraries to embrace automation because the facilities provided by automated libraries go far beyond the activities of traditional libraries. It was recommended that the library management should provide effective solution to the problems faced in the digitization unit by purchasing more equipment for the services such as digital camera, Photoshop software, a standby generating set, standardization on the supplied paper size and CD-ROMs, upgrading of the systems in other to meet the needs of modern day's technologies.

DOI: 10.4018/978-1-5225-0296-8.ch011

INTRODUCTION

All libraries were established for the purpose of acquiring information resources and making them available for their customers. Due to the fragile nature of some library resources, their age, values, type of chemical components or materials used for the production, sizes and shapes of information resources could really determine the condition under which they could be stored. The need for storage and preservation of electronic resources also required specialized methods and skills to be able to preserve its values and contents. Meanwhile, for the purpose of preserving contents of valuable resources in the libraries, this opened up different ways, ideas and methods of preservation of library resources in all form. Association of Research Libraries (ARL) (1995) defines digital libraries as libraries whose collections are all stored in digital format and accessible via computer, the internet.

This digital content can be stored locally or be accessible remotely. Furthermore, Pearow (2000) defines a digital library as: “a library in which a significant proportion of the resources are available in machine readable format accessible by means of computers. The digital contents may be locally held or accessed remotely via computer networks. Reitz (2007) opined that in the libraries process of digitization began with the catalog, moved to periodical indexes and abstracting services, then to periodicals and large reference works and finally to book publishing.

Association of Research Libraries (1995) further emphasized that digital library is not a single entity and therefore required technology to link the resources of many, the linkage between digital libraries and information services are transparent to end users, also, digital collections are not limited to document surrogates and therefore extends to digital artifacts formats. With the above description by Association of Research Libraries (1995), it suggests that digital library can also be referred to as electronic library or virtual library since their collections can both be accessed electronically via internet resources. Having all these resources at its disposal suggest that virtual library is not only exciting but also an improvement of what obtains in the past due to better utilization of resources and faster speed of accessibility. In agreement with the above statement, Cleveland (1998) referred to digital libraries as organizations that provide resources such as specialized staff, to select, structure, offer intellectual access to interprets, distribute, preserve the integrity of and ensure the persistent over time of collections of digital works so that they are readily and economically available for use by a defined community or set of community.

This suggests that digital libraries specifically required both the skills of librarians as well as those of computer scientists to be able to contribute their part for the libraries to achieve their goals. Without specialized skilled librarians who are adequately trained to use the digitization resources, the process may not function well. Digital libraries may not need to be a single, completely digital system that provides instant access.

The World Wide Web (www) is a powerful platform for providing access to multimedia information. Consequently, the WWW has been used as the platform for the deployment of digital libraries (DLs). The concept of digital library refers to collections of electronic resources consisting of text, audio, visual, graphics, and animations in nature that are accessible through the aid of digital technologies. Ideally, a digital library should provide users access to electronic information resources via electronic means. However, this definition also includes electronic resources (such as databases on standalone PCs, information on CD-ROMs, etc.) that may not be accessible through the Internet or other networks. Digital library collections may be born (digital originated or through the process of digitisation from existing print materials).

Digital libraries are increasingly being implemented by several agencies, both in government and the private sector. This impetus is attributed to, among other factors, the fact that DLs might make research easier for scholars, and may also ease budgetary constraints associated with the acquisition of print resources. Moreover, DL might solve preservation problems, or help libraries extend collections into new media. In addition, it is believed that DLs will help society to make information more available, raise its quality, and increase its diversity.

There are several examples of digital libraries. For example, Bartleby Library – Great Books Online (http://www.bartleby.com/) is the preeminent Internet publisher of literature, reference and verse. Similarly, Library of Congress (http://www.loc.gov/) provides entrance to the catalogue and a number of collections, projects and a large directory of links. On the other hand, the Collaborative Digital Reference Service (CDRS) (http://lcweb.loc.gov/rr/digiref/) is a DL project involving several institutions, and provides professional reference service to researchers through an international, digital network of libraries and related institutions. The other well-known digital library is the New York Public Library (http://digital.nypl.org/), which provides a rich site, mostly concentrating on digitised special collections of texts and images. Similarly, he United States National Library of Medicine (NLM) (http://www.nlm.hih.gov/hinfo.html) is the world's largest medical library and online system. It includes MEDLINE, MEDLINEplus, and links to numerous other health-related resources, including research programs for computational biology and medical informatics. Similarly, University of California, Berkeley (http://sunsite.berkeley.edu/), provides a wealth of digitised collections.

Digital libraries emerged largely in the 1990s, because of the revolution in Internet and WWW technologies. However, the foundation stone for digital libraries may have been laid in 1945 when Bush envisioned an automated system that would store information, including books, personal records and articles. Bush developed a system known as memex system that would allow a user to view stored information from several different access points and look at several items simultaneously. Similarly, in 1950, while driving to work, Douglas (1950) started thinking about how complicated civilisation had become and what humans were going to do about managing this complex new world that technology had helped create. He hypothesised at the time that computers could be used to automate symbol-handling tasks, and thus help people think faster, better, about more complex problems. The ideas of Bush and Engelbert led Ted Nelson to coin the term hypertext to describe a system that linked bits of knowledge in the ways that people think, rather than in hierarchical groupings (Allard, 2000). The evolution of the digital library is tied to hypertext searching.

Information and Communication Technology have greatly improved library services. Everyday new technological advances affect the way information is handled in libraries and information centers. The impacts of new technologies are felt by libraries in every aspect. Computing technology, communication technology and mass storage technology are some of the areas of continuous development that reshape the way libraries access, retrieve, store, manipulate and disseminate information to users. The terms digital library, electronic library, cybrary and virtual library are used to refer to vast collections of information to which people gain access remotely.

Usability is the ease of use and learnability of a human-made object. The object of use can be a software application, website, book, tool, machine, process, or anything a human interacts with. A usability study may be conducted as a primary job function by a *usability analyst* or as a secondary job function by designers, technical writers, marketing personnel, and others. It is widely used in consumer electronics, communication, and knowledge transfer objects (such as a cookbook, a document or online help) and mechanical objects such as a door handle or a hammer.

Usability includes methods of measuring usability, such as needs analysis and the study of the principles behind an object's perceived efficiency or elegance. In human-computer interaction and computer science, usability studies the elegance and clarity with which the interaction with a computer program or a web site (web usability) is designed. Usability differs from user satisfaction and user experience because usability also considers usefulness.

STATEMENT OF THE PROBLEM

Digitization of library resources and operations ensures quick services delivery and faster information accessibility. Digitization of library resources also provides both the librarians and users of resources the opportunity to have a convenient access to typically large amount of digital information resources such as e-journals, e-books, internet resources, databases and among others. Digitization of resources opened up opportunities in Nigerian University libraries for an improved searching and manipulation of information, improved facilities for information sharing, timely access to information and improved collaboration.

However, observation has shown that in Francis Idachaba Library, University of Agriculture Makurdi, library resources are not digitized. Interaction with most of the students in the university revealed that students' poor academic performance is also attributed to poor library resources. Students still relay on non-digitized resources such as books on shelves and catalog. The resources that facilitate information access to students are adequately put in place and information is not easily made available to students. This has posed a lot of difficulties to students. The study and reading habits of students become dull. This reflects on their examination results.

Therefore, it is a bid to explore the usability of digital resources institution: A study of Francis Sulemanu Idachaba Library University of Agriculture Makurdi that the study becomes necessary.

Objectives of the Study

The broad objectives of the study will be:

1. Identify types of library resources digitized in Francis Sulemanu Idachaba library that enhance students' academic performance in University of Agriculture Makurdi.
2. Ascertain the criteria used for the selection of library resources digitized that enhance students' academic performance in Francis Sulemanu Idachaba Library, University of Agriculture Makurdi.
3. Investigates the processes of digitization of library resources that enhance student's academic performance in in Francis Sulemanu Idachaba Library, University of Agriculture Makurdi.
4. Find out the challenges and problems face in the process of digitization of library resources that enhance students' academic performance in Francis Sulemanu Idachaba Library of University of Agriculture Makurdi.
5. Solution to curb the problems of digitization of library resources that enhance students' academic performance in Francis Sulemanu Idachaba Library of University of Agriculture Makurdi

Research Questions

The following research questions will be answered in the study.

1. What types of library resources are digitized to enhance students' academic performance in Francis Sulemanu Idachaba library?
2. What are the criteria for the selection of library resources for digitization digitized to enhance students' academic performance in Francis Sulemanu Idachaba Library University of Agriculture, Makurdi
3. What are the processes of digitization of library resources digitized to enhance students' academic performance in Francis Sulemanu Idachaba Library, University of Agriculture Makurdi?
4. What type of challenges and problems faced in the process of digitization of library resources digitized that enhance students' academic performance in Francis Sulemanu Idachaba Library?
5. What are the solutions to curb the challenges and problems of digitization of library resources digitized that enhance students' academic performance in Francis Sulemanu Idachaba Library, University of Agriculture Makurdi.

Materials and Methods

The research covers University of Agriculture Makurdi with the population of 90 library staff. The University of Agriculture, Makurdi (UAM) is one of the two Universities of Agriculture established by the Federal Government in January, 1980.

There will be no sampling technique for the study. The entire population 90 library staff of University of Agriculture, Makurdi will be used in the study as sample size because the population size could be handled effectively.

Data was collected using a structured questionnaire titled "Usability of Digital Resources and Academic Performance Questionnaire 'UDRAPQ". The questionnaire was divided into two parts; 1 and 2. Part 1 deals with demographic data of respondents. Part 2 has 5 sections and was used to elicit information on usability of digital resources and academic performance. The questionnaire was an open-ended-structured with restricted responses options of strongly agree (SA), agree (A), disagree (D) and strongly disagree (SD) with corresponding values of 4, 3, 2 and 1 respectively.

The instrument was validated by 2 experts in Library science in University of Agriculture Makurdi. In order to ensure the reliability of the instrument, a sample size of 20 library staff of the Benue state University who were not included in the sample for the main study were used. The purpose of this was to test-try the instruments that will be used in the study. A reliability coefficient of 0.89 was found ideal for the study.

Data collected was analyzed using descriptive statistics; precisely arithmetic mean. Bench mark for decision making was 2.50 (4+3+2+1=10/4=2.50).

Presentation of Results

Table 1 shows the demographic data of respondents. The result on sex revealed that majority were male (74.8%) and the women were 25.2%. Those who were ages ranged 40-45 were majority (62.2%) while

Table 1. Biodata of respondents

S/N	Item	Frequency (f)	N	Percentage (%)
Sex				
1	Male	61	90	74.8
	Female	29		25.2
Age				
2	25-30	5	90	4.2
	30-35	6		6.0
	35-40	11		9.2
	40-45	46		62.2
	45-50	11		9.2
	51 and above	11		9.2
Educational Qualification				
3	SSCE	30	90	33.9
	OND	50		53.3
	NCE	2		1.7
	HND	2		2.6
	B. Sc	4		3.0
	M. Sc	2		2.6
	MBA	1		1.9
Marital Status				
4	Married	89	90	94.1
	Divorce	1		5.9

Source: Field survey, 2015.

4.2% were age ranged between 25-30. The result on educational qualification show that OND forms majority with 53.3% while 1.9% had MBA. Finally, 94.1% were married while only 5.9% divorced.

Results in Table 2 show types of resources digitalized in Francis Sulemanu Idachaba library, University of Agriculture Makurdi. The most available resources were book scanner (3.54), digital audio (3.62), digital television (3.67) and graphic tablets. This indicates that the types of resources digitalized that enhance students' academic performance in Francis Sulemanu Idachaba library, University of Agriculture Makurdi are grossly inadequate

In Table 3, respondents rated all the items with mean above 2.50. Overall purpose and educational significance had a mean of 3.04, validity, timeliness or permanence, and appropriateness of material (2.76), contribution the subject matter makes to the curriculum and the interests of the students (2.86), high artistic quality and /or literary style (2.88), high artistic quality and /or literary style (2.88), religious, ethnic and cultural backgrounds (2.60), critical reading, listening, viewing and thinking (2.72), Variety of format (2.71), value commensurate with cost and /or need (3.15), collection needs (3.07), quality of information (4.87) and price 2.75). This means that there are criteria for used for the selection of library resources digitized that enhance students' academic performance.

Table 2. Respondents mean rating on the types of resources digitalized that enhance students' academic performance in Francis Sulemanu Idachaba library, University of Agriculture Makurdi

S/N	Item Statement	SD	D	A	SA	N	Mean	Std. Dev.	Remarks
1	Book scanner	6	6	9	97	90	3.54	.83	Agree
2	Analog digital converter	71	9	2	8	90	1.41	.91	Disagree
3	Digital audio	7	14	13	84	90	3.62	.84	Agree
4	Digital reformatted	22	16	28	24	90	1.70	1.13	Disagree
5	Digital television	9	9	11	89	90	3.67	.79	Agree
6	Frame grabber	22	16	28	24	90	1.70	1.13	Disagree
7	Graphic tablets	10	5	4	99	90	3.47	.92	Agree
8	Raster grapher	71	9	2	8	90	1.41	.91	Disagree
9	Raster image	75	5	2	8	90	1.36	.90	Disagree

Source: Field survey, 2015.

Table 3. Respondents mean rating on the criteria used for the selection of library resources digitized that enhance students' academic performance

S/N	Item Statement	SD	D	A	SA	N	Mean	Std. Dev	Remarks
1	Overall purpose and educational significance	13	8	28	41	90	3.04	1.05	Agree
2	Validity, timeliness or permanence, and appropriateness of material	17	12	26	35	90	2.76	1.09	Agree
3	Contribution the subject matter makes to the curriculum and the interests of the students	19	10	37	24	90	2.86	1.14	Agree
4	High artistic quality and /or literary style	22	16	28	24	90	2.88	1.13	Agree
5	Religious, ethnic and cultural backgrounds	19	15	29	27	90	2.60	1.13	Agree
6	Critical reading, listening, viewing and thinking	13	8	21	48	90	2.72	1.08	Agree
7	Variety of format	13	8	31		90	2.71	1.11	Agree
8	Value commensurate with cost and /or need	19	15	29	27	90	3.15	1.09	Agree
9	Collection needs	16	12	30	32	90	3.07	1.06	Agree
10	Quality of information	21	17	24	28	90	4.87	1.91	Agree
11	Price	17	12	26	35	90	2.75	1.09	Agree

Source: Field survey, 2015.

Table 4 shows the process of digitization. Respondents rated policy enactment with mean of (2.76), planning (2.86), acquisition of appropriate technology (2.88), administrative decision on the procedure to be adopted (2.73), sensitization, psychological preparation and retraining of staff (2.60). This is an indication that there are processes of digitalization of library resources that enhance students' academic performance.

In Table 5, all respondents rated the items with mean above 2.50. Deadline had 2.87, technical and Financial Challenges (2.80), manpower (2.66), power supply (2.90) and knowledge Gap had 3.73). This result indicates that the items are problems and challenges of digitization of library resources that enhance students' academic performance.

Table 4. Respondents mean rating on the respondents mean rating on the process of digitalization that enhance students' academic performance

S/N	Item Statement	SD	D	A	SA	N	Mean	Std. Dev	Remarks
1	Policy enactment	17	12	26	35	90	2.76	1.09	Agree
2	Planning, budgeting and monitoring	19	10	37	24	90	2.86	1.14	Agree
3	Acquisition of appropriate technology	22	16	28	24	90	2.88	1.13	Agree
4	Administrative decision on the procedure to be adopted	71	8	3	8	90	2.73	.91	Agree
5	Sensitization, psychological preparation and retraining of staff	19	15	29	27	90	2.60	1.13	Agree

Source: Field survey, 2015.

Table 5. Respondents mean rating on the challenges of library digitization that enhance students' academic performance in Nigeria

S/N	Item Statement	SD	D	A	SA	N	Mean	Std. Dev	Remarks
1	Deadline	21	17	24	28	90	2.87	1.09	Agree
2	Technical and Financial Challenges	17	12	24	37	90	2.80	1.14	Agree
3	Manpower	19	11	31	29	90	2.66	1.15	Agree
4	Power Supply	17	16	29	28	90	2.90	1.14	Agree
5	Knowledge Gap	4	3	9	74	90	3.73	.74	Agree

Source: Field survey, 2015.

Table 6 shows that respondents agreed framework that world separate broadcast content providers from the content distributers (2.72), sensitization of government policy maker's stakeholders and officials will contribute positively to the process (2.71),

Government should help subsidize the cost of acquiring new sets or the set top boxes to create greater accessibility (3.16), distance learners program (3.04), library cooperation (2.96) and multiple users at

Table 6. Respondents mean rating on the solution to curb the problems of digitization of library resource that enhance students' academic performance

S/N	Item Statement	SD	D	A	SA	N	Mean	Std. Dev.	Remarks
1	Framework that world separate broadcast content providers from the content distributers.	13	8	21	48	90	2.72	1.08128	Agree
2	Sensitization of government policy maker's stakeholders and officials will contribute positively to the process.	13	8	31	38	90	2.71	1.11420	Agree
3	Government should help subsidize the cost of acquiring new sets or the Set Top Boxes to create greater accessibility	19	15	29	27	90	3.16	1.09042	Agree
4	Distance learners program	13	8	28	41	90	3.04	1.04839	Agree
5	Improved searching for the user	16	12	30	32	90	3.08	1.06241	Agree
6	Library cooperation	16	12	30	32	90	2.96	1.06961	Agree
7	Multiple users at a time without purchasing multiple copies	18	15	24	33	90	2.66	1.12341	Agree

Source: Field survey, 2015.

a time without purchasing multiple copies (2.66) were solutions to curb the problems of digitization of library resource that enhance students' academic performance in Francis Sulemanu Idachaba library, University of Agriculture Makurdi.

DISCUSSION OF FINDINGS

Results on question one in Table 2 shows that the types of resources digitalized that enhance students' academic performance in Nigeria in Francis Sulemanu Idachaba library, University of Agriculture Makurdi. The most important type that enhance students' academic performance had a mean rating of 3.67 while the fewer type was 1.36. The findings confirm with a study conducted by Chimah and Nwokocha (2015) on Categories, Availability and Awareness of Electronic Information Resources by Postgraduate Library Users in South East Nigerian Federal Universities. The finding shows that one of the Universities (University of Nigeria Nsukka) has most of the electronic information resources investigated in this study. The figures and percentages are as follows: UNN – 28 (70%); FUTO – 13 (32%); NAUA – 11 (27%); and MOUAU – 6 (15%). Generally, the data shows that while UNN has most of the electronic information resources, other universities have just few of them. However, the interview with head of ICT Unit at UNN shows that most of the EIRs of University of Nigeria Nsukka are available at the Digital Library of the university being co-sponsored by Mobile Telephone Network (MTN) and UNN.

The study has clearly confirmed that e-journals, e-books, etc., through the digital library for academic staff's and research student's use. This may be due to the policy of the universities to drive all their activities with information and communication facilities. This corroborates Mutula and Ojedokun's [7] view that highlighted databases, e-journals, e-newspapers, e-books, e-mail and Internet facilities as information resources available through e-library.

Result on question two in Table 3 that there are criteria for used for the selection of library resources digitized that enhance students' academic performance in Nigeria. The major criteria was the quality of information 4.87 while the least was religious, ethnic and cultural backgrounds (2.60). The findings are similar to Guidelines for the Selection of Digital Resources as revealed by Harward-Tilton Memorial Library on (2013). These guidelines were:

- **Policy Criteria:** Overall, the selection of digital formats should reflect the library's other practices for collection development and acquisitions.
- **Service Criteria:** Overall, the selection of a digital resource should conform to Tulane University's general plans for establishing a digital information environment. Staffing and training levels should be considered.
- **Technical Criteria:** Overall, the selection of electronic databases should reflect the library's current or planned level of technical resources, as well as its current or planned level of in house technical support.
- **Cost Criteria:** Costs are an important concern and potential purchases should also be assessed with regard to the relative value of the format considered versus access through some alternative means, availability of options or price differences relative to consortium availability, lease and specified number of users.

- **Licensing Criteria:** The full list of licensing criteria from the Association of Research Libraries (ARL) Principles for Licensing Electronic Resources, to which the library adheres, can be found at http://www.arl.org/sc/marketplace/license/licprinciples.shtml.

Result on question 3 Table 4 shows the process of digitization. Acquisition of appropriate technology was the highest process (2.88) while sensitization, psychological preparation and retraining of staff (2.60) was the least process. This finding is similar to a study conducted by Ayodeji, Matthew Paris and Fabunmi on digitization of library resources: Challenges and implications for policy and planning (2002). They submitted that Administrative decision on the procedure to be adopted in digitizing library resources. Decision has to be made on the mode of operation, whether to just establish links with existing digital libraries or to digitize in-house or to contract it out. There is a need to establish time limit for the project. Similarly, the authors noted that sensitization, psychological preparation and retraining of staff *i*s another process of digitizing library resources in most places the staff will like to resist the digitization project. It is a common thing for people to resist change, just for the fear of the unknown. The library staff may fear that the success of the project may affect their jobs adversely. Those who are not computer literate may not be willing to adjust. All these categories of people have their genuine reasons to resist. It is the responsibility of the library management to educate them and allay their fears.

Results on question five in Table 5 knowledge Gap was the major problem of library digitization with mean of 3.73 while the least problem was manpower with mean rating of 2.66). he findings are in line with a study carried out by Ihechu and Uwaoma (2000) on the Challenges of Digitization of Broadcasting in Nigeria. The findings revealed that manpower and power supply are the major challenges of digitization in Nigeria. According to the authors, as the complex and fragile equipment are coming in, there is need for matching manpower. The task of training and retraining personnel to fit into the digital process pose a challenge to the race. On the other hand, the process will definitely increase the number of stations. Thus, the existing broadcast personnel who may likely fit in may not be enough to fill the spaces and as such, pose an initial challenge. However, some of the existing personnel may be adversely affected too. Those who may not be able to understand the flexibility and, or, cope with the fragility of the new technology may be thrown to the labour market. That will eventually add to the burden of unemployment that has bedeviled the nation in recent times. The authors further stressed that the power sector in the country is nothing to write home about. The country has spent huge sums of money, though not accountably, to revive the power supply to no avail. Consequently, the sound of generators at every corner of a Nigerian street calls for alarm. But the people have to use these generators to at least, "live life". Also, all the companies in the country - petrol stations, telecom, banks, manufacturers, broadcast organizations, etc., rely on standby generators to carry on their businesses. In the long run, it impacts on the cost of production or service rendering costs. The charges are later transferred to the consumers. It would be apt to point here, that the epileptic power supply and the invariable dependence on generators pose big challenges to the digitization process. It would create high cost of programme production and presentation.

Results of question five in Table 5 show that Government should help subsidize the cost of acquiring new sets or the set top boxes to create greater accessibility 3.16 while the least solution was multiple users at a time without purchasing multiple copies with mean of 2.66 was solutions to curb the problems of digitization of library resource in Francis Sulemanu Idachaba library, University of Agriculture Makurdi. The finding confirms the findings of Ihechu and Uwaoma (2000. According to the authors, government should help subsidize the cost of acquiring new sets or the Set Top Boxes to create greater accessibility. The position of Ibulubo, (2008:2) corroborates the above submissions, thus: "Stakeholders would discuss how to implement digital mode of broadcast, best sensitization methods to employ as well as adopt a policy draft that would serve as a guide to the activities in the digital era".

CONCLUSION

This study will attempt to evaluate the services of digitization unit in the Francis Sulemanu Idachaba Library. The challenges faced in the process of digitization and the way forward. The latest advancement in the field of information technology have compelled libraries to embrace automation as the facilities provided by automated libraries go far beyond the activities of traditional libraries. Digitization has immensely enhanced the effectiveness of library services including efficient organization and retrieval of information resources.

RECOMMENDATIONS

Findings from this study will necessitated the following recommendations for efficient digitization services in the Library:

1. The library management to provide effective solution to the problems faced in the digitization unit by purchasing more equipment for the services such as digital camera, Photoshop software, a standby generating set, standardization on the supplied paper size and CD-ROMs, upgrading of the systems in other to meet the needs of modern day's technologies.
2. They also need to provide enough money for the rebinding of materials and to also purchase additional modern computers.
3. To effectively tackle the problems and challenges faced by the staff of the unit, more training opportunities should be provided for the staff of digitization unit such as workshops and seminars, conferences on digitization of resources, training on software management, maintenance of server and the D-space database management. Training will afford them opportunity to acquire skills, such as the technical skills needed to perform their duties efficiently, interpersonal skills needed to interact with fellow staff and users of the library resources. When conceptual skills are acquired it will afford them the opportunity to acquire holistic knowledge and an understanding of their tasks and be able to devise a means to achieve organizational goals.
4. Digitization unit needed more staff to efficiently handle the workload in the section.
5. Provision should be made to acquire more UPS to sustain the power failure. While more money should be made available for the expansion of limited available space in other to facilitate activities and work in the library.
6. The library should develop a copyright mechanism that will allow them to provide information without violating copyright law called copyright management by restricting users from duplicating intellectual contents from the web. The library does not own the copyright of the materials they hold and may not ever be able to freely digitize and provide access to the organization digital repositories. Therefore, libraries need to obtain permission from the authors to fully publish the content to the web.

7. The Library management authority should acquire the right model of Scanner or Book Scanner and also carry out detail or comprehensive assessment of resources both in print and in softcopies before digitization process takes place.
8. Adequate fund should be made available by the management to enable the librarian in charge purchase further necessary resources for the progress of the unit

REFERENCES

Aina, L.O., & Mutula, S.M. (2007). Opportunities for Electronic Publishing In T. Mkandawire & A. Mlambo (Eds.), Africa Scholarly Publishing. Oxford: INASP.

Association of Research Libraries. (1995). *Appendix II. Definition and Purpose of a Digital Library.* Retrieved from http://www.arl.org/resources/pubs/mmproceedings/1 26mmappen2.shtml

Borgman, C. L. (2003)Designing Digital Libraries for Usability. In A.P. Bishop, N.A. Van House & B.P. Buttenfield (Eds.), Digital Library Use Social Practice in Design and Evaluation (pp. 86 -118). Cambridge: The MIT Press.

Candela'L. et al. (2008) *The DELOS digital library reference model- foundations for digital libraries.* Retrieved from http://www.delos.info/files/pdf/ReferenceModel/DELOS_DLReferenceModel_0.98.pdf

Chepesuik, R. (1997). The future is here: America's libraries go digital. *American Libraries*, *2*(1), 47–49.

Ibulubo, T. G. (2008). Nigeria to switch to digital broadcasting. *Africa News.*

Ihechu, I.I. Uwaoma Uche (2000). The Challenges of Digitization of Broadcasting in Nigeria.

National library of Australia. (2009) *Collection digitization policy.* Retrieved from www.nla.gov.au/policy/digitization.html

Pearrow, M. (2000). Website Usability Handbook. Rockland, MA: Charles River media.

Reitz, J. (2007). Digital library ODLIS: Online Dictionary for Library and Information Science. Retrieved From http://www.iu.com/odlisd.cf

ADDITIONAL READING

Barnard, T. D. F. (Ed.), (1967, April 21-23). Library Buildings: design and fulfillment. Papers read at the Week-end Conference of the London and Home Counties Branch of the Library Association, Hastings. London: Library Association (London and Home Counties Branch)

Belanger, T. (1983). Lunacy & the Arrangement of Books. New Castle, Del.: Oak Knoll Books.

Bieri, S., & Fuchs, W. (2001). *Bibliotheken bauen: Tradition und Vision Building for Books: traditions and visions*. Basel: Birkhäuser.

Ellsworth, R. E. (1973). *Academic Library Buildings: a guide to architectural issues and solutions*. Boulder: Associated University Press.

Fraley, R. A., & Anderson, C. L. (1985). *Library Space Planning: how to assess, allocate, and reorganize collections, resources, and physical facilities*. New York: Neal-Schuman Publishers.

Irwin, R. (1947). The National Library Service [of the United Kingdom]. London: Grafton & Cox.

Lewanski, R. C. (1967). Library Directories [and] Library Science Dictionaries, in Bibliography and Reference Series. Santa Barbara, Calif.: Clio Press.

Mason, E. (1980). *Mason on Library Buildings*. Metuchen, N.J.: Scarecrow Press.

Monypenny, P., & Garrison, G. (1966). *The Library Functions of the States [i.e. of the U.S.A.]: Commentary on the Survey of Library Functions of the States.*

KEY TERMS AND DEFINITIONS

Digital Library: A library in which a significant proportion of the resources are available in machine readable format accessible by means of computers. The digital contents may be locally held or accessed remotely via computer networks. Reitz (2007) opined that in the libraries process of digitization began with the catalog, moved to periodical indexes and abstracting services, then to periodicals and large reference works and finally to book publishing. Association of Research Libraries (1995) further emphasized that digital library is not a single entity and therefore required technology to link the resources of many, the linkage between digital libraries and information services are transparent to end users, also, digital collections are not limited to document surrogates and therefore extends to digital artifacts formats. With the above description by Association of Research Libraries (1995), it suggests that digital library can also be referred to as electronic library or virtual library since their collections can both be accessed electronically via internet resources. Having all these resources at its disposal suggest that virtual library is not only exciting but also an improvement of what obtains in the past due to better utilization of resources and faster speed of accessibility. In agreement with the above statement, Cleveland (1998) referred to digital libraries as organizations that provide resources such as specialized staff, to select, structure, offer intellectual access to interprets, distribute, preserve the integrity of and ensure the persistent over time of collections of digital works so that they are readily and economically available for use by a defined community or set of community. This suggests that digital libraries specifically required both the skills of librarians as well as those of computer scientists to be able to contribute their part for the libraries to achieve their goals. Without specialized skilled librarians who are adequately trained to use the digitization resources, the process may not function well. Digital libraries may not need to be a single, completely digital system that provides instant access.

Usability: The ease of use and learnability of a human-made object. The object of use can be a software application, website, book, tool, machine, process, or anything a human interacts with. A usability study may be conducted as a primary job function by a *usability analyst* or as a secondary job function by designers, technical writers, marketing personnel, and others. It is widely used in consumer electronics, communication, and knowledge transfer objects (such as a cookbook, a document or online help) and mechanical objects such as a door handle or a hammer. Usability includes methods of measuring usability, such as needs analysis and the study of the principles behind an object's perceived efficiency or elegance. In human-computer interaction and computer science, usability studies the elegance and clarity with which the interaction with a computer program or a web site (web usability) is designed. Usability differs from user satisfaction and user experience because usability also considers usefulness.

Chapter 12
Information Need and Seeking Behavior of Farmers in Laduba Community of Kwara State, Nigeria

Femi Titus Akande
Librarian, Nigeria

Akinade Adebowale Adewojo
Nigerian Stored Products Research Institute, Nigeria

ABSTRACT

The chapter present the report of a study that examined information needs and seeking haviour of farmers in Laduba community, Kwara State, Nigeria. This study adopted a survey research design using simple sampling technique to select 28 respondents from the population. Structured questionnaire was designed for the collection of data. It was discovered from the findings that majority of the farmers were illiterate of the middle aged group between 31-40. The farmers plant many crops, but it is noticeable that the farmers plant cassava mostly, the area which the farmers indicated they need information most is on agriculture, it was also observed that the farmers access information from colleagues (co-farmers), friends and relatives, agricultural extension workers. The information needs of the farmers in this study on agriculture includes how to prevent diseases for their crops on the farm and after harvesting, the farmers also stated that they need information on how to seek for loan, where to get the best market to sell their farm produce and how to get the best agro-chemical for effective use. In this study it was discovered that the challenges the farmers face in acquiring information includes, the inability to read and write in English language, lack of constant electricity supply, conflict among members of various associations and lack of access to agricultural extension workers. It is recommended that the farmers should be given effective adult education, provision of information centre with necessary personnel and information media to boost information accessibility. Also the government was encouraged to negotiate with mobile telecommunication operators to subsidize services so that the farmers who form majority in the rural areas can access information and communicate easily through their mobile phones.

DOI: 10.4018/978-1-5225-0296-8.ch012

INTRODUCTION

Information is quite indispensable to the progress of any business (Aziagba & Okede, 2011). The case of farmers is not an exceptional. Availability, accessibility of timely, concise and accurate information is a tool that has the capacity to reduce uncertainty. Hence it is an important resource in an economic planning and other life endeavor.

According to Swanson, (2008) information needs assessment give programme designers the ability to develop interventions that target users with specific information needs. (Swanson & Rajalahli, 2010) explained that the level and effort to search for information either local, national and global information depend on the aspiration of the searchers and the authors added that farmers' ability to search for information depends on the sources that are available to them. Hence, it is expected that local information needs of the farmers could be met by well-organized information acquisition and dissemination system that uses traditional and modern methods.

In Nigeria, according to (Okunade & Williams, 2014) quite a number of Nigerians are rural farmers living in small farming communities. In line with Okunade's view, Laduba is one of the Nigerian rural communities dominated by farmers. The community is subdivided into smaller clans and budoagun which has highest concentration of farmers in the community is one of them. The farmers' population in this community is about 500, it is located in Asa Local Government Area of Kwara State, Nigeria. The farmers in this community practice subsistence agriculture, which (Okunade & Williams, 2014) described as small scale farming using simple implements like hoes and cutlasses to meet the farmer's household needs and with very little for sale.

However, the advantage of availability of vast land in Laduba community and its nearness to Ilorin, the Kwara State capital made the community to attract different categories of elite who wants to engage in farming from Ilorin. In view of its strategic location, the community was selected as an adopted village by Nigerian Stored Products Research Institute (NSPRI), a Research Institute with the national mandate to research into post-harvest management of agricultural crops. Hence, the Research Institute do give her developed technologies through research to farmers at Laduba to use, while personnel from the Institute do regularly visit the farmers using the technologies to determine the efficiency of their research work. This further made Laduba community an attractive farming and research environment.

STATEMENT OF PROBLEM

Nigerian farmers are essentially rural dwellers; they live their lives based on their experiences and traditions that have been passed to them. However, the desire to increase productivity and make a better living through farming is making the scope and source of information required to extend beyond experience and tradition, so, it is observable that farmers now appreciate other sources to get information to improve their life, hence, there is a need to identify these sources and the type of information they get, so that their usage could be maximized or discouraged to enhance the productivity of farmers in Laduba and other similar communities, because without farming, man's existence on the earth would have been a mirage rather than reality (Okunade & Williams, 2014). This study therefore wishes to further support existence of farming and increase in productivity of farmers through determination of information required by them to enhance their productivity.

LITERATURE REVIEW

Effort had been made through different studies to determine information needs and information seeking behavior of different groups of people and professionals. Momoh, et al. (2015) conducted a study on information seeking behavior in central hospitals in Delta State, Nigeria. The study showed that nurses needed information to carry out their professional duties like health development and current approach to medical treatment. Friends, colleagues, libraries and internet were the identified sources where the nurses got their information.

(Aziagba & Okede, 2011) conducted a study on information seeking behavior of cassava farmers in Upata clan, Ekpeye community of Rivers State of Nigeria. The study confirmed that friends and colleagues are major sources of information for the cassava farmers. Discussion over the radio broadcast were equally strong source of information for the cassava farmers, most especially when it is broadcasted in their languages. The library, seminars, workshops and television broadcast, were revealed as sources where cassava farmers do not get needed information. The findings, equally established that these cassava farmers are still involved in sourcing for information mostly from friends and relatives within the locality.

In the study conducted by Babu, et al. (2012) on information needs and search behavior among farmers in Tamil Nadu, India, the authors grouped the different information sources accessed by farmers into four searching groups based on type of medium which include: print, broadcast, electronic and interpersonal. The findings showed how searchers relied on interpersonal sources such as imprint dealers, state department of agricultural extension workers, family and relatives. Semi medium searchers, according to the authors, accessed all media with most of them using electronic sources. High and medium searchers are revealed to also get information through print and broadcast media. Irrespective of the source used by farmers to obtain information, Babu, (2012) highlighted that the major constraints to information access were poor availability and unreliable information. Also, noticeable constraint that cut across was lack of awareness of information sources available and untimeliness of information the farmers do get. Saravan R. et al (2008) carried the study on information pattern and information need of the tribal farmers in Arunachal Pradesh, India indicated that most of the farmers need information on various topics such as pest management, disease management. Tologbonse D, et al. (2008) carried the study of information need of rice farmers' community in Niger state disclosed that majority of farmers need information about crop production. Meitei & Devi (2009) also conducted a study with farmer's community in Manipur, India to find out the information need of rural farmers' community in Manipur state. This result of the study shows that majority of the farmers did not get access to needed information for their activities. Hence, the farmers requested that ICT based agricultural information support systems should be developed for them. Byamugisha et al. (2009) conducted a study on information seeking and use of urban farmers in Uganda, the researchers found out from the study, that the information needs of the urban farmers in studied area seemed to be as varied as the farming activities and also appeared to vary from one urban farmer to another. Achugbue & Anie, 2011 carried the study in Delta State, Nigeria on Rural Female farmer's information need and importance of ICT in delivering information needs of female farmers. The findings from the research shows that the female farmers do not have enough skills to access information through ICT. Akanda & Roknuzzaman Md (2012) surveyed agricultural information literacy of 160 farmers in the northern region of Bangladesh. The survey shows that farmers need information for various purposes of agricultural activities, and they use different sources and media to access information. The researchers, therefore concluded that conceptualizing information need is a very difficult task. This is because the needs of individuals usually vary from time to time due to several factors.

UNDERSTANDING INFORMATION SEEKING BEHAVIOUR OF USERS

According to Wilson (1999, 2000), information-seeking behavior includes those activities a person may engage in when identifying his own information needs, searching for such information in any way, and using or transferring that information makes up the processes of information seeking behavior of an individual. Kakai, et al., (2004) have defined information-seeking behavior as an individual's way and manner of gathering and sourcing for information for personal use, knowledge updating, and development. This author explained further that information-seeking behavior of students, researchers, and professors has been the focus of enquiry for decades. He added further that initially, user studies were conducted in libraries and information centres primarily to evaluate library collections. These were said to be followed by studies of the research on habits of individuals or groups that would lead to the design of appropriate information systems and services. According to Kakai, et al., (2004) in mid 1980s, the focus of research shifted to holistic approaches to information-seeking behavior. However, Adereti, et al, (2006), and Aina, (2004) described information need as a piece of information, whether recorded or not, which an individual or a member of a group requires for effective functioning in their daily activities. Information needs can be seen as a set data which enables the user to make appropriate decisions on any related problem facing him or her at a particular time (Solomon, 2002).

In other words, information is needed because it enables individuals to make a decision that affects their living, just as Opeke, (2004) suggest that information represents an ordered reality about the nature of the world people live in. The need for information in any society is individualistic. Individuals need information depending on the motive for such information. Taking the right decisions depends on access to information on all the alternatives and their implications (Ajayi, 2003). Zhang (2001) is of the opinion that a thorough understanding of user information needs and information-seeking behavior is fundamental to the provision of successful information services. Anwar (2007) also reiterates that it is important to understand the information-seeking behaviours of different groups of people, as it helps in the planning, implementation, operation, designing of new information systems and the development of service programmes in the work environment for optimal performance. According to Line (2000), new studies of information users and their needs are even more necessary in the age of the Internet. Researchers such as (Callison, 1997, Devadason and Pratap, 1997, and Ellis, 1993) have explored quantitative and qualitative methodologies for user studies on how Information-seeking behavior differs among user groups. Librarians must understand the information needs of user in order to address those needs. This study explores the information-seeking behavior of farmers. Knowledge about the information-seeking behaviour and information use of individuals is crucial to effectively meet their information needs. The first basic user study in the broader sense was undertaken by Menzel in1966 and he defined information seeking behavior from three angles and they include; when approached from the point of view of the scientists or technologists, these are studies of scientists' communication behaviour; when approached from the point of view of any communication medium, they are user studies; and when approached from the science communication system, they are regarded as studies in the flow of information among scientists and technologists.

MODEL ON INFORMATION SEEKING

The Information seeking behavior is sub-discipline within the field of library and information science. It describes how people need, seek, manage, give and use information in different contexts. It may also be described as information-seeking behavior or human information behaviour. Information carriers may be in different forms based on the ISB and information-needs studies of various groups. The Information carriers may include a variety of channels, a variety of sources within the channels, and a variety of messages contained within these sources Johnson et al. (2006).

Wilson (1981) has noted that the information seeking results from the recognition of some need perceived by the user. The behavior may take several forms, such as demanding information from the library or from other people who know. The approach has however been criticized because of insufficient theories, concepts and research methods, and because it has not taken into consideration the needs of the information seekers (Dervin & Nilan, 1986; Wilson, 1994). Dervin illustrated information seeking behavior diagrammatically as shown below, illustrating it triangularly with situation for seeking for information at the peak, the base of the triangle has the gap and the outcome sections. The situation, is the information needed or being sought for, the gap is the challenge in retrieving or searching for the information and the outcome is the result of the whole process. However, Dervin explained this process further by using the illustration in Figure 2, according to him, it may be preferred to use the bridge metaphor more directly as presented in the model. The model revealed that the process of seeking for information has a bridge between the situation and outcome, which spans between time and space, which implies that the process of seeking for information has no time limit

Meho & Tibbo (2003) revise Ellis's study and give new model with more features. Among the researchers, Kuhlthau (1993) has conducted empirical research about students' information seeking behavior and developed a general model of the information search process (ISP). The ISP consists of

Figure 1. Dervin's 'sense-making' triangle

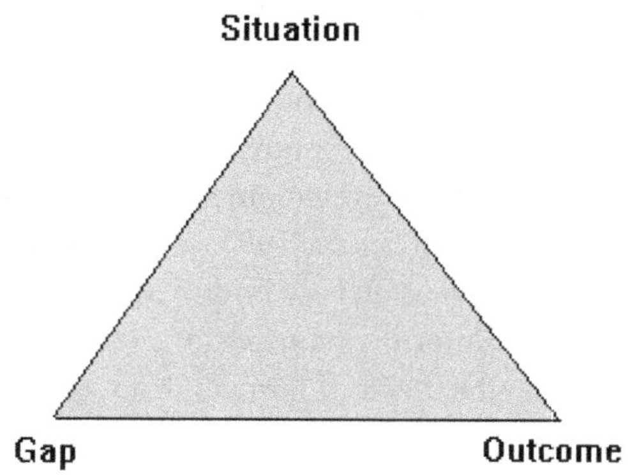

Figure 2. Dervin's 'sense-making' model re-drawn

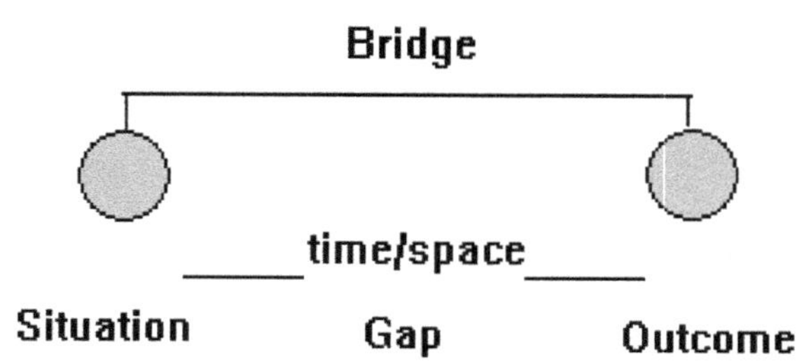

6 stages as: initiation stage, selection stage, exploration stage, formulation stage, collection stage and presentation stage.

Wilson (1999) believes in the strength of Ellis' and Kuhlthau's models as they are based on empirical research and have been tested in subsequent studies. Wilson, however reviewed Ellis model and created an illustration, it is diagrammatical explained in Figure 3.

The aim of Wilson's model was to outline the various areas covered by what the writer proposed as information-seeking behaviour, as an alternative to the models indicated in Figures 1 and 2, but it is clear that the scope of the diagram is much greater and that it attempts to cover most of what is included here as information behaviour. The model also shows that part of the information-seeking behaviour may involve other people through information exchange and that information perceived as useful may be passed to other people, as well as being used (or instead of being used) by the person himself or herself. The limitation of this kind of model, however, is that it does little more than provide a map of the area and draw attention to gaps in research: it provides no suggestion of causative factors in information behaviour and, consequently, it does not directly suggest hypotheses to be tested (Figure 4).

Hayden (1999) has studied the different information seeking models like Wilson's model of 1981, Krikelas model of 1983, Kuhlthau model of 1992, Big Six Skills model of 1992 proposed by Eisenberg and Berkowitz. The author says that we need to question who the library community is; we also need to question how we can provide information skills that leads the students towards information literacy. Borgman (2000) defines information seeking as a continuous process, involving active and

passive behaviors, and formal and informal communication. She points out the cycle of creating, using and seeking information which can be viewed as series of stages which people move back and forth, and they may be actively, creating, using and seeking information concurrently. Therefore, information seeking behavior refers to the pattern of response to the information need by person or group of persons. (Jarvelin & Wilson, 2003) discuss the functions of conceptual models in scientific research, in IS&R research in particular. What kind of models are there and in what ways may they help the investigators? What kinds of models are needed for various?

Figure 3. Wilson's information behaviour model

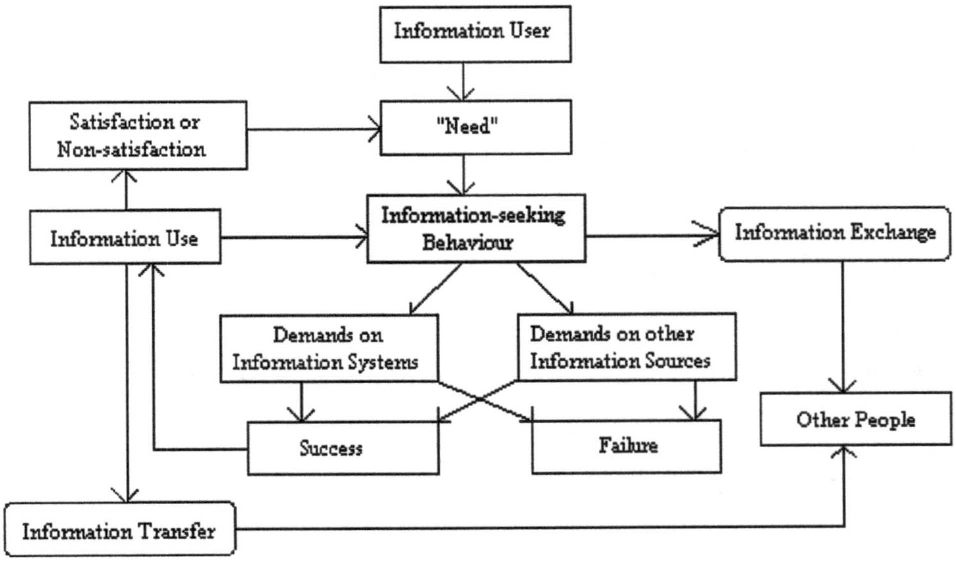

Figure 4. Wilson's information-seeking behaviour model

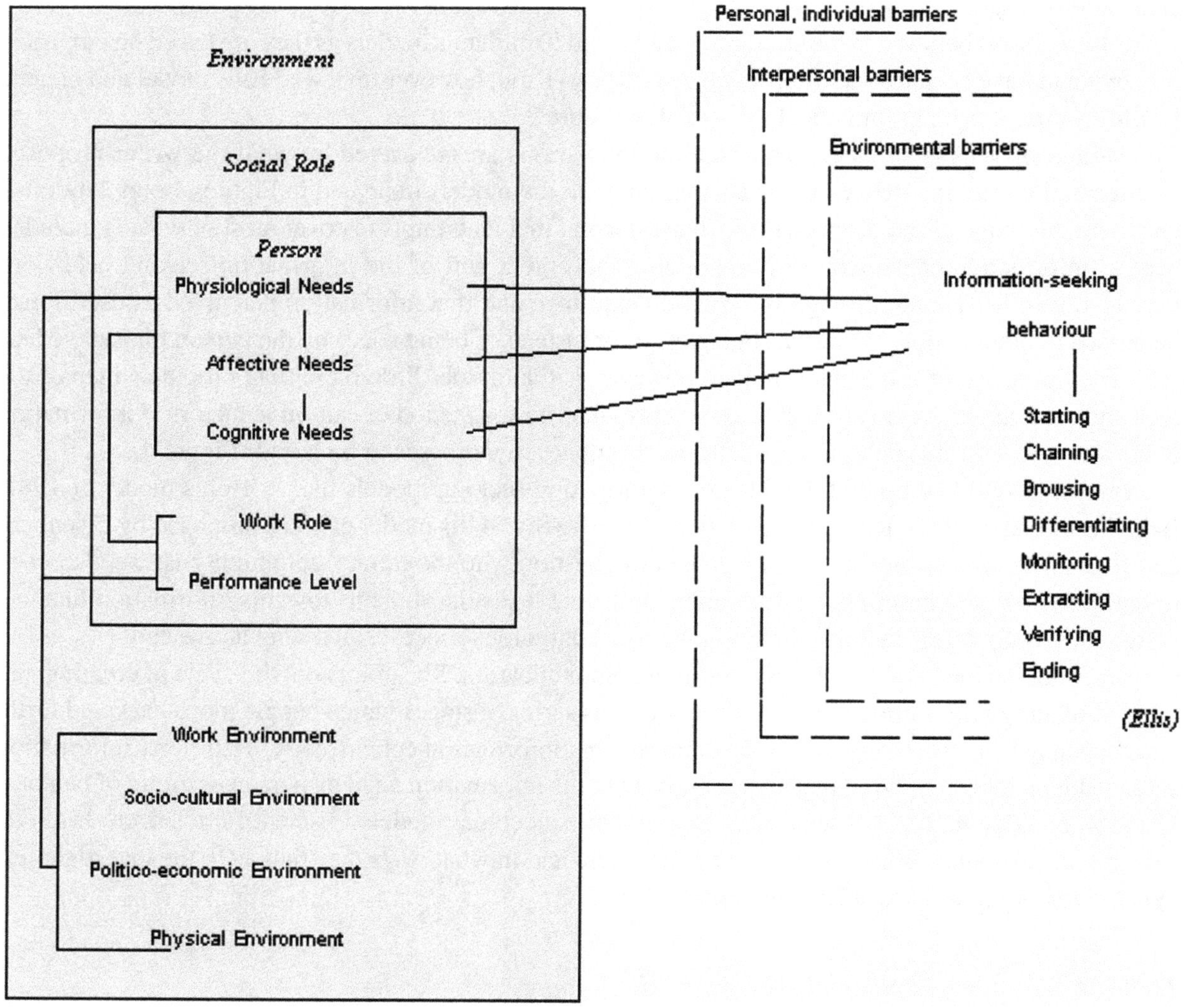

Loeber and Cristea (2003) have made an attempt at investigating, analyzing and modelling the visitor and website. Weiler (2004) observes that the first model for study of information-seeking behavior in the general population was developed by James Krikelas in 1983. This model suggestes the steps of information seeking as follows:

1. Perceiving a need,
2. The search itself,
3. Finding the information, and
4. Using the information, which results in either satisfaction or dissatisfaction.

Based on Krikelas' model, people begin to seek for information when they perceive that the current state of knowledge is less than that needed to deal with some issue (or problem). Butterworth (2006) argues that typically Information seeking and retrieval behaviour is a strongly social, but weakly collaborative leisure activity. He discusses how these assumptions fit with the existing information seeking and retrieval (IS&R) models and proposes path for future work. The author touches on the browsing behaviour and searching behaviour and has made a sketch of the characteristics of 'personal history' researchers.

Shah (2008) proposes a model that helps us to understand the requirements for a successful collaboration. The author attempts to formalize the notion of collaboration and proposes a model of Collaborative Information Seeking (CIS) that put collaboration in perspective. His model consists of four layers such as information, tools, user and results.

Of all the models, Ellis model is very much applicable to the 21st century mode of seeking for information, it is in this mode that we adopt the Ellis model on information seeking behavior. Ellis et al. (1993) model on information seeking behaviour includes six generic features. (Ellis & Haugan, 1997) have attempted to propose and describe the characteristics of a general model of information seeking behaviors based on the studies of the information seeking

patterns of social scientists, research physicists and chemists, engineers and research scientists in an industrial firm. Ellis's elaboration model describes the features of information seeking activities as generic. These features are: Starting, Chaining, Browsing, Differentiating, Monitoring, Extracting, Verifying, Ending.

- **Starting:** The means employed by the user to begin seeking information, for example, asking some knowledgeable colleague;
- **Chaining:** Following footnotes and citations in known material or 'forward' chaining from known items through citation indexes;
- **Browsing:** 'Semi-directed or semi-structured searching' (Ellis, 1989: 187);
- **Differentiating:** Using known differences in information sources as a way of filtering the amount of information obtained;
- **Monitoring:** Keeping up-to-date or current awareness searching;
- **Extracting:** Selectively identifying relevant material in an information source;
- **Verifying:** Checking the accuracy of information;
- **Ending:** Which may be defined as 'tying up loose ends' through a final search.

INFORMATION SEEKING IN DIGITAL LIBRARIES

Digital Information Resources

There are various researches have been conducted on information seeking of digital information resources by different researchers around the world. In 2013 Gakibayo et al. carried out a study at Mbrarar University Library Uganda regarding the use of digital information resources by university students. Results were tabularized and it shows that a large number of respondents were aware with the full use of technology in utilizing digital resources. Natarajan et al. (2008) revealed the users of Annamalai University library were aware of digital journals only among all the other digital resources and 50% of the users are fulfilled from digital resources and it was also observed that digital journals were only source used comprehensively by users and the digital dictionaries and digital encyclopedias were the digital resources with the least usage. The study tells that users are not well aware with the provided resources and they cannot identify their actual need properly because of which the satisfaction is below average. The use of internet based digital resources at Manipur University, India. This study identified the utilization, rationale, difficulties and satisfaction level of users about internet based digital resources services provided by the library and they conclude that low speed internet, irregular power supply and lack of required full text journals. According to findings the use of internet based digital resources by the students of Manipur University is not found very significant. The reason might be those problems which they are facing while accessing these resources (Singh, et al., 2007). In 2008 a survey was completed by H.R. and Mudhol was completed a survey at College of Fisheries, India. The research study revealed that respondents were highly satisfied about the level of access for the use of digital information sources. The study confirmed that the digital information sources users are very satisfied with their retrieved results and as the sample is limited to faculty, research scholars and post graduate students to the main reason for using digital information sources is the research in which they are currently involved. It seems that they are well aware with the usage of such digital resources. Mostafa (2013) carried out a survey at some selected private universities of Bangladesh about the use and impact of digital resources. According to results, majority of the respondents gave preference to digital thesis among all other digital resources likewise digital books, digital newspapers and digital magazines. The study exposed the fact there are sufficient digital resources available in the campus and students use those digital resources frequently but is need to modify infrastructure and training courses as well. Okiki et al. (2011) had conducted a survey in Nigeria to determine the use of digital information sources by post graduate students in Nigeria. Results showed that a large number of respondents use digital information sources daily they are motivated to use digital information sources for their research projects. According to tabulated results show connection in a major problem faced by the respondents. The post graduate students in Nigeria are being motivated for the utilization of digital information resources because of which the use of digital information is found extraordinary among them. Information Needs: Fabritius (1997) investigated the information seeking behaviour of journalists. The main purpose of the study was to investigate the role of digital information in journalism, how journalists use latest information technology and how new digital technologies sustain news reporting. The journalists' information searching behaviour was examined by means of major hierarchical aspects. Fabritius places information seeking and salvage into a wider framework which have an effect on the loom to information sources and application of information.

Digital Information Seeking Behavior

Research in the domain of information needs, information seeking and information seeking behaviour started in early twentieth century. Whereas tracing the history of information seeking and behavioral studies, few studies were carried out in the early 1900s, Ayres and McKinnie in 1916 revealed the information seeking at the Cleveland Public Library. Tibbo informs that a distinguished production of studies on the subject take placed in the 1960s [e.g. a study by the American Psychological Association, 1963 -1969 and Earle and Vickery's study in 1969]. Wilson (2000) discovered an early importance on the use of information systems with a more person-oriented approach growing later in the 1980s. Although early user-centred research concerted on the scientific community, it rapidly expanded to integrate educational institutions to investigate students and staff's actions and inspirations when using the technology. According to Francis (2008), "Researchers and practitioners in the field of LIS have long held an importance in the information-seeking behaviour of diverse patron groups. Research in this part dates back to the 1940s and the deliberate was on scientists." Since then, studies rapidly improved, preliminary with those proposed to get better collection development, followed by folks that investigated the research behavior of individual's approach that observed the system as seen by the user Studies on web information seeking behaviour emerged afterward, and many pen down the mid-90s as the exact initial point. Jansen & Spink (2004) propose that the most primitive studies of web searching behaviour in the mid -90s occurred as web search engine and web browser use began to grow, mainly in academic environments. Author discovered the behavioral outline with special reference to electronic databases and the World Wide Web. Different models of information seeking behaviour were presented and the complexities in the procedure of searching were explored. These researches offer insight into the seeking behaviour in the course of electronic systems (Wilson, 2006). Asemi (2005) agreed to understand the information searching habits of internet users at the Medical University of Isfahan. The purpose of the study was to examine the position of information searching character of the users on internet. Data was collected using a questionnaire trailed by interview with users from five faculties. 188 users responded to the study. Study revealed that students use internet extensively, and it inhabits an important position with diverse sources. Study also revealed that electronic media has not substitutes print media. A study of Brazilian social sciences scholars found that, while print resources are still the most frequently used, electronic resources are becoming more and more accepted. Access to networked computers is the main barrier to the use of databases and other electronic resources. Francis (2005) focused on a study that explained the information seeking behavior of social sciences faculty at the University of the West Indies (UWI). One of this 2005 study's findings was that social scientists have a preference journal articles in electronic format over print. Wang (2007) wrote about disciplinary and cultural differences among information seekers in the Internet age, concluding that there are distinctions across disciplines and cultures in terms of how they rank the importance of these resources and how much they use them. Wang further discussed the information needs, information-seeking behaviors, and resource use of selected special interest groups. Electronic Information retrieval skills as noted by Tsakonas & Papatheodorou (2006), digital libraries, e-journal platforms, portals, e-prints and other web-based information systems provide services supporting users to perform intense work tasks that require complex interaction activities. This implies that users cannot access e-resources without adequate computer skills. According to Toner (2008), advances in technology have made possible virtual classrooms, online courses, and distance learning. This, coupled with the growth in society's access to information via ICT, has altered student perceptions of what the library has to offer. If libraries are to maintain their relevance in the cycle of student needs, then they must adapt and change (Toner 2008). MacWhinnie, (2003) and Thachill (2008), argue that students sometimes lack technical and research skills and so do not find the best and appropriate information, tempting them to use whatever information they can find first, fast and full text. More importantly, even with a good easy to use integrated system, students very often need the expertise of a librarian to apply search techniques and find the information they need (Thachill 2008). Tella et tal (2007) argued that the students' ability to find and retrieve information effectively is a transferable skill useful for their future life as well as enabling the positive and successful use of the electronic resources whilst at school. They noted that in this digital era any student at the higher level who intends to better achieve should have the ability to explore the digital environment. Students are increasingly expected to use electronic information resources whilst at the university. To make use of the growing range of electronic resources, students must acquire and practice the skills necessary to exploit them (Okello-Obura & Magara, 2008). Skills learning is essential in a technology driven environment but can be enhanced tremendously through the use of innovative learning strategies (Lawson 2005). Ray & Day (1998) suggested that the skills required to access the maximum potential of electronic resources are much greater than those required for searching printed sources. These skills include knowledge of the structure of the database and the instructions which must be input into the computer by the searcher – as well as an understanding of the ways in which the instructions are linked to one another. Okon (2005) asserts that the core skills traditionally associated with information professionals, which include information handling skills, training and facilitating skills, evaluation skills and concern for the customer, are all still relevant. The ability to find and retrieve information effectively is a transferable skill for enabling the positive and successful use of electronic resources by students while they are at university - as well as in their future lives. As Brophy (1993) argues, libraries must "reach a position where the acquisition of information skills is acknowledged as one of the key learning objectives for every student entering a university, so that no student leaves without being fully equipped to cope up with the information intensive world – the information society - as an end-user." The library has not only ready and free information highway, but also the adequate and efficient information transport means, which allows the readers to use the tools and obtain the information they need (Shuling, 2007). The literature highlights the advantages of electronic over printed sources of information, but also suggests the need for certain skills in order to access and use electronic resources effectively. Given their apparent lack of use of electronic resources, this study set out to determine if LIS postgraduate students at Makerere University have the required skills and ability to access and use electronic resources.

Why Electronic Information Resources?

Higher education is changing rapidly with the advent of technology. According to Shuling (2007), in recent years, electronic information has gradually become a major resource in every university library. The growth and diversity of electronic resources, especially e-journals, in the past few years has led many to predict the extinction of the printed journal (Okello-Obura & Magara, 2008). It has been suggested that a new paradigm is sweeping scholarship (Liew, Foo and Chennupati, 2000; Harper et al, 2006). Majid et al (1999) argue that technological advancements opened up new horizons for the creation, storage, access, distribution and presentation of information. In the global information communications technology (ICT)-dominated world, "place" is much less important (Ferguson, 2006). "The impact of moving from text-based to resource-based learning has involved heavier use of library materials and a demand for more and varied media sources" (Kinengyere, 2007). This makes the provision and use of Electronic Information Systems (EIS) in academic libraries a critical issue for those working in information and library services (Armstrong....et al, 2001; Elam, 2007). The pace at which information resources are being produced and converted into an electronic form is greater today than in previous years (Armstrong ... et al 2001). In today's information age it would seem that library users would not only be eager to take advantage of the convenience electronic resources have to offer, but would be fully immersed in the new technologies (Elam 2007). Electronic information resources offer today's students different opportunities compared to their predecessors. Liew, Foo and Chennupati (2000:302) argued that while reading an e-journal is not the same as reading a printed one, many are beginning to acknowledge the possibility that electronic documents (e-documents) offer users advanced features and novel forms of functionality beyond what is possible in printed form. Years ago Brophy (1993), noted that the advantages of electronic resources over print include speed, ease of use, ability to search multiple files at the same time, ability to save, print and repeat searches, more frequent updating and the ability to access from outside the library (a particular advantage for the distance learner). According to Dadzie (2005), electronic resources are invaluable research tools that complement print-based resources in any traditional library. Their advantages include access to information that might be restricted to the user because of geographical location or finances, access to current information, and provision of extensive links to additional resources or related content (Dadzie 2005). E-resources could be stored electronically thereby saving space, the risk of lost, theft or damage is lessened and costs significantly reduced. Attitude towards e-resources Academic libraries now live in a superior new world. The rapid advancement of Information and Communication Technology (ICT) has brought a revolutionary change in the information scenario giving rise to a number of options to the users' community to handle varied information sources conveniently and effortlessly. As a result, e-resources have become the lively substance to the modern library's reserves in satisfying varied needs of students, teachers, and researchers with minimum risk and time (Swain and Panda, 2009). For better planning, it is vital to have knowledge on the attitudes of users towards e-resources. Swain and Panda (2009), say the library users' attitude to information is gradually shifting from the printed documents to electronic resources and thus, it has been their prerogative to know the details of the availability and organization of e-resources like online journals and databases, electronic theses and dissertations (ETDs), government publications, online newspapers, etc. in libraries. Given technology increased use, it is important to understand how technologically rich environments are influencing student attitudes toward e-resources access. Many factors influence attitudes. The introduction of open access journals and other resources for instance is creating another attitudinal tendency towards e-resources. Open access is one of the cheapest routes to electronic resources and over the last few years' open access resources have grown and provided an affordable way to provide access to some journal content (Price, 2009). Supporters of open access argue that, when academic articles, dissertations and theses are put online and open to all, it helps in fighting duplication and plagiarism of other people's intellectual works. Although the open access movement has brought access to many valuable resources, and provided libraries with an invaluable amount of resources, many open access projects still face an uncertain future (Price, 2009). Many critics are not sure that the open access model can survive because some are not considered "financially viable" or as high quality as traditionally purchased or subscribed content (Robinson 2006; Shao and Scherlen, 2007; Turk and Bjork 2008). Where do LIS postgraduate students fall in this case? What are their attitudes towards open access electronic resources? Attitudes towards e-resources access could be attributed to problems faced when accessing e-resources. For instance, in a situation where there are inadequate computer technologies to access e-resources or poor Internet connections, student's positive attitudes could be affected. That is why the problems that affect e-resources access are addressed in higher learning institutions libraries. The arguments for students using electronic resources are compelling. An adequate knowledge of computers and retrieval techniques is desirable to search these resources effectively. It is necessary to establish what computer skills students require to access electronic information resources in libraries. Amidst all the efforts to access e-resources, LIS postgraduate students face a number of challenges. These are reported in another paper by the same author.

SCOPE OF THE STUDY

The study is limited to farmers that cultivate land in Laduba community. Other inhabitants that engaged in other trades and other forms of farming apart from tilling ground were not included.

Objective of The Study

The specific objectives of the study are to:

1. Identify the information needs of farmers in Laduba community of Kwara State.
2. Determine the source of information and their preferences with regard to sources available to them.
3. Identify constraints the farmers face while searching for information.

Methodology

The Laduba Community is located in Kwara State of Nigeria. They have various occupations, but the main occupation of the natives is farming. This study adopted a survey sampling technique. Structured questionnaire was designed as the instrument for data collection and was supplemented by personal interview with the expertise of the extension personnel of Nigerian Stored Products Research Institute (NSPRI). The population of this study is about 500 farmers who dwells in Budoagun Clan of Laduba community of Kwara State, Nigeria. The Budoagun clan is where this study is based, because the clan is a section of the Laduba community where farmers that cultivates land settled. To obtain information from the respondents, 40 copies of questionnaire were administered to the respondents while 28 copies were recovered and used for analysis. Agricultural extension workers from the Nigerian Stored Products Research Institute (NSPRI) were used as the research assistants to administer the questionnaire. The questionnaire was administered to the respondents who are mostly illiterate on one- to -one basis. The research assistants read the content of the questionnaire and the options available to each of the respondent and the answers from the respondents were reflected on the questionnaire. The questionnaire was divided into two broad sections. Section one deals with the bio data of the respondents. The other section has other units that examined the information seeking behavior of the respondents. The unit in the second section of the questionnaires are five and the sub heading of the units are arranged as follows from B to F respectively; types of crops planted, area of information needs, information need of farmers, medium of accessing information and challenges faced while seeking for information. Also the head of the community, noticeable leaders among the farmers and some youths were interviewed to compliment information gathered from the respondent through the questionnaire. Data collected for the study were subjected to analysis using frequency count, simple percentage and bar charts.

RESULTS AND DISCUSSIONS

Bio Data of the Respondents

- **Age of the Farmers:** The age of the farmers in the community of Laduba shows that 42.9% are between 31-40 years of age, followed by 32.1% of the respondents which is between 41-50 years of age, the research shows that 7.1% of the farmers are between 20-30 (Table 1 and Figure 5).
- **Gender of the Farmers:** From the result shown, 60.7% of respondents were male and 39.3% were females (Table 2 and Figure 6).

Table 1. Age of the farmers

Age Range	Frequency	Percent	Valid Percent	Cumulative Percent
20-30	2	7.1	7.1	7.1
31-40	12	42.9	42.9	50.0
41-50	9	32.1	32.1	82.1
51 and above	5	17.9	17.9	100.0
Total	28	100.0	100.0	

Figure 5.

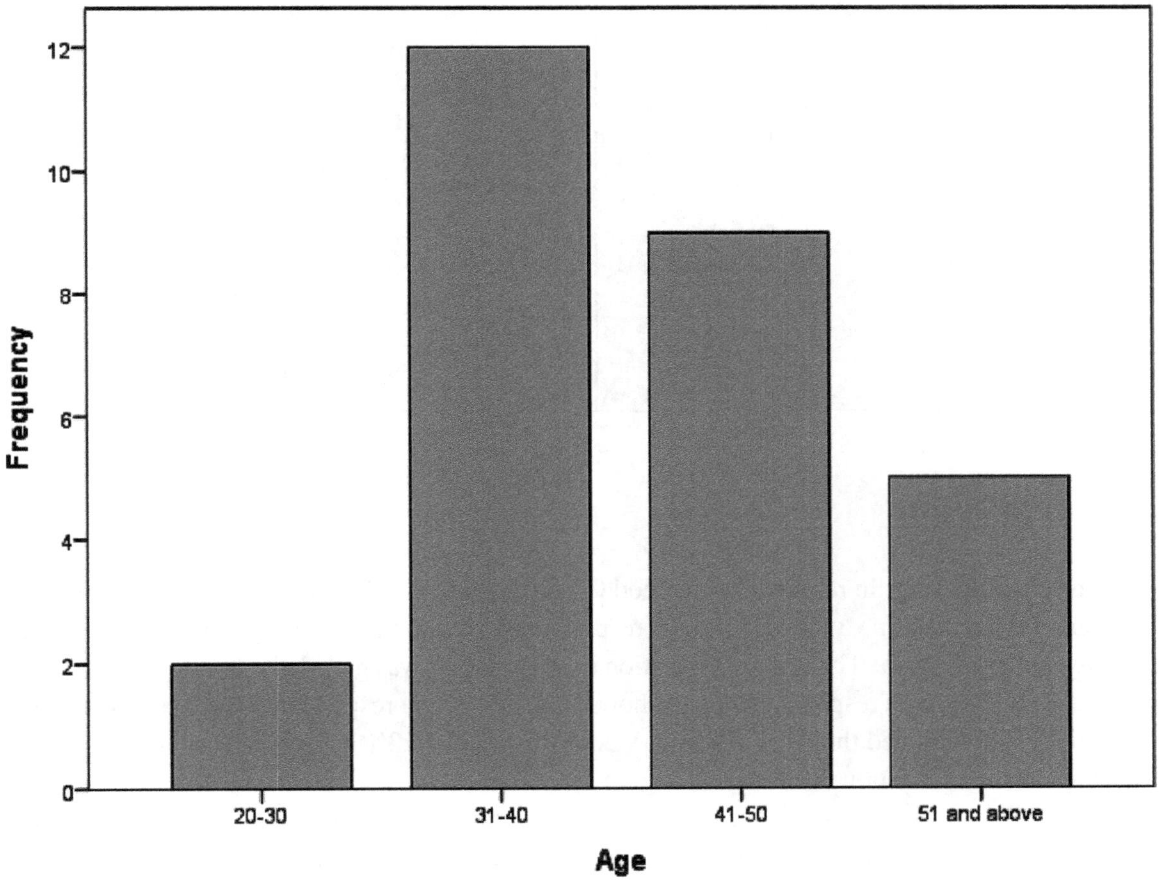

Table 2. Gender of the farmers

Gender	Frequency	Percent	Valid Percent	Cumulative Percent
Male	17	60.7	60.7	60.7
Female	11	39.3	39.3	100.0
Total	28	100.0	100.0	

Figure 6.

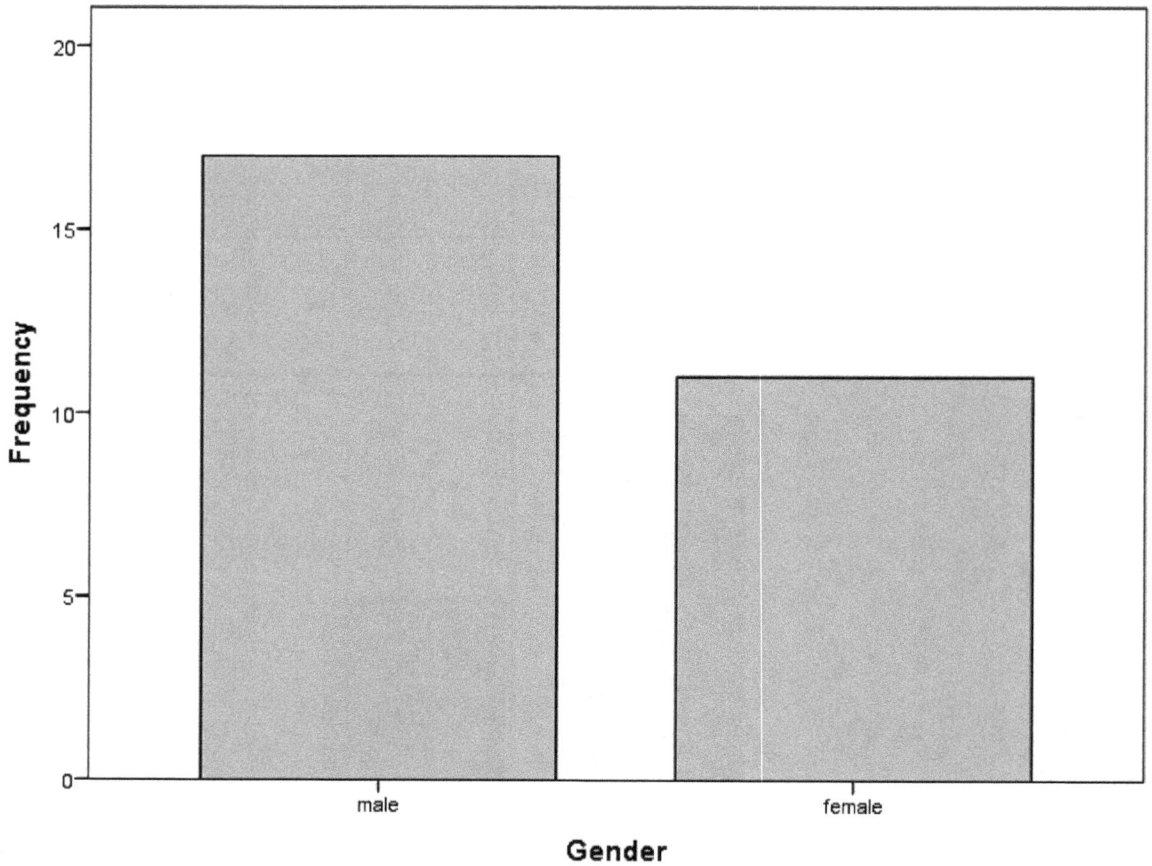

- **Mode of Farming:** In response to the mode of farming, it was discovered that 75% of the respondents are into fulltime, while 25% of the respondents are part-time farming (Table 3 and Figure 7).
- **Level of Education:** The level of education of respondents was grouped into non formal, primary and secondary. The response obtained shows that 50% of the respondents belongs to non-formal, while 35.7% attained the level of primary education, and 14.3% being the least attained the level of secondary education (Table 4 and Figure 8).
- **Size of Farm:** Majority of the farmers' size of farm ranges from 1-2 acres (60.7%), the other size of farm used by other farmers include 2-4 and 4-6 acres with both with a percentage of 17.9% (Table 5 and Figure 9).

Table 3. Mode of farming

Mode	Frequency	Percent	Valid Percent	Cumulative Percent
Full time	21	75.0	75.0	75.0
Part time	7	25.0	25.0	100.0
Total	28	100.0	100.0	

Figure 7.

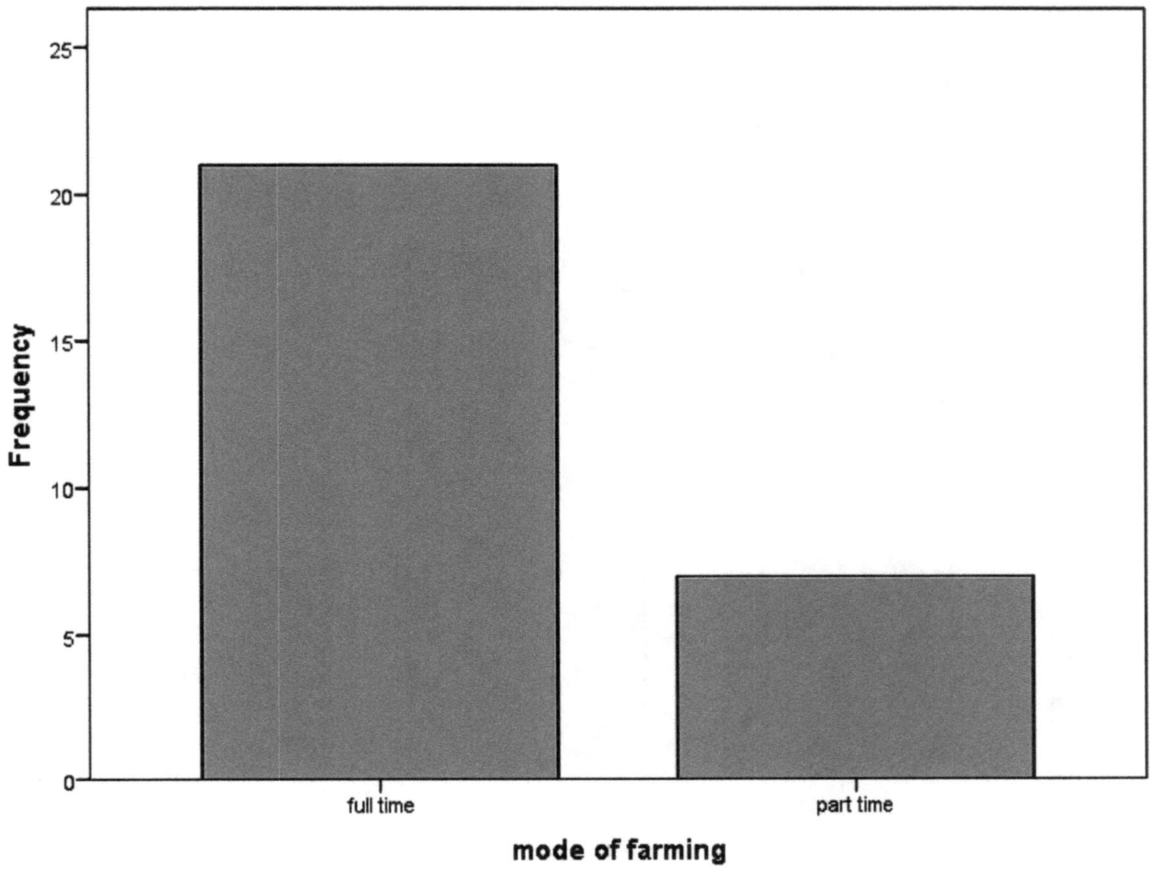

Table 4. Level of education

Education Level	Frequency	Percent	Valid Percent	Cumulative Percent
Non formal	14	50.0	50.0	50.0
Primary education	10	35.7	35.7	85.7
Secondary education	4	14.3	14.3	100.0
Total	28	100.0	100.0	

- **How Frequent Do You Go to the Farm:** Asked about how frequent they go to the farm, 92.9% of the respondents say they go to the farm every day, 3.6% of the respondents goes to the farm weekly and another 3.6% goes to the farm monthly (Table 6 and Figure 10).

Information on Other Types of Farming Apart from Tilling the Ground

- **Type of Livestock:** In response to types of livestock reared if any, 46.4% of the respondents engage in goat rearing, 39.3% of the respondents are into poultry farming, the percentage of those

Figure 8.

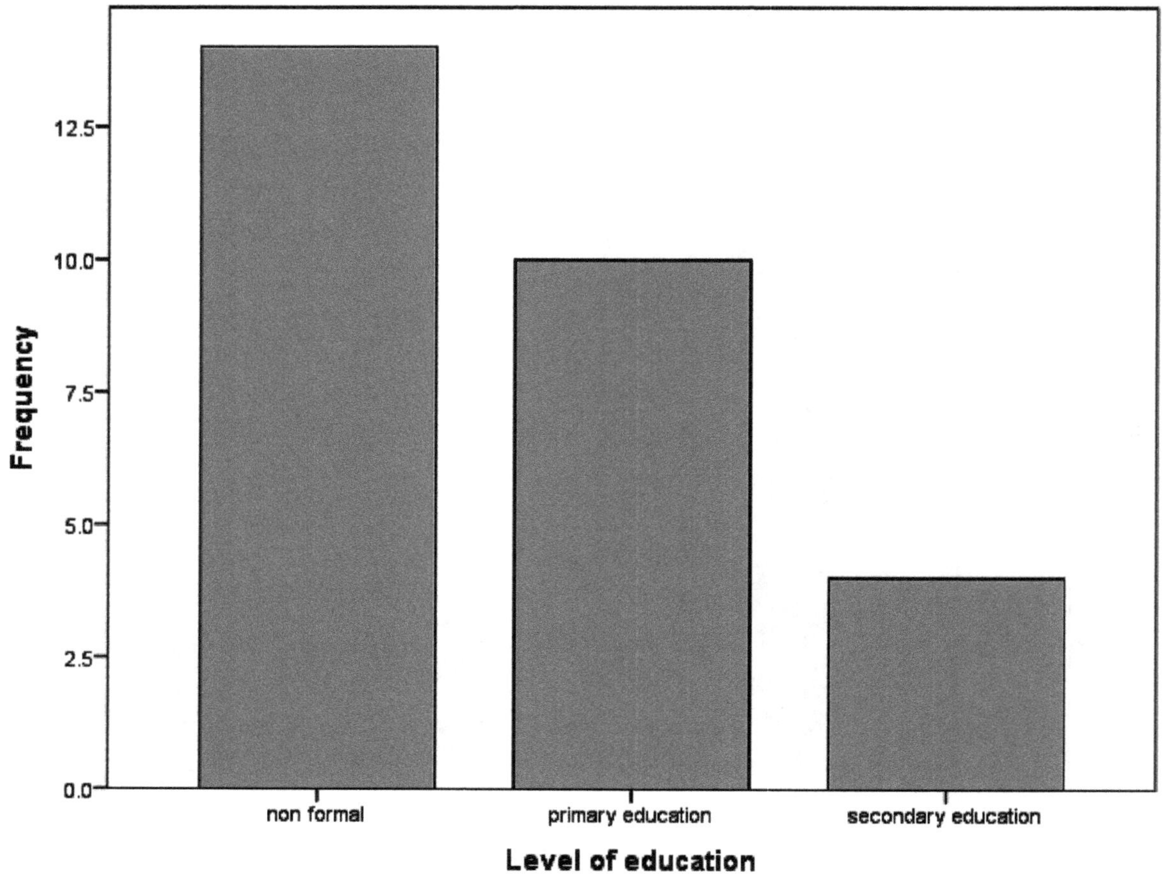

Table 5. Size of farm

Farm Size	Frequency	Percent	Valid Percent	Cumulative Percent
1-2 acres	17	60.7	60.7	60.7
2-4 acres	5	17.9	17.9	78.6
4-6 acres	5	17.9	17.9	96.4
6 acres and above	1	3.6	3.6	100.0
Total	28	100.0	100.0	

who are engaged in fish farming, pig rearing and cattle rearing is on the low side with 3.6%, 10.7% and 10.7% of the respondents respectively (Table 7 and Figure 11)

- **Type of Crops Planted:** Majority of the farmers' plants cassava (71.4%), they also plant grain crops and melon with results stating 67.9% and 57.1% respectively, other crops planted include vegetables (50%), yam (42.9%), fruits (42.9%) and groundnut (32.1%) the least crop planted is rice (3.6%) (Table 8 and Figure 12)

Figure 9.

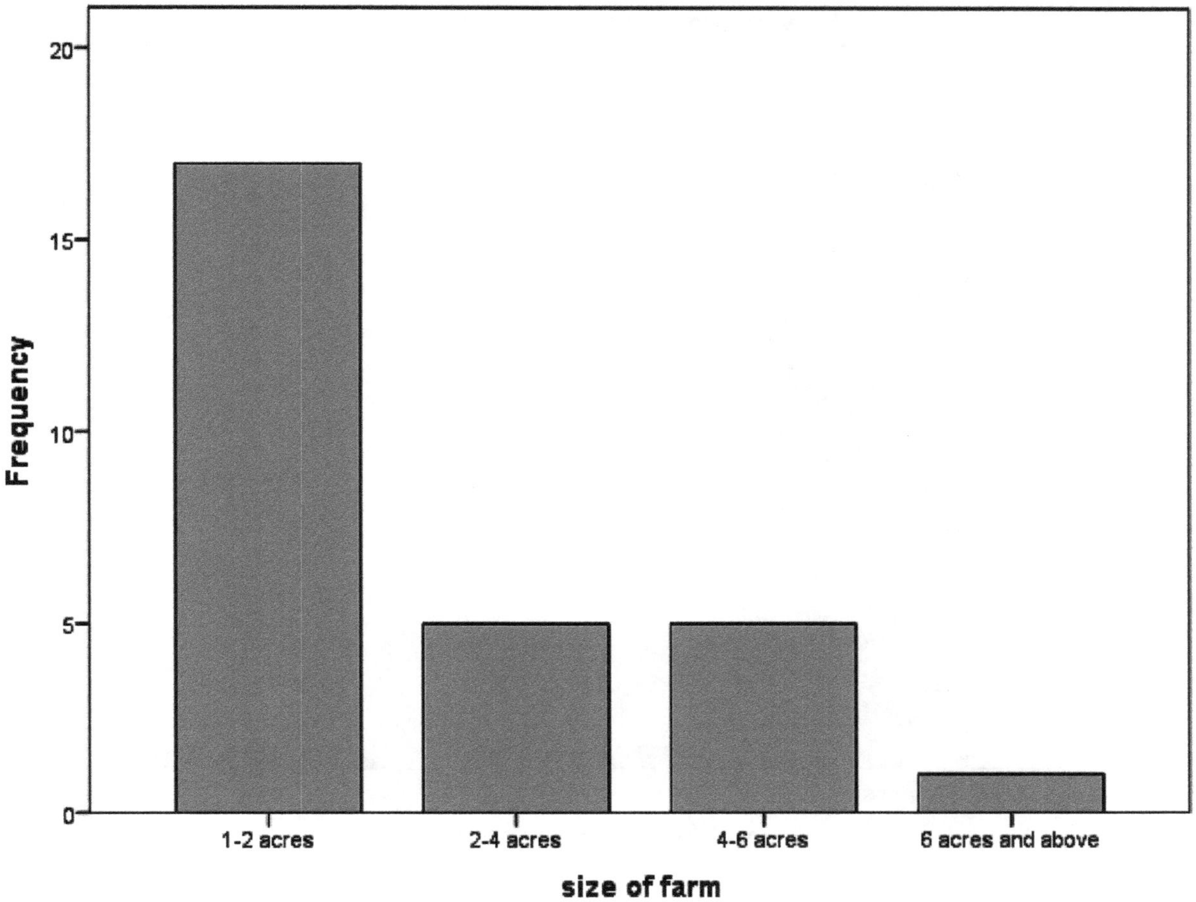

Table 6. How frequently do you go to the farm?

Time	Frequency	Percent	Valid Percent	Cumulative Percent
Everyday	26	92.9	92.9	92.9
Weekly	1	3.6	3.6	96.4
Monthly	1	3.6	3.6	100.0
Total	28	100.0	100.0	

Areas of Information Needs

Majority of the farmers stated that the area they need information most is on agriculture, about 89% of the respondents stated they needed information on agriculture, followed by education where 75% of the respondents also stated they need information in that aspect, about 71% of the farmers also stated they need information on health, 32.1% of the respondents stated they need information about community and rural development, 25% of the farmers said they need information on politics (Table 9 and Figure 13).

Figure 10.

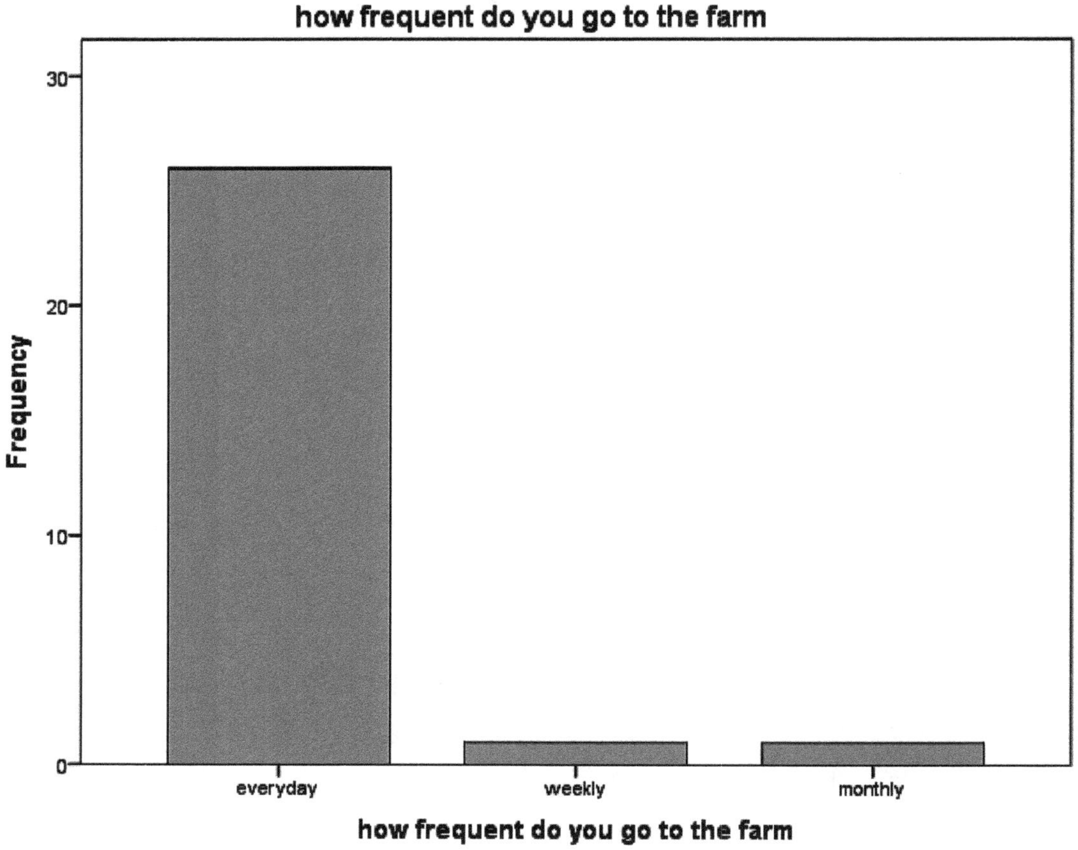

Table 7. Type of livestock

Type of Livestock	Rating of Type of Livestock				Total
	Very Highly	Highly	Fairly	Not at All	
Cow	10.7%	7.1%	7.1%	75.0%	100.0%
Ram	21.4%	25.0%	17.9%	35.7%	100.0%
Pig	10.7%	7.1%		82.1%	100.0%
Goat	46.4%	21.4%	14.3%	17.9%	100.0%
Poultry	39.3%	28.6%	21.4%	10.7%	100.0%
Fish	3.6%	3.6%	7.1%	85.7%	100.0%
Total	22.0%	15.5%	11.3%	51.2%	100.0%

Information Need of Farmers on Agriculture

The information needs of the farmers on agriculture which is their major area of information needs are categorized into disease prevention, knowledge of price of farm produce in the market, source of loan for farming, how to obtain fertilizer, location of market to sell their agricultural produce, best mode of storage, labour cost and land maintenance (Table 10). 82.1% of the farmers agreed that they need to

Figure 11.

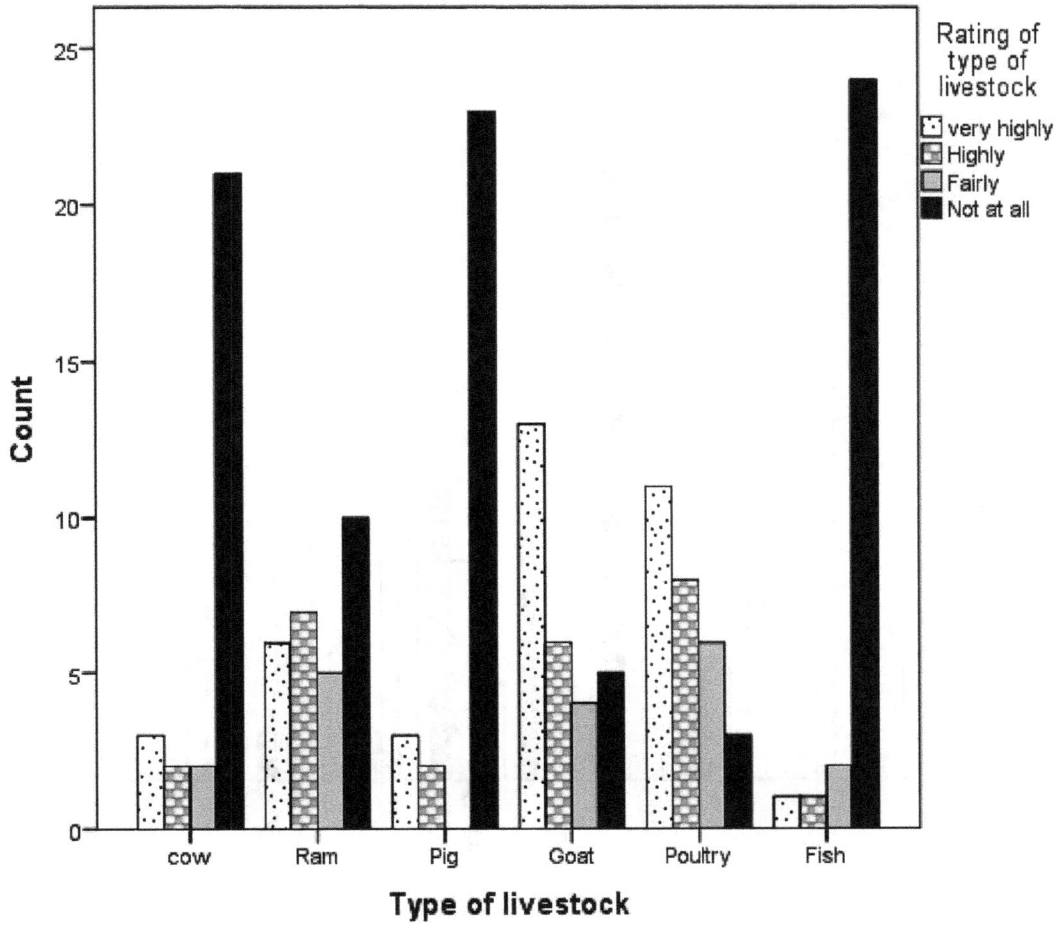

Table 8. Type of crops planted

Crops	Rating of Crops Planted				Total
	Very Highly	Highly	Fairly	Not at All	
Cassava	71.4%	21.4%	3.6%	3.6%	100.0%
Grains	67.9%	28.6%	3.6%		100.0%
Melon	57.1%	7.1%	17.9%	17.9%	100.0%
Rice	3.6%		3.6%	92.9%	100.0%
Groundnut	32.1%	21.4%	7.1%	39.3%	100.0%
Beans	14.3%	10.7%	32.1%	42.9%	100.0%
Yam	42.9%	39.3%	7.1%	10.7%	100.0%
Fruits	42.9%	25.0%	25.0%	7.1%	100.0%
Vegetable	50.0%	28.6%	17.9%	3.6%	100.0%
Total	42.5%	20.2%	13.1%	24.2%	100.0%

Figure 12.

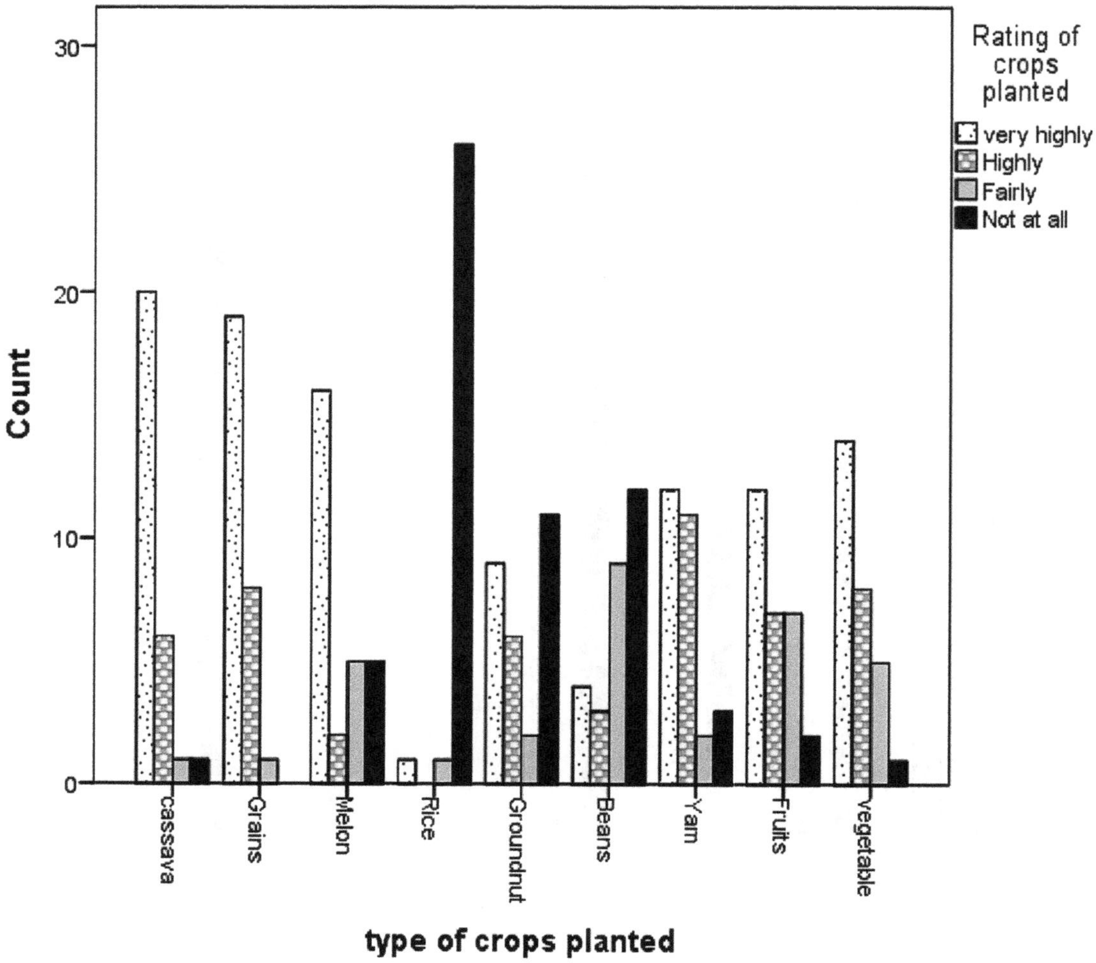

Table 9.

	Rating of Areas of Information Needs				Total
	Very Highly	Highly	Fairly	Not at All	
Politics	25.0%	39.3%	28.6%	7.1%	100.0%
Health	71.4%	25.0		3.6%	100.0%
Agriculture	89.3%	7.1%		3.6%	100.0%
Education	75.0%	21.4%		3.6%	100.0%
Community and rural development	32.1%	57.1%	10.7%		100.0%
Total	58.6%	30.0%	7.9%	3.6%	100.0%

Figure 13.

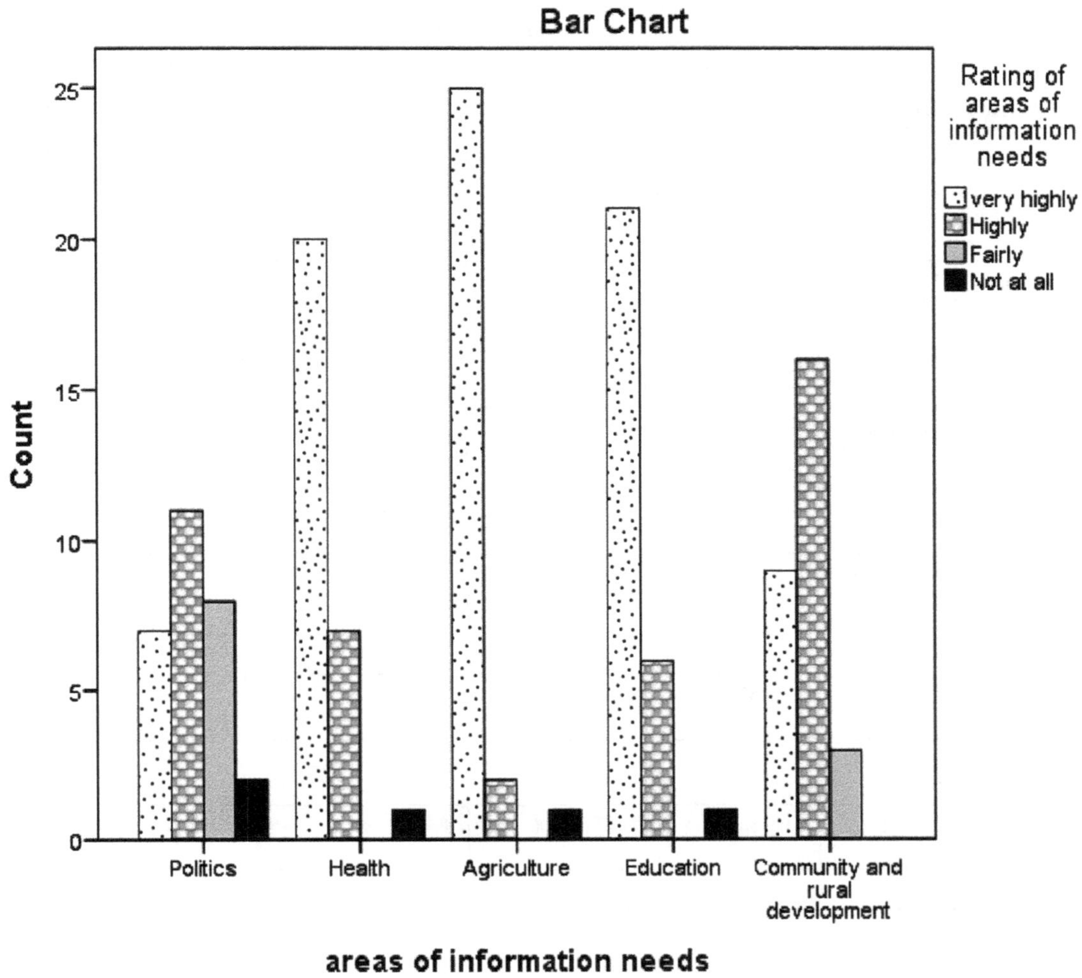

know how to prevent diseases affecting their farm produce. 64.3% of the respondents claimed they need information on how to get best price for their farm produce, 53.6% of the respondents indicated they need information on the best place to seek for loan. 71.4% of the respondents stated they need information on how to get effective agro-chemicals to apply on their farms. 64.3% of the respondents claimed they need information for more locations to sell their agricultural produce. 75% of the respondents indicated they need information on the best available mode of storage for their farm produce. 50% of the respondents indicated that they need information on how they can get labour to till the ground for them. 64.3% of the respondents claimed they need information on how to get tractors to clear their land for farming (Table 10 and Figure 14).

Medium of Accessing Information

On the topic of accessing information, the farmers were asked orally whether they were aware of the presence of the information center and the library in their locality and if they used the places to seek

Table 10. Information needs of farmers on agriculture

	Rating of Need of Farmers				Total
	Very Highly	**Highly**	**Fairly**	**Not at All**	
How to take care of livestock	57.1%	21.4%	7.1%	14.3%	100.0%
Best price available for my farm produce	64.3%	21.4%	10.7%	3.6%	100.0%
How to prevent diseases for my farm produce	82.1%	17.9%			100.0%
How to get loans	53.6%	28.6%	7.1%	10.7%	100.0%
Best fertilizer for my farm	64.3%	25.0%	10.7%		100.0%
how to marketing my farm product	64.3%	25.0%	10.7%		100.0%
how to store my farm produce	75.0%	14.3%	7.1%	3.6%	100.0%
Cost of labour in my farming	50.0%	32.1%	14.3%	3.6%	100.0%
How to get tractors to clear my land	64.3%	21.4%	3.6%	10.7%	100.0%
How to get agro chemicals	71.4%	21.4%	7.1%		100.0%
How to treat myself from ailments	64.3%	32.1%	3.6%		100.0%
Education of my children	57.1%	39.3%	3.6%		100.0%
Where to get good treatment for my health problem	57.1%	39.3%	3.6%		100.0%
Political situation of the local/ state/federal government	39.3%	42.9%	17.9%		100.0%
Available workshop and capacity building	50.0%	28.6%	21.4%		100.0%
Total	61.0%	27.4%	8.6%	3.1%	100.0%

information. The response from them shows that a majority are aware of the presence of the building but do not go there to seek for information. the response from the respondents from the questionnaire shows that, (see Table 11) 17.9% of these farmers' access information through the information center. 10.7% of the respondents were not aware of the information centre, 35.7% of the respondent who knew of the information centre occasionally use it. Another 35.7% said they don't use the centre at all. On information seeking behavior of the farmers, 57.1%, 60.7% and 60.7% of the respondents claim that they mostly collect information through their colleagues(co-farmers), friends and Association Members, respectively (Table 11). Further results showed that there are other sources where the respondents obtain information apart from the ones earlier stated. The usage of such other means like Radio, community heads, Extension Workers, Newspapers and Magazines by the respondents was 57.1%, 50%, 34.5% and 28.6% respectively. (Table 11). From the oral interview conducted with the respondents, it can be noted that the discussion over the radio broadcast was a strong information source. The respondents value radio broadcasts highly, especially when the broadcast is delivered in their local languages. As shown in (Table 11) seminars and workshop were not popular medium for gathering information by the respondents, only 25.9% of the respondents indicated that seminar and workshop had been a medium of getting information (Table 11 and Figure 15).

Figure 14.

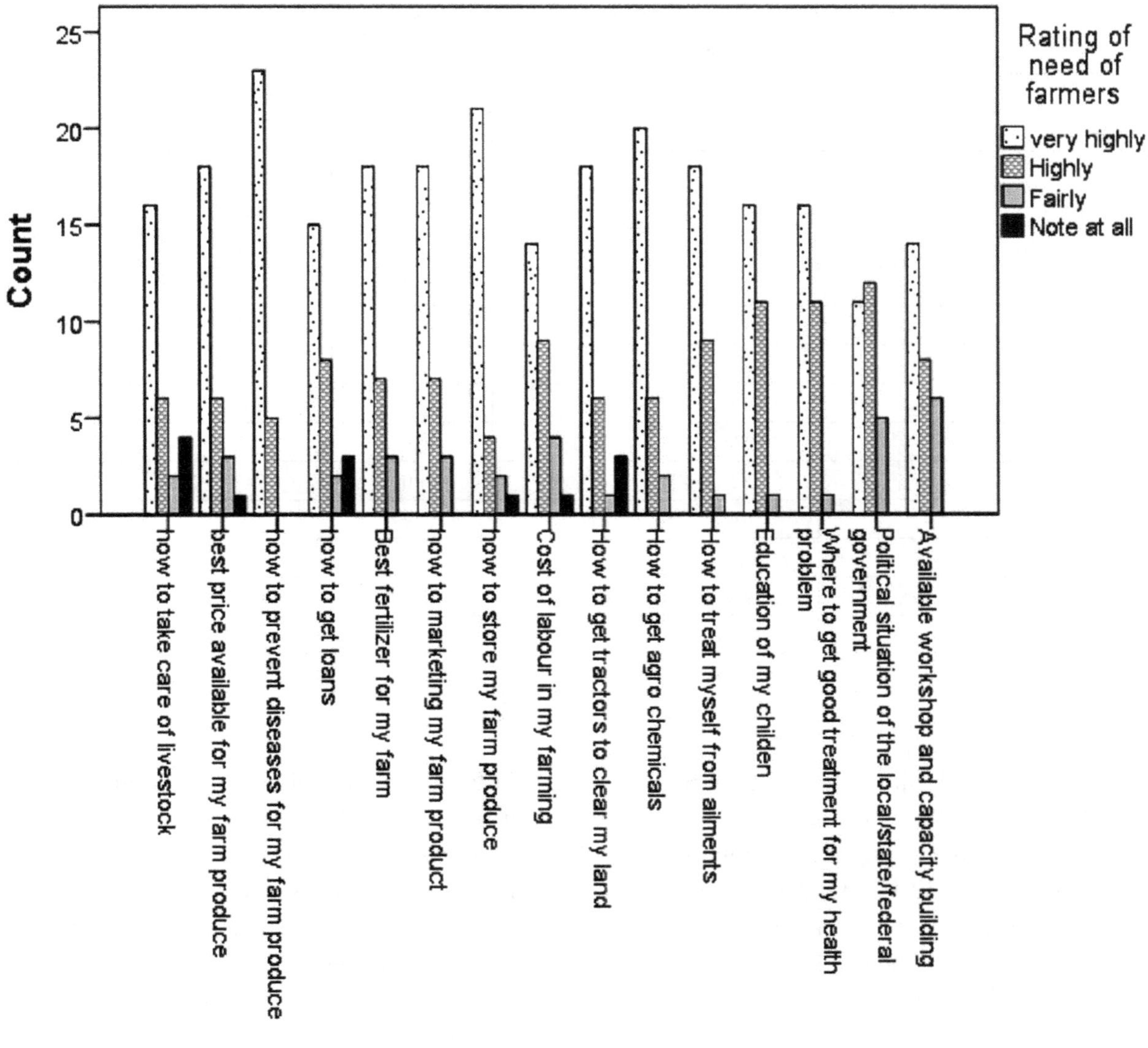

Challenges/Problems Highlighted by Respondents When Seeking Information

On challenges faced by the respondents when seeking for information (Table 12) shows that the most common problem the respondents experienced in getting information from other sources apart from their colleagues, friends and relatives is the inability to read and write, with 67.9% of the respondents indicating that they cannot read and write, hence they are constrained in using any information that is in English language. Availability of limited time after farm work is also seen as a constraint to farmers to seek for needed information 46.4% of the respondent agreed very highly to it, while 32.1% of the respondent also agreed highly to it, making a total of 78.5% of the respondents. also other challenges faced by the farmers; another noticeable constraint faced by the farmers is the lack of money to purchase airtime for their mobile phone to obtain information. 32.1% of the respondents agreed very highly to this problem, while 10.7% agreed to it highly and 32.1% said it is occasional and 25.0% of the respondents

Table 11. Medium of accessing information

	Rating of Medium of Accessing Information				Total
	Very Highly	Highly	Fairly	Not at All	
Cyber café	3.6%			96.4%	100.0%
Colleagues	57.1%	39.3%	3.6%		100.0%
Friends	60.7%	32.1%	7.1%		100.0%
Member	60.7%	28.6%	7.1%	3.6%	100.0%
Newspaper/magazine	28.6%		21.4%	50.0%	100.0%
Radio	57.1%	25.0%	17.9%		100.0%
Centre's in the town	17.9%	35.7%	10.7%	35.7%	100.0%
Television	42.9%	21.4%	17.9%	17.9%	100.0%
Library	10.7%	10.7%		78.6%	100.0%
seminar and workshop	25.9%	1.1%	8.5%	64.4%	100.0%
Extension office	34.5%	31.0%	31.0%	3.4%	100.0%
Community head	50.0%	32.1%	17.9%		100.0%
Religion	53.6%	39.3%	7.1%		100.0%
opinion leaders	39.3%	25.0%	28.6%	7.1%	100.0%
political leaders	28.6%	25.0%	42.9%	3.6%	100.0%
Total	38.1%	23.8%	15.5%	22.6%	100.0%

did not agree at all. Similarly, 39.3% of the respondents indicated that inability to use mobile phone is a challenge, with 14.3% of the respondents agreeing to it highly and 32.1% of the respondents agreeing to it fairly, we can say the inability to use mobile phones can be seen as a challenge to accessing information. Also, 32.1% of the respondents indicated that language barrier is a hindrance because from the oral interview, it is noticeable that most of the information available to the respondents from radio, newspapers and documents from government extension officers are written in English language. 39.3% of the respondents indicated very highly that lack of constant electricity is a challenge, while 32.1% of the respondents indicated highly, 25% of the respondents indicated fairly, 3.6% of the respondents did not see it as a challenge at all. From the oral interview, the constraint of electricity was attributed to contribute to their inability to charge their mobile phones, watch television and listen to radio broadcast, 42.9% of the respondents agreed very highly that the fear of going to urban areas to seek for information is a challenge, while 25% of the respondents agreed highly, 25% of the respondents agreed fairly, 7.1% of the respondents did not agree at all. 42.9% of the respondents claimed very highly that lack of reliable source of information in the community is a challenge to accessing information, 25% of the respondents agreed highly, while 21.4% of the respondents agreed to it fairly, while 10.7% of the respondents did not agree at all. The next variable is to confirm how satisfactory the respondents get access to government extension worker so as to get information on issues relating to their farm, the results shows that 17.9% of the respondents indicated very highly that they do not have access to extension workers, while 10.7% of the respondents also agreed highly to it, 28.6% of the respondents also agreed fairly to it, while 42.9% of the respondents indicated that they have access to government extension workers. The study also tried to find out if conflict among various associations that exist in the community has ever been a hindrance

Figure 15.

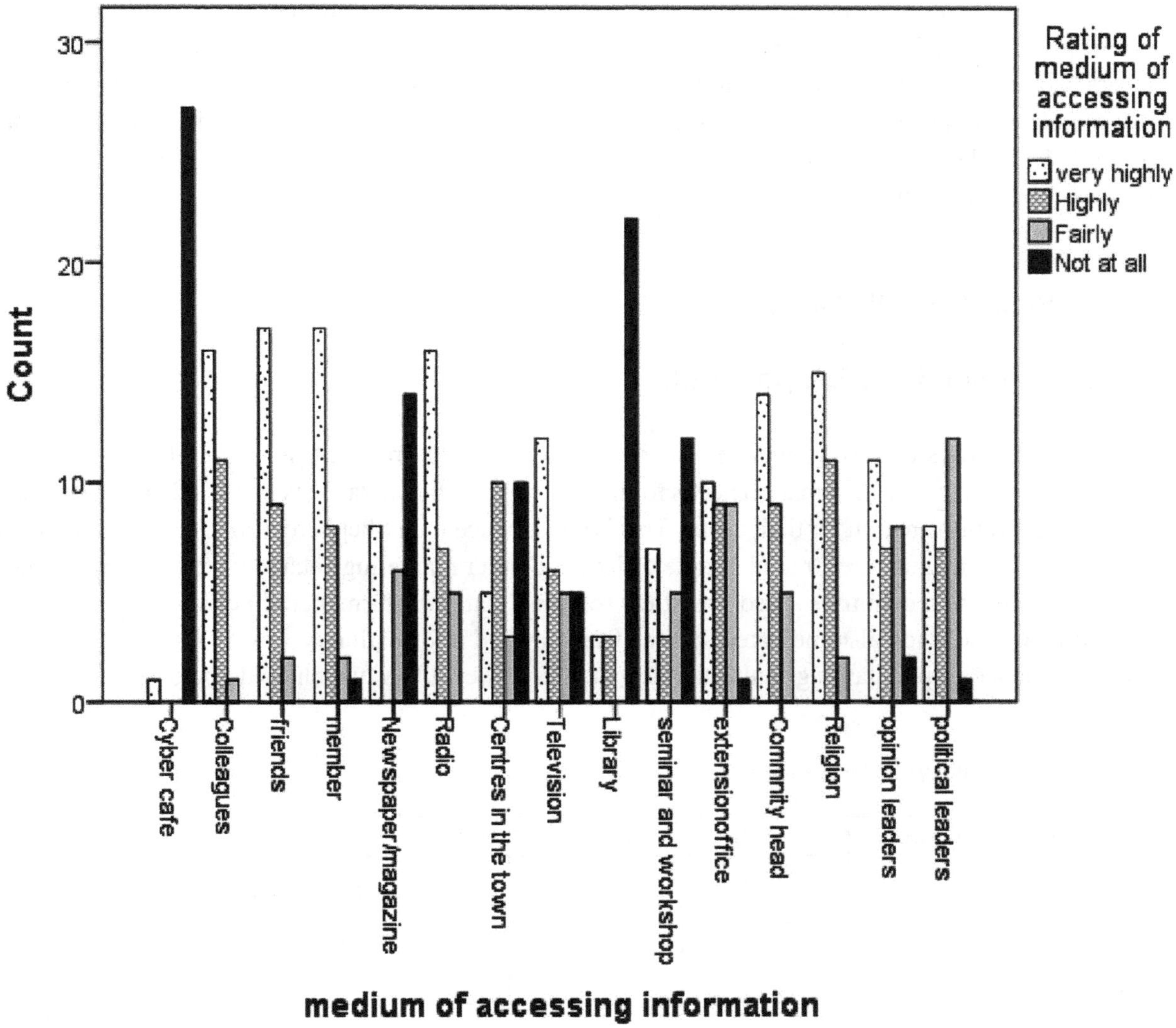

to seeking information by the respondents, the findings in this case shows that 28.6% of the respondents indicated very highly that conflict among association of farmers can prevent information from getting to each other, 15.7% of the respondents agreed highly to it, 10.7% of the respondents agreed fairly to it, while 45% of the respondents did not agree at all. It could be observed that cumulatively, the conflict in association could be a hindrance to seeking and accessing information. However, despite all the identified problems, it is noticeable that about three of the variables does not constitute any hindrance to the process of accessing information to the respondents. For example, availability of network for mobile communication was not seen as a problem for getting information, only 25% of the respondents agreed very highly that lack of network for mobile communication is a challenge, while 10.7% of the respondents also agreed to it highly, 7.1% of the respondents agreed to it fairly, and 57.1% of the respondents did not agree to it at all. Similarly, body disability of any form was not accepted by the respondent as hindrance to seek information, from the analysis, 3.6% of the respondents indicated very highly that body disability is a challenge, 10.7% of the respondents also agreed highly that it is a challenge, while 3.6% of the respondents agreed to it fairly. However, 82.1% did not agree at all that body disability hinders them from seeking information. The study also endeavored to find out if cultural difference among the farmers has been a hindrance to seek information, the respondents' response to this shows that 25% of the respondents indicated highly that cultural difference is a challenge faced by them in accessing information, 5.7% of the respondents also agreed highly, 15% of the respondents agreed fairly to it, however 54.3% of the respondents did not agree at all (Table 12 and Figure 16).

DISCUSSION OF FINDINGS

Information Needs of Respondents

Information on crops disease prevention, marketing agricultural products, agricultural loan and agro chemicals were the major information needs for farmers in the study area. This implies that farmers lack access to market information for their crops. This is consonance with Shepherd, (2000), who pointed out that information on, quantities traded, market prices and other marketing-related matters rarely reaches farmers in developing countries. Also, the study revealed that most farmers did not know where to get loans, similarly the study also indicated that the farmers need information on how to hire tractors to for land maintenance or purchase agricultural tools such as power tillers, which could be used to improve

Table 12. Challenges/problems faced

Challenges/Problems Faced	Rating of the Challenges Faced				Total
	Very Highly	Highly	Fairly	Not at All	
Mobile communication	25.0%	10.7%	7.1%	57.1%	100.0%
Purchase credit	32.1%	10.7%	32.1%	25.0%	100.0%
Inability to use phone	39.3%	14.3%	32.1%	14.3%	100.0%
Body disability	3.6%	10.7%	3.6%	82.1%	100.0%
Extension workers	17.9%	10.7%	28.6%	42.9%	100.0%
Language barrier	32.1%	3.6%	35.7%	28.6%	100.0%
No electricity	39.3%	32.1%	25.0%	3.6%	100.0%
Inability to read and write	67.9%	25.0%	7.1%		100.0%
Limited time to seek for information	46.4%	32.1%	7.1%	14.3%	100.0%
Fear of going to urban areas	42.9%	25.0%	25.0%	7.1%	100.0%
Conflict among association member	28.6%	15.7%	10.7%	45.0%	100.0%
Lack of information center	35.7%	28.6%	17.9%	17.9%	100.0%
Unreliable source of information	35.7%	39.3%	17.9%	7.1%	100.0%
Lack of authentic transfer information	42.9%	25.0%	21.4%	10.7%	100.0%
Cultural difference	25.0%	5.7%	15.0%	54.3%	100.0%

Figure 16.

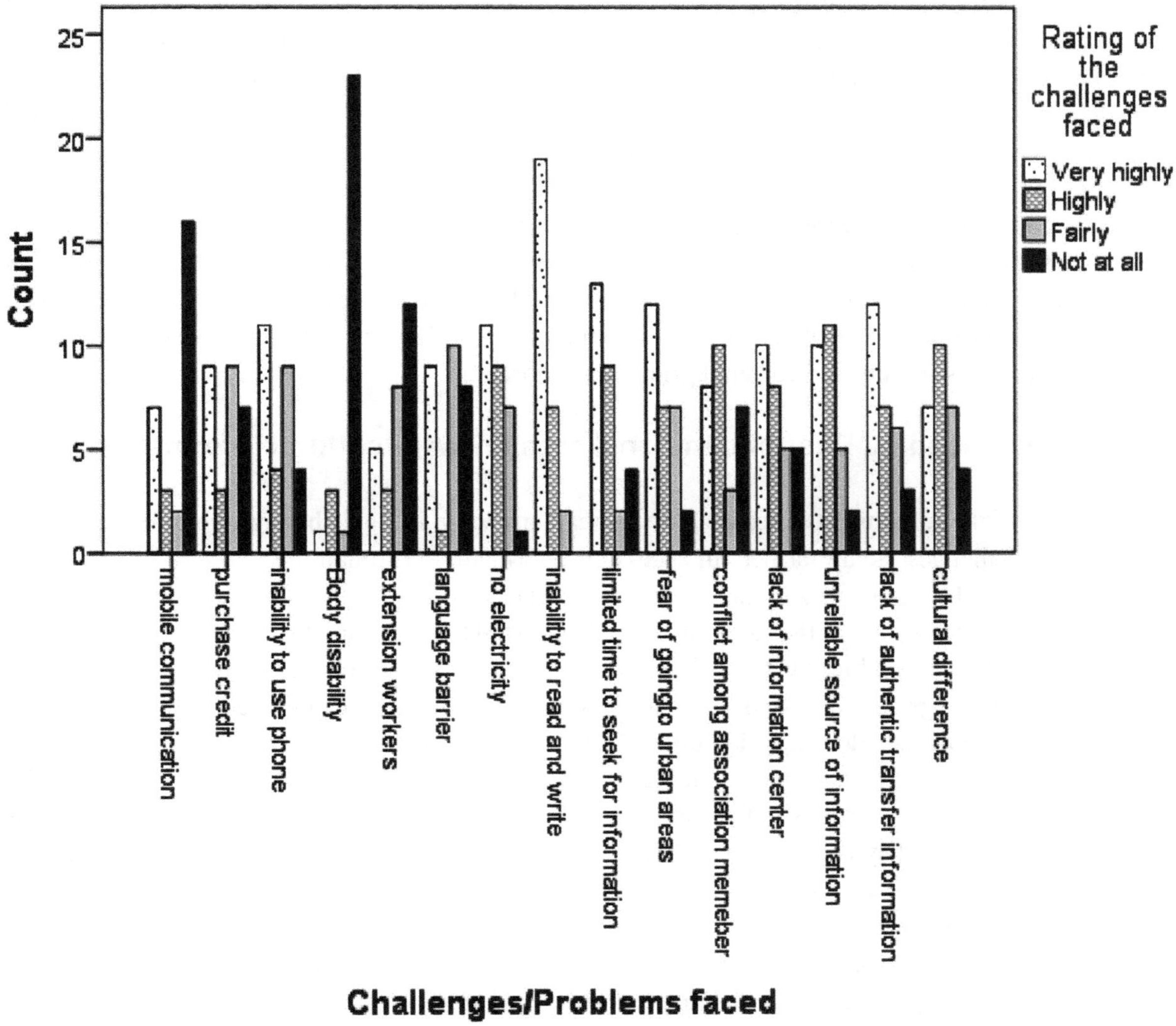

their agricultural productivity. Munyambonera et al., (2012) adds that availability and access to adequate, timely and information on low cost credit from different institutional sources is of great importance especially to small and marginal farmers.

Medium of Accessing Information

Colleagues (co-farmers), personal experience, neighbors or friends and agricultural extension officers were the major sources of information used by the farmers in accessing agricultural information. The implication here is that most of the respondents relied on interpersonal sources in accessing agricultural information, probably because of their regularly availability and accessibility. Lwoga et al., (2011) for instance stressed that interpersonal sources such as friends, relatives and neighbours are all the time become the main providers of the agriculture information due to their credibility, reliability and most of all, they are trusted by the rural community. However, none of the respondents reported to use neither internet nor library and information centres in accessing agricultural information. This is probably because of low level of education, lack of electricity, lack of libraries or information centres in the rural areas, lack of of the role of internet in provision of agricultural information to farmers and lack of lack of ICTs infrastructure in rural areas. Finding of this study are not surprising as they are in line with what have been reported previously by Benard (2011), Mtega and Benard (2013); Shaffril et al. (2010) and Samah et al. (2011). For instance, have established a few reasons why farmers are reluctant to use advance technology in accessing agricultural information such as internet, and among the reasons are do not know the benefits of the advance technology; they are illiterates: do not have skills or expertise in using the advance technology; lack of time spent on ICT and difficulties in using ICT. This therefore, calls for the government to create enabling environment for the farmers to use this modern technology so as they can access timely and current agricultural information.

Challenges Faced by Respondents in Accessing Agricultural Information

The majority of the respondents cited inability to read and write in English language in the study area was one the challenges facing farmers in accessing information. Through the oral interview with the key informants and personal observation via the researcher it was noted that there were no information services available in the area of the study such as village/ward libraries and the information centre in the community is only present but it is not utilized by the farmers. This is a common problem in most rural farmers. Therefore, agricultural extension workers should regard it as a challenge and provide farmers with access to current and relevant agricultural information. The findings further revealed the inadequate numbers of extension agents as major challenges constraining farmers from accessing information. For instance, in the study, the farmers indicated that lack or non-availability of extension officers is a challenge. In view of this, they do not have enough information to access from the agricultural extension officers. This also is in line with what have been found by Aina's (2006) findings, which revealed that the ratio of agricultural extension workers to the population in Africa is low. Similarly, inadequate funds were another challenge hindering farmers from accessing agricultural information as it was pointed by majority of the respondents. Due to financial problems, some of the farmers cannot afford to buy airtime, also, due to lack of electricity, the farmers are usually unable to charge their mobile phones to access and communicate information. Therefore, agricultural information sources and services where they exist should be widely published and promoted, not only to create awareness but also to promote and encourage usage by farmers.

CONCLUSION

According to Sarah et al (2012) in recent decades the value of information has increased considerably as the agricultural systems in developing countries become knowledge intensive. Therefore, the need to determine how farmers access information, the medium they use and the constraint that hinders their free access to required information is very important because like any other business farmers need concise, timely and comprehensive information to avoid loss of their farm produce, both on the farm and storage level, and also require appropriate environment to sell their produce for profit, all these and others are important factors to increase farmers productivity and consequently availability of food for citizens and sustenance of the nation. It is in this regard that this research is very important and findings can be of immense importance to guide research institute, state agricultural policy makers and international agencies who are also interested in the farming system in Nigeria.

RECOMMENDATIONS

It could be observed that from the age group, majority of farmers in laduba community are within the age range of 31-40, it is important that necessary incentives and encouragement is given to attract the youths of younger age to farming for availability of food for the nation.

It is noticeable that females form part of the farming population in Laduba, this is quite encouraging, for the population of the female to be improved, adequate access to information that will educate them and invoke their interest in farming is necessary.

The education status of farmers in in this study reveals that great percentage of them does not have formal education, only 14.3% of them had secondary education, this may hinder access to vital farming information from documentaries of national and international agricultural agencies. Hence, there is need for the farmers to be introduced to formal education through adult education programme on radio and television using the laduba information centre effectively.

From the study, the farmers significantly declared that information in agriculture is their major area of interest, therefore it is now important that all media that will assist the farmers to get concise, accurate and comprehensive information be made available to them. This may increase their interest in farming and consequently boost their economic level and consequently eradicate poverty among them and the nation in general.

Concerted effort should be made by government extension workers to provide the farmers information on how to prevent diseases on their crops on the field and also the best storage method for their farm produce, also they should be provided information on the best agro-chemicals to apply on their farm.

The information centre presently in the village should be improved for farmers to use it, human resource personnel that will promote its usage should be employed, the information center should have medium of disseminating information like radio and television and a well-stocked library could be developed in the centre, stocked with information materials to promote adult education programmes and enlightenment on different areas of farming. The documents acquired for these purpose should be in local languages and those written in simple understandable English language words.

The government should improve on the electricity in some of the rural areas including Laduba community and negotiate with operators of mobile communications, so that they can have subsidized airtime to communicate and receive information.

The group of extension workers like those from Kwara State Agricultural development project (ADP) and Nigerian Stored Products Research Institute (NSPRI) should interact effectively to give the farmers timely and necessary information they require and the extension workers should endeavor to sustain friendliness among the members of associations that exist in the community so that any conflict will not arise among them that will disrupt information sharing.

REFERENCES

Adereti, F. O., Fapojuwo, O. F., & Onasanya, A. S. (2006). Information on utilization on cocoa production techniques by farmers in Oluyole Local Government Area of Oyo State, Nigeria. *European Journal of Soil Science*, *3*(1), 1–7.

Aina, L. O. (2006, August 20-24). Information Provision to Farmers in Africa: The Library- extension service linkage. *Proceedings of the World library and information congress, 72nd IFLA general conference and council '06*, Seoul, Korea. Retrieved from http://www.ifla.org/iv/ifla72/index.htm

Ajayi, O.O. (2002). African Response to the Information Communication Technology Revolution: A case study of the ICT development in Nigeria (ATPS Special Paper Series No 8).

Anwar, M. A. (2007). Research on information seeking and use in Pakistan: An assessment. *Pakistan Journal of Library and Information Science*, *8*, 15–32.

Aziagba, P. C., & Okede, G. W. (2011). information seeking behavior of cassava farmers in Upata clan, Ekpeye community of Rivers State, Nigeria.

Babu, S. C., Glendenning, C. J., Asenso-Okyere, K., & Govindarajan, S. K. (2012). Farmer's information needs and search behaviors. IFPRI Discussion paper 01165.

Borgman, C. L. (2000). *From Gutenberg to the global information infrastructure: access to information in the network world.* Cambridge, MA: MIT Press.

Brophy, P. (1993). Networking in British academic libraries. *British Journal of Academic Librarianship*, *8*(1), 49–60.

Butterworth, R. (2006, June 15). Information seeking and retrieval as a leisure activity. DL-CUBA 2006 - Workshop on digital libraries in the context of users' broaden activities, Chapel Hill, USA. *Proceedings of JCDL '06*. Retrieved from http://www.uclic.ucl.ac.uk/events/dl-cuba2006/papers/Butterworth.pdf

Dadzie, P. S. (2005). Electronic resources: Access and usage at Ashesi University College. *Campus-Wide Information Systems*, *22*(5), 1065–0741. Retrieved from http://www.emeraldinsight.com/Insight/ViewContentServlet doi:10.1108/10650740510632208

Devadason, F. J., & Pratap, P. L. (1997). Methodology for the identification of information needs and uses of users. *IFLA Journal*, *23*(1), 41–51. doi:10.1177/034003529702300109

Ellis, D. (1993). Modeling the information-seeking patterns of academic researchers: A grounded theory approach. *The Library Quarterly*, *63*(4), 469–486. doi:10.1086/602622

Ellis, D., Cox, D., & Hall, K. (1993). A Comparison of the Information Seeking Patterns of Researchers in the Physical and Social Sciences. *The Journal of Documentation*, *49*(4), 356–369.

Ellis, D., & Haugan, M. (1997). Modelling the Information Seeking Patterns of Engineers and Research Scientists in Industrial Environment. *The Journal of Documentation*, *53*(4), 384–403. doi:10.1108/EUM0000000007204

Hayden, K.A. (1999). Information Seeking Models. Retrieved from http://www.ucalgary.ca/~ahayden/seeking.html

Järvelin, K., & Wilson, T. D. (2003). On conceptual models for information seeking and retrieval research. *Information Research*, 9(1). Retrieved from http://InformationR.net/ir/9-1/paper163.html

Kakai, J. M., Ikoja-Odongo, R., & Kigongo-Bukenya, I. M. N. (2004). A study of the information seeking behavior of undergraduate students of Makerere University, Uganda. *World Libraries*, 14(1). Retrieved from http://www.worlib.org/vol14no1/print/kakai_print.html

Krikelas, J. (1983). Information-seeking behaviour: Patterns and concepts. *Drexel Library Quarterly*, 19(2), 5-20, 78.

Kuhlthau, C. C. (1993). *Seeking meaning: a process approach to library and information services*. Norwood, NJ: Ablex Publishing.

Lwoga, E. T., Stilwell, C., & Ngulube, P. (2011). Access and use of agricultural information and knowledge in Tanzania. Retrieved from http://ir.muhas.ac.tz:8080/jspui/bitstream/123456789/1368/1/library_review_paper_lwoga_Stilwel_Ngulube.pdf

Meho, L. I., & Tibbo, H. R. (2003). Modeling the information-seeking behavior of social scientists: Ellis's study revisited. *Journal of the American Society for Information Science and Technology*, *54*(6), 570–587. doi:10.1002/asi.10244

Menzel, H. (1996). Information needs and uses. In C.A. Cuadra (Ed.), Annual Review of Information Science and Technology (ARIST) (Vol. 1, pp. 41-69). USA: Interscience Publishers.

Momoh, A. U, Osaheni, O & Oshioneb, F. (2015). Information seeking behavior of nurses in central hospitals in Delta State. *Pyrex Journal of Library and Information Science*, 1(3), 26.

Mtega, W., & And Benard, R. (2013). The state of rural information and communication services in Tanzania: A meta-analysis. *International Journal of Information and Communication Technology Research*, *3*(2), 64–73.

Munyambonera, E., Nampewo, D., Adong, A., & Mayanja, M. (2012). Access and Use of Credit in Uganda: Unlocking the Dilemma of Financing Small Holder Farmers. Retrieved from http://ageconsearch.umn.edu/bitstream/150229/2/policybrief25.pdf

Okunade, O. S. & Williams, J. O. (2014). *Agriculture in Nigeria: problems, consequences and the way forward*. Ilorin: Adewumi press.

Price, A. C. (2009). How to make a dollar out of fifteen cents: Tips for electronic collection development. *Collection Building*, *28*(1), 31–34. doi:10.1108/01604950910928493

Ray, K., & Day, J. (1998). Student attitudes towards electronic information resources. *Information Research*, 4(2). Retrieved from http://informationr.net/ir/4-2/paper54.html

Robinson, A. (2006). Open access: The view of a commercial publisher. *Journal of Thrombosis and Haemostasis*, *4*(7), 1454–1460. doi:10.1111/j.1538-7836.2006.02009.x PMID:16839337

Saravan,, R., & Raja,, P., & Tayeng, S. (2009). Information input pattern and information need of Tribal Farmers in Arnuchal Pradesh, *Indian Journal of Extension Education*, *45*(1&2), 51-54

Shaffril, H. A. M., Samah, B. A., Hassan, M. A., & Silva, J. L. (2010). Socio-economic factors that impinge computer usage in administration works among village leaders in Malaysia. *Scientific Research and Essays*, *5*, 3623–3633.

L. Shanta Meitei & Th. Purnima Devi. (2009). Farmers information Needs in Rural Manipur: an assessment. *Annals of Library and information studies*, 56(2), 35-40

Shao, X., & Scherlen, A. (2007). Perceptions of open access publishing among academic journal editors in China. *Serials Review*, *33*(2), 114–121. doi:10.1080/00987913.2007.10765105

Sharma, P. S. K. (1990). *Universe of knowledge and research methodology*. Delhi: Ken Publications.

Shuling, W. (2007). Investigation and analysis of current use of electronic resources in university libraries. *Library Management*, *28*(1/2), 72–88. Retrieved from http://www.emeraldinsight.com/Insight/ViewContentServlet?Filename=Published/EmeraldFullTextArticle/Articles/0150280107.html doi:10.1108/01435120710723563

Solomon, P. (2002). Discovering information in context. *Annual Review of Information Service and Technology*, *36*(1), 229–264. doi:10.1002/aris.1440360106

Stigter, C. J. (2002). Opportunities to improve the use of seasonal climate forecasts. Bangkok, Thailand: Asian Disaster Preparedness Center (ADPC).

Swain, D. K., & Panda, K. C. (2009). Use of electronic resources in business school libraries of an Indian state: A study of librarians' opinion. *The Electronic Library*, *27*(1), 74–85. doi:10.1108/02640470910934605

Swain, D. K., & Panda, K. C. (2009). Use of electronic resources in business school libraries of an Indian state: A study. *Collection Building*, *28*(3), 108–116. doi:10.1108/01604950910971134

Swanson, B. (2008). Global review of good agricultural extension and advisory service systems. Food and Agricultural Organization, Rome.

Swanson, B., & Rajalahti, R. (2010). *Strengthening agricultural extension and advisory systems: procedures for accessing, transforming and evaluating extension systems. Agricultural and rural development discussion* (p. 45). Washington, DC: World Bank.

Tella, A., Tella, A., Ayeni, C. O., & Omoba, R. O. (2007). Self-Efficacy and Use of Electronic Information as Predictors of Academic Performance. *Electronic Journal of Academic and Special Librarianship*, 8(2). Retrieved from http://southernlibrarianship.icaap.org/content/v08n02/tella_a01.html

Thachill, G. (2008). Academic Libraries Redefined: Old Mission with a New Face. Scroll, 1(1).

Tologbonse, D., Fashola, O., & Obadiah, M. (2008). Policy Issues in Meeting Rice Farmers Agricultural Information Needs in Niger State. *Journal of Agricultural Extension*, *12*(2), 84–94.

Toner, L. (2008). Non-use of Library Services by Students in a UK Academic Library. *Evidence Based Library and Information Practice*, 3(3). Retrieved from http://ejournals.library.ualberta.ca/index.php/EBLIP/article/view/1330/1241

Tsakonas, G., & Papatheodorou, C. (2006). Analysing and evaluating usefulness and usability in electronic information services. *Journal of Information Science*, *32*(5), 400–419. doi:10.1177/0165551506065934

Weiler, A. (2005). Information-Seeking Behavior in Generation Y Students: Motivation, Critical Thinking, and Learning Theory. *Journal of Academic Librarianship*, *31*(1), 46–53. doi:10.1016/j.acalib.2004.09.009

Wilson, T. D. (1999). Models in information behavior research. *The Journal of Documentation*, *55*(3), 249–270. doi:10.1108/EUM0000000007145

Wilson, T. D. (2000). Recent trends in user studies: Action research and qualitative methods. *Information Research*, 5(3). Retrieved from http://informationr.net/ir/5-3/paper76.html

Zhang, Y. (2001). Scholarly use of internet-based electronic resources. *Journal of the American Society for Information Science*, *52*(8), 628–654. doi:10.1002/asi.1113

ADDITIONAL READING

Lenz, E. R. (1984). Information seeking: A component of client decisions and health behavior. *ANS. Advances in Nursing Science*, *6*(3), 59–72. doi:10.1097/00012272-198404000-00010 PMID:6426379

Okwu, O. J., & Umoru, B. I. (2009). A study of women farmers' agricultural information needs and accessibility: A case study of Apa Local Government Area of Benue St. Retrieved from http://www.academicjournals.org/AJAR

Saima Sadaf, Asif Javed, & Muhammad Luqman. (n. d.). Preferences of Rural Women for Agricultural Information Sources: A Case Study of District Faisalabad–Pakistan. *Journal of Agriculture & Social Sciences*. Retrieved from http://www.fspublishers.org

Sharma, A. K. (2007). Information Needs and Sharing Pattern among Rural Women: A Study. *IASLIC Bulletin*, *52*(3), 156–167.

KEY TERMS AND DEFINITIONS

Community: A group sharing a common understanding and often of the same language, manners, tradition and law.

Farming: The act of cultivating land for the purpose of planting desired agricultural crops for sustenance of life and profit making.

Information: A processed data being searched for to use to enhance occupation and other things that sustains life.

Information Need: A piece of information, whether recorded or not, which an individual or a member of a group requires for effective functioning in their daily activities.

Information Seeking Behavior: An individual's way and manner of gathering and sourcing for information for personal use.

Chapter 13
Role of Social Networking for Information Seeking in a Digital Library Environment

Ganiyu Ojo Adigun
Ladoke Akintola University of Technology, Nigeria

Oluwole Akanmu Odunola
Ladoke Akintola University of Technology, Nigeria

Adewale Joel Sobalaje
Ladoke Akintola University of Technology, Nigeria

ABSTRACT

This chapter discusses how to use social networking tools for information seeking in a digital library environment. Social networking is an evolutionary development of online participation, where people of common interest communicate, share and contribute content on the social cyberspace. The role of social networking for information seeking in libraries, most especially digital library is still evolving and cannot be over-emphasized. There is the need for libraries to exploit the advantages presented by these new media in providing better services. Social networking tools enable librarians and other information professionals to communicate, network and share documents with many clients regardless of location, and at little or no expense and viz. The chapter looks at: information seeking / search process; digital libraries; social networking as a concept; relationship between web 2.0, library 2.0, social media and social networking; role of social networking in digital library environment; role of information professionals in using social networking; social media platforms in digital library environment; challenges and prospects of integrating social networking with digital libraries and ways to improve the use of social networking for information seeking and dissemination in the future.

DOI: 10.4018/978-1-5225-0296-8.ch013

INTRODUCTION

Social Networking can be seen as an evolutionary development of online participation, where people of common interest communicate, share and contribute content on the social cyberspace. As seen by Adigun, et.al (2015), Social networking also referred to as Social Media, is a new way of providing library and information services through new Internet technologies, with emphasis on '**user-centred**', two-way interaction and communication of information. The term social networking or media encompasses all Internet-based or mobile applications which operate for the purpose of collaboration, where participants can connect, create, comment, view, share, rate, discover, profile, and exchange user-generated content (Bradley & McDonald, 2011 cited in Onwuchekwa, 2015). According to Oladokun (2015), for reasons of its resourcefulness, adaptability and expediency, social networking has become an integral part of modern world, and constitutes a very dynamic aspect of the mass media that has not only grow in popularity, but also become mainstream. Amuda (2015) who cited Michael (2010) also defined social networking as the wide range of Internet-based and mobile services that allow users to participate in online exchanges or join online communities such as Facebook, MySpace, LinkedIn, Twitter, Delicious, Flickr, Live Journal, etc. Though the definitions of social networking or media are diverse and relative, all laid emphasis on two-way interaction, content creation and sharing as well as user-centeredness.

Every human being is engaged in information seeking in one form or the other either to augment an existing knowledge or to discover new ones and it has been well documented that information seeking and use varies by discipline, profession, task, situation, and context. Where an individual encounters a problem or task for which their current knowledge is inadequate, they may engage in information-seeking in order to change their knowledge state.

Digital libraries on the other hand are constructed by and for a community of users, and their functional capabilities support the information needs and uses of that community in which they are to be found. They are a component of communities in which individuals and groups interact with each other, using data, information, and knowledge resources and systems. In this sense they are an extension, enhancement, and integration of a variety of information institutions as physical places where resources are selected, collected, organized, preserved, and accessed in support of a user community. The content of digital libraries includes data, metadata that describe various aspects of the data (e.g., representation, creator, owner, reproduction rights), and metadata that consist of links or relationships to other data or metadata, whether internal or external to the digital library (Borgman, et.al, 2001).

LITERATURE REVIEW

Information Seeking/Search Process

Every human being is engaged in information seeking in one form or the other either to augment an existing knowledge or to discover new ones. Where an individual encounters a problem or task for which their current knowledge is inadequate, they may engage in information-seeking in order to change their knowledge state (Belkin, 2000 in Heath, 2008). Seeking information is one of the most common activities people perform on the Web (Haythornthwaite, 2001 cited by Oladokun, 2015) as well as in the library whether digital or not. Search engines such as Google attempt to support this process using complex algorithms that take account of the content of documents and their patterns of linkage to other documents

(Page, et al., 1999 in Heath, 2008), in an attempt to identify documents that are most relevant to a user's search query. However, despite the vast extent of digital and online resources, locating the required piece of information can still present challenges to the user. These challenges according to Heath (2008) may take a number of forms, for example:

1. That user may not be able to identify suitable keywords that lead him to documents containing the information he requires, due to issues with synonymy (where two different terms are used to refer to the same concept) or polysemy (where one word has many meanings), or because he is unsure of exactly what he is looking for;
2. That required information may not yet be available online because it is sensitive in nature or stored in a legacy format or system; and
3. That user's search query may yield so many results that identifying those most relevant to the original information need is not always possible (Heath, 2008).

The last problem is an example of what is referred to as information overload (Denning, 2006 in Heath, 2008), where the vast numbers of documents on the Web or digital archive that may be somewhat relevant to a query, overwhelm the smaller subset of those of greatest relevance. In many cases, just one of the documents linked to from a search engine results page may be sufficient to meet the user's information need, but this document may not be easily identifiable among the many hundreds or thousands listed in the results. Ordinary human beings are not well equipped to quickly process and differentiate such large amounts of information, whereas machines are more adapted to this task.

It has also been well documented that information seeking and use varies by discipline, profession, task, situation, and context (e.g., Borgman, 2006; Hansen & Järvelin, 2005; Savolainen, 2006a, 2006b; Vakkari, 2006; Vakkari & Talja, 2005). Consequently, a substantial body of literature exists on information seeking behavior, information seeking and scientific communication. Due to space limitations, this review is extremely brief but readers are directed to several excellent reviews and monographs for this line of research (Case, 2002; Bates, 2005; Fisher, Erdelez & McKechnie, 2005; Spink & Cole, 2005; Kuhlthau, 1991, 2007; Kuhlthau, Heinström, & Todd, 2008).

Kuhlthau (1991, 2007) conducted research on student activities for affective, cognitive, and physical dimensions of information behavior in the traditional library setting and also in technology-rich online environments. The Information Search Process (ISP) Model, devised by Kuhlthau, depicts six stages of student information activity: initiation, selection, exploration, formulation, collection, and presentation. Together these six stages can help explain student information behavior and also allow educators to guide students in search activities (Kuhlthau, 1991).

Kuhlthau's (2007) research, an updated review of the literature and extensive inquiry project among n = 574 students, indicated that the ISP model for dimensions of information behavior continues to be useful in explaining the search process in the digital and technology-pervasive information environment of the Web 2.0 world (Kuhlthau, 2007; Kuhlthau, Heinström, & Todd, 2008). Validation of Kuhlthau's (1991) ISP model for student information behavior in technology-rich environments provides direction for instruction designed to guide student inquiry (Kuhlthau, Maniotes, & Caspari, 2007) beyond the traditional library to the Internet realm of digital information. Viewed as an instructional model, guided inquiry can direct teachers' and students' information behavior to educationally meaningful activities that will support knowledge construction. One approach to guided inquiry focuses on a teacher and curriculum connection to each individual student's learning environment. Kuhlthau (2007) cited Maniotes (2005) who conceptualized three spaces that are important for teaching and learning - the first space, the students' current experience and knowledge; the second space, the curriculum; and the third space, the teachers' and students' learning environment. Maniotes' model is based on the premise that educational social interaction and intellectual discourse in the teachers' and students' third space can interconnect their experience and knowledge with curriculum (Kuhlthau, Maniotes, & Caspari, 2007). ICT, especially social media communications tools, offer new options to support teacher and student learning interaction and guide their information behavior in digital information settings of the 21st century. The third space for curriculum-driven intellectual communication employs ICT to advance learning interactions via social dimensions of student-teacher systems of communications.

Digital Libraries

Digital libraries are an emerging concept, despite over a decade of research and development (Borgman, 1999; Borgman, 2000a). This work builds upon the definition established in Borgman, et al. (2001) that:

1. Digital libraries are a set of electronic resources and associated technical capabilities for creating, searching, and using information. In this sense they are an extension and enhancement of information storage and retrieval systems that manipulate digital data in any medium (text, images, sounds; static or dynamic images) and exist in distributed networks. The content of digital libraries includes data, metadata that describe various aspects of the data (e.g., representation, creator, owner, reproduction rights), and metadata that consist of links or relationships to other data or metadata, whether internal or external to the digital library (Borgman, et.al, 2001).
2. Digital libraries are constructed (collected and organized) by and for a community of users, and their functional capabilities support the information needs and uses of that community. They are a component of communities in which individuals and groups interact with each other, using data, information, and knowledge resources and systems. In this sense they are an extension, enhancement, and integration of a variety of information institutions as physical places where resources are selected, collected, organized, preserved, and accessed in support of a user community. These information institutions include, among others, libraries, museums, archives, and schools, but digital libraries also extend and serve other community settings, including classrooms, offices, laboratories, homes, and public spaces (Borgman, et.al, 2001).

There are several other definitions of what a digital library is as proposed by several other authors. Notable among them is Smith (2001) who defined a digital library as an organized and focused collection of digital objects, including text, images, video and audio, with the methods of access and retrieval and for the selection, creation, organization, maintenance and sharing of collection. Though the focus of this definition is on the document collection, it stresses the fact that the digital libraries are much more than a random assembly of digital objects. According to Smith's definition the main targets of digitalization are easy, fast, and convenient access to the world's information (regardless of where that information is stored) at any time, from anywhere in the world effective storage and organization of massive amounts of text, multimedia and data beyond the bounds of what even the largest single library could provide. Daniel (2001) on the other hand, diligently listed digitalised material in the library environment to include but not limited to: books, journals, paper-based archives, video, film, and sound recordings that are as visible in the digital library service environment as are online catalogs, finding aids, abstracting and indexing services, e-journal and e-print services, digitized collections, geographic information systems, Internet resources, and other "electronic" holdings.

As digital libraries quickly increase in number and size, researchers are continually developing improved public access methods for the many different types of digital library information. The primary user interface approach, especially for libraries containing unstructured collections of heterogeneous documents, is the keyword query method. In this case as opined by North, et.al (1996), Information Retrieval systems pre-process documents in the library, usually using automated algorithms, to generate comprehensive indices (meta-data). Then, when a user enters a query, the system can quickly generate a list of matching documents.

Social Networking as a Concept

As observed by Adigun, Adegbore and Amuda (2015), social networking is an evolutionary development of online participation where people of common interest communicate, share and contribute content on the social cyberspace. The term "Social Networking" refers to a range of Internet/information technology-enabled software programs that allow users to interact and work collaboratively with other users. It is a viable tool for cooperation and sharing of knowledge in an open access platform. In the Social Network Space (SNS) according to Adigun, et.al (2015), people with common interests are able to share information with each other via a huge variety of social networking sites (sites created specifically to make sharing, communicating, and creating information as simple and efficient as possible). Social networking is a new way of providing library service through new Internet technologies, with emphasis on "user-centered", two-way interaction and communication of information.

With new networking tools, information can now flow in a multi-faceted dimension (library to user, user to library, library to library, and user to user), rather than the one-way stereotype form of library to user (Adigun, et.al, 2015). It is constantly expanding the world of participatory and collaborative scholarly communication and learning. It is a new model of online service that encourages an increased flow of information from library to users and from the user back to the library. Online participation and content contribution are core issues in the present social networking practices. Social networking tool is a platform where users are both consumers and producers of online content (Cowling, 2012). With these tools, librarians can constantly evaluate and update content to meet the changing needs of users most especially in a digital library environment. These tools are used for collaboration and sharing of ideas and it is becoming an integral part of library services.

It also calls for libraries to encourage users' participation and feedback mechanism in the development and maintenance of library services. The active participation of users in a social media-enabled digital library environ, enables them to contribute content, establish communication links, and stay informed of new developments in the social network space. With information and ideas flowing in both directions – from the library to the user and from the user to the library – library services have the ability to evolve and improve on a constant and rapid basis. It includes ability to browse, search, invite friends to connect and interact, share film reviews, comments, blog entries, favourites, discussions, events, videos, ratings, music, classified ads, tag and classified information and more. A social network allows individual to join and create a personal profile, then formally connect with other users of the systems as social friend.

It can be expressed as social connecting sites among the social user in web 2.0 domain. Social network sites (SNSs) are web-based services that allow individuals to:

- Construct a public or semi-public profile within a bounded system,
- Articulate a list of other users with whom they share a connection, and
- View and traverse their list of connections and those made by others within the system (Boyd, 2007).

Social networking media is also defined by Kim, et.al (2014), as forms of electronic communication (as Web sites for social networking and microblogging) through which users create online communities to share information, ideas, personal messages, and other content (as videos). While there are different ways to categorize social media, its typology is often based on the main function and purpose of use, such as for blogging, microblogging (such as Twitter), social networking (for instance, Facebook), collaborative knowledge production and sharing (like Wikipedia), multimedia sharing (example: YouTube), and sharing reviews and opinions (such as social Q&A, user reviews).

The advent of social media has brought about significant impacts on daily life, not only changing the ways in which people stay connected but also presenting considerable opportunities and challenges for librarians and educators. It is already known that social networking sites (SNS) such as Facebook are widely used; in fact, about 66 percent of online adults use SNS. College students are particularly heavy users of social media. For example, one 2011 Pew report found that over 80 percent of the college students surveyed used SNS (Smith, et.al, 2011 cited in Kim, et.al, 2014). With the increasing popularity of social media, librarians have actively leveraged these online forums to communicate with users and to reach out to potential audiences. Some librarians have also explored ways to use social media for teaching information literacy skills.

In addition to affecting communication, marketing, and instruction, social media seem to have changed researchers' and students' information-seeking behaviors. Some studies suggest that faculty and students may be using various social media platforms to satisfy their academic and everyday-life information needs. Such changes in information-seeking behavior make it increasingly urgent to understand faculties' and students' evaluation and use of information obtained from social media. Therefore, the time seems ripe to review (and potentially expand) the scope of information literacy education to include different media and contexts. In turn, this may further increase the value that librarians can bring to their clients' education and lifelong learning.

Social network analysis views social relationships in terms of nodes and ties. Nodes are the individual actors within the networks, and ties are the relationships between the actors. There can be many kinds of ties between the nodes. In its simplest form, a social network is a map of all of the relevant ties between the nodes being studied. The network can also be used to determine the social capital of individual actors. These concepts are often displayed in a social network diagram, where nodes are the points and ties are the lines. Before introducing social network in library, let have look on conceptual approach to web 2.0 and library 2.0 in digital library scenario.

Web 2.0, Library 2.0, Social Media, and Social Networking

This work will not be complete if it failed to trace the roots of social media back to the principles upon which social media is founded. The literature is used to contextualize how the terms web 2.0, library 2.0, social networking and social media relate to each other. Web 2.0 is characterised by open communication, participation, collaboration and content creation (Abram, 2005 cited in Adigun, et.al, 2015). The term social networking is often mentioned in conjunction with social media (Kaplan & Haenlein, 2010), whereby users can create a profile with the purpose of building a personal network to connect with others (Lenhart & Madden, 2007). The term social media encompasses any internet-based or mobile application which operates for the purpose of collaboration, where participants can connect, create, comment, view, share, rate, discover, profile and exchange user-generated content (Bradley & McDonald, 2011; Hanna, Rohm, & Crittenden, 2011). Web 2.0, social networking and social media are inextricably linked, and have in fact often been used synonymously (Cook & Hopkins, 2006).

The term web 2.0 precedes the terms social networking and social media in the research literature. Web 2.0 has been in usage since 2005, when it was defined by Tim O'Reilly and Dale Doherty (O'Reilly, 2005). Chu & Du (2008) state that social media can be taken to mean any collaborative environments employing web 2.0 technologies. Thus, web 2.0 is the platform upon which social networking and social media is based (Kaplan & Haenlein, 2010) and from which it has evolved from. For the purposes of this paper, the term social media will encompass all web 2.0 and social networking tools that enable content creation, sharing, discovering and exchange of user-generated content, with the main focus on their participatory nature. The interrelatedness of these terms means that the web 2.0 research that has paved the way for social networking and social media literature is still valid.

Library 2.0 can be seen as the library sector's response to web 2.0. and as such, many papers have focused on the notion of library 2.0 as a service model, which relates to the delivery of library programmes and services in innovative ways (Cho, 2008). It also relates to how library and information professionals are translating the principles of web 2.0 into the design and delivery of library services most especially in a digital library environment (Farkas, 2008; Partridge, 2011). How are libraries becoming 2.0 organisations? By considering libraries on a spectrum that ranges from the traditional brick and mortar library model to the library 2.0 model, libraries which adopt social media tools are moving towards the library 2.0 end of this spectrum. One way to consider where libraries sit on this spectrum is through the analysis of how social media is incorporated into library strategy. How are libraries future-planning for the inclusion of social media and incorporating it into their strategic or operational plans? Before an analysis of how social media is incorporated into library strategy, social media must first be contextualised against the broader context in the non-library sector (Adigun, et.al, 2015).

Social media is now in the mainstream and is expected by library users and client groups (O'Dell, 2010). For examples, Adigun, et.al (2015), submitted that: there are 845 million monthly active users on Facebook (Facebook, 2012); Twitter reported that they reached the 100 million user mark in 2011 (Kiss, 2011), and there are increasing numbers of new social media tools entering the market. There are also many organisations in the non-library sector that have already incorporated social media into service models to enhance relationships with customers. This incorporation of social media is no longer novel. Organisations are even moving beyond the use of social media in this way and expanding its use further to drive innovation in products and services (KPMG, 2011 cited in Adigun, et.al, 2015).

ROLES OF SOCIAL NETWORKING IN DIGITAL LIBRARY ENVIRONMENT

The roles of social networking for information seeking and dissemination in a digital library environment cannot be over-emphasized. Social networking seems to be an excellent way of reaching out to people of like mind in order to take advantage of individual or collective creativity and innovation. Some of the roles of social networking media for information seeking a in digital library environment are:

1. **Easy to Keep in Contact with People of Similar Interests:** Social networking in a digital library environment provides a platform for researchers and students that have similar interest to interact together. Researchers would be able to know what other researchers have carried out on the field through their publications. The contact of researchers in some of these social media are made available so that interested person could contact them for more information and for sharing of information resources if need be. This above is supported by Casia (2013) who stated that it is now easier than ever to keep in contact with colleagues. He stressed further that the potential of this enhanced connectivity is huge; whereas in the time past, researchers and students face the challenge of sorting through business cards in order to connect with another researcher of like mind trying to remember details about each person, it is now easier to look up a connection's credentials and research interests on their social media profile.
2. **Broader Connectivity:** The use of social networking media software in a digital library environment provides wide connectivity of people and information resources. Donna (2014) states that no matter what you are searching for, whether former college roommate, your first grade teacher, or an international friend, there is no easier or faster way to make a connection than via the social network. Although Facebook, Twitter, LinkedIn and MySpace are probably the most well-known social networking communities, there are new websites popping up regularly that are dedicated to allowing people to connect and to interact via the Internet. Through such sites, individuals make new friends or connections or extend their personal base by connecting and interacting with friends of friends and so forth for information resources. He stated further that in many ways, social communities are the virtual equivalent of meeting at the general store or at other socials places to exchange news and get update on friends and families. Likewise, this is achievable and a useful information seeking and dissemination platform in digital library environment.
3. **Common Interest:** When you opt to participate in a social network community, you can pick and choose those individuals whose likes and dislikes are similar to yours and build your network around them. For instance, if you are a book lover, you can find and interact with those who share your interest. Because you are connecting digitally instead of having to physically attend meetings, you have the luxury of joining many more groups and communities. You can meet with your friends anytime you have an Internet connection and whenever you find them online (Donna, 2014).
4. **Real-Time Information Sharing:** Many social networking sites incorporate an instant messaging feature, which means you can exchange information in real-time via a chat. This is a great feature for faculty and students when facilitating classroom discussions. In addition, the Internet is the ultimate online textbook. Researchers and Students no longer need to take out six library books at a time. Much of what they need to know, they can find online. Schools and academics are not the only settings where this type of real-time information sharing can be beneficial. Social networking can provide a tool for managers to utilize in team meetings, for conference organizers to use to update attendees and for business people to use as a means of interacting with clients or prospects (Donna, 2014).

ROLE OF INFORMATION PROFESSIONALS IN USING SOCIAL NETWORKING MEDIA IN A DIGITAL LIBRARY ENVIRONMENT

The potentiality and credibility of librarian and other information professionals is a question mark in the age of information landscape where technology is changing drastically. The answer to the ongoing debate on role of libraries becoming "inefficient, limited and obsolete" (Crawford, 2006 cited in Kim, et.al, 2014), may be "Yes" for libraries and librarians more importantly, but they need to change. The geometric increase in the quantity and quality of information, greater access, easy and quick retrieval of information are most crucial issues in scenario of knowledge management. Also the virtual presence of libraries seems to be great debate for future. Web 2.0 and its implication in library should be considered as huge challenge among the professionals. But on the other hand it would be a unique opportunity among the librarians to raise their visibility in information world by applying these new technologies in library activities. Every library (opined Kim, et.al, 2014) should have attained library 2.0 status by 2010. Therefore, the role of librarian cannot be ignored in library 2.0 community for winning the massive expectation of user in digital library environment. According to Kim, et.al (2014), librarian and other information professionals in the age of web 2.0 should perform the following roles for catering for the needs of user 2.0:

1. **Information Broker:** As an information broker he should identifies, retrieve, organize, repackage and provides electronic access to digital information resources by various means.
2. **Change Agent:** ICTs has posed a great challenge. For proper access to digital and e-information, librarian should work as technology application leader. He should have the time to evaluate systems that would facilitate e-access.
3. **Information Facilitator:** Accessing timely and easy retrieval of information is major issues in libraries. Librarian as information facilitator should make information access easier by providing easy network access, adopting suitable software, follower of social networking tools, e-journals licenses, and designing portal.
4. **Knowledge Educator:** User awareness on web 2.0 tools (SNS) is crucial for successfully implementing web 2.0 in the library. Librarian should train clients on internet use (i.e. tools, search engines, e-journals, e-databases, using of information portal, online tutorials etc.) to user so that these can be used for accessing potential information from various web resources.
5. **Innovative Manager:** Librarians can become innovative manager through the activities like web site or knowledge portal design, by giving various links from various information sources, providing information awareness on what library services are available in the website with their effective use to the user. As far the librarian is concerned, he should time to time evaluate websites on user centric approach.
6. **Effective Collaborator:** To become an effective and suitable collaborator it required the activities like expanding of collaboration not just with fellow librarian but information technology (IT) people who have experienced on using of recent SNS and web 2.0 tool so that some knowledge can be gained from them on how and when to use web 2.0 resources in the library. Libraries not only should examine how social software can improve services to their patrons, but they should also consider how these tools can improve internal communication and collaboration.

7. **Policy Maker:** Web 2.0 policy should be strictly followed and framed for the organization ensuring total or selective access to all information resources. However, if possible it should be effectively analyse before implementing in the library.
8. **Image Maker:** Add value to the library to gain management support and project a positive image to the outside world.
9. **User Interaction:** Finally, librarians often talk about providing outreach to their patrons. This usually means getting out of the library and providing services where patrons congregate. Libraries should be aware of their patrons' online social worlds, whether these are Massively Multiplayer Online Games (MMOGs), social networking sites, or other online communities. First and foremost, Librarian 2.0 understands his or her users at a deep level – not just as pointers and clickers (Habib, 2006). Librarian 2.0 understands end users deeply in terms of their goals and aspirations. Accordingly, action plan should be framed for implementing the concept of web 2.0 in library field (Kim, et.al, 2014).

SOCIAL MEDIA PLATFORMS IN A DIGITAL LIBRARY ENVIRONMENT

There are so many social networking or media platforms that could be employed for information seeking and dissemination in digital library environment, among these are the following:

- **Academia/Research Gates:** Either of these two academic social network can be used by both librarian and clients in their information dissemination and seeking process in a digital library setting. Users can be linked with other researchers in his/her area of study. The librarian having belonged to these other researchers' network will be able to refer the users to connect with other researchers with which they will be able to follow their research output. By doing so, his other colleagues who are following him or those he his following will have the opportunity of having access to his work, consult, reference and improve his impact factors.
- **Facebook:** Facebook can be utilized for communicating with the library by clients on a frequent basis. This platform can also be used by our library so that we can communicate with our researcher easily and provide means for the researcher to consult and ask any questions concerning any information they need. Facebook will provide a cheaper means of communication that is fast and thus keep the researcher updated on the current happenings both in the library as well as in their individual connections.
- **LinkedIn:** LinkedIn is also one of the leading professional social platforms which bring academics, technocrats and professionals together where each member's profile such as professional and academic accomplishments can be accessed. Information seekers as well as librarians can use the platform as a means of carrying referral services whereby a leading researcher can be linked to aspiring or upcoming ones for the purpose of advancing the frontiers of knowledge. It provides a platform to communicate with other researchers: LinkedIn allows creating of networks, in this case, a network of various research groups can be created for the researchers. Librarians can get patrons connected with specialists in their particular field of interest via LinkedIn and can use this platform to render specialized services such as Strategic Dissemination of Information (SDI).

- **Creating an ORCID:** Open Researcher and Contributor ID (ORCID) is an open, non-profit organization that maintains an international registry of unique researcher identifiers and a method of linking research activities to those identifiers. Libraries most especially digital ones, can include its client's ORCID ID on LinkedIn to make the research output more visible for upcoming researchers to use.
- **Google+:** Google+ is a social networking and identity service that is owned and operated by Google Inc. Google has described Google+ as a "social layer" that enhances many of its online properties, and that it is not simply a social networking website, but also an authorship tool that associates web-content directly with its owner/author (Adigun, et.al, 2015). It is easy for researchers and students to be on Google+ and access other Google accounts such as Google Scholar where he keeps track of his research outputs, citations, alerts, and index. In addition, other Google cloud services are within the user's reach and he does not have to sign in and out to access them. A good example here is Google drive which allows him to save and retrieve his articles on the 'go', allows him to share his findings with co researchers and students.

Some of the other Social Networking Sites (SNS) popularly used by librarians to meet the information needs of their users include but not limited to:

- **Blogs:** With this opportunity, the available resources of the digital library and information services, access and details about them will be blogged and uploaded unto World Wide Web. This will not only promote, disseminate and advertise library resources but also improve the impact of the library to clients through social media. Here, librarians can periodically post messages; share information on a particular subject or issue, and allow users to contribute to content. They can write articles, news on topical issues and expect an instant reaction from their users.
- **Flickr:** Librarians can use this tool to share and distribute new images of library collections. Cover page of new arrivals of both books and journals can be disseminated to users via Flickr.
- **Library Thing:** A tool that enriches the library OPAC. Once an account is created, a list of books with ISBNs is sent to Library Thing which sends back a piece of code which is pasted into the footer of the Library OPAC. Librarians can utilize this to send a list of current publications to users.
- **Micro-Blogging:** Twitter is very useful here. It offers the opportunity to recommend clients to research articles through short messages and links. Twitter can send a researcher's research output to those readers 'on the go' who does not have time to sit and read. These sets of readers can download the articles through their mobile devices, read, use, and reference thereby improving the impact of the library.
- **Myspace:** In Academic institutions where the researchers and students are; libraries have taken advantage of this site to post, calendar, custom catalog search tools, and blog features to improve their presence.
- **Ning:** Librarians can get connected with users, library associations, and more. The Nigerian Library Association (NLA) utilizes this platform to discuss topical issues among the members.
- **Twitter:** A micro blogging application, to keep staff and patrons updated on daily activities, like frequently updated collections. Users can utilize this platform to type in short messages or status update. Users can send Instant Messages (IM) on complaints or ask questions on a particular issue and get a feedback on the spot using twitter.

- **Wikis:** A free online encyclopedia that gives a background knowledge and definition of concepts. It offers a platform for users to access, edit and contribute to content. This is a collaborative web page for developing web content.
- **YouTube:** In institutions in Nigeria, events such as important highlights of inaugural lectures, conferences and workshops are disseminated via the YouTube.

CHALLENGES AND PROSPECTS OF USING SOCIAL NETWORKING IN DIGITAL LIBRARIES

The following (but not limited to) are some of the anticipated disadvantages of using social networking for information seeking and dissemination in a digital library environment:

- **Slow Speed of Internet:** Internet is a platform on which social media rest. Without the internet, social networking in a digital library environment may become practically impossible. Parmeshwar and Patil (2009) reported while examining use of the internet by Faculty and Research Scholars of Gulbarga University Library that the speed of the internet is slow in most cases. If the networking, transfer and sharing information resources are slow, it could discourage users to use the services no matter how good the services maybe.
- **Power Outage:** Electricity is one of the problems confronting social networking in a digital library environment. In Nigeria for example, electricity is one of the major problem confronting business organization, institutions and even government parastatals. Most of the alternatives to electricity like sola power, generator, inverters, etc. are not always sustainable.
- **Off-Topic:** Users may discuss discussing off the topic which may be an eventual waste of time and resources. If care is not taken, social networking in a digital library environment may also lead to dating which may attract which would have defeated the objective of using the platform.
- **Shallowness:** Justin (2014) reported that social media does promote a kind of intellectual and social shallowness but could have long-term negative consequences for researchers and learners. He stated further that Twitter, instant messages, and other social media tools focus on brief, quick, "shallow" interactions that do not encourage either deep social engagement or intellectual exploration. Most of the information is shared on the surface which could be partly because of bandwidth problem.
- **Distraction:** Justin (2014) stated that this is not concerned about the momentary distraction of an isolated text message, but rather the way in which social media involvement provides an acceptable diversion from intellectual pursuits.
- **Pressure to Conform:** Justin (2014) cited examples of students confiding in him that one of the main reasons behind their 24/7 connection is a fear of not keeping up with peers or appearing "like a loser in public". Because of the pressure to conform, social networking could turn many researchers and learners to "busy body."

Just like the open Web resources, the use of social media as an information source is of concern to information literacy (IL) librarians and educators, in part due to the varying quality of the information available via these media. User preference toward Web and digital resources has drawn considerable attention from librarians in the past decade and has led to information literacy programs covering digital and Internet information source evaluations. Social networking / media, however, may bring additional challenges to information evaluation when compared to traditional digital library resources. Quite a few social media platforms, such as the microblogging platform Twitter, have intentionally limited the length of messages that can be transmitted (for example, 140 characters for each Twitter message). Messages sent out via SNS (social networking sites) also tend to be short as well as informal. These may contribute to fragmented information that lacks details or context, which can complicate the evaluation of information quality. Furthermore, many social media platforms, including video sharing sites like YouTube, lack important cues such as citations that researchers and students typically use when evaluating scholarly resources or traditional Web resources. All of these factors make it challenging to evaluate the quality of the information gained in a social media-enabled environment.

In addition, partly due to the ease of forwarding messages with a single click, information can be forwarded almost instantly via one's social networks. Undiscerning social media users may therefore unwittingly contribute to the spread of misinformation. Rumours and inaccurate information can quickly and easily be distributed to a large number of users worldwide. Seeing the same information on many sites, and being posted by many different individuals, unsuspecting readers may misjudge the information as being credible. While raising some concerns among information literacy educators, social media also offer exciting opportunities for users. They facilitate interactive and collaborative knowledge production and sharing. Social media can also provide local and current information and serve as outlets for viewpoints and voices that are not typically conveyed by traditional or dominant media outlets. If used properly and with care, social media can be powerful and transformative tools. In this day and age, being information literate inevitably involves a level of expertise in navigating a variety of media platforms, evaluating the information obtained from various sources, and effectively disseminating quality information via social media. As with digital and Web resources, the popularity of social networking media has again prompted the need for reflective discussions about the goal, definition, and scope of information literacy education.

CONCLUSION

In conclusion, this chapter has tried to examine the concept of social networking and its potential usefulness as a tool for information seeking in a digital library environment. It has been observed that many libraries and librarians have not fully embraced these social networking tools in providing effective and efficient library services. As such, there is a need for a pro-active awareness and training to educate both users and the librarians on the invaluable importance of utilizing social networking for the purpose of information seeking and dissemination in digital library settings.

RECOMMENDATIONS

For libraries whether digital or otherwise, that may be interested in entering or forging forward in this exciting social media environment for information provision services, there are a number of ways to incorporate social media into their structure. The list though not an exhaustive one, libraries may need to:

- Be ready and make provision for dedicated Internet service as well as alternative power source before implementing plan for using social networking capabilities.
- Deploy dedicated staff members that will be using social media to keep abreast of professional development articles, papers etc., that can be shared with users and colleagues.
- Have dedicated staff explore new ways of reaching users or providing services via social media e.g. providing an aggregator service based on information needs and user profiles or setting up social media feeds for users.
- Include social networking/media into strategic and/or communication plans of digital libraries
- Implement a policy for social media which provides loose guidelines for staff doing social media tasks.
- Empower professionals and paraprofessionals to complete relevant training in the use of social media, and the provision of guidelines in order to prepare staff to communicate the library brand.
- From time to time, train and re-train digital library clients on the pros and cons of using social media platforms for effective information seeking.
- Dedicate work time and staff to build a library's brand or presence online to increase engagement and to build rapport and positive relationships.
- Support professionals and paraprofessionals to use social media to engage with library users, to engage with other colleagues, and/or for professional learning purposes.

There is a great deal of potential inherent in social networking software (SNS) for professional development and professional networking purposes. This is particularly true for the library and information industry which is already embracing web 2.0 technologies across many of its core activities. However, at the same time, there is a significant level of confusion, skepticism, resistance and even fear surrounding the use of these technologies within the workplace by many librarians and other information professionals. A suitable plan and strong evaluation needs to be look while pioneering social networks in digital and all kinds of libraries. User required being aware and sufficient training should be imparted to staffs to accomplish the task of planning social software in library.

Lastly, there is the need for encouragement and user empowerment on technologies used in social networking media. The possible implication of social networking can be successful by conducting maximum research and experiment on social networking from different point of view on library. Librarian is the solely responsible for accomplishing the task of planning, organizing and implementing social networks in library and information centre. In this context sufficient training and more expertise need to be gain by him to furnish an absolute shape to social networks in the library.

REFERENCES

Abram, S. (2005). Web 2.0 - huh?! Library 2.0, librarian 2.0. *Information Outlook*, *9*(12), 44–46.

Adigun, G. O., Adegbore, A. M., & Amuda, H. O. (2015). The Social library: integrating social networking into library reference services. In A. Tella (Ed.), *Social media strategies for dynamic library development* (pp. 140–154). Hershey, PA, USA: IGI Global. doi:10.4018/978-1-4666-7415-8.ch008

Amuda, H. O. (2015). Social Networking and the promotion of library services: what does the future hold? In A. Tella (Ed.), *Social media strategies for dynamic library development* (pp. 113–125). Hershey, PA, USA: IGI Global.

Bates, M. (2005). An introduction to metatheories, theories, and models. In K. Fisher, S. Erdelez, & L. McKechnie (Eds.), *Theories of Information Behavior*. Medford, NJ: Information Today.

Belkin, N. (1980). Anomalous states of knowledge as a basis for information retrieval. *Canadian J. of Inf. Sci.*, *5*, 133–143.

Borgman, C. (2001). Where is the librarian in the digital library? *Communications of the ACM*, *44*(5), 66–67. doi:10.1145/374308.374344

Borgman, C. (2006). What can studies of e-learning teach us about collaboration in e-research? Some findings from digital library studies. *Computer Supported Cooperative Work*, *15*(4), 359–383. doi:10.1007/s10606-006-9024-1

Borgman, C. L. (1999). What are digital libraries? Competing visions. *Information Processing & Management*, *38*(3), 227–243.

Borgman, C. L. (2000a). Digital libraries and the continuum of scholarly communication. *The Journal of Documentation*, *56*(4), 412–430. doi:10.1108/EUM0000000007121

Borgman, C. L., Leazer, G. H., Gilliland-Swetland, A. J., & Gazan, R. (2001). Iterative design and evaluation of a geographic digital library for university students: A case study of the Alexandria Digital Earth Prototype (ADEPT). In P. Constantopoulos & I.T. Solvberg (Eds.), *Research and Advanced Technology for Digital Libraries: 5th European Conference, LNCS* (Vol. 2163, pp. 390–401). New York: Springer.

Boyd, D. M., & Ellison, N. B. (2007). Social network sites: Definition, history, and scholarship. *Journal of Computer-Mediated Communication*, *13*(1), 1. http://jcmc.indiana.edu/vol13/issue1/boyd.ellison.html doi:10.1111/j.1083-6101.2007.00393.x

Bradley, A., & McDonald, M. (2011). *The Social Organization*. Boston, Massachusetts: Harvard Business Review Press.

Case, D. (2002). *Looking for Information: A Survey of Research on Information Seeking, Needs, and Behavior*. San Diego, CA: Academic Press.

Cho, A. (2008). Library 2.0 and the new librarianship: new ways of understanding libraries. *Suite101*. Retrieved from http://allan-cho.suite101.com/library-20-and-the-new-librarianship-a86278

Chu, S. K.-W., & Du, H. S. (2012). Social networking tools for academic libraries. *Journal of Librarianship and Information Science*, *13*(1), 69–85.

Martin, R.S. (2004). Libraries and librarians in the 21st century: Fostering a learning society. *College & Research Libraries News*, *65*(11), 668–671.

Cook, T., & Hopkins, L. (2006). *Social media: or, "how I learned to stop worrying and love communication": An introduction to the power of "web2.0"*. Retrieved from: http://www.leehopkins.net/2006/10/30/social-media-for-business-101-free-white-paper/

Cowling, D. (2012). *Facebook Australia 2012 [Infographic]*. Retrieved from http://www.socialmedianews.com.au/facebook-australia-2012-infographic/

Crawford, W. (2006). Library 2.0 and 'Library 2.0:Cites and Insights, *Journal of Libraries, Policy, Technology and Media,* 6(2). Retrieved from http: //www.cites.boisestate.edu/civ6i2.pdf

Denning, P., Horning, J., Parnas, D., & Weinstein, L. (2006). Wikipedia Risks. *Communications of the ACM*, *48*(12), 152. doi:10.1145/1101779.1101804

Donna, C. (2014). *Advantages and Disadvantages of Social Networking.* Retrieved from http://www.lovetoknow.com/member/347~donna-cosmato

Facebook. (2012). *Newsroom: Factsheet.* Retrieved from http://newsroom.fb.com/content/default.aspx?NewsAreaId=22

Farkas, M. (2008). The essence of Library 2.0. *Information wants to be free*. Retrieved from http://meredith.wolfwater.com/wordpress/2008/01/24/the-essence-of-library-20/

Fisher, K., Erdelez, S., & McKechnie, L. (Ed.), (2005). Theories of Information Behavior. Medford, NJ: Information Today.

Fitzpatrick, M. (2006). The Deleting Online Predators Act of 2006. *Journal of Tech Law*. Retrieved from http://www. techlawjournal.com/cong109/bills/house/hr5319/hr5319ih.asp

Habib, M.C. (2006). Toward Academic Library 2.0: Development and Application of a Library 2.0 Methodology. North Carolina University, Chappe Hill. Retrieved from http://etd.ils.unc.edu/dspace/bitstream/1901/356/1/michaelhabib.pdf

Hanna, R., Rohm, A., & Crittenden, V. L. (2011). We're all connected: The power of the social media ecosystem. *Business Horizons*, *54*(3), 265–273. doi:10.1016/j.bushor.2011.01.007

Hansen, P., & Järvelin, K. (2005). Collaborative information retrieval in an information-intensive domain. *IPM*, 41(5), 1101-1109.

Heath, T. (2008). Information-seeking on the Web with Trusted Social Networks – from Theory to Systems [Unpublished PhD Thesis]. UK: Knowledge Media Institute, The Open University.

Justin, M. (2014). The pros and cons of student social media use. Retrieved from http://www.teachthought.com/uncategorized/the-pros-and-cons-of-student-social-media-use/

Kaplan, A. M., & Haenlein, M. (2010). Users of the world, unite! The challenges and opportunities of Social Media. *Business Horizons*, *53*(1), 59–68. doi:10.1016/j.bushor.2009.09.003

Kasia, M. (2013).Advantages and Disadvantages of Social Networking: Should You Spend More Time Connecting Online? Retrieved from https://blog.udemy.com/author/kasiamikoluk/

Kim, K. O., Sin, S. J., & Yoo-Lee, E. Y. (2014). Undergraduates' Use of Social Media as information Sources. *College & Research Libraries*, *75*(4), 442–457. doi:10.5860/crl.75.4.442

Kiss, J. (2011). *Twitter reveals it has 100m active users*. Retrieved from http://www.guardian.co.uk/technology/pda/2011/sep/08/twitter-active-users

KPMG. (2011). *Social media: the voyage of discovery for business*. Retrieved from http://www.kpmg.com/NZ/en/IssuesAndInsights/ArticlesPublications/Pages/social-media-discovery.aspx

Kuhlthau, C. (2007). The 'information search process' revisited: Is the model still useful? *Information Research*, 13(4).

Kuhlthau, C., Heinström, J. & Todd, R. J. (2008). The 'information search process' revisited: Is the model still useful? *Information Research*, 13(4).

Kuhlthau, C., Maniotes, L., & Caspari, A. (2007). *Guided inquiry: Learning in the 21st century*. Westport, Connecticut: Libraries Unlimited.

Kuhlthau, C. C. (1991). Inside the search process: Information seeking from the user's perspective. *Journal of the American Society for Information Science*, *42*(5), 361–371. doi:10.1002/(SICI)1097-4571(199106)42:5<361::AID-ASI6>3.0.CO;2-#

Lenhart, A., & Madden, M. (2007). Social Networking Websites and Teens: An Overview. Retrieved from http://www.pewinternet.org/Reports/2007/Social-Networking-Websites-and-Teens.aspx

North, C., Shneiderman, M., & Plaisant, C. (1996). Visual Information Seeking in Digital Image Libraries: The Visible Human Explorer. *Proceeding of ACM DL 96 - Conference in Digital Libraries* (pp. 74-82).

O'Dell, S. (2010). Opportunities and Obligations for Libraries in a Social Networking Age: A Survey of Web 2.0 and Networking Sites. *Journal of Library Administration*, *50*(3), 237-251. doi:10.1080/01930821003634989

O'Reilly, T. (2005). What is Web 2.0: Design Patterns and Business Models for the Next Generation of Software. Retrieved from http://www.oreillynet.com/pub/a/oreilly/tim/news/2005/09/30/what-is-web-20.html?

Oladokun, O. (2015). The Potential and utilization of social media in library and information centres. In A. Tella (Ed.), *Social media strategies for dynamic library development* (pp. 24–40). Hershey, PA: Information Science Reference (an imprint of IGI Global). doi:10.4018/978-1-4666-7415-8.ch002

Onwuchekwa, E. (2015). The Role of social media and social networking in information service provision: a practical view. In A. Tella (Ed.), *Social media strategies for dynamic library development* (pp. 126–139). Hershey, PA, USA: IGI Global. doi:10.4018/978-1-4666-7415-8.ch007

Parmeshwar, S., & Patil, D. B. (2009). Use of the Internet by Faculty and Research Scholars of Gulbarga University Library. *Library Philosophy and Practice*. Retrieved from http://digitalcommons.unl.edu/cgi/viewcontent.cgi?article=1268&context=libphilprac

Partridge, H. (2011). Being "librarian 2.0": it's all in the attitude. *Library Connect, 9*(3). Retrieved from http://libraryconnectarchive.elsevier.com/lcn/0903/lcn090303.html

Savolainen, R. (2006). Information use as gap-bridging: The viewpoint of Sense-Making methodology. *Journal of the American Society for Information Science*, *57*(8), 1116–1125. doi:10.1002/asi.20400

Savolainen, R. (2006). Time as a context of information seeking. *LISR*, *28*(1), 141–163.

Smith, A. (2001), *Strategies for Building Digitized Collection.* Washington, D.C. Digital Library Federation, Council on Library and Information Resources. Retrieved from http://www.clir.org

Solomon, P. (1997). Discovering information behavior in sense making: I. Time and timing; II. The social; III. The person. *Journal of the American Society for Information Science*, *48*(12), 1097–1108. doi:10.1002/(SICI)1097-4571(199712)48:12<1097::AID-ASI4>3.0.CO;2-P

Spink, A., & Cole, C. (Eds.), (2005). *New Directions in Human Information Behavior.* Dordrecht, The Netherlands: Springer.

Vakkari, P. (2006). Trends in the use of digital libraries by scientists in 2000-2005: A case study of FinELib. In A. Grove (Eds.), *Proceedings 69th Annual Meeting of ASIST*, Austin, TX, USA. doi:doi:10.1002/meet.1450430132 doi:10.1002/meet.1450430132

Vakkari, P., & Talja, S. (2005). The influence of the scatter of literature on the use of electronic resources across disciplines: A case study of FinELib. *Proceedings of the 9th European Conference on Digital Libraries* (pp. 207-217). Berlin & Heidelberg: Springer.

ADDITIONAL READING

Ezeani, C.N. (2010). Network literacy skills of academic librarians for effective services delivery: The case of the University of Nigeria, Library Systems. *Proceedings of Second Professional Summit on Information Science and Technology (PSIST)* (pp. 56-66), Nsukka, Nnamdi Azikiwe Library.

Ezeani, C. N., & Igwesi, U. (2012). Using social media for dynamic library service delivery: the Nigeria experience. *Library Philosophy and Practice.* Retrieved from http://digitalcommons.unl.edu/libphilprac/814

KEY TERMS AND DEFINITIONS

Digital Library: An organised and focused collection of digital objects, including texts, images, video and audio, with the methods of access and retrieval. The main objectives of digitalization are easy, fast and convenient access to the world's information.

Information Seeking: The mode in which individuals articulate their information needs, search, recognize, retrieve, evaluate and use information.

Library 2.0: This generally means the application of web 2.0 technologies in a library setting.

Social Media: A Web-based means for social interaction using highly accessible publishing techniques that transforms people from only content consumers to content producers.

Social Media Platforms: Online means of communication that are used by large group of people to share information and to develop social and professional contacts. Examples: Facebook, Twitter, LinkedIn, Academia/Research Gates, Google+, etc.

Social Networking: A platform where people from diverse cultural backgrounds can connect and interact with one another via the Web to create and share content.

Web 2.0: The read/write web which enables its users to contribute content, socialise, communicate, interact, collaborate and network with other in a virtual environment.

Chapter 14
Barriers to Information Seeking in the Digital Libraries

Ajayi Ayo Oluwaseun
University of Ibadan, Nigeria

ABSTRACT

Adequate knowledge about the information needs and seeking behaviour of users is vital for developing digital library collections, services and facilities to meet their information needs effectively. Information seeking as an underlying feature in research cannot be done without an enabling environment where needed resources and services are provided. The available literature reveals that although librarians have made good progress in adapting primary values of librarianship which are to support intellectual freedom and equitable access to information, information seeking process in the Digital Libraries has, however, been found not to be without limitations. Seeking scholarly information in the Digital Libraries is limited by the availability of reliable and affordable information and communication technologies. Information seeking in the Digital Libraries has been found to be limited to those scholars who are affiliated with organisations which have the money and skills to provide access. It has been found limited to those who are literate, information literate and have a command of the major languages of commerce and scholarship (English in particular). Infrastructure, education and skills as well as content were the three spheres identified in this Chapter as preconditions that must be satisfied if broad digital scholarly information is to be sought without restrictions. Provision of effective service in the Digital Libraries as recommended in this Chapter requires sufficient understanding of the real needs of information users and making precise efforts to satisfy them. This can best be achieved through formal in–depth studies of the information needs and seeking behaviour of users. Librarians, especially those involved in bibliographic instruction should be interested in ways individuals approach the library (be it digital or physical) and the methods they use to search for needed information. Strategies intended to improve the provision of library services should be redesigned towards information skills development and information resource awareness.

DOI: 10.4018/978-1-5225-0296-8.ch014

INTRODUCTION

Library services and activities have been enhanced expeditiously in the advent of modern technology. Formerly considered as activities involved in physical collection of information found in books, library activities, in our day, are shifting from traditional collections housed within bricks and mortar to a new focus on digital materials that exist outside the physical and administrative bounds of any one library.

Librarians, in the 21st century, are expected to be familiar with and sustain new online information-seeking behaviors and user expectations precipitated by the electronic networks, while instantaneously continuing to acquire – and find space to store – traditional materials with the incorporation and/or exploitation of innovative technologies.

Users no longer have to enter the library to use journals or search the catalog to find books, contemporary technologies have realistically moved the library beyond its physical space to reach a greater numbers of users. Substantiating this, Byrne (2003) asserts that access, shorn of geographical limitation, to the prevailing combination of digital publications, dedicated and generalist databases, sophisticated search systems and portals has created unique remote access to scholarly information. In his words, it was affirmed further that the combination had recently provided a digital library which enables scholars as well as learners to rapidly examine a great wealth of the scholarly literature in their own disciplines and those new to them.

The primary principles of digital libraries are to support intellectual freedom and equitable access to information. Fulfilling this task and safeguarding these values are not without challenges.

The debate continues on whether barriers to information seeking are in terms of physical limits to access, that is, lack of information resources or the means to retrieve them but it has been discovered that information seeking can be hindered in several ways.

It is in this perspective that this chapter undertakes a review of issues and some empirical studies on what constitutes hindrances to effective information seeking in the digital libraries and proffer ways of addressing them.

Human Information Behaviour

The Information behaviour is a sub-discipline within the field of library and information science. It describes how people need, seek, manage, give and use information in different contexts. It may also be described as information-seeking behaviour or human information behaviour.

The belief that information is indispensible in the functioning and interaction of individuals, social groups, organizations, and societies, and to the ongoing improvement of the quality of life is in tandem with the Latin and Greek origins of the word: information: inform.ere informo, informare, informavi, informatus as "inward forming. Supporting this credence is the opinion that information has the potential to modify what people already know and to shape their decisions and actions.

Todd (2003) succinctly defined human information behavior as the study of the interactions between people, the various forms of data, information, knowledge, and wisdom that fall under the rubric of information, and the diverse contexts in which they interact. His search light was further beamed on the key dimensions of human information behaviour including such concepts as people's information contexts, information needs, information seeking behaviours, patterns of information access, retrieval and dissemination, human information processing, and information use.

The central focus of reviewing human information behaviour is to gain understanding of inter-correlation among the areas (especially information seeking process and information seeking behaviours) covered in human information behaviour.

Information Seeking

Previous studies have provided direction on the conflicting views regarding the information needs, information search process and information seeking behavior of users of information services (Todd, 2003, Kuruppu, 1999 and Baran and Davis 1995). Empirical researchers of human information behavior, however, often contend with a dilemma in an information-intense society whereby focus is always on understanding how people and information come together and how information professionals respond.

Andersen (2002) noted that studies on information seeking have looked at how individuals go about finding the materials that they need in order to satisfy information needs. A number of models such as Ellis' 1993 model, Eisenberg and Berkowitz's 1992 model, and Kuhlthau's 1992 model had been developed in this respect. How information could be sought scientifically and the patterns used in seeking information have been explained in a number of situations by these models.

Kuruppu (1999) submitted further that people seek information depending upon their respective functions and tasks, the level of their knowledge and experience (in the specific field of specialization and in the use of information systems and services), their particular interest and need to satisfy for which they seek information, on the breadth and depth of their interest profiles, and on the nature of the subject or field of specialization or interest. Information needs of a user have been observed to vary considerably depending upon his/her current activity, for instance, when entering a new field of research as compared to when seeking a solution to a specific problem in a field already familiar to the person. An information seeking behaviour of a user may result from the recognition of some information need (Kuruppu, 1999).

Hence, information seeking is defined as a basic activity indulged in by all people and manifested through a particular behavior (Kakai et.al, 2004). According to Wright and Guy (1997), information seeking is undertaken to identify a message that satisfies a perceived need. This activity may be actively or passively done when taking steps to satisfy a felt need (Ikoja–Odongo, 2002). It is also being regarded as an aspect of scholarly work of most interest to academic librarians who strive to develop collections, services, and organizational structures that facilitate information seeking.

Kakai, et.al (2004), in their studies, reported Mann (1993) as observing most researchers, even with computers, finding only a fraction of the sources available to them. He explains that researchers tend to work within one or another mental framework that limits their basic perception of the universe of knowledge available to them. Students according to him use a subject–disciplinary method that leads them to a specific list of sources on a particular subject.

He points out that while this method allows students and researchers to find more specific sources, it is limiting in that they may not realize that work of interest to their own subject appears within the literature of many other disciplines. This impinges on how much they get out of the library system.

Information seeking is a multi-dimensional process, diverse, dynamic, and complex activity and one shaped by many situational, personal, social, and organizational factors. Therefore, information seeking is defined, for the purpose of this study, as activities, attempts and actions carried out by an individual or group to solve an information need or problem through cognitive, emotional and physical actions done in any environment of his search.

Information Seeking Behaviour

Indisputably, literature is awash with empirical studies and models of information seeking behavior. Most of which had addressed various concepts and aspects of information-seeking behaviour. The various aspects of information seeking behaviour examined by Sridhar (1989) include the motives and purposes of seeking information, nature and type of information sought, delegation of information gathering work, and the time spent on in gathering activity. In the study 'Information-Seeking Behaviour: Pattern and Concepts', Krikelas (1983) examines the elements of user studies and presents them as unified concepts within a model of information-seeking behaviour. The concept of information-seeking behaviour, information needs, information gathering, information giving and source preference are discussed.

Information seeking behaviour, put concisely, refers to the way people search for and utilize information (Fairer–Wessels, 1990). Information seeking behaviour of people, most times, involves active or decisive information seeking as a result of the need to perform some tasks, prepare for seminars, workshops, conferences, or carry out researches. Most unfortunate incidence is the report that most information seekers do not learn the basic information skills required to make purposeful information seeking that can satisfy their needs. From a study of the information seeking behaviour of undergraduate students, Kakai, et.al (2004) found that, most often than not, students end up using trial and error methods of enquiry that limits their proficiencies to satisfy their needs. It has been observed that enquirers encounter barriers in the quest to satisfy their information needs especially in this digital age. This will be adequately addressed in the subsequent section.

Barriers to Scholarly Information Seeking in the Digital Libraries

Digital Library is a complex, multi-faceted notion that defies a simple definition. A comprehensive depiction capturing all possible perceptions is therefore desirable. As a concept, it has attracted a great deal of misperceptions arising from the fact that digital libraries are at the focal point of many different areas of research and that there are many things, on the internet, being referred to as "digital libraries", which from information professionals' point of view are not. For instance; what many people consider to be a digital library today is the World Wide Web, an online version of a catalogue, databases and electronic document delivery services, collections of computer algorithms or software programs or document management systems that control business documents in electronic form.

According to Nurnberg, et al, (1995), features of a digital library differ depending upon the research community that is describing it. To some, it is an application of the Web, one particular application of hypertext methods, a large database and to others in the library science; it is another step in the continuing automation of libraries that began about three decades ago. In reality, these different research approaches add to the development of digital libraries. A digital library is all of these things but not a single, completely digital system that provides instant access to all information, for all sectors of society, from anywhere in the world. Instead, they will most likely be a collection of disparate resources and disparate systems, catering to specific communities and user groups, created for specific purposes. They also will include, perhaps indefinitely, paper-based collections.

According to Clifford Lynch, one of the leading scholars in the area of digital library research. Lynch (1997) states:

One sometimes hears the Internet characterized as the world's library for the digital age. This description does not stand up under even casual examination. The Internet and particularly its collection of multimedia resources known as the World Wide Web was not designed to support the organized publication and retrieval of information as libraries are. It has evolved into what might be thought of as a chaotic repository for the collective output of the world's digital "printing presses." In short, the Net is not a digital library.

A working definition of "digital library", put forward by Cleveland (1998), which makes sense to librarians: digital libraries are libraries with the same purposes, functions, and goals as traditional library's collection development and management, subject analysis, index creation, provision of access, reference work, and preservation.

He further described digital libraries as organizations that provide the resources, including the specialized staff, to select, structure, offer intellectual access to, interpret, distribute, preserve the integrity of, and ensure the persistence over time of collections of digital works so that they are readily and economically available for use by a defined community or set of communities.

With the assumption that digital libraries are libraries in the first place, the following characteristics are then gleaned from various discussions about digital libraries, both online and in print (See Arms, 1995; Graham, 1995; Chepesuik, 1997; Lynch and Garcia-Molina, 1995) as reported by Gary Cleveland in his paper to International Federation of Library Associations and Institutions' occasional paper.

These characteristics are:

- Digital libraries are the digital face of traditional libraries that include both digital collections and traditional, fixed media collections. So they encompass both electronic and paper materials.
- Digital libraries will also include digital materials that exist outside the physical and administrative bounds of any one digital library.
- Digital libraries will include all the processes and services that are the backbone and nervous system of libraries. However, such traditional processes, though forming the basis digital library work, will have to be revised and enhanced to accommodate the differences between new digital media and traditional fixed media.
- Digital libraries ideally provide a coherent view of all of the information contained within a library, no matter its form or format
- Digital libraries will serve particular communities or constituencies, as traditional libraries do now, though those communities may be widely dispersed throughout the network.
- Digital libraries will require both the skills of librarians and well as those of computer scientists to be viable.

Presently, the term 'Digital Library' is used to connote systems that are very diverse in scope and yield varied functionality. These systems range from digital object and metadata repositories, reference-linking systems, archives, and content administration systems, which have been mainly developed by industry, to complex systems that integrate advanced digital library services, which have chiefly been developed in research environments.

This heterogeneous backdrop is not devoid of constraints. It brings significant impediments, particularly to interoperability and the re-use of both content and technologies that would open up new horizons for the private and public sectors alike and empower a broad spectrum of communities. A daunting set of challenges, associated with reinvention of the role of librarians, digitization as well as investments in digital technology, is steering librarians and other information professionals in the face. And this could be responsible for the initial enthusiasm surrounding the development of the digital library being rapidly replaced by sober second thought. Digital Libraries, nonetheless, have been found to be means of providing more equitable access to content from anywhere at any time and Digital Libraries are cheaper tools than physical libraries (Candela et al., 2011).

Information seeking as an underlying feature in research is not done without an enabling environment where needed resources and services are provided. Information seeking/information search process in the Digital Libraries has, however, been found not to be without limitations. Access to scholarly information in the Digital Libraries, going by the word of Byrne (2003), is limited by the availability of reliable and affordable information and communication technologies. Information seeking in the Digital Libraries has been found to be limited to those scholars who are affiliated with organisations which have the money and skills to provide access. It has been found limited to those who are literate, information literate and have a command of the major languages of commerce and scholarship (English in particular). In addition, contractual and other bounds imposed by vendors exclude many potential users.

This contradiction between the technical possibilities and the economic, educational and infrastructural limitations poses many challenges for libraries and especially technological university libraries.

The three domains, as identified by Byrne (2003), in which preconditions must be satisfied if broad digital scholarly information is to be sought without temporal, spatial or other restrictions are: infrastructure, education and skills as well as content. Each has multiple levels at which Information Seeking in the Digital Libraries can emerge.

Infrastructure

Information search process in a digital library, especially in developing countries requires basic infrastructure such as consistent electricity supplies, telecommunications, computers and software, without which seeking scholarly information will be very difficult. This is an immediate problem in poor and remote areas of many African countries and Middle East, devastated by conflict as well as poor governance.

Telecommunications infrastructure is obviously vital and has many choke points at which services can become unavailable through lack of capacity, unreliable service, unsustainable cost, corporate policy or political control. While users in advanced nations are seeing ever decreasing Megabyte charges due to over capacity on intercontinental cables and the implementation of high bandwidth domestic and international fibre networks, many in poorer countries find international access costs too high and suffer very limited domestic bandwidth (Greenspan, 2002). Inadequate distribution networks deprive many parts of many countries of access, especially poorer districts of cities and poor and remote rural regions. In combination these deficiencies result in frequent service drop outs and an inability to use advanced services.

Access to computers constitutes the next level which is essential to enable use of the digital library. Whether it be from a common access Internet facility, home, school, university or workplace, ready access to a computer which reasonable capabilities is essential. Without enough computers, it is impossible to get sufficient access time. Without adequate memory, speed and storage, it is impossible to open, download or use electronic scholarly information. These problems can be compounded by ageing hardware and lack of technical support.

Up to date and efficient software is equally important. Proprietary software may be too expensive and lack compatibility with other systems. Open source software may not be readily available. In addition, software may be unsuitable for national or local conditions because it implements a North American or European solution and fails to accommodate local considerations. It is unlikely to be available in languages other than the principal European languages, and especially English, although some library systems and other software do provide user interfaces in a variety of languages (Gonzales 2003).

Education and Skills

But all the equipment, connectivity and software in the world are useless without the skills to use it. Basic computers skills are of course necessary but not sufficient. Obtaining scholarly information demands high levels of literacy and the development of information literacy. Those who do not have the opportunities to develop the necessary exhibition of skills are unable to use digital scholarly information effectively. They lack the codes to open the digital library.

Advanced skills are required to manage systems and to be able to create and make available information. Without those abilities, scholars remain consumers, their creations are locked out of contemporary scholarly communication.

Language, however, is the most important ability (Byrne, 2003). Pastore (1999) asserted that other languages are catching up to English. He stated further that many language users are invisible on the Internet including those from South Asia, all of Africa and Indonesia as well as the speakers of threatened indigenous languages.

The dominance of a few languages on the Internet continues to privilege those users who are fluent in the dominant languages. Conversely, it marginalises those without sufficient familiarity. This is of course not unique to digital information: the predominant languages of international scholarly communication have been the major European languages and English has become progressively more dominant during the twentieth century. However, the meshed systems of content-metadata-search-access which make digital information systems so powerful also make them highly language dependent, which disables those without high levels of competency in the languages of the systems (or language, since it is usually English) as well as the languages of scholarship. Even the most highly educated scholar can be incapacitated.

In the digital environment, language has become much more important. Without good knowledge of the major languages of scholarship and of English in particular, it is impossible to both use the systems and read and comprehend the literature. Education and skills have also become more important especially computer skills and information literacy. Without those competencies, the systems can only be used ineffectively and the student or researcher is unable to access the literature.

Content

Lack of language ability can also make it very difficult to contribute to the international scholarly literature. Publications in little understood languages are inevitably ignored unless translated or cited by publications in the major languages. Without language it may be impossible to adequately convey concepts within their cultural context.

Narrowness in language can thus bring about blinkeredness in understanding. In scholarly communication it can lead to ignorance of important findings and knowledge. The dominant can conversely be ignorant because of their linguistic incompetence.

Many other issues relating to digital content stem from ownership. The commodification of scholarly literature and consequent significant and sustained increases in its cost over the last three decades has put most high-status scholarly journals out of reach of many university libraries and most individual scholars. Many university and research libraries in developing countries have been unable to purchase a journal for many years: they depend on donations. In richer countries the situation is not so dire but there can be very few academic and research libraries that are able to meet the inexorably rising costs. The problems have again been aggravated by the move to electronic scholarly information which has significantly raised the entry fee from the price of a single subscription to the price of at least a minimal aggregated set (in addition to the costs in infrastructure and skills discussed above).

Since most scholarly literature is necessarily imported in most countries, its purchase requires both funding and foreign exchange in some of the world's strongest currencies (US dollar, UK pound, Euro) which is very difficult for universities and their libraries to obtain.

Financial Constraints

The control obtained over scholarly intellectual property by major publishers acts as a significant barrier to all-encompassing intellectual freedom in seeking scholarly information. It limits the use of interlibrary loans, copying for student use and republication. This is not to decry the benefits of a balanced intellectual property regime but to describe some of the consequences of current directions in the law in most countries (under WIPO and WTO guidance). The harm to scholarship from current trends in intellectual property law is not inherent in the principles of intellectual property but has two roots. One is the narrowing of the public good: tighter conditions for fair use and postponement of succession to the public domain. The other is greed: the desire to obtain a continuing commercial return from scholarly publication (even though the commercial publishers have invested only in its distribution, not in its creation). This has shifted the emphasis in scholarly information from communication between scholars to profit for publishers and distributors.

And, finally, in this long list of professional challenges created for us by the digital library, is its vulnerability to control. Censorship can be and is applied to printed materials, although university libraries have often been exempted as in the case of South Africa under apartheid (Merrett 1994). In the digital environment, filtering and surveillance as described above can be secretly or openly applied with chilling effect on scholarship. Publishers, too, find it easier to apply post publication censorship than in the print environment.

These trends have amplified the disadvantages already suffered by many libraries and scholars, especially in poorer countries. They cannot afford access to high priced aggregations of scholarly publications nor can they or their countries afford to invest in the necessary ICT infrastructure. Previously a superseded backset of a journal could have provided useful sources for a student and for research training, but nothing is available now without subscription.

Improving information Seeking Strategies

Finding ways of intercepting the barriers to information seeking is one of the solutions to improving the scholars' information seeking behaviour. Martin and Metcalfe (2001) acknowledged that modes of informing are specific to each person's concern, as are the topics they want to be informed about. Both note that libraries in the past sought to accommodate this need by promoting current awareness services (CAS) and selective dissemination of information (SDI), either through print or electronic means. These are user outreach avenues that can still be optimally utilized in addition to customizing access points in accordance with user interests using Internet or the university intranet. Fister (1992) in analyzing and comparing the bibliographic instruction research processes taught to students and the approaches that students used in seeking information noted that students should not be left to flounder on their own.

Library skills should be put in context of the research process. Callison (1997) recommends increased efforts to expand instruction beyond the one–time experience in introducing scholars to the library. Lau (2001) observed that although librarians had assumed the role of user information educators, their work tended to occur in isolation. Teamwork was needed to make library instruction part of the learning process.

CONCLUSION

Many digital library initiatives and projects have been created by Librarians for jointly exploring key issues on the daunting set of challenges associated with digital library since the discovery of the technical and legal constraints in making a business case for digitization and investments in digital technology involved in digital library. Librarians have, however, discovered that, as with most technically inclined developments in libraries over the years, extent in digital library projects have to move forward in small, manageable, evolutionary steps, rather than in a rapid revolutionary manner.

More importantly, understanding the actual needs of information users and taking steps to satisfy them is the first step towards effective service provision. This can best be achieved through formal in–depth studies. Librarians, especially those involved in bibliographic instruction should be interested in ways individuals approach the library and the methods they use to search for needed information. Librarians could redesign strategies intended to improve the provision of library services especially towards information skills development and information resource awareness.

REFERENCES

Andersen, D. L. (2002). Communicating information across cultures: understanding how others work. Retrieved from www.pantaneto.co.uk/issue9/andersen.htm

Arms, W. Y. (1995). Key concepts in the architecture of the digital library. *D-Lib Magazine*, *1995*(July). Retrieved from http://www.dlib.org/dlib/arms.html

Baran, S., & Davis, D. (1995). *Mass communication theory: Foundations, ferment, and future*. Los Angeles, CA: Wadsworth.

Byrne, A. (2003), Digital libraries: barriers or gateways to scholarly information. *Proceedings of the-IATUL Conference*, Turkey doi:doi:10.1108/02640470310499777 doi:10.1108/02640470310499777

Callison, D. (1997). Evolution of methods to measure student information use. *Library & Information Science Research*, *19*(4), 347–357. doi:10.1016/S0740-8188(97)90025-6

Candela, L., Athanasopoulos, G.; Castelli, D.; El Raheb, K.; Innocenti, P.; et al. (2011). The Digital Library Reference Model. *DL.org Project.*

Chepesuik, R. (1997). The future is here: America's libraries go digital. *American Libraries*, *2*(1), 47–49.

Cleveland, G. (1998). Digital Libraries: Definitions, Issues and Challenges. *International Federation of Library Associations and Institutions.*

Eisenberg, M. B., & Berkowitz, R. E. (1992). Information problem solving: The Big Six Skills Approach. *School Library Media Activities Monthly*, *8*(5), 27.

Ellis, D. A. (1993). Modeling the information–seeking patterns of academic researchers: A Grounded theory approach. *The Library Quarterly*, *63*(8), 469–486. doi:10.1086/602622

Fairer-Wessels. (1990). Basic Community information needs of Urban Black Women in Mamelodi, Pretoria, South Africa. Retrieved from fromwww.cais-acsi.ca/proceedings/1995/olson_1995.pdf

Fister, B. (1992). The Research process of undergraduate students. *Journal of Academic Librarianship*, *18*(3), 163–169.

Gonzales, E. J. (2003). Language limits confront Latinos on Internet. *IM Diversity*. Retrieved from http://www.imdiversity.com/villages/hispanic

Graham, P. S. (1995). Requirements for the digital research library. Retrieved from http://aultnis.rutgers.edu/texts/DRC.html

Greenspan, R. (2002). China pulls ahead of Japan. CyberAtlas. Retrieved from http://cyberatlas.internet.com./epdf

Ikoja–Odongo, J.R. (2002). An observational study of the information seeking and communicating behavior of entrepreneurs in the informal sector of Uganda. In T. Bothma, & A. Kaniki (Eds.), *ProLISSA 2002: Proceedings of the second biennial DiSSA net conference*, Pretoria (pp. 11–28).

Kakai, M.J., Ikoja–Odongo R., & Kigongo–Bukenya, I.M.N. (2004). A study of the information seeking behavior of undergraduate students of Makerere University, Uganda. *World Libraries*, 14(1).

Krikelas, J. (1983). Information-seeking behaviour: Patterns and concepts. *Drexel Library Quarterly*, *19*(2), 5–20.

Kuhlthau, C.C. (1993). *Seeking meaning: A process approach to library and information services.* Norwood, N.J.: Ablex.

Kuruppu, D.C. (1999). Information needs and information seeking behaviour of users in organizations. *Information Studies*, *5*(1), 53–66.

Lau, J. (2001). Faculty–Librarian collaboration: A Mexican experience. *RSR. Reference Services Review*, *29*(2), 95–105. doi:10.1108/00907320110394137

Lynch, C. A. (1997). Searching the Internet. *Scientific American*, 397, 52-56. Retrieved from http://www.sciam.com/0397issue/0397lynch.html

Lynch, C. A., & Garcia-Molina, H. (1995). Interoperability, scaling, and the digital libraries research agenda: a report on the IITA Digital Libraries Workshop. Retrieved from http://www.diglib.stanford.edu/diglib/pub/reports/iitadlw/main.html

Mann, T. (1993). *Library research models: A guide to classification, cataloguing and computers*. New York: Oxford University Press.

Martin, P., & Metcalfe, M. (2001). Informing the knowledge workers. *RSR. Reference Services Review*, *29*(4), 267–275. doi:10.1108/00907320110408384

Merrett, C. (1994). *A culture of censorship: secrecy and intellectual repression in South Africa*. Cape Town: David Philip & University of Natal Press.

Nurnberg, P. J., Furuta, R., Leggett, J. J., Marshall, C., & Shipman, F. M. III. (1995). Digital libraries: issues and architectures.*Proceedings of the Second Annual Conference on the Theory and Practice of Digital Libraries*, Austin, Texas (pp. 147-153).

Pastore, M. (1999). The language of the web. *Cyber Atlas*. Retrieved from http://cyberatlas.internet.com

Sridhar, M. S. (1989). Information seeking behaviour of the Indian space technologists. *Library Science*, *26*(2), 127–132.

Todd, R. J. (2003). Adolescents of the Information Age: Patterns of Information Seeking and Use, and Implications for Information Professionals. *School Library Media Quarterly*, *9*(2), 27–46.

Wright, M., & Guy, L. (1997). Where do I find it and what do I do with it: Practical problem–solving in the data library. Retrieved from dphs.dacc.wisc.edu/types/data_reference.html

ADDITIONAL READING

Borgman, C.L. (2000). *From Gutenberg to the global information infrastructure: access to information in the network world*. Cambridge, MA: MIT Press.

Kadli, J.H., & Kumbar, B. D. (2013). Library Resources, Services and Information Seeking Behaviour in Changing ICT environment: A Literature Review. *Library Philosophy and Practice*. Retrieved from http://digitalcommons.unl.edu/libphilprac/951

Lynch, C.A., & Garcia-Molina, H. (1995). Interoperability, scaling, and the digital libraries research agenda: a report on the IITA Digital Libraries Workshop. Retrieved from http://www.diglib.stanford.edu/diglib/pub/reports/iitadlw/main.html

Meyers, E. M., Nathan, L. P., & Saxton, M. L. (2006). Barriers to information seeking in school libraries: conflicts in perceptions and practice. *Information Research*, 12(2). Retrieved from http://InformationR.net/ir/12-2/paper295.html

World Summit on the Information Society. (2003). International Telecommunications Union. Retrieved from http://www.itu.int/wsis

KEY TERMS AND DEFINITIONS

Content: This refers to the ideas that are contained in a piece of writing submitted to the international scholarly literature. The content, here, describes ideas that of defined quality and according to broad codified policies which are being comprehensively collected, managed and preserved for the long term and are offered to targeted international user communities by potentially virtual organisation.

Digital Library: The term 'Digital Library', as used in this Chapter, refers to the universal knowledge repository and communication channel that enables everyone to access all human knowledge, anytime and anywhere, in a friendly, multi-modal, efficiently and effectively by overcoming barriers of distance, language and culture and by using ICT enabled devices. Its scope covers systems ranging from digital objects and metadata repositories, reference-linking systems, archives, and content administration systems, which have been chiefly developed in research environments, to complex systems that integrate advanced automated library services.

Education and Skills: This refers to ability to read, write and use equipment, connectivity and software involved in providing or accessing digital library services. It encompasses information literacy and IT skills needed in seeking and using scholarly information.

Information Need: Information need refers to the extent to which information is required to solve problems as well as the degree of expressed satisfaction or dissatisfaction with the information. An information need arises when an individual senses a problematic situation or information gap, in which his or her internal knowledge and beliefs, and model of the environment fail to suggest a path towards the satisfaction of his or her goals. Such an identified information need may lead to information seeking and the formulation of requests for information.

Information Seeking: Information seeking refers to activities that are actively or passively undertaken to identify pieces of evidence or facts that satisfy a perceived or felt need. Information seeking is a form of human behaviour that involves seeking for information by means of the active examination of information sources or information retrieval systems to satisfy the information need, or to solve a problem. Information seeking is a cognitive exercise and it involves search, retrieval, recognition and application of meaningful content.

Information Seeking Behaviour: Information seeking behaviour is described as an individual's way and manner of gathering and sourcing for information for personal use, knowledge updating and development. It can be described as the way an information user conducts himself or acts when looking for, receiving or acquiring information.

Infrastructure: This includes telecommunications, computers and software, electricity supplies, physical access to set up services and suitable buildings (universities, libraries, telecentres, schools) without which it becomes very difficult, if not impossible, to provide or to access digital library services.

Librarian: A librarian is a person who works professionally in a library, provides and maintains information in many formats, and also provides other information services, including: information literacy instruction; computer provision and training; and assistance locating community resources.

Limitation: This is an act or anything that prevents people from gaining equitable access to digital scholarly information or content from anywhere at any time.

Chapter 15
Digital Libraries as Information Superhighway

Prakash Dongardive
Makelle University, Ethiopia

ABSTRACT

During the decade of 1990s the term digital libraries become a recognized phrase for describing libraries that offer access to digital information by using a variety of networks, including internet and world wide web. Other synonyms used interchangeably with digital libraries are library without walls and electronic and virtual libraries because every online or virtual source of information is electronic source of information but every electronic information sources are not online or virtual form, so digital or electronic library includes digital contents and that can be delivered any time anywhere to the networked computer. Digital libraries provide remote access to the contents and the services of the libraries and other information sources combining an onsite collection of current and heavily used materials in both print and electronic form with an electronic networks which provide access to and delivery for worldwide libraries and commercial information and knowledge sources. Basically the digital libraries are the metaphor for the networked libraries. In the light of this therefore, this chapter discussed digital libraries as information superhighway looking at issues like factors responsible for the emergence of digital libraries, influence internet on digital libraries, etc.

INTRODUCTION

Digital library is a relatively a new concept, the term digital library explains the nature of its collection. Digital library is understood to have the information stored in predominantly in electronic or digital medium. The digital information collections may include digital books, digital/scanned images, graphics, textual and numeric data, digitized films audio and video clips, etc. A digital library is expected to provide access to the digital information collection, direct usage of communication networks for accessing and obtaining information, and copying by either downloading or on-line/off line printing form a master file. Digital libraries enable managing a very large amount of data, preserve unique and rare collections. Provide faster access to information, facilitate dealing with data from than one location, and enhance

DOI: 10.4018/978-1-5225-0296-8.ch015

distributed learning environments. They also help to perform searches that are manually not feasible or practical and offer to protect content owner's information. The main function of digital library librarian is that, identify, select, procedure, process, organize, provide access, preservation and conservation, and management of digital information. Digital libraries playing a challenging role for advanced users satisfaction, which is a advancement of computer hardware, software, communication and networks made it economically feasible and technically possible to delivery electronic full text to the desktop.

FACTORS RESPONSIBLE FOR EMERGENCE OF DIGITAL LIBRARIES

Following are the factors are catalytic effect in the emergence of digital libraries;

1. Knowledgeable, computer literate and information literate user's base have started to demand more information at their PC or Laptop computer.
2. If library budget is not able to cope with the user's rising demands for hard copy of valuable journals which being provided by various publisher wise full text database.
3. Research community require current and updated information in their respected area of research, such information being published time to time in e-journals for the purpose of rapidly transmitting for research and development.
4. The peculiarity between library collection management and document delivery, the ownership and access approaches, are becoming increasingly unconfident.
5. The rapid growth in the internet as established the potential wealth of information resources available at the click of a mouse button as ICT and Internet technology feature.
6. Libraries and information centers started giving increased emphasis to provide access to resources available elsewhere rather than physically possessing resources e.g. library automation, inter library networks, online library catalogues, and resource sharing activities.

INFLUNCES OF INTERNET ON DIGITAL LIBRARIES

Networked computer or Internet has become backbone for obtaining, storing, processing and transmitting valuable information worldwide. Internet is enabling inter-connectivity of computer networks. Internet is the global network of number of networks with about millions of host computers spread around the world, those dealing with each other through a common set of communication protocols and reaching globally and providing connectivity to millions of users. The growth of internet has been global and continuous. Libraries have been changes their concepts as it placed into digital library e. g. electronic libraries, digital libraries, libraries without walls, shifting the libraries on to a laptop at the office or home. A variety of technologies are used for accessing the huge electronic information available in optical media, internet and on web. Opening with basic tool like e-mail, internet has been shifted to navigation aids like wide area information servers (WAIS), Netscape and Gopher; web clients such as Lynx, Win web and Cello, and more recently to the consumer oriented home pages of the web. Information resources available on the web are getting inter linked through web pages. Internet reacts for spreading of electronic and online journals. Several journals are already available on the Net e.g. Journal of Universal Computer Science, electronic letters online, journal of knowledge synthesis arid Nursing, and

Online Journal of Current Clinical trials. Publishers offering number of electronic journals on Internet is steadily increasing. Services like Uncover by Blackwell and Contents first by OCLC offer internet access to table of contents of several thousands of journals followed by online ordering of full text of paper. Digital libraries have begun to take such services into the account while planning their acquisition of online or electronic resources particularly online journal subscription. Networked computers provide seamless access digitally to specific information of the entire subject field. We can say that the thing is not exist in the block whole which information is not available on internet net, therefore digital libraries can do the fulfillment of entire user demand it is not only the dignity of digital libraries but it is a credit of Internet and Information communication technology (ICT).

DIGITIZATION

Definition for Digitization: Digitization refers to the process of translating a piece of information such as book, sound recording, image, picture, and videos into the bits, bits are the fundamental units of information in computer system, turning information into these binary digit is called digitization and such digitization process can be carried through a variety of existing technologies.

PROCESS OF DIGITIZATION

1. With the Archivist's approval, a document is selected for digitization.
2. Tracking data are compiled so that the document's whereabouts are always known.
3. Documents are then sent out to be digitized. Fragile documents are taken to Metadata and Preservation Services department, but most documents are shipped to an outside vendor.
4. A trained expert scans or digitally photographs documents to create TIFs, or Tagged Image Files. Archival digitization requires high-resolution scanners or cameras operated by skilled technicians to ensure high-quality results.
5. Documents and digital files are returned to the Archive, where the Archivist or a Student Assistant performs quality-control analysis.
6. The Archivist or Student Assistant creates metadata — electronic records maintained by the library to make digital objects searchable online — for each digitized document.
7. Digital files are then converted into appropriate formats — JPEG 2000 for photographs, maps, or slides, PDF for text — for online public access.
8. The digital files and corresponding metadata are united in an electronic database. Morgan Library uses software called DigiTool for this process.
9. Finally, files are made available online for public access through the Library's searchable Digital Repository. Files are also linked to electronic versions of archival collection finding aids.

DIGITAL PRESERVATION

According to the research libraries groups, digital preservation is defined as the managed activities necessary for the long term maintenance of the bite streams including metadata sufficient to reproduce a suitable facsimile of the original document, for the continued accessibility of the document contents through the time and changing technology. Digital Preservation refers to the series of managed activities necessary to ensure continued access to digital materials for as long as necessary. Digital preservation is defined very broadly for the purposes of this study and refers to all of the actions required to maintain access to digital materials beyond the limits of media failure or technological change. Those materials may be records created during the day-to-day business of an organization; "b o r n-digital" materials created for a specific purpose e.g. teaching resources; or the products of digitization projects. This handbook specifically excludes the potential use of digital technology to preserve the original artifacts through digitization. Following are some digitization definition;

1. **Long-Term Preservation:** Continued access to digital materials, or at least to the information contained in them, indefinitely.
2. **Medium-Term Preservation:** Continued access to digital materials beyond changes in technology for a defined period of time but not indefinitely.
3. **Short-Term Preservation:** Access to digital materials either for a defined period of time while use is predicted but which does not extend beyond the foreseeable future and/or until it becomes inaccessible because of changes in technology.

The Libraries recognize our responsibility for building and preserving print and digital collections in support of teaching, learning, scholarship, and research. To ensure the continued use of these collections, the Libraries will follow a policy of active preservation with the aim of safeguarding the authenticity and utility of all resources entrusted to its care. The specific objectives of the Library's digital preservation program are to:

1. Maintain and develop processes and systems to capture, manage, preserve, find, and make accessible digital materials now and into the future.
2. Identify collections to digitize that are unique to UMass Amherst and that have regional, state, national, and international interest.
3. Continue to develop expertise in the creation and management of digital collections and information.
4. Provide context for digital materials by creating the metadata necessary to understand them.
5. Provide authentic and reliable digital materials to our users with provenance and authorized change histories for each item.
6. Adapt preservation strategies to incorporate the capabilities afforded by new and emerging technologies in cost-effective and responsible way.
7. Serve the needs of our users by enabling persistent access to digital content over time as the technology for digital content creation and distribution evolves.
8. Demonstrate auditable compliance with the development of the standards and practice of the digital preservation community.
9. Contribute to the development of the standards and practice of the digital preservation community.
10. Explore collaborative opportunities to collect and preserve digital materials so as to make the best use of available resources and avoid duplicative efforts.

DEFINITION TO DIGITAL LIBRARY

"Digital libraries are organization that provides the resources including specialized staff, to select, structure, offer intellectual access to, internet, distribute, preserve the integrity of and insure the persistence over time of collections of digital works, so that they readily and economically available for use by a defined community or a set of community.

CHARACTERISTICS OF DIGITAL LIBRARIES

1. Networked accessibility.
2. User friendly interface.
3. Advanced search and retrieval of information.
4. Supporting Multimedia contents.
5. Accessibility from anywhere e.g. School, Library, Home even during the journey.
6. Providing access to very long collection including access to primary and secondary information.
7. Availability for long time.
8. Greater opportunity to publishing.

ADVANTAGES OF DIGITAL LIBRARIES

1. It helps in preservation of materials: Digital library preservation is to protect information of enduring value for access by present and future generations Libraries and archives have served as the central institutional focus for preservation, and both types of institutions include preservation as one of their core functions. In recent decades, many major libraries and archives established formal preservation programs for traditional materials in paper, microform, photographic, and to lesser degree audio-visual formats.
2. Saving the space: the 21 century is the age of information explosion. Information being published every minute because of the ease of the information technology, today's information become old for tomorrow. Digital Library influencing by information growth which rising problem for available place in library. Today some libraries finding the ways of digitization and electronic preservation and conservation of materials as a solution for place in libraries but it is not possible for all the budget libraries in the world
3. It also providing the facility of computer and internet for downloading, printing and universal accessibility: Digital libraries stand with number of benefits for the community for instance; it provides remote access and use can access related information anywhere anytime with the ease of internet downloading and printing.
4. Digital libraries enable one to perform searches that is not possible manually, it preserves cultural heritages and rare collection through digitization. Digital libraries enable greater access to information and provide mean to enrich the teaching and learning environment with the protection of copyright.

DIGITAL LIBRARY SERVICES

1. **Internet Services:** Online journals, online books, online encyclopedia, online conference proceeding, online newspapers, online dictionary and directory, online sample copies, online table of contents services, abstract services, online catalogue services.
2. **Newspaper Clipping Services:** Section of newspapers clipping, scanning and saving, online searching and saving, Access and retrieval.
3. **Digitization of Specialized Collection:** Digitization of specialized collection being provide in digital libraries e.g. British library, National library of Australia.
4. Service examination cell.
5. **Digital Reference Services:** Digital reference services include e-mail services, telephone or online enquiry services, chat based services, virtual references.
6. **Enquiry Service Section:** Online enquiry services include inquiry about information sources, reference information and referral services about collection which is not available online for the user.
7. Inter Library lone services.

DIGITAL LIBRARY PROJECTS/INITIATIVES

Several projects and initiatives taken up to create digital libraries e.g. communication of ACM, April 1995; DESIDOC bulletin of information technology, November 1997; journal of American Society for Information Science, September 1993, and October 1994; and SIGLINK Newsletter, February 1995 to name a few). Important amongst the many initiatives launched is the joint initiatives of Advanced research Project Agency, National Aeronautics and Space Administration, and National science Foundation of the USA who announced several digital library projects involving Carnegie Melon University, Stanford University of Michigan (Ann Arbor), University of California (Banta Barbara), University of Illinois (Urbana Champaign) and University of California (Berkeley), to advance the means to collect, store and organize in digital format and to make it available for searching, retrieval, and processing via communication networks, many other Universities and also OCLC have undertaken project involving digital libraries. The Library of Congress is making efforts to transfer traditional print collection into versatile electronic resources under its National Digital Library Program which had aim to digitize5 million items. Also in the United Kingdom, the British Library, the Electronic Library Project of De Montfort University, University of west Anglia, University of Bath, University College London, University of Wales, University of Ulster, University of Surrey etc. are making efforts towards electronic or digital libraries are making efforts towards electronic or digital libraries. On the publisher observation, in the recent past many reference books and scholarly periodicals were brought out in digital form. Major databases like INSPEEC, MEDLINE, BIOSIS, ERIC, and CAB abstracts, Compendex plus, Metade, Mathsci. ABI Inform, AIDSLINE, Agricola, Chemical Abstracts, NTIS, ASIT, etc. Are available on CD-ROM and printed format. On the journals fronts, many commercial publishers like Elsevier science, HW Wilson, silver platter, Wiley, McGraw-Hill, Academic, Kluwer, etc. and professional societies like IEEE, IEE, ACM, ACS, American Institute of Physics, etc., are bringing out electronic versions of journals. There are many journals available online only through networks. In many libraries and Information centers, the electronic information component added is progressively increasing.

DIGITAL LIBRARIES AND THE CYBER LAW

Leaving apart technical and other problems to escort in digital libraries, the most important problem is the copyright in cyber places. Existing copyright laws have not caught up with the technological developments cyberspaces. Cognizant users are confused as to which is right and which is wrong. At present there is no clarity about whether the content of electronic resources on internet is free or rapid. Although the copyright statements appear in many cases, they are elusive to locate in some cases. It can be argued that publishers of promotional materials, especially, advertising and marketing materials, on the web implicitly encourage downloading, printing and copying the material for redistribution to more than one in the same organization. One can see copyright notices on advertising and situation further. Even if an electronic resource is a free journals or a newspaper, there is no clear cut law whether it is violation to forward the items from them to colleagues, friends or through list serve. Many electronic papers on internet allow personals and fair use; many more lacks explicit statements if it is free or priced. It is a copyright violation to e-mail a web page by an intermediary to a colleague or a user; strictly for information sake no financial gain is involved. The best way can be to provide information about the URL where the piece of information appears. Even downloading e-mail is an offence under copyright law. It is observable that many authors and publishers turning to legal issue. This is one reason that the copyrighted books and other material are not expected to be readily available in cyber places as they are available in traditional libraries.

PROBLEMS ASSOCIATED WITH DIGITAL LIBRARIES

Library and information centers may have to face many challenges while transforming to digital libraries, addition to more electronic and digital information, providing access to the digitized information, sorting out issues like access to information versus ownership and appropriation of budget toward maintaining computer system, databases etc., as well as the problems and issues associated with digital information like acceptability, accuracy, accountability, authenticity, standardization, copy right and pricing, some important problems discussed below;

1. **Information Accuracy:** Most of the digitizing projects employ optical character recognition (OCR) technology which is only 95 percent accurate. So there is 5 percent error remain. Because of this dean may become clean, river may be read naiveté, etc. thus there is no fully accuracy in digital project work.
2. **Compatibility of Hardware/Software:** The use of digital collections will pose compatibility problems as witnessed while using IEEE/IEE electronic library (IEL)
3. **Shelf Life:** Another concern is the storage life of electronic media. As against a print-on-paper (acid free) document or a microfiche/film which have a much longer shelf life, the durable CD-ROMs survive about a generation. But, floppy disks, computer tapes hard disks lost only a few years.
4. **Other Issues:** Apart from these, problem like developing electronic catalogues that can retrieve information scattered across digital libraries over a network finding a cost-effective way to digitize the materials without spoiling the original in the process, and making the digital material available while protecting the literary rights of articles, writers and publishers are to be addressed.

MEKELLE UNIVERSITY DIGITAL LIBRARY

EIS Access Policy for EIS E-Information Sources in Mekelle University Digital Library

Mekelle University Library web portal (URL: http://www.mu.edu.et/index.php/library-e-resources) growing collection of Electronic Resources. Over 74 electronic databases are available in the Library and can be accessed either from the digital library in each campus Library or online in the Library Web Page. Assistance in using electronic resources in general and databases in particular can be obtained through email (getahun.assefa@mu.edu.et) or (Cell phone: (+251) 911 165515) and from computer labs in the Digital Libraries of each campus Library.

Mekelle University Digital Library subscribed to the following electronic information resources: Acoustical Society of America, AERA SIG Communication of Research, AGORA, American Chemical Society, American Institute of Physics, American Physical Society, American Society of Agricultural & Biological Engineers (ASABE), American Society of Civil Engineers, Animal Health and Production Compendium, Annual Reviews, Aquaculture, Compendium, Cambridge University Press (CUP), Canadian Science Publishing (was NRC Press), Cochrane Library (Web), Conrnel University Library, Crop Protection Compendium, Directory of Open Access Books., DOAJ (Directory of Access Journals), Duke University Press, EBSCO Host, Econport, Edinburgh University -direct from EUP, Emerald Group publishing ltd EM120, Forestry Compendium, Free books for medical doctors, Gale CENGAGE learning: expanded academic resources, Gale CENGAGE Learning: health and wellness Resources, Geological Society Geology, Earth Science. Health and Medical Journals, HINARI Access to Research in Health Programme, Institute for Operations Research and Management Sciences (INFORMS), Institute of Electrical and Electronics Engineers (ASPP, POP), Institution of Engineering Technology (IET), International journal of Teaching and Learning in Higher Education, IOP science (Journals from Institute of physics), JSTOR, Law and public policy, Mary Ann Liebert, NPG – Nature, NPG - Palgrave Macmillan Journals, OARE, On-line books, Open Access Dissertations and Theses (PQDT Open), Optical Society of America (OSA), Organization for Economic Cooperation & Development (OECD), Over 4000 journals (All Subject), Oxford University Press E-journals, PLOS (public library of science), Policy Press, Project MUSE, Royal College of Physicians, Royal Society, Royal Society of Chemistry, Royal Society of Chemistry Archive, Sage, Sage IMechE (was PEP), Scientific Commons, Springer Basic Package 1349 titles, Springer Lecture Notes in Computer Science series (per institution) (annual subscription), Symposium Journals, Taylor & Francis Journals, Teeal (on LAN), The International Publishers Association (IPA), The Ptolemy project, University of Chicago Press, University of Wollongong, WHO for Africa (world health organization). Wiley Online Library full collection (1,360 titles), World Bank e-library, World Bank: World Development Indicator (WDI)/ World Development Finance (GDF)/African Development Indicator (ADI)/ Global Economic Mentor (GEM). This survey has been undertaken to know the level of awareness and use as well as the availability of EIS to the IEGDS field. Thus, the study is an attempt to evaluate e-resources awareness, attitude and usability by the academic staff members of IEGDS, Mekelle University and to find out problems encountered by the users in accessing the e-resources (Mekelle university Annual Report, 2014).

FUTURE PERSPECTIVE OF DIGITAL LIBRARIES

The number of digitization projects is underway at Google, the Million Book Project, and Internet Archive. With continued improvements in book handling and presentation technologies such as optical character recognition and e-Books, and development of alternative depositories and business models, digital libraries are rapidly growing in popularity. Libraries have ventured into audio and video collections, so have digital libraries such as the Internet Archive. Google Books project recently received a court victory on proceeding with their book-scanning project that was halted by the Authors' guild. This helped open the road for libraries to work with Google to better reach patrons who are accustomed to computerized information. One factor that gave Google an advantage is the library's fair use argument. All the problems associated with digital libraries are wrapped up in archiving." "If in 100 years people can still read your article, we'll have solved the problem." (Daniel Akst, 2003) author of The Webster Chronicle, proposes that "the future of libraries and of information is digital." (Peter Lyman and Hal Varian) information scientists at the University of California, Berkeley, estimate that "the world's total yearly production of print, film, optical, and magnetic content would require roughly 1.5 billion gigabytes of storage." Therefore, they believe that "soon it will be technologically possible for an average person to access virtually all recorded information."

CONCLUSION

Digital libraries considered as libraries without walls which providing remote information access to users with number of advanced features therefore it serving as a information superhighway to the community. Digital libraries providing online information resources which include hypertext hypermedia and multimedia compositions which are illustrate difficult data and provide related link to information sources. Digital libraries provide rapidly transmission and remote access thus it is very beneficial for academician in their Research and Development activities.

RECCOMENDATION FOR PUBLIC PRIVATE PARTNERSHIPS FOR THE DIGITISATION AND ONLINE ACCESSIBILITY OF CULTURAL HERITAGE

Digital libraries playing a vital role in digitization worldwide, digitization process can preserve and conserve cultural diversity around the world. Public can have access to cultural information to know their custom, even we can learn many things and improvise many things on the base of past information and therefore digitization is essential. In this context number of ancient record going to destroy which is waiting to being digitized. Digitization is not only difficult but it is very expensive and time taking process. Public private partnership PPPs can help in digitization in libraries; here achievements and recommendations Public private partnerships (PPPs) can have an important role in helping the development of digital libraries and in implementing a strategy for digitization, online accessibility and digital preservation of Europe's collective memory. Libraries, archives, museums and galleries have preserved this collective memory and have experience of resource discovery and user requirements, private partners can bring to the table funding, technology, software and expertise required for large-scale digitization. By working together public access can be enhanced. Most of the partnerships investigated as case studies were still in their preliminary stages of development, and therefore it was too early to make ultimate conclusions as to the key elements of success. Lessons could be learnt by continuing the observation of the development of ongoing partnerships analyzed. While there is broad consensus on the potential usefulness and on the need to promote PPPs, there is also evidence of difficulties, conflicts and failures related to PPPs.

Recommends for Public Private Partnership [PPPs]

1. Partners should clearly state their strategic objectives and the benefits for the citizen to be achieved through the project.
2. The partnership should fully utilize the experience and expertise of the partners and bring complementary contributions.
3. The partnership should maximize public access and take into account long-term preservation and sustainability issues.
4. **Financial Environment:** Legislation aimed at supporting finance of cultural heritage through the provision of fiscal benefits to private partners should be more extensively applied to digitization projects.
5. **IPR:** Partnerships should be established within the framework of applicable copyright law.
6. **Public Domain:** Public domain content in the analogue world should remain in the public domain in the digital environment. If restrictions to user's access and use are necessary in order to make the digital content available at all, these restrictions should only apply for a limited period of time.
7. **Exclusivity:** Exclusive arrangements for digitizing and distributing the digital assets of cultural institutions are to be avoided. Where exclusive agreements are necessary to provide a service in the public interest, that such exclusive arrangements are time-limited, regularly reviewed and transparent.
8. **Re-Use:** Cultural institutions should aim to stand by the principles Ethiopian National Archive and Agency Library Proclamation No. 179/1999 on the re-use of Public Sector Information".
9. **Governance:** Public Private Partnerships should be transparent and accountable, and have formal governance arrangements enshrined in a formal contract between parties.

SUGGESTIONS FOR FUTURE RESEARCH IN DIGITAL LIBRARY ARENA

Digital Libraries are a new research topic, opening up important opportunities for a multi-faceted approach spanning information seeking behavior and social processes such as learning and knowledge sharing, in addition to Digital Libraries as collections of content that need curation; collection, description, preservation, retrieval and so forth. As such, Digital Libraries research opens up important opportunities for a multi-faceted approach spanning information seeking behavior and social processes such as learning and knowledge sharing, in addition to Digital Libraries as collections of content that need curation, ranging from collection and description to preservation and retrieval, among others.

REFERENCES

Lakshmana Moorthy, A., & Karisiddappa, C. R. (1998). Transformation to virtual libraries: Real or Virtual? *Proceedings of the Society for Information ScienceAnnual Conference*, University of Hyderabad.

Mayank, T., & Patel, S. (2010). *Digital Libraries: Functionality, usability, and accessibility*. Library Philosophy and Practice.

Akst, D. (2003). The Digital Library: Its Future Has Arrived. *Carnegie Reporter*, *2*(3), 4–8.

Mekelle University Annual Report. (2014). Electronic Information Resources. Retrieved from http://www.mu.edu.et/index.php/library-e-resources

ADDITIONAL READING

Lennon, L. (n. d.). The Practice of Digital Libraries. *Corporation for National Research Initiatives.*

Oliver, G., & Knight, S. (n. d.). Storage is a Strategic Issue. *Digital Preservation in the Cloud.*

Bishoff, L., & Smith, C. (n. d.). Managing Digital Collections Survey Results. *DuraSpace.*

Lea Moulaison, H., Dykas, F., & Gallant, K. (n. d.). *Open DOAR Repositories and Metadata Practices.* University of Missouri

Schöpfel, J., Prost, H., Pirotrowski, M., Hilf, E.R., Severiens, T. (n. d.). *A French-German Survey of Electronic Theses and Dissertations: Access and Restrictions.* GERiiCO Laboratory, University of Lille 3, France.

Houghton, B. (n. d.). Trustworthiness: Self-assessment of an Institutional Repository against ISO 16363-2012.

Park, O. N. (n. d.). *Development of Linked Data for Archives in Korea.*

McCown, F., Yarbrough, M., & Enlow, K. (n. d.). *Tools for Discovering and Archiving the Mobile Web.*

Hiernet, D., Sawitzki, F., & Mayr, P. (n. d.). Digital Library Research in Action: Supporting Information Retrieval in Sowiport. Leibniz Institute for the Social Sciences, Germany.

Sorensen, J. B. (n. d.). Reconstructing the Past through Utah Sanborn Fire Insurance Maps: A Geospatial Approach to Library Resources. J. Willard Marriott Library. *University of Utah.*

KEY TERMS AND DEFINITIONS

Born Digital: Born digital is referring to denoting texts or recordings produced in digital form, rather than having been converted from print or analogue equivalents.

Cyber Law: Cyberlaw or Internet law is a term that encapsulates the legal issues related to use of the Internet. It is less a distinct field of law than intellectual property or contract law, as it is a domain covering many areas of law and regulation.

DigiTool: DigiTool are a collection of computer devices, input technologies, and software tools that help us communicate with each other. New DigiTool - speech and handwriting recognition, mobile tablet PCs, Pocket PCs, Palm Pilots, and wireless networking - are now indispensable to professional, academic, and economic success. These emerging DigiTool have placed our business curriculum under terrific pressure to evolve and change.

E-Resources: An electronic resource is any information source that the library provides access to in an electronic format. The library has purchased subscriptions to many electronic information resources in order to provide you with access to them free of charge or on pay basic.

Compilation of References

Aaker, D. A., Batra, R., & Myers, J. G. (1992). *Advertising Management* (4th ed.). Englewood Cliffs, NJ: Prentice Hall.

Abiala, E. O. (2011). *Trade Union Laws and Practice in Nigeria: The Travails*. Ibadan: St Paul's Publishing House.

Abram, S. (2005). Web 2.0 - huh?! Library 2.0, librarian 2.0. *Information Outlook*, *9*(12), 44–46.

Adams, L. E. (2009). Information seeking behaviour of Generation Y students at the Stellenbosch University Library and Information Service. Retrieved from http://etd.uwc.ac.za/usrfiles/modules/etd/docs/etd_gen8Srv25Nme4_7779_1275522114.pdf

Adams, L.E. (2009). *Information seeking behaviour of Generation Y students at the Stellenbosch University Library and Information Service* (Magister Bibliothecologiae). University of the Western Cape. Retrieved from http://etd.uwc.ac.za/handle/11394/2715

Adebisi, A. (2010). Labour Relations and Industrial Harmony in Nigerian Tertiary Educational Institutions In Omotoso Femi, Agagu A. A. and Abegunde Ola (Eds.), Governance, Politics and Policies in Nigeria: An Essay in Honour of Prof. Dipo Kolawole (pp. 438-464). Porto Novo: Editions SONOU d'Afrique.

Adereti, F. O., Fapojuwo, O. F., & Onasanya, A. S. (2006). Information on utilization on cocoa production techniques by farmers in Oluyole Local Government Area of Oyo State, Nigeria. *European Journal of Soil Science*, *3*(1), 1–7.

Adigun, G. O., Adegbore, A. M., & Amuda, H. O. (2015). The Social library: integrating social networking into library reference services. In A. Tella (Ed.), *Social media strategies for dynamic library development* (pp. 140–154). Hershey, PA, USA: IGI Global. doi:10.4018/978-1-4666-7415-8.ch008

Adomi, E. E. (2005). The effects of a price increase on cybercafés in Abraka, Nigeria: The bottom-line. *Managing Library Finances*, *18*(2), 78–86. doi:10.1108/08880450510597523

Adusei, P. (2010). Ghana. In C. Armstrong (Ed.), *Access to knowledge in Africa: the role of copyright* (pp. 57–82). UCT Press.

Agarwal, R., Krudys, G., & Tanniru, M. (1997). Infusing learning into the information systems organization. *European Journal of Information Systems*, *6*(1), 25–40. doi:10.1057/palgrave.ejis.3000257

Agarwal, R., & Venkatesh, V. (2002). Assessing a firm's web presence: A heuristic evaluation procedure for the measurement of usability. *Information Systems Research*, *13*(2), 168–186. doi:10.1287/isre.13.2.168.84

Agosto, D. E. (2001). Propelling young women into Cyber Age: gender considerations in the evaluation of Web-based information. *School Library Media Research* 4. Retrieved from http://www.ala.org/ala/aasl/aaslpubsandjournals/slmrb/slmrcontents/volume42001/agosto.htm

Agosto, D.E., & Hughes-Hassell, S. (2005). People, places, and questions: An investigation of the everyday life information-seeking behaviors of urban young adults. *Library & Information Science Research*, 27(2), 141–63.

Aguirre, V. V. (2010). Ensuring access to information: A librarian's dilemma. *Journal of Philippine Librarianship, 30*(1), 10–21.

Aina, L. O. (2006, August 20-24). Information Provision to Farmers in Africa: The Library- extension service linkage. *Proceedings of the World library and information congress, 72nd IFLA general conference and council '06*, Seoul, Korea. Retrieved from http://www.ifla.org/iv/ifla72/index.htm

Aina, L.O., & Mutula, S.M. (2007). Opportunities for Electronic Publishing In T. Mkandawire & A. Mlambo (Eds.), Africa Scholarly Publishing. Oxford: INASP.

Aina, L. O. (2004). *Library and Information Science Text for Africa*. Ibadan: Third World Information Services Limited.

Aina, L. O. (2004). *Library and information science text for Africa*. Ibadan: Third World Services Limited.

Aina, L. O. (2004). *Library and information science text*. Ibadan: Stirlin-Horden.

Ajayi, O.O. (2002). African Response to the Information Communication Technology Revolution: A case study of the ICT development in Nigeria (ATPS Special Paper Series No 8).

Ajiboye, J. O., & Tella, A. (2007). University undergraduate students' information seeking behaviour: implications for quality in higher education in Africa. *The Turkish Online Journal of Educational Technology*, 6(1). Retrieved from http://www.tojet.net/articles/v6i1/614.pdf

Ajiboye, J.O., & Tella, A. (2006). Class attendance and gender effects on undergraduate students' achievement in a social studies course in Botswana. *Essays in Education, 18*(1), 1–11.

Akester, P. (2010). *The new challenges of striking the right balance between copyright protection and access to knowledge, information and culture*. Intergovernmental Copyright Committee, UNESCO. Retrieved from http://unesdoc.unesco.org/images/0018/001876/187683E.pdf

Akst, D. (2003). The Digital Library: Its Future Has Arrived. *Carnegie Reporter, 2*(3), 4–8.

Alavi, M. (1994). Computer-mediated collaborative learning: An empirical investigation. *Management Information Systems Quarterly, 8*(4), 159–174. doi:10.2307/249763

Albanese, A. R. (2001). Revolution or evolution. Retrieved from http://www.libraryjournal.com/article/CA178186.html

Alemna, A. A., & Skouby, K. E. (2000). An investigation into the information needs and information seeking behavior of members of Ghana's legislature. *Library Management, 21*(5), 235–240. doi:10.1108/01435120010324815

Allen, B. (1997). Information Needs: A Person in-Situation Approach. *Proceedings of an international conference on Information seeking in context ISIC '96*, Tampere, Finland (pp. 111–122). London: Taylor Graham Publishing. doi:doi:10.1108/S1876-0562(1996)0000096004 doi:10.1108/S1876-0562(1996)0000096004

Al-Suqri, M., & Al-Aufi. (2015). Information-seeking behavior and technology adoption: theories and trends. Hershey, Pennsylvania, USA: IGI Global.

Al-Suqri, M. N. (2011). Information-seeking behavior of social science scholars in developing countries: A proposed model. *The International Information & Library Review, 43*(1), 1–14. doi:10.1080/10572317.2011.10762875

American Library Association. (2008). Serving non-English speakers: 2007 Analysis of library demographics, services and programs. Retrieved from http://www.ala.org/offices/olos/nonenglishspeakers

Amuda, H. O. (2015). Social Networking and the promotion of library services: what does the future hold? In A. Tella (Ed.), *Social media strategies for dynamic library development* (pp. 113–125). Hershey, PA, USA: IGI Global.

Ananaba, W. (1979). The Trade Union in Africa. C. Nigeria: Nwamife Publishers Ltd..

Anandarajan, M., Igbaria, M., & Anakwe, U. (2000). Technology acceptance in the banking industry: A perspective from a less developed country. *Information Technology & People*, *13*(4), 298–312. doi:10.1108/09593840010359491

Andersen, D. L. (2002). Communicating information across cultures: understanding how others work. Retrieved from www.pantaneto.co.uk/issue9/andersen.htm

Andrup, S., Fagerjord, K., & Magnussen, M. T. (1995). Fagbibliotekets rolle i problembasert læring (PBL). Oslo: RBT/Riksbibliotektjenesten. (Skrifter fra RBT/Riksbibliotektjenesten, Nr. 69).

Anwar, M. A. (2007). Research on information seeking and use in Pakistan: An assessment. *Pakistan Journal of Library and Information Science*, *8*, 15–32.

Anwar, M. A., Al-Ansari, H., & Abdullah, A. (2004). Information seeking behaviour of Kuwaiti journalists. *Libri*, *54*(4), 228–236. doi:10.1515/LIBR.2004.228

Anzsi.org. (2015). Types of indexing. Retrieved from https://anzsi.org/resources/about-indexers-and-indexing/types-indexing/

Appelbaum, S. (1990). Training managers to reduce fear and love the machines. *Industrial and commercial training*, 22(6), 9-16.

Applegate, R. (2008). Whose Decline? Which Academic Libraries are "Deserted" in Terms of Reference Transactions? *Reference and User Services Quarterly*, *40*(2), 176–188.

Aregbesola, A., & Oguntayo, S. (2014). Use of Electronic Resources by Faculty Members in Landmark University. *Computing, Information Systems. Development Informatics and Allied Research Journal*, *5*(2), 53–58.

Arm, W.Y. (n. d.). *Digital Libraries*. Cambridge: MIT Press.

Arms, W. Y. (1995). Key concepts in the architecture of the digital library. *D-lib Magazine*, URL: http://www.dlib.org/dlib/July95/07arms.html

Arms, W. (2000). *Digital libraries*. Cambridge: M.I.T. Press.

Arms, W. Y. (1995). Key concepts in the architecture of the digital library. *D-Lib Magazine*, *1995*(July). Retrieved from http://www.dlib.org/dlib/arms.html

Ascensão. José de Oliveira. (2008). Sociedade da informação e liberdade de expressão. In Direito da Sociedade da Informação (7th ed., Coimbra ed., pp. 51-73).

Association of College and Research Libraries. (2010). *Information literacy competency standards for higher education*. Retrieved from http://www.ala.org/ala/mgrps/divs/acrl/standards/informationliteracycompet ncy.cfm

Association of Research Libraries. (1995). *Appendix II. Definition and Purpose of a Digital Library*. Retrieved from http://www.arl.org/resources/pubs/mmproceedings/1 26mmappen2.shtml

Ayamunda, J., & Nwabachili, C. (2015). Copyright exceptions and use of educational materials in universities in Kenya. *Journal of Law. Policy and Globalization*, *39*, 104–116.

Ayre, L. B. (2008). The extensible library: library 2.0 and patron 2.0. Retrieved from http://galecia.com/included/docs/2007/LoriAyre_SSP_june8_2007.pdf

Azami, M., & Fattahi, R. (2010). Matching database user interfaces with Ellis model of information seeking behavior: results of a qualitative survey. *Proceedings of the QQML2010*, Chania, Crete, Greece. Retrieved from http://www.researchgate.net/profile/Mohammad_Azami/publication/228965938_Matching_database_user_interfaces_with_Ellis_model_of_information_seeking_behavior_results_of_a_qualitative_survey/links/00b7d521cf0b43da95000000.pdf

Aziagba, P. C., & Okede, G. W. (2011). information seeking behavior of cassava farmers in Upata clan, Ekpeye community of Rivers State, Nigeria.

Babu, S. C., Glendenning, C. J., Asenso-Okyere, K., & Govindarajan, S. K. (2012). Farmer's information needs and search behaviors. IFPRI Discussion paper 01165.

Badhusha, K. N. (2008). *Digital library architecture*. New Delhi: Ane Books.

Baeza-Yates, R., & Ribeiro-Neto, B. (Eds.), (2011). *Modern information retrieval: the concepts and technology behind search* (2nd ed.). England: Pearson Education Limited.

Bailin, A., & Grafstein, A. (2005). The Evolution of Academic Libraries: The Networked Environment. *Journal of Academic Librarianship*, *31*(4), 317–323. doi:10.1016/j.acalib.2005.04.004

Bajpai, S. K. (1999). *Modern information retrieval*. New Delhi: Ess Ess Publications.

Baran, S., & Davis, D. (1995). *Mass communication theory: Foundations, ferment, and future*. Los Angeles, CA: Wadsworth.

Baro, E. E., Onyenania, G. O., & Osaheni, O. (2010). Information seeking behaviour of undergraduate students in the humanities in three universities in Nigeria. *South African Journal of Library and Information Science*, *76*(2), 109–117. doi:10.7553/76-2-74

Bates, M. (1996). Learning about the information seeking of interdisciplinary scholars and students. *Library Trends*, *45*(2), 155–164.

Bates, M. (2005). An introduction to metatheories, theories, and models. In K. Fisher, S. Erdelez, & L. McKechnie (Eds.), *Theories of Information Behavior*. Medford, NJ: Information Today.

Bates, M. J. (2010). Information behavior. In M. J. Bates & M. N. Maack (Eds.), *Encyclopedia of Library and Information Sciences* (pp. 2381–2391). New York: CRC Press.

Bawden, D., & Rowlands, I. (1999). Digital libraries: Assumptions and concepts. *Libri*, *49*(4), 181–191. doi:10.1515/libr.1999.49.4.181

Bawden, D., & Vilar, P. (2006). Digital libraries: To meet or manage user expectations. *Aslib Proceedings*, *58*(4), 346–354. doi:10.1108/00012530610687713

Belkin, N. J. (1980). Anomalous states of knowledge as a basis for information-retrieval. *Revue Canadienne Des Sciences De L Information [Canadian Journal of Information Science]*, 5(May), 133–143.

Belkin, N. J. (1996). Intelligent information retrieval: whose intelligence? In Proceedings of the Fifth International Symposium for Information Science (Vol. 96, pp. 25–31). Konstanz: Universitätsverlag Konstanz. Retrieved from http://core.kmi.open.ac.uk/download/pdf/11540431.pdf#page=23

Belkin, N. (1980). Anomalous states of knowledge as a basis for information retrieval. *Canadian J. of Inf. Sci.*, *5*, 133–143.

Belkin, N. J. (1980). Anomalous states of knowledge as a basis for information retrieval. *The Canadian Journal of Information Science*, *5*, 133–143.

Berkman Centre for internet and Society. (2012). Copyright for librarians: the essential handbook.

Bernal, J. D. (1960). Scientific information and its users. *Aslib Proceedings*, *12*(12), 423–438. doi:10.1108/eb049779

Bertino, E., Casarosa, V., Crane, G., Croft, B., Del Bimbo, A., & Fellner, D. (2001). Digital libraries: future directions for a European Research Programme. San, Cassiano: DELOS.

Bertot, J. C. (2009). Public access technologies in public libraries: Effects and implications. *Information Technology and Libraries*, *28*(2), 81–92.

Bian, G., & Chen, H. (2000). Cross-language information access to multilingual collections on the Internet. *American society for information science*, 51(3), 281-296.

Bilal, D., & Kirby, J. (2001). Factors Influencing Children's and Adults' Information Seeking on the Web: Results of Two Studies. *Proceedings of the ASIST Annual Meeting* (Vol. 38, pp. 126–40). Retrieved from http://eric.ed.gov/?id=EJ637598

Blazek, R., & Aversa, E. (1994). The humanities: A selective guide to information resources. (4th ed.). Library Science Text Series. Englewood, CO: Libraries Unlimited.

Blomberg, O. (2011). Concepts of cognition for cognitive engineering. *The International Journal of Aviation Psychology*, *21*(1), 85–104. doi:10.1080/10508414.2011.537561

Book Industry Study Group. (2010). *Consumer attitudes toward e-book reading*. New York, NY: The Author.

Bordeianu, S., Carter, C. E., & Dennis, N. K. (2000). Delivering electronic resources with Web OPACs and other Web-based tools: Needs of reference librarians. *RSR. Reference Services Review*, *28*(2), 111–119. doi:10.1108/00907320010326683

Borgman, C. L. (2003)Designing Digital Libraries for Usability. In A.P. Bishop, N.A. Van House & B.P. Buttenfield (Eds.), Digital Library Use Social Practice in Design and Evaluation (pp. 86 -118). Cambridge: The MIT Press.

Borgman, C. L., Bates, M. J., Cloonan, M. V., Efthimiadis, E. N., Gilliland-Swetland, A., Kafai, Y., Maddox, A. (1996). Social aspects of digital libraries. Final report to the National Science Foundation. http://dli.grainger.uiuc.edu/national.htm

Borgman, C. L., Leazer, G. H., Gilliland-Swetland, A. J., & Gazan, R. (2001). Iterative design and evaluation of a geographic digital library for university students: A case study of the Alexandria Digital Earth Prototype (ADEPT). In P. Constantopoulos & I.T. Solvberg (Eds.), *Research and Advanced Technology for Digital Libraries: 5th European Conference, LNCS* (Vol. 2163, pp. 390–401). New York: Springer.

Borgman, C. (2001). Where is the librarian in the digital library? *Communications of the ACM*, *44*(5), 66–67. doi:10.1145/374308.374344

Borgman, C. (2003). Designing digital libraries for usability. In *A. Bishop, N. Van House, & B. Buttenfield, Digital library use: social practice in design and evaluation* (pp. 85–118). Cambridge, Massachusetts: MIT Press.

Borgman, C. (2006). What can studies of e-learning teach us about collaboration in e-research? Some findings from digital library studies. *Computer Supported Cooperative Work*, *15*(4), 359–383. doi:10.1007/s10606-006-9024-1

Borgman, C. L. (1999). What are digital libraries? Competing visions. *Information Processing & Management*, *38*(3), 227–243.

Borgman, C. L. (2000). *From Gutenberg to the global information infrastructure: access to information in the network world*. Cambridge, MA: MIT Press.

Borgman, C. L. (2000). *From Gutenberg to the Global Information Infrastructure: Access to Information in the Network World*. Cambridge, MA: MIT Press.

Borgman, C. L. (2000). *From Gutenberg to the global information infrastructure: Access to information in the networked world.* Cambridge: M.I.T. Press.

Borgman, C. L. (2000). *From Gutenberg to the Global Information Infrastructure: Access to Information in the Networked World.* Cambridge: MIT Press.

Borgman, C. L. (2000a). Digital libraries and the continuum of scholarly communication. *The Journal of Documentation, 56*(4), 412–430. doi:10.1108/EUM0000000007121

Boyd, D. M., & Ellison, N. B. (2007). Social network sites: Definition, history, and scholarship. *Journal of Computer-Mediated Communication, 13*(1), 1. http://jcmc.indiana.edu/vol13/issue1/boyd.ellison.html doi:10.1111/j.1083-6101.2007.00393.x

Bradley, A., & McDonald, M. (2011). *The Social Organization.* Boston, Massachusetts: Harvard Business Review Press.

Bramley, P. (1989). Effective training. *Journal of European Industrial Training, 13*(7), 2–33. doi:10.1108/EUM0000000000203

Brennan, K., Kelly, D. & Arguello, J. (2014). The Effect of Cognitive Abilities on Information Search for Tasks of Varying Levels of Complexity. ACM. doi:10.1145/2637002.2637022

Brindley, D. L. J. (2009). *Challenges for great libraries in the age of the digital native.* Amsterdam: IOS Press.

British Library. (2010). *2020 vision.* London, UK: The British Library Board. Retrieved from http://www.bl.uk/aboutus/stratpolprog/2020vision/2020A3.pdf

Brophy, P. (1993). Networking in British academic libraries. *British Journal of Academic Librarianship, 8*(1), 49–60.

Brosnan, M. (1999). Modelling technophopia: A case for word processing. *Computers in Human Behavior, 15*(2), 105–121. doi:10.1016/S0747-5632(98)00020-X

Buchanan, G., Cunningham, S. J., Blandford, A., Rimmer, J., & Warwick, C. (2006). Information seeking by humanities scholars. Retrieved from www.ucl.ac.uk/slais/claire-warwick/articles/ECDL2.doc

Buckland, M. (1991). *Information and Information System.* New York: Praeger.

Budapest Open Access Initiative. (2012). Retrieved from http://www.soros.org/openaccess/read.shtml

Bunning, C. (1992). The reflective practitioner: A case study. *Journal of Management Development, 11*(1), 25–38. doi:10.1108/EUM0000000001388

Burke, J. (2010), Discovery versus disintermediation: the new reality driven by today's end-user. Retrieved from http://www.vala.org.au/vala2010/papers2010/VALA2010_57_Burke_Final.pdf

Butterworth, R. (2006, June 15). Information seeking and retrieval as a leisure activity. DL-CUBA 2006 - Workshop on digital libraries in the context of users' broaden activities, Chapel Hill, USA. *Proceedings of JCDL '06.* Retrieved from http://www.uclic.ucl.ac.uk/events/dl-cuba2006/papers/Butterworth.pdf

Byrne, A. (2003), Digital libraries: barriers or gateways to scholarly information. *Proceedings of theIATUL Conference,* Turkey doi:doi:10.1108/02640470310499777 doi:10.1108/02640470310499777

Callison, D. (1997). Evolution of methods to measure student information use. *Library & Information Science Research, 19*(4), 347–357. doi:10.1016/S0740-8188(97)90025-6

Campbell, J. D. (2006). Changing a cultural icon: The academic library as a virtual destination. *EDUCAUSE Review*, *41*(1), 16–31. Retrieved from http://www.educause.edu/EDUCAUSE+Review/EDUCAUSEReviewMagazineVolume41/ChangingaCulturalIconTheAcadem/158029

Candela, L., & Nardi, D. (2011). Digital library technology cookbook: an introperability framework best practices and solutions. Brussels: European Commission Information Society and Media. Retrieved from http://www.dlorg.eu

Candela, L., Athanasopoulos, G.; Castelli, D.; El Raheb, K.; Innocenti, P.; et al. (2011). The Digital Library Reference Model. *DL.org Project.*

Candela'L. et al. (2008) *The DELOS digital library reference model- foundations for digital libraries.* Retrieved from http://www.delos.info/files/pdf/ReferenceModel/DELOS_DLReferenceModel_0.98.pdf

Carmen, L. (2006). My Computer, My Doctor: A Constitutional Call for Federal Regulation of Cybermedicine. *American Journal of Law & Medicine*, *32*(4), 585–609. PMID:17240732

Carroll, J. B. (1993). *Human cognitive abilities: a summary of factor-analytic studies*. N.Y.: Cambridge University press. doi:10.1017/CBO9780511571312

Case, D. O. (2002). *Looking for information: a survey of research on information seeking, needs, and behavior*. Amsterdam: Academic Press.

Case, D. O. (2007). *Looking for Information: A Survey of Research on Information Seeking, Needs, and Behavior* (2nd ed.). Amsterdam: Elsevier.

Case, D. O. (2008). *Looking for information: A survey of research on information seeking, needs, and behavior* (2nd ed.). Bingley, UK: Emerald.

Casey, M., & Savastinuk, L. C. (2006). Library 2.0: service for the next generation library. Retrieved from http://www.libraryjournal.com/article/CA6365200.html

Casey, M., & Savastinuk, L. C. (2007). *Library 2.0: a guide to participatory library service*. Medford: Information Today.

Chad, K., & Miller, P. (2005). Do libraries matter? The rise of library 2.0. Retrieved from http://www.talis.com/downloads/white_papers/DoLibrariesMatter.pdf

Chahale, S. (n. d.). The publishing industry in Kenya. *Copyright News*, 9, 3.

Chakrabortty, A. R., & Chakrabarti, B. (1984). *Indexing: Principles, Processes and Products*. Calcutta: The World Press Private Limited.

Challener, J. (1999). *Information seeking behaviour of professors of art history and studio art* [Unpublished Master's Thesis]. Kent State University.

Chen, H., & Schatz, B. (1999). Guest Editors' Introduction: Digital Libraries—Technological Advances and Social Impacts. *Computer, 32*(2), 0045–50.

Chepesuik, R. (1997). The future is here: America's go digital. *American Libraries*, *2*(1), 47–49.

Chepesuik, R. (1997). The future is here: America's libraries go digital. *American Libraries*, *2*(1), 47–49.

Cho, A. (2008). Library 2.0 and the new librarianship: new ways of understanding libraries. *Suite101*. Retrieved from http://allan-cho.suite101.com/library-20-and-the-new-librarianship-a86278

Choo, C., Detlor, B., & Tumbull, D. (2000). Information Seeking on the Web: an integrated model of browsing and searching. First Monday, 5(2). Retrieved from http://firstmonday.org/ojs/index.php/fm/article/view/729/638

Choo, C. W., Detlor, B., & Turnbull, D. (2000). Information seeking on the Web: An integrated model of browsing and searching. *First Monday*, *5*(2). doi:10.5210/fm.v5i2.729

Chowdhury, G. G. (2010). *Introduction to Modern Information Retrieval* (3rd ed.). London: Facet Publishing.

Chowdhury, G. G., & Chowdhury, S. (2003). *Introduction to digital libraries*. London: Facet Publishing.

Christian, G. E. (2008). Issues and challenges to the development of open access institutional repositories in academic and research institutions in Nigeria. Available at: http//idl-bnc.idrc.ca/dspace/bitstream/10625/36986/1/127792pdf

Chu, H. C., Hwang, G. J., Huang, S. X., & Wu, T. T. (2008). A knowledge engineering approach to developing e-libraries for mobile learning. *The Electronic Library*, *26*(3), 303–317. doi:10.1108/02640470810879464

Chu, S. K.-W., & Du, H. S. (2012). Social networking tools for academic libraries. *Journal of Librarianship and Information Science*, *13*(1), 69–85.

CIBER. (2008). Information behaviour of the researcher of the future. Retrieved from http://www.ucl.ac.uk/infostudies/research/ciber/downloads/ggexecutive.pdf

CJEU. (2014). Court of Justice of the European Union - opinion of Advocate General Jääskinen - Case C-117/13, Retrieved from http://curia.europa.eu/juris/document/document.jsf?text=&docid=153306&pageIndex=0&doclang=en&mode=lst&dir=&occ=first&part=1&cid=77241

Clark, C. (1996). The answer to the machine is in the machine. In P. Bernt Hugenholtz (Ed.), *The future of copyright in a digital environment*. The Hague: Kluwer Law International.

Cleveland, G. (1998). Digital Libraries: Definitions, Issues and Challenges. *International Federation of Library Associations and Institutions*.

Cleveland, G. (2003). Digital libraries: definitions, issues and challenges. Retrieved from http://www.ifla.org/archive/udt/op/udtop8/udtop8.htm

Cleveland, D. B., & Cleveland, A. D. (2000). *Introduction to indexing and abstracting* (3rd ed.). U.S.A.: Libraries Unlimited.

CLIR. (2008). No brief candle: reconceiving research libraries for the 21st century. Retrieved from http://www.clir.org/pubs/reports/pub142/pub142.pdf

Cohen, L.B. (2006). A librarian's 2.0 manifesto. Retrieved from http://liblogs.albany.edu/library20/2006/11/a_librarians_20_manifesto.html

Computer Science and Telecommunications Board. (1997). *More than Screen Deep: Toward every-citizen interfaces to the nation's information infrastructure*. Washington, DC: National Academy Press.

Cook, T., & Hopkins, L. (2006). *Social media: or, "how I learned to stop worrying and love communication": An introduction to the power of "web2.0"*. Retrieved from: http://www.leehopkins.net/2006/10/30/social-media-for-business-101-free-white-paper/

Copyright Working Group. (2008). Works created under a federal contract or grant. *Frequently asked questions about copyright issues: Issues affecting the S. government*. Retrieved from http://www.cendi.gov/publications/04 8copyright.pdf

Courtney, N. (2007). *Library 2.0 and beyond*. London: Libraries Unlimited.

Cowling, D. (2012). *Facebook Australia 2012 [Infographic]*. Retrieved from http://www.socialmedianews.com.au/facebook-australia-2012-infographic/

Crawford, W. (2006). Library 2.0 and 'Library 2.0:Cites and Insights, *Journal of Libraries, Policy, Technology and Media,* 6(2). Retrieved from http: //www.cites.boisestate.edu/civ6i2.pdf

Dadzie, P. S. (2005). Electronic resources: Access and usage at Ashesi University College. *Campus-Wide Information Systems, 22*(5), 1065–0741. Retrieved from http://www.emeraldinsight.com/Insight/ViewContentServlet doi:10.1108/10650740510632208

David, K. (1995). The importance of information. *Library Management, 16*(5), 6–15. doi:10.1108/01435129510772283

Davis, C. (2000). Managing expert power in information technology. *Journal of Database Management, 11*(2), 34–36.

Davis, C. H., & Shaw, D. (Eds.). (2011). *Introduction to information science and technology*. New Jersey: Association for Information Science and Technology.

Davis, F. (1989). Perceived usefulness, perceived ease of use and user acceptance of information technology. *Management Information Systems Quarterly, 13*(3), 319–340. doi:10.2307/249008

Davison, R. B. (1977). *Industrial Relations Decree: Questions and Answers to Explain the Law* (pp. 2–6). Zaria: Ahmadu Bello University Press.

DeBell, M., & Chapman, C. (2006). *Computer and internet use by students in 2003 (NCES 2006-065). U.S. Department of Education*. Washington, DC: National Center for Education Statistics.

Denning, P., Horning, J., Parnas, D., & Weinstein, L. (2006). Wikipedia Risks. *Communications of the ACM, 48*(12), 152. doi:10.1145/1101779.1101804

Dervin, B. (1992). From the mind's eye of the user: The sense-making qualitative-quantitative methodology. In J.D. Glazier & R.R. Powell (Eds.), Qualitative Research in Information Management (pp. 68-70). Englewood, CO: Libraries Unlimited.

Dervin, B., & Nilam, M. (1986). Information needs and uses. *Annual Review of Information Science, 21*, 3–33.

Dervin, B., & Nilan, M. (1986). Information needs and uses. In M. E. Williams (Ed.), *Annual Review of Information Science and Technology* (Vol. 21, pp. 3–33). New York: Knowledge Industry Publications.

Devadason, F. J., & Lingman, P. P. (1997). A methodology for the identification of information needs of users. *IFLA Journal, 23*(1), 41–51. doi:10.1177/034003529702300109

Digital divide basics fact sheet. (2015). Retrieved from Lifeline Fact-Sheet: http://centerformediajustice.org/wp-content/uploads/2015/12/lifelinefact-sheet-1.pdf

Digital library Federation. (1998). Retrieved from https://old.diglib.org/about/dldefinition.htm

Ding, C. (2000). Access to digital information: Some breakthroughs and obstacles. *Journal of Librarianship and Information Science, 32*(1), 26–32. doi:10.1177/096100060003200104

Donna, C. (2014). *Advantages and Disadvantages of Social Networking*. Retrieved from http://www.lovetoknow.com/member/347~donna-cosmato

Dresang, E. (1999). More research needed: Informal information-seeking behavior of youth on the Internet. *Journal of the American Society for Information Science, 50*(12), 1123–1124. doi:10.1002/(SICI)1097-4571(1999)50:12<1123::AID-ASI14>3.0.CO;2-F

Du Preez, M., & Fourie, I. (2009). The information behaviour of consulting engineers in South Africa. *Mousaion, 27*(1), 137–158.

Durkey, E. (2008). Academic libraries and copyright issues in Ghana. *International Journal of Legal information*, 36, 432-448.

Dussin, M., & Ferro, N. (2009). Managing the knowledge creation process of large scale evaluation campaigns. Retrieved from http://lekythos.lib.ucy.ac.cy/bitstream/handle/10797/13871/ECDL015.pdf?sequence=1

Eason, K., Richardson, S., & Yu, L. (2000). Patterns of use of electronic journals. *The Journal of Documentation*, *56*(5), 477–504. doi:10.1108/EUM0000000007124

Egghe, L. (2006). Theory and practice of the g-index. *Scientometrics*, *69*(1), 131–152. doi:10.1007/s11192-006-0144-7

Eisenberg, M. B., & Berkowitz, R. E. (1992). Information problem solving: The Big Six Skills Approach. *School Library Media Activities Monthly*, *8*(5), 27.

Electronic Information for Libraries (EIFL). (2006). EIFL-IP handbook on copyright and related issues for libraries.

Ellis, A. (1994). *Reason and emotion in psychotherapy*. Secaucus, NJ: Birch Lane.

Ellis, D. (1989). A behavioral approach to information retrieval system design. *The Journal of Documentation*, *45*(3), 171–212. doi:10.1108/eb026843

Ellis, D. (1989b). Behavioural approach to information retrieval system design. *The Journal of Documentation*, *46*, 191–213.

Ellis, D. (1993). Modelling the information-seeking patterns of academic researchers: A grounded theory approach. *The Library Quarterly*, *63*(4), 469–486. doi:10.1086/602622

Ellis, D. (2005). Ellis's model of information-seeking behavior. In *K. Fisher, S. Erdeles, & L. MacKechnie, Theories of information behavior* (pp. 138–142). Medford, New Jersey: Information Today.

Ellis, D., Cox, D., & Hall, K. (1993). A comparison of information-seeking patterns of researchers in the physical and social sciences. *The Journal of Documentation*, *49*(4), 356–369. doi:10.1108/eb026919

Ellis, D., Cox, D., & Hall, K. (1993). A Comparison of the Information Seeking Patterns of Researchers in the Physical and Social Sciences. *The Journal of Documentation*, *49*(4), 356–369.

Ellis, D., & Haugan, M. (1997). Modelling the information-seeking behavior of engineers and research scientists in an industrial environment. *The Journal of Documentation*, *53*(4), 384–403. doi:10.1108/EUM0000000007204

Ellis, D., & Oldman, H. (2005). The English literature researcher in the age of the Internet. *Journal of Information Science*, *31*(1), 29–36. doi:10.1177/0165551505049256

Encyclopedia of Library and Information Science. (1974). In A. Kent & H. Lancour (Eds.), Vol. I, pp. 16–37). New York: Marcel Dekker Inc.

Encyclopedia of Library and Information Science. (1974). In H. Lancour & J. E. Daily (Eds.), *Kent, A* (Vol. II, pp. 286–298). New York: Marcel Dekker Inc.

Entezaryan, N., & Fattahi, R. (2009). The study of user`s understanding of the interface environment of database on the basis of Nilson models. *Library & Information Science Research*, *47*(3), 43–64.

Eskola, E. (1998). University students' information seeking behaviour in a changing learning environment - How are students' information needs, seeking and use affected by new teaching methods? *Information Research*, 4(2). Retrieved from http://www.shef.ac.uk/~is/publications/infres/isic/eeskola.html

Europe and the Global Information Society. (1994). *Recommendations to the European Council ("the Bangemann Report")*. Brussels: European Council.

Eysenbach, G. (2007). From intermediation to disintermediation to apomediation: New models for consumers to access and assess the credibility of health information in the age of Web 2.0. *Studies in Health Technology and Informatics*, *129*(1), 162–166. PMID:17911699

Eysenbach, G. (2008). Medicine 2.0: Social networking, collaboration, participation, apomediation, and openness. *Journal of Medical Internet Research*, *10*(3), e22. Retrieved from http://www.ncbi.nlm.nih.gov/pmc/articles/PMC2626430/ doi:10.2196/jmir.1030 PMID:18725354

Facebook. (2012). *Newsroom: Factsheet.* Retrieved from http://newsroom.fb.com/content/default.aspx?NewsAreaId=22

Fairer-Wessels. (1990). Basic Community information needs of Urban Black Women in Mamelodi, Pretoria, South Africa. Retrieved from fromwww.cais-acsi.ca/proceedings/1995/olson_1995.pdf

Fallows, D. (2005). How women and men use the Internet. Washington, DC: Pew Internet & American Life Project. Retrieved from http://www.pewInternet.org/pdfs/PIP_Women_and_Men_online.pdf

Farkas, M. (2008). The essence of Library 2.0. *Information wants to be free*. Retrieved from http://meredith.wolfwater.com/wordpress/2008/01/24/the-essence-of-library-20/

Farkas, M. (2008). The essence of library 2.0. Retrieved from http://meredith.wolfwater.com/wordpress/index.php/2008/01/24/the-essence-of-library-20/

Fashoyin, T. (1980). *Collective Bargaining in the Public Sector in Nigeria*. Nigeria: Macmillan Publishers.

Fast, K., & Campbell, D. (2004). I still like Google: university student perceptions of searching OPACs and the web. *Proceedings of the 67th American Society for Information Science and Technology*, 4(1), 138-146. Retrieved from http://onlinelibrary.wiley.com/doi/10.1002/meet.1450410116/pdf

Fatoki, O. C. (2012). *Individual and system factors predicting user acceptance of digital libraries in Nigerian universities of agriculture* [Unpublished M.Phil Thesis]. University of Ibadan.

Ferber, R., & Thiel, U. (1996). Digital libraries and information retrieval. *ERCIM News No.27*. Retrieved from http://www.ercim.eu/publication/Ercim_News/enw27/ferber.html

Festinger, L. (1957). *A Theory of Cognitive Dissonance*. Stanford, California: Stanford University Press.

Fialkoff, F. (2012). Libraries should be what users want - with a little help from librarians. *Library Journal*, Retrieved from http://lj.libraryjournal.com/2012/05/opinion/editorial/owning-up-to-the-future-libraries-should-be-what-users-want-with-a-little-help-from-librarians/

Fidel, R. (1986). The possible effect of abstracting guidelines on retrieval performance of free-text searching. *Information Processing and Management.* 22(4), 309-316. Retrieved from faculty.washington.edu/fidelr/RayaPubs/PossibleEffectofAbstractingGuidelines.pdf

Fidel, R., Davies, R., Douglass, M., Holder, J., Hopkins, C., Kushner, E., & Toney, C. et al. (1999). A visit to the information mall: Web searching behavior of high school students. *Journal of the American Society for Information Science*, *50*(1), 24–37. doi:10.1002/(SICI)1097-4571(1999)50:1<24::AID-ASI5>3.0.CO;2-W

Fidel, R., & Pejtersen, A. M. (2004). From information behaviour research to the design of information systems: The Cognitive Work Analysis framework. *Information Research*, *10*(1), 10–11.

Fidzani, B. T. (1998). Information needs and information-seeking behaviour of graduate students at the University of Botswana. *Library Review*, *47*(7), 329–340. doi:10.1108/00242539810233459

Fisher, K., Erdelez, S., & McKechnie, L. (Ed.), (2005). Theories of Information Behavior. Medford, NJ: Information Today.

Fishman, S. (2008). *The copyright handbook: What every writer needs to know*. Berkeley, CA: Nolo.

Fister, B. (1992). The Research process of undergraduate students. *Journal of Academic Librarianship*, *18*(3), 163–169.

Fitzpatrick, M. (2006). The Deleting Online Predators Act of 2006. *Journal of Tech Law*. Retrieved from http://www.techlawjournal.com/cong109/bills/house/hr5319/hr5319ih.asp

Fluid Dynamics Software Corporation. (2015). FDSC. Retrieved from https://www.xav.com/scripts/search/help/1123.html

Ford, N., Miller, D., & Moss, N. (2001). The Role of Individual Difference in Internet Searching: An Empirical Study. *Journal of the American Society for Information Science and Technology*, *52*(12), 1049–1066. doi:10.1002/asi.1165

Foster, A. (2004). A nonlinear model of information-seeking behavior. *Journal of the American Society for Information Science and Technology*, *55*(3), 228–237. doi:10.1002/asi.10359

Fourie, I. (2002, October 24–25). A Review of Web Information-Seeking/Searching Studies (2000-2002): Implications for Research in the South African Context. In T. Bothma & A. Kaniki (Eds.), *Progress in Library and Information Science in South Africa:Proceedings of the Second Biennial DISSAnet Conference* (pp. 49–75). Pretoria: Infuse.

Fourie, I. (2006). Learning from web information seeking studies: some suggestions for LIS practitioners. *The Electronic Library*, 24(1), 20-37. doi:10.1108/02640470610649227

Fox, E. A., & Urs, S. R. (2002). Digital Libraries. In B. Cronin (Ed.), *Annual Review of Information Science and Technology* (Vol. 36, pp. 503–589).

Fox, E., Akscy, R., Furuta, R. L., & Legget, J. (1995). Digital libraries. *Communications of the ACM*, *38*(4), 23–28. doi:10.1145/205323.205325

Fox, E., & Marchionini, G. (1998). Towards a world-wide digital library. *Communications of the ACM*, *41*(4), 29–32. doi:10.1145/273035.273043

Fox, E., Suleman, H., Madalli, D., & Cassel, L. (2004). Digital libraries. In M. Singh (Ed.), *Practical handbook of Internet computing* (pp. 61–76). New York: CRC. doi:10.1201/9780203507223.ch4

Ge, X. (2005). Information-seeking Behavior of Social Sciences and Humanities Researchers in the Internet Age [Master Thesis]. University of Tennessee, Knoxville. Retrieved from http://trace.tennessee.edu/utk_gradthes/1899/

Gefen, D., Karahanna, E., & Straub, D. (2003). Trust and TAM in online shopping: An integrated model. *Management Information Systems Quarterly*, *27*(1), 51–90.

Gefen, D., & Straub, D. (1997). Gender difference in the perception and use of e-mail: An extension to the technology acceptance model. *Management Information Systems Quarterly*, *21*(4), 389–400. doi:10.2307/249720

Geiger, C., ... (2008). A balanced interpretation of the "three-step test" in copyright law. Max Planck Institute for Intellectual Property, Competition and Tax Law. Retrieved from http://www.ip.mpg.de/shared/data/pdf/declaration_three_step_test_final_english.pdf

Geiger, C., Hilty, R., Griffiths, J., & Suthersanen, U. (2010). Declaration: A Balanced Interpretation of The "Three-Step Test" In Copyright Law. Journal of Intellectual Property, Information Technology and E-Commerce Law, 1(2), 119-122.

Geiger, C. (2010). The future of copyright in Europe: Striking a fair balance between protection and access to information. *Intellectual Property Quarterly*, *1*, 1–14.

Ge, X. (2010). Information-seeking behavior in the digital age: A multidisciplinary study of academic researchers. *College & Research Libraries*, *71*(5), 435–455. doi:10.5860/crl-34r2

Ginman, M. (1995). Paradigm och trender inom biblioteks- och informationsvetenskap. In: Biblioteken, kulturen och den sociala intelligensen. Aktuell forskning inom biblioteks- och informationsvetenskap. Ed. Lars Höglund. Stockholm: Forskningsrådsnämnden, FNM, 9-18.

Glossary of Cognitive Skills. (n. d.). Retrieved from http://www.learningrx.com/what-are-cognitive-skills.htm

Goldstein, P. (2003). *Copyright's highway: from Gutenberg to the celestial jukebox*. Stanford University Press.

Goncalves, M., Fox, E., Watson, L., & Kipp, N. (2004). Streams, structures, spaces, scenarios, societies (5S): a formal model for digital libraries. ACM transactions on information systems (TOIS), 22(2), 270-312.

Goncalves, M. (2011). Digital Libraries. In R. Baeza-Yates & B. Ribeiro-Neto (Eds.), *Modern information retrieval: the concept and technology behind search* (2nd ed.). England: Pearson Education Limited.

Gonzales, E. J. (2003). Language limits confront Latinos on Internet. *IM Diversity*. Retrieved from http://www.imdiversity.com/villages/hispanic

Graham, P. S. (1995). Requirements for the digital research library. Retrieved from http://aultnis.rutgers.edu/texts/DRC.html

Graham, P. S. (1995). *Requirements for the Digital Research Library*. Retrieved from http://aultnis.rutgers.edu/texts/DRC.html

Green, A. (2011). Africa: failure to adopt technology in libraries results in fewer users. Retrieved from http://www.globalissues.org/news/2011/11/11/11841

Greenberg, D. (1998). Camel drivers and gatecrashers: quality control in the digital research library. In B. Hawkins & P. Battin (Eds.), *The mirage of continuity: reconfiguring academic information resources for the 21st century* (pp. 105–116). Washington, DC: Council on Library and Information Resources and Association of American Universities.

Green, D. (2000). The evolution of web searching. *Online Information Review*, *24*(2), 124–137. doi:10.1108/14684520010330283

Greenspan, R. (2002). China pulls ahead of Japan. CyberAtlas. Retrieved from http://cyberatlas.internet.com./epdf

Grimes, B. F. (1996). *Ethnologue: Language of the world* (13th ed.). Dallas: Summer Institute of Linguistics.

Grover, V., & Rammanlal, P. (1999). Six myths of information and market information technology networks, electronic commerce and the battle for consumer surplus. *Management Information Systems Quarterly*, *23*(4), 465–495. doi:10.2307/249486

Guenette, D. R., Trippe, B., & Golden, K. (2010). *A blueprint for book publishing transformation: Seven essential processes to re-invent publishing*. Cambridge, MA: Gilbane Group.

Gunasekera, C. (2010). Students' usage of an academic library: A user survey conducted at the main library, University of Peradeniya. *Journal of the University Librarians Association of Sri Lanka*, *14*(1), 43–60.

Gwizdka, J. (2002). TaskView - Design and Evaluation of a Task-based Email Interface. CASCON Conference. *IBM*.

Gwizdka, J. (2004). Email Task Management Styles: The Cleaners and the Keepers. In *Extended Abstracts of ACM Conference on Human Factors in Computing Systems CHI'2004* (pp. 1235 – 1238). ACM Press.

Gwizdka, J., & Chignell, M. H. (2004). Individual differences and task-based user interface evaluation: A case study of pending tasks in email. *Interacting with Computers*, *16*(4), 769–797. doi:10.1016/j.intcom.2004.04.008

Haastrup, A. A. (2012). Current Trends in Employee and Industrial Relations in Nigeria: Challenges for HR.

Habib, M.C. (2006). Toward Academic Library 2.0: Development and Application of a Library 2.0 Methodology. North Carolina University, Chappe Hill. Retrieved from http://etd.ils.unc.edu/dspace/bitstream/1901/356/1/michaelhabib.pdf

Hamzat, D. (2012). Fundamentals of Archives Management. Proceedings of Records and Information Management Awareness Foundation Quarterly Training (Q3), Lagos.

Hanani, U., & Frank, A. (2000). The parallel evolution of search engines and digital libraries: their mega portal. *Proceedings of the Kyoto International Conference on Digital Libraries* (pp. 269-276). Kyoto: Kyoto University. Retrieved from http://u.cs.biu.ac.il/~ariel/download/ird665/kyoto.pdf

Hanna, R., Rohm, A., & Crittenden, V. L. (2011). We're all connected: The power of the social media ecosystem. *Business Horizons*, *54*(3), 265–273. doi:10.1016/j.bushor.2011.01.007

Hansen, P., & Järvelin, K. (2005). Collaborative information retrieval in an information-intensive domain. *IPM*, 41(5), 1101-1109.

Hargittai, E. (2001). Second-level digital divide: Mapping differences in people's online skills. TPRC. Retrieved from http://arxiv.org/ftp/cs/papers/0109/0109068.pdf

Harper, G. K. (2001). The Copyright Crash Course. The University of Texas Library. Retrieved from http://copyright.lib.utexas.edu/l-108abc.html

Harris, M. (2012, March). What is a digital library? Retrieved from Writing on information studies. Retrieved from next-nexus.info/writing/infostudies/digital_libraries.php

Harris, R. M., & Dewdney, P. (1994). *Barriers to information: how formal help systems fail battered women*. Westport, CT: Greenwood Press.

Harris, R., & Davison, R. (1999). Anxiety and involvement: Cultural dimensions of attitudes towards computers in developing societies. *Journal of Global Information Management*, *7*(1), 26–38. doi:10.4018/jgim.1999010103

Haruna, I., & Mabawonku, I. (2001). Information Needs and Seeking Behavior of Legal Practitioners and the Challenges to Law Libraries in Lagos, Nigeria. *The International Information & Library Review*, 2011, 33.

Harzing, A.W. (2009). Harzing's Publish or Perish. *Herpetology Notes*, *3*, 239–245.

Harzing, A.W.K., & Wal, R. (2008). Google Scholar as a new source for citation analysis. *Ethics in Science and Environmental Politics*, *8*, 61–73. doi:10.3354/esep00076

Hauroo, P. (nd*). Copyright issues for Libraries in Mauritius.

Hawkins, D.T. (2001). Bibliometrics of electronic journals in information science. *Information Research*, 7(1). Retrieved from http://www.informationr.net/ir/7-1/paper120.html

Hayashi, R. (2013). Language specific mobility difference in sub-Saharan Africa. *Proceedings of the XXVII IUSSP International Population Conference.* Tokyo: National Institute of Population and Social Security Research. Retrieved from http://iussp.org/sites/default/files/event_call_for_papers/LongAbstract%20iussp1308%20MobilitySSA%20Reiko%20Hayashi130813.pdf

Hayden, K.A. (1999). Information Seeking Models. Retrieved from http://www.ucalgary.ca/~ahayden/seeking.html

Hayes, C. J. (2008). Changing the rules of the game: How video game publishers are embracing user-generated derivative works. *Harvard Journal of Law & Technology*, *21*(2), 567–587.

Head, A. (2008). Information literacy from the trenches: How do humanities and social science majors conduct academic research? *College & Research Libraries*, *69*(5), 427–446. doi:10.5860/crl.69.5.427

Heath, T. (2008). Information-seeking on the Web with Trusted Social Networks – from Theory to Systems [Unpublished PhD Thesis]. UK: Knowledge Media Institute, The Open University.

Helberger, N., & Hugenholtz, P. B. (2007). No place like home for making a copy: Private copying in European copyright law and consumer law. *Berkeley Technology Law Journal*, *22*, 1061–1098.

Hetland, P. (2011). Science 2.0: bridging science and the public. *Nordic Journal of Digital Literacy* 6(Special Issue), 326-339. Retrieved from http://www.uv.uio.no/intermedia/personer/adm/perhet/dokumenter/dk_2011_special_issue_art05_Norwegian.pdf

Hewins, E.T. (1990). Information need and use studies. *Annual Review of Information Science*, *25*, 145–172.

Hirsch, J. E. (2005). An index to quantify an individual's scientific research output. Retrieved from http://arxiv.org/pdf/physics/0508025v5.pdf

Hopkins, R. (1989). The information seeking behaviour of literary scholars. *Canadian Library Journal*, *46*(2), 113–115.

Ibulubo, T. G. (2008). Nigeria to switch to digital broadcasting. *Africa News.*

Idowu, B., Adagunodo, R., & Idowu, B. (2004). Gender difference in computer literacy among Nigerian undergraduate students: A case study of Obafemi Awolowo University students, Nigeria.*The African Symposium: An Online Educational Research Journal,* 4(3), 24-30.

IFLA. (2004). Limitations and exceptions to copyright and neighbouring rights in the digital environment: an international library perspective. Retrieved from http://archive.ifla.org/III/clm/p1/ilp.htm

IFLA. (2010). *IFLA Manifesto for Digital Libraries*. Retrieved from http://www.ifla.org/en/publications/ifla-manifesto-for-digital-libraries

Igbo, U. H., & Imo, N. T. (2010). Challenges of Accessibility of Information Resources by the Post Graduate Library Users of a Nigeria University. *An International Journal of Information and Communication Technology*, *7*(2), 1–10.

Igwe, K. N. (2012). A Survey of the Information Literacy Skills of Students in Federal Polytechnic Offa, Kwara State, Nigeria. *Information Technologist*, *9*(2), 8–19.

Ihechu, I.I. Uwaoma Uche (2000). The Challenges of Digitization of Broadcasting in Nigeria.

Ikoja–Odongo, J.R. (2002). An observational study of the information seeking and communicating behavior of entrepreneurs in the informal sector of Uganda. In T. Bothma, & A. Kaniki (Eds.), *ProLISSA 2002: Proceedings of the second biennial DiSSA net conference*, Pretoria (pp. 11–28).

Ikoja-Odongo, R., & Ocholla, D. N. (2004). Information seeking behavior of the informal sector entrepreneurs: The Uganda experience. *Libri*, *54*(1), 54–66. doi:10.1515/LIBR.2004.54

Inbun, B. Y., & Ngangan, K. (2012). The Disclosure of Information in Paupa New Guinea. *Labour Management in Development,* 2(4). Retrieved from http://ncdsnet.anu.edu.au

Ingwersen, P., & Järvelin, K. (2005). Information retrieval in context: IRiX. In ACM SIGIR Forum (Vol. 39, pp. 31–39). ACM. Retrieved from http://dl.acm.org/citation.cfm?id=1113351

Ingwersen, P. (1996). Cognitive perspectives of information retrieval interaction: Elements of a cognitive IR theory. *The Journal of Documentation*, *52*(1), 3–50. doi:10.1108/eb026960

International Digital Publishing Forum. (2010). *Industry statistics.* Seattle, WA: The Author. Retrieved from http://www.idpf.org/doc_library/industrystats.htm

International Encyclopedia of Information and Library Science. (1997). In J. Feather & P. Sturges, Eds.). London: Routledge.

International Labour Organization. (2001). *World Employment Report 2001: Life at Work in the Information Society.* Geneva: International Labour Office.

International Telecommunication Union. (2013). Study on international Internet connectivity in sub-Saharan Africa. Geneva. Retrieved from https://www.itu.int/en/ITU-D/Regulatory-Market/Documents/IIC_Africa_Final-en.pdf

International Telecommunications Union (ITU). (2003). World telecommunication development report. In Access Indicators for the information society (pp. 12-30).

International Telecommunications Union (ITU). (2007). ICT Statistics Database, Geneva: ITU. Retrieved from http://www.itu.int/ITU-D/icteye/Indicators/Indicators.aspx

Ioannidis, Y. (2005). Digital libraries at crossroads. *International Journal on Digital Libraries, 5*(4), 255–265. doi:10.1007/s00799-004-0098-4

Ioannidis, Y., Mair, D., Abiteboul, S., Buneman, P., Davidson, S., & Fox, E. (2005). Digital library information-technology infrastructures. *International Journal on Digital Libraries, 5*(4), 266–274. doi:10.1007/s00799-004-0094-8

Isaacson, D. (2006). BackTalk: serve their needs, not their wants. Retrieved from http://www.libraryjournal.com/article/CA6396343.html

Islam, M. A., Abdul Rahim, A., Tan, C. L., & Momtaz, H. (2011). Effect of demographic factors on e-learning effectiveness in a higher learning Institution in Malaysia. *International Education Studies, 4*(1), 4–7. doi:10.5539/ies.v4n1p112

Issa, A. O. (2011). A Study of Public Library status in Rural Information Dissemination. Retrieved from http://unilorin.edu.ng/publications/issaao

Jain, P. (2012). Promoting open access to research in academic libraries. Retrieved from llunllib.unl.edu/LLP/

Jaja, C.A. (2012). Knowledge Management and its Enabling Resources for Transformative Development. *Proceedings of the Annual National Workshop of NLA*, Ilorin.

Jamali, H. R. (2013). Citation relations of theories of human information behaviour." Webology, 10(1). Retrieved from http://www.webology.org/2013/v10n1/a106.html

Järvelin, K. & Vakkari, P. (1981). Tiedontarpeiden ja kirjaston käytön tutkimisesta. Kaksi tutkielmaa. Tampereen yliopisto. Kirjastotieteen ja informatiikan laitos. Julkaisuja A Tutkimusraportit nro 15.

Järvelin, K. (1987). Kaksi yksinkertaista jäsennystä tiedon hankinnan tutkimista varten. *Kirjastotiede ja informatiikka*, 6(1); 18-24.

Järvelin, K., & Wilson, T. D. (2003). On conceptual models for information seeking and retrieval research. *Information Research*, 9(1). Retrieved from http://InformationR.net/ir/9-1/paper163.html

Järvelin, K., & Wilson, T. D. (2003). On conceptual models for information seeking and retrieval research. *Information Research, 9*(1). Retrieved from http://InformationR.net/ir/9-1/paperl63. html

Jega, M. (1994). *Nigerian Academics under Military Rule.* Stockholm: Department of Political Science, Stockholm University.

Jerabek, A. J., Meyer, L. S., & Kordinak, T. S. (2001). Library anxiety and computer anxiety: Measures, validity, and research implications. *Library & Information Science Research*, *23*(3), 277–289. doi:10.1016/S0740-8188(01)00083-4

John-Okeke, R. (2008). Developing institutional repositories: Considering copyright issues. *Journal of Applied Information Science and Technology*, *2*(8), 11–18.

Johnson, J. D., & Meischke, H. (1991b). Cancer Information: Women's Source and Content Preferences. *Journal of Health Care Marketing*, *11*, 37–44. PMID:10110080

Julien, H. (1996). A content analysis of recent information needs and uses literature. *Library & Information Science Research*, *18*(1), 53–65. doi:10.1016/S0740-8188(96)90030-4

Julien, H., & Duggan, L. J. (2000). A longitudinal analysis of the information needs and uses literature. *Library & Information Science Research*, *22*(3), 291–309. doi:10.1016/S0740-8188(99)00057-2

Julien, H., Pecoskie, J., & Reed, K. (2011). Trends in information behavior research, 1999-2008: A content analysis. *Library & Information Science Research*, *33*(1), 19–34. doi:10.1016/j.lisr.2010.07.014

Justin, M. (2014). The pros and cons of student social media use. Retrieved from http://www.teachthought.com/uncategorized/the-pros-and-cons-of-student-social-media-use/

Kaddu, S. (2007). Information Ethics: A student perspective. *International Review of information. Ethics*, *7*, 2–6.

Kakai, J. M., Ikoja-Odongo, R., & Kigongo-Bukenya, I. M. N. (2004). A study of the information seeking behavior of undergraduate students of Makerere University, Uganda. *World Libraries*, 14(1). Retrieved from http://www.worlib.org/vol14no1/print/kakai_print.html

Kakai, M.J., Ikoja–Odongo R., & Kigongo–Bukenya, I.M.N. (2004). A study of the information seeking behavior of undergraduate students of Makerere University, Uganda. *World Libraries*, 14(1).

Kakai, M., Ikoja-Odongo, R., & Kigongo-Bukeny, I. M. N. (2004). A study of the information seeking behavior of undergraduate students of Makerere University, Uganda. *World Libraries*, *14*, 544–564.

Kaplan, A. M., & Haenlein, M. (2010). Users of the world, unite! The challenges and opportunities of Social Media. *Business Horizons*, *53*(1), 59–68. doi:10.1016/j.bushor.2009.09.003

Kasia, M. (2013).Advantages and Disadvantages of Social Networking: Should You Spend More Time Connecting Online? Retrieved from https://blog.udemy.com/author/kasiamikoluk/

Katz, W. A. (2002). *Introduction to reference work* (Vol. II). Boston: McGraw-Hill.

Kawooya, D. et al.. (2010). Uganda. In C. Armstrong (Ed.), *Access to knowledge in Africa: the role of copyright* (pp. 281–316). UCT Press.

Kelly, G. (1963). *A theory of personality: The psychology of personal constructs*. New York, NY: Norton.

Kennedy, T., Wellman, B., & Klement, K. (2003). Gendering the digital divide. *IT and Society*, 1(5), 72-96. Retrieved from http://www.stanford.edu/group/siqss/itandsociety/v01i05/v01i05a05.pdf

Kerins, G., Madden, R., & Fulton, C. (2004). Information Seeking and Students Studying for Professional Careers: the Cases of Engineering and Law Students in Ireland. *Information Research: An International Journal, 10*(1). Retrieved from http://arrow.dit.ie/ittsupart/3/

Khati, P. (2009). Information seeking behavior of undergraduate students at the University of Western Cape. Retrieved from http://www.slideshare.net/2548233/info-seeking-behaviour-of-students-at-uwc

Khey, D. N., Jennings, W. G., Higgins, G. E., Schoepfer, A., & Langton, L. (2011). Reranking the top female academic "Stars" in criminology and criminal justice using an alternative method: A research note. *Journal of Criminal Justice Education*, *22*(1), 118–129. doi:10.1080/10511253.2010.517655

Kibirige, H., & DePalo, L. (2001). The education function in a digital library environment: A challenge for college and research libraries. *The Electronic Library*, *19*(5), 283–295. doi:10.1108/02640470110408869

Kim, C. (2003). A comparison of perceived importance of information systems development strategies by developers from the United States and Korea. *Information resources management*, 16(2), 1-18.

Kim, K. O., Sin, S. J., & Yoo-Lee, E. Y. (2014). Undergraduates' Use of Social Media as information Sources. *College & Research Libraries*, *75*(4), 442–457. doi:10.5860/crl.75.4.442

Kirk, M., & Zander, C. (2004). Narrowing the digital divide: In search of a map to mend the gap. *Journal of Computing Sciences in Colleges*, *20*(2), 168–175.

Kirriemuir, J. (2007). Digital games in libraries in information science. Retrieved from http://www.slideshare.net/silver-sprite/digital-games-in-libraries-and-information-science

Kiss, J. (2011). *Twitter reveals it has 100m active users.* Retrieved from http://www.guardian.co.uk/technology/pda/2011/sep/08/twitter-active-users

KPMG. (2011). *Social media: the voyage of discovery for business.* Retrieved from http://www.kpmg.com/NZ/en/IssuesAndInsights/ArticlesPublications/Pages/social-media-discovery.aspx

Krikelas, J. (1983). Information-seeking behaviour: Patterns and concepts. *Drexel Library Quarterly*, 19(2), 5-20, 78.

Krikelas, J. (1983). Information seeking behavior: Patterns and concepts. *Drexel Library Quarterly*, *19*, 5–20.

Krikelas, J. (1983). Information-seeking behavior: Patterns and concepts. *Drexel Library Quarterly*, *19*(2), 5–20.

Krikelas, J. (1983). Information-seeking behaviour: Patterns and concepts. *Drexel Library Quarterly*, *19*(2), 5–20.

Krikelas, J. (1983). Information-Seeking Behaviour: Patterns and Concepts. *Drexel Library Quarterly*, *19*(2), 5–20.

Kuhlthau, C. (2007). The 'information search process' revisited: Is the model still useful? *Information Research*, 13(4).

Kuhlthau, C. C. (1983). *The research process: Case studies and interventions with high school seniors in advanced placement English classes using Kelly's theory of constructs* [PhD dissertation]. Rutgers University, New Brunswick.

Kuhlthau, C. C., Heinström, J., & Todd, R. J. (2008). The 'information search process' revisited: is the model still useful? *Information Research, 13*(4).

Kuhlthau, C., Heinström, J. & Todd, R. J. (2008). The 'information search process' revisited: Is the model still useful? *Information Research*, 13(4).

Kuhlthau, C. (2004). *Seeking meaning: A process approach to library and information services* (2nd ed.). Westport, CT: Greenwood Press.

Kuhlthau, C. C. (1991). Inside the search process: Information seeking from the user's perspective. *Journal of the American Society for Information Science*, *42*(5), 361–371. doi:10.1002/(SICI)1097-4571(199106)42:5<361::AID-ASI6>3.0.CO;2-#

Kuhlthau, C. C. (1993). A principle of uncertainty for information seeking. *The Journal of Documentation*, *49*(4), 339–355. doi:10.1108/eb026918

Kuhlthau, C. C. (1993). *Seeking meaning: a process approach to library and information services.* Norwood, NJ: Ablex Publishing.

Kuhlthau, C. C. (1993). *Seeking Meaning: A Process Approach to Library and Information Services.* Norwood, NJ: Ablex Publishing.

Kuhlthau, C. C. (2005). Towards collaboration between information seeking and information retrieval. *Information Research, 10*(2), 10–12.

Kuhlthau, C., Maniotes, L., & Caspari, A. (2007). *Guided inquiry: Learning in the 21st century.* Westport, Connecticut: Libraries Unlimited.

Kumar, V., & Rao, p. (2014). Digitization of library resources and the formation of digital libraries: a practical approach. *International Journal and Magazine of Engineering, Technology, Management and Research*, 1(12). Retrieved from http://www.ijmetmr.com/oldecember2014/VVijayKumar-DrPRamaMohanRao-14.pdf

Kuny, T., & Cleveland, G. (2008). The Digital Library: Myths and Challenges. Retrieved from http://web.simmons.edu/~chen/488_sp2008/kuny.pdf

Kupersmith, J. (1998). Technostress in the bionic library. Retrieved from http://www.jkup.net/bionic.html

Kupersmith, J. (2003). Library technostress. Retrieved from http://www.jkup.net/tstress-survey-2003.html

Kuruppu, D.C. (1999). Information needs and information seeking behaviour of users in organizations. *Information Studies, 5*(1), 53–66.

Kwanya, T. (2011). The potential of Library 2.0 for research libraries in Kenya. Retrieved from http://researchspace.ukzn.ac.za/xmlui/bitstream/handle/10413/5025/Kwanya_Tom_Joseph_Mboya_2011.pdf?sequence=1

L. Shanta Meitei & Th. Purnima Devi. (2009). Farmers information Needs in Rural Manipur: an assessment. *Annals of Library and information studies*, 56(2), 35-40

Lagoze, C., & Van de Sompel, H. (2001). The open archives initiative: building a low-barrier interoperability framework. *Proceedings of the 1st ACM/IEEE-CS Joint Conference on Digital Libraries, Virginia, United States of America* (pp. 54-62). New York: ACM. Retrieved from http://www.openarchives.org

Lakshmana Moorthy, A., & Karisiddappa, C. R. (1998). Transformation to virtual libraries: Real or Virtual? *Proceedings of the Society for Information ScienceAnnual Conference*, University of Hyderabad.

Larney, T. (1996), The McDonaldisation of information. Retrieved from http://web.simmons.edu/~chen/nit/NIT%2796/96–171-Larney.html

Laryea, K. A. (2013, June 25-29). Mutation is a must: a perspective on collection development for academic libraries. *Paper presented at 2nd Annual International Interdisciplinary Conference*, Catholic University of Eastern Africa (CUEA), Nairobi, Kenya.

Lau, J. (2001). Faculty–Librarian collaboration: A Mexican experience. *RSR. Reference Services Review, 29*(2), 95–105. doi:10.1108/00907320110394137

Leckie, G. J., Pettigrew, K. E., & Sylvain, C. (1996). Modeling the Information Seeking of Professionals and Lawyers. *The Library Quarterly, 66*(2), 161–193. doi:10.1086/602864

Lee, G. T., & Dahlan, N. (2005). Impact of Interface Characteristics on Digital Libraries Usage. *Malaysian Online Journal of Instructional Technology, 2*(1), 10–15.

Legris, P., Ingham, J., & Collerette, P. (2003). Why do people use information technology? A critical review of the technology acceptance model. *Information & Management*, *40*(3), 191–204. doi:10.1016/S0378-7206(01)00143-4

Lenhart, A., & Madden, M. (2007). Social Networking Websites and Teens: An Overview. Retrieved from http://www.pewinternet.org/Reports/2007/Social-Networking-Websites-and-Teens.aspx

Lepi, K. (2014). What happens in an Internet minute. Retrieved from http://www.edudemic.com/internet-minute-infographic/

Lesk, M. (n. d.). (B. a. London, Producer) Retrieved from http://lesk.com/mlesk/follett/follett.html

Lesk, M. (2005). *Understanding digital libraries* (2nd ed.). San Francisco, CA: Morgan Kaufman.

Lester, J., & Koehler, W. C. (2007). *Fundamentals of information studies: understanding information and its environment*. New York: Neal-Schuman Pub. Inc.

Limb, P. (2004). *Digital dilemmas and solutions*. Oxford: Chandos Publishing. doi:10.1533/9781780630649

Line, M. B. (1969). Information requirements in the social sciences: Some preliminary considerations. *Journal of Librarianship*, *1*(1), 1–19. doi:10.1177/096100066900100101

Loren, L. P. (2000). The purpose of copyright. *Open Spaces Quarterly, 2*(1). Retrieved from http://www.open-spaces.com/

Lorica, M. D. V. (2010). Information Seeking Behavior: Its relevance to the LIS Profession. Retrieved from http://mlorica.blogspot.com/2011/02/introduction-this-paper-aims-to-provide.html

Lucas-Schloetter, A. (2011). Digital Libraries and Copyright Issues: Digitisation of Contents and the Economic Rights of the Authors. In I. Iglezakis, T. Synodinou, & S. Kapidakis (Eds.), *E-Publishing and Digital Libraries: Legal and Organizational Issues* (pp. 159–179). Hershey, PA, USA: IGI Global. doi:10.4018/978-1-60960-031-0.ch009

Lwoga, E. T., Stilwell, C., & Ngulube, P. (2011). Access and use of agricultural information and knowledge in Tanzania. Retrieved from http://ir.muhas.ac.tz:8080/jspui/bitstream/123456789/1368/1/library_review_paper_lwoga_Stilwel_Ngulube.pdf

Lynch, C. A. (1993). Accessibility and integrity of networked information collections (Background Paper No. BP- TCT-109). Office of Technology Assessment, Washington.

Lynch, C. A. (1997). Searching the Internet. *Scientific American*, 397, 52-56. Retrieved from http://www.sciam.com/0397issue/0397lynch.html

Lynch, C. A. (1997). Searching the Internet. *Scientific American*, 52-56. Retrieved from http://www.sciam.com/0397issue/0397lynch.html

Lynch, C. A., & Garcia-Molina, H. (1995). Interoperability, scaling, and the digital libraries research agenda: a report on the IITA Digital Libraries Workshop. Retrieved from http://www.diglib.stanford.edu/diglib/pub/reports/iitadlw/main.html

Lynch, C. A., & Garcia-Molina, H. (1995). *Interoperability, Scaling, and the Digital Libraries Research Agenda: A Report on the May 18-19, 1995 IITA Digital Libraries Workshop*. Retrieved from http://www-diglib.stanford.edu/diglib/pub/reports/iita-dlw/main.html

Lynch, C., & Garcia-Molina, H. (1995). Interoperability, scaling, and the digital libraries research agenda (Research workshop). Retrieved from http://www.hpcc.gov/reports-nco/iita-dlw/main.html

Lynch, C., & Garcia-Molina, H. (1995). Interoperability, scaling, and the digital libraries research agenda http://www.hpcc.gov/reports/reports-nco/iita-dlw/main.html

Lynch, C., & Garcia-Molina. (1995, May 18-19). Interoperability, scaling and the digital libraries. *Proceedings of the 1995 IITA Digital Libraries Workshop*. Retrieved from http://www-diglib.stanford.edu/diglib/pub/reports/iita-dlw/main.html

Lynch, C. (1993). *Accessibility and integrity of networked information collections. Background Paper No. BP-109.* Washington, DC: Office of Technology Assessment.

Lynch, C. (1997). Searching the Internet. *Scientific American*, *276*(3), 52–56. doi:10.1038/scientificamerican0397-52 PMID:8972618

Lynch, C. A. (1994). *The integrity of digital information: Mechanism and definitional issues*. Silver Spring, MD: ASIS.

Mahajan, P. (2009). Information seeking behaviour: a study of Punjab University, India. Library Philosophy and Practice. Retrieved from http://www.webpages.uidaho.edu/~mbolin/mahajan4.htm

Mahmood, M., Burn, J., Geornoets, L., & Jacquez, C. (2000). Information technology end-user satisfaction: A meta-analysis of the empirical literature. *International Journal of Human-Computer Studies*, *52*(4), 751–771. doi:10.1006/ijhc.1999.0353

Majchrzak, A., Rice, R., Malhotra, A., King, N., & Ba, S. (2000). Technology adaptation: The case of a computer-supported inter-organizational virtual team. *Management Information Systems Quarterly*, *24*(4), 569–600. doi:10.2307/3250948

Majid, S., & Kassim, G. M. (2000). Information-seeking behaviour of International Islamic University Malaysia Law Faculty Members. *Malaysian Journal of Library & Information Science*, *5*(2), 1–17.

Makri, S., Blandford, A., & Cox, A. (2008a). Using information behaviors to evaluate the functionality and usability of electronic resources: From Ellis's model to evaluation. *Journal of the American Society for Information Science and Technology*, *59*(14), 2244–2267. doi:10.1002/asi.20927

Makri, S., Blandford, A., & Cox, A. (2008b). Investigating the information-seeking behavior of academic lawyers: From Ellis's model to design. *Information Processing & Management*, *44*(2), 613–634. doi:10.1016/j.ipm.2007.05.001

Manda, P. A., & Mulkangara, F. (2007). Gender Analysis of Electronic Information Resources Use: A Case of the University of Dares Salaam Tanzania. *University of Dares Salaam Library Journal*, *9*(1), 31–52.

Maness, J. A. (2006). Library 2.0 theory: web 2.0 and its implications for libraries. *Webology,* 3(2). Retrieved from http://www.webology.ir/2006/v3n2/a25.html

Manley, W. (1981). Facing the public'. *Wilson Library Bulletin*, *55*(10), 762–763, 798.

Mann, T. (1993). *Library research models: A guide to classification, cataloguing and computers*. New York: Oxford University Press.

Marcella, R., & Baxter, G. (1999). The information needs and information-seeking behavior of a national sample of the population in the United Kingdom. *The Journal of Documentation*, *55*(2), 159–183. doi:10.1108/EUM0000000007142

Marchionini, G. (1995). *Information seeking in electronic environment*. Cambridge: Cambridge University Press. doi:10.1017/CBO9780511626388

Marchionini, G. (1998). *Research and development in digital libraries. Encyclopedia of Library and Information Science* (Vol. 63). New York: Dekker.

Marchionini, G., Plaisant, C., & Komlodi, A. (1998). Interfaces and tools for the Library of Congress National Digital Library program. *Information Processing & Management*, *34*(5), 535–555. doi:10.1016/S0306-4573(98)00020-X

Marshall, A. B. (1998). *Trafficking in old books*. Ann Arbor: Lost Domain.

Martin, R.S. (2004). Libraries and librarians in the 21st century: Fostering a learning society. *College & Research Libraries News*, *65*(11), 668–671.

Martin, P., & Metcalfe, M. (2001). Informing the knowledge workers. *RSR. Reference Services Review*, *29*(4), 267–275. doi:10.1108/00907320110408384

Mayank, T., & Patel, S. (2010). *Digital Libraries: Functionality, usability, and accessibility*. Library Philosophy and Practice.

McClure, C. R., Bertot, J. C., & Jaeger, P. T. (2011). The ever changing impacts of internet access on libraries and their communities. In J. C. Bertot, C. R. McClure, & P. T. Jaeger (Eds.), *Public libraries and the internet: Roles, perspectives, and implications* (pp. 261–281). Santa Barbara, CA: Libraries Unlimited.

McKechnie, E.F., Goodall, G.R., Lajoie-Paquette, D. and Julien, H. (2005). How human information behaviour researchers use each other's work: a basic citation analysis study. *Information Research*, 10(2). Retrieved from http://InformationR.net/ir/10-2/paper220.html

Medical Library Association. (2007). The copyright law and the health sciences librarian. Available at: www.mlanet.org

Meho, L., & Tibbo, H. (2003). Modelling the information-seeking behavior of social scientists: Ellis's study revisited. *American Journal of the society for Information and Technology*, 54(6), 570-587.

Meho, L. I., & Tibbo, H. R. (2003). Modeling the information-seeking behavior of social scientists: Ellis's study revisited. *Journal of the American Society for Information Science and Technology*, *54*(6), 570–587. doi:10.1002/asi.10244

Mekelle University Annual Report. (2014). Electronic Information Resources. Retrieved from http://www.mu.edu.et/index.php/library-e-resources

Menzel, H. (1996). Information needs and uses. In C.A. Cuadra (Ed.), Annual Review of Information Science and Technology (ARIST) (Vol. 1, pp. 41-69). USA: Interscience Publishers.

Merrett, C. (1994). *A culture of censorship: secrecy and intellectual repression in South Africa*. Cape Town: David Philip & University of Natal Press.

Meso, P., Musa, P., & Mbarika, V. (2005). Towards a model of consumer use of mobile information and communication technology LDCs: The case of sub-Saharan Africa. *Information Systems Journal*, *115*(2), 119–146. doi:10.1111/j.1365-2575.2005.00190.x

Metz, R. F. (2002). *Coaching in the library: a management strategy for achieving excellence*. Chicago: American Library Association.

Miller, P. (2005). Web 2.0: building the new library. Retrieved from http://www.ariadne.ac.uk/issue45/miller/

Miller, P. (2006). Library 2.0 – the challenge of disruptive innovation. Retrieved from http://www.talis.com/resources/documents/447_Library_2_prf1.pdf

Mnubi-Mchombu, C., & Mostert, J. (2011). Information seeking behaviour of orphaned and vulnerable children's caregivers in Namibia. *Library Review*, *60*(5), 396–408. doi:10.1108/00242531111135308

Momoh, A. U, Osaheni, O & Oshioneb, F. (2015). Information seeking behavior of nurses in central hospitals in Delta State. *Pyrex Journal of Library and Information Science*, 1(3), 26.

Morgan, E. L. (2009). Technology trends and libraries: so many opportunities. Retrieved from http://infomotions.com/musings/trends-and-opportunities/

Mostert, B. J., & Ocholla, D. N. (2005). Information needs and information seeking behavior of parliamentarians in South Africa. *South African Journal of Libraries and Information Science, 71*(2), 136.

Mtega, W., & And Benard, R. (2013). The state of rural information and communication services in Tanzania: A meta-analysis. *International Journal of Information and Communication Technology Research, 3*(2), 64–73.

Mullen, T., & Lyles, M. (1993). Toward improving management development's contribution to organizational learning. *Human resources planning[HRP]*, 16(2), 35-49.

Munyambonera, E., Nampewo, D., Adong, A., & Mayanja, M. (2012). Access and Use of Credit in Uganda: Unlocking the Dilemma of Financing Small Holder Farmers. Retrieved from http://ageconsearch.umn.edu/bitstream/150229/2/policybrief25.pdf

Mutshewa, A. (2007). A theoretical exploration of information behaviour: A power perspective. *Aslib Proceedings: New Information Perspectives, 59*(3), 249–263. doi:10.1108/00012530710752043

Mwita, D. (1999, September 22). Freedom of information access in Kenya: a publishing perspective in a changing environment. *Paper presented at the13th Kenya Library Association Annual Seminar.*

Nakonecny, M. (1998). *Psychologie osobnosti. 2. vyd.* Prague, Czech Republic: Academia.

National library of Australia. (2009) *Collection digitization policy*. Retrieved from www.nla.gov.au/policy/digitization.html

Nicholas, D., Huntington, P., Willians, P., & Dobrowolski, T. (2004). Re-appraising information seeking behavior in a digital environment: Bouncers, checkers, returnees and the like. *The Journal of Documentation, 60*(1), 24–43. doi:10.1108/00220410410516635

Niedzwiedzka, B. (2003). A proposed general model of information behaviour. *Information Research, 9*(1), 9–1.

Nigeria Department of Labour. (1955). Annual Report *1954/55*

NOLO. (2010). *The 'fair use' rule: When use of copyrighted material is acceptable.* Retrieved from http://www.nolo.com/legal-encyclopedia/article30100.html

North, C., Shneiderman, M., & Plaisant, C. (1996). Visual Information Seeking in Digital Image Libraries: The Visible Human Explorer. *Proceeding of ACM DL 96 - Conference in Digital Libraries* (pp. 74-82).

Noruzi, A. (2005). Google Scholar: The New Generation of Citation Indexes. *Libri, 55*(4), 170–180. doi:10.1515/LIBR.2005.170

Nurnberg, P. J., Furuta, R., Leggett, J. J., Marshall, C., & Shipman, F. M. III. (1995). Digital libraries: issues and architectures.*Proceedings of the Second Annual Conference on the Theory and Practice of Digital Libraries*, Austin, Texas (pp. 147-153).

O'Connor, D. (2010). Apomediation and ancillary care: Researchers' responsibilities in health-related online communities. *International Journal of Internet Research Ethics, 3*(12). Retrieved from http://ijire.net/issue_3.1/7_OConnor.pdf

O'Day, V., & Nardi, B. (2003). An ecological perspective on digital libraries. In *A. Bishop, N. Van House, & B. Buttenfield, Digital library use: social practice in design and evaluation* (pp. 65–82). Cambridge, Massachusetts: MIT Press.

Obawusi, L. (2001). An Address" Delivered at the opening ceremony of The 5th National Delegate Conference of the Senior Staff Union of Colleges of Education held at the Niger State College of Education, Minna. November 7.

OCLC. (2002). *How Academic Librarians can Influence Students' Web-Based Information Choices*. Retrieved from http://www.mnstate.edu/schwartz/informationhabits.pdf

Odedra, M., Lawrie, M. B., & Goodman, S. (n. d.). University of Pennsylvania- African Studies. Retrieved http://www.africa.upenn.edu/Comp_Articles/Information_Technology_117.html

Odedra, M., Lawrie, M., Bennet, M., & Goodman, S. (n. d.). University of Pennsylvania - African Studies. Retrieved from http://www.africa.upenn.edu/Comp_Articles/Information_Technology_117.html

O'Dell, S. (2010). Opportunities and Obligations for Libraries in a Social Networking Age: A Survey of Web 2.0 and Networking Sites. *Journal of Library Administration*, *50*(3), 237-251. doi:10.1080/01930821003634989

Odini, C. (2005). Information seeking and communication behaviour of Kenya Railways' engineers. *University of Dar es Salaam. Library Journal*, *7*(2), 98–111.

Ogba, C. O. (2013). Information Seeking Behaviour of Final Year Law Students in South Western Nigerian Universities. *Information & Knowledge Management*, 3(5).

Okafor, G. O., & Malizu, C. F. (2013). The Media, Democracy and Trade Unionism in Nigeria. *Challenges and Prospects New Media and Mass Communication*, *17*, 2224–3275.

Okiki, O.C and Asiru, S.M. (2011). Use of Electronic Information Sources by Postgraduate Students in Nigeria: Influencing Factors. *Library Philosophy and Practice 2011.*

Okonkwo, R. (1993). The Nigeria Civil Service Union, 1919-*1922. The International Journal of African Studies*, *26*(3), 609–622.

Okunade, O. S. & Williams, J. O. (2014). *Agriculture in Nigeria: problems, consequences and the way forward.* Ilorin: Adewumi press.

Oladokun, O. (2015). The Potential and utilization of social media in library and information centres. In A. Tella (Ed.), *Social media strategies for dynamic library development* (pp. 24–40). Hershey, PA: Information Science Reference (an imprint of IGI Global). doi:10.4018/978-1-4666-7415-8.ch002

Olatokun, M. W. (2009). Analysing Socio-Demographic Differences in Access and Use of ICTs in Nigeria Using the Capability Approach. *Issues in Informing Science and Information Technology*, *6*(3), 34–40.

Olorunfemi, D. Y., & Mostert, J. (2012). Information seeking behaviour of law students in a developing country: a literature review. Retrieved from http://www.lis.uzulu.ac.za/research/2012/Yemisi%20and%20Mostert%20SCECSAL,%20UZ,%207.pdf

Olusoji, J.G., Oluwakemi, O., & Uche, O. (2012). Trade Unions and Unionism in Nigeria: A Historical Perspective.

Omwansa, T. (2014). Re-introduction of VAT on ICT equipment in Kenya: special focus on mobile phones. School of Computing and Informatics, University of Nairobi, Nairobi, Kenya. Retrieved from http://www.c4dlab.ac.ke/wp-content/uploads/2014/04/VAT_TKO.pdf

Ono, H., & Zavodnty, M. (2003). Gender and the Internet. *Social Science Quarterly*, *84*(1), 111–121. doi:10.1111/1540-6237.t01-1-8401007

Onwuchekwa, E. (2015). The Role of social media and social networking in information service provision: a practical view. In A. Tella (Ed.), *Social media strategies for dynamic library development* (pp. 126–139). Hershey, PA, USA: IGI Global. doi:10.4018/978-1-4666-7415-8.ch007

O'Reilly, T. (2005). What is Web 2.0: Design Patterns and Business Models for the Next Generation of Software. Retrieved from http://www.oreillynet.com/pub/a/oreilly/tim/news/2005/09/30/what-is-web-20.html?

Osang, W. (2002). *The Trade Unions and their Impact on University Education in Nigeria* [M.Ed. Thesis]. University of Ibadan.

Otike, J. (2011, August 24-26). Kenya Libraries and Information Services Consortium (KLISC). *Presented at the Copyright Advocacy Workshop*, Nairobi, Kenya.

Otike, J. (2012, June 4 – 8). Copyright: the challenges posed by Reproduction Rights organizations (RROs) in the provision of information to users with special reference to Kenya. *Presented at the Standing Conference for East, Central and Southern African Librarians (SCESCAL)*, Nairobi, Kenya.

Otike, J. (2012, June 4-8). Copyright: challenges posed by reprographic rights organizations (RROs) in the provision of information to users with special reference to Kenya. *Presented at the Standing Conference of East, Central and Southern African Librarians (SCECSAL)*, Nairobi, Kenya.

Otike, J. (1996). Provision of legal information to rural populations in Anglophone Africa. *Libri*, *46*(4), 228–231. doi:10.1515/libr.1996.46.4.226

Otike, J. (1997). Legal information needs of the general public; with special reference to developing countries. *Library Review*, *46*(1), 28–33. doi:10.1108/00242539710160866

Otubelu, N. J. (2011). E-Learning through digital libraries: the case of National Open University. *Library Philosophy and Practice.* Retrieved from unllib.unl.edu/LPP/

Ouma, E., & Sihanya, M. (2010). Kenya. In C. Armstrong (Ed.), *Access to knowledge in Africa: the role of copyright* (pp. 83–125). UCT Press.

Owolabi, S. E. (2013). Socio-demographic factors as determinants of access and use of ICT by staff of university libraries in Oyo State. *Library Philosophy and Practice.* Retrieved from http://digitalcommons.unl.edu/libphilprac/947

Pachat, J., & Manjula, M. (2011). Collaboration in corporate libraries. In L. E. Kelsey & M. J. Porter (Eds.), *Best practices for corporate libraries* (pp. 65–79). Santa Barbara: Libraries Unlimited.

Pareek, A., & Rana, M. (2013). Study of information seeking behavior and library use pattern of researchers in the s University. Library philosophy and practice. Retrieved from http://digitalcommons.unl.edu/librphilprac/887

Park, N., Roman, R., Lee, S., & Chung, J. E. (2009). User acceptance of a digital library system in developing countries: An application of the TAM. *International Journal of Information Management*, *29*, 196–209. doi:10.1016/j.ijinfomgt.2008.07.001

Parmar, Arvind Kumar, S., Sanghmitra, A. & Prakash, T. (2004). *Bibliometric analysis of information seeking behaviour related literature.*

Parmeshwar, S., & Patil, D. B. (2009). Use of the Internet by Faculty and Research Scholars of Gulbarga University Library. *Library Philosophy and Practice.* Retrieved from http://digitalcommons.unl.edu/cgi/viewcontent.cgi?article=1268&context=libphilprac

Partridge, H. (2011). Being "librarian 2.0": it's all in the attitude. *Library Connect, 9*(3). Retrieved from http://libraryconnectarchive.elsevier.com/lcn/0903/lcn090303.html

Pastore, M. (1999). The language of the web. *Cyber Atlas.* Retrieved from http://cyberatlas.internet.com

Paul, J. (2002). Narrowing the digital divide: Initiatives undertaken by the Association of South-East Asian Nations. *Program*, *36*(1), 13–22. doi:10.1108/00330330210426085

Pauly, D., & Stergiou, K. I. (2005). Equivalence of results from two citation analyses: Thomson ISI's Citation Index and Google's Scholar service. In *Ethics in Science and Environmental Politics* (pp. 33–35). Retrieved from www.int-res.com/articles/esep/2005/E65.pdf

Pearrow, M. (2000). Website Usability Handbook. Rockland, MA: Charles River media.

Petros, M. F., & Rugare, M. (2013, June 25-29). The impact of social networks on teaching and learning: the Great Zimbabwe University experience. *Paper presented at 2nd Annual International Interdisciplinary Conference, held at the Catholic University of Eastern Africa CUEA)*, Nairobi, Kenya.

Pettigrew, K. E., & McKechnie, L. E. F. (2001). The use of theory in information science research. *Journal of the American Society for Information Science and Technology*, *52*(1), 62–73. doi:10.1002/1532-2890(2000)52:1<62::AID-ASI1061>3.0.CO;2-J

Pharo, N. (2004). A new model of information behaviour based on the search situation transition schema. *Information Research*, *10*(1), 10–11.

Phil, P. (2014, January 22). City-Data Forum. Retrieved from http://www.city-data.com/forum/africa/2035113-language-sub-saharan-africa.html#ixzz3wCUAxBlz

Phillips, D. (2006). *Quality of Life: Concept, Policy and Practice* (pp. 1–39). Oxon: Routledge. doi:10.4324/9780203356630

Piccoli, G., Ahmad, R., & Ives, B. (2001). Web based virtual learning environments: A research framework and a preliminary assessment of effectiveness in basic IT skills training. *Management Information Systems Quarterly*, *25*(4), 401–426. doi:10.2307/3250989

Pienaar, H., & Smith, I. 2007). Development of a Library 2.0 service model for an African library. *Proceedings of the73rd IFLA General Conference and Council*, Durban, South Africa.

Piper, P. S., & Collamer, B. E. (2001). Male librarians. *Journal of Academic Librarianship*, *27*(5), 406–411. doi:10.1016/S0099-1333(01)00226-9

Prabhakaran, A., & Mishra, H. K. (2012). Technological change in libraries: the evolution of technostress. Journal of Arts, Science & Commerce, 2(1), 131-135. Retrieved from http://www.researchersworld.com/vol3/Paper_14.pdf

Price, A. C. (2009). How to make a dollar out of fifteen cents: Tips for electronic collection development. *Collection Building*, *28*(1), 31–34. doi:10.1108/01604950910928493

Primus, S. (2009). Distance learning library services: Keeping up with the times. *Distance Learning*, *6*(1), 22–30.

Quinn, B. (2000). The McDonaldisation of Academic Libraries?'. *College & Research Libraries*, *61*(3), 248–261. Retrieved from http://crl.acrl.org/content/61/3/248.full.pdf doi:10.5860/crl.61.3.248

Rafiq, M., & Ameen, K. (2009). Information Seeking Behavior and User Satisfaction of University Instructors: *A Case Study. Library Philosophy and Practice*. Retrieved from http://www.webpages.uidaho.edu/~mbolin/rafiq-ameen.htm

Rainie, L. (2009). The nine tribes of the Internet. Retrieved from http://www.slideshare.net/lrainie/the-nine-tribes-of-the-internet-1555624

Ramos, M. M. (2007). The role of librarians in the 21st century. Retrieved from http://www.slideshare.net/plaistrlc/the-role-of-librarians-in-the-21st-century

Rana, H. K. (2009). Impact of Information and Communication Technology on Academic Libraries in Punjab. Retrieved from http/www.goarticles.com/cgi-bin/showa/cgi=1239032

Rasmussen, E. (2011). Library systems. In R. Baeza-Yates & B. Ribeiro-Neto (Eds.), *Modern information retrieval: the concept and technology behind search.* (2nd ed.). England: Pearson Education Limited.

Ray, K., & Day, J. (1998). Student attitudes towards electronic information resources. *Information Research*, 4(2). Retrieved from http://informationr.net/ir/4-2/paper54.html

Reitz, J. (2007). Digital library ODLIS: Online Dictionary for Library and Information Science. Retrieved From http://www.iu.com/odlisd.cf

Reitz, J. M. (2004). *Dictionary for Library and Information Science*. Westport: Libraries Unlimited.

Riding, R., & Rayner, S. G. (1998). *Cognitive styles and learning strategies*. London: David Fulton Publisher.

Robinson, A. (2006). Open access: The view of a commercial publisher. *Journal of Thrombosis and Haemostasis*, *4*(7), 1454–1460. doi:10.1111/j.1538-7836.2006.02009.x PMID:16839337

Rogers, E. M. (1983). *Diffusion of Innovation* (3rd ed.). New York: The Free Press.

Rose, G., Evaristo, R., & Straub, D. (2003). Consumer responses to web download time: A four-continent study of mono and polychronism. *IEEE Transactions on Engineering Management*, *50*(1), 31–44. doi:10.1109/TEM.2002.808262

Rose, G., & Straub, D. (1998). Predicting general IT use: Applying TAM to the Arabic world. *Journal of Global Information Management*, *6*(3), 39–46. doi:10.4018/jgim.1998070104

Ross, S. (2003). *Digital library development review*. Wellington: National Library of New Zealand.

Rothman, D. (2006). Library 2.0. Retrieved from http://davidrothman.net/2006/11/30/library-20/

Rouse, M. (2005, April). Wireless definition. Retrieved from http://whatis.techtarget.com/definition/digital

Rowley, J., & Farrow, J. (2000). *Organizing knowledge: An introduction to managing access to information*. USA: Ashgate Publishing Ltd.

Rowley, J., & Hartley, R. (2008). *Organizing knowledge: an introduction to managing access to information* (4th ed.). England: Ashgate Publishing Limited.

Rubin, R. E. (2010). *Foundations of library and information science* (3rd ed.). New York: Neal-Schuman Publishers, Inc.

Rupp-Serrano, K., & Robbins, S. (2013). Information-seeking habits of education faculty. *College & Research Libraries*, *74*(2), 131–142. doi:10.5860/crl-322

Saleh, A. G., & Lasisi, F. I. (2011). Information needs and information seeking behavior of rural women in Borno State, Nigeria. Retrieved from http://www.webpages.uidaho.edu/~mbolin/saleh-lasisi2.pdf

Salwasser, J., & Murray-Rust, C. (2002). Assessing the need for a natural resources digital library. Retrieved from http://www.istl.org/02-winter/article2.html

Saravan,, R., & Raja,, P., & Tayeng, S. (2009). Information input pattern and information need of Tribal Farmers in Arnuchal Pradesh, *Indian Journal of Extension Education*, *45*(1&2), 51-54

Savolainen, R. (2006). Information use as gap-bridging: The viewpoint of Sense-Making methodology. *Journal of the American Society for Information Science*, *57*(8), 1116–1125. doi:10.1002/asi.20400

Savolainen, R. (2006). Time as a context of information seeking. *LISR*, *28*(1), 141–163.

Savolainen, R. (2007). Information behavior and information practice: Reviewing the 'umbrella concepts' of information-seeking studies. *The Library Quarterly*, *77*(2), 109–127. doi:10.1086/517840

Schatz, B. R. (1997). Information retrieval in digital libraries: Bringing search to the net. *Science*, *275*(5298), 327–333. Retrieved from www.canis.illinoi.edu/archive/papers/science-irdl-journal.pdf doi:10.1126/science.275.5298.327 PMID:8994022

Selvam, M. (2014). An introduction to semantic information retrieval in digital libraries. Retrieved from http://www.liscom.org/postContent/fullPaper/pdf/paper%20presented/P%20O%2014%20An%20Introduction%20to%20Semantic%20Information%20Retrieval%20in%20Digital%20libraries.pdf

Senftleben, M. (2004). *Copyright, Limitations and the three-step Test. An Analysis of the Three-Step Test in International and EC Copyright Law*. The Hague: Kluwer Law International.

Shaffril, H. A. M., Samah, B. A., Hassan, M. A., & Silva, J. L. (2010). Socio-economic factors that impinge computer usage in administration works among village leaders in Malaysia. *Scientific Research and Essays*, *5*, 3623–3633.

Shakeel, G. T., & Vinayagamoorthy, P. (2013). Information seeking behaviour of business school students: A special study of universities and colleges located in Academic City, Dubai, UAE. *International Journal of Library and Information Science*, *5*(11), 447–456.

Shao, X., & Scherlen, A. (2007). Perceptions of open access publishing among academic journal editors in China. *Serials Review*, *33*(2), 114–121. doi:10.1080/00987913.2007.10765105

Sharma, A. K., & Bhardwaj, S. (2009). Marketing and promotion of library services. Retrieved from http://crl.du.ac.in/ical09/papers/index_files/ical-79_73_172_2_RV.pdf

Sharma, P. S. K. (1990). *Universe of knowledge and research methodology*. Delhi: Ken Publications.

Shuling, W. (2007). Investigation and analysis of current use of electronic resources in university libraries. *Library Management*, *28*(1/2), 72–88. Retrieved from http://www.emeraldinsight.com/Insight/ViewContentServlet?Filename=Published/EmeraldFullTextArticle/Articles/0150280107.html doi:10.1108/01435120710723563

Shuman, B. A. (2001). *Issues for libraries and information science in the internet age*. Englewood: Libraries Unlimited.

Sihanya (n. d.). Promoting access through legal reform: Kenya case study. *Presented in a workshop on exceptions and limitations for education and research environments in Ghana.*

Singer, P. M., & Griffith, G. (2010). *Succession planning in the library: developing leaders, managing change*. Chicago: American Library Association.

Skyes, J. (2001). The value of indexing. A white paper prepared for Factiva, a Dow Jones and Reuters Company. Retrieved from www.4info-management.com/pdf/indexingwhitepaper.pdf

SLA (Special Libraries Association). (1999). Seven easy ways to promote your library. Retrieved from http://units.sla.org/division/dleg/Newsletter/v5no3_seven.htm

Smith, A. (2001), *Strategies for Building Digitized Collection.* Washington, D.C. Digital Library Federation, Council on Library and Information Resources. Retrieved from http://www.clir.org

Smith, A. (2001). Strategies for building digitized collections.: Digital Library Federation, Council on Library and Information Resources, Washington, DC. Retrieved from http://www.clir.org

Solomon, P. (1997). Discovering information behavior in sense making: I. Time and timing; II. The social; III. The person. *Journal of the American Society for Information Science*, *48*(12), 1097–1108. doi:10.1002/(SICI)1097-4571(199712)48:12<1097::AID-ASI4>3.0.CO;2-P

Solomon, P. (2002). Discovering information in context. *Annual Review of Information Service and Technology*, *36*(1), 229–264. doi:10.1002/aris.1440360106

Sorrentino, R., & Short, J. (1986). Uncertainty Orientation, Motivation, and Cognition. In R. Sorrentino & E. Higgins (Eds.), *Handbook of Motivation and Cognition*. New York: The Guilford Press.

Spink, A., & Cole, C. (2006). Human information behavior: Integrating diverse approaches and information use. *Journal of the American Society for Information Science and Technology*, *57*(1), 25–35. doi:10.1002/asi.20249

Spink, A., & Cole, C. (Eds.), (2005). *New Directions in Human Information Behavior*. Dordrecht, The Netherlands: Springer.

Sridhar, M. (1987). Information-seeking behavior of the Indian space technologists. Retrieved from http://elis.da.ulcc.ac.uk/10887/2/J_26_ISB_OF_IST.pdf

Sridhar, M. (1989). Information-seeking behavior of the Indian space technologists. *Library Science*, *26*(2), 127–132.

Sridhar, M. S. (1989). Information seeking behaviour of the Indian space technologists. *Library Science*, *26*(2), 127–132.

Stahl, B. (1995). Trends and challenges for academic libraries and information services. *CAUSE/EFFECT*, 18(1). Retrieved from http://www.educause.edu/ir/library/text/cem951a.txt

Stebbins, L. (2015). Markers of quality: the role of librarians in everyday life information literacy – peer to peer review. Retrieved from http://lj.libraryjournal.com/2015/12/academic-libraries/markers-of-quality-the-role-of-librarians-in-everyday-life-information-literacy-peer-to-peer-review/#_

Steinerová, J., & Susol, J. (2006). Users' information behaviour-a gender perspective. *Information Research*, *12*(3), 13.

Stephens, M. (2004). Technoplans vs. technolust. *Library Journal*. Retrieved from http://www.libraryjournal.com/article/CA474999.html

Stephens, M. (2008). Taming technolust: Ten steps for planning in a 2.0 world. *Reference and User Services Quarterly*, *47*(4), 314–317. doi:10.5860/rusq.47n4.314

Sternberg, R. J., & Sternberg, K. (2009). *Cognitive psychology* (6th ed.). Belmont, CA: Wadsworth, Cengage Learning.

Stigter, C. J. (2002). Opportunities to improve the use of seasonal climate forecasts. Bangkok, Thailand: Asian Disaster Preparedness Center (ADPC).

Stoan, S. K. (1991). Research and information retrieval among academic researchers: Implications for library instructions. *Library Trends*, *39*(3), 238–257.

Suowari, D. U. (2005). *Contribution to Sectoral Development. The Roles and Responsibilities of the Senior Staff Association of Nigerian Universities*. SSANU.

Supply and Demand in ARL Libraries, 1986-2011. (2011). Association of Research Libraries.

Swain, D. K., & Panda, K. C. (2009). Use of electronic resources in business school libraries of an Indian state: A study of librarians' opinion. *The Electronic Library*, *27*(1), 74–85. doi:10.1108/02640470910934605

Swain, D. K., & Panda, K. C. (2009). Use of electronic resources in business school libraries of an Indian state: A study. *Collection Building*, *28*(3), 108–116. doi:10.1108/01604950910971134

Swanson, B. (2008). Global review of good agricultural extension and advisory service systems. Food and Agricultural Organization, Rome.

Swanson, B., & Rajalahti, R. (2010). *Strengthening agricultural extension and advisory systems: procedures for accessing, transforming and evaluating extension systems. Agricultural and rural development discussion* (p. 45). Washington, DC: World Bank.

Tamine-Lechani, L., Boughanem, M., & Daoud, M. (2010). Evaluation of contextual information retrieval effectiveness: Overview of issues and Research. *Knowledge and Information Systems*, *24*(1), 1–34. doi:10.1007/s10115-009-0231-1

Tanui, T. (2013, June 25-29). Reconstructing and redefining the university library: the exploitation of underlying library resources. *Paper presented at 2nd Annual International Interdisciplinary Conference, held at the Catholic University of Eastern Africa (CUEA)*, Nairobi, Kenya.

Tarulli, L. (2010). Mobile devices and library catalogues. Retrieved from http://laureltarulli.wordpress.com/2010/06/21/mobile-devices-and-library-catalogues/

Taylor, A. G. (2004). The organization of information (2nd ed.). Library and Information Science text series. Westport: Libraries Unlimited Inc.

Taylor, A. G., & Joudrey, D. N. (2009). *The organization of information* (3rd ed.). Cincinnati: Libraries Unlimited.

Taylor, R. S. (1962). The Process of Asking Questions. *American Documentation*, *13*(4), 391–396. doi:10.1002/asi.5090130405

Taylor, R. S. (1968). Question negotiation and information seeking in libraries. *Journal of College and Research Libraries*, *29*(3), 178–194. doi:10.5860/crl_29_03_178

Tella, A., Tella, A., Ayeni, C. O., & Omoba, R. O. (2007). Self-Efficacy and Use of Electronic Information as Predictors of Academic Performance. *Electronic Journal of Academic and Special Librarianship*, 8(2). Retrieved from http://southernlibrarianship.icaap.org/content/v08n02/tella_a01.html

Tella, A. (2009). Correlates of Undergraduates' Information-Seeking Behavior. *College & Undergraduate Libraries*, *16*(1), 1–19. doi:10.1080/10691310902754221

Thachill, G. (2008). Academic Libraries Redefined: Old Mission with a New Face. Scroll, 1(1).

Thanuskodi, S. (2009). *(June). Information-Seeking Behavior of Law Faculty at Central Law College*. Salem: Library Philosophy and Practice.

Thompson, C. J., & Zeynep, A. (2004). The Starbucks Brandscape and Consumers' (Anticorporate) Experiences of Glocalization. *The Journal of Consumer Research*, *31*(12), 631–642. doi:10.1086/425098

Thórsteinsdóttir, G. (2005). The information seeking behaviour of distance students: a study of twenty Swedish library and information science students (PhD dissertation). Sweden: University of Boras; Retrieved from http://bada.hb.se/handle/2320/2573

TNS Global. (2012, June 15). Connected world. Retrieved from http://www.tnsglobal.be/sites/default/files/whitepaper/TNS_In_Focus_digital_media_SSA.pdf

Todd, R. J. (2003). Adolescents of the Information Age: Patterns of Information Seeking and Use, and Implications for Information Professionals. *School Library Media Quarterly*, *9*(2), 27–46.

Tologbonse, D., Fashola, O., & Obadiah, M. (2008). Policy Issues in Meeting Rice Farmers Agricultural Information Needs in Niger State. *Journal of Agricultural Extension*, *12*(2), 84–94.

Toner, L. (2008). Non-use of Library Services by Students in a UK Academic Library. *Evidence Based Library and Information Practice*, 3(3). Retrieved from http://ejournals.library.ualberta.ca/index.php/EBLIP/article/view/1330/1241

Trade Union (Amendment) Act 2005. (2005).

Trivedi, M. (2010). Digital libraries: functionality, usability and accessibility. Library philosophy and practice. Retrieved from http://www.webpages.uidaho.edu/~mbolin/trivedi-diglib.htm

Trivedi, M. (2010). Digital Libraries: Functionality, Usability, and Accessibility. *Library Philosophy and Practice. ISSN 1522-0222.*

Troll, D. A. (2001). How and why are libraries changing. Retrieved from http://old.diglib.org/use/whitepaper.htm

Troll, D. (2002). How and why libraries are changing: What we know and what we need to know. Portal. *Libraries and the Academy*, *2*(1), 99–123. doi:10.1353/pla.2002.0023

Tsakonas, G., & Papatheodorou, C. (2006). Analysing and evaluating usefulness and usability in electronic information services. *Journal of Information Science*, *32*(5), 400–419. doi:10.1177/0165551506065934

Turner, K. (2007). Information seeking, retrieving, reading and storing behaviour of library-users. Retrieved from http://std.kku.ac.th/4830802252/Programme/Greenstone/examplegreenstone/Word_and_PDF/Documents/rtf02.rtf

Tury, S., Robinson, L., & Bawden, D. (2015). The Information Seeking Behaviour of Distance Learners: A Case Study of the University of London International Programmes. *The Journal of Academic Librarianship*.

Uhegbu, A. H. (2007). *The Information User: Issues and Themes*. Okigwe Whytem Publishers.

Ukachi, N. B. (2004). Information needs, sources, and information seeking behaviour of rural women in Badagry, Lagos, Nigeria. Retrieved from http://www.unilag.edu.ng/opendoc.php?sno=15750&doctype=doc&docname=$

United States Copyright Office. (2008). *Copyright basics*. (Circular 1). Retrieved from http://www.copyright.gov/circs/circ01.pdf

United States Copyright Office. (2010). *Fair use*. (Circular FL-102). Retrieved from http://www.copyright.gov/fls/fl102.html

Urquhart, C., Thomas, R., Lonsdale, R., Spink, S., Yeoman, A., Fenton, R., & Armstrong, C. (2003). Uptake and use of electronic information services: Trends in UK higher education from the JUSTEIS project. *Program*, *37*(3), 168–180.

Vakkari, P. (2006). Trends in the use of digital libraries by scientists in 2000-2005: A case study of FinELib. In A. Grove (Eds.), *Proceedings 69th Annual Meeting of ASIST*, Austin, TX, USA. doi:doi:10.1002/meet.1450430132 doi:10.1002/meet.1450430132

Vakkari, P. (2008). Trends and approaches in information behaviour research. *Information Research, 13*(4). Retrieved from http://www.informationr.net/ir/13-4/paper361.html

Vakkari, P., & Talja, S. (2005). The influence of the scatter of literature on the use of electronic resources across disciplines: A case study of FinELib. *Proceedings of the 9th European Conference on Digital Libraries* (pp. 207-217). Berlin & Heidelberg: Springer.

Vakkari, P. (2001). A theory of the task-based information retrieval process: A summary and generalisation of a longitudinal study. *The Journal of Documentation*, *57*(1), 44–60. doi:10.1108/EUM0000000007075

Vaughan, L., & Shaw, D. (2008). A new look at evidence of scholarly citation in citation indexes and from web sources. *Scientometrics*, *74*(2), 317–330. doi:10.1007/s11192-008-0220-2

Venkatesh, V., & Morris, M. (2000). Why don't men ever stop to ask for directions? Gender, social influence, and their role in technology acceptance usage behavior. *Management Information Systems Quarterly*, *24*(1), 115–139. doi:10.2307/3250981

Von Wright, J. (1994). *Oppimiskäsitysten historiaa ja pedagogisia seurauksia. 2. muuttamaton p.* Helsinki: Opetushallitus.

Walshman, G. (2002). Cross-cultural software production and use: A structurational analysis. *Management Information Systems Quarterly*, *26*(4), 350–380.

Walshman, G., & Sahay, S. (1999). GIS for district-level administration in India: Problems and opportunities. *Management Information Systems Quarterly*, *23*(1), 39–65. doi:10.2307/249409

Wang, P., Hawk, W. B., & Tenopir, C. (2000). Users' interaction with World Wide Web resources: An exploratory study using a holistic approach. *Information Processing & Management*, *36*(2), 229–251. doi:10.1016/S0306-4573(99)00059-X

Warlick, D. (2010). Patron 2.0. Retrieved from http://davidwarlick.com/wordpress/?p=1143

Waters, D. J. (1998). What are Digital Libraries? *CLIR Issues*, July/August. Retrieved from http://www.clir.org/pubs/issues/issues04.HTML

Weigts, W., Widdershoven, G., Kok, G., & Tomlow, P. (1993). Patients' information seeking actions and physicians' responses in gynaecological consultations. *Qualitative Health Research*, *3*(4), 398–429. doi:10.1177/104973239300300402

Weiler, A. (2005). Information-Seeking Behavior in Generation Y Students: Motivation, Critical Thinking, and Learning Theory. *Journal of Academic Librarianship*, *31*(1), 46–53. doi:10.1016/j.acalib.2004.09.009

Wells, H. (1938). *World brain*. New York: Doubleday.

Werra, J. (2001). Le régime juridique des mesures techniques de protection des oeuvres selon les Traités de l'OMPI, le Digital Millennium Copyright Act, les Directives Européennes et d'autres legislations (Japon, Australie). *Revue Internationale du Droit d'Auteur*, *189*, 66–213.

Wheeler, A., & Harris, P. (2006). Creativity & personalization: freshman orientation for the millennial generation. Retrieved from http://www.emich.edu/public/loex/handouts/wheeler/FreshmanOrientationSlides.pdf

White, M. D. (1975). The communication behavior of academic economists in research phases. *The Library Quarterly*, *45*(5), 337–354.

Widharto, L. (2002). Challenges in accessing information in Indonesia during the economic crisis. *Bulletin of the American Society for Information Science and Technology*, *28*(4), 25–27. doi:10.1002/bult.243

Wikipedia. (2015, October 27). Information needs. Retrieved from https://en.wikipedia.org/wiki/Information_needs

Wilson, T. D. (1994). Information needs and uses: Fifty years of process? A Journal of Documentation Review, 1994, 15-51.

Wilson, T. D. (2000). Recent Trends in User Studies: Action Research and Qualitative Methods. *Information Research*, *5*(3). Retrieved from http://information.net/ir/5-3/paper76html

Wilson, T. D. (2000). Recent trends in user studies: Action research and qualitative methods. *Information Research*, 5(3). Retrieved from http://informationr.net/ir/5-3/paper76.html

Wilson, T. D. (2008). Human information behavior. Retrieved from http://inform.nu/Articles/vol.3/v3n2

Wilson, T. (2000). Human information behavior. *Informing Science*, *3*(2), 49–55.

Wilson, T. D. (1981). On user studies and information needs. *The Journal of Documentation*, *37*(1), 3–15. doi:10.1108/eb026702

Wilson, T. D. (1997). Information behavior: An interdisciplinary perspective. *Information Processing & Management*, *33*(4), 551–572. doi:10.1016/S0306-4573(97)00028-9

Wilson, T. D. (1999). Models in information behavior research. *The Journal of Documentation*, *55*(3), 249–270. doi:10.1108/EUM0000000007145

Wilson, T. D. (2000). Human information behavior. *Informing Science*, *3*(2), 49–55.

Wilson, T. D. (2000). Human information behaviour. *Informing Science*, *3*(2), 49–55.

Wilson, T. D. (2006). A re-examination of information seeking behavior in the context of activity theory. *Information Research*, *11*, 4.

Witten, I. H., Bainbridge, D., & Nichols, D. M. (2010). *How to Build a Digital Library* (2nd ed.). Burlington, MA: Morgan Kaufmann.

Witten, I., & Bainbridge, D. (2003). *How to build a digital library*. San Francisco: Morgan Kaufmann Publishers.

Worcman, K. (2002). Digital division is cultural exclusion. But is digital inclusion cultural inclusion? *D-Lib Magazine*, *8*(3). Retrieved from http://www.dlib.org/dlib/march02/worcman/03worcman.html doi:10.1045/march2002-worcman

World Bank. (2013). Fact sheet: infrastructure in sub-Saharan Africa. Washington, DC: World Bank. Retrieved from http://go.worldbank.org/SWDECPM5S0

Wright, M., & Guy, L. (1997). Where do I find it and what do I do with it: Practical problem–solving in the data library. Retrieved from dphs.dacc.wisc.edu/types/data_reference.html

Wu-Jun, Y., & Peng, Z. (2010). Computer application and system modelling. *ICCASM, International conference*. Retrieved from ieeexplore.ieee.org/xpi/login.jsp?tp=&arnumber=5622829*url=http%3A%2F%Fieeexplore.ieee.org%Fxpls%2Fabs_ail_jsp%3Farnum

Xie, H. (2000). Shifts of interactive intentions and information-seeking strategies in interactive information retrieval. *Journal of the American Society for Information Science*, *51*(9), 841–857. doi:10.1002/(SICI)1097-4571(2000)51:9<841::AID-ASI70>3.0.CO;2-0

Yakovleva, S. (2014). Public libraries: the right to digitise and the right of reproduction. *Kluwer Copyright Blog*. Retrieved from http://kluwercopyrightblog.com/2014/10/17/public-libraries-the-right-to-digitise-and-the-right-of-reproduction/

Yazit, N., & Zainab, A. N. (2007). Malaysian publication contributions to the field of Library and Information Science. In Abdullah, A., et al. (Eds.), Proceedings of ICOLIS '07, Kuala Lumpur (pp. 407-420).

Yesufu, T. M. (1982). *The Dynamics of Industrial Relations: The Nigerian Experience*. Ibadan: University Press Limited.

Youngman, D. C. (2002). Re-shaping library service programming: new strategies for the new millennium. Retrieved from http://www.iatul.org/doclibrary/public/Conf_Proceedings/2002/Youngman.pdf

Zainab, A. N. (2007). Women's studies in Malaysia: A bibliometric study with implications for its bibliographical control. In Abdullah, A., et al. (Eds.), Proceedings of ICOLIS '07, Kuala Lumpur (pp. 385-396).

Zhang, H., & Salvendy, G. (2001). The Implication of Visualization Ability and Structure Preview Design for Web Information Search Tasks. *International Journal of Human-Computer Interaction*, *13*(1), 75–95. doi:10.1207/S15327590IJHC1301_5

Zhang, W. (1998). Analyzing faculty and staff's information needs and use of electronic technologies: A liberal arts college's experience. *Journal of Education Media and Library Sciences*, *35*(3), 218–241.

Zhang, Y. (2001). Scholarly use of internet-based electronic resources. *Journal of the American Society for Information Science*, *52*(8), 628–654. doi:10.1002/asi.1113

Zimmerman, N., & Tu, F. (2003). It is not just a matter of ethics II: an examination of issues related to the ethical provision of consumer health services in public libraries. In B. Rockenbach, T. Mendina, & S. Almagno (Eds.), *Ethics and electronic information: a festschrift for Stephen Almagno* (pp. 119–130). Jefferson: McFarland.

About the Contributors

Adeyinka Tella is a senior lecturer in the Department of Library and Information Science, Faculty of Communication and Information Sciences, University of Ilorin, Nigeria. Tella is a commonwealth scholar who finished his PhD in September 2009 from the Department of Library and Information Studies; University of Botswana. Tella was rated as the no 28th scientist in Nigeria and first in his University in the ranking of scientist in Nigeria released by Webometrics in March, 2015. In 2007, he was awarded a small grant for thesis writing for the PhD students' category by the council for the development of social science research in Africa (CODESRIA). He has written and published articles mostly in international reputable refereed journals together with chapters in books. He is one of the contributors to an information science reference 'Cases on Successful E-learning Practices in the Developed and Developing World: Methods for the Global Information Economy.' Currently, he is the Associate Editor International Journal of Library and Information Science, and Editor-in-Chief- International Journal of Information Processing and Communication (IJIPC). His research areas include e-learning, information literacy, information communication technology, psychology of information, etc.

* * *

Adewojo Akinade Adebowale is presently a librarian at the Nigerian Stored Products Research Institute, he holds a bachelor's degree in library and information science from university of Ilorin in 2013.

Ganiyu Ojo Adigun is a Chattered Librarian and an Executive Member, Nigerian Library Association (NLA), Oyo State Chapter; he has a number of publications in reputable local and international journals. He is presently a Librarian II with Olusegun Oke Library, Ladoke Akintola University of Technology, Ogbomosho, Oyo State, Nigeria. He attended Ahmadu Bello University, Zaria, Nigeria between 1994 – 1997, 1998 – 2002 and 2008 – 2011 where he obtained Diploma in Library Science (DLS), Bachelor of Library and Information Science (BLIS) and Masters of Information Science (MIS) respectively. He also attended University of Ilorin between 2005 – 2007 for Masters of Business Administration (MBA). He is currently a research student with the Department of Library and Information Science, University of Ilorin, Nigeria. Adigun's research interest cut across: Scholarly Information Environment and Communication, Online Information Environment, Information Organisation, Use of Information Communication Technology (ICT), Digital Librarianship, and Information Support Services to Distance Learning. Adigun is married and blessed with children.

Joel Olawale Afolayan holds National Diploma (2005) and Higher National Diploma (2008) both in Library and Information Science, Federal Polytechnic, Offa and Post Graduate Diploma in Education (PGDE), National Teachers' Institute (NTI), Kaduna (2015). He currently works with Michael Imoudu National Institute for Labour Studies (MINILS), Nigeria as Senior Library Officer. His research areas of interest include Information Resources Management; Organization of Knowledge; Records and Archive Management; Information Services in Industrial and Labour Relations; Community Development and Value Reorientation. He is also a member of professional bodies like The Institute for Information and Record Management of Nigeria (TIIREM), Abuja; Records and Information Management Awareness Foundation (RIMAF) Lagos. He is the Public Relations Officer of the Kwara State Chapter of Nigeria Library Association (2013-2016). He is married to Victoria and blessed with a baby.

Seyedali Ahrari is currently completing a PhD programme in the field of youth studies at Institute for Social Science Studies, Universiti Putra Malaysia. He obtained his Master of Science in sociology from Science and Research Branch of the Islamic Azad University (Tehran SRBIAU). To date, he is involved in different research projects.

Ayoola Oluwaseun Ajayi holds a first degree in Guidance and Counselling and a Master of Information Science degree from the University of Ibadan, Nigeria. He is an administrative staff in the Registry of the same University. His research interests cover Social Informatics, Information Systems, Knowledge Management and ICT for development.

Akakandelwa Akakandelwa is a senior lecturer in the Department of Library and Information Studies, School of Education, University of Zambia. He holds a Bachelor of Arts with Library and Information Studies (University of Zambia), a Master of Library and Information Studies (University of Botswana), and a PhD in Political and Social Sciences (University of Antwerp, Belgium). He lectures in a number of courses at both undergraduate and postgraduate levels. He has published widely in peer refereed journals and has written a number of book chapters. His major areas of research include Informetrics (bibliometrics, citation analysis, webometrics, and scientometrics), E-government, Information ethics, Information Literacy, Information Seeking Behavior, Information Systems, Data and Knowledge Management, Information Retrieval, and Organization of Knowledge and Information Resources (Cataloguing and Classification).

Aregbesola Ayooluwa is the Collections Development Librarian of the Centre for Learning Resources, Landmark University, Omu-Aran, Nigeria. He holds Bachelor Degree in Economics and Education from the University of Ado-Ekiti, and M.Inf.Sc. in Information Science from the University of Ibadan. He has a considerable number of publications in reputable local and international journals. He is a Member of the Nigerian Library Association (NLA), Member of the Information Technology Section of the Nigerian Library Association and a Certified Librarian of Nigeria (CLN).

Kwaghga Beetseh is a library staff at the Federal University of Agriculture Makurdi. He is a part time lecturer at the College of Advance and Professional Studies Makurdi. Mr. Beetseh has published locally and internationally. He is member of Association of Nigerian Teachers (ASSONT), member Collaboration of Education Faculties in West Africa (CEFWA) and member Nigerian Political Association (NPSA). He is happily married.

Jusang Bolong is an Associate Professor, a senior lecturer and currently acts as the Deputy Dean of Research and Innovation at Faculty of Modern Language and Communication, Universiti Putra Malaysia. He gained his Ph.D. in Human Communication from Universiti Putra Malaysia and most of his research focus on technology usage among the community.

Okiki Olatokunbo Christopher is the Systems Librarian in the University Library, University of Lagos, Akoka, Lagos, Nigeria. He holds a Ph.D in Library Science from the University of Ibadan, Ibadan, Nigeria. His research focus is on information literacy, Knowledge management, Data Mining, Development and installation of retrieval system & information services

Prakash Dongardive was born in 15 June 1976, at 'Mera BK' a small town in India located in the state Maharashtra. Mr. Prakash hold M.A. in (Sociology), MLIS (Library and Information Science), from Nagpur University, India. He earned a certificate in information Technology from Technical Board Mumbai, MS, India as well as qualified UGC SET. He is an Electronic Resource Librarian in King Abdullah University of Science and Technology, Saudi Arabia, and presently an Asst. Professor in Mekelle University, Ethiopia. He has published a number of book chapters and research papers.

Toluwani Adeyimika Eyiolorunshe has a Master's degree in Library and Information Studies (MLIS). She is a librarian in the readers' services unit at the Centre for Learning Resources (CLR), Landmark University, Omu-Aran.

Olaronke O. Fagbola, Ph.D. is a Librarian with the Library/ Learning Resources, National Open University of Nigeria, Lagos, Nigeria. Her research interest covers users studies, Information for organisational development and management.

Okocha Foluke currently serves as the Serials Liberian of the Centre for Learning Resources, Landmark University, Nigeria. She holds a B.Sc. in Management Information Systems from the Covenant University, M.Sc. in Information Science, in University of Ibadan .She is an Oracle Certified Associate and an Oracle Certified Professional.

Idachaba Joy A is a Chartered Librarian working at the University of Agriculture Library Makurdi. She is a Principal Librarian, holds BLS, MLS (NIG) and currently running a Ph.D. programme in the Department of Library and Information Science University of Nigeria, Nsukka. She has published scholarly works including Journal articles and Abstracts of Ph.D. Thesis and Dissertation of University of Agriculture Makurdi. Idachaba J.A has a very strong passion for Librarianship as a profession.

Tom Kwanya is a Knowledge Management specialist with several years of practical experience. He has developed and implemented Knowledge Management strategies; conducted knowledge audits; developed models and frameworks for knowledge elicitation and representation; and conducted knowledge management capacity building and mentoring consultancies in the South, East, West and Horn of Africa regions. He has also taught knowledge and information management; technology-mediated communication; and infopreneurship in public and private universities in Kenya. He is a published author of several refereed journal articles, conference papers and two monographs. His current areas of research interest include social networkps analysis; infodemiology and infoveillance; library innovations;

knowledge management; and infopreneurship. He holds PhD in Information Studies from the University of KwaZulu-Natal in South Africa. He is currently a senior lecturer in the Department of Information and Knowledge Management at The Technical University of Kenya.

Stella C. Nduka is an acquisition Librarian at the University of Lagos Library. She is a certified librarian and a member of Nigeria Library Association. She has passion for rendering library services to users and also meeting user's information needs. Her research areas are; Innovative Technologies, ICT tools and Use, Digital Libraries, Library management and women & Gender issues in Librarianship.

Oluwole Akanmu Odunola is a part time Lecturer at Professional Accountancy Training. He has been lecturing Information Technology (IT) and Management Information System (MIS) for over 8 years. He has produced more than 100 qualified candidates of Account Technician Scheme of the Institute of Chartered Accountants of Nigeria. Odunola holds B.Sc Computer Science with Second Class Upper Division and Master of Library and Information Studies with PhD grade from University of Ilorin and University of Ibadan. He is working at Olusegun Oke Library as System Analyst in Ladoke Akintola University of Technology Ogbomoso. He is currently a doctoral student in the Department of Library and Information Science, University of Ilorin. Odunola research interest cut across: System Analysis, Library Automation, Information Technology used in the library, use of library, library patronage, library management and information use.

Ojo Olubukola James was born 36 years ago in Lagos Nigeria and has a Ph.D. in Educational Management from the University of Ilorin, Nigeria where he is currently a lecturer. His research interest is on ICT. He has taught courses at both undergraduate and graduate levels.

E Ondari-Okemwa, PhD, Professor and Head, Department of Library and Information Science, University of Fort Hare, Alice, South Africa. Research interests: Knowledge management, Digital libraries, knowledge production, Scholarly communication, Information resources management and Open access publishing. Author of several journal articles, one book and two book chapters.

Japhet Otike is a professor in the Department of Library, Records Management and Information Studies, School of Information Sciences at Moi University, Eldoret in Kenya. He had his university education in library and information studies at Makerere University in Uganda and Loughborough University in the United Kingdom. The author has served as Head of the Department of Library and Information Studies; and until August 2014, he was Dean, School of Information Sciences at Moi University. His research and teaching interests are in legal information with particular reference to copyright; marketing of library and information services; and disaster management.

Sola Owolabi is currently the Readers' Services Librarian, Centre for Learning Resources, Landmark University. He has worked with United Bank for Africa, Olaniwun Ajayi (Law Firm), KPMG Professional Services and Synergy Sparks. He holds DLS, BLIS and MLIS in Library and Information Studies, University of Ibadan. He has considerable number of publications in reputable local and international journals. He is a member of Nigerian Library Association (NLA), member Information Technology Section of the Nigerian Library Association and a Certified Librarian of Nigeria (CLN).

Oguntayo Adebisi Sunday is a Resource Officer 1 in the Centre for Learning Resources, Landmark University, Omu Aran. He holds Bachelor of Library Science degree from Ahmadu Bello University, Zaria and Master of Library of Information Science from Delta State University, Abraka. He has published some papers in professional journals. He is a registered member of Librarian's Registration Council of Nigeria (LRCN), member, Nigerian Library Association; member Nigerian Library Association Cataloguing, Classification and Indexing section and member Nigerian Library Association Medical Library section. He is the Head Technical Services Landmark University Omu aran.

Pedro Pina is a lawyer and a law teacher at the Polytechnic Institute of Coimbra - ESTGOH, in Portugal. He holds a law degree from the University of Coimbra Law School and a post-graduation in Territorial Development, Urbanism and Environmental Law from the Territorial Development, Urbanism and Environmental Law Studies Center (CEDOUA) at the University of Coimbra Law School. He holds a master degree in Procedural Law Studies from the University of Coimbra Law School and is currently a Ph.D. student in the Doctoral Programme 'Law, Justice, and Citizenship in the Twenty First Century' from the University of Coimbra Law School and Economics School.

Oyeniran Saheed was born 46 years ago in Osun State, Nigeria and has a Ph.D. in Educational Management from the University of Ilorin. He is a Lecturer in the Department of Educational Management, University of Ilorin, Nigeria. His research interest is on Economics of Education. He has taught courses at both Undergraduate and Graduate levels.

Bahaman Abu Samah started his career as a lecturer at Universiti Putra Malaysia in 1982. Currently he serves as director at Institute for Social Science Studies (IPSAS). His teaching focuses in statistic and computer application in Human Resource Development. As a researcher, he is actively involved in different research projects.

Adewale Joel Sobalaje is a Librarian at Olusegun Oke Library, Ladoke Akintola University of Technology, Ogbomoso, Oyo State, Nigeria. He holds Bachelor of Technology in Agric-Econs and Extension (B.Tech.) from the same university and Master of Information Science (M.Inf.Sc.) in Africa Regional Centre for Information Science from the university of Ibadan, Ibadan, Oyo-State, Nigeria. His area of interest is in Information Communication Technology, Cataloguing and Classification.

Akande Femi Titus is presently Director Information and Documentation at Nigerian Stored Product Research Intitute, Ilorin. He holds a Bachelor's Degree in Science Education from Ahmadu Bello University Zaria in 1987. He has a Master degree in Information Library and Archival Studies from the University of Ibadan. He also has a Master degree in Public Administration MPA from University of Ilorin in 1993 and PGD Certificate in Mass Communication at University of Lagos. He has scholarly publications to his credit. He is married and blessed with children.

Michael T. Upev is a Senior Librarian, Head of Collection Development at Francis Sulemanu Idachaba Library, University of Agriculture, Makurdi, Nigeria. He holds Master of Library Archival information Studies Degree from the University of Ibadan in2004. His research interest includes information resources management, knowledge management, and information searching and retrieval.

Felicia Yusuf is the pioneer University Librarian (Director of the Centre for Learning Resources), Landmark University. She holds a B.A degree in Library Science/Sociology from Bayero University, Kano and a Master degree in Library and Information Science from the University of Ibadan. Before she was redeployed to Landmark University in 2011, she had worked for eight years at the Centre for Learning Resources, Covenant University, Ota where she received an award for singularly automating the Serials Section of the Library. She has published substantially in a number of reputable local and international journals. Yusuf, Felicia is a member of the Nigeria Library Association (NLA) and a Certified Librarian of Nigeria (CLN).

Zeinab Zaremohzzabieh is the corresponding author of the paper and currently doing PhD programme in the field of youth studies at Institute for Social Science Studies, Universiti Putra Malaysia. She obtained her Master of Science in sociology from Science and Research Branch of the Islamic Azad University (Tehran SRBIAU). To date, she has completed a number of research projects related to the community development and ICT.

Index

R

S

T

U

V

W

www.ingramcontent.com/pod-product-compliance
Lightning Source LLC
LaVergne TN
LVHW062141200926
848484LV00007B/1842